PABLO NERUDA

PABLO NERUDA

A Passion for Life

ADAM FEINSTEIN

BLOOMSBURY

For my family

First published in Great Britain in 2004

Copyright © 2004 by Adam Feinstein

The moral right of the author has been asserted

Bloomsbury Publishing Plc, 38 Soho Square, London W1D 3HB

A CIP catalogue record for this book
is available from the British Library

ISBN 0 7475 7192 9

10 9 8 7 6 5 4 3 2 1

Typeset by Hewer Text Ltd, Edinburgh
Printed in Great Britain by Clays Ltd, St Ives plc

All papers used by Bloomsbury Publishing are natural,
recyclable products made from wood grown in well-managed
forests. The manufacturing processes conform to the
environmental regulations of the country of origin.

Contents

Acknowledgements

It is no exaggeration to say that I could not have written this biography without the generous support of Professor Robert Pring-Mill of St Catherine's College, Oxford. I owe him an immense debt of gratitude for his friendship and his hospitality, his kindness in lending me invaluable documents, in sharing his time, his research, advice, list of contacts in Chile and personal anecdotes from his own friendship with Pablo Neruda. Robert also read the manuscript of this book, made copious notes and corrected some infelicities in my translations. Any errors that remain are, of course, my own.

I am also enormously grateful to the Fundación Pablo Neruda in Santiago for putting me in touch with other friends and relatives of Neruda who helped me while I was in Chile.

Support from the Wingate Foundation and the Leverhulme Trust allowed me to travel to, and research the archives in, Chile, Spain and Russia.

I am grateful to José Miguel Varas, editor of the Chilean cultural magazine *Rocinante*, for his insights and for providing me with further useful names and telephone numbers.

I appreciate the help given to me by Juan Camilo Lorca at the Biblioteca Nacional in Santiago in guiding me through the many files on Neruda at the library, and to staff at the Biblioteca Municipal in Barcelona and the National Archives in London for their patience in locating various relevant documents.

I am immensely indebted to Kathleen Boet-Herbert in The Hague for her remarkable investigation into the life of Neruda's first wife, Maruca, and her discovery of many previously unpublished details. I am also very grateful to Anabel Torres for help in this area.

My thanks go to Julio Gálvez in Chile for supplying information about Neruda's time in Spain and to Frances Stonor Saunders for sharing her documentation on the successful campaign to prevent Neruda winning the 1964 Nobel Prize.

For their willingness to share their insights and their memories of Neruda in Chile, I must thank: Volodia Teitelboim, Margarita Aguirre, Aída Figueroa, Sergio Insunza, Inés Valenzuela, Inés Figueroa; Póli Delano, Francisco Velasco, Marie Martner, Sara Vial, Víctor Pey, Roser Bru, José Balmes, Maria Gálvez, Victoria Lago, Federico Schopf, Rodolfo Reyes and Irma Pacheco in Santiago; Francisco Velasco and Marie Martner in Valparaíso; Juan Carlos Reyes, Bernardo Reyes and Lidia Herrera in Temuco and Nicanor Parra in Las Cruces.

I have to pay particular tribute to Neruda's friend, secretary and biographer Margarita Aguirre, whom I met on several occasions in Santiago and who sadly died in December 2003.

Special thanks must also go to the Chilean poet and journalist, Sara Vial, for many hours of delightful and illuminating conversation in Viña del Mar and her help in acquiring valuable documentation.

I am immensely grateful to Arthur Miller for sharing his experiences of organising the 1966 PEN Congress in New York and his personal impressions of Pablo Neruda during his stay in the United States.

Vera Kuteishikova in Moscow also gave me invaluable insights into Neruda's many visits to the former Soviet Union, and this help is much appreciated. I am also grateful to the staff of the National Archive Centre in Moscow for their help.

I also acknowledge, with gratitude, the help given to me by Liu Hongbin, who translated various Chinese texts relating to Neruda.

I would like to thank the staff members at Neruda's three houses in Chile – La Chascona, Isla Negra and La Sebastiana – who allowed me to make lengthy tours of the buildings and their surroundings and to take photographs.

I am also grateful to Professor Jason Wilson, professor of Latin American literature at London University, for many stimulating discussions while writing this book and for lending me a number of useful documents.

I must pay tribute to Hernán Loyola's new edition of Neruda's *Complete Works*, which has proved a constant source of information and delight.

I should also like to thank Liz Calder and Alexandra Pringle for their unwavering enthusiasm for this project, my agent Victoria Hobbs, and my editors at Bloomsbury, Bill Swainson and Victoria Millar, whose task it has been to smooth out the rough edges.

ADAM FEINSTEIN

List of Illustrations

Unless otherwise stated, these photographs form part of the personal archive of one of Chile's best-known poets and journalists, Sara Vial, who kindly lent them to the author. Most appeared in Vial's illuminating book, *Neruda en Valparaíso*, first published in 1983, and in its four subsequent editions. Vial was a close friend of Neruda, who was a witness at her wedding and wrote a prologue to her 1958 book, *La ciudad indecible*. Many have also appeared in the following Chilean magazines: *Hoy*, *Siembra*, *Sucesos*, *Zig-Zag*, *Hechos Mundiales*, *Vistazo*, *Aurora de Chile* and *Anales de la Universidad de Chile*.

Introduction

Of very few poets can it be said that they enriched the lives of millions around the world, and continue to do so more than thirty years after their death. The Chilean poet Pablo Neruda is such a man. Neruda was one of the greatest Spanish-language poets of the twentieth century, and the beauty of his work, together with his passion for social justice and his love of life are as vital today as they ever were.

Nearly half a century before he won the Nobel Prize for Literature in 1971, lovers everywhere wooed one another with verses from Neruda's *Twenty Love Poems*. Many more have been entranced by the elegant and touching simplicity of the *Elementary Odes*, the hermetic beauty of *Residence on Earth*, the epic power of the *Canto general*, the gloriously witty self-mockery of *Estravagario*, and the overpowering lyricism of the later love poetry.

Neruda's political convictions – he was a long-time Stalinist, although he was increasingly troubled by events from 1956 onwards – may no longer hold up. But his underlying humanism remains relevant as we approach the centenary of his birth in July 2004.

Neruda spanned the century and the globe and he was close friends with some of the most fascinating and influential personalities of the twentieth century, including Lorca, Picasso, Eluard, Aragon and Ehrenburg.

His life story is extraordinary. Neruda was not just a poet, diplomat and politician. He was an energetic lover of wine (Chilean, above all), women (he had three wives and numerous mistresses) and song. He sacrificed his diplomatic posting in Madrid to take a courageous pro-

Republican stance during the Spanish Civil War, and saved the lives of 2,000 Republicans by shipping them out to Chile on an old fishing boat, the *Winnipeg*. His year in hiding from his own country's tyrannical leader and his death-defying escape on horseback across the Andes into Argentina would make a book in themselves. It is significant that, during that escape, and often afterwards, the power of his poetry and his sheer pleasure in being alive earned him the devoted support of not only close friends but also political foes. His three years in exile in Europe included a successful flight from the Italian authorities by gondola in Venice. Back in Chile, he was nominated as candidate for the Presidency, only to stand down in favour of Salvador Allende.

He wove a spell over most people he met. Lorca memorably called him 'closer to blood than to ink'.

Neruda was also an immensely complex man. He acknowledged the contradictions within himself, calling 'Pablo Neruda . . . my most perfidious enemy'. This is the first fully referenced English-language biography to attempt to untangle these contradictions. The only other full biography, by Neruda's close friend Volodia Teitelboim, was written in 1984, in Moscow, where Teitelboim had no access to essential documents, and markedly glosses over the less attractive aspects of Neruda's character and political affiliations.

Pablo Neruda was the antithesis of Jean-Paul Sartre. While Sartre felt nausea at the world around him, Neruda felt joy even at the height of his painful and protracted final illness. While Sartre attempted to teach us to find individual freedom through accepting the essential meaninglessness of life, Neruda felt that man – and writers, above all – had a duty to embrace life and commit to seeking social justice. In the global village we live in today, Sartre's message is alienatingly empty and difficult to read, while Neruda's call for human solidarity has more potency than ever.

The Russian poet Yevgeny Yevtushenko – who turned against Stalinism at the time of Khrushchev's Thaw but remained a close friend of Neruda – wrote his moving 'Epistle to Neruda' just days after the Chilean's death in 1973:

> . . . today I see Neruda –
> he's always right in the centre
>   and, unfaltering,
> he carries his poetry to the people
>   as simply and calmly
>   as a loaf of bread.[1]

I

Secrets, shadows, wine and rain

1904–20

Pablo Neruda was born Ricardo Eliecer Neftalí Reyes Basoalto on 12 July 1904, in Parral, in central Chile's wine country, 'where the vines curled their green heads of hair'.[1] His schoolteacher mother, Rosa, was already thirty-eight years old. On 14 September 1904, just two months and two days later, she was dead, probably from puerperal fever, but certainly weakened by labour. He never knew the woman who brought him into the world.

Neruda's father, José del Carmen Reyes Morales, had likewise lost his own mother, the quiet, demure Natalia Morales Hermosilla, at birth. José del Carmen's father had remarried a woman of quite different temperament and constitution. Encarnación Parada was robust, with an impish sense of humour, who bore José del Carmen's father no fewer than thirteen children, all given biblical names.

At the age of twenty, José del Carmen, a strongly built, bearded man with an imposing presence, left the biblical tribe of step-siblings behind in the small, oddly named Belén (Bethlehem) family estate in Parral to seek work in the port of Talcahuano, some 150 miles away. Talcahuano had become a site of bustling industry after the construction of a dam ordered by President José Balmaceda.

Neruda's father was not a *roto*. Not quite. The *roto* is unlike anyone else in South America: he is the link between the backward peasant of the Chilean *campo* and the specialised worker of the Santiago suburbs, someone who leaves an estate to become an artisan, a miner or even an electrician. But he is also, by tradition, sharp-witted and astute in business. Such epithets, unfortunately, could hardly be applied to José del Carmen, as he criss-crossed Chile in search of work. His wanderings even took him across the border into Argentina at one point.

In the Talcahuano boarding house where he stayed, José del Carmen struck up a friendship with a talkative, would-be entrepreneur of North American origin, Carlos Mason Reinike, who was interested in becoming involved in the burgeoning Chilean rail network, with its tentacles stretching rapidly southwards. Mason became a confidant to José, and was soon a frequent visitor to the Belén estate back in Parral, especially after meeting Micaela Candia, one of the daughters of the local Candia Marverde family, whom he married.

After the wedding, Mason decided to extend his enterprises. He bought a number of properties near the railway station in Temuco, a burgeoning frontier town of 10,000 inhabitants. Here, with characteristic energy, Mason launched himself into several businesses, including a small hotel.

It was at this Temuco hotel that his young friend José del Carmen would stay on his comings and goings between the work in Talcahuano and his father's estate in Parral, and it was here that he felt himself drawn to Carlos's sister-in-law, Micaela's sister, Trinidad. On one of these fleeting visits to Temuco, it seems, José made Trinidad pregnant. The child, born in the spring of 1895, was Pablo Neruda's half-brother: Rodolfo Reyes Candia.

This scandal could not be made public, so the birth took place far from Temuco – in Coipúe, on the banks of the River Toltén. Rodolfo was left there, to be brought up by his midwife, Ester, until the age of eleven. The relationship between Rodolfo's parents – such as it was – stopped there. It became a family secret. Until quite recently Rodolfo was believed to be Neruda's younger brother.[2]

Four years later, the 29-year-old José del Carmen began courting another woman in earnest. Rosa Neftalí Basoalto Opazo was six years older than he and a schoolteacher in Parral. Mariano Latorre Elordouy, father of the Chilean writer, Mariano Latorre Court, was a pupil of Neruda's mother at Parral's School Number Two. His wife, Fernandina Court, also met Rosa Neftalí Basoalto Opazo, and remembered her as 'stiff, haughty, of iron-fisted discipline, although extremely affectionate with her pupils'. Rosa apparently liked to encourage the schoolchildren to write poems and compositions, and when she corrected these, she showed 'the rare gift of finding the correct word to describe emotion or beauty'. Fernandina recalled her as a cultured woman, and even remembered hearing her reciting a classical text. With her black clothes, her high voice and her inquisitive, greenish eyes, she was, in Fernandina's words, 'a woman of style'.[3]

José del Carmen had met Rosa from time to time at social gatherings, while still under the spell of Trinidad Candia in Temuco, but had not pursued his interest any further. The only surviving photograph of Rosa shows an intriguing, rather than beautiful face: her dark eyes, black, curly hair and a tender, silent, reserved expression may have reminded José of his own mother.

They married in the autumn of 1903 and set up home in the Calle San Diego in Parral, where the future poet would be born a year later. Mariano Latorre Elordouy describes turn-of-the-century Parral as

> a grey, dirty dump. If it had any character at all, I think it was its total lack of character. It gave the impression of being a recently set-up camp. Solid houses without style, whose walls were like a map of winter, with their flakiness and traces of squalls. Dust in summer and mud in winter . . . [But] at festival times, the town had a Dionysiac fury. The horse races attracted people from all over Chile, and in the Social Club, people played for fantastic amounts day and night. Its singers and women of easy virtue were famous.[4]

Money was tight. José, hard-working man though he was, could not eke out a living from a small vine-filled area of land, and teaching was a poorly paid profession. But the couple were happy. Rosa enjoyed reading poetry to herself, and may even have tried writing verse, although none has survived.[5]

The Chile Neruda was born into was in severe economic difficulties and wracked by social unrest, especially in the north, after decades of prosperity and political stability. 'It had more castes than India, and there was a pejorative term to set every person in his or her rightful place: *roto, pije* [toff], *arribista* [upstart], *siútico* [poser] . . . Birth defined status: it was easy to descend in the social hierarchy, but money, fame or talent was not sufficient to allow one to rise, that required the sustained effort of several generations.'[6]

Yet for the average Chilean at the beginning of the twentieth century, the country where Communism would become more active than anywhere else in Latin America was anything but a hotbed of social conflict. 'Everyone immediately knew their precise place. In Chile, the upper classes generally look European, but as you move down the social and economic ladder, the indigenous features are accentuated. Class consciousness is so strong that I never saw anyone cross the boundaries of his position.'[7]

The future Pablo Neruda, still known as Neftalí (his mother's second name), had more pressing problems to deal with than switching classes. He had to make it through the first, difficult years of life. His father later recalled: 'As a child, Neftalí was very shy and very sickly. He spent most of the time in bed. He was so weak that we even feared for his life.'[8]

Unable to look after the infant himself, José del Carmen left Neftalí in the hands of his grandfather, José Angel Reyes Hermosilla, who was better off financially, despite having to feed his thirteen recognised children. José's stepmother Encarnación Parada, quickly set about a search for a wet-nurse. She found a healthy young wife, María Luisa Leiva, who had a child of her own but who was willing and able to supply milk to the new arrival. A wet-nurse was routine in Chile at the time, provided the family could afford one.

In this house full of children, Neftalí had to compete for attention. His grandfather was affectionate enough, if a little pompous and severe in his moral sermons, which in Neftalí's case fell on uncomprehending, youthful ears.

While many migrants moved towards the nitrate-rich areas in northern Chile for work, José del Carmen once again decided to head southwards, back to work on the Talcahuano dam project. He stayed at the same boarding house where he had met Carlos Mason years earlier, run by the Tolrá family, of Catalan origin, and spent longer and longer periods away from Parral, to escape the grief of losing his wife just a year after marrying her. During his stays at the boarding house, he opened up his heart to one of the three Tolrá daughters, Aurelia, telling her about the pain of losing Rosa, about his son, Rodolfo, in Coipúe – whom he had barely seen in the ten years since his birth. It was Aurelia, barely an adult, who advised him to talk to Rodolfo's mother, Trinidad, in Temuco, with a view to 'normalising' the situation.

Trinidad accepted everything in her usual, resigned way. Lidia Herrera, who was married to Rodolfo's son Raúl, told me in Temuco: 'She was very quiet, she listened all the time. I thought she was too submissive.'[9]

However, José's visit to Rodolfo was less successful – son refused to recognise father and ran off into the thick undergrowth next to the River Toltén. Rodolfo's son, Rodolfo Reyes, today the head of a major Chilean copper company, recalls:

> My father told me that, in the countryside, he got to know the animals. He said he had looked a puma in the eyes. He understood the natural language of life, but when they came to fetch him, he was scared, and didn't want to leave.[10]

In 1906, two years after Rosa's death, Neftalí's father decided to marry Trinidad Candia Marverde. The newly-weds moved into Carlos Mason's house in Temuco. Rodolfo – a 'little semi-savage of twelve or thirteen' – joined them soon afterwards.[11]

The relationships between the young Neruda and his half-brother, and between Rodolfo and his father, were not easy. 'My father always told me that my grandfather, José del Carmen Reyes, was a very strict man indeed,' said Bernardo Reyes.

> When he arrived home, he gave the orders, accompanied by train whistles, and everyone rushed around, making sure that those orders were carried out to the letter. He was very authoritarian, especially to my father, Rodolfo, because he gave him missions as the eldest child. My father told me that one of those missions was to take Pablo to school in the mornings. My father said that, on those walks to school, Pablo was so 'slow and stupid' that this really came to irritate him, and he would virtually push Pablo into the school building.[12]

Eighty years later, Lidia Herrera recalled that José del Carmen 'was a very affectionate man, very fond of his friends – most of them from the railway – and they all liked him. But he was very strict with his children. Laurita told me that he wouldn't allow anyone to sit down at table until they had washed their hands or combed their hair.'[13]

But Trinidad proved to be the most loving of stepmothers. Young Neftalí always called her his '*mamadre*' (mo-mother). It was to her that he dedicated his first affectionate attempts at poetry, and later he recalled her as 'sweet like the shy coolness of the sun in stormy lands, like a shining lantern, in her noisy wooden-soled shoes'.[14] She was 'diligent and gentle, she had a peasant's sense of humour, an active and indefatigable goodness'.[15]

Gilberto Concha Riffo – soon to be Neftalí's schoolfriend and himself a poet in later years, under the name of Juvencio Valle – visited the Reyes household a number of times. He found Trinidad's attitude to Pablo

> totally different from what you would normally assume a step-mother's to be . . . Pablo's father, José del Carmen Reyes, was an elegant man, with a distinguished air. He had a little beard with a whitish tip to it . . . He was cordial, generous, but very strict with Pablo. Doña Trinidad was short, thin and affectionate to her stepson. She spent her life worrying about Pablo's health, which was pretty frail.[16]

Trinidad proved a wonderful choice for her new husband, also. She was not only devoted to him, but brought hope of financial gain through her wealthy relatives. José del Carmen had always been a willing businessman – but never a very competent one. In his memoirs, Neruda recalled him trying to bargain with an Araucanian Indian at a railway station who wanted to sell him a hen.

> His blond goatee was something to watch as he picked up a hen in front of an impenetrable Araucanian woman who would not lower the price of her merchandise by a single centavo.[17]

Through his friend and now relative Carlos Mason, José del Carmen was offered work on the new railroad in Temuco.

Temuco today is a bustling modern commercial town made up of grids of streets lined with shops and stalls selling clothing and food – although even now if you walk just a few hundred yards outside the centre you find a district where Mapuche Indians on cattle-drawn wagons vie coolly with buses spewing out exhaust fumes for right of way across the main roads. The Temuco that Neftalí grew up in was

> a pioneer town, one of those towns without a past, but with hardware shops. Since the Indians cannot read, the hardware shops put up conspicuous signs in the streets: an immense saw, a gigantic pot, a colossal padlock . . . And over there, the cobbler's, with a huge boot.[18]

The descendants of the Araucanian Indians, the Mapuche, lived in the fields on the outskirts of Temuco, in their own settlements. They would go into Temuco to sell their goods (lambs, eggs, textiles) and then retreat to their huts in the evening, the men on horseback while the women walked beside them.

Whenever Neruda later looked back on his early childhood in Temuco, he said that the 'only unforgettable character' was the rain.

> It rained for months on end, years on end. The rain fell in threads like long glass needles which shattered on the roofs, or lashed against windows in transparent waves, and each house was a ship which reached port only with the greatest of difficulty on that winter ocean. That cold rain from the south of America does not come in impulsive warm squalls falling like a whip and passing, leaving a blue sky behind. On the contrary, the southern rain is patient and continuous, endlessly falling from a grey sky.[19]

His was a childhood of 'wet shoes, broken tree trunks in the forest, devoured by lianas and beetles,' and his father's 'golden beard'.

His father's new job was as driver of a ballast train on the burgeoning railroad. It was a job José del Carmen seemed born to. 'He was a bad farmer, a mediocre worker on the Talcahuano dam, but a good railwayman. My father was a railwayman at heart. My mother could tell, at night, which of the trains arriving or leaving Temuco station was my father's,' Neruda later recalled.[20] On José's return home from his shift at four in the morning, 'the door shook, the whole house shook, the stairs groaned, a loud voice uttered hostile recriminations'.[21] At times his father seemed so dictatorial that Neftalí and his half-sister, Laura, even discussed the possibility of killing him.

Sometimes, his father would pull Neftalí out of school and take him with him on those long train journeys, through the rain and the mud, into the midst of the forest. It was a magical experience. The trains carried stones and sand which they left between the sleepers to prevent the powerful rain from shifting the rails. Because the workers had to dig ballast from the quarries, the train sometimes stood still for weeks on end, and Neftalí would stay with his father in this 'little house, which stopped alongside the spring forest, a virgin jungle which held the most splendid treasures for me, immense ferns, dazzling beetles, strange wild birds' eggs'.[22]

It opened up a world of wonder to him.

Nature made me feel inebriated. I must have been about ten years old, but I was already a poet. I was not yet writing verse, but I was attracted to the birds, the beetles, the partridge eggs. It was a miracle to find them [the eggs] in the ravines, greasy, dark and gleaming, the colour of the barrel of a shotgun. I was stunned by the perfection of the insects.[23]

Those train journeys brought Neftalí into contact not only with nature but with strange human beings, whose sinister, violent pasts he could only guess at. These people may have coloured his early attempt at prose fiction, the 1926 novella *El habitante y su esperanza* (The Inhabitant and His Hope), with its tales of adultery and violent revenge. Neftalí had met one of the railway workers, Monge, who had a vertical scar from a knife-wound across his face. José had warned him that Monge was the most dangerous of men, but as it turned out, he had a fondness for the young boy, feeding his inquisitiveness by bringing him hairy spiders, baby wood pigeons and – most impressive of all – a multicoloured beetle which he placed in the boy's hands until it slipped away, leaving behind the memory of red, violet, green and yellow. One day, Monge, too, slipped away. When Neftalí asked his father where he'd gone, he learnt of Monge's appropriately violent end: he had fallen from the train and rolled down a precipice to his death. Neftalí cried for a week after hearing the news.

Back home in Temuco, the house was never quiet. Firstly, because, as in so many other large frontier buildings at the time, the various family quarters were inter-connected. The Reyes (José del Carmen's side), the Candias (his wife's) and the Masons (his wife's relatives) all shared tools, umbrellas, tables and chairs.

Some of the most memorable occasions were the feasts held in the Mason section of the household, with roast lamb, kidney-bean salad, flowing wine and guitar music. The lamb was killed in the morning and, to young Neftalí's horror, he was often asked to drink the blood, which dripped into a basin. The patriarch himself, Carlos Mason, with his long white hair, bearing a striking resemblance to the poet Emerson, would preside at the head of a never-ending table, alongside his wife, Micaela Candia.

The second reason for the bustling atmosphere in the house was José del Carmen's unusual degree of sociability: if none of his drinking railroad colleagues or other friends was available, he would invite people in off the street to share a meal. This cannot have been easy for the less gregarious Trinidad, who, in her husband's presence, was quiet and reserved, cowed but supremely dignified.

She needed all the dignity she could muster: another secret was about to endanger her marriage.

During some of his lengthy absences from home, José del Carmen continued to visit Aurelia Tolrá at the boarding house in Talcahuano. Whereas in the early years, Aurelia, barely out of her teens, had been no more than a close friend to him, she had now blossomed into an enticing young woman. The forty-year-old José fell for her charms – once again, with unexpectedly speedy results. Aurelia became pregnant, and gave birth to Laura.

Neruda's beloved sister, Laura (the 'Laurita' to whom he would write so often from around the world, nicknaming her *Conejita*, 'Little Rabbit'), was actually his half-sister, something that was kept hidden from him. 'Trinidad, the gentle, silent one, never knew, or didn't want to know, about this relationship. Like a spirit, she moved around the house, lavishing love on little Neftalí and on Rodolfo . . .'[24]

At first, Laurita was kept well away from the rest of the family, in a small town called San Rosendo, where from time to time she would ask her mother, Aurelia, where her father was. Meanwhile, the relationship between Aurelia and José seems to have deteriorated with Aurelia's growing determination to make something of her life. She eventually broached the possibility that Trinidad could bring Laurita up as her own daughter in Temuco.

To José's astonishment, when he returned to his wife and confessed all, she took the news, and the idea of adopting Laurita, with total equanimity. Neftalí and Laurita quickly became very close. Whenever he was sick, Neftalí would ask her to look out of the window and describe every little detail of what was going on outside. But did he realise the truth about Laurita?

He must have suspected. He once tried to raise the subject with her, according to his third wife, Matilde Urrutia, but Laurita suddenly broke off the conversation and ran to her room in tears. Neruda never brought up the topic again, appalled at having hurt his beloved Laurita.[25]

In winter, the house was freezing cold. The wooden building, like so many others in Temuco, had been raised hurriedly, and the rain fell constantly on the zinc roofs. From time to time, Neftalí would wake up, look out of the window, and find that the house opposite had lost its roof to the wind. It became a routine event.

At the age of six, in 1910, Neftalí entered the Boys' Lyceum in Temuco. The range of his schoolmates revealed the cosmopolitan extent of Chilean society, even in the provinces, thanks to the major influx of immigrants from Europe. 'My fellow pupils had names like Schnake, Scheler, Hauser, Smith, Taito, Serani . . . There were Sephardim, Albalas, Francos. There were Irish, McGuintys, there were Poles, Yanichewskys . . . And we fought with acorns in the large covered shed. You have to be hit by an acorn to realise how much it hurts.'[26]

Gilberto Concha Riffo – the future poet Juvencio Valle – recalled Neftalí as absent-minded, a daydreamer, quiet, very thin (his nickname was 'Shinbone') and melancholy, and yet clearly his stepmother had already taught him to read and he was even then an alert observer of nature.

Valle remembered Neftalí always being left out of the schoolchildren's racing games 'because he was so small and so very thin. And when it came to playing ball games, no one chose him for their team. He was a quiet, peaceful child, who would sit in a corner reading little books of stories . . . He had an insatiable curiosity for little things (strange stones, pieces of wood, insects). And he never lost that curiosity.'[27]

Another classmate, Luis Humbero Cerda, shared this impression. 'Neftalí was terrible at football. He couldn't get a touch of the ball at all. We went on excursions, down to the river, to look for herbs, insects. He loved books, especially Jules Verne. He was very bad with his fists.'[28]

He was equally poor at mathematics, but fortunately he was helped by his schoolfriend, Alejandro (Sasha) Serani.

A fourth fellow pupil, Gerardo Seguel, would later become one of Chile's first Communist intellectuals. Neftalí's first observation of politics was at ten, when the First World War broke out, and he saw his schoolmates split between those who supported the Allies and those children of German immigrants who took the opposing side. However, politics made no great impact on the very young Neruda's life at this time – not even the upheaval of the 1917 Russian Revolution, although ripples did cross the oceans.

As another schoolfriend, Diego Muñoz, who recalled these times in his memoirs, wrote:

> We did not have a clear idea of what it [the Revolution] was, nor could we have until years later. But we enjoyed one of its consequences: the circulation, in our own language, of the work of the greatest Russian writers, which was widely distributed with the aim, certainly, of revealing all that civilised humanity was 'losing'. This literature had a major influence on us.[29]

Neftalí's major concern was to keep warm.

> We would walk to school, treading on one stone after another along the path, fighting the cold and rain. The wind snatched our umbrellas away. Raincoats were expensive, I didn't like wearing gloves, shoes became drenched. I will always remember the wet socks by the fireplace and all the shoes steaming, like little locomotives. Then came the floods, which swept away the villages where the poorest people lived, by the river. And the earth also shook, trembled.[30]

He took to wearing a bright green hat belonging to his father, until it blew away and was lost for ever.

But in spring, Temuco was enchanting. Far from attempting to escape the wet, he and his classmates would run down to dip their toes in the River Cautín.

Summer in Temuco was 'yellow and scorching'.[31] His father would often take them away to the cooler coast, at Puerto Saavedra, carrying the mattresses out of the house with them so they had something to sleep on when they arrived. Neruda never forgot Puerto Saavedra. It was there that he first saw his penguins, the wild swans of Lake Budi, and ate sandy figs.

> On the shores of the lake we fished, or hunted, for mullet, using harpoons or spears. It was hypnotising to watch those motionless stalkers, lances held high, to see the flashing spear and then a thrashing fish. There, too, I often saw the rosy flight of flamingos across virgin territory.[32]

The Reyes family were put up at the Puerto Saavedra home of Horacio Pacheco, a farmer friend of José del Carmen – years later Neruda looked back fondly to those stays in the Pacheco household in his 1964 collection, *Memorial de Isla Negra*.[33] Horacio Pacheco recalled observing Neruda's father, a whistle to his lips, marching Neftalí and Laura, nervously holding hands, into the cold, wild sea.[34]

One of the few survivors from that time, Horacio Pacheco's daughter, Irma, told me that she remembers Neftalí playing with her around the house in Puerto Saavedra:

> He lifted me up and my mother was terrified that he would drop me. She cried: 'You're going to kill her.' And he did drop me once, which put a stop to those games. But in later years, Neruda, when he saw me, would tell me to come and sit on his lap, because that was what he had done back in Puerto Saavedra. He was very affectionate.[35]

Irma Pacheco also recollects that Neftalí was already writing poetry at this time, and that his father was disgusted. 'He would write on the beach and on the small boats, His father was always saying: "He's a fanatic" as he tried to call his son in to have lunch.'[36]

Another of the pleasures of Puerto Saavedra was riding a horse along the beach. In his early teens, riding provided Neftalí with sensual enjoyment: 'There is nothing more beautiful in my homeland than galloping on a horse beside the sea.'[37]

Even more enticing for young Neftalí was the library in Puerto Saavedra, run by a poet, Augusto Winter, a small man with a 'shabby, short yellow beard, and, above the beard, a pair of eyes full of love'.[38] When Puerto Saavedra was virtually destroyed in the terrible 1960 earthquake and huge tidal wave, books were found strewn in the sand.

Augusto Winter was a major influence on the young Neftalí's thinking. He was an easy-going, free-thinking man, very unlike the stern, disciplinarian traditionalist, José del Carmen. Before taking up his librarian's post he had been a boat mechanic responsible for tending to the little steamers navigating the Imperial River. Winter, who also acted as secretary and treasurer of Puerto Saavedra's municipality, was a highly cultured man, in regular correspondence with many of the leading poets of the day.

> Don Augusto Winter admired my voracious literary appetite. 'Have you read it already?' he asked, passing me a new Vargas Vila, an Ibsen, a Rocambole. Like an ostrich, I swallowed everything without discriminating. Don Augusto Winter was the librarian at the best library I've ever known. He had a sawdust stove in the the middle of the room, and I settled down there as if I'd been condemned to read, in those three months of summer, all the books that had ever been written in the long winters of the world.[39]

Neftalí was a ravenous reader of any book he could lay his hands on – from Victor Hugo to Maxim Gorky, from Cervantes to Baudelaire. He claimed to have devoured three books a day. He read accounts of Buffalo Bill's feats. He didn't like the Wild West hero because he killed Indians, but admired the skills of a fellow horseman.

Later on, the greatest charm that Puerto Saavedra would hold for the impressionable young Neftalí was a girl who, like him, would spend summers by the sea with her family: Teresa Vázquez – the 'Terusa' who would inspire eight of the *Twenty Love Poems*, and whom Neruda would recall elsewhere as 'Terusa, open among the poppies, black spark of first pain'.[40]

In fact, Neftalí wrote his first love letters, Cyrano-like, as a favour for a schoolfriend who was madly in love with Blanca Wilson, daughter of the local blacksmith. When she became suspicious and asked Neftalí whether he was he really the author, he could not summon up the courage to deny it. As a reward for his loving words, she presented him with a quince which he didn't eat but treasured. 'Having thus replaced my friend in the girl's heart, I went on writing interminable love letters to her and receiving quinces.'[41]

If we believe Neruda's memoirs – among the most exhilarating ever written but also, in places, not to be entirely trusted – his first serious introduction to the charms of the opposite sex was probably with two girls, 'as precocious and wicked as I was shy and silent',[42] who lived in the house opposite him in Temuco. Once, despite his timidity, he could not help looking over at them, because he was intrigued by something they were holding in their hands. Approaching, he found it was a wild bird's nest, with some tiny turquoise eggs inside. As he reached out to grasp the nest, one of the girls told him that first he must let her feel in his clothes. Seized by panic, Neftalí fled, only to be chased down an alleyway and into a baker's shop. The two girls tracked him down and were beginning to remove his trousers when they heard his father's steps approaching. Neftalí and his two assailants crouched down and hid behind the counter, holding their breath.

Two weeks before his eleventh birthday, 'seized by profound anxiety, a feeling I hadn't had before, a kind of anguish and sadness',[43] he wrote his first poem. It was dedicated to his 'angelic' stepmother. Unsure of the quality of what he had written, he rushed to his parents brandishing the piece of paper.

> They were in the dining-room, immersed in one of those hushed conversations which, better than any river could, separate the world of children from the world of grown-ups. I held out the piece of paper carrying my verses, still trembling from the first visit from the muse. My father took the paper absent-mindedly, read it absent-mindedly and returned it to me absent-mindedly, saying: 'Where did you copy that from?' Then he went on talking to my mother in a lowered voice about his important and remote affairs. That, I seem to remember, was how my first poem was born, and that was how I received the first example of absent-minded literary criticism.[44]

That first poem, dated 30 June 1915, still exists. It ran:

> From a landscape of golden regions
> I chose
> to give you, dear Mama,
> this humble postcard. Neftalí

His stepmother, unlike the men in the household, was religious, but she did not thrust her faith on her stepson. Once, when he was twelve, she offered Neftalí her hand to take him to church. He recalled

Temuco's Iglesia del Corazón smelling of lilacs. 'Since I was not religious, I did not follow the rituals . . . I never learnt to cross myself, and no one ever paid any attention . . . to the irreverent little boy standing up in the midst of the faithful. Perhaps that is why I have always entered churches with respect.'[45]

He later said it was in that Temuco church that he experienced his first feelings of love, for a girl called María. 'That whole, confused first love, or something like it, was shattering, painful, full of commotion and torment and impregnated with all the traces of a penetrating aroma of convent lilac.'[46]

Not long afterwards, Neftalí had his first genuine sexual encounter. By his own account, it occurred under some hay on a threshing floor, surrounded by workers. He was asleep when he felt a body beneath the straw moving closer to his.

I was afraid. The thing was slowly drawing closer. I could hear the wisps of straw snapping, crushed by the unknown shape that kept moving toward me. My whole body stiffened, waiting. Maybe I ought to get up and yell. I remained stock still. I heard breathing right next to my head. Suddenly, a hand slid over me, a large, calloused hand, but it was a woman's. It ran over my brow, my eyes, my whole face, tenderly. Then an avid mouth clung to mine, and I felt a woman's body pressing against the whole of mine, all the way down to my feet. Little by little, my fear turned into intense pleasure. My hand slid over her braided hair, her smooth brow, her closed eyelids, soft as poppies, and went on exploring. I felt two breasts that were large and firm, broad, rounded buttocks, legs that locked around me, and I sank my fingers in her pubic hair like mountain moss. Not a word came from that anonymous mouth. How difficult it is to make love, without making a noise, in a mountain of straw burrowed by the bodies of seven or eight other men, sleeping men who must not be awakened for anything in the world! And yet, anything is possible, if you take infinite care over it. A little while later, the stranger suddenly fell asleep beside me, and worked into a fever by the situation, I began to panic. It would soon be daybreak, I thought, and the first workers would discover a naked woman stretched out beside me on the threshing floor. But I also fell asleep. When I woke up, I put out a startled hand and found only a warm hollow, a warm absence.[47]

The sheer intensity of this experience must have inspired his headily erotic teenage verse only recently published in the *Cuadernos de Temuco* (Temuco Notebooks).[48] He even refers specifically to crossing 'wheatfields in search of your silken hands and your golden ponytails . . .'[49]

> Like fallow ground I felt your body open up
> to receive all that I can offer you.
> . . . To feel, to tremble, oh land, to sink, sink, sink
> like the sun at dusk[50]

There is a quiet longing in many of these poems that reflects the tormented nature of Neftalí's early, fleeting love affairs in Temuco.

Inés Valenzuela, the widow of Diego Muñoz, told me she believed Neftalí was also in love with another girl at this time – Amalia Alviso, the daughter of a Temuco family that was responsible for supplying electricity to the town.

Inés Valenzuela recalls Amalia, whom she later met and became good friends with, despite a twenty-year age gap, as 'very good-looking, very dark with black eyes. She was very charming and full of life. Pablo was in love with her when he was a child. He invited her in later years to his house in the Avenida Lynch in Santiago, but by then it was just friendship.'[51]

Young Neftalí often felt the profound loneliness of being 'a little child poet, dressed in black'. Overcome, at times, by a sense that no one fully appreciated his precocity, he would escape his everyday existence by 'taking a pinch of salt, leaping up a cherry tree, making himself comfortable and eating a hundred cherries at a time'.[52]

Some of Neftalí's early influences were the French poets – Baudelaire, Rimbaud, Mallarmé, Apollinaire – whose verse he copied out from collections lent to him. And, as Diego Muñoz, pointed out,

Pablo Neruda was born when a new phenomenon was hitting Spanish-language poetry: Rubén Darío. The [modernist] Nicaraguan poet was everywhere: he was discussed, he was commented on, he was listened to and he was praised – and attacked – passionately, as had happened three centuries earlier with Góngora and Quevedo. For those of us who studied literature in the schools in those days, Rubén Darío took on the proportions of a colossus.[53]

Neftalí had his first work published at the age of thirteen, in 1917. It was not a poem, but an article, entitled 'Entusiasmo y perseverancia', signed Neftalí Reyes, which appeared in the Temuco daily newspaper, *La Mañana*, on 18 July. In the article, he called for people to follow their desires with enthusiasm and perseverance: 'Examples such as those of Columbus and Marconi and so many others should not be discarded, because they lead to a more honourable life, and without them it is impossible to live.'[54]

The editor of *La Mañana* was the man Neruda believed to be his uncle, Orlando Mason, one of Neruda's first heroes. In provincial Temuco, 'among these bourgeois in a tranquil village where a poet is treated almost like a thief',[55] Mason was the inspiration young Neftalí needed. Mason would read his poetry aloud at public recitals in Temuco, including in Neftalí's own home.[56] He was also a fighter for social justice, the kind of fighter Pablo Neruda would become years later.

Under the pretext of exterminating bandits, the colonisers dispossessed the inhabitants of their land, and Indians were killed as if they were rabbits ... After independence, after 1810, the Chileans devoted themselves to killing Indians with the same enthusiasm as the Spanish invaders. Temuco was the last heart of the Araucanian Indian. Orlando Mason protested about all this. It was beautiful to see his newspaper among barbaric and violent people, defending the just against the cruel, the weak against the powerful.[57]

Mason refused to conform. From the pages of his newspaper, he condemned abuses, and named names. One of these names was probably responsible for burning down the offices of *La Mañana*, an event which left Neftalí shocked and appalled. Although the perpetrator was never found, the fire at *La Mañana* certainly looked like a revenge attack, rather than an accident, and stirred in the future Neruda the angry desire to follow in his uncle's footsteps.

There was one more astonishing secret in the Reyes family past. Orlando Mason was not Neruda's uncle at all. Orlando was the offspring of a love affair years earlier between Neruda's future stepmother, Trinidad Candia Marverde, and Rudecindo Ortega, a young man whom Carlos Mason had met at the Belén estate in Parral and, admiring his energy, had summoned to Temuco to help co-ordinate his various business schemes. In other words, Orlando Mason – the 'uncle' that Neruda always looked up to – was in fact his elder stepbrother, although Orlando was brought up tenderly in the Mason household, believing his father to be Carlos.

But, as with Laurita, these remarkable new revelations should take nothing away from the influence and importance Orlando had in Neruda's early life. What they may change is our attitude to Trinidad, the *mamadre*: she, too, had a past that had to be concealed and which could explain her quiet, subdued behaviour around the house and her seemingly placid acceptance of her husband's frequent lapses.

Meanwhile, Rodolfo, after his early years living virtually in the wild in Coipúe, had found work at a hardware store in Temuco. One day, José del Carmen was summoned to an urgent meeting at the Temuco school. There, to his astonishment, the music teacher informed him that Rodolfo had been accepted as a singer at the Music Conservatory in Santiago, on a full scholarship. As Rodolfo's son Bernardo later recalled,

> All his life, my father, Rodolfo, loved to sing. He was a lyrical singer, but he did not have Pablo's luck in being sent to study when still young. Pablo was always the privileged one. He went to Santiago, and his lodgings and university were paid for. My father wanted to do the same – he wanted to study singing at the Santiago conservatory. But when José del Carmen heard of these plans, he cried out: 'Haven't I got enough troubles with one idiot who wants to be a poet – and now you want to be a singer!' He was furious. He beat Rodolfo with pointed boots, and my father told me that the pain was so acute afterwards that he couldn't sit down for several days.[58]

After Orlando Mason, Neruda's other major early influence in Temuco was Gabriela Mistral, then known as Lucila Godoy, who arrived to head the girls' school in 1919. From his first meeting, as a fifteen-year-old, with the great Chilean poet – in 1945, Mistral would become the first Latin American to win the Nobel Prize for Literature – Neftalí recalled her as a tall, badly dressed woman with sunburnt face, brilliant white teeth and a full, generous smile who, when the women of Temuco suggested she put a hat on, replied: 'Why? It would be ridiculous, like putting a hat on the Andes.' He was too shy to show her his early writings. Instead, she gave him reading material which he avidly consumed: Tolstoy, Dostoyevsky, Chekhov.

The teenager had already started to write poems in earnest, signing them Neftalí Reyes. Sixteen of them were published in a Santiago general-interest magazine, *Corre-Vuela*, in late-1918 and early-1919, and others in a number of student journals. Many are simply and heavily autobiographical, with titles like 'These Fifteen Years of Mine' and 'About My Life as a Student'. The first, published in *Corre-Vuela* on 10 October 1918, when Neftalí was fourteen, was called 'Nocturne':

> It's night time: I'm alone and sad,
> thinking in the light of a flickering candle,
> about joy and pain,
> about tired old age
> and handsome, arrogant youth . . .
>
> When night arrives, as dark
> as a wolf's mouth, I lose myself
> in reflections full of bitterness . . .[59]

Neruda himself, in later years, described these as 'my execrable first poems'.[60] Yet, though many are mannered, others reveal fascinating insights into his state of mind as an adolescent and some of the themes which would dominate his mature verse: love, solitude, rain, bells.

He was undoubtedly feeling his way. In 1919, his poem entitled 'Communión ideal' (Ideal Communion) was awarded third prize in the Maule Floral Games, in Cauquenes, near Parral, and a year later, another of his early efforts won him first prize in the Temuco Spring Games Competition.

In a poem written in May 1920, he described himself as 'drunk with love' – but this was no non-sexual romanticism. It is overtly physical:

> Give me two warm breasts and two lovely eyes.
> If you don't give me those, what good will my love be?[61]

In another interesting poem, written in July 1920, he recognised that it was unlikely that poetry alone would ever keep him alive. It is

almost as if he were feeling guilt, however temporary, at ignoring his
father's desire for him to do something 'useful' with his life:

> . . . Tomorrow or the day after.
> I'll be as bourgeois as any lawyer,
> as any little doctor wearing glasses with
> his route blocked to the new moon . . .
> What the hell, in life, like in the magazines,
> a poet has to graduate as a dentist![62]

One of Neruda's most intriguing – if little-noted – poems, 'Los
rosales de la soledad', (The Rosebuds of Solitude), likewise written in
1920, refers to the healing power of the rose. Some critics have made
something of a cottage industry out of the importance of the rose in
Neruda's poetry throughout his life, pointing out that Rosa was the
name of his real mother and claiming that he felt an obsessive pain
every time he recalled that his birth had caused her death. Many of
these critical interpretations may be fanciful, but others have some
force, and in this 1920 poem, rose bushes can nourish man with 'sweet
branches of humility'. According to Volodia Teitelboim, his friend and
biographer, 'Neruda always felt like an orphan. Some say he spent his
life looking for his mother. This may be a psychoanalyst's interpretation, but I believe that there could be some truth in it. He was always a
big child who missed his mother.'[63]

Neruda's father was more than absent-mindedly unimpressed with
Neftalí's early verses; he could not stomach the idea of his son
sacrificing his studies to poetry, let alone considering such a bohemian
activity as a future career. In a fit of helpless rage, José del Carmen ran
to Neftalí's bedroom, threw his notebooks out of the window and
burnt them in the patio below.

Tensions with his father were growing so hurtful that Neftalí
realised drastic measures were needed. In October 1920, at the age
of sixteen, he decided to change his name to Pablo Neruda. It was not
an official move – he would not alter his name by deed poll until 28
December 1946 – but from now on, his writings would be signed
Pablo Neruda, in an attempt to gain independence, once and for all,
from his father's clutches.

The 'Pablo' may have been inspired by Neruda's love of the Italian
name Paolo from Italian poetry.[64] His new surname, it is generally

believed, was taken from the great Czech writer, Jan Neruda – Neftalí had read and admired a translation of one of his *Stories of Mala Strana* in a Santiago journal. However, at least one critic has speculated that it may have come from the pianist Wilhelmina Norman-Neruda, a real violinist who was mentioned in the Sherlock Holmes story, *A Study in Scarlet*. The poet was an avid reader of detective novels – and the Conan-Doyle stories – at the time, and remained so all his life. *A Study in Scarlet* had appeared in a Spanish translation in Santiago (as *Un crimen extraño*) in 1908, whereas Jan Neruda's best-known work was not translated into Spanish until 1923, long after Neftalí chose his new name.[65] And in an astonishingly bizarre but intriguing piece of recent detective work, of which Sherlock Holmes himself would have been proud, a Temuco-born doctor, Enrique Robertson Alvarez, has unearthed what he sees as 'evidence' that Neruda actually did take his name from the woman violinist. Neftalí would certainly, Robertson feels, have seen posters advertising her concerts in Temuco – and violins do, indeed, appear at the most unexpected moments in Neruda's verse, including the beautiful reference to 'a violin-coloured insect' in the *Odas elementales* (Elementary Odes), 'El hombre invisible' [The Invisible Man].[66]

However, interviews with Neruda, and his intense curiosity to visit the birthplace of his namesake during his later trips to Prague, indicate that the Czech origin is the more likely one. In his memoirs, Neruda claimed that he picked the name out of a newspaper because he liked the sound of the word, without knowing it belonged to a writer.[67]

The first poem Neruda signed with his new name was called 'Lost Love'. Like so many of his poems at the time, it is preoccupied with fleeting passion. Rudecindo Ortega Mason – a son of the Rudecindo who had had a brief affair with his stepmother, Trinidad – who was a student at Santiago University at the time, had the bright idea of taking some of Neruda's poems back to the capital and managed to persuade the Students' Federation journal, *Claridad*, to publish them. Pablo's promise was recognised, but for the moment it was as a prose-writer that he was in demand.

1920 was a bloody year in Chile. Although the country had remained neutral in the First World War and the boom in Chilean export commodities had fuelled a resurgence in general economic activity and industrial expansion, the prosperity was short-lived. The worldwide post-war depression was exacerbated in Chile by the fall in demand for natural nitrate – one of Chile's main sources of revenue – as hostilities ceased, and the development in Germany of synthetic nitrate production. Much of Chile's labour force migrated south, away from the mining areas, in search of work. Labour agitation grew markedly in 1918 and 1919 with strikes and massive demonstrations, as well as violent clashes with the police. A strike in Puerto Natales in February 1919 was brutally put down at a cost of fifteen dead. Although the formation of the Communist Party did not take place until 1922, the FOC (Chilean Workers' Federation) was already extremely active (it mustered a gathering of 100,000 people in Santiago in 1919). The Communist movement in Chile would become one of the most active in all Latin America, due to the lengthy tradition of trade union representation in the copper and nitrate mines.

In 1920, Chile's outgoing President Juan Luis Sanfuentes, presided over a brutal repression of the student uprisings in Santiago on 21 July. The Students' Federation headquarters in the capital were destroyed and a young student poet, José Domingo Gómez Rojas, was beaten and tortured so severely in custody he went mad and died in a mental hospital later that year.

In the midst of this political turmoil, the seventeen-year-old Neruda was appointed president of the Ateneo Literario in Temuco and secretary of the Cautín Students' Association. In October 1920, he also became a correspondent in Temuco for *Claridad*, and as the grim news of the crushing of the student rebellion in Santiago reached him, he was deeply saddened. The seeds of genuine political commitment stirred within him. He became directly involved when a student leader, José Santos González-Vera, sought refuge in Temuco after the assault on the student headquarters and turned to Neruda for support.

The first article he signed as Neruda reflected not only his struggle to escape from his provincial life but, also his anger at 'exploitation, capital, abuse'.

His next stop would be university in Santiago, where he would begin, he said, to feel repulsion towards the bourgeoisie, and to identify with restless, dissatisfied people, artists and criminals.

2

A bohemian in Santiago

1921–27

When the sixteen-year-old Pablo Neruda stepped off the night train from Temuco into the warmth of Santiago in March 1921, wearing a black suit, a wide-brimmed hat and a striking black cape which his father had given him, he found a city that 'smelled of gas fumes and coffee. Thousands of buildings housed strangers and bedbugs. Public transport was handled by small, rickety trams that struggled along with a loud clanking of iron and bells.'[1]

The Chilean capital, which had grown dramatically in size in the early years of the twentieth century (the population had doubled every twenty years since the 1865 census)[2] was wracked by political upheaval and student and worker riots in 1920 and the aftermath both fascinated and horrified Neruda.

The fate of the student poet José Domingo Gómez Rojas inspired Neruda to write a poem, 'La canción de la fiesta' (The Festival Song) which won the 1921 Students' Federation poetry competition, earning him some renown but no money – a situation that was going to be his lot for some time to come.

When Neruda was asked to read his winning poem in public, a fellow poet, Roberto Meza Fuentes, was so afraid that Pablo would be made fun of for his thin voice that he agreed to read the prize verse instead. (Neruda himself claimed that he had been too nervous to read the lines; he did, however, acknowledge that his voice was 'monotonous, typical of men from the south who have listened to the rain falling for so long.')[3]

Instead of attending classes at the Pedagogical Institute, where he was studying to become a teacher of French, Neruda spent much of his initial period in Santiago listening to the speeches of celebrated anarchists like Juan Gandulfo at the Students' Federation headquarters. Gandulfo was small and balding but totally fearless: once, a soldier who had a reputation as a brutal killer challenged him to a duel; he accepted, learned to fence in two weeks, and easily won the contest.

At the offices of the student magazine, *Claridad*, for which he was soon writing a weekly political column and poems, Neruda met the chief editor, Alberto Rojas Giménez, who wore a large hat, striking ties and imposing side-whiskers, a man who managed to dress like a dandy without having a peso to his name. A lover of books, wine and women, he was, in Neruda's words, 'a joyously persistent and spontaneous bohemian'. Rojas also wrote poetry, even founding his own school of poetry called 'agu', which, he said, rose out of man's primal scream, the first verse of the newborn.

Rojas taught the young Neruda – who admitted that he was still a 'boy' when he arrived in Santiago – to dress less sombrely, to smoke and to make birds out of paper. He lit up Neruda's life. Although Pablo insisted that he had avoided being infected by Rojas's cynicism and love of alcohol, another friend of Neruda's, Orlando Oyarzún, thought that Pablo's friendship with Rojas Giménez was decisive in persuading him to give up any intention of becoming a French teacher and to dedicate himself instead to literature. 'The whitewashed mud walls of Pablo's room were covered in [Rojas Giménez's] drawings, verses and sentences of comic solemnity, all of which were aimed at pulling Pablo out of his melancholic withdrawal.'[4]

Among the books on the tiny bookshelf in Neruda's student room were many by the Russian poet, Pushkin, as well as poems by the French Communist poet, Paul Eluard, a novel by Leonid Andreyev and works by the Spanish novelist, Pío Baroja. 'And I have never forgotten,' wrote Tomás Lago, a poet who later became a critic and essayist and who was one of Pablo's closest friends at the time, 'the reproduction of the body of Chatterton, an English adolescent poet, after he had committed suicide, lying on his bed in his attic,' which Neruda had on his wall. Lago thought it showed something of the inner world of a poet about to be born.[5]

Meanwhile, Neruda was starting to write confident political poetry, such as 'A los poetas de Chile' calling for the release of the ailing student, Joaquín Cifuentes Sepúlveda, from jail.

Neruda had arrived a very shy young man in Santiago, but an article he wrote for *Claridad* less than four months after settling in the capital shows the sixteen-year-old's uninhibited attitude to sex. 'Young and strong, he [male youth] is an animal simply looking for an outlet for his natural power . . . The streets are full of hundreds of eager, vigorous women, and man goes off on his quest again . . .'[6]

Other companions, all equally impoverished, included Rubén Azócar, a short, witty man who quickly became a close friend; Homero Arce, who later worked for years as Neruda's loyal secretary, and Alvaro Hinojosa, who spoke English perfectly after studying at a New York University and smoked Havana cigars. Alvaro was doggedly full of extravagant financial schemes to make them all rich, including trade in sea-wolf skins. To Neruda's immense delight, he soon also met up again with fellow school pupils from Temuco: Diego Muñoz, Gerardo Seguel and Juvencio Valle.

The nights were spent in Santiago bars, talking about literature with his new-found friends. 'For a provincial like me, finding people who spoke about Baudelaire, who knew the French poets, attracted me enormously. We spent whole nights exchanging discoveries.'[7]

He could no longer count on his father for his monthly allowance, however: that had been cut off when José del Carmen found out that his son was wasting his time writing poems rather than studying. In difficulties, Neruda wrote back to his half-sister, Laurita: 'I'm too young not to eat every day.'[8] The little money Neruda did possess in Santiago came from his beloved stepmother, Trinidad, who surreptitiously passed it on to him via Laurita.

Homero Arce recalled Pablo as one of the key members of the group:

Tall, thin, dark-clothed, naturally friendly; the presence of this young poet set the tone for the atmosphere. In spite of the immensity of his verse, he spoke without pretentiousness. Only those friends present, with their petty concerns, seemed to have any importance for him. There was frivolous humour in his conversation . . . and he had a lazy voice which many people imitated comically.[9]

For his part, Tomás Lago wrote:

> Every day, the young Reyes . . . could be seen strolling with his thin
> face and his imperturbable eyes, accompanied by a girlfriend. There
> are portraits at the time which show what he was like in those days.
> A pensive boy, dressed in black, obsessed by great ideas about which
> he did not speak, silent, studious and lost in thought.[10]

According to Lago, Neruda drank only coffee at the time, and put all
his energy into reading and writing poetry.

But Lago's view of the bohemian Neruda as an essentially sober,
serious creature is strikingly at odds with that of Diego Muñoz, who
accompanied him to cabaret bars, and on at least one occasion went
home with one of the singers while Pablo took home the other: 'The
writers of the time did not usually gather in the soda bars or cafés, but
preferred the beer halls and the bars.' When they weren't reciting
Baudelaire, Rimbaud and Verlaine by heart, they 'sang in French,
English or German, drinkers' or sailors' songs'.

Orlando Oyarzún remembered eating at a Chinese restaurant,
oddly named El Tokio, with Pablo and Tomás Lago. The first thing
they did when they sat down was to cover the bread with salt and olive
oil and eat ravenously. On one visit, the waiters refused to serve them:
'You're using all our oil up,' they complained.

At one stage, a bossy interloper invaded the circle: Pablo de Rokha,
a young Chilean poet who attempted to set himself up as the leader of
the group – with later repercussions. De Rokha went on to become a
ferocious, lifelong enemy of Neruda. He devoted a whole book to a
savage attack on his fellow Chilean poet: *Neruda y yo* (Neruda and
Me).

It was, however, an exciting time to be in Santiago if you were
young. Despite the political tensions, there was a new flamboyance.
The tango had recently crossed the border from Argentina into Chile –
though Neruda never learnt it. Diego Muñoz recalled,

> At the time of our bohemian period, we danced the tango, the
> foxtrot, the charleston. Rojas Giménez, Orlando Oyarzún and I
> were the great dancers. But Pablo never danced. He also liked song,
> but he could never sing even moderately in tune. He would remain
> seated with his face in one hand and a melancholy air. Rojas
> Giménez made fun of him. He told him that a poet had to be
> cheerful.[11]

Chileans were rediscovering poetry at this time. 'They knew lots of poets' verse by heart,' Neruda said later. 'Chileans have always had a weakness for poetry. Maybe this is due to the isolation of the country, which is both volcanic and maritime.'[12]

In an interesting essay on Neruda's poetry, the Soviet writer Ilya Ehrenburg, who in later years became a great friend of the Chilean and translated his works into Russian, described the state of Latin American literature at the time Neruda arrived in Santiago:

> The poetry of Latin America was at a crossroads. In 1916, Rubén Darío, the last, masterful representative of the so-called 'Modernista' current, had died – the poet who knew how to combine Verlaine's autumn violins with the sounding of the summer drums in Nicaragua. After Darío's death, various schools and literary circles tried to prolong the poetry of the past . . . Some eagerly imitated the latest fashions from Paris . . . Pablo Neruda absorbed the concerns of the old Spanish-language poetry, without neglecting the poetic and spiritual experiences of the French *poètes maudits* – principally Baudelaire and Arthur Rimbaud. The poet also understood the vitality of popular Chilean poetry.[13]

Ehrenburg reminds us that Neruda confessed to marvelling at the resonance of the poetry of the Soviet poet, Mayakovsky. In his youth, writes Ehrenburg, Neruda was influenced by Mayakovsky's 'sincerity, his rejection of conventions, his thunderous voice'.[14]

The first place Neruda lived in Santiago was a boarding house he had been recommended, at number 513 Calle Maruri. It was an address he never forgot. Not because of its luxury – quite the contrary: it was situated in a rough area of Santiago, on the north side of the Mapocho River. But it offered magnificent sunsets. It was Neruda's daily, mesmerising encounters with the multicoloured dusk which were to feed so much of his first book, *Crepusculario* [Book of Twilights], published in 1923.

'At that time, living in a rooming-house for students meant starvation. I wrote a lot more than I had up until then, but I ate much less. Some of the poets I knew in those days broke down under the strict diet of poverty.'[15]

Even worse: tuberculosis was rife in the capital, and had no cure. Neruda quickly lost several friends to the terrifying disease, and though he never mentioned the illness specifically in his poems or his memoirs, the black threat constantly hanging over student life can be read in much of *Crepusculario*. Neruda himself managed to avoid tuberculosis, which, given that he was living in extreme poverty and that he had been burdened with ill-health from childhood, was remarkable.

Diego Muñoz, who was studying law at the university, recalled one of Neruda's various abodes:

> It was a room at the back, with no more furniture in it than an iron bed with mattresses and some blankets, a box with a candle on it and another box with a flowerpot and a water-jug on top. Although it wasn't late, the candle was already lit and Pablo was writing . . . We greeted each other and I started chatting to him. Pablo went on writing and spoke to me from time to time. It wasn't out of disrespect: he did the same thing up to the last days of his life. It seems that not only did it not disturb him to have someone next to him interrupting his work – he enjoyed it. Rather than it getting in his way, it appeared to help him.[16]

Neruda's first well-appointed room was on the Avenida España. He shared it with Alejandro Serani, the schoolfriend from Temuco who had sat down with him so patiently by the River Cautín and coached him in mathematics. But they didn't stay long there. Quite apart from the expense of these lodgings, the landlady turned out to be a character out of a Balzac novel, spying on her residents and their visiting girlfriends.

So Neruda moved to a cheaper tenement house, which he rented with the poet Rubén Azócar and the writer and critic Tomás Lago. This home too was short-lived. Pablo heard from Laurita that his father was due to arrive in Santiago for surgery. Fearful that José del Carmen would track him down and reproach him, he moved back to the Avenida España until he was sure that his father had returned to Temuco.

One night, when Neruda joined his friends at a restaurant in Santiago's Calle General Mackenna to see Rubén Azócar off on a trip to Mexico, they found that, even though it was a cheap eating-place, they did not have enough money to pay the bill and they all had to leave their jackets behind. Azócar never forgot the sight of all his friends leaving the restaurant in shirtsleeves. Rubén would soon have other matters to occupy his mind, however. During his time abroad, he was arrested by the Peruvian police in Callao, on suspicion of being a leftist, and locked up in Lima's Panóptico Prison for twenty-one days.

Neruda was meanwhile reviewing books in the student journal, *Claridad*. He was bowled over by *Desolación*, the first collection of poems by his fellow Chilean poet, Gabriela Mistral – whom he had met as a school headmistress back in Temuco. He also reviewed poetry collections by Rubén Azócar and by the Uruguayan Carlos Sabat Ercasty, who was to have an influence on Neruda's own poetic development shortly afterwards.

By now, Neruda was in love – with at least two women at once. In the spring of 1920, he had met a girl called Teresa Vázquez in Temuco; she had just been crowned queen of the town's Floral Games. She later changed her name to Teresa León Bettiens, when her mother married for the second time. Before leaving for Santiago, Neruda met Teresa on the beach in Puerto Saavedra, and they shared a delight in dressing up in Mapuche or Andalusian costumes.

Neruda clearly missed Teresa in Santiago. From 1922 to 1924, he continued to write passionate letters to her and was delighted when she replied. 'How sweet and lovely it is to receive letters from one's faraway beloved, from you, and to love once again and to feel happiness again.' He called Teresa the 'Queen of the Spring, whereas I am King of Autumn and Winter'.

Between 1921 and 1923, Neruda wrote a number of poems dedicated to Teresa, his 'Terusa'. These have recently been collected in Hernán Loyola's new edition of Neruda's complete works, under the title of 'Album Terusa'.[17]

Loyola believes that, as the poet first met Teresa in the spring of 1920 (the same spring in which he began to use the pseudonym Pablo Neruda), he could have been hiding his own adolescent passion behind the literary masks of the names Paolo and Francesca. Half a century later, he would use the same device, with the names Rhodo and Rosía, to conceal another illicit love. There was a part of Pablo Neruda that never grew up.

From Santiago Neruda bombarded Teresa with letters full of love, need and self-doubt.

You know, I suddenly fall into a fit of loneliness, fatigue, sadness, which prevent me from doing anything and embitter my life. Why should I write to you at those moments! And then, at the most unexpected times, how sweet, how beautiful it is to receive letters from afar, from the woman I love, from you, and to love life again and find new joy! . . .

In the holidays Pablo left Santiago to meet Teresa in Temuco and Puerto Saavedra, but things were no longer the same. Too much had happened to him in the capital, and by 1924, the twenty-year-old was writing: 'We're so far apart, aren't we, Terusa? We're growing apart, aren't we? Or is it just my impression?'[18]

His impression was correct – but what really separated them, even more than the large geographical distance, was the opposition of Teresa's parents. According to her niece, Rosa León Muller, the León Bettiens family considered themselves high-class in Temuco, and regarded the Reyes family as inferior, almost outside society altogether. 'What's more, they had a nickname for him – "Buitre" [Vulture], because of the cape and wide-brimmed hat he wore.'[19]

Neruda never forgot Terusa.

I'm no longer in love with her, it's true, but maybe I love her.
Love is so short, and forgetting is so long,

he wrote, in a beautiful depiction of adolescent turmoil, in the celebrated Poem 20, devoted to her. He dedicated two poems to her forty years later in *Memorial de Isla Negra*. And despite her family's fervent opposition, she too seems to have taken a long time to get over Neruda. She married a typewriter repairman years after her split from Pablo, and died a year before Neruda, in 1972.

But while he was writing passionate letters and poems to Teresa, Neruda was also in love with another woman: Albertina Rosa Azócar, the sister of his friend, Rubén. They met, soon after Pablo's arrival in Santiago, in the corridors of the Pedagogical Institute. Albertina recalled their first encounter in a 1978 interview: 'He was sixteen and I was eighteen. We were both studying French and we became very close friends . . . We enjoyed talking to poets who were friends, like Romeo Murga, my brother Rubén, Tomás Lago . . . With Romeo, we became much closer and that's when things really started . . .'[20]

Albertina Azócar, like Pablo, had arrived in the capital from the south of Chile – though not from Cautín province, but from Arauco, in Lota Alto, near the coal mines. Her parents were both teachers.

> He was very quiet, like me. We enjoyed walking in silence and broke that silence only to exchange ideas. But we liked to walk beside one another, living in our own world. We were different with other people. We would go to the students' ball at the Palacio de Bellas Artes, and there were also recitals and concerts at the Pedagogical Institute on Saturdays . . . My sister, Adelina, couldn't stand him [Pablo], because in those days, poets did not have a good image – they were seen as eccentric and bohemian.[21]

As early as 10 November 1921, when his passion for Teresa was still at its peak, and he was meeting her in the holidays, Neruda was also writing a love poem to Albertina, calling her a 'butterfly . . .

> at the hour of the roses
> the hour that never ceases.
> Harass,
> kiss,
> the powerful head
> of the one who seizes you,
> brushes against you,
> kisses you everywhere,
> sweet
> Albertina
> Rosa.'

It was a passionate juggling act that Neruda was to repeat many times in his life. Indeed, the 111 letters that he wrote to Albertina stretched into July 1932, by which time he had already been married to his first wife for two years. He continued to write to Albertina after she left Santiago to pursue her studies at the University of Concepción. In a letter dated 16 September 1923, he referred to a poem dedicated to her which had been published in a newspaper. He calls it 'The poem of the absent one'. This would later become the famous Poem 15 of the *Twenty Love Poems*.

The letters to Albertina reinforce the sense of Neruda as a young man in a confused, almost unstable frame of mind. His was a long-lasting adolescence. Sometimes, he could be very loving, calling Albertina 'Netocha Neruda' (her favourite epithet), while at other times he used violent, hate-filled names, his anger fuelled by the belief that she was rejecting him. The truth was that it was, indeed, a one-sided relationship much of the time. This was due in part to the fact that Albertina's family – like Teresa's – had great difficulty in accepting Neruda as an appropriate suitor.

As Albertina recalled years later:

> I was physically with Pablo for just two years, which was the time I spent at the Pedagogical Institute in Santiago. After the holidays, I wasn't allowed to return and my father enrolled me at the University of Concepción, where I finished my French teaching course. I think my sister [Adelina] had a lot to do with it. He wrote lots of letters to me, and came to see me as much as he could . . . I loved Pablo intensely, but at that time things were very different from now . . . He wrote more often than I did and he became very indignant when more than ten days passed without receving news from me. I loved him greatly, but I am not a very demonstrative person. Just imagine it: I had to pick up his letters without my parents seeing me and the same went for my replying to him, because they controlled my every movement – I couldn't even leave the house to walk around the corner. It was a terrible situation.[22]

Nevertheless, the couple still found ways to travel by train together in the university holidays. They would separate at San Rosendo – the small town where Neruda's half-sister had been kept hidden away after her birth – and Albertina would continue on to Concepción while Pablo would return to the family home in Temuco.

Albertina and Teresa were not Neruda's only girlfriends at this time. Among those who visited Pablo's lodgings in Echaurren Street was Laura Arrué. Although she was one of a number, there is some evidence that this relationship may have been quite significant. Laura kept a remarkable album which included informal sketches by Neruda and a list of recommended reading for the girl he called 'Lala' or 'Milala'.[23]

But more than anything else, Neruda was sitting watching the twilight and writing the poems that would comprise his own first book. He had to make many personal sacrifices to ensure that

Crepusculario saw the light of day at all. It was published in 1923 by Editorial Claridad (the Chilean Students' Federation publishing house) and illustrated by the student leader, Juan Gandulfo.

> I had setbacks and successes every day, trying to pay for the first printing. I sold the few pieces of furniture I owned. The watch which my father had solemnly given me, on which he had had two little flags enamelled, soon went off to the pawnbroker's. My black poet's suit followed the watch. The printer was adamant and, in the end, when the edition was all ready and the covers had been pasted on, he said to me, with an evil look: 'No. You are not taking a single copy until you pay me for the whole lot.'[24]

Financial help to publish this first book also came from a most improbable source: the right-wing critic, Hernán Díaz Arrieta, better known as 'Alone', who recognised his talent at once. Recklessly, however, Neruda signed away the rights to his book to the publisher for 500 pesos – the equivalent of less than five dollars in those days – and then treated his friends, who were waiting outside the notary's door, to a lavish meal at Santiago's best restaurant, La Bahía.

Crepusculario is a precocious, if uneven, collection. Although it appeared in 1923, when Neruda was only nineteen years old, it contains some poems written in May 1920, before he even arrived in Santiago. Some poems are virtually direct descendants of the outpourings in his Temuco notebooks. Others, however, reveal a new maturity and confidence.

The book consists of forty-eight poems distributed across five sections. They are metrically traditional, but all kinds of influences can be felt. Neruda had not severed his emotional ties with the French poetry he had loved from schooldays. Verlaine's *Poèmes Saturniens* had been published more than half a century earlier, in 1866, but it had contained poems such as 'Crépuscule du soir mystique' and 'Soleil couchant' which find an instant echo in Neruda's own dazzled reactions to the dusk from his boarding-house balcony. Like Verlaine, Neruda sometimes invokes a deity. But in his collection, Verlaine specifically says that he does not believe in God. Like Verlaine, Neruda includes a poem with an English title (the celebrated 'Farewell') – Verlaine had called one 'Nevermore'.

Closer to home, Rubén Darío's modernism still cast a huge shadow over young poets. The Modernists' view of the poet as an outcast from bourgeois society fitted in well with Neruda's own experience of those Santiago bohemian days. And, atheist (actually, in later years he called himself an agnostic) though he was, Neruda – in his troubled state of mind – was well aware of Pythagoreanism, the belief that man is part of a great chain of being which evolved form the humblest rocks to the divine. Darío thought the poet's duty was to transcend the contradictions of ordinary man and point up that universal harmony. And just as Rubén Darío alludes to figures from Greek mythology in *Prosas Profundas*, Neruda's *Crepusculario* refers to Helen of Troy.

But *Crepusculario* is not a typical Modernista book: the rhythms are too traditional, for one thing, and the themes too diverse. And, as the authority on Latin American literature, Jean Franco, has pointed out, 'whatever [Neruda's] reading of other poetry may have been, he had a strong personal statement to make, for which he appropriated and developed new forms and techniques . . . For him, poetry was always intuition, "physical absorption of the world".'[25]

If the themes in *Crepusculario* are varied, a single tone runs through this first collection, and it is one of melancholy, sadness, even depression. As the Chilean critic Hugo Montes has noted, Neruda frequently uses variations of the verb *caer* (to fall), and describes the sensation of departure.[26] Indeed, one entire poem, 'La tarde sobre los tejados' (Evening over the Roofs) is built on the verb *caer*. But melancholy is something Neruda seems to enjoy, as if he feels it is an appropriate mood for poets. He took years to shake off this conviction: in a letter to the Argentinian critic, Héctor Eandi, from the Far East in 1928, Neruda was still writing: 'That depressing moment, so unfortunate for many, was noble material for me.'

Love and eroticism also infuse many of the poems in *Crepusculario*, but, as in his earlier writing, the love is full of tension, doubts, and frustrated yearnings for communion, for escape from solitude. Many girlfriends came to share Neruda's bed in his various lodgings, but they were brief adventures which satisfied him sexually rather than emotionally.

> Curve of the belly, hidden
> and open like a fruit
> or a wound.

Sweet naked knee
leaning against my knees
sweet naked knee.

Tangle of hair
between the round offerings
of your breasts.

A trace that lingers in the bed
a trace that sleeps in the soul,
crazed words[27]

But what kind of love was Neruda looking for at this time? *Crepusculario* is full of feelings of emptiness and loneliness. Was it this hollowness that induced so much easy promiscuity? Or was it his Don Juan-like existence that gave him such feelings of inner hollowness?

I like the love of sailors
who kiss and go their own way.

They leave behind a promise.
And never come back.

In every port a woman waits:
the sailors kiss and go their own way.

One day they sleep with death
on the sea bed.

I love the love that is handed out
in kisses, bed, bread.

Love that may last for ever
or is fleeting.

Love that wants to free itself
to love some more.[28]

Such a restless seaman's life seems to prefigure Neruda's own urge to leave Santiago and Chile, to explore other lands. It is also a lament for the sea of his youth, written in a town surrounded by mountains. He appears only to find a sense of harmony in the sunset which gives the book its title. The euphoria this engenders even leads him to thank a God he does not believe in:

> God – where did you find, to light up the sky,
> this marvellous copper sunset?
> It taught me how to fill myself with joy again.[29]

For an atheist, there are a surprisingly large number of references to God, even if his attitude to God is hardly positive. In the poem 'El padre' (The Father), Neruda writes:

> Ask God why I was given
>   what I was given and why then
> I came to know such loneliness on earth and in heaven.

It could be that Neruda was consciously following a literary trend of the time in his invocation of a deity, but even if he was not religious in any way, Hugo Montes points out a biblical simplicity in many of the utterances in this first collection: 'I'm sad, but I'm always sad . . . As if crying was a seed and I the only furrow in the earth . . . If you're hungry, eat from my bread . . .'[30]

What is surprising – in view of the many hours Neruda spent listening to radical leaders speaking at the Students' Federation headquarters – is the total absence in *Crepusculario* of any political poems, or even political references. It is as if, for now at least, he had consciously decided to reserve political ideas for articles in journals such as *Claridad* and *Zig-Zag*. The only overt sign of his commitment comes in the dedication: to Juan Gandulfo, who had played a leading role in getting *Crepusculario* published, by helping with the wood engravings.

As soon as it was published in Santiago in 1923 *Crepusculario* was well received by Chilean readers, many of whom learnt the famous poem, 'Farewell', with its oft-cited first lines: '*Desde el fondo de tí, y arrodillado / un niño triste, como yo, nos mira*' (From the depths of you kneeling / a sad boy, like me, looks at us) by heart and recited it in the street.

The critics, by and large, were also impressed. Neruda must have been proud to find among his admirers a Chilean poet from the previous generation, Pedro Prado, whom he had admired as a Temuco schoolboy. Prado predicted a great future for Neruda, whom he compared to 'a tree that grows slowly, firm and tall . . . I can assure you that I know of no other poet in this land who has reached similar heights at his age.'[31] *Claridad* heaped acclaim on *Crepusculario* and its author, saying: 'With this book, Neruda places himself at the head of a literary generation holding out fruitful promise for our backward and humdrum intellectual milieu.'

Was Neruda really as unhappy in Santiago as he implies in some of these poems? Not if his fellow bohemians are to be believed. He would joyfully join in their all-night discussions: in practically the same breath, they would move from the French poet Apollinaire, to Chilean seafood. They would recite Baudelaire, Verlaine and Rimbaud by heart, and argue about James Joyce and Marcel Proust. 'Neither was yet translated into Spanish at that time, so we read them in French, which was then the universal language of culture,' recalled Diego Muñoz. 'Pablo read James Joyce with great devotion. It was *Ulysses*. And Pablo lent me Proust's *A la recherche du temps perdu*, recommending many of its pages.'[32]

For all the extrovert conversation, Neruda remained shy: 'I sought refuge in poetry with the intensity of someone timid,' he later wrote in his memoirs;[33] and he would remain shy for the rest of his life. Perhaps the nocturnal sessions in the bars hid a basic insecurity, dissatisfaction, isolation.

Oddly, this did not prevent him being a great success with women – although not all his friends could fathom why. 'Pablo had a lot of luck with women, but I think that this was through his poetry and his prestige as a triumphant poet rather than his looks, because he was thin, consumptive-looking, and he wore his hair disconcertingly long,' said Diego Muñoz.[34]

During one of his visits back to Temuco, during the summer holidays in January 1923, Pablo was preparing to go to sleep at midnight when he decided to take a last look out at the night. There, staring back at him, was the stunning southern Chilean night sky, vast and clear, covered in stars. 'I rushed to my desk and wrote, with heart beating high, as if I were taking dictation, the first poem of a book which would have many titles and would end up as *El hondero entusiasta* [The Ardent Slingsman].'³⁵

But the magic of that moment did not last long. When he read the poem to his friend Aliro Oyarzún, Orlando's brother, Aliro immediately asked him whether Pablo had not been directly influenced by another poet. Shocked, Neruda asked who he could mean. 'Sabat Ercasty,' said Aliro, referring to the well-known Uruguayan poet. Still stunned, Pablo sent the poem to Sabat Ercasty, who replied: 'I have rarely read such a magnificently successful poem, but I have to tell you: there are echoes of Sabat Ercasty in your verse.'³⁶

This was Neruda's first jolting literary setback as an adult, comparable to the response he had received from his father when he showed him his first poem scrawled on a postcard. He put *El hondero entusiasta* away in a drawer and would not allow the book to be published for another decade. However, there are lines from the beginning of the book that provide an insight into his unsettled state of mind in the early 1920s – particularly the repeated: *Grito. Lloro. Deseo.* (I shout. I weep. I desire.), and the graphic sexual imagery reflects both his physical appetite and his continued yearning for satisfaction beyond the purely sexual: 'Fill yourself with me. Desire me, exhaust me . . .'

The night-long drinking and womanising seems to have done little to impair Neruda's literary drive and ambition, although for a time Ercasty's letter put an end to his ambition to write grand poetry. 'Looking for more unpretentious qualities, for the harmony of my own world, I began to write another book. *Veinte poemas* was the result.'³⁷

In June 1924, *Veinte poemas de amor y una canción desesperada* (Twenty Love Songs and a Song of Despair), the book which decisively made Neruda's name, appeared – and it remains the one from which people around the world can still quote copiously. Certain poems became engraved on the minds and on the lips of readers throughout Chile, and later the whole of the Spanish-speaking world, and remain so to this day. There's the first line of Poem 15: *Me gustas cuando callas, porque estás como ausente* (I like you when you're silent, because it's as though you're absent) and the beginning of Poem 20: *Puedo escribir los versos más tristes esta noche . . .* (I can write the saddest lines tonight).

Yet, Neruda's publisher, Carlos George Nascimento, was initially reluctant to publish *Twenty Love Poems,* and some of the admirers of *Crepusculario* felt cheated by the new book.

From the obscurity of *El hondero entusiasta* Neruda had gone back to what he – and most of his readers – at the time, at least, thought he did best: the simple, direct appeal to the emotions. Throughout his life he would be asked to recite poems from this book, and to explain their influences. Who were the women who inspired him? He refused to give names. He said they were many different loves. He told friends they corresponded to Marisol and Marisombra. Marisol represented the provinces, nature, sunlight, while Marisombra represented the woman in the grey beret. We know that Marisol was Teresa Vázquez and Marisombra was Albertina Azócar. But Poem 6 ('You were the grey beret . . .'), as Neruda himself stated, belongs to the nature in the south. On many occasions Neruda declared that the *Twenty Love Poems* belonged both to the atmosphere in the south of Chile (the abandoned wharfs, the seagulls) and also to the heady bohemian nights of conversation and sex in Santiago.

The British Neruda expert Professor Robert Pring-Mill believes that Poem 2 from *Twenty Love Poems* was composed with Laura Arrué in mind, because of the similarity between the girl described in the manuscript version and a picture of 'Milala' on the following page of the album – although Poem 2 is usually said to be addressed to Albertina. The first entry in Laura's album is the text of the first version of Poem 2.[38]

One of the strengths of *Twenty Love Poems* is that, although the collection is monothematic, Neruda finds so many different ways to explore the love between a man and a woman. And though Neruda's own confused, desperate, unfulfilled state of mind emerges throughout, the women he loves seem equally complex, equally plagued by contradictions. A woman is variously an object of sexual pleasure, a place of refuge, a dominator and dominated, a cosmic force and a very real physical presence, a woman in the poet's arms, and yet again unreachable. In Poem 14, Neruda describes his loved one before she even exists – that is, when she is merely a series of images sustained by his desire for her.

In broader terms, Woman, the loved one, forms a bridge between the lonely isolated individual and the warmth of the universe's mystery.

You are like the night, silent and starry
Your silence is like a star's, so distant and simple (Poem 15)

The 'Canción desesperada' (Song of Despair) at the end of *Twenty
Love Poems* is a cry of recognition that he can never reach the one he
loves.

Abandoned like a wharf at dawn,
Only the trembling shadow curls up in my hands.
Ah, beyond everything. Beyond everything,
It's time to leave. I'm abandoned.

What is hard to appreciate today is the extent to which *Twenty
Love Poems* scandalised many contemporary readers: Neruda was
communicating an erotic experience and an image of woman and
sexual relations which had simply not appeared before in Chilean
poetry.

Another kind of scandal surrounded one of the other poems in the
book: Poem 16, which begins:

In my sky at dusk you are like a cloud
and your colour and shape are the ones I love
You are mine, you are mine, sweet-lipped woman,
and my dreams are alive in your life.

Neruda's literary enemies – who included Pablo de Rokha and Vicente
Huidobro – were quick to claim that this was a plagiarisation of a
poem by the Indian poet, Rabindranath Tagore. Poem 30 from
Tagore's *The Gardener* does begin very similarly indeed: 'You are
the crepuscular cloud of the sky of my / fantasies. Your colour and
shape are those of / my love's yearning. You are mine, you are mine,
and you live / in my infinite dreams.' Both poems refer to 'harvester of
my song' and 'lonely dreams'. The Chilean poet Vicente Huidobro
spent the rest of his life repeating this accusation, and at one point
Neruda responded so heatedly that the International Association of
Writers in Defence of Culture wrote a letter to both men in 1937
urging them to mend their differences for the sake of the anti-fascist
struggle. They never did.

Tomás Lago and Diego Muñoz and a third loyal friend, Antonio

Rocco del Campo, leapt to Neruda's defence, but in the 1937 edition of *Twenty Love Poems*, Neruda felt compelled to write an explanatory note: 'One final word: Poem 16 is, in the main, a paraphrase of a poem by Rabindranath Tagore, from *The Gardener*. This has always been publicly known, and the fact has been published. Those bitter people who tried to take advantage of this circumstance, in my absence, have found themselves deservedly neglected in the face of the enduring vitality of this adolescent book.'

Despite what Neruda himself said about *Twenty Love Poems*, it would be a major mistake to see the book as only a direct appeal to the emotions, an attempt to escape the hermeticism of *El hondero entusiasta*, which he had put aside in a drawer. Some of the *Twenty Love Poems* are by no means easily interpreted. In Poem 9, he writes:

Between lips and voice something is dying
   something with a bird's wings, a thing of anguish and oblivion

Hernán Loyola has written:

Like the novels of Kafka, Proust and Joyce, the *Twenty Love Poems* shed the nineteenth century's psychological model in order to propose the embryo of a total vision of existence. The poet's interior is no longer placed in opposition to the world but encompasses it in the disjointed flow of consciousness (and the subconscious).[39]

As Robert Pring-Mill has pointed out, although there are two very different forms of poem in this book – highly structured quatrains on the one hand, and free verse on the other – 'even poems of the second kind show, on closer inspection, a pattern of unobstrusive echoes which is largely responsible for their poetic force.'[40]

Crepusculario and *Twenty Love Poems and a Song of Despair* had quickly earned Neruda what Diego Muñoz described as, 'the greatest fame ever witnessed in Chile, surpassed only by that still enjoyed by Rubén Darío.'[41] Literary critics fought with each other to gain interviews with the new celebrity, whose verse was now known by heart by youths all over Latin America. Everyone was talking about *Twenty Love Poems*.

You often found young people in the streets or public ways carrying the notorious volume – it was well-known because of its square format – reading and re-reading in a low voice, visibly striving to learn the verses by heart . . . Because they calculated that no normal girl could resist the spell of those verses which transformed them into a real woman. For these youths, the book became a love-bible . . .[42]

Not that Neruda took his new-found fame that seriously. Not yet.

Pablo did not appreciate those two books in the same way as he would later in life. For the moment, they were merely the expression of his personal, intimate feelings . . . More than one of us dared to suggest that both *Crepusculario* and *Twenty Love Poems* . . . would be translated into every language and would enjoy unimaginable circulations . . .

Fame did bring some rewards. Luis Enrique Délano, who later shared a house in Mexico City with Neruda for three years, remembered a night in September 1924 when Pablo invited fourteen of his friends to the Teatro Esmeralda cinema to see a Cecil B. De Mille film 'with sensational cardboard biblical reconstructions'. The cinema owner took one look at the large group, then another, admiring, glance at Neruda, and refused to accept an entrance payment from any of them.

Despite his fame, Neruda felt a lingering sense of dissatisfaction. As the tensions grew with Albertina, so they did with his father, and he turned to drinking copiously. His unhappiness did not stop him writing, however. By the age of twenty-two, quite apart from two collections of poems, he had published 108 articles in *Claridad*, and had also contributed to the literary sections of the dailies *El Mercurio* and *La Nación*, as well as journals such as *Zig-Zag, Atenea, Juventud* and *Alí Babá*.

In 1926 – a very productive year in Neruda's early literary career – three books were published. The first, *Tentativa del hombre infinito*, (Endeavour of the Infinite Man) published in January by Nascimento, in Santiago, was stunningly different from his two previous collections. It was misunderstood, if it was understood at all, and not well received, but Neruda himself remained proud of it for the rest of his life.

'In its small way, and within its minimal expression, it steered me more than other works of mine towards the path I was to follow. I've always seen *Tentativa del hombre infinito* as one of the true nuclei of my poetry.'[43]

The book certainly represented an experiment for Neruda: the absence of punctuation feeds the free flow of subconscious images. One critic, Alberto Cousté, sees the book as a single poem, a journey beginning and ending in the night. On this journey, Neruda 'tries out technical pirouettes which are not undetectable in other books of the time (combination of metres, of blank and free verse, trust in spontaneous association, phonetic link-ups).'[44]

Tentativa marked the beginning of a new and hermetic poetry. Gone are the pledges Neruda made to write simpler poetry after Sabat Ercasty's comments on *El hondero entusiasta*. Gone is the direct, romantic appeal to the senses. And yet the dominant tone is still one of sadness and solitude. At one point, he repeats the words: *Mi corazón está triste* (My heart is sad) and asks: 'Who did I buy the loneliness from that I possess tonight?'

There are moments of joy, as in the striking lines:

> I feel the contented baker's joy and then
> dawn breaks weak and violin-coloured
> with the sound of a bell with the smell of distance

And once again, love for a woman is the only thing that appears to give him unmixed pleasure.

With the money his publisher sent him for *Tentativa*, Neruda at last managed to furnish his room with a desk and some cushions, and even a live tortoise. But he did not really want to put down roots in Santiago. The more success he achieved, the more restless Neruda appeared to become. It was clear to his friends that he wanted to leave Chile, to travel – to Paris, they thought, since that was where most young poets wanted to go.

From 1925 onwards, Neruda began to write poems that would eventually form part of *Residencia en la tierra* (Residence on Earth), which many have come to regard as among the greatest collections of verse ever composed in the Spanish language. The very first, 'Madrigal escrito en invierno' (Madrigal Written in Winter), was probably written during a visit to Puerto Saavedra in the summer holidays of 1925.

He was still writing to Albertina. In March 1925, he discovered that Augusto Winter, his librarian friend in Puerto Saavedra, had a type-writer. 'I've found that you can lie more easily on a typewriter,' Neruda told Albertina in a proudly typed letter that month. 'Have you ever met a penguin? Careful – they bite!' He then signed off with 'tontatontatontatontatontatonta' (stupidstupidstupidstupidstupidstu-pid).

In July 1925, Albertina's brother, Rubén – who had returned to Chile from his adventures abroad two months earlier – invited Neruda to Ancud, on the beautiful southern Chilean island province of Chiloé. Rubén had been appointed as a Spanish teacher there, so Neruda accepted with alacrity, keen to escape Santiago for a while, and also hopeful of passing through Temuco and patching up the tensions with his father.

The visit home was not, however, a happy one. It was marked by a shouting match between Pablo and José del Carmen, with father accusing son of wasting his life in trivialities and pig-headedly persist-ing in his ambition be a poet, while his son screamed back in defiance. Neruda must have found it galling that his father did not feel the same pride as his friends in his poetic achievements, which by now were even spreading far outside Chile.

Being away from Santiago and enjoying Rubén's intelligent and witty company once again revived Neruda's spirits, however. They talked at length, and Neruda helped his friend to mark his school pupils' homework. And then there was the exquisite seafood. Food was to become one of Neruda's lifelong passions, and, thanks to a new law, the Maza Law, teachers' pay (including Rubén's) had improved considerably, so Neruda was able to fill his stomach as he had not done during his whole time in Santiago.

Oddly, despite Neruda's improved state of mind on this trip, it was in Ancud that he wrote his dark novella, *El habitante y su esperanza* (The Inhabitant and His Hope), the second of his books to appear in 1926, again published by Nascimento. In this first major venture into prose fiction, he explores the baser human instincts: violence and vengeance. Surreal dreams merge with lyrical descriptions. In a sense, it can be seen as the prose cousin of *Tentativa del hombre infinito*. The novella tells the story of a jailed horse-thief in love with Irene, the wife of his fellow felon, Florencio Rivas. Once freed, the horse-thief visits Irene, but Rivas, who is aware of their affair, kills Irene and flees. This synopsis does no justice to the dream-like quality of the narrative. Most of the action, indeed, takes place inside the characters' minds.

The brooding atmosphere of the story has vague echoes of the remarkable Mormon revenge section in the Sherlock Holmes story *A Study in Scarlet*, which Neruda knew well.

When Pablo received a telegram at Ancud's Hotel Nilsson, where he was staying, asking him to return to Santiago, the first thing he did was to find a tailor in Ancud, and told him to make him 'a pair of trousers, Oxford-style'. When the bewildered man merely shrugged uncomprehendingly at him, Neruda said, good-humouredly: 'Don't panic. This is what I want, more or less.' And he drew a pair of trousers on the page of a newspaper. Impoverished he may have been, but his dandyish love of clothes – which had led students to follow him down the streets of Santiago in matching black capes, forming the so called '*banda de Neruda*' – remained with him for the rest of his life. The Chilean critic, Federico Schopf, said that the first thing Neruda did on meeting him was admire his jacket so fervently that he thought he was going to offer to buy it.[45]

As if to emphasise the contrast between his father's icy scorn for his chosen calling and his widespread acclaim, 150 of Ancud's most prominent citizens thronged Neruda's hotel for a farewell celebration to see Chile's most illustrious poet back on his way to Santiago.

Celebrity could not yet buy him prosperity, however. In the second half of 1926, despite the year's prodigious output, Neruda was still living in poverty, this time sharing lodgings at 25 Calle García Reyes with Tomás Lago and Orlando Oyarzún. Oyarzún recalled:

> when Pablo returned from Chiloé, we three friends of few means decided to join forces and rent a room together. We found one on the second floor of Doña Edelmira's fruit stall. During the day, you had to negotiate watermelons, pumpkins and lettuces. But when night fell, the woman opened a door on to a stairway. She found it hard to understand the adventures we three got up to, but little by little, she became a sort of kindly aunt. Our furnishings could not have been more basic: an iron bed, a few blankets, a night table with a candlestick and candle, a washstand and a jug.[46]

Neruda and Lago began to translate Joseph Conrad's *The Nigger of the Narcissus* into Spanish – a project which was sadly never completed. Neruda wrote to Laurita: 'Tell them to send me money by telegraph, because I'm only eating once a day.'[47]

He continued to read voraciously and write feverishly, despite the pangs of hunger. He retranslated a section of *The Notebooks of Malte Laurids Brigge* by the great German poet, Rainer Maria Rilke, whom he had read in French translation, into Spanish for the October–November edition of the student journal, *Claridad*. Schopenhauer and Proust held a tight hold over him at this time. He also enjoyed Pierre Loti's novel, *Mon Frère Yves*. In a letter to Albertina Azócar, he claimed that he was quite capable of devouring two novels a night.

Neruda and Tomás Lago collaborated again, this time more productively. They wrote a short collection of lyrical prose poems, *Anillos*, once again published by Nascimento. According to Enrique Anderson-Imbert, in this book, the last of his three works published in 1926, Neruda

> leapt from impressionism to expressionism; that is, the poet, excited by the same sensory stimuli, instead of remaining in a passive attitude, took the initiative and expressed himself dynamically; objects lost their nature, reality was deformed into a violent explosion of imagination, feeling and desire.[48]

Between 1925 and 1927, Neruda made several trips to the beautiful port of Valparaíso, northwest of Santiago, with its vast sweeping bay, to see his friend, Alvaro Hinojosa. These flights from Santiago to a city he would grow to love dearly, and eventually buy a home in, restored Neruda's strength and state of mind.

Alvaro Hinojosa's sister, Sylvia Thayer, recalled Neruda's visits in the late 1920s: 'He stayed for weeks, even months. He went out to look at the sea, strolled through the markets, wharfs and hills during the day, and at night he walked through the port's forbidden districts.'[49]

Despite the plangent tone of his pleas for money in his letters to Laurita, Neruda was not passively waiting for a windfall. Clearly realising that poetry – even poetry as successful as his – was not going to make him a rich man in Latin America, he began to think up wild schemes to become wealthy. With Alvaro Hinojosa, he produced sets of *faciógrafos* – comic postcards which they designed and printed themselves, including one showing an Apache whose face could be moved by a tiny metal chain. Armed with these postcards, he and Alvaro stood in streets, passed through trams, trains and restaurants, vainly attempting to attract buyers.

This humiliating failure cannot have been easy for the timid Neruda – but a sign that he also had a certain eloquence was the fact that he managed to persuade the owner of a Santiago cinema to buy two hundred of the postcards, convincing him that they would provide invaluable publicity for the film he was showing at the time: Lon Chaney as *The Man of a Thousand Faces*. For a time, Neruda had fantasies of setting himself up as a businessman in Santiago. His dream of a business career was short-lived, however. In a letter to Laurita on 9 March 1927, he confessed that 'the business has produced only inconveniences, and I have no money, barely enough to live'. Perhaps he was afraid that his father had been right after all.

It seems outrageous that the man who was by now fêted throughout Chile and Latin America for the *Twenty Love Poems* could still be living such a precarious existence. But he was. Orlando Oyarzún wrote:

> Our economic situation was deteriorating. I remember once, perhaps at the beginning of 1927, we were walking back in silence to our lodgings in the early hours of the morning. Our poverty made us sad. Suddenly, Pablo stopped and, in the silence of the night and the solitude of the street, began to shout at the top of his voice an exalted imprecation against his bad luck. Tomás [Lago] joined in, in just as loud a voice. It was up to me to cheer them up. 'Boys,' I told them, 'this is going to change . . . it can't go on much longer like this.'[50]

Oyarzún was right – but not in the way he might have predicted. Neruda was restless, and waiting to escape abroad.

> In the twenties, cultural life in our [Latin American] countries depended exclusively on Europe . . . A cosmopolitan élite was active in each and every one of our republics, and the writers who belonged to the ruling class lived in Paris . . . In fact, as soon as I had acquired the first bit of youthful fame, people in the street started asking me: 'What are you doing here? You must go to Paris.'[51]

One day, encouraged by some of his friends, Neruda, with great trepidation, made his way to the head of the consular department at the Foreign Ministry, and tentatively asked the tall official whether there were any vacant consular postings abroad. There were not, the official replied, expressing huge admiration for Neruda's poetry, but they would let him know when one came up. He heard nothing for some time, and his depression deepened. But as luck would have it, he bumped into a friend of the Foreign Minister's, Manuel Bianchi, brother of the artist, Víctor. As soon as he heard of Pablo's wish to go abroad, Bianchi arranged a meeting with the Minister, who handed the poet a list of vacant positions overseas. 'Choose one,' he told Neruda. The name of the Burmese capital, Rangoon, meant nothing to him – and perhaps for that very reason, he chose it.

It would be the setting for one of his most desolate periods – and a love affair that was to scar him for life.

3

Asian desolation

1927–32

Although he was desperate to leave Santiago, before his long sea voyage, Neruda had some important loose ends to tie up. Some sources[1] claim that he proposed marriage to Laura Arrué before leaving for Rangoon. He certainly sent her drawings, poems, letters and an edition of *Twenty Love Poems*, telling her that she had been the chief muse and influence for that collection.

He had told Albertina exactly the same thing, and he continued to try and win back her affections. Pablo was genuinely in love with both women at the same time. Unfortunately, he could have neither.

It was not just personal unhappiness, however, that drove him away from his own country in 1927. Carlos Ibáñez del Campo, an Army hard man who had already revealed dictatorial tendencies as Interior Minister, took over as President from Emiliano Figueroa Larraín on 7 April 1927. Two months earlier, Ibáñez had ordered mass detentions declaring that there was a need for a serious purge to rid the nation of 'anarchists and Communists'. Once he became head of state, Ibáñez immediately called elections for 22 May, at which, unsurprisingly – given that he was the only candidate – he secured 98 per cent of the vote.

Meanwhile, Chile's economy continued to suffer. The nitrate industry in the north was dwindling, workers were being laid off, causing huge discontent. The four million inhabitants of the country were about to feel the full consequences of relying on a single source of export.

Neruda had written to Laurita at the end of 1926, telling her that he was leaving for Europe on 3 January. 'I'm so bored of fighting with my father. If you could see how my head's driving me crazy. For the past fifteen days, I've had only enough money to cover the trip. What will I eat in Gerona? Steam? I wonder if you could find me something?'[2]

That trip to Europe never materialised, though Paris would have been a more likely destination for the young poet. Another Chilean poet, Vicente Huidobro, was enjoying a successful exile there. But Neruda wasn't interested.

'He said he didn't want to choose the same route taken by all other poets and artists: namely, Paris, capital of culture. He didn't want that. In any case, no one would have offered him the prestigious post of consul in Paris at that time,' said his biographer, Volodia Teitelboim.[3]

So Rangoon it was. Although Neruda had never heard of the place, and could only find it as a dent on the Chilean Foreign Ministry globe, he could see it was in Asia. And after all, Rimbaud had fled a European existence to live thousands of miles from home.

At least two months of sea voyage lay ahead of Neruda. He arranged a series of farewell parties with his friends, who were all envious that he was achieving so great an escape. At one of these raucous gatherings, in Valparaíso, his old friend Alvaro Hinojosa came out with a surprising suggestion: Pablo could exchange his first-class boat ticket for two third-class tickets, and let him, Alvaro, come along too. After all, not long before, the painter Paschín Bustamente and Alberto Rojas Giménez had done something very similar on a trip to Buenos Aires. Neruda accepted the plan immediately. He was very fond of Alvaro, whose ideas often nearly succeeded – if never entirely. He would be a resourceful companion, and that was exactly what Neruda felt he needed in the face of the dauntingly long voyage ahead of him. Alvaro, unlike Pablo himself, was already an experienced traveller who had spent some time in New York.

Diego Muñoz recalled the companions eating, drinking and ex-changing information about Burma, about Rangoon, 'its climate, inhabitants, the beauty of the Burmese women, with their Oriental costumes. We painted a very exotic picture and we all dreamt about that distant country where our friend was going to live.'[4]

Envied Pablo might have been, but neither he nor Alvaro had any money. Rescue arrived in the form of some unexpected funds from Neruda's publisher, Nascimento. Neruda asked Alvaro to pick the money up for him while he continued preparations for the trip. On the way back with the money, Alvaro took it into his head to gamble with it. He asked Neruda's permission, and the poet – unwilling to upset his friend – professed to be delighted with the idea. Alvaro took Neruda's hard-won funds to the Club de Septiembre and began to win at the roulette table. Like so many gamblers before and since, he could not leave while he was ahead. When he walked into Pablo's bedroom the poet was deep in a book but he scarcely needed to ask what had happened: 'You lost, didn't you?' 'Every bit of it,' came Alvaro's mournful reply. 'Not just your 500 pesos, but the two million I was up.' But when the shame-faced Alvaro dared to raise his eyes to meet Neruda's, the two friends burst out laughing.[5]

Armed with Neruda's brand-new diplomatic passport, but little money, they set out from Valparaíso to catch the Transandino train across the Andes to Mendoza in Argentina. It was from Mendoza, on 15 June that Neruda wrote to Laurita: '*Conejita*, Tell my father and mother how sorry I am that I couldn't give them a goodbye hug because I had my tickets booked and the Transandino was about to leave . . . I felt genuine sorrow and anguish, but I think this separation will not last long.'[6]

An exhausting train journey took Neruda and Hinojosa from Mendoza to Buenos Aires. Here Neruda had his first and only meeting with the Argentinian writer, Jorge Luis Borges. Neruda does not mention their two-hour conversation in his memoirs, but Borges often recalled the details of that bizarre encounter in interviews. 'For two hours, we played at trying to out-dazzle one another,' Borges told the French daily, *Le Monde*. 'He said to me: "It simply isn't possible to write in Spanish." I replied: "You're right. That's why no one has ever written anything in that language." Then he suggested: "Why not write in English or French?" "Fine, but how can we be so sure that we deserve to write in those languages?" In the end, we decided that we would have to resign ourselves to writing in Spanish, after all.'[7]

Neruda and Hinojosa boarded the steamer *Baden* on 18 June, bound for Lisbon, Portugal. It was not much of a ship. 'It was a German boat which claimed to be single-class. If so, it was fifth-class.'[8] Alvaro Hinojosa, Neruda claimed in his memoirs, spent the journey chatting up the lady passengers incessantly until some, at least, were forced to give in to his advances. Neruda himself was far less out-wardly assured at this time, despite his sexual successes in Santiago.

Indeed, he tended to be shy with the opposite sex, and they usually came chasing after him. Once aboard the *Baden*, he became captivated by 'a young Brazilian woman, infinitely Brazilian, who had boarded the ship with her parents when the boat docked at Rio de Janeiro.' He gave an account of their meeting in one of the articles he wrote for the Santiago daily, *La Nación*, during the journey.

> That day, a Brazilian family came on board: a father, mother and a girl. The girl was very beautiful. Much of her face was taken up by her eyes, profound, black, unhurriedly looking, abundantly radiant . . .[9]

Whether there was any physical relationship between them, we do not know. 'Possibly,' is Volodia Teitelboim's view. 'Boat journeys were long in those days – it took between twenty and twenty-five days to reach Europe from Santiago – and a lot could happen in that time!'[10] The girl's name was Marinech, and Neruda described how she liked to sit in her chair on deck, talking to him. 'She's a friend of mine. She speaks in the musical Portuguese language, and she enjoys playing with her language like a toy. Fifteen suitors surround her. She's haughty, pale, shows no preference for any of them. Her look, loaded with darkness, flees them.'[11]

As the boat approached the shores of Portugal, on 12 July 1927, Neruda celebrated his twenty-third birthday, but he was anxious because he had not paid off a tailor's bill before leaving Chile; in a letter to Laurita he asked her to see if his father would bail him out. Money continued to worry him:

> I hope to be in Paris in six days' time, and then leave for the Orient at the end of the month. I'm a little afraid of arriving, because here on board I've learnt that life is extremely expensive there, that the cheapest boarding house costs 600 pesos a month, and I'm arriving in a very bad state [financially]. On top of that, they've got plagues, tertian fever, fevers of all kinds. But what is there to do? We have to submit to life and struggle with it, in the belief that nobody else will look after us. Hugs for my father and my beloved mother . . .[12]

From Lisbon he moved on to Madrid, where he stayed only three days. While there he managed to track down Guillermo de Torre, the influential critic and secretary of the fortnightly literary journal, *La Gaceta Literaria* and showed him nine of the poems which would later form part of *Residencia en la tierra*. The Spanish luminary's reaction, however, was disappointingly negative.

> He read the first poems and, in the end, he told me, with a friend's frankness, that he could not see or understand anything in them, and that he couldn't even see what my intentions were. I had planned to stay longer, but seeing the impermeability of this man, I took it as a bad sign and I departed for France, leaving shortly afterwards from Marseille for India. I had recently turned twenty-three, and it was natural that my place was not in Spain in the dying stages of Ultraism . . . The generation of Alberti and Lorca was as yet unknown . . . Out of this boastful, but vain, climate emerged Ortega y Gasset's book, *The Dehumanisation of Art . . .*[13]

When these critical comments of Neruda's were published in 1950, Guillermo de Torre wrote a reply to *Cuadernos Americanos* in the form of an 'Open Letter to Pablo Neruda', in which the Spanish critic provided his own impression of that brief Madrid meeting in 1927.

> We did indeed speak, very rapidly, once, since you were leaving the very next day . . . you handed me copies of your books, some of which I already knew. Because, despite the incriminating 'lack of understanding' and 'impermeability', I had already committed the contradictory act of getting hold of [these books] for myself or through friends in Chile. Well now, I cannot possibly imagine that *Residencia en la tierra* was among those books . . . The only thing I can be certain of is that I did not pronounce the word that you perhaps hoped to hear: '*genial*' (works of genius).[14]

In Paris, Neruda failed to find the French poets he had dreamed of meeting, but he did have a critically important encounter with the Peruvian poet César Vallejo, among the greatest of all Latin American poets.

Vallejo treated Neruda with awe, telling him that he had no equal in Spanish-language poetry other than Rubén Darío. This must have been music to Neruda's ears, but he playfully reproached Vallejo for being too respectful, and for not giving him a brotherly hug.

Together with Alvaro Hinojosa, Neruda made the most of the social delights that the fortnight's stopover in Paris could offer. In his memoirs, he recalled a lavish champagne party given by his wealthy Chilean compatriot, Alfredo Condon, a writer and the son of the owner of Chile's largest shipping company. During the party Neruda was dramatically reminded that even such wealth was no guarantee against financial embarrassment when Condon fell down unconscious. The owner of the club heartlessly insisted on being paid for the evening's festivities immediately nevertheless, and locked the door to stop anyone leaving. None of the guests was able to help, however. 'We escaped from his custody only by leaving my brand-new diplomatic passport as security.'[15]

Outside, they found one of the nightclub hostesses waiting for them in a taxi. She was the only person who had not abandoned them in their hour of need. Pablo and Alvaro invited her for onion soup in Les Halles as dawn broke, and bought her flowers in the market.

> We invited her back to our seedy hotel, and she had no objection to coming with us. She went with Alvaro to his room. I dropped into bed exhausted, but all at once I felt someone shaking me, roughly. It was Alvaro. His harmless maniac's face seemed a bit odd. 'Listen,' he said, 'that woman's something special, she's fantastic. I can't explain it. You've got to try her right away.' A few minutes later, the stranger got into my bed, sleepily but obligingly. Making love to her, I received proof of her mysterious gift. It was something I can't pin down with words, something that rushed up from deep within her, something that went back to the very origins of pleasure, to the birth of a wave, to the erotic secrets of Venus.[16]

From Paris, Pablo and Alvaro took the train south to Marseille. On 1 August 1927, the two men caught the boat taking them on the last part of their long voyage to the Orient.

On that same day, unbeknownst to Neruda, an article appeared in the Madrid journal, *La Gaceta Literaria*, by one Guillermo de Torre, in which he assessed contemporary Chilean poetry. De Torre acknowledged Neruda as a fine poet, whose *Twenty Love Poems* 'represent a point of perfection and equilibrium'. However, the writer, continued, 'dissatisfied, the poet then tried to go one better, and exceeding the limits of Huidobro's poetry, he threw himself into an abstract, naked lyricism.'[17]

We know quite a lot about Neruda's impressions of the final stage of his sea voyage from his regular articles for *La Nación*. We have his colourful descriptions of stop-offs at Port Said in Egypt, with its narrow streets full of bars, where 'even the air . . . the light, shout out prices and invitations', and retracing Rimbaud's footsteps in Djibouti, in the heat of the midday sun, 'at a time when even the camels' humps shrink and they turn their tiny eyes away from the desert'.[18] Volodia Teitelboim claims that, 'Something very odd happened in Djibouti. Neruda danced with prostitutes in brothels, but they couldn't speak any language other than Arabic – so Neruda observed that they "understood each other" in other ways.'[19]

His articles also convey his first impressions of Colombo, in Ceylon (now Sri Lanka), and Singapore, both of which would later become diplomatic postings.

Disembarking at Singapore in October 1927, they thought they had finally reached their destination. It was a huge psychological blow to be told otherwise, and to discover that 'ahead of us lay several days on board a ship, and to make matters worse, the only one making the regular run had left for Rangoon the previous day. We had no money to pay the hotel or our fares. More funds were waiting for us in Rangoon.'[20]

In desperation, Pablo and Alvaro turned to the Chilean consul on Singapore, a man named Mansilla. Initially, he refused to lend the two Chileans the money they needed. However, when Neruda threatened to give a series of talks about Chile in Singapore to raise the funds, Mansilla agreed to help. After another two or three days in Singapore, Neruda and Hinojosa set sail for Rangoon, sharing the trip with tradesmen and colonial civil servants. They finally arrived in Burma around 25 October 1927.

The first letter we know of that Neruda sent from Rangoon was addressed, not to his family in Temuco, nor to Albertina Azócar, but to the Argentinian writer, Héctor Eandi. Neruda had struck up an epistolary friendship after Eandi sent him a copy of his own collection of short stories, *Errantes*, accompanied by an article in which Eandi praised *Twenty Love Poems*. This series of letters is of huge importance in understanding the poet's state of mind in the Orient and his plans for the future.

In this first letter, dated 25 October 1927, Neruda apologises for the delay in writing back to the Argentinian, blaming this on the 'miserable circumstances of every day'. He hopes that the correspondence with Eandi will continue. Not only does it continue, but it provides a lifeline for the fifteen desolate months he spends in Rangoon.

Three days later, he sent a letter to Laurita, in which he told her: 'Here the women are black. Don't worry, I won't be getting married.'[21]

Burma was still an administrative part of British-ruled India in 1927, but the Burmese – who had been a gentle people and easy to govern – were beginning to resent the degree to which they were being exploited commercially by the Indians and the Chinese, and by British and other European mercantile interests. Neruda told Tomás Lago years later that not only had he quickly felt mystified by the native culture in Burma but he was also alienated from the British colonial atmosphere there. 'I led a life which was separate from the English. I attended their parties only very rarely, because there was no one interesting among the colonials. They were monotonous and even ignorant.'[22] He was, however, far less politically percipient than George Orwell, who arrived in Burma just months after Neruda left.

Neruda soon found himself in a suffocating bureaucratic routine.

> My official duties demanded my attention only once every three months, when a ship arrived from Calcutta bound for Chile with hard paraffin and large cases of tea. I had to stamp and sign documents with feverish speed. Then another three months of doing nothing followed, of solitary contemplation in markets and temples. This was the most painful period for my poetry.[23]

Unlike the Mexican poet Octavio Paz, who was captivated by the mystical Oriental religions he discovered while he was posted in the Far East, Neruda found the religious element brutally inhuman and alienating.

> There in Rangoon I understood that the gods
> were as big an enemy as God
> to the poor human being . . .
> elegant naked buddhas
> smiled at the cocktail party
> of empty eternity . . .[24]

But at least the street life was vibrant:

> The street became my religion. The Burmese street, the Chinese quarter with its open-air theatres and paper dragons and splendid lanterns. The Hindu street, the humblest of them, with its temples operated as a business by one caste, and the poor people prostrate in the mud outside. Markets where the betel leaves rose up in green pyramids like mountains of malachite. The stalls and pens where they sold wild animals and birds. The winding streets where supple Burmese women walked with long cheroots in their mouths. All this engrossed me and drew me gradually under the spell of real life.[25]

Real life, for the newly arrived Neruda, and his friend, Alvaro Hinojosa, was bewildering. They were astonished to discover that it was the consul's responsibility to find lodgings for himself in advance. So there was nowhere for them to live except for YMCA youth hostels (neither man believed in the Christian ethic, but rather in a cheap pillow for the night), brothels or even opium parlours. It was an unusual beginning for a diplomatic posting.

Neruda was as restless in Rangoon as he had been in Santiago, but without the stimulus of close friends (apart from Hinojosa) to keep his spirits up. Diego Muñoz, who was now living in Ecuador, received a letter saying that 'he felt very lonely, he had no friends; there was not a single person he could talk to in Spanish. Imagine! He remembered our daily gatherings and he asked me to write to him often . . . I wrote him other letters, but I received only one back, even more bitter.'[26]

Neruda found himself in a social ghetto, as well, since the locals were not allowed in premises run by the English colonials – when he was seen riding the local wheeled vehicle, the *gharry*, he was warned by the British that a consul should not be seen in one of these because it was generally used for shady assignations with women. He was also warned not to frequent the Persian restaurants, difficult advice to heed – this was where Neruda said he enjoyed the best tea in the world out of small transparent cups. 'These were final warnings. After that, they stopped greeting me at all. The boycott couldn't have pleased me more . . . Those intolerant Europeans were not very interesting and, after all, I had not come to the Orient to spend my life with transient colonisers, but rather with the ancient spirit of that world, with that large, hapless human family.'[27]

In a little-known letter, which Neruda wrote to a Chilean friend, Yolando Pino Saavedra, in Hamburg, Germany, on 7 December 1927, Neruda declared that he and Alvaro were seriously considering leaving Rangoon and were looking at Germany as their next destination. 'We are beginning to get bored with a life of such enclosed isolation, so far from the great whirlwinds of people, from the good big cities. The women . . . are dark-skinned, they wear high hair stiff with lacquer, rings in their noses and have a different smell. All this is charming for the first week. But the weeks pass, time passes!'

This letter also contains an illuminating reference to the genesis of *Residencia en la tierra*: 'I am writing less and less. For a couple of years, I've been thinking of a book of which I've written about twelve things. So that is my only work. Let's see if I can finish it in the tranquillity of these days in Burma. It will be called "Nocturnal collection" and I really hope that it gives a good idea of my inner feelings.'[28]

In fact, Pablo and Alvaro left Burma not for Germany, but for China and Japan. Neruda knew that he would not be missed much in Rangoon for a few months, and a voyage would be no more expensive than life back on land. At the beginning of 1928, they set off for Shanghai in China and Yokohama in Japan. Their first port of call was Bangkok in Siam (now Thailand). From there, Neruda sent a postcard to Laurita dated 20 January 1928, telling her that he was heading for Japan and planned to be away from Burma for about two months. From Shanghai, he sent her another card on 7 February, complaining of the bitter cold, 'a cold that I have never felt before, with snow, rain and wind'. Then comes a surprise: 'My plans are to leave for Europe in March and continue my studies in France and Spain. It's not possible to live a long time in the Orient.'[29]

In Shanghai, he and Alvaro tried to visit one nightclub after another, but were dismayed to discover that, because it was midweek, they were either closed or deserted. Returning to the boat on a rickety rickshaw in the pouring rain, they found themselves being clearly taken out of their way by the driver. He suddenly stopped and demanded money. They were soon surrounded by seven or eight other Chinese demanding the same thing. When Alvaro pretended that he had a weapon concealed in his trousers, both he and Neruda received a blow to the back of the head. As he lay on the ground, Neruda could feel them searching all his pockets 'with a juggler's skill.

They didn't leave a centimetre of clothing unsearched, nor a penny of the little money we had. But one thing: with the traditional consideration of Shanghai thieves, they scrupulously respected our papers and our passports.'³⁰ Some kind Chinese helped them back to the boat.

In Yokohama, the two men learnt, to their distress, that a sum of money that should have been awaiting them was not available. After several nights of impoverished time-wasting in the Japanese city, they were infuriated to find that the Chilean consul had indeed had the funds on him all along, without realising it.³¹

With the money in their pockets, they lost no time in enjoying themselves. From Tokyo, Neruda informed Laurita, in a postcard bearing the photograph of a Japanese girl, that Japanese women were 'very nice and smiling, I will always remember them. They are the most feminine, the prettiest in the world. I learnt a few words of Japanese. I ate in a purely Japanese restaurant, and it wouldn't have taken much for me to have married one of these dolls. Take a good look at her, because she could have been your sister-in-law.'³²

While in Yokohama, Neruda took in a Noh play. 'I didn't understand a thing.' But in the preliminary note to the only play he wrote in his life, *Fulgor y muerte de Joaquín Murieta* (Radiance and Death of Joaquín Murieta), Neruda claimed that he had been influenced by this early visit to a Japanese theatre, especially in the funeral scene.

The poet was clearly dreading the prospect of returning to Rangoon. On the boat journey back, he sent Laurita a long letter from Shanghai, in which he informed her:

> I am quite bored in Rangoon, and I'm thinking of leaving there shortly. I can't describe the heat there – it's like living in an oven day and night. Everyone ends up going down with malaria, but luckily the fevers I had soon went away . . . Life in Rangoon is a terrible exile, I wasn't born to spend my life in such a hell. So, what am I going to live on in Europe? I could eat and live there with very little money, but where am I going to get that little money? Everything's difficult for me, and I feel tired and ill.³³

Too tired and ill to write any poetry, it seems. As far as is known, there is not a single poem to emerge from Neruda's voyage to China and Japan at the time, although he did recall the trip in later collections of verse.

In March 1928, back in the oven of Rangoon, Neruda learnt of the death of Augusto Winter, the librarian and poet from Puerto Saavedra responsible for so many of his early literary influences through the books he lent the young Neftalí. From Rangoon, a saddened, chastened Neruda sent *La Nación* a moving tribute to his old mentor, whose poetry had finally been published shortly before his death. 'I remember his house, his tobacco, his theosophy, his Catholicism, his atheism, and I can see him lying down, sleeping, accompanied by anxieties and habits.'[34] This was the first of a long list of articles and poems Neruda would write in honour of dead friends.

In the famous 1961 edition of *Twenty Love Poems* marking the sale of the millionth copy of the book, Neruda told his readers that Winter had helped him to type out the whole book on special brown paper.[35]

On 11 May 1928, Neruda renewed his correspondence with Héctor Eandi in Buenos Aires. His outlook was bleak: 'I want to escape from a truly miserable state of mind . . . As life has passed, I have made my literary life harder and harder.'[36]

In contrast to the unstable letters Neruda wrote to Albertina Azócar, from both Santiago and the Far East, which can strike readers as slightly posturing accounts of a self-consciously modish anguish, these letters to Héctor Eandi are among the most honest Neruda ever wrote. He bared his soul to a man he had never even met face to face.

Speaking about this period, Volodia Teitelboim told me that

Neruda found a very closed civilisation, and never allowed himself to be seduced by the religiosity he saw around him. He was inspired by the joy of living, and participation in life. A life of contemplation represented misery to him. He found his greatest consolation in writing and in a woman's love. He looked for this love everywhere – in brothels, in the street.[37]

Desolate and empty Neruda may have been, but it is astonishing to discover that, even while he was writing so bitterly and desperately back to Latin America, he was in the grips of an extraordinarily passionate love affair which was to change his life for ever. It was a love affair that left him even more isolated from Burmese high society, a society which knew him as Ricardo Reyes, not Pablo Neruda, which saw him as a diplomat from a distant land, not as a famous poet, and which soon ostracised him mercilessly for publicly daring to take a native into his bed.

Josie Bliss was her name. Or rather, it was the only name Neruda used when referrring to her. She was a beautiful, dark-skinned Burmese woman who, as was the custom, adopted a simpler pseudonym when dealing with the British colonials or other Europeans passing through. Neruda said in his memoirs that she used her real name when at home with him – but he never revealed what that name was.

Josie, who worked in an office in Rangoon, and was Neruda's secretary for a while,[38] became his 'love terrorist'. In the street, she wore English clothes, but around the house with Neruda, she changed into her native costume. She was a passionate and knowledgeable lover. In the seven or eight months they were together (from April or May 1928 until he left for Calcutta at the beginning of November of that year), she brought him to sexual maturity. The intimacy between the two of them was new and disconcerting. She was a woman with very strange ways. A Mexican friend of Neruda's claimed that the poet had told him Josie always refused to sleep in the same bed after making love, but insisted on sleeping on the floor nearby.[39]

This 'Burmese panther' became intensely jealous of any other females attempting to grow close to Neruda – and there were many. At the same time, when the white colonials learnt of his affair with Josie, they refused him admission to their clubs. He does not appear to have minded this – it was scarcely a sacrifice for him to be forced to avoid the company of people he largely despised for their snobbery, their deliberate act of distancing themselves from the society in which they lived. The fact that Josie never learnt Western rituals was, for once, a source of attraction for Neruda, who in many other ways found the exoticism of the Orient tiresome.

Who was Josie Bliss? Frustratingly, Neruda does not mention her once in his letters to Héctor Eandi. He did provide brief glimpses in conversations with friends. And, according to Inés Valenzuela, the widow of Diego Muñoz, her memory stayed with Neruda to the end of his life.[40]

Meanwhile, tensions were growing between Neruda and Alvaro Hinojosa. 'He ended up making my life impossible,' Neruda recalled in his memoirs.[41] Yet previously unpublished writings by Hinojosa claim that it was Neruda's intransigence which led to a rise in tensions.

'In matters which affected both of us, he operated as if I didn't exist,' wrote Alvaro.

> One night, I returned to the house quite cheerful and in the mood for a chat. Pablo took a book and, replying to me against his will, he looked for a way to end my superficial, alcohol-laden chatter. I tried out various topics to interest him. Nothing. Then I told him: 'I'm leaving tomorrow for Calcutta.' I didn't have the slightest intention of carrying out this plan from one day to the next, but my aim was to force him to speak. His only response was: 'That's crazy.' And he went on reading.[42]

Neruda continued to work towards the collection he had started in Santiago. On 6 August 1928, in a letter to his friend José Santos González Vera, we find his first reference to *Residencia en la tierra* by that name: 'My scanty recent works, for more than a year, have reached a great perfection (or imperfection), but in any case they lie within my ambitions . . . My new book will be called *Residencia en la tierra* and it will be forty verse poems which I want to publish in Spain.'[43]

To Eandi in September, Neruda, now in a more positive frame of mind, pinpoints his aim as to 'benefit from the struggle' against 'difficulties and impossibilities encountered in life'. He accompanied this letter with three poems which would be included in *Residencia*: 'Juntos nosotros' (We Together), 'La noche del soldado' (The Soldier's Night) and 'Sonata y destrucciones' (Sonata and Destructions).

Towards the end of 1928, Neruda decided once again to leave Rangoon – which at least one critic[44] sees as the poet's equivalent of Rimbaud's *Une saison en enfer*, hence the number of times Neruda referred to 'hell' in his letters of the time – in order to travel to Calcutta, where he enjoyed a friendly reunion with Alvaro Hinojosa and attended the meeting of the Indian National Congress.

Writing home from Calcutta on 12 December, Neruda had some important news to impart: 'I have to inform you that the [Chilean] government has transferred me to Colombo, on the island of Ceylon, to the south of India. I'll have the same salary as in Rangoon, and the climate there is just as bad, or even worse, than here [in Rangoon], but it was becoming unbearable and tiring for me to live in the same place for so long, and I accepted my transfer with joy.'[45]

What Neruda did not tell his family, of course, was that the move to Colombo would also provide a means of escaping the clutches of the ever more desperately possessive Josie Bliss.

Sweet Josie Bliss gradually became so brooding and possessive that her jealous tantrums turned into an illness. Except for this, perhaps I would have stayed with her for ever. I loved her naked feet, the white flowers brightening her dark hair. But her temper drove her to savage paroxysms. The letters I received from abroad made her jealous and furious. She hid my telegrams without opening them; she glowered at the air I breathed. Sometimes, a light would wake me up, a ghost moving on the other side of the mosquito net. It was her, dressed in white, brandishing her long, sharpened native knife. It was her, walking around and around my bed for hours at a time, without quite making up her mind to kill me. When you die, she used to say to me, my fears will end. The next day she would carry out mysterious rituals to make me remain faithful. She would have ended up killing me.[46]

Neruda left their house in secret and took a boat from Rangoon to Colombo. No sooner had the boat entered the Gulf of Bengal, than he sat down to write a key poem in *Residencia en la tierra*, one of the most heartfelt he ever penned: 'Tango del viudo' (Widower's Tango). For three decades, readers would not realise to whom the poet was referring in this poem – this was revealed only when Neruda disclosed Josie Bliss's existence in the autobiographical articles he wrote for the Brazilian magazine, *O Cruzeiro Internacional*, in 1962.

In this poem, Neruda refers to Josie Bliss as as La Maligna (the Evil One) and Hernán Loyola sees the poem as a kind of exorcism. I do not feel that so much should be made of this choice of adjective. After all, in one of his letters to Héctor Eandi, on 24 April 1929, he curses stray dogs in the street as *los malignos*. But the poem does feel like an exorcism of a kind: expunging not so much Josie from his life as his own guilt at leaving her. This explains why he calls the poem 'Widower's Tango', as if *he* were the one who had been abandoned.

Oh, Evil One, by now you'll have found the letter, cried with fury,
and insulted my mother's memory
calling her rotten bitch and mother of dogs,

you'll have drunk tea alone, in solitude, at dusk
looking at my old shoes empty for ever,
and you can no longer remember my illnesses, my dreams at night,
   my meals
without cursing me out loud as if I were still there . . .

Buried next to the coconut palm you'll find
the knife I hid because I feared you'd kill me
and now suddenly I would like to smell its kitchen steel
so accustomed to the weight of your hand and the shine of your
   foot . . .

I would give the wind off the giant sea for your hoarse breathing.
. . . and to hear you urinating, in the darkness, at the back of the
   house . . .

When he arrived in Ceylon, Neruda looked for a place to live in
Colombo. He found a small bungalow in the suburbs of Wellawatta,
facing the sea. He was unaware how close he had come to losing out
on the Colombo posting; it was one of the fifty consulates which the
Chilean Foreign Ministry was contemplating closing to save money.
   Ceylon in 1929 had the same colonial structure as Burma and India.

   The English had entrenched themselves in their neighbourhoods and
   their clubs, hemmed in by a vast multitude of musicians, potters,
   weavers, plantation slaves, monks in yellow and immense gods
   carved into the stone mountains. Caught between the Englishmen
   dressed every evening in dinner jackets, and the Hindus, whom I
   couldn't hope to reach in their fabulous immensity, I had only
   solitude open to me, so that time was the loneliest in my life.[47]

Nevertheless, the Ceylon period was far calmer than Rangoon.
Neruda appears happier than he had been. In a letter to his step-
mother, written soon after his arrival, he told his *mamadre* that
Wellawatta reminded him of his beloved Puerto Saavedra.

   I get up early and walk along the beach in a bathing suit for a couple
   of hours, taking advantage of the only cool time of day. Then I bathe
   in the water, which is always warm, and I try to swim, an art in

which I am making progress little by little. Then I return home, where my servants have prepared an excellent (?) lunch for the 'master', as they call me. Then I work. At times, the work is tiring. At others, there is nothing to do but sleep.[48]

His residence was basic. He slept on a campbed 'like a soldier, an explorer'. His only campanions were a dog, a tame mongoose named Kiria, and a servant boy called Brampy. The boy did not speak, but 'smiled with big horse-teeth'. But as in Rangoon, he was appalled by the 'terrible gap' between the British masters and the 'vast world of the Asians . . . It ensured an inhuman isolation, a total ignorance of the values and lives of the Asians.'[49]

Into this calm solitude broke a totally unexpected storm: Josie Bliss. She had followed him from Rangoon, and had tracked him down to his bungalow. She arrived, laden with a rug, a sack of rice and some Paul Robeson records, to which she and Neruda had loved listening during their life together in Rangoon. 'I can see her now,' Neruda wrote at the end of his life, 'consumed by her overwhelming jealousy, threatening to burn down my house, and attacking a sweet Eurasian girl who had come to pay a call. The colonial police . . . warned me that she would be thrown out of the country if I didn't take her in . . . I didn't dare let her set foot in my house. She was a love-smitten terrorist, capable of anything.'[50]

For a few days, Josie was allowed to stay in the house of the neighbour opposite, a Ceylonese gentleman by the name of Mr Fernando whom Neruda mentioned in letters from time to time. Astonishingly, Mr Fernando managed to convince Josie of the impossibility of staying in Ceylon, and she made one final request of him: that he talk to Pablo and persuade him to accompany her to the dock to see her off.

Neruda agreed. As the boat was about to leave, Josie suddenly turned round and,

seized by a gust of grief and love, she covered my face with kisses and bathed me with her tears. She kissed my arms, my suit, in a kind of ritual, and suddenly slipped down to my shoes, before I could stop her. When she stood up again, the chalk polish of my white shoes was smeared like flour all over her face. I couldn't ask her to give up her trip, to leave the boat that was taking her away for ever and come with me instead. My better judgment stopped me, but my heart received a scar which is still part of me. That unrestrained grief, those terrible tears running down her chalky face, are still fresh in my memory.[51]

There were some unusual, and more pleasant, surprises in Ceylon. One was his encounter with Leonard Woolf, husband of the writer Virginia Woolf. Leonard was a civil servant at the time, who was sacked soon after Neruda arrived and shipped back to England where he wrote what Neruda called 'one of the best books ever written about the Orient',[52] *The Village in the Jungle*. We know that Neruda was reading a great deal of English-language literature in Ceylon, especially D. H. Lawrence, thanks to a large library owned by the painter, photographer, critic and film director, Lionel Wendt, who received all the latest literature from England.

Neruda praised Lawrence as 'the greatest of them all', a fact that seems to indicate that he was not yet interested in adopting a stance in favour of the Russian Revolution. Otherwise, I feel that Neruda would have made some comment on Lawrence's political poems, especially his 'Now It's Happened', in which Lawrence condemns the Revolution for the way it portrayed the great Russian artists of the nineteenth century.

Politics could not have been further from Neruda's mind in his Ceylonese isolation. In a letter to Eandi dated 27 February 1930, he declared: 'The sexual question is [a] tragic matter . . . Perhaps it is the most important reason for my misery.'

Indeed, it was, as he wrote in his memoirs, what finally ended his love affair with D. H. Lawrence's writings. Neruda read the first edition of *Lady Chatterley's Lover* in Ceylon. 'It soon became clear to me that, for all his genius, he was frustrated by his passion for instructing the reader; like so many other great English writers, D. H. Lawrence sets up a course in sexual education that has almost nothing to do with what we learn spontaneously from love and life.'[53]

It seems Neruda's own sex life in Ceylon was not quite as barren as he made out in his correspondence. Even after the brutal ending of the Josie Bliss affair, Neruda had many women visitors who passed briefly through his bedroom, helping to assuage his boredom and guilt.

The most beautiful woman he saw in all his time in Ceylon, by his own account, was a Tamil whose job it was to empty the buckets bearing human waste every day.

She was so lovely that, regardless of her humble job, I couldn't get her off my mind. Like a shy jungle animal, she belonged to another kind of existence, to a different world. I called out to her, but it was no use. After that, I sometimes put a gift in her path, a piece of silk or some fruit. She would go past without hearing or looking . . . One morning, I made up my mind, took a firm grip of her wrist and stared into her eyes. There was no language I could talk with her. Unsmiling, she let herself be led away and was soon naked in my bed. Her waist, so very slim, her full hips, the brimming cups of her breasts made her look just like one of the thousand-year-old sculptures from the south of India. It was the coming together of a man and a statue. She kept her eyes wide open, all the while, completely unresponsive. She was right to despise me. The experience was never repeated.[54]

All the time, he was being asked: 'Are you married, Mr Reyes?' And little by little – after so many months of insisting in his letters back to Laurita that marriage was the last thing on his mind – Neruda was coming to crave domestic happiness. In an interesting chapter of his book, the Chilean writer Edmundo Olivares Briones makes a comparison between Rimbaud's letters home to his family from Harar in 1883 and Neruda's own new search for stability. Where Rimbaud wrote: 'Alas, what are all these comings and goings for, this fatigue and these ventures in the midst of strange races . . . if I do not manage, after some years, to rest in a place which I love, form a family and have at least one child whom I can bring up for the rest of my life?' Neruda was writing to Héctor Eandi on 5 October 1929, 'I, who continually made a doctrine out of irresponsibility and movement for my own life and others', now feel an anguished desire to settle down, to fix my conditions, to live or die in peace. I also want to marry, but soon, tomorrow even, and live in a big city. These are my own persistent desires, perhaps I'll never be able to achieve them.'[55]

His need for marriage was also prompted by his frustration over the lack of response to his many letters back to Chile. We now know that he was writing not only to Albertina Azócar, asking her to marry him, but also to Laura Arrué, proposing the same thing. Neither replied – but for for very different reasons.

By 1929, Albertina was no longer in Chile: she had been awarded a scholarship to travel to Brussels to study the Decroly Audio-visual

System for teaching children French. She did eventually renew contact with Neruda, writing to the Chilean consulate in Colombo from Brussels. He replied, begging her to give up her career, her grant, her studies, everything, to come and live with him in Ceylon.

Their relationship remained largely a one-sided romance throughout. That letter from Albertina no longer exists, but we do know it that it brought back all Neruda's emotional insecurity, reviving new hopes and banishing any feelings of peace he was starting to feel in Wellawatta, Ceylon.

On 10 December 1928, he sent her a miserable postcard:

I live anxious to receive your reply. Have you got all my cards? Have you done anything yet? Why don't you write? Where were you in Paris? Be intelligent and quick, act, come . . . All my love, Pablo.[56]

Silence from Albertina.

My little Netocha, I wasn't planning to write to you until you answered my earlier letters, but it's night-time, it's hot and I can't sleep . . . I'm growing tired of solitude, and if you do not come, I will try and marry some other woman.

This was as clear an ultimatum as he could summon.

Does that seem brutal to you? No, what would be brutal would be if you didn't come. You ought to know that I have a little social situation connected with my 'Señor Consul' [status] and I can't help noticing that this produces certain expectations among the mothers (who sometimes have attractive daughters). But listen to me! I have never loved anyone but you, Albertina. In my eyes, no other woman can be compared to you. Are you happy?[57]

The very next day, Neruda dashed off another desperate letter to Albertina in Brussels. This time, he was prepared to pay out the extra cash for an airmail message, a rare gesture for him in his dismal financial condition:

Albertina darling, two hours ago, I received your letter and I learnt of your problem with the University . . . Don't think I can come to

Europe. I have no money for that, nor can I leave my post for the moment . . . My idea is this: that you come any way you humanly can . . . When we're married, I'll write to Molina [the rector of the University of Concepción, to which Albertina was still attached] or whoever, and I will try to pay for your tickets and your expenses down to the last centavo . . . I'm tired of living alone, and if this time you disappear, I will never seen you again. Of that you can be sure . . . You'll like my house a lot. It's small and it's almost in the sea, and the fresh smell of the sea fills it. I hope, my love, that you will do what your heart commands you. I kiss you a thousand times and a thousand more. Your Pablo . . . Did you receive my letters? Do you think I look old and ugly in my portrait? . . . Do you really love me? Can you feel the caresses that you will receive? Do you feel naked in my arms? My love! Isn't it true that we have loved, adored, each other, like no one else? P.[58]

Neruda seems to have regretted the force with which he'd written his two previous letters, especially the ultimata they both contained, and anxious not to seem as though he was pressuring Albertina into a decision against her will, he sent her another letter on 19 December:

In no way do I want to force you to come with me. I cannot put myself in your situation, and after reading your only letter for the hundredth time, I note that perhaps you want to go back to Chile . . . You do as you want. Yours, Pablo.[59]

But what of Laura Arrué? Why her silence? Neruda was still sending her letters begging her, too, to marry him. She never received a single letter. The reason was simple: Pablo sent his letters to 'Milala' via his friend, Homero Arce, to keep them from falling into the hands of Laura's family. However, Homero had himself fallen in love with Laura during Pablo's absence and had decided to keep the letters arriving for her from the Far East to prevent her seeing them.

As 1930 began with silence from the two women he loved, Neruda felt both despair and anger well up inside him. He wrote another letter to Albertina on 12 January:

My Albertina, I can hardly control my fury enough to write to you calmly. Yesterday they returned my important registered letter from your famous rue Jourdain with the note: 'Parti sans laisser adresse.' I must say that I see this as a cruel lack of responsibility on your part and I don't know how to take it . . . I've been waiting anxiously for a word from you, and when I thought it had come, I find it's my own letter returned to me, because you did not think it was worth leaving [forwarding] instructions. Yesterday, I thought I was going mad with anger, disappointment and sadness . . . So where should I send this letter? Can I be sure of anything with you? And naturally, one postcard in a month. After five years of absolute silence, all you can say to me fits on a postcard! Tell me, Albertina, must I doubt you? If you receive any of my letters, you will see how much I love you. I'm furious, irritated, I don't want to say more things that will make you suffer.[60]

Dissatisfied with the tone of this letter, Neruda sent Albertina a second one the same day to ask her forgiveness for his unpleasantness: 'Look, I lead a very solitary life here, in general I do not talk to anyone except my servant for weeks on end . . . You know that I have quite a temper.'[61]

Albertina remained silent.

Years later, she gave her own account:

I kept Pablo's address with me and when I arrived in Belgium, I sent him a photograph in an envelope, without writing a word. Immediately, he started to write me letter after letter, and sent me cables asking me to come out and marry him as soon as possible . . . I have never been very effusive, although my feelings run very deep. I thought a lot about marrying Pablo and I concluded that I couldn't do it . . . I was still very influenced by my parents' attitude. So I made the mistake of not accepting him. I also felt I had a duty to return to university to justify the money they were sending me every month . . . After that, I spent Christmas in London at a friend's house. At the same time, letters arrived from Pablo at the house where I had been living in Brussels and they were returned to him with the message 'Left without providing forwarding address.' The poor man was furious and wrote to tell me that I had shown a lack of interest in him. But he still insisted that I change my return ticket to Chile for one for Ceylon. I thought that proposal was improper and I refused.[62]

In the end, Albertina said, she had never even completed her university studies, because the director of the school, a Bolivian, had opened some of Pablo's letters to her. 'I felt violated and gave up the course . . . it was very painful for me . . . I had sacrificed the love of my life out of loyalty to the university, only to lose it all for nothing. It was terrible.'[63]

Yet, February 1930 saw two important developments in Neruda's life. The first occurred far from Ceylon, in Madrid. The second edition of the journal, *Bolívar*, dedicated to Latin American culture, appeared with a brief article, signed Alfredo Condon (the host whose sudden drunken slump into unconsciousness had left Neruda and Alvaro Hinojosa in the lurch during their stopover in Paris), announcing the imminent publication in Spain of a book of poems called *Residencia en la tierra*. It was described as 'without doubt one of the most important books of modern poetry'. Condon, now secretary at the Chilean embassy in Madrid, was rather ahead of events – the book would not see the light of day for another three years.

That same month, on 11 February, Neruda wrote to Héctor Eandi to say:

> It seems they are going to transfer me to Singapore . . . the Consul General has put forward my name for the vacant position, and I'm going to accept. I'm tired of Ceylon, of this deadly idleness. Singapore means the magical Malayan archipelago, beautiful women, beautiful rituals. I've already been twice to Singapore and Bali. I've smoked many opium pipes there, I don't know if I like that, but it's different, anyhow [the word 'anyhow' appears in English]. I've sent my book to Spain and I still do not know its fate.[64]

He was unaware of the Spanish magazine article.

Despite the anguished letters back to Albertina Azócar in Brussels and Laura Arrué in Chile, Neruda appears to have satisfied himself sexually in Ceylon, as he had in Burma. On 27 February 1930, he wrote to Eandi saying as much, but also making clear that sexual fulfilment was not the same thing as emotional fulfilment. He confided that 'a woman I loved greatly (I wrote almost all my *Twenty Love Poems* for her) . . . [and with whom I had] arranged her coming here, we were going to get married, and for a time I lived full of her arrival, sorting out the bungalow, thinking about the kitchen, well, about everything. And she couldn't come, at least not for the moment.'[65]

In this same letter, Neruda expressed satisfaction over the possibility of a transfer to Singapore and Java. His moods swing alarmingly within the letter to Eandi, as they do in so many that he wrote to Albertina: 'I'm undoubtedly contented. In the evenings, sitting with my few books and my whisky soda, I feel happy. And yet, my dear friend, I'm not short of bitter worries. Luckily, on the first of April, I finally pay off a debt with the bank (2,000), which it has cost blood to pay off with barely enough money to buy rice with.'[66] To this letter, he attached a moving poem, 'Ausencia de Joaquín,' (Joaquín's Absence) a tribute to another great Chilean friend who had died a few months earlier, Joaquín Cifuentes Sepúlveda.

A dilemma faced him as he came to pack his bags and leave Ceylon for Singapore: what to do with his beloved long-tailed pet mongoose? He knew he would have to say farewell to his dog, Kuthaka, who had played a vital role in ensuring that one of the greatest twentieth-century poets survived long enough to write his masterpieces. One night, near his Wellawatta home, Neruda tumbled during a night-time stroll and fell on to the rails in front of an oncoming train. It was only Kuthaka's loud barking that alerted the train driver to stop in time. (In honour of his canine saviour, Neruda called the pet dogs he owned in later years in Chile by the same name.)

At least, as Neruda recalled in his memoirs, the telegram confirming his transfer to Singapore and Java meant a slight rise in salary: he would no longer have to sleep on a campbed. There can be no doubt that he was sorrier to leave Ceylon than Rangoon. He told Eandi, 'My last days on the island are almost happy. To think that this is coming to an end, and I am enjoying the sun and the sea that I won't have in Malaysia. Singapore is very urban, very full of noise and dust and Chinese cafés. I know little about Java but I'm anxious to see it.'[67]

In the end, Neruda could not bear to part with either his mongoose or his servant, Brampy. Both of them joined him on board the boat bound for Singapore in June 1930 – even though he knew that they would cause complications at the customs. It shows a sense of loyalty that Neruda would retain all his life, to those closest to him, to the people who really mattered in his life.

When Neruda arrived in Singapore on 12 June, he did at least have a room waiting for him at the celebrated Raffles hotel. But where was the consulate of Chile? He had no idea of its whereabouts, and when he consulted the hotel telephone directory, there was nothing listed. Asking around, he was shocked to hear the news: there was no such thing as a Chilean consulate on the island of Singapore. When he asked for the name of the former consul, Mansilla – the man who had lent him and Alvaro Hinojosa money on their previous stay – he was told that no such man existed.

The beginning to Neruda's new posting might have been written by Kafka.

> I was devastated. I scarcely had enough money to pay for a day in the hotel and my laundry. Then it struck me that the phantom consulate must have its headquarters in Batavia [now Jakarta, the Indonesian capital] and I decided to get back on the same boat that I had arrived on, since it was going on to Batavia and was still in port. I ordered my clothes to be removed from the tub, where they were soaking. Brampy made a wet bundle out of them and we dashed down to the docks. They were already drawing up the ship's ladder. I clambered on board, panting.[68]

Returning to the ship, out of breath, had its compensations. He met a Jewish girl named Kruzi on board. After the cruise's farewell party, Neruda said, 'We spent that last night making love in my cabin, in a friendly way, knowing that chance had brought us together for this brief time only. I told her about my misadventures. She comforted me gently and her light-hearted tenderness touched me. Kruzi, in turn, confided the true nature of the job awaiting her in Batavia. There was an organisation, more or less international, which placed European girls in the beds of respectable Asians.'[69]

In Java, he found not only a real, solid Chilean consulate, but a building bearing his country's coat of arms. But he also found a consul already in place. The man, who happened to be an irascible Dutchman with not an ounce of Chilean blood in him, refused to budge: 'There is no room for two Chilean consuls on Java, and I am the only accredited consul,' said the official. Neruda finally found out the extraordinary truth:

Mansilla had never assumed his duties as consul in Batavia at all. He had lived in Paris for some time and had come to an arrangement with the Dutchman to have him perform the consular duties and to send him, Mansilla, the papers and the fees every month. Mansilla promised to pay him a monthly stipend for his work, but he never did. Hence the indignation of this naive Dutchman, which fell on my head like a collapsing roof.[70]

Neruda had no choice but to return to his hotel. That, at least, was a good one: the internationally renowned Hotel der Nederlanden. He was exhausted and still upset by the stream of abuse the Dutchman had heaped on him, even though he had discovered the explanation. Shivering with fever, and unable to speak either Dutch or Malay, he struggled to acquire pen and ink. A telegram was eventually dispatched to Chile and Neruda was able to assume his position as consul on Java – although he remained for a while at the Hotel der Nederlanden while a residence was sorted out.

Neruda felt less alone in Java than in his previous postings – and was able to buy books such as Shakespeare's sonnets which, he said, kept him in touch with Western culture. He could mostly be found sitting on his own in the outdoor cafés, sipping a beer as he looked out at the canals, 'I resumed my life of desperate tranquillity.'[71]

Not too tranquil, however, to become embroiled in a little literary spat with his old Chilean adversary, Hernán Díaz Arrieta (Alone). Neruda had been sent a May 1930 edition of La Nación in which Alone referred snidely to the Uruguayan poet, Carlos Sabat Ercasty as 'known among us for his influence on Pablo Neruda and, through him, on the young writers of Chile'. Neruda had already freely acknowledged Sabat's influence on his book, El hondero entusiasta, which he had not yet even published. But Alone's assertions angered him so much that, on 15 July 1930, Neruda wrote a furious refutation.

It is very true that Sabat had an influence on a certain period of my production. But it is outrageous to say that indirectly Sabat has influenced the new poets. Other than me, no poet of Chile has undergone this influence . . . I have never found a young Chilean poet who felt sympathy for Ercasty's work or for the intellectual situation of his writings . . . My literary language in recent times is

beginning to smell of Foreign Ministry decrees and reports. I want to
warn you of this sinister fact.[72]

Despite his solitude, Neruda retained the strength for a fight. He
always would.

Meanwhile, Neruda's tribulations continued. His beloved mongoose, Kiria, somehow escaped and, even though the distraught poet
placed an advertisement in the local newspaper for any knowledge
of his whereabouts, the creature was lost for ever. Neruda's servant,
Brampy, felt personally responsible and could not even bear to
look his master in the eyes. One day, he took off and was never
seen again.

Neruda, minus servant and pet, moved into his new residence in
Probolingo Street. The house had a garage, although Neruda had no
car (he never did learn to drive). He was given a Javanese cook ('an
old, charming, egalitarian peasant woman') and a boy to serve his
meals and wash his clothes. And for the first time in his life, the poet,
still known diplomatically as Ricardo Reyes, had to buy a dinner
jacket.

Some time between June and October 1930, Neruda met the
woman who was to become his first wife. María Antonieta Hagenaar
Vogelzang, aged thirty, was born in Batavia to Indonesian parents –
Richard Pieter Fedor Hagenaar and Antonia Helena Vogelzang – on 5
March 1900.[73] When Neruda met her, she was an employee at the
Bataviascha Afdelingsbank. Her real, Dutch, name was Maryka, but
Pablo was not fond of that and Hispanicised it to Maruca, the name he
used from then on.

In his memoirs, Neruda described her as 'a tall, gentle woman,
totally alien to the world of the arts and letters'. There are few
objective descriptions of her at the time, but later on, when she
returned to Chile with Neruda, Diego Muñoz would write: 'She
was a strange, hermetic creature, who could only talk in English.'[74]

They were married in Batavia on 6 December 1930, and the
photograph of the wedding is captioned 'Maruca de Reyes'.

Neruda's future secretary and biographer, Margarita Aguirre, said
that Maruca was very proud to be the wife of a consul and had quite
an exotic idea of [Latin] America. She did not speak Spanish but was
beginning to learn it, but there is no doubt that it was not just the
language that she did not understand. Despite everything, her senti-

mental attachment to Neruda was very strong and they were always seen together.'[75]

Neruda himself made it quite clear later in a well-known poem that he had married Maruca out of loneliness.[76] Nevertheless, that was far from the message he transmitted to his family back in Temuco. In a letter to his father on 15 December he informed them:

> My wife is of Dutch nationality and belongs to a distinguished family settled in Java for many years. My desire was to communicate my decision to marry and await your consent, but owing to numerous circumstances, our marriage was confirmed much earlier than the date we thought. But I believe that, even so, if you had been fortunate enough to meet the woman who is now my wife, you would have been as proud of her as I am, and you would love her as much as I do. As soon as Maruca – that's the name of your new daughter – learns Spanish, she will write to you often . . . From now on, you will no longer have to be concerned that your son is alone and far from you, since I have someone who is with me for ever . . . She has no personal fortune: her father was ruined after some unwise speculation. We are poor, but happy . . .[77]

Photographs of this period show a white-suited Neruda with his arm around Maruca, a tall attractive woman. He seems to have been genuinely content to find some new stability in his life, but the stability meant that he had little material to feed his creative imagination, and his poetic writings dried up at this stage. One of the few things he wrote at the time was an article entitled 'Introduction to the Poetry of Angel Cruchaga,' which would become a prologue to Cruchaga's 1933 book, *Afán del Corazón*. Cruchaga had taken Neruda's part against Alone in October 1930, calling him 'the greatest poet alive in the Spanish language'.

Life did not run smoothly for long, however. In March, Maruca fell seriously ill. As Pablo wrote back to Laurita on 23 March 1931, the doctor's fees cost a hundred pesos a visit, which came as an even more severe blow when accompanied by the bad news that his salary had been halved, as part of an across-the-board budget cut by the Chilean Foreign Ministry in the aftermath of the 1929 Wall Street Crash.

Despite these new difficulties, Neruda's newly married status magically opened doors into society that had remained shut to him as a bachelor consul. He provided a good account of married life in those early months in a letter to Héctor Eandi on 5 September:

> My wife is Dutch, we live extremely well together, extremely happy in a house smaller than a thimble. I read, and she sews. Consular life, protocols, meals, dinner jacket, dress coats, morning coats, uniforms, dances, cocktail parties, all the time: a hell. The house is a refuge but the pirates are surrounding us. We break the siege and flee, with a thermos flask and cognac and books to the mountains or the coast. We lie down on the sand and look at the black island, Sumatra, and the underwater volcano, Krakatoa. We eat sandwiches. We return. I'm not writing. I read the whole of Proust for the fourth time. I like him more than before. I've discovered a surrealist painter. We go out with him, eat in Chinese restaurants, drink beer . . .[78]

What Neruda did not directly tell Eandi was that his marriage was probably already in trouble. At the same time that he was writing about how happy home life was, he was also writing a poem, 'Lamento lento' (Slow Lament), expressing his unhappiness at losing Albertina (she is not named, but the allusion is clear).

But perhaps the problems did not start this early. A well-known Chilean visitor to Java in 1931 provided a far more cheerful picture of Pablo and Maruca's marriage. The children's writer Elvira Santa Cruz Ossa, better known under the pen name of 'Roxane', reported for *El Mercurio*:

> Pablo Neruda . . . recently married an attractive Javanese woman of Dutch origin . . . Pablo Neruda's house is in Weltebreden; only two rooms are closed and even these have little holes in the walls for the birds to make their nests in. The Chilean consul's tiny house is his love nest . . . Maruca laces her conversation with the charm of her stuttering Spanish, like a child learning to speak. The pretty Javanese woman has a vast culture and acts as the poet's secretary.[79]

If Maruca really did act as Neruda's 'secretary', she cannot have had much work to do: Neruda had scant commercial correspondence to deal with at the consulate.

That period came to an abrupt end at the beginning of 1932, when a telegram arrived announcing that the Chilean Foreign Ministry had abolished the post of consul on Singapore and Java. There was now nowhere else to go but back to Chile, to an uncertain future with a wife he was no longer sure he loved.

Neruda himself was later often at pains to emphasise that his poetry had not been as dramatically shaped by his experiences in the Far East as critics tended to suggest. Jorge Edwards has written of Neruda's years in self-imposed 'exile' in the Orient:

> The title [*Residencia en la tierra*] is a hidden allusion. Residence on earth is actually residence in the language . . . In his letters from the Far East, he repeatedly explained that his only territory, his only certainty in those years, was the Spanish language. Actually, his Spanish became quite odd. It was very much influenced by solitude. He heard chiefly English, as spoken in the English colonies, and his use of verbs is not altogether Chilean or Spanish. It was something new, and he made of it something very creative in the Spanish language. All his accounts of this period, for him a very creative one, indicate anguish and anxiety, isolation and a very critical personal state.[80]

In fact, there seems little odd about the language Neruda used in his letters from Asia; they are direct and honest about his sense of desolation and loneliness. But his experiences in the Far East would feed many of the hermetic poems he wrote there, later to be incorporated in *Residencia en la tierra*, which Robert Pring-Mill has called 'the finest collection of Surrealist poetry in the Spanish language'.[81]

4

Back home, new battles – and Buenos Aires

1932–34

There was a frosty reception awaiting Pablo Neruda and his new wife Maruca when the poet returned home to Chile after his five-year diplomatic exile in the Far East. The two-month sea voyage had been physically exhausting. The couple first boarded the Dutch boat, *Pieter Corneliszoon Hooft*, on or around 15 February 1932, and it took them from Batavia to Colombo. From there, they took the cheapest vessel they could find, a cargo ship under a British flag, the *Forafric*, which ferried them around the coasts of Africa, through the Strait of Magellan, stopping for a day in Buenos Aires. Pablo and Maruca landed at Puerto Montt in rain-soaked southern Chile on 18 April 1932. From there, they took a train to Temuco. Maruca did not need to speak Spanish to sense the hostility of Neruda's family, over both his choice of spouse and the fact that he was returning with no job, no money and no savings.

Of that long journey, Neruda wrote only two sentences in his memoirs but, in a letter to Héctor Eandi on 26 September that year, Neruda said: 'I took the trip in a terrible cargo boat which took 75 days in bringing me home. I saw my Ceylon prison again, then Mozambique, and the ocean.'[1]

Indirectly, of course, those seventy-five days at sea with a new wife, gazing out at the Indian and Atlantic oceans, fed much of his writing. He was no longer in love with Maruca, and this contributed to many of his poems, especially those devoted to describing the sea as an ally, as a teacher. Moreover, on board that cargo boat, Neruda wrote one of the last poems to appear in the first volume of *Residencia en la tierra*: 'El fantasma del buque de carga' (The Phantom of the Cargo Ship). It is one of Neruda's bleakest – and greatest – poems about the sea, which he normally considers a life-enhancing element, but which is seen as a trap on his long voyage home. The phantom – the vacant shell staring out over the ocean – could well be Neruda himself, full of a gnawing sense of the hollowness of his life.

> All that's left is time in the cabins:
> time in the wretched solitary dining-room . . .
> The phantom watches the sea with his eyeless face:
> the circle of the day, the ship's cough, a bird
> in the rounded, lonely equation of space,
> and descends once again to life on the boat
> falling on dead time and wood . . .

Hernán Loyola sees this poem as highly significant, particularly because Neruda decided to include it in the third section of *Residencia*, the section that relates to sexual isolation or conflict. The poem reflects the sexual loneliness he was already feeling in his relationship with his new wife.[2]

The couple did not stay long in Temuco, but hurried off to Santiago, the capital of a Chile now under a new dictator, President Carlos Dávila, who was struggling to maintain control over the chaos left by his right-wing, authoritarian predecessor, Carlos Ibáñez del Campo. (Ibáñez had been toppled by a 'general strike of intellectuals' on 25 July 1931, and fled into exile in Argentina.) Immediately following the overthrow of the Ibáñez regime, a leftist junta had taken control as the República Socialista de Chile, with the exotically named Marmaduke Grove as leader. But his rule lasted just twelve days, before Dávila, who had been a respected Chilean Ambassador to Washington, became provisional President and exiled Grove to Easter Island, the Chilean outpost in the Pacific.

So political unrest welcomed Neruda home. But there were compensations. Pablo was delighted to find himself reunited with his old friends, and behaved as if he had never been away and as though he were not married, plunging enthusiastically back into his old bohemian lifestyle.

Sadly, his friends' opinion of Maruca was no better than his family's. Diego Muñoz, who by now had a law doctorate, wrote:

As soon as we learnt of his arrival, we visited him at his apartment in the Huneena passageway, on the Calle Catedral. He was living there with his wife, María Antonieta Hagenaar. We friends gathered to comment on the situation. Of course, none of us liked the wife. She was an unfriendly creature, who did not show the slightest interest in meeting Pablo's old friends. Moreover, she spoke only English, and hadn't learned a single word of Spanish. On the other hand, we all noticed that Pablo had changed a great deal. He was no longer the sombre, melancholic, absent young man. Now he talked a lot, laughed for the strangest reasons . . .[3]

Escorting Pablo back home in the early hours of the morning,

there was the *gringa* [foreigner], at a third-floor window, leaning on the balcony. That was how she waited for him every night. I immediately sensed Pablo shiver. There was going to be a conflict. The same one as always. He'd have to explain, he'd be falsely cheerful, resort to my help and laugh. The *gringa* remained hermetic, evidently disgusted. Suddenly, she let out a torrent of English like a stream of cold water . . . She had been brought up in a colonial world, used to extremely formal receptions where people would no doubt complain of the heat and fan themselves, drink whisky and speak English. That was the civilised thing to do. Come and join us in one of our bars? Never! Speak Spanish, learn Spanish? Never! The *gringa* was still living in Batavia, completely absent in our country . . . That woman did whatever she could to distance Pablo from all his friends.[4]

Others were kinder towards Neruda's first wife. Lavinia (Lala) Andrade – the wife of Neruda's friend, Rubén Azócar – used to see a lot of Pablo and Maruca, joining them in a goulash at the Viena restaurant. 'She was very tall, taller than Pablo, she whistled nicely. I thought that was very strange in her. She could whistle like a bird. But most of the time she was silent. She was like that, timid and silent. Maybe proud . . . maybe semi-indifferent.'[5]
Neruda's friend Homero Arce wrote:

Relaxed and athletic, he [Pablo] arrived on the arm of Maruca Hagenaar . . . She was very tall and attractive, naturally beautiful, and she communicated with him in English only. Soon after they arrived, they moved into lodgings in the Calle Catedral, opposite the Congress, two blocks from the Plaza de Armas . . . In his rather forlorn suitcase, he brought presents for a few friends, little knives and Asiatic masks. Maruca, in her suitcase, brought dozens of pairs of shoes which she placed in long rows on the bedroom floor.[6]

Arce, of course, never wrote a word about the fact that he had married Neruda's love, Laura Arrué, while Pablo was in the Far East. Nor did he mention the fact that Neruda was still in love with Laura and may have begun courting her again, even though both he and she were married to others. It is unclear whether Maruca was aware of her husband's affection for Laura.

Despite the fact that Maruca had met with an icy reception from Neruda's father and stepmother in Temuco, she wrote at least four letters to Neruda's half-sister Laurita between May 1932 and April 1932, and these letters do suggest that she had more command of Spanish than Pablo's friends believed, or chose to believe.

And although some people remember Maruca as spending her time moaning about lack of money, her letters to Laurita reveal a more cheerful temperament. 'I like Santiago a lot, what a big city! The climate is very good, not as cold as Temuco,' she wrote to Laurita on 2 May 1932.[7] She told Laurita: 'What a pity that you can't be with us.'

Thanks to the efforts of friends, the Chilean Foreign Ministry was persuaded to create a new, part-time post especially for Neruda at a Ministry library, but his financial difficulties persisted. 'My money situation is worse than bad,' he explained in a letter to Héctor Eandi on 26 September.

Only the pleasure of my recent arrival stops me from dashing off in search of a country with less bankruptcy and less misery. I'm going to try and leave Chile by next autumn. My years of service in the consular corps and the thousand miseries that gnawed at my bones there got me nowhere. I returned to Chile without a cent, without a job and without being dismissed. Recently, they made me librarian in a library which doesn't exist, with a salary that also hardly exists.[8]

His marriage proving no consolation, Neruda sought other women: not only Laura Arrué, but his other great love, a relationship which had appeared moribund but which he felt a need to resuscitate, Albertina Rosa Azócar. It is as if he craved the passion that had already drained from his marriage.

On 15 May 1932, Pablo wrote to Albertina:

I would like to see you. Would you like to write me a long letter? There's so much to talk about, so much to remember. I don't want to torment you, but I believe you made a big mistake. My telegrams, my letters, told you that I was going to marry you as soon as you arrived in Colombo. Albertina, I already had the marriage licence, and I had asked for the necessary money. You know this, I repeated it in every one of my letters to you, in great detail. Now my sister tells me that I asked you to come and live with me, without getting married, and that that was what you said. Never! Why do you lie? On top of the terrible bitterness over your not understanding me, I have the bitterness at your slandering me. I've loved you dearly, Albertina, you know it, and you've behaved badly. You were silent when I most needed you, just like you were when you didn't answer a single one of my letters from Llanquihue in 1926. When you left Belgium, even when you knew you were coming back, you didn't write to me to explain. Why not? Only you know that. Your letter from Concepción which I received 10 months late gave me strange reasons, as if you could ever explain such silence. But anyway, let's forget the harm we've done to each other and let's be friends. Let's have hope . . . You can write to me at the Ministry of Foreign Affairs where I work. You will know that I have been married since December 1930. The loneliness that you did not want to cure became more and more unbearable to me. You will understand if you think of so many years in exile. I would so love to kiss your forehead a little, caress your hands which I've loved so much, give you a little of the friendship and affection which I still hold for you in my heart. Don't show this letter to anyone. And no one must know that you are writing to me. Can you come to Santiago for a day? Kisses from your old friend, Pablo.[9]

Nearly two months later, on 11 July, after not a word from Albertina, Neruda wrote to her again with new reproaches:

Always the same, how can I ever trust you? Rubén tells me that you have written to him, so why not a line for me? The same, just the same as before! I know that you tell him that you could come to Chillán. Don't do it, I beg you. Come to Santiago. It's very easy to arrange a transfer. When are you coming, can you come in September? I'm finding it so hard to write to you, I have so much to say, to talk to you about, to reproach you about, to tell you. I remember you every day, I thought you would write me a letter every day, but you are as ungrateful as ever. I still can't understand what happened to you in Europe. I still don't understand why you didn't come [to me]. Why don't you write me a long letter, for the first time in your life, telling me things?[10]

Albertina never replied to this letter, and it was the last Pablo ever sent her expressing his love. He asked his friend, the writer, Angel Cruchaga, to publish a prominent photograph of himself and Maruca, newly married, in the journal, *Zig-Zag*, which Cruchaga edited – presumably with the aim of hurting Albertina. She did not respond – but five years later, she married Cruchaga. In later years, when Neruda met Albertina, he treated her with the affection of a friend, but not a close friend. But just as with Josie Bliss, and with his other great loves in his life, he never forgot the depth of his previous feelings for her, as can be seen in the two beautiful poems dedicated to her in his 1964 collection, *Memorial de Isla Negra*.

His growing fame as a poet compensated for his personal strife. Neruda's name attracted huge crowds in Santiago. When he gave a recital of poems for the Amigos del Arte [Friends of Art] on 11 May 1932, the hall, the Posada del Corregidor, was packed. The audience was dazzled by the beauty of the poem 'Arte poética' (Poetic Art):

In shadow and space, between garrisons and ladies,
armed with a strange heart and gloomy dreams
I'm suddenly pale, my forehead's wrinkled,
and like a furious widow in mourning for every day.
With every drop of invisible water that I sip at drowsily
and every sound that I take in trembling,
I feel the same absent thirst and the same chill fever . . .

More interesting, however, is the list of poems that the Chilean poet Roberto Meza Fuentes states were read by Neruda at the recital. They include well-known poems from what was to be *Residencia en la tierra* such as 'Lamento lento' (Slow Lament) and 'Alianza (Sonata)' (Alliance), but also two mysterious titles: 'Prothalamio' (Prothalamium) and 'Oda tórrida' (Torrid Ode). The choice of the word Prothalamio shows how familiar Neruda was with old English poetry; Edmund Spenser had coined it more than 300 years earlier, in 1597. Unfortunately, no record exists of Neruda's poem, or why he left it out of *Residencia*.

'Oda tórrida' was written in Java in 1931, and, as Edmundo Olivares Briones has pointed out,[11] its oppressive tone is similar to that of poems like 'El joven monarca' (The Young Monarch). But there is also an epic quality foreshadowing one of Neruda's greatest works, *Alturas de Macchu Picchu* (The Heights of Macchu Picchu) – maybe it was this that persuaded Neruda that it did not fit in with the intensely personal poems of *Residencia*. The poem appeared only in June 1935, in a short-lived Chilean publication called *Revista del Pacífico*.

Two days after Neruda's Santiago poetry recital, Maruca wrote to Laurita, referring to the successful reading but also complaining about the parlous state of their finances: Pablo, she said, 'is working at the Foreign Ministry for 400 pesos, just enough to pay for our lodgings. It's very little and we can't afford to buy wine or grapes, but it's a transitory job, while he waits for something better. We are looking for a cheap little house or flat with a bathroom. We don't like the boarding house any more, the bathroom is very bad and we go to the public baths where we each pay 4.40 pesos.'[12]

That same month, on 29 May, many of Chile's leading writers arranged a homage to their great compatriot, on his return from the Orient. Among those present at the glittering occasion at Santiago's Giovinezza restaurant was his old foe, Pablo de Rokha, as well as loyal friends like Diego Muñoz, Tomás Lago, Rubén Azócar, Angel Cruchaga and Alberto Rojas Giménez. He thanked them for their 'rock-solid friendship'.[13]

Yet one of his enemies was already sharpening his literary knife. When, just a few weeks later, the second edition of *Twenty Love Poems* was published, Hernán Díaz Arrieta (Alone) – the man who had helped Neruda to get his first book, *Crepusculario*, published – spotted his chance:

After eight years, Pablo Neruda's *Twenty Love Poems* reappear, magnificently adorned in violet, as if for a consecration . . . If we pick up his book, after eight years, and compare the impression it made on us at the time and today, we hardly need to change our response at all, except for the hope that the poet might soon evolve in the direction of clarity. Well, he's evolved, all right – but he's become even more obscure.[14]

Alone grudgingly conceded that some of Neruda's poems 'have such beauty, audacity and transparency that they drip and dazzle with sea water . . . You cannot hide this light. What's serious, what's tragic, is the entirety of his poetry, its direction, the course which it is taking not away from chaos but towards chaos . . . We do not know what precise point *Residencia en la tierra* will reach, but we can guess at it from from the reading he gave of some of the poems at a literary centre. They seem terrible.'[15]

As can be seen by Alone's final comment, rumours were abounding about an imminent publication of Neruda's next book, *Residencia en la tierra* (Residence on Earth) – although the poet himself was less confident about where and how it could be published. Undaunted by the failure of his attempt to get the collection produced in Spain, he was still more keen to have it appear outside Chile because of the terrible economic plight facing his homeland. In a letter to Héctor Eandi on 5 September 1932, he expressed the hope that an Argentinian novelist, Elvira de Alvear, would be able to publish *Residencia* in Barcelona. However, Alvear disappeared with the manuscript. At which point, Neruda threatened to produce a copy of the corrections, as well as letters from influential allies, and send them to a literary journal in Buenos Aires so that Elvira was portrayed in the worst possible light. It seems this was bluster born out of extreme frustration. In the end, as Neruda told Eandi: 'I never even summoned up the strength to write to the girl Alvear. Let her go to hell!'[16] He turned back to Chile and to his first publisher, Nascimento.

By now, Pablo and Maruca had moved from their boarding house in the Calle Santo Domingo, with its dreadful bathroom, into the tiny apartment at Calle Catedral 1155. On 8 October 1932, Maruca wrote to Laurita again to say that she wished the new place were bigger 'so that you could come and live with us'. She was trying her hardest to adapt to her husband's lifestyle, despite what his friends said of her.

And the letter, in stumbling but by no means non-existent Spanish, has glimpses of a sense of humour which others failed to spot.

> We are very well. I'm thinner, I've lost 8 kilos, which I'm very pleased about. Neftalí is a little fatter, which he's not pleased about. We have so many friends, we are great friends with the Spanish Ambassador, Ricardo Baeza, and his wife, especially the Ambassador, who is a writer. He has great affection for Neftalí. His wife is very nice, I like her a lot . . . PS: A friend of Neftalí's has brought for you in Temuco a book of the new edition of the *Twenty Love Poems*. He is a very good poet.[17]

This was the only time Maruca ever wrote about her husband's poetry.

On 10 November, Neruda gave a second recital, this time at the Teatro Miraflores in Santiago. In his regular Thursday column in the Chilean daily, *La Nación*, Joaquín Edwards Bello, wrote: 'In countries like Chile, where lapidaries and similar experts do not exist, the reconstituted ruby may be taken for genuine. Fortunately, we do have some literary experts and many of them concur in declaring Neruda the greatest young poet in America.'[18]

The recital went down well. But the very next day – to Neruda's disgust – Pablo de Rokha launched a particularly vicious assault in the Chilean press. He said that, with the exception of *Tentativa del hombre infinito*, none of Neruda's works deserved the praise the critics had heaped on them. He called *Crepusculario* 'supremely stupid, appallingly mediocre', and *Twenty Love Poems* 'very ordinary'. For de Rokha it was 'an old, mangled bicycle, with pedals moving with lamentable rhythm, without boldness, without shape, without greatness, without universal appeal . . .'[19]

Two weeks later, even more bilious criticism came Neruda's way – from the same source.

> A friend told me that 'Neruda's hand is a cold hand, soft and sticky, like a lizard's belly.' Yes, indeed. And so is his presence, his spirit, his literature . . . The fact is that Neruda belongs to the family of batrachians or molluscs. He's a warm-water animal. He's an animal with only one stomach, like a snake, without a mouth, without a life, without a tongue, with gills, with lungs in the half-light, lined

with gourd-skin, slippery, sticky, suspicious. His poetry is the poetry of a fish, lamentable poetry, insulting poetry from a literary crocodile.[20]

Neruda was acquiring a very jaundiced view of the literary world, despite the popular success of the new edition of *Twenty Love Poems*. When asked by the magazine, *Lecturas*, to comment on the state of literary criticism in Chile, he hit back at Alone, whom he called 'a critic from a backward culture who has always been in conflict with his times, and the product of this conflict has been sterile work'.[21] However, he did not fully defend himself against de Rokha and Alone until he wrote the long poem, 'Aquí Estoy' (Here I Am) years later.

At this time, Neruda's orientation was not political – or certainly not directed towards praising Russian Communism and its people, even though the Russian Revolution was already sixteen years old. Fads and fashions in Chile were not sufficient to sway him. It would take the experience of the Spanish Civil War to bring him firmly into the Communist camp, and this lay a few years off. One of the most fascinating letters in all the early correspondence is one that Pablo wrote to Eandi on 17 February 1933, in which he refers much more concretely to his political views than he had done previously – and distances himself from Soviet Communism.

> It seems that a wave of Marxism is criss-crossing the world. Letters I receive [from] Chilean friends are pushing me towards that position. In reality, politically speaking, you cannot be anything but a Communist or an anti-Communist today . . . A few years ago, I was an anarchist, editor of the anarchist trade union journal, *Claridad*, where I published my ideas and things for the first time. And I still retain the anarchist's distrust of the forms of the state, of impure politics. But I believe that my romantic intellectual's point of view is not important. What is true is that I hate proletarian, proletarianising art. In any period, systematic art can tempt only the lesser artist. There has been an invasion here of odes to Moscow, tanks, etc. I continue to write about dreams.

This same letter also reveals how hurt he had been by the criticisms of Alone and Pablo de Rokha. 'I've been the object of both appalling insults (from fellow writers, of course) and extreme praise. I've tried to return to a diplomatic career, but my country is too poor and it wasn't possible.'[22]

Neruda's depressed state of mind imbues a letter he wrote to Laurita on 27 November: 'I can't send you a book for the school because I'd have to buy it, and I never have any money. Life in Santiago is becoming more and more expensive.'[23] He also informed his family that it would be difficult to find a job in Santiago for his brother, Rodolfo, as they had requested. But at least Neruda was delighted to hear that an operation his stepmother had undergone on her leg had turned out well. And soon there was a good piece of political news: Arturo Alessandri Palma won the 30 October presidential elections in Chile with a clear majority. His victory – and second stint as President – was hailed as a return to a stable and constitutional society.

The year 1933 began with Neruda as impoverished as ever. He wrote to Laurita on 4 January to say that he and Maruca had spent a happy New Year's Eve, despite his wife's bout of poor health, but that he couldn't help the family financially after the death of his Uncle Manuel 'because I myself am very poor. My salary is not enough to live off, life is incredibly expensive in Santiago . . . Maruca is still very weak.'[24]

Residencia en la tierra, as it happened, was not Neruda's next book to be published. On 24 January 1933, *El hondero entusiasta* (The Ardent Slingsman) was published by Letras. This was the volume of poetry that Neruda had shelved in Temuco in 1926 after the Uruguayan poet Carlos Sabat Ercasty had confirmed his own influence on the writing – and because he himself thought it was 'excessive'.

The critics were generally kind to *El hondero*. The Chilean daily, *El Mercurio*, wrote: 'These are poems in which the form remains that of which Neruda acquired mastery in *Crepusculario*. Long, violent, superb lines, their tone lit up with eroticism . . .'[25]

At last, however, on 16 February 1933, Neruda was able to write to Héctor Eandi to say: '*Residencia en la tierra* is being printed at this very moment in a luxury edition of just 100 copies, by Nascimento. It will be a stupendous edition. You can count on one copy, the only one I'll be able to send to Argentina. It will cost 50 Chilean dollars and I don't think that it will be on sale in Buenos Aires.'[26]

The idea was to follow this large-format edition quickly with a normal, commercial edition of *Residencia*, but the publication of that first edition was vitally important for Neruda. It meant more than the culmination of a struggle lasting nearly five years across continents. 'These poems indicated that I had at last found my voice. With great serenity, I discovered that I was coming to possess a territory which was indisputably mine.'[27]

The luxury edition of *Residencia en la tierra* met with a mixed reception. For many, it was simply too expensive to buy. Some felt offended that they had not received a signed copy. The publisher, Nascimento, thought that the cost was too high to send out publicity copies. One of the first to review the book, predictably, was Pablo de Rokha. As the title of his article – 'Epitaph to Neruda' – indicates, de Rokha remained determined to demolish Neruda both as a man and as a poet. In his lengthy article in *La Opinión*, he implied that Neruda was a fake. He took as his theme the 'mask', and made capital out of the fact that page four of the luxury edition of *Residencia* featured a photograph of a plaster cast of Neruda's face made by the Chilean sculptor Totila Albert a few years earlier – and from the masks Neruda had used in his recitals in Santiago's Posada del Corregidor and Teatro Miraflores the previous year. 'Pablo Neruda. Yes indeed, the mask. Neruda is both the owner and the victim of the mask; of that "poet's mask" which begins and defines *Residencia en la tierra . . .*' De Rokha claimed that Neruda's 'words hang like rags'.[28]

Fortunately, the Chilean author Norberto Pinilla wrote a far more favourable review of *Residencia* in *La Nación*: 'Neruda's work is a beautiful, definitive, singular contribution to Chilean literature . . . Neruda possesses his very own poetic language. The words submissively obey the poet's inspiration and are moulded gently, meekly, to the theme of his song . . . Neruda has reached intellectual maturity, has acquired a mastery over his creative work.'[29]

The Chilean critics were still divided over Pablo Neruda the poet. As his great friend, Luis Enrique Délano, wrote in a Chilean newspaper article at the time:

> Surely few things have been so argued over as Neruda's poetry. While some have condemned him blindly, others have proclaimed him like a new faith and shared his literary journey, hoisting him up as their flag. And yet no one can have failed to recognise that the voice of Pablo Neruda has influenced a whole generation in Chile and has even sounded out among other people far from America.[30]

In some ways it is ironic that, after the immense effort he had put into seeing *Residencia* into print, Neruda himself became ambivalent about many of the poems in later years. In 1950 he told his Mexican friend, the writer and critic Alfredo Cardona Peña, 'Looking back at them now, I consider the poems of *Residencia en la tierra* to be harmful. These poems must not be read by young people in our countries. They are poems which are soaked in atrocious pessimism and anguish, they do not help you to live, but to die.'[31]

One of the best-known poems in the book, bearing the English title, 'Walking Around', and seen by some critics as among the most pessimistic poems in the Spanish language, begins:

> It so happens that I'm tired of being a man

There was a tragically concrete reason why Neruda came to feel the power of the poems in this collection could be fatal. In 1949 he learned that a young student had shot himself dead under a tree while reading *Residencia*. The book was found open at 'Significa sombras' (It Means Shadows) which begins:

> What hope can be kept alive, what pure premonition,
> what irrevocable kiss sunk in our hearts,
> acknowledging the roots of need – and the intelligence,
> self-confident and smooth on always muddied waters

Neruda told Margarita Aguirre that the news of the student's suicide had been one of the greatest shocks he had ever received in his life.[32]

Nevertheless, when his Argentinian publisher, Losada, produced a collection of of his complete works in 1951, Neruda allowed all three volumes of *Residencia* to be included. And when the Italian critic Giuseppe Bellini was preparing an anthology of his poems in 1959, Neruda wrote personally to Bellini to recommend that he include 'quite a few poems' from *Residencia*.[33]

Bellini sees in the collection the influence of the philosophical and satirical Golden Age poet, Francisco de Quevedo, especially in Neruda's gloomy fascination with the passage of time and man's minimal place in the universe. Neruda did later write an entire essay devoted to the debt he owed the Spaniard. And he told the Spanish critic Amado

Alonso – who wrote the first major critical study of Neruda's work in 1940 – that the line from the poem 'Alianza (Sonata)'

> precedes and follows the day and its golden family

was directly influenced by a line from Quevedo's sonnet, 'Lisi's Portrait Carried in a Ring'.[34]

In 1933, Neruda's stepmother fell ill again in the aftermath of her operation, and his father was also unwell. Fearing for their health, Neruda paid two visits to Temuco. He did not take Maruca with him. The reasons he and Maruca gave were finances and Maruca's own frail health. 'I'm very sorry I couldn't come to Temuco to see you and I hope that we can see each other together next summer,' Maruca wrote to Laurita on 14 April 1933. 'Autumn in Temuco is too cold for me, and we did not have enough money to pay for my trip.'[35] It seems likely both Pablo and Maruca realised that, apart from Laurita, his family would not make her feel that welcome and it was better for all concerned if she remained in Santiago.

On his return from this visit to Temuco, in May 1933, Neruda learned that he had been given a better-paid post, at the department of cultural extension at the Ministry of Employment. The drawback was that it was a post which could soon be suppressed – so there was no financial security. The tensions continued. Creatively, the whole of this period, from April 1932 to August 1933, was a barren one: Neruda wrote just four poems, which would later form the start of Volume Two of *Residencia*. These poems were: 'Un día sobresale' (A Day Stands Out), 'Sólo la muerte' (Only Death), 'Barcarola' (Barcarole) and 'El sur del océano' (South of the Ocean)

'Un dia sobresale' provides a poignant picture of Neruda's sense of time slipping by:

> Around me the night rings out,
> the day, the month, time,
> ring out like sacks of wet bells
> or fearful mouths of fragile salt

In mid-1933, he was delighted to receive the news that he had been offered a new, and far more prestigious, diplomatic posting – as consul in Buenos Aires. He was relieved at the thought of leaving a Chile which, in the words of its own President, Arturo Alessandri Palma, was going through 'a period of true national calamity'. Alessandri's second term as President had not lived up to the expectations a change of government had aroused. He had moved towards the Right, partly under the influence of his formidable Finance Minister, Gustavo Ross. He put down strikes ruthlessly, and harassed the Left.

Whether Maruca was happy to move once again is hard to tell. She seems to have been making big efforts to settle down, and the prospect of uprooting cannot have been too appealing. As Neruda had written to Eandi back on 16 February: 'My wife is getting used to Chile and is slowly learning Spanish. She is always reminding me to write to you (she knows we are good friends), but I arrive home exhausted from the office, and I don't feel like doing anything.'[36]

On 25 August 1933, Neruda wrote to his father to inform him that he had been told to leave for Buenos Aires immediately 'hardly giving me enough time to sort out my debts and prepare my luggage. As we must leave on Sunday, I do not have time to say goodbye to you and Maruca is especially sorry, and me too, since my wandering lifestyle means I have to leave again.'[37]

Neruda would have preferred to have been posted to Spain. In fact, before the Buenos Aires posting came up, rumours had been flying that the Chilean government was planning to give him a European posting, as he informed Eandi.

Neruda and Maruca left Chile for in Buenos Aires on 28 August 1933. Maruca was ill, Neruda informed Laurita in a letter. But, in stark contrast to his desolate diplomatic postings in the Far East, Neruda was immediately made to feel at home when he arrived. His new boss, Sócrates Aguirre, the Chilean consul-general in Buenos Aires, was a remarkable human being: kind, cultured and tolerant. Sócrates' young daughter, Margarita, was destined to be his secretary, friend and biographer in later life.

She was only eight when Neruda was consul in Buenos Aires, but she still recalled those days clearly years later. She remembered him in their apartment in Caballito, on New Year's Eve 1933, in a red dressing-gown, dressed as Father Christmas with white cotton stuck to his cheeks. Margarita and her brother recognised him at once and shouted: 'You're Pablo Neruda!' He always spoke to the Aguirre children in English – probably, says Margarita, to please their old Irish governess, Miss Maria, who found the poet 'so kind . . .'[38]

That's how the young Margarita saw him, too. He was very affectionate to her when she visited his consular offices. He would call her to his side and show her his coloured pencils or a photograph of himself dressed as a sailor. He would stroke her black hair, and she 'felt protected next to him, a sensation which lasted all my life'.[39]

This time Neruda quickly found himself in the midst of a wide circle of new friends. The most intimate of these were Pablo Rojas Paz, Oliverio Girondo and his wife, Norah Lange. He also finally met Héctor Eandi, and they remained friends despite their political differences.

In August 1933, just days after Neruda and Maruca's arrival in Buenos Aires, they were joined by the Chilean writer, María Luisa Bombal, who was feeling literally suicidal after an unrequited love affair with the married Eulogio Sánchez Errázuriz, a commander in the Republican Milicians (a paramilitary, anti-Communist organisation enjoying the support of Chile's President Arturo Alessandri). Neruda had enormous affection for Bombal and, feeling deep sympathy for her emotional upheaval, invited her to join them in Buenos Aires and live at their comfortable apartment, which was twenty floors up a skyscraper. He nicknamed Bombal 'Madame Mérimée' because the French poet had been the the subject of her doctoral thesis at the Sorbonne in Paris. Other affectionate nicknames for her were 'mongoose' – in memory of Pablo's beloved pet in Java – 'Fire Bee' or 'María Piojo' ('Maria Louse' – *piojo* being a typically Chilean way of referring to beloved children).

Although Neruda often teased Bombal playfully, he respected her mind. Introducing her to his old schoolfriend, Juvencio Valle, he warned him that she was 'an elegant, witty princess, the only woman one can talk seriously to about literature'.[40] For her part, those months spent living at Neruda's Buenos Aires apartment gave Bombal a chance to observe the poet's deteriorating relationship with his wife (although Bombal got on quite well with Maruca and was much fonder of her than many of Pablo's friends). In fact, much of what she witnessed as Pablo's and Maruca's 'loneliness *à deux*' fed Bombal's great novel, *La última niebla* (The House of Mist), which she wrote in the Nerudas' Buenos Aires kitchen.

When the Chilean writer, María Flora Yáñez, visited Buenos Aires, Neruda arranged a cocktail party in her honour on 3 October 1933, and the joint hostesses were Maruca and María Luisa Bombal 'such was the degree of friendship' between the two women. Pablo, for his part, took Yáñez on to the terrace and told her: 'You're lovely, María Flor, I mean that with all my heart.' After the dinner, Yañez later recalled, Neruda suggested to the guests – who also included the Argentinian writer Alfonsina Storni – that they finish off the evening at Signo, a writers' centre in Buenos Aires.

> Then Maruca disappeared into her bedroom signalling to Neruda to follow her. Soon we could hear a screaming row. 'That's Maruca saying she doesn't want us to go to Signo,' said Storni. 'She hates late nights, but she's wrong, because an extraordinary poet like Neruda needs to be up all night.' At which point, Neruda and Maruca emerged from the bedroom. He was looking glummer than ever, and she was still convulsed with anger. 'Right, let's go to Signo,' Pablo ordered. And we left.[41]

Neruda and Maruca managed to keep up appearances in public; Sócrates Aguirre thought that Neruda and Maruca made a very good couple, as they plunged into Buenos Aires social life.

Despite their political differences and the fact that she was religious and Neruda was an atheist, Pablo had far more in common with Bombal than with Maruca. Asked once in an interview whether she feared death, Bombal replied: 'Since I'm religious, I don't, no.' Her interviewer then noted: 'How strange, Neruda once gave the same answer as you when we asked him that question. He said four words: "Death does not exist."'

'It's true,' said Bombal.

> He realised that, as well. And it is not the reply of a Marxist. It's what the Neruda whom I knew would have answered, the Neruda with whom I lived for a time in Argentina, with his wife Maruca Hagenaar. At that time, he was a man with leftist ideas, but that's all. He had no party political viewpoint . . . We loved each other. We were like brother and sister in our youth . . . Yes, Pablo is the reminder of a totally unforgettable part of my life. He was very kind, very generous to me.

For Bombal, Neruda at this time 'was the Pablo of *Residencia en la tierra*, the most valuable, poetically speaking . . .'

He taught me a lot . . . He created a language which came from the soul. It began to deteriorate when he allowed politics to enter his work. He invented an entire language. I learnt a lot from *Residencia en la tierra*. . . . I got a mysterious strength from his *Residencia*, although I expressed myself very differently, of course . . . Pablo sometimes fought with me over literary matters. He enjoyed reading me his writings. I told him: 'I like that,' or 'I don't like that,' and sometimes he got cross and said: 'You don't understand modern poetry, you get no further than Mallarmé' . . . But he always came to me with his papers, saying: 'Look, listen to this,' and he'd read it out to me.

The poems he read out included 'Walking Around'. 'I was really indignant,' recalled Bombal.

He had added a horrible phrase: '*Matar a una monja con un irrigador*' (To kill a nun with a sprinkler) . . . That's ugly, I told him. 'It's grotesque. That's not you, that's just in there to *épater les bourgeois*. I don't see why you have to put it in.' He came back a few hours later and said: 'Look, listen to this now. I've changed the sentence.' He read the poem again, and then it was his turn to get cross. He said: 'What really makes me angry is: how is it possible that an ignoramus like you is always right?'[42]

In the final version of the poem, Neruda replaced the lethal sprinkler with the surreal 'blow from an ear'.

In Buenos Aires Neruda met the genius who, in his short life, was to become one of his closest friends. The Spanish poet and play-wright Federico García Lorca had arrived in Buenos Aires on 13 October 1933, for the Argentinian première of his play, *Bodas de Sangre* (Blood Wedding). That very night, at the house of the Argentinian writer Pablo Rojas Paz, Lorca was introduced to Neruda.

Neruda was twenty-nine, Lorca thirty-five. Both men had recently spent time away from their homeland. For both men, the culture shock had been dramatic. Lorca's trip to New York had been particularly painful for him. Both men had felt all too keenly the loneliness of the outsider – not the fashionable, bohemian 'outsider among outsiders' of fellow poets, but a genuine outsider. Both had fathers who had opposed the idea of their becoming poets, but who had reluctantly paid for them to study in their respective capitals.

Both men shared a vast appetite for life – and a mutual appreciation of each other's poetry. Lorca inscribed a copy of his collection *Gypsy Ballads* with the words: 'For my dear Pablo, one of the few great poets I've had the good fortune to love and know.' Indeed, whenever he heard Neruda begin to recite his verse, Lorca would laughingly raise his arms, cover his ears, and tell the Chilean, 'Stop, stop, that's enough. Don't read any more, you'll influence me!' And although Neruda was still not openly expressing his political beliefs, there was a clear affinity between the two men in this area, as well. When Lorca told a journalist from *Crítica* that 'those who love and enjoy freedom are on the Left', Neruda would have wholeheartedly agreed.

Nothing illustrated the depth of closeness between these two remarkable men better than the tribute they paid to the great Nicaraguan poet, Rubén Darió, at a PEN Club ceremony on 28 October 1933. At the Hotel Plaza in Buenos Aires, Neruda and Lorca startled their audience by rising jointly to their feet and taking turns to read sentences *al alimón* – a bullfighting term for when two bullfighters hold a single cape between them and jointly outwit the bull.

The two poets memorably collaborated on another artistic project in March 1934, while they were in the Argentinian capital together. Lorca produced ten pen-and-ink drawings to illustrate a short series of poems (including 'Solo la muerte' (Only Death) from *Residencia*) and phrases by Neruda. They produced a single, handmade copy of the work. The harrowing final sketch shows two bleeding severed heads – one clearly Lorca's, the other Neruda's, on a table beneath a crescent moon.

The eight months Neruda spent in Buenos Aires were ones of intense sexual activity – but not with his wife. Earlier in 1933, before leaving Chile, he had fallen in love with Loreto Bombal, María Luisa's sister. One of his great poems during this period, 'Oda con un lamento' (Ode with a Lament), is probably written for her. At the same time, this poem also contains heavy nostalgia for a past love, possibly Josie Bliss in Burma.

Hernán Loyola, sees the whole of Neruda's stay in Argentina as being dominated by the erotic power of memory. I think, rather, that this poem shows Neruda trying to 'neutralise' or even erase the old erotic memories with newer, more positive ones. In other words, there has been a shift from Josie to Loreto, and to the other women passing through his life. The past memories are of death. In 'Oda con un lamento', he imagines himself kissing Loreto, with the waves of the sea at his back,

> swimming against the cemeteries floating in certain rivers
> with wet grass growing on sad plaster tombs

And while Josie 'keeps calling to me through her sobs' – a clear allusion to that tearful final goodbye between the lovers on the harbour in Ceylon – Loreto weeps not with sobs or sorrow but with 'health, onions, bees / burning alphabet-books'.

Whereas in *Twenty Love Poems*, Neruda was frequently tortured by his present love, here his current love rescues him from torment. The pain, now, comes not from his present sexual experiences – which give him joy – but from the act of wrenching himself away from past erotic recollections.

As he drifted apart from Maruca, spending long nights enjoying the same bohemian lifestyle he had led in Santiago as a bachelor, there was certainly no shortage of erotic escapades. In his memoirs, Neruda recalled an amorous adventure in which he and Lorca had been involved at the Buenos Aires home of the millionaire magnate, Natalio Botana:

> At the table, Federico and I sat on either side of the host and across from a tall, ethereal poet who kept her green eyes more on me than on Federico during the meal . . . We got up when we'd finished eating, myself, the poetess and Federico, who was enjoying every-thing . . . We climbed up to the highest lookout point on the tower . . . I took the tall, golden girl in my arms, and as I kissed her, I found her sensual, well-fleshed, all woman, perfect in every way. To Federico's surprise, we lay down on the floor of the lookout, and I was starting to undress her when I noticed Federico's enormous eyes staring at us, not daring to believe what was happening. 'Get out of here! Go and make sure that no one comes up the stairs', I shouted at him . . . Federico ran off cheerfully to fulful his mission as aide and sentinel – with such haste and such ill fortune that he tumbled down the dark tower stairway. The lady and I had to help him up, with great difficulty. He hobbled around for two weeks.[43]

Another, very different account of this whole episode has recently emerged – although its veracity is by no means proven. It purports to come from the woman who was the mysterious poetess in this episode (Neruda did not name her). The Uruguayan poet, Blanca Luz Brum, lived a full life. She was kidnapped from a convent by a Peruvian poet, Juan Parra del Riego, whom she married at seventeen but who died of tuberculosis three years later. She was a revolutionary Marxist early on, the lover of the Mexican mural painter, David Alfaro Siqueiros, before switching sides and acting as a propagandist for Juan Domingo Perón – and even for Augusto Pinochet! She became a Chilean citizen in 1981 and died four years later. After her death many of her unpublished letters, articles and interviews were collected in a book by the Uruguayan author, Hugo Achugar; these include – or so Achugar insists – Blanca Luz Brum's version of the bell-tower episode, which bears very little resemblence to Neruda's account:

> By then, I was no longer interested in Neruda and when he tried to embrace me, it was not he who asked Lorca to act as a procurer. I was the one who called Lorca asking him to rescue me. All memoirs are false memories. Neruda's, too . . . It was Lorca who shouted at him: 'Out of here! Go, and make sure you don't drink any more,' while he tried his best to come between us. Neruda tried to push him away. Lorca dodged him and tried to get him off me. I'm not certain whether it was nerves or simply bad luck, but the poor poet, who was much smaller than the Chilean, as he tried to confront him, tripped and fell down the stairwell which led down to the garden fountain, dragging Neruda behind him . . . Poor Delia del Carril and poor all the other women, shackled to a man like that.[44]

Severe doubts have been cast on this unflattering view of Neruda by a journalist, Maura Brescia de Val, who knew Blanca Luz Brum in the last years of her life and who claims to have received the Uruguayan poet's genuine and definitive memoirs from her in person. Brescia insists that Luz Brum never referred to any incident with Neruda in these memoirs.

Like several of the anecdotes and incidents in Neruda's memoirs, it is impossible to know how much he embellished them when he came to recall them in writing, decades later. His early recollection of a sexual encounter in his sleep with a mysterious, unnamed woman in a barn is very reminiscent of Proust's imaginings at the beginning of *Swann's Way*. We know that Neruda, like his fellow Santiago bohemians in the 1920s, was a keen reader of Proust, and devoured the extracts of *A la recherche du temps perdu* which were being translated in Chile in that decade. Much of Neruda's later poetry clearly shows Proust's influence in its sensuality, attention to detail and playing with memories.

Some of the best times in Neruda's Buenos Aires period were spent at the house of the remarkable poet, Oliverio Girondo, and his wife Norah Lange. At a ceremony to mark the launch of Norah's book, *45 días y 30 marineros* (45 Days and 30 Sailors), almost all those present – including Neruda – were disguised as seamen. Norah Lange herself was dressed as as a mermaid, with a long fish-tail.

Despite his sexual and social exertions, Neruda kept reading and writing. He told Pedro Juan Vignale, the editor of the Argentinian poetry magazine *Poesía*, that he was 'working on a long poem, about whose intensity he has only a general idea'. Was Neruda already thinking about his vast masterpiece, *Canto general*, at the time? Vignale certainly thought so, looking back on their conversation. So did the Italian critic, Dario Puccini. But Hernán Loyola is convinced that Neruda was actually thinking about a small cycle of poems which he had begun to write in early 1933 in Chile and which were thematically linked. They would become the second part of *Residencia en la tierra* (under the 'probable' influence, Loyola believes, of Joyce, and T. S. Eliot's *The Waste Land*).

Hernán Loyola sees 'Walking Around' as a literary 'wink' towards James Joyce's *Ulysses*, which Neruda had read in Ceylon.[45] At the same time as he was writing the poem he published his translation of Joyce's *Chamber Music* in the October/November 1933 edition of *Poesía*. Neruda wrote 'Walking Around' in Buenos Aires between October and December 1933, and both this poem and 'Desespediente' – which he wrote at about the same time – are reminders that, despite Neruda's enriching friendships and sexual adventures, there were still mind-numbingly dull bureaucratic chores to fulfil as consul. Indeed, there was far more paperwork than in the Orient, because while no Chilean set foot in Burma or Java or Ceylon for months at a time, Argentina's diplomatic relations with Chile were in a state of constant flux. 'Walking Around' begins:

It so happens that I'm tired of being a man,
it so happens that I enter a tailor's shop or a cinema
withered, impenetrable, like a swan of felt
floundering in a primeval sea of ashes

In late 1933 or early 1934, despite the fact that they saw little of each other, Maruca became pregnant with Pablo's child. And a new posting came his way – Spain. Maruca's horror at having to move again just as she was starting to settle in Buenos Aires was softened by her euphoria about becoming a mother. We know that Neruda himself wanted a child, although he had misgivings about becoming a father in such an uncertain relationship. He also loved Spain and had long sought to live there. Yet he had forebodings about the fate awaiting him when he arrived.

María Luisa Bombal recalled a startling occasion at the Nerudas' home in Buenos Aires:

Once, Pablo had a strange, prophetic nightmare. We were all together and I began to shout to him not to go to Spain. I shouted so much that he told me to be quiet and he went off to bed. And he dreamt of being surrounded by immense quantities of water, every-where. Then he woke up, and imagined that his bed was surrounded by tall clouds of smoke which were encircling him. He got up, terrified, believing the house was on fire, and he went to the kitchen to see what was going on. The kitchen had blueish-white glass panes. Through these, he saw a tall, dark shadow, in profile, a black silhouette, quite motionless. He couldn't stand it any longer and he ran to wake me up. 'I've seen death,' he told me . . . 'I've had a terrible dream. I need to go out, to talk. I'm going to die of a heart attack.' He was pale, white and trembling . . . By this time, Maruca was awake. 'Please go with him,' she said to me. We left the house and went to the Café Munich. We talked until dawn, and when he'd calmed down, we returned home. Shortly afterwards, they sent him to Europe. He had had a premonition of the war, of death, of the Spanish Civil War.[46]

5

Spanish sorrow – the turning-point

1934–37

Neruda and a pregnant Maruca boarded a ship from Buenos Aires, bound for Barcelona, on 5 May 1934. The three-week sea voyage was uneventful – except for the death of a little monkey Neruda had bought in Brazil, who 'died, while Maruca wept huge tears'.[1]

Hardly had he reached Barcelona than Neruda learned of the death back in Chile of his old friend and drinking companion, Alberto Rojas Giménez, the man who had taught him to be a genuine bohemian soon after arriving in Santiago as a student.

His grief over Alberto's death prompted his first poem written in Spain, the magnificently moving 'Alberto Rojas Giménez viene volando' (Alberto Rojas Giménez Comes Flying):

> Over cities of sunken roofs
> where tall women remove their plaits
> with wide hands and lost combs,
> you come flying . . .
>
> Amid bitter-coloured bottles, amid rings of anise and ill-luck
> raising your hands and crying,
> you come flying . . .

> The black wind of Valparaíso
> opens its wings of coal and foam
> to sweep the sky as you pass,
> you come flying . . .[2]

Neruda soon discovered that he did not particularly enjoy living in Barcelona, despite the fact that it was next to the sea, which he usually loved. He wanted to move inland, to Madrid – because he knew that it was in the capital that Spanish cultural life was flourishing.

The Chilean consul in Madrid was none other than the poet Gabriela Mistral – the woman to whom he had been too timid to show his early poems when she was a headmistress in Temuco. Nevertheless, the relationship between the two consuls was not exactly easy. If the Spanish writer and critic, Luis Rosales, can be relied on as a judge, while Neruda retained something of that same veneration for his elder compatriot,

> neither consul visited the other. Of course, Neruda didn't, or couldn't, visit Gabriela Mistral. Gabriela was intelligent, upright, generous and difficult . . . The relationship between both consuls was a distant, telephonic, highly formal one. It was always Gabriela who called. It was always Pablo Neruda who answered . . . I believe they naturally respected one another. I believe they naturally admired one another – but from a distance. And finally, I believe they envied one another, but from a distance.

Rosales, who wrote a study of Neruda's poetry, thought there were also profound poetic differences between them. 'Both represented, at their peaks, two distinct poetic schools – Mistral, post-modernism; Neruda, surrealism – and even more importantly, two distinct eras. In the fifteen years which separated them, poetry had changed greatly, but social life had changed even more.'[3]

Finally, Neruda decided to make a protracted trip to the capital, leaving Maruca behind in Barcelona. As he stepped off the train in Madrid on 1 June 1934, Neruda was delighted to be reunited with Federico García Lorca, who met him at Madrid's Estación del Norte with his lover, Rafael Rodríguez Rapún – a handsome young engineering student, committed socialist and great womaniser who had fallen under Lorca's spell.

Carlos Morla Lynch, the Chilean Ambassador to Spain at the time, met Neruda, Lorca and the others at the Bar Barrera in the Calle de Alcalá and took them back home to eat. In his diary he gives a delightfully vivid physical description of Pablo Neruda, a month short of his thirtieth birthday. Neruda was 'palid, an ashen pale, with big, narrow eyes, like black, crystal almonds, which are constantly laughing . . . His hair is very black, too, badly groomed. His hands are grey. No elegance. Pockets full of documents and newspapers. What captivates us is his voice: it's slow, monotonous, nostalgic, as if tired, but suggestive and full of charm.'[4]

The following day turned out to be a busy one. Neruda visited the Ambassador's residence again. As the poet was not feeling too well after the celebrations of the night before, Morla Lynch offered Neruda a bed, which the poet accepted with alacrity. After he had rested, Gabriela Mistral came to see him. And that night it seemed that most of Madrid's most important personalities arrived at the Chilean Ambassador's residence to meet the illustrious poet.

The party was memorably uproarious. Carlos Morla Lynch recalled in his diary that Lorca danced in a rug; Bebe Vicuña (Carlos's wife) played a guitar and sang her husband's songs (with words based on poems by Lorca, Rafael Alberti, Luis Cernuda, Manuel Altolaguirre and Juan Ramón Jiménez). It was not until the very early hours of the morning that Neruda stood up and read poems from *Residencia en la tierra*. Neruda's reading held his audience transfixed with 'a poetry of profound truth within a modern colouring of naturalistic character. Talent of a unique, unmistakable personality'.

Spain, and especially Madrid, was a revelation for Neruda. 'Within a few days, I was one with the Spanish poets. Spaniards and Latin Americans are different, of course – a difference that is borne with pride, or in error, by either side. The Spaniards of my generation were more brotherly, closer-knit and and better-spirited than their counterparts in Latin America.'[5]

Maruca soon joined Pablo in Madrid. Rafael Alberti, the Spanish Communist poet, reacted with a mixture of astonishment and amusement when a man dashed up the stairs of his Madrid home and said: 'I am Pablo Neruda . . . I have come to say hello. My wife is downstairs, but don't be afraid because she's almost a giant.' Neruda had sent Alberti an early draft of *Residencia en la tierra* from the Far East and Alberti had tried in vain to get it published in Spain.

Alberti found Neruda and Maruca a home in western Madrid. It was situated on the fifth floor of a block on the Calle de Rodríguez San Pedro, looking out on the Guadarrama mountain range. There were geraniums growing on the window sills, and the apartment quickly came to be known as the Casa de las Flores (House of Flowers). It was ideally placed for Neruda: nearby was the Argüelles market, and the poet, a lifelong market-lover, would delightedly trawl the stalls for fruit and vegetables (especially his favourite hot peppers).

The Casa de las Flores quickly became like any of Neruda's homes: open to friends who wanted to join him in drink, food, literary (or other) conversation twenty-four hours a day and host to manic sleeping arrangements (sometimes guests lay crosswise on the floor, in order to fit). Lorca was an almost daily visitor. He and Neruda were virtually inseparable. When they weren't drinking and talking, Neruda would sit in on Lorca's theatre rehearsals, and they often combed Madrid together for suitable props for Federico's plays, or those of other authors he was putting on with his company, La Barraca.

In a famous speech in Madrid on 6 December 1934, Lorca referred to the Chilean as one of the greatest of all Latin American poets, 'closer to death than to philosophy, closer to pain than to intelligence, closer to blood than to ink'. Lorca added that Neruda 'lacks the two elements with which so many false poets have lived: hatred and irony'.[6]

A few months later, in the spring of 1935, Neruda returned the compliment, in a great poem, 'Oda a Federico García Lorca'. This has odd premonitions (similar to the Spaniard's own) of Lorca's imminent death, although Hernán Loyola surprisingly reads the references to death and blood as marking Neruda's response to the brutally repressed miners' rebellion in Asturias, northern Spain, in October 1934:

> When you fly, dressed as a peach tree,
> when you laugh with a laugh like rice tossed in a hurricane,
> when you sing, with a tremble in your arteries and teeth,
> throat and fingers,
> I would die for your gentleness,
> I would die for the red lakes
> where in the depths of autumn you live
> with a fallen steed and a blood-spattered god.[7]

Despite the fact that Maruca had become very weak towards the end of her pregnancy, Neruda continued to party as wildly as ever. Every afternoon, he and his friends would meet up at the Cervecería de Correos bar to plan that evening's activities. Neruda would enjoy plentiful supplies of the Spanish aniseed drink, *chinchón*, to which he had become devoted. They talked about the rapidly deteriorating political situation in Spain. It was a time when to be on the Left seemed the only honourable path, with Hitler's rise to power in Germany the previous year, and Spain hit by repeated waves of repressions (as in Asturias) and atrocities committed by fascist thugs.

Alberti recalled Neruda telling him soon after his arrival in Madrid: 'I don't know anything about politics. I'm a little bit "anarchoid" . . . I want to do whatever I like.' But if Neruda was still clinging to the anarchistic, anti-bourgeois tendencies he had shown as a Santiago student writing for *Claridad*, many of his friends were prepared to commit themselves more decisively. Some, like Rafael Alberti and Miguel Hernández, had already visited the Soviet Union to see at first hand – and gain a taste for – the Communist experiment there. Not so Neruda. Interestingly, one of these friends, the Argentinian Communist poet Raúl González Tuñón, had certainly become more radical since the Asturias uprising, and at least one critic has claimed that Tuñón's book of verse, *La rosa blindada* (The Armour-Plated Rose), which expresses the hopes and sufferings of working people, had a considerable influence on Neruda at the time.[8]

Miguel Hernández, the goat farmer, quickly became a very close friend of Neruda.

> Miguel was a peasant with an aura of earthiness about him. He had a face like a clod of earth or a potato that has just been pulled up from the roots and still has its underground freshness . . . He was the kind of writer who emerges from nature like an uncut stone, with the freshness of the forest and an irresistible vitality. He would tell me how exciting it was to put your ear against the belly of a sleeping she-goat. You could hear the milk coursing down to the udders, a secret sound that no one but that poet of goats has been able to hear. At other times, he would talk to me about the nightingale's song. Eastern Spain, where he came from, swarmed with blossoming orange trees and nightingales. Since that bird, that sublime singer, does not exist in my country, crazy Miguel liked

to give me the most vivid imitation of what it could do. He would shinny up one of the trees in the street and, from its highest branches, would whistle or warble like his beloved native birds.[9]

For Neruda, Hernández was the man who toiled with his hands. (Years later, Neruda lamented the fact that he himself hadn't done anything worthwhile with his hands. Why didn't I make a broom? / Why was I given hands? / What use were they / if all I did was hear the sound of cereal / if all I did was listen to the wind?)[10]

The critic María de Gracia has suggested that, for Miguel Hernández, 'Neruda meant not only a poet who created with blood and mud, capable of touching the world, but also a good, understanding man, closer to a man's heart than to his wisdom.'[11]

Hernández himself wrote a tribute to Neruda – a lengthy, very strange poem called 'Oda entre sangre y vino a Pablo Neruda' (Ode amidst Blood and Wine to Pablo Neruda). In it, Hernández captured the social whirlwind that made up the Chilean's day-to-day existence: 'Around you, Pablo / everything is crazy chatter, closeness / bursting out in song and solstices / until there's sudden silence from exhaustion / and then kisses of purity, arms that understand / their ring-like, bracelet-like fate: embracing.'

On 18 August 1934, Maruca gave birth to a daughter, whom the couple named Malva Marina Trinidad, in honour of Pablo's beloved *mamadre*, the purple flower that Neruda liked and the marine environment of his childhood, which he never forgot. Neruda had cards specially printed and sent them off to all his friends around the world, announcing the happy event.

In Madrid, Lorca was ecstatically happy for his friend, and wrote a great poem, 'Verses on the Birth of Malva Marina Neruda'. It is sad that, unlike Neruda's 1934 poem to Lorca, which the latter had the chance to read with immense joy, Neruda was unaware of Lorca's poem to his newborn daughter – the manuscript came to light only when Lorca's family were sorting through his papers fifty years later. It was published by the Spanish daily, *ABC*, on 12 July 1984.

Unfortunately, it soon became clear that Malva Marina was not growing normally. Her head was too big, and the rest of her body was scrawny. Hence Neruda's memorable description of his daughter as 'a kind of semi-colon, a three-kilo vampire', in a letter to his Argentinian friend Sara Tornú, wife of Pablo Rojas Paz, on 19 September 1934.

Soon after her birth, Neruda wrote a touchingly helpless tribute to the sickly girl, 'Enfermedades en mi casa' (Sickness in My House):

> Like a grain of wheat in the silence, but
> who to beg for pity for a grain of wheat?
> Look at how things are: so many trains,
> so many hospitals with broken knees,
> so many stores with dying people:
> so who? When?
> Who to beg for eyes the colour of a cold month,
> for a heart the size of tottering wheat?
> . . . I'm drowning in the damp of the dew rotting in the shade,
> and for a smile that doesn't grow, for a sweet mouth . . .
> I wrote this poem that is no more than a lament,
> no more than a lament.[12]

Neruda subverts his usual symbols in this poem: the tree, for instance, usually a source of vital energy, now takes on 'vampire-like qualities', sucking his daughter's blood and trapping her little hand in its roots.

In this poem, too, as Hernán Loyola has noted, Neruda also becomes fully aware of himself 'in an almost irrational, mythical sense'[13] as an American and, from Spain, makes his first direct, and desperate, appeal for help to the 'landscape gods' of Temuco:

> Help me, leaves and rain of the South

Neruda wrote to his father (affectionately and uncharacteristically calling him 'dear Papa') a week after his daughter's birth, on 25 August 1934, to say:

> Not everything has gone well. It seems that the child was born prematurely and she nearly died. She has had to have doctors looking after her all the time, and they have forced her to eat with a probe, to have injections of serum and to take spoonfuls of milk, because she wouldn't breast-feed. There were moments of great danger, when the little kid was dying and we did not know what to do. She's had to do without sleep at night, and even during the day, so she could be fed every two hours, but the doctor has just told us

that there is no longer any danger, although the creature will need a lot of care. I think that, as I too have given her a lot of attention, we can bring her up. In twenty days' time, we'll start giving her cod-liver oil, just like I had to take. It's the only solution for rachitic children. The child is very little, she was born weighing 2 kilos and 400 grammes, but she is very pretty, like a little doll, with blue eyes like her grandfather. She has Maruca's nose (fortunately) and my mouth. Everyone thinks she's very pretty and I'll send you a photograph of her soon. Of course, the fight is not yet over, but I think that the worst is past and that she'll now put on weight and will soon be plump.[14]

Miguel Hernández immediately took to little Malva Marina. He held her in his arms, arranged little parties in her honour. One day, Miguel took his young niece, Elvirita, to play with Neruda's daughter. When it became clear that Malva Marina had been born seriously ill, Hernández tried to do everything he could. He scoured Madrid for doctors who could help and, when that proved fruitless, he conceived the idea of taking Malva Marina with his parents to a beach in his native part of eastern Spain. He wrote to two friends in Alicante, Antonio Oliver and Juan Guerrero, in 1934 to arrange it. However, the dreamt-of trip never took place.

Neruda's optimism initially seemed to be justified. In the letter to Sara Tornú, on 19 September 1934, he wrote:

You can't imagine how much I've suffered. The doctors told me the girl was dying, and the little thing was suffering horribly, from a haemorrhage which appeared on her brain at her birth. But cheer up, fair Sara, because everything is going well. The girl has started to breast-feed, and the doctors are coming round less often. She's smiling and putting on grammes every day with leaps and bounds.[15]

He was determined to remain busy. He translated William Blake's 'Visions of the Daughters of Albion' and 'The Mental Traveller', which he published in the journal *Cruz y Raya*. He made clear his debt to the great satirical Spanish Golden Age poet, Francisco de Quevedo, by publishing a series of fifteen of Quevedo's *Sonetos de la muerte* (Sonnets of Death). As Robert Pring-Mill has pointed out, Quevedo was 'perhaps the most disillusioned author of a disillusioned age'.[16]

The fact that Neruda so deeply immersed himself in the writer at precisely this time (he did, of course, return to Quevedo many times in later years) is, I believe, a sign of how disenchanted he was with the state of his own life, and the direction the Spanish political scene was taking.

In September 1935, Neruda's long-held dream of seeing *Residencia* published in Spain was finally realised. Cruz y Raya printed the collection in two volumes. Neruda's friends celebrated the 'new arrival' with expressions of euphoria. Miguel Hernández expressed his 'tempestuous admiration' for the book and declared himself ready to publicise it by putting a foot inside every door or climbing the highest, trickiest pine trees to shout out the poet's merits to anyone willing to listen.

In his letter to Sara Tornú on 19 September 1934, Neruda was able to announce with delight that his efforts to move permanently to Madrid had proved successful:

> I spent weeks in this coming or going, without knowing whether I was going to be allowed to live in Barcelona or Madrid. I stayed on in Madrid in any case, but completely lost in uncertainty . . . Tomorrow, [Gabriela Mistral] is heading for Barcelona, giving great leaps of joy, and I am staying on as consul in Madrid, screaming with joy like a centipede. These images come to me because last night, at a great national festival, September 18, Peruvians, Cubans, the Argentinian Delia del Carril, Mexicans, came to my house, where they drank frenetically.

Buried away in this list, with the discretion which Neruda often – but not always – showed, was the name of a woman with whom he was already deeply in love. While Maruca spent hours lovingly and dutifully singing lullabies in Dutch to her sick baby daughter, Neruda was secretly meeting his new love, Delia del Carril, who at fifty was twenty years his senior. She was to become his second wife and companion for more than two decades.

At the same time, Neruda was recalling his harrowing harbour farewell in Ceylon to his Asian mistress, the Burmese panther, Josie Bliss, in a poem written in the first few months of 1935, making her name public for the first time in its title:

Colour blue of extinguished photographs
colour blue with petals and sea-strolls
a definite name falling on weeks
with a blow of steel that kills them . . .

There they are, there they are,
the kisses swept away in the dust by a sad ship.[17]

Delia del Carril might have been approaching her fiftieth birthday, but she remained an attractive, vital woman. She was also a
militant Communist. She was born on her family estate in Pola-
verdas, Saladillo, Argentina, and was the youngest and most in-
dependent-minded of thirteen children. Her father, Víctor, was the
son of a politician, and her mother, Julia, who had married at
fourteen, was a cultured woman who passed on her musical and
literary sensibilities to Delia. Rafael Alberti's wife, María Teresa
León, herself a militant Communist, wrote in her memoirs, *Memoria
de la melancolía*: 'If you're looking for an image of beauty and wit,
look no further than Delia.'[18]

When Delia was just eight, the huge family moved as one to Paris by
boat. Once in Paris, Delia spent a time in a convent, which she hated.
Her father was soon appointed deputy governor of the province of
Buenos Aires, but Delia stayed on in Paris. The following year, her
father killed himself, and her mother journeyed back and forward
between Buenos Aires and Paris, taking care of the Argentinian estate
while bringing up her children.

In Paris, Delia made friends with the Argentinian poet, Oliverio
Girondo, and his brother, Alberto. Back in Buenos Aires, she came to
know the visiting Spanish philosopher, José Ortega y Gasset, and also
befriended Victoria Ocampo, the influential founder and director of
the Argentinian magazine *Sur*.

In 1916, at the age of thirty-two, Delia married Adán Diehl, an
Argentinian writer and hotelier. But the marriage was a stormy one.
Diehl appears to have been frequently unfaithful, and in the end, Delia
left him. There followed several unhappy years: one of Delia's brothers was accidentally killed during a hunting expedition, her sister Julia
also died, as did three other relatives. A distraught Delia decided to
flee Argentina and return to Paris. Here, life looked up when she met
the painter, Fernand Léger, who not only taught her to paint but, as a

member of the French Communist Party, encouraged a dramatic shift leftwards in her politics.

With Léger, Delia met Picasso, Le Corbusier, and the poets Blaise Cendrars, Louis Aragon and Paul Eluard – all committed left-wingers. To the horror of her family back in Buenos Aires, Delia soaked herself in Marxist thinking. Establishing herself as a painter in her own right, she became an active member of the Association of Revolutionary Writers and Artists.

When she realised that her family's hostility to her hardening political position made a return to Argentina impossible, she decided – on the urging of Rafael Alberti and his wife – to go to Spain. Delia arrived in Madrid in the winter of 1934, and took up art studies at the San Fernando Academy.

It is still unclear where Delia first met Neruda. It could have been at the Cervecería de Correos in the Calle de Alcalá, at Rafael Alberti's home or in Carlos Morla Lynch's house. Lola Falcón, the wife of Neruda's friend and consular colleague, Luis Enrique Délano, remembered:

> On one occasion, Delia asked me: 'Do you know that Neruda?' The truth is that there wasn't much I could tell her about him at that time. We had only just become friends at the consulate. Pablo seemed to be marked by his solitary years in India and Indonesia [sic]. He spoke little, he was very ordered and serious in the fulfilling of his functions . . . I believe that Pablo and Delia first met at a restaurant, at one of the many dinners they offered to celebrate the appearance of some book or other, some prize or the birthday of one of their writer friends . . . At first, we thought that it was just a literary friendship.[19]

Falcón, like Delia's biographer, Fernando Sáez, was certain that it was Delia's influence which finally convinced Neruda to become a Communist. 'She was an attractive woman of fifty with very clear ideas, with a very clearly defined left-wing commitment. I believe she was very important in Neruda's political shift, although the terrible experience in Spain, the annihilation of the Republic and of democracy, was a tragic prelude to what came next in Europe in the Second World War, and was also decisive.'[20]

Neruda himself never gave Delia much credit for his growing alignment with the Communist cause. He told one interviewer:

I began to become a Communist in Spain, during the civil war . . . That was where the most important period of my political life took place – as was the case for many writers throughout the world. We felt attracted by that enormous resistance to fascism which was the Spanish war. But the experience meant something else for me. Before the war in Spain, I knew writers who were all Republicans, except for one or two. And the Republic, for me, was the rebirth of culture, literature, the arts, in Spain. Federico García Lorca is the expression of this poetic generation, the most explosive in the history of Spain in many centuries. So the physical destruction of all these men was a drama for me. A whole part of my life ended in Madrid.[21]

Rafael Alberti, who already knew Delia quite well from Paris, described her as being 'as agile as a ship's boy clambering up a mast. She adored Pablo immediately. She penetrated, with her slight soprano's voice – she sang marvellously – into the poet's night-time circle, mixing with the jokes, stories and theatre scenes.'[22]

Photographs of Delia at the time show an alluring woman, with bright, intelligent eyes. Neruda was immediately captivated by her energy, her mind and her looks. Right from the very beginning, Delia seems to have enjoyed the prospect of mothering Pablo. Maruca was certainly too busy being a genuine mother to their very ill daughter to pay much attention to her husband. Delia's inclination to assume the role of mother figure, on top of the fact that she was a warm, good-hearted person who was his intellectual equal, made her instantly seductive.

Delia herself said later in life: 'Pablo was a child. His health improved a lot because I looked after him. He was born to a mother who died of tuberculosis three days after giving birth [sic]. So the little one spent nine months in his mother's sick body.'

Delia had acquired the nickname 'La Hormiga' or 'La Homiguita' (the Ant or the Little Ant) – probably because she was always bustling about brimming with political energy – and the name stuck. Delia often referred to Pablo as *'arrieré mental'* (mentally retarded) – an allusion to his childish weakness for collecting things.

As early as the end of 1934, not long after Delia arrived in Madrid, Neruda had probably already made up his mind that there was no future in his marriage to Maruca. From New Year's Eve onwards, he made a conscious decision to be more open about his relationship with Delia.

How much Maruca knew about her husband's increasingly passionate love affair with Delia is unclear. She may have refused to see what was going on in front of her nose. But other people were aware of it. Delia's friends were turning up from Argentina – notably, another committed Communist, the poet Raúl González Tuñón and his wife, Amparo Mom, whom Neruda had got to know well during his stay in Buenos Aires.

In a letter to Delia's sister, Adelina – married to Ricardo Güiraldes, the Argentinian author of the popular 1926 novel *Don Segundo Sombra* – Neruda spelt out his feelings explicitly: 'I adore Delia and cannot live without her.' He also pointed out a feature of Delia's character which her friends found endearing, rather than irritating. Although she was a very focused Communist and an extremely hard-working political activist, she was totally absent-minded in domestic matters: 'I often have to tell her off,' Neruda told her sister. 'A few days ago, when she was in charge of the kitchen for a few minutes, she brought us match soup – after lighting the gas, she'd absent-mindedly thrown the matches into the cooking-pot. She's always losing gloves on the trams, she calls all the stocking-sellers *mijito* [my son] and tries to pay the bus fare with keys and buttons.'[23]

Miguel Hernández, who at twenty-three was even younger than Neruda, felt as charmed by Delia as Pablo, though he did try to encourage him to persist with his marriage to Maruca. Miguel wrote a beautiful poem to Delia called 'Tale Which I Dedicate to My Friend Delia'. In it, he praised the Hormiguita's human warmth and called her 'Delia, she of the speechless eyes / with the same gestures and elegance as goats . . . Your tenderness could hug a thistle.'

While Neruda was pursuing Delia, Maruca was pleased with what appeared to be an improvement in the health of their daughter. She wrote to Laurita and Pablo's father and stepmother to inform them of the move to Madrid, which, she said, made them happy (despite the fact that Pablo was still not well-paid) 'because Madrid is the most important place for his books'.

Malva Marina, Maruca wrote,

is five-and-a-half months old and she is lovely. She's grown taller and put on a lot of weight, She's 71 cms high, whereas she was only 47 when she was born, which scares me a lot because I'll be sorry to see her end up as tall as me. She's a girl who is always happy, she never cries, she's smiling all the time. Everyone loves her a lot and finds her very pretty and intelligent . . . She's having ultra-violet treatment to strengthen her bones, and this helps her health in general.

However, in January or February 1935, when Maruca's mother came to stay with her daughter on the fifth floor of the Casa de las Flores, meeting her son-in-law and seeing her granddaughter for the first time, the atmosphere – and Malva Marina's condition – had deteriorated.

By early 1936, little Malva Marina's health had taken a dramatic turn for the worse. It seems, too, that her parents had been trying to hide the worst from themselves and others for many months. Maruca wrote to Neruda's stepmother on 2 May to say: 'We have some bad news about our Malvita. When she was just a few months old, we discovered that, as a result of her difficult birth (although I didn't suffer at all), her little head began to grow too fast: a disease that the best doctors in Madrid and Paris could not cure, which was desperate for us.'[24] The official diagnosis was hydrocephaly.

In the midst of this personal unhappiness, Neruda managed both to keep up with his consular business (still signing his official correspondence 'Ricardo Reyes') and to stay active in the literary arena. He indulged one of his great passions: starting up magazines. When a friend, the Malaga-born poet Manuel Altolaguirre, turned up at the Casa de las Flores and offered Neruda the editorship of a beautifully produced new cultural journal, he accepted with alacrity. And thus was launched *Caballo Verde Para la Poesía* (Green Horse for Poetry), which ran for five issues (the sixth edition was due to appear on 19 July 1936, but the day before saw Franco's uprising). Neruda made full use of Altolaguirre's considerable typographical skills. (Many years later, Neruda recalled: 'Manolito honoured poetry with his own verse and with his manual craft, the hands of a hard-working angel.')[25]

Rafael Alberti didn't understand the title of the journal. 'Why a green horse? Why not a *red* one?' he is said to have asked Pablo indignantly. Some reports claim that Alberti's annoyance at the title of the new journal was so vehement that Neruda felt he needed to pacify his friend and made Alberti a present of a dog. Alberti's own version is rather different. He recalled the Chilean telephoning him one autumn day to say: 'Look, comrade, last night, I found a marvellous dog in the midst of a thick mist. He's lame in one leg. He followed me back to the door of the house, limping, begging me to help him or take him in. And so here he is with me. He's very big. I can't keep him here. My house is small. You've got a large terrace. He'll get better there and be able to run around. We'll take him to a vet beforehand.' Alberti accepted the idea at once and told Pablo to bring the dog round to him immediately.[26]

Under Neruda's editorship, *Caballo Verde* published surrealist texts, poems by Lorca, Hernández, Luis Cernuda, Vicente Aleixandre and Jorge Guillén, and became embroiled in a controversy with the Spanish poet, Juan Ramón Jiménez. Jiménez espoused a 'pure' poetry and called Neruda a 'great, bad poet'. In response, Neruda took his opportunity to lay out his poetic agenda in the prologue to the very first edition of *Caballo Verde* to appear in 1935. It was called 'On a Poetry without Purity', and in it, he wrote:

> This is the poetry we should be after, worn away, as if by acid, by the labour of hands, impregnated with sweat and smoke, smelling of lilies and of urine, splashed by the variety of what we do, legally or illegally. A poetry as impure as old clothes, as a body, with its food stains and its shame, with wrinkles, observations, dreams, wakeful-ness, prophecies, declarations of love and hate, stupidities, shocks, idylls, political beliefs, negations, doubts, affirmations, taxes . . .[27]

But note that Neruda still refrains in this or his other prologues for editions of *Caballo Verde* from insisting that poetry should be politically engaged.

Another illuminating insight to how mature and attentive Neruda had already become in his use of poetic language comes down to us from the Spanish Communist poet Gabriel Celaya who, as a student, met both Neruda and Federico García Lorca in Madrid in 1935. Celaya showed both men the same poem, which he later included in his book *La soledad cerrada*. Lorca merely made a verbal com-ment about the essential aim of the poem, its composition, its structure.

> Neruda, on the other hand, paid no attention whatsoever to any of that. And I can be quite sure of that in his case because I still have the

poem with the notes in his handwriting. They are almost excessively meticulous notes, almost like the marks of an old professor, but always – and this is what seems their chief characteristic – referring to details. He didn't like 'nieve' [snow] at the end of a line because the word has two 'e's', which he underlined, with the note: 'Assonance!' He stopped at 'perfect polyhedra' and said 'Neutral, ineffective adjective'. He found the word 'culminate' 'bad!', while he said 'La luna delira' was 'Good!' 'Polished by the cold' was 'Very good!' 'I feel an absence' was 'Bad, elemental' 'low eyelids,' he didn't like, etc. I would say, in short, that Neruda, in total contrast to Lorca, showed himself to be, as in his own poetry, more concerned with the minimal units of the poem, the right adjectives, no wasted images, functional sounds, than with the form and overall structure of the poem. The accumulation of correct words or lovely details takes precedence for him, like a primitive, over the general concept.[28]

Neruda was still not officially named consul in Madrid, despite his permanent move to the capital and it was only due to an unfortunate incident that he was confirmed in the position. On 2 October 1935, a Chilean magazine, *La Familia*, published a private letter from the Chilean consul in Madrid, Gabriela Mistral, to her friend Armando Donoso, in which she appeared to be insulting Spain and the Spaniards. Appalled and offended Spaniards prompted an order in November 1935 for Mistral to leave Madrid immediately by train for Lisbon, and Neruda was appointed her replacement as consul in Madrid, with his old friend, Luis Enrique Délano, as his assistant.

As 1936 began, political tensions grew in Spain, but Neruda was able to see more of Delia because she had moved into a little house in Cascares belonging to Délano and his wife, Lola Falcón, who were on a trip to Portugal. Neruda also persuaded Maruca that it would be better to take Malva Marina back to Barcelona, where his consular boss Tulio Maqueira had promised that they would be safer from the growing political danger than in Madrid. While Neruda was genuinely concerned for the safety of his family, this step resembles one Neruda was to make years later, when he persuaded Delia to return to Latin America from Europe to arrange his return from exile – allowing him to spend more time with his third wife-to-be, Matilde Urrutia.

Back in Madrid, Neruda, Delia and their friends were debating their response to the assassination of a left-wing lieutenant, José Castillo, on 12 July 1936, followed the next day by the disappearance and murder of the monarchist leader, José Calvo Sotelo. Delia's Stalinism was hardening – La Hormiga was quickly gaining a second nickname: 'El ojo de Molotov' (Molotov's Eye – a reference to Stalin's Foreign Minister). Neruda, however, was still wavering. Since the Chilean President, Arturo Alessandri Palma, backed Franco, Neruda, as one of the leading diplomatic representatives in Spain, was obliged, at the very least, to remain neutral – despite the ceaseless pressure on him from friends to adopt the Republican cause openly.

But events were moving fast. On 11 July, exactly a week before Franco's uprising, a group of Falangists seized control of Radio Valencia and announced that the fascist revolution was imminent. That same day, Lorca was eating at Neruda's flat and declared that he wanted to return home to Granada. A socialist member of Parliament, also at Neruda's house, advised Lorca against leaving Madrid, telling him he was safer in the capital. Two days later, ignoring all his friends' advice, Federico left for his home province – and his own death.

It was the murder of Federico García Lorca on 17 or 18 August 1936, more than anything else, which pushed Neruda into deciding that support for the Republican side was worth the inevitable sacrifice of his diplomatic position. Neruda had been expecting to meet Lorca at a wrestling match on 19 July. They were keenly looking forward to watching bouts between men with names like the Masked Troglodyte, the Abyssinian Strangler and the Sinister Orang-Utang. But Federico never turned up: Franco's uprising, the day before, had changed the face of Spain.

Neruda did not find out about the loss of his great friend until 9 September when the news reached Madrid. Franco himself confirmed, in an interview with the Buenos Aires newspaper *La Prensa*, that Lorca had died. 'These are the natural accidents of war,' said Franco. But Neruda knew that Lorca's death had been a brutal execution, not an accident.

What a poet he was! I have never seen combined, as in him, wit and genius, a winged heart like a crystalline waterfall. Federico García Lorca was all devastating wit, centrifugal gaiety which gathered and irradiated joy of life like a planet. Ingenuous and an actor, cosmic and provincial, a singular musician, a splendid mime, fearful and superstitious, radiant and gentle, he was a kind of résumé of the ages of Spain, of popular flourishing, an Arab-Andalusian product which illuminated and perfumed like a jasmine tree the whole Spanish stage of his time – and, alas, he is gone![29]

Neruda started writing his great hymn to the victims of the Spanish Civil War, *España en el corazón* (Spain in My Heart). The first poem he wrote in this impassioned collection, was 'Canto a las madres de los milicianos muertos' (Song of the Mothers of Dead Militiamen). It was the first poem in which Neruda clearly laid down his commitment to social and political justice.

The poem took shape in the first days of September 1936, just weeks after Lorca's death, and two months after Franco's uprising. Neruda's friend and consular assistant, Luis Enrique Délano, looked back on the gestation of the poem in his memoirs of this period, *Sobre todo Madrid*.

One day, someone, I don't remember who, said to Neruda: When are you going to write something for *El Mono Azul*? Pablo gave a vague reply. But no doubt he was already working over the idea in his head. And how could it be otherwise? The stimulus of the war was too strong for a poet like him. One day in September, when I arrived at the office, Pablo passed me a typewritten piece of paper, with some corrections in ink, and I began to read the following, with a mixture of astonishment and excitement:

> They have not died! They're standing, in the gunpowder,
> like burning wicks.
> Their shadows have joined
> in the copper-coloured meadow
> like a curtain of armour-plated wind . . .

'It's my first proletarian poetry,' Pablo told me.[30]

Délano had the poem typed out neatly and personally took it to the offices of *El Mono Azul* (The Blue Monkey Suit), the journal published by the Alianza de Intelectuales and edited by Rafael Alberti. (The surreal title plays on the two meanings of the word 'mono': the worker's blue 'dungarees' and 'monkey'.) Although Neruda's name appeared on the poem when Délano handed it over, it was published anonymously. 'I think it was Rafael Alberti who provided the explanation: they thought that the reactionary government in Chile could take reprisals against a civil servant in the consular service who showed himself so determinedly to be on the side of the Republic.'[31]

And so, on 24 September 1936, the first, fervent poem of *España en el corazón* appeared, unsigned, in issue number five of *El Mono Azul*. Not long afterwards, on 12 October, Neruda read the poem at an event organised by the Alianza de Intelectuales and the Federación Universitaria Hispanoamericana, in Cuenca, to demonstrate the support of Latin American intellectuals for the cause of the Spanish Republic. No one, now, could mistake where Pablo Neruda stood on the Spanish Civil War.

On 7 November 1936, with Franco's forces approaching Madrid, Neruda and Luis Enrique Délano decided that the time had come to abandon the capital. Delia del Carril travelled to Valencia, where the Republican government had set up its headquarters, while Neruda, Délano and Délano's wife, Lola, continued northwards to Barcelona.

Although this meant Pablo's rejoining Maruca and Malva Marina, the reunion was very short-lived. Neruda knew the marriage was over. By now, he was profoundly in love with Delia, and needed to be with her openly. Maruca seems to have understood this, or at least felt powerless to prevent it. She and Malva Marina boarded the same train north to Paris from Barcelona as Pablo, Délano and Lola. Neruda first saw Délano and Lola off on a ship to Chile from Marseille, then continued on with Maruca and their daughter to Monte Carlo. They hoped that a clinic there would be able to improve their daughter's health. Neruda would never see his first wife or daughter again.

On 10 December 1936, he wrote to Delia from Marseille to inform her that he had left Maruca for good. He told her that the plan was for Maruca and Malva Marina to stay at a small apartment in Monte Carlo owned by a Dutch family, the Van Trichts, at a cost of 25 French francs a day, on top of Malva Marina's medical expenses. 'Fortunately, the little girl was feeling better, and I left her singing and laughing just like she used to. Now the thing is to make sure that Maruca has enough money every month, so that she won't have any worries.'

Neruda chastised Delia for not joining him, now that he had made the break from Maruca.

Dearest Ant, I don't know why you're going to stay in Barcelona for months. You had plans. I've left Maruca. The situation is resolved with her departure; I'm at a very old hotel down by the port. Every morning, I look out at the sailing ships. How good we would be together! I hug you with all my heart and I love you every day. I hope to see you, which is the only thing I want.[32]

The tone of childish incomprehension is reminiscent of the letters he wrote to Albertina Azócar begging her to join him in the Far East. Delia, like Albertina, was a strong woman who appeared determined to follow her own course, not that dictated by a man. Neruda was both attracted to this strength in women and frustrated by it. Another sign of his childishness was a request he made in the same letter to Delia: for her to buy him a miniature boat he had seen in a shop in Barcelona. Unlike Albertina, however, Delia was ready to indulge Pablo's whims. She *did* buy him that little boat and she did agree to change her plans, turn her back on Spain and join Neruda in Paris.

Before Delia arrived, Pablo's energy had found another direction. He collaborated with Nancy Cunard, the great-granddaughter of the founder of the Cunard shipping line, in publishing the first issue of another new journal (it more ressembled a leaflet) at her home in Réanville. Each edition of *Los Poetas del Mundo Defienden al Pueblo Español* (Poets of the World Defend the Spanish People) contained several poems, in English and French as well as Spanish, and was sold in London and Paris to raise money for the cause. Neruda recalled this endeavour in his memoirs:

Nancy had a small printing press in her country house, in the French provinces, I don't remember the name of the place, but it was far from Paris. . . . I started setting type for the first time, and I am sure there has never been a worse typesetter. I printed 'p's upside down and they turned into 'd's through my typographical clumsiness. A line in which the word *párpados* [eyelids] appeared twice ended up as two *dárdapos*. For years afterwards, Nancy punished me by calling me that. 'My dear Dárdapo,' she would begin her letters from London. But it turned out to be an attractive publication, and we managed to print six or seven issues.[33]

Contributors to the journal included Rafael Alberti and Raúl González Tuñón, but also the Afro-American poet, Langston Hughes, and the British poets W. H. Auden and Stephen Spender. 'These English gentlemen will never know how much my lazy fingers suffered setting their poems,'[34] Neruda remembered.

In fact, the most famous poem in Cunard's series of leaflets was W. H. Auden's 'Spain' – the most influential poem in English about the Spanish Civil War – which appeared in the fifth edition. Cunard had met Auden briefly in Paris, and was delighted with what she thought was an 'extremely beautiful' poem, written by Auden on his return from his one visit to Spain with a medical team in January 1937.

While she was working on these campaigning cultural leaflets, Cunard conceived another idea: to ask all the English-speaking writers and poets she could think of where they stood on the Spanish question, and then to publish the results. Of the entries, 126 supported the Spanish Republic, five were for Franco and sixteen were neutral. The neutrals included Aldous Huxley, T. S. Eliot, Ezra Pound, H. G. Wells and Vita Sackville-West. The Franco supporters were Edmund Blunden, Arthur Machen, Geoffrey Moss, Eleanor Smith and Evelyn Waugh. The shortest answer came from Samuel Beckett, who merely replied with 'Up the Republic!'

Cunard collected eleven other signatures, alongside her own, including those of Neruda, Stephen Spender, Tristan Tzara, W. H. Auden and Louis Aragon. The *Left Review* published the questionnaire as a separate booklet in November 1937.

At the start of the year Delia joined Pablo and they set up 'home' in a cheap Paris hotel. Those first days of reunion were darkened by sad news from Buenos Aires: the death of Delia's mother, Julia, in January 1937.

Quite apart from her grief, Delia, unlike Pablo, didn't particularly like what she saw in Paris. Everything had become much more expensive since she had lived there previously, and she found things backward – fifty years behind Spain! Despite the fact that France had a new, socialist President, Léon Blum, his determination not to intervene in the Spanish Civil War was deeply disappointing for the Left.

Meanwhile, Neruda was keeping busy in his new base. On 21 January he gave a very important and moving lecture honouring the memory of Lorca. In the talk, he made both his love and admiration for Federico and his total commitment to justice and the working-class abundantly clear – while still, remarkably, claiming to maintain his distance from active politics.

> How does one dare select one name to stand out from all the others amid the vast forest of our dead! The humble tillers of Andalucía, murdered by enemies older than memory, the dead miners in Asturias, the carpenters, the bricklayers, the salaried workers in city and country, as well as each of the thousands of murdered women and slaughtered children – each of these fiery shadows has the right to appear before you as a witness from a great, unhappy land, and each, I believe, has a place in your hearts, if you are free of injustice and evil . . . Yes, how dare we choose one name, one alone, among so many who have been silenced? Because the name I am going to utter among you holds in its dark syllables such mortal richness, is so weighted and so fraught with significance, that to utter it is to utter the names of all those who fell defending the very essence of his poems, for he was the sonorous defender of Spain's heart. Federico García Lorca! He was as much a part of the people as a guitar, happy and melancholy, as profound and lucid as a child, as the people themselves.

Neruda must have startled many of his listeners in that Paris auditorium when he concluded his speech by saying: 'I am not a political man, nor have I ever taken part in political contention, but my words, which many would have wished to be neutral, have been coloured by passion. You must understand, understand that we, the poets of Spanish America and the poets of Spain, cannot forget or ever forgive the murder of the one who we know to be the greatest among us, the guiding spirit of this moment in our language.'[35]

Delia introduced Neruda to many leading intellectuals in Paris who were to become his great friends, including two French Communist poets, Paul Eluard and Louis Aragon. Aragon headed a committee for the defence of culture, in which Pablo became very active.

At this point, the Chilean government – having finally lost patience with Neruda's overtly pro-Republican stance – decided to cut off his source of income by closing down the consulate in Madrid, using the bombardment of the Spanish capital by Franco's forces as an official pretext.

How did Pablo and Delia manage to live from now on? In his

memoirs, Neruda claims that he was the main breadwinner: 'She always had the reputation of being a rich ranch-owner, whereas in fact she was poorer than I was.' Delia's biographer, Fernando Sáez, believes that this was simply untrue. He maintains that the couple survived on the income reaching Delia from Buenos Aires from her property – although it only ever arrived after huge delays.

Either way there was very little money around. Neruda apparently worked for Louis Aragon's association for the defence of culture for just 400 old francs. 'For months, we ate very little and badly.'[36] Neruda's shoes had holes in them. On 31 January 1937, his cultured consular boss, Tulio Maqueira, wrote from Bayonne in southern France urging the poet to be prudent: 'Once again, I must deplore the bad timing of your Paris lecture [the one dedicated to Lorca] and all I can do is intercede with the [Chilean Foreign] Ministry to try to get them not to take it too badly.'[37] Maqueira told Neruda that, as far as future prospects were concerned, his only hope was to be put in charge of the Chilean consulate in Marseille.

Neruda's abandoned wife Maruca suffered the most: Pablo was unable to send her the money she needed to help with their sick daughter. From Monte Carlo Maruca wrote to President Arturo Alessandri Palma – probably unaware of the depth of Alessandri's disenchantment with Pablo over his siding with the Spanish Republicans – asking him to reinstate Neruda as a Chilean consul in Spain so that at least he would have a salary. Presumably, she hoped that he would be able to send her the funds she so urgently needed and deserved. If that wasn't possible, Maruca said, could Alessandri please arrange for herself and Malva Marina to be repatriated to Chile.

Alessandri does not seem to have replied to Maruca's desperate pleas, and she decided to return with her daughter to her family home in Holland.

Meanwhile, France and the intellectual Left had been rocked by a book by the French novelist, André Gide, *Retour de l'URSS*. Gide had travelled to see the Soviet Communist experiment for himself – and had not been impressed. He wrote that the Revolution had not helped the poor working-classes at all – they remained as poor as ever, Gide insisted, while basic liberties and human rights were being systematically stamped out.

Gide's book was a bombshell. Immediately after the book came out at the end of 1936, Gide came under ferocious attack as a traitor. It lent an added impetus to a massive conference of intellectuals against fascism that Pablo, Delia, Raúl González Tuñón and Amparo Mom were organising for July 1937. It had been planned for Madrid, but with the capital clearly threatened with imminent defeat at the hands of Franco's troops, it was switched to Valencia, where the provisional Republican government had also moved.

Suddenly, a considerable sum of money came Neruda's way. In his memoirs, he wrote that he had received the bank draft from the Spanish government, to cover expenses for the writers' congress. Pablo was bewildered to be in possession of such large funds, but Rafael Alberti – gazing down at the Chilean's threadbare shoes and reminding him that the Chilean consular service had washed its hands of him – recommended that Pablo use some of the money for his basic needs.

Thousands of famous poets were either living in, or descending on, Paris, prior to the Valencia congress. Neruda was working again with César Vallejo, the Peruvian poet he had first befriended on his way to the Far East. With Vallejo, Neruda set up the Spanish-American Committee for the Defence of the Spanish Republic. In this last year before he died, Vallejo himself wrote one of the most harrowing of all laments to the victims of the Spanish Civil War, the posthumously published *España, aparta de mí este cáliz* (Spain, Take This Cup from Me). Neruda was not so pleased when Vicente Huidobro, the Chilean poet with whom he rarely saw eye to eye, also arrived in the French capital.

But he was happy to see the Mexican poet Octavio Paz, whom he had personally invited to Spain for the congress. Paz later recalled that, as he got off the train on his initial arrival in Madrid, 'a tall man came towards me, shouting: "Octavio Paz, Octavio Paz!" It was Neruda. When he saw me, he said: "But how young you are!" We immediately became friends.'[38] It was a friendship which was to blow up explosively not long afterwards, but for now they were allies. The two men met at the Spanish consulate to arrange visas. Emerging from the building, they came across the Spanish film director, Luis Buñuel, who was also joining them on the train to Valencia. Fellow passengers included André Malraux, Stephen Spender (who crossed the Spanish border with a forged passport in the name of Ramos Ramos) and Ilya Ehrenburg. When the train set out for Valencia and then Madrid, Neruda noted with pride, 'Never had a train left Paris packed with so many writers.'[39]

The Valencia congress, which began on 4 July 1937 and concluded in Madrid on 6 and 7 July, was one of the most remarkable gatherings of writers in history – and remains so to this day. The fact that about two hundred writers from thirty countries – from Algeria to Peru, from Iceland to China – attended the conference was seen as a major moral victory for the Republican government, because it seemed to provide irrefutable proof that many of the world's most prestigious intellectuals were willing to stand up and express their support for a Spanish Republic which appeared to be on the brink of collapse. In fact, some French and Spanish writers, as Nancy Cunard's question-naire had shown, took the opposite side and supported the fascists. Neruda was appalled when the Spaniards Gerardo Diego and Dámaso Alonso backed the Franco forces and he remembered them later in some vituperative lines from *Canto general*: 'The Dámasos, the Gerardos, the sons of bitches, silent accomplices of the executioner!'.

However, despite its auspicious start and unparalleled attendance, the congress turned out to be bitterly disappointing for Neruda and many others. The squabbling and in-fighting overshadowed the gen-eral purpose of the meeting: to rally concerted oppposition to Franco. Although the areas of discussion – the role of the writer in society; humanism; nationhood and culture; aid to the Spanish Republican writers – were virtually identical to those on the agenda at the first Congress of Intellectuals in Paris in 1935 (which had, ironically, been presided over by André Gide), the pro-Soviet line seemed to impose itself from the start, spearheaded by Ilya Ehrenburg, Alexis Tolstoy and Alexei Fadeyev.

The new Spanish Prime Minister, Juan Negrín, gave the inaugural address on 4 July 1937. His speech sought to persuade those advocat-ing a non-interventionist approach to the Civil War to come in on the Republic's side. But after Negrín's speech, even though all delegates expressed their deepest sympathy for the Republican cause, and declared their unconditional support for the heroism of the Spanish people, and although writers killed in action in the Civil War, such as John Cornford and Ralph Fox, were solemnly commemorated, the blatantly pro-Soviet, and pro-Stalin, line dominated.

There was considerable concern in some quarters at what appeared to be Stalin's increasing efforts to manipulate the political scene in Spain, now that he had begun sending arms to the Republican side.

As one writer has put it:

The Soviets had wanted to turn this Congress into a trial of André Gide first because his *Retour de l'URSS* was a coarse thorn in their flesh, and also because they had, at all costs, to divert attention as noisily as possible away from the international scandal provoked by the assassination of Andrés Nin, the leader of the POUM [the Trotskyist faction among the anti-fascist fighters], who everyone knew had been kidnapped and liquidated by agents of the NKVD [the Soviet secret services] in Spain. Very little was said about Nin [at the Valencia congress], and much more about Gide, the other 'Hitlero-fascist'.[40]

One major decision taken in Valencia was to create an international network of writers' organisations to combat the fascist uprising in Spain. Neruda instinctively felt that it was his role to be responsible for setting up the Chilean 'branch' of this literary war.

When the train stopped off in Madrid, Neruda was determined to return to the house where he had lived so many intense months. He was accompanied to the Casa de las Flores by Miguel Hernández, wearing his Republican army uniform. Miguel had somehow managed to find a van to carry away all the books and other belongings that Neruda had been forced to leave behind when he and Délano fled Madrid hastily for France almost a year earlier.

However, when Pablo and Miguel reached the fifth-floor apartment, they were horrified to find that whole chunks of the walls had been gouged out by gunfire and the floor was strewn with books and rubble. Saddest of all, the invaders had carried off some of the possessions Neruda had most prized – his Polynesian masks, knives from the Far East and the tailcoat he had worn at consular functions. Digging around, in what was more like an archaeological excavation, Hernández located some of Pablo's manuscripts, but the Chilean shook his head: 'I don't want to take anything with me.' Astounded, and perhaps a little hurt after the effort he had taken to procure a special vehicle, Miguel replied: 'Not even one single book?' The two poets left the Casa de las Flores for the very last time in an empty van.

Neruda set sail for Valparaíso, with Delia at his side, in October 1937. It would be the first time he had set foot in his homeland for five years. Deeper personal tragedy awaited him there.

6

A life-saving mission

1937–40

Neruda arrived home in Chile on 12 October 1937. Waiting for him were some of his old friends from his bohemian days in Santiago. While Alberto Rojas Giménez, once their leader, had died, there were many others to welcome Pablo and Delia as they stepped off the train at Santiago's Mapocho station.

Delia was wearing an elegant blue two-piece suit, with her fair hair emerging from a pink hat. Certainly she made a much better first impression than Maruca had on Neruda's previous return. Diego Muñoz reported: 'He had separated from *la gringa*. We had heard very good things about the Hormiguita. She was a charming, cultured woman. We all became friends immediately.'[1] That same night, true to form, the friends gathered for a long, uproarious reunion party at Santiago's Hotel City – and unlike Maruca, Delia was happy to join the celebrations.

The first place the couple lived was a sixth-floor apartment on the Calle Merced, near the Parque Forestal. They moved in with Raúl González Tuñón and his wife, Amparo Mom. But the flat was not suitable.

As Muñoz put it: 'It had to be something like the Casa de las Flores in Madrid . . . After a lengthy search, we found what Pablo wanted, in the Avenida Irrarázabal, near Pedro de Valdivia.'[2] It was a large house, notable for a big fig tree outside, and soon – like its Madrid forerunner – it became open to any friends who happened to be nearby. For Delia, absent-minded as a hostess though she could certainly be, loved company every bit as much as Pablo and would never turn away a guest, whether invited or not. And although she remained as poor a cook as ever, they did have a willing helper in Delia's great friend, Lavinia Andrade, who was able cheerfully to prepare meals for as many as eighty guests at a time. Neruda would get up early in the morning and visit the market to buy his favourite ingredients, including sea bass.

Delia was not a weak woman. She could be a severe mother to her 'son'. If she disapproved of how Neruda was behaving, she came out, firm but smiling, with her mantra: '*Eso no, Pablo. Usted es un retrasado mental*' ('Not that, Pablo. You're mentally retarded'). Visitors found the couple devoted, close and very affectionate.

Having found somewhere to live, Neruda immediately got to work helping to create the Chilean Alianza de Intelectuales, which was formally established less than a month later, on 7 November 1937. Neruda himself was the association's first president. On 13 November the Chilean publisher, Ercilla, printed the first edition of his book, *España en el corazón.* (Spain in my Heart). This edition combined Neruda's text with sixteen photo-montages by Pedro Olmos – reminiscent of Josep Renau's famous Spanish Civil War posters – to produce what Robert Pring-Mill has called a 'multi-art propaganda weapon. The visual aspect of this edition plays almost as important a part in its overall effect as the poetry.'[3]

It was a good time to be a poet in Chile. According to Diego Muñoz, writers' reputations had soared. 'The writer was no longer seen as a tramp, a madman, a lazybones. Now, we were received everywhere with great interest and respect, because the people had discovered that we were useful, [even] indispensable, at that moment in our history, when the clear aim was to raise the cultural level of the popular masses.'[4]

Delia took a trip to Argentina – to sort out her financial affairs and to see her sister, Adelina, who was about to leave for a long stay in India. But most importantly, to clarify the state of her marriage to Adán Diehl. When she discovered that he had gone bankrupt, Delia ordered a lawyer to draw up divorce papers. Meanwhile, Neruda travelled up and down Chile, giving poetry readings, for the first time, to ordinary working people rather than to intellectuals, and raising funds and other aid for the Spanish Republican cause.

Although he had delivered lectures abroad, it seems he was not yet a natural orator when it came to speaking to his countrymen. At one of these fund-raising events, at which he was due to address the porters' union in Santiago's central market, he suddenly found himself frozen with nerves as he looked out at the workers, with 'hard features on their faces, and their huge hands on the backs of the benches'. At a total loss for politically meaningful words, he took out his new collection, *España en el corazón*, and read practically every poem in it.

According to his own account, the porters stared back at him in stony, Chilean silence. 'Those who have never come into contact with our people cannot know what the Chilean silence is like. It's total silence and you can't tell whether it's a silence of reverence or absolute disapproval. No face says anything. If you try to sniff out the slightest clue, you're lost. It is the heaviest silence in the world.'[5]

He came to the end of that Santiago reading with great trepidation. He needn't have worried. In what he described as 'the most important event in my literary career', some of the listeners applauded, others lowered their heads, and then they all looked towards one man, who may have been the union leader.

> This man, with a sack around his waist like the others, got up, leaning with his large hands on his chair, looked at me and said: 'Comrade Pablo, we are totally forgotten people. And I can tell you that we have never been so greatly moved. We would like to say to you . . .' And he broke down in tears, his body trembling with the sobs. Many of those around him were also crying. I felt a knot form in my throat . . .[6]

Robert Pring-Mill rightly singles out that evening in Santiago, talking to the porters' union, as a formative experience for Neruda. It was the workers, from now on, who would be his readers, not the intellectuals. Gone was any desire for obscurity and complexity; from now on, he wanted to reach out to ordinary people and touch them as profoundly as he had in that Santiago market. Anything he wrote after that, he wrote for them.

Politically, it was an even more difficult time for Neruda to be living in Chile than when he left. The government of Arturo Alessandri Palma (the 'Lion of Tarapacá') had taken a depressingly pro-Nazi line, and the now overtly pro-Republican Neruda was regarded with great suspicion by the authorities. Apart from the poetry readings and political rallies, he became the editor of a new journal, *Aurora de Chile*, the organ of the Alianza de Intelectuales, which first appeared in August 1938. Much of its content was devoted to attacks on the Nazis.

As Neruda wrote later in his memoirs:

> In Latin America, there were no eminent writers, like Céline, Drieu la Rochelle or Ezra Pound, who turned traitor to serve fascism, but there was a strong fascist movement nurtured, with or without financial aid, by Hitlerism. Groups sprang up everywhere whose members dressed like storm troopers and raised their arm in the fascist salute. And they weren't just small groups. The old feudal oligarchies of the continent sided, and still side, with anti-Communism of any kind. What's more, let's remember that people of German descent make up the bulk of the population in some parts of Chile, Brazil and Mexico. These areas were easily seduced by Hitler's meteoric rise and by the fabled millennium of German greatness. More than once, on those days of Hitler's resounding victories, I literally had to walk through a street, in some small village or town in the south of Chile, under forests of flags bearing a swastika. Once, in a small southern town, I was forced to pay an involuntary tribute to the Führer in order to use the telephone. The German owner of the establishment, which had the only telephone in town, had managed to place the instrument so that, to take the receiver off the hook, you had to raise your arm to a portrait of Hitler, whose arm was also raised.[7]

Neruda received death threats. One Nazi-inspired Chilean publication claimed that Neruda was Jewish. Copies of the pornographic Nazi propaganda sheet, *Der Stürmer*, were sent to Neruda's offices at *Aurora de Chile*.

But a double tragedy struck which put political events firmly in the shade. On 7 May 1938, Neruda's father died. On the train journey to Temuco for the funeral, as Pablo sat in his solemn black suit, his mind raced back to those thrilling journeys he had taken as a child with his train-driver father through the forests of southern Chile.

He sat next to his father's body for a while, and from those moments emerged the moving lines he wrote to a man whom he had never understood and who had never understood him, but who had been a permanent presence in his life. José del Carmen had, unwittingly, shaped his son's destiny. Those train rides had awakened both Neruda's lifelong love of nature and the sensibility which had driven him to write poetry. And it was a debt Neruda acknowledged – although he had had to change his name to be able to do so freely.

The day after his father's funeral, he wrote a poem, 'Almagro', which at least one critic – the Uruguayan, Emir Rodríguez Monegal – considered to be the earliest poem included in Neruda's masterpiece, *Canto general*.[8] 'Almagro', known in *Canto general* as 'Descubridores de Chile' (Discoverers of Chile), has a description of a bearded man which could be a portrait of the poet's father. (His father was an 'uncoverer' of sorts, as his ballast train headed through the forest, and in this poem, Diego de Almagro is described as 'sitting one day near a rose / near oil, near wine.' Could Neruda have been thinking of his real mother, Rosa, and the vine-rich lands of his birthplace, Parral?) Others believe that the earliest poem in *Canto general* is 'Oda de invierno al río Mapocho' (Winter Ode to the Mapocho River), which was certainly the first to be published in *Aurora de Chile* on 1 August 1938.

Twenty years later Neruda tenderly recalled his father:

> How can I live so far
> from what I loved, from what I love?
> From the stations shrouded in steam and cold smoke?
> Although he died so many years ago,
> my father must still be walking there
> with his cape covered in raindrops
> and his beard the colour of leather.[9]

On 18 August, 1938, just two months and eleven days after his father's death, another telegram brought an even greater shock. Neruda's beloved stepmother, his *mamadre*, had died. He returned once again with a heavy heart to Temuco. With his brother, Rodolfo, and some of his father's old railway colleagues, they hacked open the sealed cement vault containing José del Carmen's coffin so that the *mamadre* could lie side by side with him. To their horror, his father's casket, already covered in fungi, was leaking liquid. Pablo thought that his father's body fluid was flowing out of the coffin, but the truth was more prosaic: the constant rains of Temuco had seeped into the vault and saturated the coffin. It was an image that was to haunt Neruda for many years to come.

Neruda continued to dedicate poetry to his stepmother for the rest of his life.

> Oh, sweet mamadre
> – I could never call you
> stepmother –
> now
> my mouth trembles as I try to define you,
> because as soon I was old enough to understand,
> I saw goodness dressed in dark rags,
> I saw the most useful saintliness:
> that of water and flour.
> That's what you were:
> life made bread of you
> and we consumed you there
> Oh Mama, how could I go on living
> without remembering you
> every single minute?[10]

As if the deaths of his father and *mamadre* were not terrible blows enough, as Neruda came to publish that first edition of *Aurora* in Santiago on 1 August 1938, he learned that César Vallejo had died in Paris. The great Peruvian poet, with whom, just a year earlier, Neruda had worked on the Valencia congress, had succumbed to his long illness. Neruda recalled his friend in that issue of *Aurora*:

In Europe, spring is burgeoning over yet another unforgettable friend among the dead: our greatly admired, our greatly beloved César Vallejo . . . The tragedy of Spain was gnawing at your soul . . . You were a great man, Vallejo. You were private and great, like a glorious palace of subterranean stone with a vast, mineral silence and copious essences of time and matter. And deep within, the implacable fire of your spirit, coal and ashes . . .[11]

Neruda realised that life had, nevertheless, to go on. Not only was he now at the cultural centre of Chile, he also found himself working as public relations manager for the Popular Front candidate, Pedro Aguirre Cerda, in the forthcoming presidential elections.

These were remarkable times in Chile. On 5 September 1938, the so-called Nacista (Nazi) Party, led by Jorge González von Maráes, attempted a coup d'état. His supporters shot a policeman outside the Moneda (the presidential palace in Santiago). President Alessandri Palma witnessed the shooting from his office window, rushed out into the street and personally dragged the dying policeman into a doorway. He then ordered out the troops. The Nacistas hid in the headquarters of the state security apparatus, but the Alessandri government commanded the soldiers to storm the building. Every Nacista member inside was killed. González von Maráes and his major political ally in Chile, Carlos Ibáñez del Campo – the dictator deposed as President in 1931, who was also planning to stand for President in the 1938 elections – were jailed.

The regime of the incumbent, Alessandri, had moved to the Right since coming to power in 1932. Some blamed the influence of his Finance Minister, Gustavo Ross. Strikes were brutally repressed, and the Left's activities were stamped out. It was natural that, when the Frente Popular (Popular Front) – a coalition of Socialists and Communists, together with the powerful Radical Party – was created especially to fight the Right's candidate (Ross himself) in the 25 October 1938 elections, Neruda was asked to help out, and that he would find the request impossible to resist.

It is easy to see why working with Aguirre Cerda appealed to Neruda on a personal level. The presidential candidate's father had been a farmer of modest means. Pedro himself had grown up, like Miguel Hernández, feeling close to the soil and to the poor. By the 1920s, he was also president of the Chilean Wine Growers' Association – a position that certainly must have endeared him to Neruda. And Aguirre Cerda and Neruda had something further in common: both had wives (or companions) who were, if anything, even more committedly left-wing than they were. Aguirre Cerda was easy to get on with: he was accessible, unassuming and cheerful. He liked writers. He told the American journalist, John Gunther, that he would like to see an essay contest held in every country of the world, with the winner the student who best described his own country. Then these essays should be exchanged, printed cheaply and distributed as a pamphlet for workers and students everywhere.[12]

Aguirre Cerda had his enemies, however: on the extreme Left, he was condemned for being 'bourgeois', while the Right denounced him as a Bolshevik. Fittingly, Aguirre Cerda announced that, if he won the presidential elections, Chile would remain neutral in the Second World War, just as it had in the First.

No one gave the Popular Front a chance. Everyone predicted a Ross landslide. In the end – Neruda joining the throngs on the Alameda, one of Santiago's main thoroughfares, to hear the results – the election was very close, but Aguirre Cerda emerged victorious by just 4,111 votes. Some claim that what made the victory possible was the fact that, behind their prison bars, the Nacista leader González von Maráes and Carlos Ibáñez del Campo had thrown their weight, improbably, behind the Popular Front. Whatever the truth of this, Neruda was ecstatic and invited his friends around to his home on the Avenida Irrarázabal, where they celebrated long into the night.

Pedro Aguirre Cerda officially took over the reins of the country on Christmas Eve, 1938. One of his first moves was to summon Neruda and inform him that he was sending him back to Europe, to Paris, where he would take up the post of special consul for Spanish emigration.

There was considerable concern in Chile, and other parts of Latin America, over reports of the terrible plight facing more than half a million Spanish Republicans who had crossed the Pyrenees, mostly on foot, from Spain into France to escape the Franco onslaught. The refugees believed that they were fleeing to safety, but the French government, anxious to solve the problem of a sudden influx of immigrants, asked Franco to set up a neutral zone on Spanish territory, between Andorra and Port Bou, where the refugees could remain until they were accepted by other nations prepared to grant them asylum. Franco rejected the French request. On 28 January 1939, the French Interior Minister, Albert Serraut, gave an order for women and children to be allowed to cross the border into France – and for the men to be returned to Spain. It was not until 5 February that the French Prime Minister, Edouard Baladier, relented and agreed to permit Spanish Republican soldiers to enter the country, provided they handed over their weapons at the frontier. Little did the soldiers know that waiting for them in France were squalid concentration camps without the most basic hygiene or medical facilities. They were to be considered prisoners of war, surrounded by barbed wire, carefully guarded, living in tents without a roof over their heads to protect them from the harsh winter. They were fed little more than bread and water. Similar camps were opened in Algeria and Morocco. Back in Chile, Neruda read the press reports with horror.

These were heady days in his literary life. *Espagne au coeur*, the French translation of his hymn to Spain, had been published in July 1938, with a prologue by his Communist friend Louis Aragon. Then, to Neruda's enormous delight, he heard that the book had also been published in remarkable conditions in Spain itself – in the midst of the raging Civil War.

The Spanish publication of *España en el corazón* is the stuff of legend. And like all legends, at least some of the truth has become distorted. What is known is that, during the Civil War, the Generalitat (the Catalan Parliament) handed over the administration of the monastery of Montserrat to a Republican deputy, Carles Gerhard. Part of the monastery contained a print workshop founded more than 450 years before (in 1499), which is still operating to this day. During the Civil War, it was run by Neruda's friend from *Caballo Verde* days, the poet Manuel Altolaguirre. Under his guidance, the presses produced three books of poetry in the heat of battle: Neruda's *España en el corazón*, César Vallejo's *España, aparta de mí este cáliz*, and *Cancionero menor para los combatientes*, by the Spanish poet, Emilio Prados.

The first Spanish edition of *España en el corazón* appeared on 7 November 1938. It had a very limited circulation, and was distributed to the Republican authorities, policemen and soldiers. The second edition, begun in January 1939, never reached the binding stage. Franco's troops entered the monastery at the beginning of February and destroyed almost the whole run, taking with them all the other Republican books they found there.

In a letter, Altolaguirre claimed that the paper for the second edition 'was manufactured by soldiers who worked at the mill. Not only did they use raw materials (cotton and pieces of cloth) supplied by the commissariat, but the soldiers added to the mixture clothes, bandages, war trophies, an enemy flag and the shirt of a Moorish prisoner.' If so, the resultant paper was of surprisingly high quality.

Neruda repeats this extraordinary version of the story in his memoirs. Sadly, however, according to Jordi Torra, who works at the library of the Universidad Autónoma in Barcelona, which owns a copy of the second edition of *España en el corazón*, 'what Altolaguirre says about the way the paper was produced and its composition seems to be something of a myth. We've searched the whole region, and there is no trace of any village with a mill which could have produced it.'[13]

All that is important, ultimately, is the poetry itself. In the key poem, 'Explico algunas cosas' (Let Me Explain a Few Things), Neruda reveals that he has disowned his previous, inward-looking self, together with any romantic, unworldly lyricism, and is now fully committed to his new role of truth-teller and exposer of the world's injustices – specifically, here, the horrors being committed by Franco's forces. But his new verse, of course, possesses a striking lyricism of its own:

> You will ask: And where are the lilacs
> And the metaphysics petalled with poppies
> And the rain repeatedly spattering
> its words, filling them with holes and birds? . . .
> You will ask why his poetry
> does not speak of dreams and leaves,
> and of the great volcanoes of his birthplace?
>
> Come and see the blood in the streets.
> Come and see
> the blood in the streets.
> Come and see the blood
> in the streets!

Many critics see this book as marking Neruda's dramatic conversion from anguished self-obsession to social commitment. The Spanish scholar, Amado Alonso, was one of the first to make this point in 1940.[14] The Uruguayan critic Emir Rodríguez Monegal wrote that *España en el corazón* represented a shift from the frenetic individualism of *Residencia en la tierra*, through the horrific experiences of living in war-torn Spain, to a concept of these experiences as part of a wider solidarity. For Monegal, all Neruda's earlier poetry had been obscure and shapeless by comparison.[15]

The Chilean specialist Jaime Concha sees things rather differently. He believes that *España en el corazón* marked not so much a definite farewell to obscure poetry as a change in mood. Paradoxically,

Concha writes, while *Residencia en la tierra* had contained some of the most pessimistic lines in twentieth-century Spanish-language poetry, Neruda's Civil War writings are actually full of hope in the midst of despair (in contrast to César Vallejo's harrowing *España, aparta de mí este cáliz*, for instance, written at the same time). Neruda, as Concha correctly points out, often expresses hope – hope and respect for decency and for humanity.[16]

In fact, there are already signs of this shift earlier, in some of the poems in *Residencia en la tierra*, those written in his first months in Spain long before the fascist uprising. Also, as Hernán Loyola has noted, Alonso's theory does not explain the fact that Neruda was also writing poems at this time which had no immediate political significance. Some techniques, too, remain similar. As in *Residencia*, so in *España en el corazón*, Neruda repeats phrases to emphasise them, almost like a Greek chorus ('Come and see the blood in the streets').

Nevertheless, he saw the world and his role as a poet in it differently. What is new is his intense feeling of betrayal – not an embittered, personal disillusionment over a failed love affair but a sense of a betrayal of a broader human, decent society (of which he now feels a part, rather than alienated from) by brutal, unintelligent, inhumane forces (Franco and his fascist troops). Neruda denounces the traitors relentlessly, the 'bandits' who 'came from the sky to kill children / and through the streets the children's blood / flowed simply, as children's blood does.'

España en el corazón is clearly imbued with a passion for something other than himself. As the Mexican poet, Octavio Paz, wrote admiringly at the time, it goes 'beyond the anecodotal and wounds us, wounds itself, in the place where voices resound terribly throughout the centuries: in the heart'.[17]

Prior to his departure from Chile for Europe, Neruda started looking around for a place in Santiago where he and Delia could live in tranquillity on his return from his European mission. He came across a small old building, covered with vines, on the Avenida Lynch, and bought it, thanks largely to a generous loan from the Public Employees' and Journalists' Pension Fund. Delia was busy obtaining equipment and clothing for the Spanish Republican refugees they were hoping to save. Just before they were due to leave for Paris, Neruda seriously hurt his leg in an accident and had to undergo an operation. He boarded the boat, *La Campana*, at Valparaíso with his leg in plaster, but with the words of the new President of Chile ringing in his ears: 'Bring me thousands of Spaniards. We have work for all of them. Bring me fishermen, bring me Basques and Castillians, people from Extremadura.'

On reaching Paris at the end of April 1939, Neruda and Delia were delighted to be reunited with their friends, Rafael Alberti and his wife María Teresa León. The two couples shared an apartment by the River Seine, on the Quai de l'Horloge.

With Franco's victory in Spain on 19 May 1939, Neruda knew that every day counted. He had the help of French friends and that of the Spanish government-in-exile, presided over by Juan Negrín. It was Negrín who found the boat to transport 2,000 Spanish refugees across the ocean to Chile.

Busy as he was, Neruda still needed fun – and as his constant companion at this time, Rafael Alberti, recalled, he found plenty.

> Neruda remained the Neruda of old: a terrible child, capricious, dangerous . . . He squeezed you. He made you drink at his whim. It was impossible to drink just one bottle; you had to join him in every bottle he drank. Not to mention the countless whiskies.[18]

Neruda had also lost none of his childish passion for unusual objects. He and Alberti were walking down the rue du Chat qui Pêche in Paris one day when Neruda noticed a shoemaker's shop with a huge iron key nailed above the doorway. As Alberti remembered: 'Pablo immediately fell into a state of ecstasy. "Oh, *confrère*, do you see that magnificent key? I want to take it back with me to Chile for my collection." '

Alberti desperately tried to dissuade Pablo from such a pointless exercise. But Neruda was not to be thwarted. When the shopkeeper refused to contemplate parting with the key, Neruda returned in the company of a bricklayer, a member of the French Communist Party, who broke the key away from the wall. Pablo took the key with a triumphant smile and paid the shopkeeper 500 francs for it – an offer the man was happy to accept.

Reports quickly began to circulate in France that the great Chilean poet had returned to Europe on a rescue mission. Alberti recalled that thousands of letters arrived for Pablo from inmates of French concentration camps. Some made transparent attempts at flattery in a bid to secure a place on board the poet's ship. One letter, from a soldier, declared: 'Great poet Pablo Neruda. I know that your wife is like a little bird, a small nightingale who sings every morning.' Neruda was entranced by the mixture of innocence and guile in the letter and did indeed make sure that its author was among those saved.

Neruda was given a small office at the Chilean consulate in Marseille and set to work enthusiastically. However, his work did not go unhindered.

> My country's government and political situation were not what they had been, but the Embassy in Paris was still the same. The idea of sending Spaniards to Chile infuriated our smartly dressed diplomats. They set me up in an office next to the kitchen, they harassed me in every way they could, even going so far as to deny me writing paper. The wave of undesirables was already beginning to reach the doors of the Embassy: wounded veterans, lawyers and writers, professionals who had lost their practice, all kinds of skilled workers. They had to make their way through hell and high water to get to my office, and since it was on the fourth floor, our Embassy people thought up a fiendish scheme: they cut off the elevator service. Many of the Spaniards had war wounds and were survivors of the African concentration camps. It broke my heart to see them come up to the fourth floor with such painful effort, while the cruel officials gloated over my difficulties.[19]

The Chilean Foreign Ministry responded to Neruda's request for a secretary by sending him a chargé d'affaires, Arellano Marín, who was bright and could be very charming, but disconcerted Neruda with his love of luxurious cars and rented homes and the striking blonde on his arm. During a brief trip to Brussels, Neruda tried to warn Marín that his extravagant behaviour was inappropriate. The advice appears to have fallen on deaf ears. Neruda learnt a few years later in Mexico that, while in Brussels, Marín had informed two Spaniards that Neruda was preparing to turn them in to the Gestapo as dangerous Communists. Moreover, Marín had persuaded the two men to leave their suitcases with him for safe keeping. The cases contained 90,000 dollars, which the hapless Spanish pair never saw again. (Still later, Neruda discovered that the stunning blonde at Marín's side was actually a fair-haired male student from the Sorbonne.)

Just as the final preparations for Neruda's rescue mission were being made, startling news arrived from Chile. President Pedro Aguirre Cerda had changed his mind: he didn't want the boat to leave France for Chile, after all. Neruda was appalled. Some sources claim that he went as far as to threaten to commit suicide if the boat were not allowed to depart for Chile with the Spanish refugees on board. However, it is likely that Aguirre Cerda was more convinced by a threat of resignation from his Foreign Minister, Abraham Ortega.

Víctor Pey, a Spanish civil engineer, was one of the men who was rescued on the *Winnipeg*. He told me,

> I was a very close friend of Ortega. He was a Radical. When the Second World War broke out, Aguirre Cerda did indeed order Ortega to suspend the arrival of the *Winnipeg*. There are many versions of how Neruda reacted. What is certain is that Ortega threatened to resign and it was this threat that convinced Aguirre Cerda to rescind the suspension of the operation. Neruda must have exerted pressure as well, of course. But Ortega's Radical Party was a key member of the Popular Front government, and he had a lot of influence over the President.[20]

So the mission was saved, and the refugees began to make their way down to Bordeaux.

Neruda swiftly persuaded Juan Negrín – Prime Minister of the Spanish Republican government-in-exile – to establish the Service for the Evacuation of Spanish Refugees (SERE). Writing later, Neruda noted that assistance also came from another, surprising, source:

> The SERE was set up as a solidarity organisation. Help came, on the one hand, from the last funds available to the Republican government and, on the other hand, from an institution which remains a mystery to me: the Quakers. I admit that I am abominably ignorant as far as religions are concerned. That struggle against sin in which these religions specialise alienated me in my youth from all creeds, and this supercifial attitude – one of indifference – has persisted all my life. But the fact is that, at the harbour, those magnificent sectarians turned up and paid for half of every Spanish [boat] ticket to freedom, without discriminating between atheists and believers, between 'pecadores' and 'pescadores' [sinners and fishermen]. From

then on, whenever I read the world 'Quaker' anywhere, I mentally
bow in reverence.[21]

Thanks to Negrín and to the SERE, the boat, the *Winnipeg*, was
hired to take the 2,000 refugees to Chile. It was not an ideal vessel: it
was an old ship which had been used to go back and forward between
Marseille and the African coast with a crew of just seventeen, and it
stank of fish. It had, however, seen active military service: it had
transported troops during the First World War. Workmen quickly
began transforming the interior of the *Winnipeg*, converting the six
floors of storerooms into three levels of wooden bunk beds.

Unfortunately, there were still obstacles to the rescue mission back
in Chile. The opposition press – notably *El Diario Illustrado* – claimed
that Chile could not afford to allow so many refugees into the country.
In response, the government daily, *Frente Popular*, exclaimed: 'The
Spanish refugees must have put up with a life of tremendous depriva-
tion in the concentration camps and other parts of the world. Now the
opportunity has arisen for Chile – the democratic hope of America – to
help them, while at the same time the country will benefit from the best
immigrants it could ever have signed up.' The debate soon hit the
Chilean Parliament, with heated discussions in the Chamber of
Deputies between those who supported the *Winnipeg* mission for
bringing in 'honourable, hard-working people' and opponents who
claimed that the operation would 'fill the country with vagrants'.

Neruda, though thousands of miles away in Paris, was well aware
of the controversy back home. But he was more concerned that the
money was running out for his mission. Those final days leading up to
the departure of the *Winnipeg* were extraordinary ones, as concentration camp inmates arrived in Bordeaux, in third-class train car-
riages, weak from fatigue, hunger and thirst. From Bordeaux, they
were transferred to Pauillac, to prepare for the final checking of their
papers before boarding at the Trompeloupe docks.

One of the passengers chosen by Neruda to board the *Winnipeg*
with her mother was Roser Bru, now among Chile's leading painters.

The first image I had of them was of Delia, the Hormiguita, who
later became a great friend of mine. She was dressed in white. I was
very young, just sixteen, and they looked very old! They were in a
café, a bistrot. My father went off to Paris. Neruda didn't want

people who were 'intellectuals'. He wanted peasants, people who worked with their hands.[22]

Neruda sat at a long table, selecting a list of passengers. According to Víctor Pey, Neruda did not choose all 2,000 passengers to be shipped to safety himself. Most were selected by the SERE, and Neruda personally picked only a few hundred.[23] While Pablo was busy with the paperwork and the interviews, Delia was distributing dresses, shoes and shirts – though some of the men politely refused the flowery ones she offered them.

The late Chilean author and artist, Leopoldo Castedo, claimed in his memoirs that he had run into difficulties with Neruda when it was discovered that he was not an active member of any political party, but Pey vigorously rejected this suggestion. He pointed out that the vast majority of those allowed on board the *Winnipeg* were not Communists at all. Pey also described as 'totally false' a rather snide claim by the late Galician painter, Eugenio Granell, that he had been turned away from boarding the boat because he was a Trotskyist; Granell was particularly hostile to Spanish writers and painters, such as Alberti and Picasso, who had sided with Stalin.

At one point, an old Spaniard presented himself to Neruda, who asked him: 'What's your speciality?' 'Well, I work in cork, from the moment it is removed from the cork tree to the time it's handed over, ready to be used for bottling. I can be very useful in Chile, because . . .' Neruda interrupted the old man and said: 'What a pity! There's no cork production in Chile. There are no cork trees.' 'What do you mean, Comrade Neruda? No cork trees in Chile? Well, you just leave it to me, and I'll make sure there are.' Convinced that this was the kind of man Chile needed, Neruda added him to the list of passengers.

The *Winnipeg* left Pauillac, the port of Bordeaux, on 4 August 1939. Neruda stood alongside Delia on the dock, in his white hat, to wave the boat off. Everything was very well-organised during the one-month voyage. Women and children had the cabins below deck, and men those on deck. There were rotas for breakfast, lunch, tea and dinner, as well as cleaning rotas. There were even organised talks, chess games and a choir formed by Basque passengers. During the trip, a boy and a girl were born.

It was stiflingly hot on board, especially below deck, Roser Bru told me. 'Imagine it: one whole month, with lots of us packed into chairs. It was very hot. The atmosphere on board was terrible. We each grabbed a space and tried not to lose it. My mother told us never to sleep below deck, because it was suffocating.'[24]

Another passenger, José Balmes, who, like Bru, is among Chile's finest contemporary painters, told me that his abiding memory of the trip was of the stench of 'rotten fish and vomit' on board.

Was there enough to eat? 'Look,' Víctor Pey recalled, 'the fact is that we had just emerged from concentration camps where we had no food, no washing facilities, nothing, so the *Winnipeg* seemed like a luxury! We had three good, healthy meals a day. And we had something priceless: our freedom.'[25]

They had their freedom, but also boredom. There were no books on board the boat at all, but the passengers quickly organised a mural newspaper.

> We would write down notes on the wall about the Civil War in Spain. Lots of discussions started every day. But even though the debates got heated, we never came to blows, despite what has sometimes been reported. Never. We discussed the French Socialist government's refusal to send arms to help the Spanish Republicans, despite its previous agreement to do so. We discussed the attitude of the Spanish Republican Prime Minister, Juan Negrín, a Europeanist, a doctor who, right in the middle of the Civil War, attended a scientific congress in Switzerland.[26]

Others remember things differently. There were physical confrontations, particularly after the news came through of the signature of the Nazi-Soviet pact on 23 August 1939, which was a devastating blow to the Communists on board. What must Delia del Carril, back in France, have felt on learning that the man from whom she took one of her nicknames – the Soviet Foreign Minister, Vyacheslav Molotov – had signed a pact of non-aggression with his German counterpart, Joachim von Ribbentrop? Especially as Molotov had also come out with some astounding comments to the Supreme Soviet, lashing out at all the anti-fascist and anti-Nazi slogans, which he now called 'inapplicable and outmoded', even going so far as to say: 'It is not only senseless but criminal to wage this war against fascism with the aim of destroying Hitlerism, under the pretext of defending democracy.'

There were rumours on board ship that the captain had received orders to turn around and return to France. The boat was also held up for several days in Panama because a fee had not been paid to pass through the canal.

The *Winnipeg* finally arrived in Valparaíso on 3 September 1939. It was a date no one would forget – the Second World War broke out that very day. Chileans watching the ship pull in cheered the refugees' arrival, waving white handkerchiefs and singing songs of welcome. According to some reports, among those waiting on the dock was the Chilean Health Minister and future President, Salvador Allende.

The refugees were divided up according to which region of Spain they came from, and some remained in Valparaíso while others were put on a train to Santiago. Arriving in the Chilean capital, they were fêted once again. José Balmes noted: 'I was just twelve years old and I could still clearly remember the feeling of being up to my knees in snow as I crossed the Pyrenees from Spain into France. Here [in Chile] the people loved us immediately.'[27]

As Neruda proudly wrote in his memoirs: 'Let the critics wipe out all my poetry. No one will wipe out the poem of the *Winnipeg*.' That, he said, had been 'the most important mission of my life'.[28]

Mission accomplished, he and Delia stayed on in Paris for a further two months. The world was at war, and they waited to see whether Paris would fall to the Nazis in the same way as Madrid had tumbled to the fascists. 'From my window in Paris, I looked out on Les Invalides and saw the first contingents leaving, youngsters who had not yet learned how to wear their soldiers' uniforms but were marching straight into death's gaping mouth.'[29]

Chile remained officially neutral during the Second World War, as it had in the First. Neruda's friend, the Communist poet Louis Aragon, took refuge in the Chilean Embassy in Paris, fleeing from pro-Nazi forces. There, according to Neruda, Aragon completed his novel, *Passengers of Destiny*. After five days, Aragon left the Embassy to join the fight against the Germans.

The Chilean Embassy in Madrid had become a haven for refugees seeking a flight to safety. Although the role of the Chilean Ambassador, Carlos Morla Lynch remains unclear, the suggestion that he denied Miguel Hernández asylum in the Chilean Embassy seems to be false: Hernández himself apparently rejected the idea of asylum, seeing it as an act of desertion. Isolated in the French capital, Neruda tried to ensure that his friend was given safe passage out of Spain. But the Franco regime was unmoved. Hernández was arrested and held at Torrijos jail. Neruda arranged to send Miguel and his wife a monthly pension via the attaché at the Chilean Embassy in Madrid, Germán Vergara, but his friend's plight remained perilous. Neruda, together with a number of Spanish and French colleagues, appealed to a friend of Franco, Cardinal Baudillart, to plead for Miguel's release. The cardinal, who was almost totally blind, listened in admiration as some of Hernández's poetry was read out to him – and the plan worked. Franco's government relented and freed Hernández in mid-1939.

It looked as though Neruda's intervention from Paris had done the trick. Miguel was free to leave Spain. Misguidedly, he chose not to, because his second child was due to be born at any moment. The regime seized its chance and put him back in jail. This time, he would not come out alive. If Neruda considered the *Winnipeg* as among his finest achievements, he always viewed his inability to save Miguel Hernández's life as one of his greatest failures.

Neruda had scarcely written a line of verse since he had arrived back in Europe. His hands had been occupied writing out details and filling in the paperwork for the *Winnipeg* mission. Now he felt the need to resume his literary work.

He and Delia returned to Chile in January 1940. Neruda needed somewhere quiet where he could write. The royalties from his various books were now starting to bring in larger sums, enough to encourage Neruda to purchase a modest stone house on the Pacific coast, on the border of Valparaíso province in an undeveloped part of Chile. The house's owner was a Spaniard, Eladio Sobrino – according to Delia, a guitar-playing sea captain who had lost his ship – and he, in turn, approved of Neruda's actions during the Spanish Civil War.[30] The house was to be turned into one of the most beautifully situated homes in Latin America, called Isla Negra – not because it was an island, but because it looked out on to a large black rock in the ocean.

The house had problems: it was lit only by precarious paraffin lamps, and the water in the building was never more than lukewarm. But the couple loved the tranquillity and the view of the Pacific from their bedroom window. They would often stroll on the beach. Like all Neruda's houses, it became a hive of activity, with friends arriving unannounced. Delia, too, cultivated friendships. They included Neruda's half-sister Laurita and Pablo's former lover Albertina Azócar, now married to Angel Cruchaga.

Just as Neruda and Delia were settling into to their new life by the ocean, and Pablo was beginning to write the first poems of what was to become his uneven but undoubted masterpiece, *Canto general*, the Chilean Foreign Ministry – now much more amicably disposed towards him – summoned Neruda again. This time, he was being posted to Mexico City.

7

Mexican magic, marriage, a tragic telegram and a mordant badger

1940–43

Neruda and Delia set out from Valparaíso on the Japanese boat, the *Rakuyu Maru* (sunk by a torpedo just a few months later in the Second World War).

On board, Delia wrote a letter, dated 29 July 1940, to the Cuban writer Juan Marinello, in which she explained that Pablo was very keen to visit Cuba for the first time.[1] She told Marinello that Neruda 'had made good progress on his *Canto general*' and that he was not writing personally because he was too busy with the 'annoying and unpleasant' duty of writing a number of letters back to Chile. Nevertheless, Neruda did add a postscript in his own hand, saying: 'I'm dying to visit Cuba' and asking Marinello to send his best wishes to those in Havana – 'except that old bastard, Juan Ramón Jiménez'. (It was in Havana, where he had lived between 1936 and 1939, that Jiménez had written his famous attack on Neruda as a 'great bad poet'.) Their reconciliation would not occur until 1942, when Jiménez wrote an 'Open Letter to Pablo Neruda' praising his 'exhuberant . . . authentic Latin American poetry'.[2]

Pablo and Delia arrived at the Mexican port of Manzanillo, with Luis Enrique Délano, Luis's wife, Lola Falcón, and their six-year-old son, Poli, on 16 August 1940.

While war was raging in Europe, Mexico was a haven of

political and economic stability under the outgoing President Lázaro Cárdenas. Neruda initially intended to keep a low public profile in Mexico City. He and Delia lived for a while at the Hotel Montejo, on the Paseo de la Reforma. But eight days after his arrival, Pablo could not resist giving a mischievously ambiguous interview to the Mexican daily, *El Nacional*, in which he praised Mexico's poets: 'I wish Chile had poets like those here, whose peculiarity lies in form . . . Not that I can talk, because I have sought to do away with form . . .'[3] A back-handed compliment, indeed, to the poets in his host country. Fortunately, it was not picked up by the Mexican literary establishment, otherwise Neruda would have ruffled feathers no sooner than he had arrived.

But it is clear that, however ambivalent Neruda may have felt towards some sections of the Mexican intelligentsia, he loved most of what Mexico had to offer. He was also hugely appreciative of the Mexican government's efforts on behalf of the Spanish Republican victims of Franco's repression. Mexico, like no other Latin American country, opened its doors wide to refugees fleeing fascism. And it was not just Spanish refugees, either. Neruda's *Winnipeg* had a 'sister ship', the *Serpa Pinto*, a Portuguese vessel that was the last boat to leave Europe bound for Mexico carrying opponents of the Nazi regime in Germany.

After their brief stay in the Hotel Montejo, Neruda and Delia moved first to an apartment on the Calle Revillagigedo, and then to a much bigger house, La Quinta Rosa María. Once again, Neruda's home became *the* venue for Mexico's leading cultural personalities, as well as artists and writers fleeing fascism in Europe.

From Spain came León Felipe, José Bergamín and Wenceslao Roces, who at the time was best known for translating Marx's works into Spanish. Among the Mexican visitors were Octavio Paz and Carlos Pellicer. There was the German novelist Anna Seghers, and the great Czech journalist Egon Erwin Kisch (described by George Steiner as 'the most gifted journalist ever to service the Marxist cause'[4]), who was constantly trying to tease Pablo into explaining how he had chosen his pseudonym.

Delia delegated most of the catering duties – this time to Lola Falcón. And, as always, there was plenty of catering to do. To celebrate the christening of Cibeles, the daughter of their friend, the Mexican novelist Andrés Henestrosa, 400 guests were invited and spent two days dancing, singing and climbing the trees. So loud were the festivities that the owner of the building asked Pablo and Delia to move.

But while Delia did not help much in the kitchen, she played a vital role in Neruda's poetic creation. He showed her every green-ink-written manuscript, had a total respect for her opinion, and if she did not approve or thought a line needed reworking, he would change it.

Nor did Delia neglect her own creativity. Lola Falcón recalled that, 'as we anxiously followed the resistance of Stalingrad, the clandestine struggle of the Maquis [underground] in Paris against the German occupation, the advances of the Third Reich in the midst of the devastation of Europe, it was there [Mexico] that I saw Delia paint. She said she was just an amateur, but we thought her works had great power, a beautiful sense of colour.'[5]

The Mexican writer Wilberto Cantón recollected the Pablo Neruda of the early 1940s in Mexico, '. . . presiding over an improvised banquet, where there was no talk of love, only literature. I recall him with his broad laugh, there among the seashells which invaded his apartment.'[6]

Neruda had already begun his lifelong habit of collecting seashells and any other objects which reminded him of the sea. Another writer, Manuel Lerín, recalled Pablo 'in the living-room of his house, surrounded by marine pieces and motifs, as if he were nostalgic for the coastline of his homeland'.

Pablo adored the markets.

Mexico is to be found in its markets. Not in the guttural songs of the movies or the false image of the Mexican in sombrero, with moustache and pistol. Mexico is a land of crimson and phosphorescent turquoise shawls. Mexico is a land of earthenware bowls and pitchers, and fruit lying open to a swarm of insects. Mexico is an infinite countryside of steel-blue century plants with yellow thorns. The most beautiful markets in the world have all this to offer. Fruit and wool, clay and weaving looms, are evidence of the incredible skill of the fertile and timeless fingers of the Mexicans . . . Mexico, the last of the magic countries, because of its age and its history, its music and its geography . . .[7]

Another of Neruda's habits, which he frequently indulged, was to disguise himself – and to encourage his guests to do likewise. Sometimes, he would emerge to greet his guests dressed as a fireman, an army general or a ticket collector. Andrés Henestrosa rather unkindly suggested that this love of disguise might have reflected Neruda's self-consciousness about the ugliness of his own appearance.

In part, these games were attempts to flee the bureaucratic burden of his consular duties. The Chilean Foreign Ministry assigned him to tasks which would have been ridiculous if they had not been unpleasantly tainted. Once, he was asked to check up on the racial origins of people attempting to obtain visas for Chile.

Ironically, it was his unilateral decision – without informing the Foreign Ministry – to grant a visa to Chile to one of Mexico's greatest painters and most controversial figures which earned Neruda a two-month suspension from the diplomatic service. It was thought of as a punishment, but in fact it was just the break he needed.

In 1937 Mexico's then President Lázaro Cárdenas, under attack from the United States and several European countries for nationalising the oil industry and accused of being a puppet of Russian Communism for his nationalist policies, had granted political asylum to the Russian revolutionary Leon Trotsky to prove his independence from Stalin's regime.

The first attempt to assassinate Trotsky was organised by one of Mexico's mural painters, David Alfaro Siqueiros. He was the leader of a group of men wearing police uniforms who attacked Trotsky's house in Coyoacán on the night of 24 May 1940. Siqueiros himself participated in the action dressed in the uniform of a major in the Mexican army. All the participants in the attack were members of the Mexican Communist Party (MCP) or related to organisations controlled by the party. They broke into Trotsky's house and shot 300 bullets into his bedroom. Trotsky and his wife Natasha miraculously survived by taking cover under their bed. Their young grandson, whose father had been killed shortly before by the NKVD (the Soviet secret police, later known as the KGB) in Paris, was wounded in the attack.

Siqueiros and eight other militants of the MCP were arrested after the failed assassination attempt. Thanks to pressure from the Soviet Union and NKVD agents in Mexico, they were given light sentences. Without consulting the Chilean Foreign Ministry, Neruda met

Siqueiros in jail and arranged for him to be granted a visa for Chile. As a mark of his gratitude, Siqueiros would paint a giant mural in Chillán, in the south of Chile.[8]

In the late afternoon of 20 August 1940, four days after Neruda arrived in Mexico, Trotsky was killed by the blow of a mountaineer's pickaxe at his home in Coyoacán. The assassin, Ramón Mercader, at that time using the pseudonym of Jacques Mornard Vanderdreschd, was an agent of the NKVD. His mission had been ordered personally by Stalin and was carried out with the aid of high officials in the Third International – the Comintern – and with the logistical and material support of the Mexican Communist Party. In ordering the assassination of Trotsky, Stalin hoped to wipe out any possibility that a Communist opposition movement would emerge to challenge the leadership of the Comintern and the Soviet Union.

For years afterwards, Neruda's political and personal enemies accused him of being an accomplice in Siqueiros' attempted murder of Trotsky, and even of some form of involvement in the actual killing. As we know, Neruda did not arrive in Mexico City to take up his consular post until 16 August, four days before the assassination and three months after the earlier attempt. The accusation against him irritated Neruda, but he refused to be drawn into any explanation or self-defence – until 1971, in an interview with the Uruguayan magazine, *Marcha*.

> In Europe, for political and literary reasons, they tried to link me with Trotsky's death. But I never saw that man, not close-up or from a distance, neither alive nor dead. But let me tell you something rather quaint. I had just arrived in Mexico, to take up my post as consul-general, when I received a visit from the Mexican Ambassador in Chile, Octavio Reyes Espindola . . . He informed me that General Manuel Avila Camacho, [the new] President of the Mexican Republic, had charged me with a confidential mission. In a word, he asked me, in a personal capacity, to grant, as quickly as possible, a visa to the painter David Alfaro Siqueiros, authorising him to enter Chile. I must confess that his request surprised me, because I thought Siqueiros was in prison. And indeed, so he was: he had been accused of machine-gunning Leon Trotsky's house. So I said to Ambassador Reyes Espindola: 'How can I grant him a visa if he's in jail?' The Ambassador replied: 'Don't you worry about that,

we'll get him freed.' I proposed that we go and visit him [Siqueiros], which we did the following day. We went to the office of Captain Pérez Rulfo, director of the prison, who received us very warmly. He summoned Siqueiros, whom I had never met, and the three of us left to have a few drinks in the city's cafés. Although I had no right to demand anything, since it was a request from the President of Mexico, I asked that, as a condition for my granting him a visa, Siqueiros donate a work of art to Chile, on behalf of the Mexican government. And that was how Siqueiros spent more than a year painting his biggest wall fresco [to date], in Chillán. That is the truth about this malicious story, which I've never told until now.[9]

Unfortunately, Neruda's account didn't stop the accusations – even from what would appear to be the most prestigious of sources. On 24 January 1988, the *New York Times Book Review* published a feature entitled 'Intellectuals and Assassins – Annals of Stalin's Killerati', accompanied by photographs of Neruda and Siqueiros, and citing American Defense Intelligence Agency research to intimate links between both men and a NKVD death squad. When an American critic, John Bart Gerald, tried to challenge the *New York Times Book Review* article in a letter to the editor, noting that 'the military sources who brought us the Vietnam War were now destroying a poet for a propaganda advantage', his letter was not published, 'and I know of no other challenge by American writers, allowed in print'.[10]

There is no evidence whatsoever to link Neruda with Trotsky's murder. What is clear, however, is that the Russians were interested in Neruda. The NKVD were keen to recruit him to their ranks during his consular stint in Mexico. I have seen a memo to this effect dated May 1944 (i.e. *after* Neruda left Mexico) in the NKVD files.[11] How Neruda responded, if at all, is not known. The NKVD had a foothold in Mexico from 1943, when the Soviet Embassy was opened in the capital.

In any case, Neruda took full avantage of the enforced two-month escape from bureaucracy to travel around Mexico and then to Guatemala. Crossing the Mexican border into Guatemala, Neruda was stunned by the lianas and gigantic leaves and then by Guatemala's 'placid lakes . . . like eyes forgotten by extravagant gods'.[12] One of the great joys of his trip to Guatemala was meeting the novelist Miguel Angel Asturias (later to win the Nobel Prize for Literature but at the time a virtually unknown writer). The two men got on immediately. They shared a physical resemblance (which may well have saved Neruda's life later on) and a love of life, especially food, which would stand them in good stead when they co-authored a book on Hungarian gastronomy in 1967.

Guatemala was governed by a brutal dictator called Jorge Ubico y Castañeda who held his country in an iron grip, executing anyone who dared to oppose him. 'The Guatemalans could not speak freely,' Neruda recollected later, 'and none of them talked about politics in front of anyone else. The walls had ears. Sometimes, to be able to chat, we stopped the car at the top of a hillside and there, quite certain that there was no one behind a tree, we greedily discussed the situation.'[13] Even so, when the government found out that Neruda had managed to snatch a few words with Ubico's secretary, the poor man was whipped.

Ubico nevertheless allowed Neruda to give a recital and he read his poems 'with delight, because they seemed to open the windows of that vast prison'. Neruda couldn't help noticing that sitting in the front row of the packed auditorium was the chief of police.

> Later, I found out that four machine-guns were trained on me and on the audience and that these would have gone off if the police chief happened to leave his seat in the middle of the recital. But nothing happened, because he sat there until the end, listening to my verse. Then they wanted to introduce me to the dictator, who was crazed like Napoleon. He let a lock of hair hang over his forehead, and frequently had his portrait done in the pose of Bonaparte. I was warned that it was dangerous to reject the suggestion to meet him, but I preferred not to shake hands with him and returned to Mexico as quickly as possible.[14]

Neruda also took trips to Panama, Colombia, Peru and the United States. It was as if the *Canto general de Chile*, as he called it at the time, was expanding geographically and spiritually, as his own experiences of Latin America deepened. It was becoming a song to the entire continent rather than to his homeland alone.

He began writing what was to become the section of *Canto general* called 'América, no invoco tu nombre en vano' (America, I Do Not Invoke Your Name in Vain), in which he tried, for the first time, to capture the nature of Latin American plurality. Neruda sketches his impressions of the continent's landscapes, creatures, cities, dictatorial personalities.

> I am, I am surrounded
> by honeysuckle and wasteland, by jackal and lightning,
> by the enchanted perfume of lilacs:
> I am, I am surrounded
> by days, months, waters that I alone know,
> by fingernails, fish, months that I alone establish,
> I am, I am surrounded
> by the slender combatant foam
> of the seaboard full of bells.
> The scarlet shirt of Indian and volcano . . .
> dark blood like autumn
> poured on the ground . . .[15]

On Neruda's return to Mexico, his circle of friends widened as he became friendly with two other great Mexican mural painters, Diego Rivera and José Clemente Orozco.

Rivera fascinated Neruda, although the relationship was not an easy one – partly because Rivera had been a Trotskyist (although he had fallen out with Trotsky after discovering that the Soviet dissident had been carrying on a year-long affair with his wife, Frida Kahlo). The Mexican was an inventive storyteller who enjoyed making up fabulous lies; his character formed the basis for Ilya Ehrenburg's wonderful novel, *Adventures of Julio Jurenito*. Neruda was easily attracted to this type of man. Rivera even told Neruda that he was the father of the Nazi 'Desert Fox', Marshal Rommel

As for the one-armed Orozco, Neruda admired him profoundly, calling him 'the Mexican Goya'. Unlike the Spanish original, however, Orozco never made any money through his work, steadfastly refusing commissions.

At the same time that Neruda was making new friends, he was falling out with others. The differences between himself and Octavio Paz had begun to surface after the 1937 Valencia congress, although Paz was as fervently anti-fascist as Neruda. Later, Paz's profound dillusionment over the 1939 Nazi-Soviet pact made him unwilling to praise Stalin. 'Neruda became more and more Stalinist, while I became less and less enchanted with Stalin,' Paz once recalled. 'Finally we fought – almost physically – and stopped speaking to each other. He wrote some not terribly nice things about me, including one nasty poem. I wrote some awful things about him.'[16]

The political differences between Paz and Neruda were not the only reason for the explosive rupture between the two men. The Paz scholar Enrico Mario Santí believes that the direct cause was an edition of the journal, *Laurel*, which Paz was preparing, along with José Bergamín, Xavier Villaurrutia and Emilio Prados, in 1941, devoted entirely to modern Spanish poetry. Santí claims that Neruda was invited to collaborate but refused. 'He broke with Bergamín for reasons that neither of them ever clarified,' wrote Santí in the introduction to his book on Paz. 'The only allusion to the matter which appears in *Canto general* . . . implies that it was because of the exclusion of Miguel Hernández from the anthology.' This is a reference to the poem entitled 'To Miguel Hernández, Murdered in the Prisons of Spain', where Neruda writes: 'And those who denied you the space in their rotten *Laurel* . . .'[17]

According to Santí, Octavio Paz was furious at Neruda's refusal – together with that of León Felipe – to participate in the special edition of *Laurel*. Paz always insisted that the edition was his personal baby. Soon, the literary world of Mexico City had split dramatically into two groups: the Nerudistas and the anti-Nerudistas (or Paz supporters).

However, Paz's own version of his split from Neruda is rather different. Neruda, he said, had quite happily collaborated with him on his magazine, *Taller* (Workshop), in November 1939, by offering his poem, 'Discurso de las Liras', as a kind of introduction to a brief anthology of seventeenth-century poets. In 1940, Neruda gave Paz another text: a short introduction to the poet, Sara Ibáñez, an unknown on whom Neruda heaped inordinate praise. At the same time, Neruda could not help reviving his old feud with the Spanish writer, Juan Ramón Jiménez. This placed Paz in a dilemma, because Jiménez was another contributor to *Taller*. The magazine's editorial board told him that he could not publish Neruda's article, but Paz went ahead and printed it anyway. Unfortunately, Neruda's name did not appear on the cover ('due to an unforgivable error', as Paz later admitted).

'Pablo was very upset and only partly accepted my explanations. He was right, but also only in part. Unfortunately, this small incident coincided with his quarrels with Bergamín, in which I found myself caught up, in spite of myself.'

Paz claimed that he and Pablo stopped seeing each other for a while. 'I didn't like several things about Neruda: his heated jealousy, his reproaches . . . The aesthetic discussions were really political, deep down. Pablo suffered from the sickness of Stalinism. Anyone who was not with him was a reactionary. All this provoked the explosion between us.'[18]

For a while, however, the two men renewed their friendship. The final, blistering quarrel between them lay two years ahead, not long before Neruda prepared to leave Mexico.

Just as in Spain – where he had been discontented with the state of the Spanish magazine industry – so in Mexico, Neruda quickly set about adding to the titles. Clearly his experiences with both *Taller* and *Laurel* had soured his view of the local magazines available. His new enterprise started off with a bang.

'I entitled it *Araucanía*, and put on the cover the portrait of a beautiful Araucanian woman laughing and showing all her teeth,' he recalled in his memoirs.[19]

Neruda may have enjoyed it, but the Chilean authorities didn't. The Foreign Ministry told him that it considered the cover an affront to Chilean dignity in featuring the image of a Mapuche native woman so prominently – even though, as Neruda pointed out, the face of the then-President of Chile, Pedro Aguirre Cerda, was a

pleasant, noble face, showing all the elements of our mixed race . . . It is common knowledge that the Araucanians were crushed and, finally, forgotten or conquered. What's more, history is written by the conquerors or by those who reap the spoils of victory. There are few races worthier than the Araucanian. Some day, we'll see Araucanian universities, books printed in Araucanian, and we'll realise how much we have lost of their clarity, their purity and volcanic energy . . .[20]

In the spring of 1941, at the Bolívar Theatre in Mexico City, Neruda recited his poem 'Un canto a Bolívar', to enthusiastic applause. However, there was a group of fascists in the auditorium, who launched a rowdy counter-demonstration, cheering Franco, crying

'Death to the Spanish Republic'. This must have appalled and repulsed Neruda. The Mexican writer Wilberto Cantón was an eye-witness to the scene: 'While the rector, the ambassadors and other authorities left in a hurry, the rest of the audience launched themselves at the rioters and soon there was a pitched battle.'[21] As an act of apology, the Universidad Nacional in Mexico City published 'Un canto a Bolívar' in a luxury plaquette illustrated by Julio Prieto.

Neruda's anti-fascist views and activities were well-known in Mexico. In 1941, as the Nazis besieged Leningrad and advanced on Soviet soil, Neruda publicly became a member of the Committee to Aid Russia at War and then wrote 'Un canto de amor a Stalingrado' (A Love Song to Stalingrad), a hymn to the courage of the Soviet troops fighting the enemy to the west. He recited the poem in the Teatro del Sindicato Mexicano de Electricistas (the Theatre of the Mexican Electricians' Union) at an event on 30 September 1941. It was then printed off and posted on walls all over Mexico City.

As was to be expected, the poem's ardently pro-Soviet views, pasted so overtly over the city, aroused great passions both in support and opposition. Newspapers came out with vicious attacks. Unfazed, Neruda responded with 'Un nuevo canto de amor a Stalingrado' (A New Love Song to Stalingrad) in early November 1941. His Russian translator, Ilya Ehrenburg, wrote to him from Moscow on 29 November to thank him for his support. But in Mexico, Neruda's political foes were gaining in strength and violent intent.

On Sunday, 29 December 1941, Neruda and Delia went to Amitlán Park in Cuernavaca to have lunch with Luis Enrique Délano, Lola Falcón and Poli. Poli Délano, now one of Chile's best-known prose writers, recalls the Cuernavaca incident vividly, even though he was still a young boy at the time.

> We were eating in a kind of covered patio, with arches on the walls, and the sun was shining powerfully, the exuberant foliage of the 'city of the eternal spring' [Cuernavaca] was shimmering. Suddenly, chaos descended. Screams . . . and blows. I had never seen anything like it . . . My father pushed me under the table, and from there, I retained certain images: Lola, my mother, and the Hormiguita fighting hand to hand, beside their men, against other men who seemed, looking back on it now, much better prepared. I saw my mother smash a huge box of fire-lighting matches on one of the

men's heads. I saw my father defending himself and I saw Neruda
with his head cut open and blood streaming from it. I'll never be able
to forget that image. I don't know how long that little piece of hell
lasted, but suddenly calm returned and the assailants vanished like
smoke. We left with Neruda in his car, heading for an infirmary and
then went to buy him a new shirt, since the one he was wearing was
covered in blood.[22]

It is still not clear how Neruda's head came to be cut open. It was
variously ascribed to a bullet or the butt of a revolver, but what we do
know is that the attackers were a group of German Nazis who had
been infuriated by the pro-Allied cheers emerging from Neruda's table
over lunch.

Violence also came from another, non-Nazi – indeed, non-human –
source. On Christmas Eve, Poli Délano was visiting Pablo and Delia's
house to give them a Christmas present: an ashtray in the form of a
heart. When Poli entered Delia's room (she was still in bed), he was
brutally attacked. The assailant this time was Neruda's pet badger,
which Pablo called 'El Niño'. The creature emerged from under
Delia's bed and proceeded to bite the unfortunate Poli deep in the
left leg. He had to spend Christmas Day at a clinic being stitched up –
his leg bears the scars to this day. Neruda and Delia reluctantly
realised that it was impossible to keep the badger, when it also bit
the maid, Virginia, in the neck, and they handed El Niño over to the
zoo at Chapultepec.

One day, a group of seven Japanese turned up at Neruda's consular
offices. They had just arrived from the United States and asked
Neruda, with anxious faces, for an immediate visa for Chile. Neruda
enquired why they were so keen to catch the first flight out of Mexico.
They told him they wanted to catch a boat to Japan from the northern
Chilean port of Tocopilla. Neruda remembered:

I countered that there was no need to travel to Chile, at the other end
of the continent, for this because that same Japanese line called at
Manzanillo, which they could reach even on foot with time to spare.
They exchanged embarrassed glances and smiles, and talked among
themselves in their own language. They consulted the secretary at
the Japanese Embassy, who was with them. He decided to be open
with me and said: 'Look, colleague, this ship happens to have

changed its itinerary and won't be coming to Manzanillo any more. So these distinguished specialists must catch it at the Chilean port.' A confused vision flashed across my mind: this was something very important. I asked them for their passports, their photographs, details about their work in the United States, etc. and told them to return the following day. They objected. They had to have their visas immediately and would be willing to pay any price.[23]

Eventually, the visitors did agree to return the next day. In the meantime, Neruda wondered why the boat, for the first time in thirty years, would be diverting from its usual course.

Then it dawned on me. Of course, this was an important, well-informed group, Japanese spies beating a hasty retreat from the United States because something critical was about to happen. And that could be nothing other than Japan's entry into the war. The Japanese in my story were in on the secret.[24]

Neruda refused to grant the visas to the group of Japanese for another two days, but they found a way to acquire diplomatic passports. A week later, the Japanese bombed Pearl Harbor.

Among Neruda's saddest duties during his Mexican stint was to bid farewell to two dear friends who died in the capital. The first was Silvestre Revueltas, a magical Mexican composer whom Neruda considered a brother. His major works were symphonic poems on Mexican themes. Although Neruda had no ear for music, he loved and admired musicians. One day, Revueltas was practically living in Neruda's house. The next, in that autumn of 1940, he was dead.

Neruda's other loss was the Italian photographer and Communist activist, Tina Modotti, one of the most remarkable women of the twentieth century. She was the wife of the legendary Italian guerrilla commander, Vittorio Vidale, at whose side she had participated in the Spanish Civil War. Modotti died in a taxi in Mexico City on 5 January 1942, in mysterious circumstances. Either she had suffered coronary failure due to indigestion and died before medication could be given, or she had been poisoned.

Neruda wrote a moving tribute to her.

Tina Modotti, sister, you do not sleep, no,
you do not sleep.
Perhaps your heart hears the rose of
yesterday
growing, the last rose of yesterday, the
new rose.
Rest gently, sister.

In 1942, Neruda paid his first visit to Cuba. He had been invited there by a Catholic writer, José María Chacón y Calvo, at the time cultural director at the Cuban Education Ministry. It was an interesting time for the island, politically. The 1940 constitution had protected individual and social rights and supported full employment and a minimum wage. General Fulgencio Batista had been elected Cuba's fourteenth President and was shortly to legalise the Communist Party. Neruda and Delia spent long hours walking along the Cuban coastline and Pablo fell in love with the multicoloured *polimyta* sea shells. Just as he had with the huge key above the Paris shop a few years earlier, he insisted on taking *polimytas* back for his collection. He emptied Delia's two suitcases of all their contents and filled them with the shells. They arrived back at Mexico City airport with their clothes in two plastic bags.

It was there that Neruda received the news that Miguel Hernández had died in prison on 28 March 1942, at the age of thirty-two, ravaged by tuberculosis, acute haemorrhages and hideous coughing fits. On the wall above his prison bed, he had scribbled the lines: 'Goodbye brothers, comrades, friends / Let me take my leave of the sun and the fields.'

Despite this bitter blow, Neruda kept himself busy working constantly on the poems which would make up his *Canto general*. And, while he was as affectionate and loving as ever to Delia, he remained keenly interested in other women – whether this was always a physical interest is not entirely clear. The beautiful Mexican poet and sexual predator, Pita Amor, told *Vogue* magazine that '*Sólo te diré que no era sólo superdotado como poeta*' ('All I will say is that he wasn't just well-endowed as a poet').

That year – 1942 – also saw Neruda's final falling out with Octavio Paz. Neruda does not mention the specific incident anywhere, but Paz remembered it all too well:

We were in the Spanish Republican Centre [in Mexico City], José Luis Martínez, Enrique González Martínez, José Clemente Orozco and myself. Pablo Neruda was also there. It was 1942. I had broken away from Marxism. That break and my criticisms hurt Neruda and Rafael Alberti deeply. They had placed a lot of faith in me. Neruda more so. And that night, Pablo stood up and, in a drunken tone of voice, said to me, looking at my white shirt-collar: 'That was how white your conscience was, Octavio. How it used to be, once. Today, you are no more than an *hijo de la tiznada* ('son of a filthy bitch'). He said worse things. He insulted my mother. I threatened to punch him. He was very drunk. He pointed to me and screamed: 'Look at the white collar on that . . . so and so,' and he tugged so hard on the collar that he ripped a piece off it. By now Neruda was very sozzled, and he went on insulting me. And I did the same to him. And yet I loved him dearly. But I couldn't stomach his insults . . . We were about to come to blows when José Luis Martínez and Enrique González Martínez separated us. We left the Spanish Republican Centre. The Republicans – quite rightly – were on Neruda's side. José Luis Martínez dragged us off to a fashionable nightclub and ordered bottles of champagne. It was so expensive! We all drank to the incident.[25]

But Paz and Neruda did not speak to each other again for twenty-five years.

At the beginning of 1943, the first fragments of *Canto general* were published in Mexico, in a private, non-commercial edition, under the title *Canto general de Chile*. Elsewhere in Latin America, a Peruvian selection, *Cantos de Pablo Neruda*, and a Colombian edition of Neruda's *Mejores poemas* (Best Poems), also appeared.

In February, Neruda flew briefly to New York to take part in a cultural meeting organised by the Voz de las Américas. On his return to Mexico, he decided to accelerate his drive to legalise his divorce from Maruca, so that he could marry Delia. He petitioned the court in Tetecala, in the Mexican state of Morelos, claiming his 'unjustified desertion of the conjugal home, [neglect] of duties inherent to marriage and incompatibility of character'. A few days later, on 8 February 1943, the divorce was confirmed because Maruca did not present herself to contest the petition. The divorce was not formally recognised in Chile, however, as divorce was illegal there at the time.

It was in the first week of March 1943 (and not 1942, as all other sources say), that Neruda received sombre news: his daughter, Malva Marina, had died, aged eight, in Nazi-occupied Holland on 2 March. The funeral took place in Gouda at 2 p.m. on Saturday, 8 March. A black-bordered announcement in a Dutch newspaper that same day – clearly placed by Maruca and her parents – read:

> We wish to express our profound gratitude for all the sincere signs of condolence received following the death of our dear daughter and granddaughter, Malva Marina.

It was signed: 'Mexico: Ricardo Reyes; The Hague: Maruca Reyes-Hagenaar; The Hague, N.O.I. [Netherlands Overseas Territories]: A. H. Hagenaar-Vogelzang [Maruca's parents who were still living in Java].[26]

It seems that Maruca was either unwilling, or felt unable, to look after her sick daughter on her own. On 6 October 1939, she put Malva Marina into foster care in a house at 4 Noothoven van Goorstraat, in the Dutch town of Gouda. The tiny building must have been very crowded: it housed Hendrik Labertus Julsing, an electrician; his wife, Gerdina Sierks; their three children; two servants – and, from 1939, Malva Marina. Meanwhile, Maruca went to live in The Hague, at 209 Groothertoginnelaan. This house was quite different: it was a large, attractive, four-storeyed terraced house in a very good neighbourhood. However, it appears to have been a boarding house, so there, too, it may have been quite crowded.

It is impossible to gauge the precise effect the news of the death of his daughter had on Neruda's state of mind. He did not – like Victor Hugo after his daughter's death at sea – stop writing for an entire year. But nor did he write any more poems to Malva Marina.

Despite a terrible few months, which had seen him lose several close friends – after Miguel Hernández's death, Amparo Mom, the estranged wife of Raúl González Tuñón, succumbed to cancer – and a daughter, Neruda resiliently attempted to continue to live life as fully as he could.

Once again he felt the itch to start up a new magazine. Once again, the enterprise was short-lived. The new publication was to be called *La sangre y la letra* (Blood and Letters), and Neruda would be the editor, publisher and fund-raiser. He managed to scramble together a thousand pesos for the first issue. He claimed that the money had come from anonymous sponsors, but his collaborators suspected that he himself was the sole sponsor. Neruda announced that the peso notes were deposited within the pages of a beautiful edition of Walt Whitman's *Leaves of Grass* on his shelves. But when he opened the book to show his team the funds, he found to his horror that the money wasn't there. Instead, someone had written in the margin of the book, as if it were a literary quotation: 'Refer to Bernal Díaz del Castillo.' So Neruda and his editorial team turned to the books by that author, where another note instructed them to refer to Milosz, then Vallejo, Dante, Rilke, Plato, Tagore, Goethe, Dostoyevsky . . .

As Wilberto Cantón, who was supposedly acting as the magazine's secretary, recalled, 'It was a voyage through world literature. The trip ended on page 213 of Hans Christian Andersen's *Fairy Tales*. That's where we discovered our treasure. We never did find out who the prankster was . . . In any case, the magazine never came out. Neruda left the country soon afterwards in the midst of literary earthquakes.'[27]

By mid-1943, as much as he loved Mexico, Neruda was growing very tired of diplomatic duties. He felt stiff and starchy in an atmosphere of formality. (In a wonderful poem published years later in his collection, *Estravagario*, he looks forward with dread to the next Embassy function and wonders: 'What am I going to do with my hands?') So, when he became embroiled in a new controversy in June 1943, which clearly threatened the future of his Mexican consular post, he did not seem much bothered. The row broke out on the occasion of the funeral of the mother of the Brazilian revolutionary leader, Luis Carlos Prestes, jailed in Rio de Janeiro. Neruda made feverish attempts to persuade the Brazilian dictator, Getulio Vargas, to allow Prestes to leave prison to attend the funeral. When Vargas refused, Neruda wrote a satirical poem: 'The little tyrant wants to conceal fire beneath his tiny cold bat-wings and he wraps himself in the unsettled silence of rats / which he steals from the corridors of the palace at night . . .'

The Brazilian Ambassador to Mexico was furious. Prestes, he insisted, had been convicted of common crimes, not political ones. The Brazilian government demanded that Neruda be stripped of his consular post. Neruda himself responded:

As Consul General of Chile (and not as diplomatic representative) my duty is to work towards the intensification of commercial relations between Mexico and my country. But as a writer, my duty is to defend freedom as an absolute norm of the civil and human condition, and no complaints or incidents of whatever sort will change my actions or my poetry . . . I am a man who is not used to retracting his actions, still less when it's a question of fulfilling my obligations as a free man . . .[28]

While the Chilean government dithered, unwilling to dismiss such a prestigious figure as Neruda from the diplomatic corps, the poet himself simplified matters by requesting six months' leave, during which time he prepared his return to Chile.

At 1 p.m. on 2 July 1943, the 39-year-old Neruda married Delia, twenty years his senior but looking far younger, in Tetecala. It was a very hot day, and apart from the witnesses – Oscar Schnake Vergara, the Chilean Ambassador to Mexico, and Luis Enrique Délano for Neruda, and Wenceslao Roces and Enrique de los Ríos for Delia – there were some troubling visitors: vast numbers of gnats pestering everyone present. But the outdoor lunch was a joyous occasion, with cheerful conversation, songs and poetry. Pablo's wedding present to the Hormiguita was an elegant silver necklace made in Oaxaca.

The three years Neruda spent in Mexico – and his travels through the region – were very important in maturing him as a poet and as a man. Neruda was learning to broaden his perspectives, geographically and historically.

Politically, he was moving further to the Left. His contact with Spanish and Mexican Communists was pushing him inexorably towards joining the Party – though that formal commitment was still a couple of years away.

As the Chilean artist, Julio Escámez, put it:

They were years that enriched his work and his ideas. There [in Mexico] he wrote a lot of *Canto general* and he lived the worst years of the Second World War. Not counting the diplomatic formalities, which he did have to fulfil, he committed himself to the world campaign to open a second front to help the Soviet Union to defeat Hitler. He wrote his unforgettable love songs to Stalingrad . . . I believe that those years helped him to discover in depth the roots of American essence which are present in all his later poetry. Above all, in *Canto general* the dazzling popular Mexican culture, the lively and decisive indigenous life there, the great challenges of nature and cultural colonisation, converted him into an epic and cosmic poet . . . It is not possible to speak about Neruda after *España en el corazón* without considering what he lived through and learned in Mexico.[29]

Neruda was determined not to leave Mexico with a whimper. In August 1943, he gave an interview to the Mexican magazine, *Hoy* (Today), in which he made a number of what must have been deliberately provocative comments to the Spanish journalist, Alardo Prats.

'For me,' he said, 'the best thing about Mexico are the agronomists and the painters . . . I consider that in [Mexican] poetry, there is a truly impressive lack of direction or civic morality . . . The Mexican novel is its greatest representative – Juan de la Cabada, Emilio Abreu Gómez, José Revueltas and Andrés Henestrosa have successfully expressed a new classicism . . . The essay [in Mexico] has been perverted by an anaemic generation . . .'[30]

Paz did not take long to respond to this withering attack. Just a few days later, on 15 August, the 29-year-old Mexican offered this 'Farewell' to Neruda, ten years his senior, in the journal *Letras de México*:

> What separates us from his person are not political convictions but simply vanity . . . and salary. The vanity which obliges him to accept, every six months, banquets and homages from those same people whom he accuses of lacking civic morals, and the salary which allows him to offer bed and board to a pack of hounds who flatter him in his bitterness . . .[31]

As Jason Wilson has pointed out, Paz was convinced of the ineptitude of political poetry. Poetry, he felt, was incapable of bringing about political change: better a text by Lenin than a bad poem by Mayakovsky or Neruda.[32] Years later, Paz still believed that politics 'empoverishes poetry, rather than enriching it'.[33]

This mutual mud-slinging must have hurt both men. After a

reconciliation of sorts in London in 1967, Paz looked back on these troubled times and recollected:

> Before our dispute – which began at the sad dinner in his honour at the Centro Asturiano – Neruda and I enjoyed a friendship which maybe I couldn't call intimate but was certainly close. We visited each other's homes continuously. I remember the Sunday lunches in the large house at Michoacán which, I don't know why, Pablo insisted once belonged to López Velarde. He loved to live surrounded by people and his parties were amusing and tumultuous. There were always three of four 'parasites' – in the original, Roman, sense of the word: those whose job it was to amuse the rich and shared their table. His 'parasites' were professional wits and they helped Delia del Carril (La Hormiguita) to attend to the numerous guests. There was also a more picturesque and terrible guest – a badger, who went around drinking the red wine and destroying the women's tights. Pablo was generous and, at the same time, tyrannical. He was very loyal to his friends, but he didn't like it when they were too independent.[34]

Neruda's enduring love for Mexico – if not for all its people – and especially his passion for the Mexican state of Michoacán, whose name he would borrow for his Santiago home, shines brightly in a magnificent speech he made at the Universidad de San Nicolás de Hidalgo in Morelia, where he was given an honorary doctorate on 17 August 1943.

> Perhaps the beauty of this land, its splash of green shadow, recalls deep within me a similar landscape, the southern territory of Chile, with its lakes and its skies, with its volcanoes and its silence: the landscape of my childhood and adolescence. Perhaps my wandering heart rediscovered the silhouette of light and shade which flees and endures, the language of wet leaves, the lofty example of the pure countryside.[35]

But Neruda the poet, lover of nature and fanatical lover of life, was also becoming increasingly politically committed. His brush with death at Cuernavaca had served only to heighten his loathing of the Nazis. In fact, in his Morelia speech, he saw Latin America as Hitler's potential next victim:

> The terrifying threat of the Nazi-fascist conquistadors [fascinatingly, Neruda here deliberately employs the word *conquistadores*, which of course is normally reserved for the Spanish Christian conquerors and converters of pre-Colombian Latin American civilisation] was more serious for us Americans than anyone else. If other nations were going to lose power and splendour, we were going to lose everything: we were destined to be the newest slaves, the semi-humans for the new, great Germany. Racially despised . . . [we would be] highly coveted as producers and as cheap meat in the new, immense market of slavery which the Nazis were preparing, we were the true victims dreamt of by the terrible terrorists of the modern age.[36]

Just how prestigious a figure Neruda had become could be seen in the send-off he was given on his departure from Mexico. The act of homage, attended by some three thousand people, took place on 27 August 1943 in the Frontón de Mexico. Yet Neruda's ambivalence towards Mexico lingered to the end:

> Mexico is the touchstone of America, and it was no accident that the solar calendar of ancient America, the node of irradiation, wisdom and mystery, was carved there. Anything could happen, anything did happen there. The only opposition newspaper was subsidised by the government. It was the most dictatorial democracy anyone could imagine . . . Mexican dramas are so clothed in the picturesque that one comes away astounded by all the allegory that is every day more remote from the essential throb of life, the blood-spattered skeleton.[37]

8

From the rich heights of Machu Picchu down to the poverty of the driest place on Earth

1943–48

Neruda and Delia did not return directly to Chile from Mexico. Neruda had become an inveterate and permanently curious traveller. So, after being fêted on 3 September 1943 in Panama – where he made two speeches emphasising the duty of the writer to play a key role in society – the couple flew first to Colombia on 9 September, on the invitation of the Liberal President, Alfonso López Pumarejo. López was a man with similar political views to Neruda's. In his first term as President, he had put through laws introducing workers' compensation and free hot meals for schoolchildren. He had also revised the constitution and done more for education than any Colombian for at least a generation. There was considerable political tension, nevertheless, arising from the United States' commercial involvement in the country, particularly through the United Fruit Company. Shortly before Neruda's arrival, the municipality in Barranquilla had passed a resolution to expropriate the American firm that operated its public utilities. The authorities in the capital, Bogotá, were threatening to do likewise. It may well be that during his stay in Colombia the seeds of Neruda's bitterness against the US economic presence in Latin America – which were to emerge in *Canto general* – were fully sown.

On being met at Bogotá airport, Neruda was informed: 'We have four hundred poets waiting to greet you.' Horrified, he replied: 'What on earth am I going to do among so many poets?' Not only friends, however, awaited Neruda on Colombian soil. The leader of the extreme Right in Colombia, Dr Laureano Gómez, was one of the poet's most determined adversaries. Gómez was extremely religious, ardently clerical and fervently pro-German. A hot-headed nationalist, he was convinced that the United States had 'swindled' Colombia out of the Panama Canal.

In 1936, Gómez had founded a newspaper, *El Siglo* (not to be confused with the Chilean Communist Party organ of the same name), which he used as a mouthpiece for his fanaticism. At the time of Neruda's visit, Gómez's *El Siglo* launched a series of vicious attacks on the poet, both in prose and in verse. One deeply unpleasant poem, entitled 'Escarabajo lírico' (Lyrical Beetle), began:

> Mendicant, vagabond poetaster
> who, to the sounds of your gypsy drum
> goes around infesting the American world
> with your howl of an irate satirist

Another poem stormed, even more unpleasantly:

> Don't go on, no, don't go on believing you're a poet.
> Your style is tomato sauce
> manufactured in atrocious slums
>
> In you, there's nothing left even as a bargain,
> don't show your face around here again, dirty cheat,
> because you're filthy, and, on top of it all, ungrateful[1]

In response, Neruda published a poem in which he called the Colombian politician 'a little anti-Christian anti-Christ':

> Just like you, with their whips in their hand,
> the assassin Franco trembles in Spain,
> and in Germany your bloody brother
> reads his destiny written in the snow.[2]

The visit to Colombia was not an entirely enjoyable one, but there, as elsewhere, his fame attracted adoring admirers to his poetry readings. He took these opportunities to lament the fate of writers who had fallen victim to European oppressors.

Where are they? Where are Romain Rolland, Aragon, Malraux? Where are Antonio Machado, Federico García Lorca and Miguel Hernández? Where are they? The last three have been beneath the ground for some time. They paid with their lives for the beam of light they shone on human life with their poetry. The others, the French, the Germans, the Italians, the Norwegians, the poets of Czechoslovakia, of Prague and Romania, paid for having spoken out, for having named and defied the tyrants, with bloody prison or lengthy exile . . .[3]

He was silent, however, on the Soviet writers who had paid for speaking out. From Colombia, Neruda and Delia flew to Peru on 22 October. He had briefly visited the country during his two-month suspension from consular service in Mexico 1941, but this time he planned to see the remarkable Inca fortress city of Machu Picchu high up in the Andes.

Many have written that this encounter with ancient civilisation in October 1943 changed Neruda's outlook for ever. Arguably, his earlier travels, especially in Guatemala, had already launched this process. But the Machu Picchu visit was the culmination. As Robert Pring-Mill put it, 'When Neruda does reach Machu Picchu, its heights turn out to be the place from which all else makes sense, including his own continent.'[4]

This is how Neruda recalled the long journey up to the Andean fortress accompanied by Delia and by the Peruvian writer, José Uriel García. They were supplied with mules and provisions for the trip by the Peruvian government of President Manuel Prado.

There was no highway then and we rode up on mules. At the top, I saw the ancient stone structures hedged in by the tall peaks of the verdant Andes. Torrents hurtled down down from the citadel, eaten away and weathered by the passage of the centuries. White fog drifted up in masses from the Wilkamayu river. I felt infinitely small in the centre of that navel of rocks, the navel of a deserted world, proud, towering high, to which I somehow belonged. I felt that my own hands had laboured there at some remote point in time, digging furrows, polishing the rocks. I felt Chilean, Peruvian, American. On those difficult heights, among those glorious, scattered ruins, I had found the principles of faith I needed to continue my poetry.[5]

Some sources claim that Neruda commented: 'What a wonderful place for a roast.'[6] If he did make this flippant remark, it seems likely it was a device to conceal the depth of his response: it took Neruda nearly two years of meditation to produce one of his most famous poems, *Alturas de Macchu Picchu* (The Heights of Macchu Picchu). He added a 'c' to the first part of the name, perhaps to imprint his own stamp on the miraculous site, to forge that long link he saw between pre-Columbian civilisation and his own existence.

A few years later, Neruda wrote:

After seeing the ruins at Macchu Picchu, the fabulous cultures of antiquity seemed to be made of cardboard, papier mâché. India itself seemed minuscule, daubed, banal, a popular god-fest, compared with the haughty solemnity of those abandoned Inca towers. I could no longer separate myself from those constructions. I understood that, if we trod the same hereditary soil, we had something to do with those lofty efforts of the American community, that we could not ignore them, that our ignorance or silence were not merely a crime but the continuation of a defeat. Our aristocratic cosmopolitanism had led us to revere the past of the most remote peoples and had blinded us to discovering our own treasures . . . I thought about ancient American man. I saw his ancient struggles intermeshed with present-day struggles. That was where the seeds of my idea of an American *Canto general* began to generate, a kind of chronicle . . . Now I saw the whole of America from the heights of Macchu Picchu. That was the title of the first poem of my new conception.[7]

In the poem, which he began to write at Isla Negra in September 1945, Neruda felt a mission to reveal the greatness of his ancestors, just as he had sensed a mission to expose Franco's atrocities to the world in *España en el corazón*. But *Alturas* marks a new synthesis of personal crusade and public chronicle. He was genuinely reaching outside himself in an effort to embrace a vast cosmic universe.

In a much later, very beautiful poem, 'Primeros viajes' (First Journeys) from *Memorial de Isla Negra* (1964), Neruda wrote that his early adolescent state was one of self-obsessed, semi-blindness: '*No sabía leer sino leerme*' ('I didn't know how to read, only to read myself'). In *Alturas* Neruda discards the introverted sense of anguish of *Residencia en la tierra*. While that book was infused with desolation, here there is an ultimately optimistic desire for renewal, for order, which Robert Pring-Mill rightly calls Neruda's 'personal cosmology'.[8]

Yet there are moments of youthful melancholy reminiscent of *Tentativa del hombre infinito*. Hernán Loyola has described the line '*Alguién que me esperó entre los violines*' ('Someone waited for me among the violins') as one of the most enigmatic in the whole of Neruda's oeuvre. Neruda apparently told Loyola that the line was a reference to 'an amorous experience'. In the notes to his new edition of the poet's complete works, Loyola is more specific, saying: 'This amorous experience . . . could only be the beginning of his relationship with Matilde Urrutia.'[9] This would make sense only if we accept Loyola's assumption that, because of the weather, Neruda met Matilde at an open-air concert in Santiago's Parque Forestal in late-1945 – when he was still writing *Alturas* – rather than in 1946, as is generally assumed and as Matilde herself claimed in the Spanish daily, *El País*, on 23 May 1983.[10]

Alturas renews Neruda's emotional links, too, with Quevedo, especially with that poet's obsession with the transitoriness of the human condition seen against the vastness of time.

In Lima, Neruda and Delia were surprised to meet Victoria Ocampo, founder of the Argentinian magazine, *Sur*. Pablo had criticised several of the contributors to *Sur* – especially the French writer, Drieu la Rochelle – for their fascist sympathies. But for Neruda, friendship was usually stronger than political differences. As soon as he learnt that Ocampo was staying at their Lima hotel, he and Delia not only took time to meet her but gave her a present.

What has not been noted elsewhere about Neruda's visit to Peru, amidst the understandable attention paid to his visit to Machu Picchu, is how it reinforced his awareness, already aroused in Colombia, of the United States's commercial investment in Latin American society. The US controlled 80 per cent of Peru's oil production through the International Petroleum Corporation, and close to 100 per cent of Peru's mineral output.

But it was the pre-Columbian fortress in the Peruvian Andes that made the most permanent impression on him. In an article written while he was still in Peru in 1943, Neruda wrote: 'The Incas left more than a small crown of fire and martyrdom and the amazed hands of history; they left a vast, expansive ambience chiselled by the most delicate fingers, by hands that could coax melancholy and reverence from sound, and raise colossal stones to last throughout infinity.'[11]

How interesting that word 'melancholy' is in this context. It is as if, even through the infinity of time and the rediscovery of his pre-Columbian roots, he was also recalling his own memory: that melancholy of the solitary, Far Eastern diplomat. He may be referring to that desolation in these lines from *Alturas de Macchu Picchu*

> How many times in wintry city streets, or in
> a bus, a boat at dusk, or in the denser solitude
> of festive nights, drenched in the sound
> of bells and shadows, in the very lair of human pleasure,
> have I wanted to pause and look for the eternal, unfathomable
> truth's filaments I'd fingered once in stone, or in the flash a kiss
>   released[12]

He may also be recognising that the boozy, chatty late-night sessions of his bohemian, Santiago student days had been fundamentally empty. As in so many of his poems – and this is what gives them their extraordinary depth and richness – Neruda works on both direct sensory experiences and memories of previous sensations. I believe this reflects the influence of Marcel Proust, among Neruda's favourite reading as a young man, whose work bears the same loving attention to detail and sensual use of memory.

After leaving Peru, Pablo and Delia stopped off in Uruguay and Argentina, arriving back in Santiago on 3 November 1943. Neruda was nearly forty years old, and a much wiser man than when he had left Chile for Mexico three years earlier. Work was still going on at the house at 164 Avenida Lynch – which Neruda now nicknamed Michoacán in memory of his time in Mexico – so for the first few days, the couple stayed at the Hotel Carrera in the capital, and then they moved into the apartment of Sylvia Thayer at 40 Avenida Vicuña Mackenna. Sylvia was the sister of

Alvaro Hinojosa, Pablo's companion during the long sea voyage to the Orient in 1927.

Antonia Ramos, a young Argentinian student at the Universidad de Chile, provides a valuable insight into life with Pablo and Delia at the time:

> Pablo was already chubby and virtually bald. She [Delia] was slim, very delicate, with magnificent manners. She moved her hands, her neck, her voice, in a marvellous way . . . She was very preoccupied with her looks, but she wanted someone else to deal with them. A hairdresser came who dyed her hair fair, because it was going grey. I myself helped her many times to put waves in her hair, to comb it . . . They would arrive back home at two in the morning, waking everyone up, and then they would go on talking until four or five in the morning. The house was transformed into an ant's nest full of Spanish refugees, people from Mexico . . . She was the sober one, she handled the vulgarity of their shared life with great patience and style. She was elegance, he was the *enfant terrible*.[13]

Delia remained a vital influence on Neruda and an essential support. In her role as literary critic she continued to look over most of what he wrote, making valuable criticisms which he heeded and acted upon. Diego Muñoz's widow, Inés Valenzuela, recalled: 'I remember once, we were in the car, on the way to lunch at the Czech Embassy in Santiago. Pablo was reading Delia part of the *Canto general* and Delia told him: "No no, Pablo, that's really bad, you can't say that," and Pablo immediately took her advice to heart.'[14]

Although Delia was demonstrative towards Pablo, it is not clear whether they still had a sexual relationship. Their friend Aída Figueroa told me that she had once asked Delia at around this time whether she thought Pablo still had strong physical urges and she had said she thought he did not. How wrong the Ant was. Neruda's eye was constantly wandering.

And yet the affection between them was as strong as ever. Delia's attention was unwavering. She was worried about Pablo being over-weight. So worried, indeed, that she bought a set of small weights, and tried to control Neruda's food intake – no easy task when dealing with such a committed epicurean. During mealtimes Delia – who had turned herself into an expert on proteins, vitamins, fats – would recommend that he chew his meat more than sixty times, eat slowly and refrain from more than a single spoonful of '*dulce de alcayota*' (sweet marrow). Slightly piqued, Pablo would reply: 'Hormiga, I will eat all the alcayota, until I turn into an alcayota!'

Delia, to be fair, was just as concerned with her own health. She was about to turn sixty. She booked herself into Santiago's Clínica Santa María to try to wean herself off smoking – cigarettes were making her voice hoarse.

Most importantly, Delia backed Neruda in his crucial decision: to join the Chilean Communist Party. Spain, he said, had taught him that Communism was the only effective way of fighting fascism. It was Delia, of course, who had played a vital role in pushing him in this direction – and it was she who would support his move to commit himself at last, and help him prepare his speeches.

But first, the couple would have to learn the new political map in Chile, which had altered considerably in the three years they had been away. Chile's stable, multi-party political system bore more resemblance to Western European than to Latin American models. Chileans took great pride in their representative democracy. The Conservatives and the Liberals had grown closer together as the combined forces on the Right, and were now more fearful of socialism than of their traditional enemies in the anti-clerical camp. The Radicals had replaced the Liberals as the swing party in the centre, now that they were outflanked on the Left by the growing Communist Party and the Socialist Party.

The Chilean Communists had backed away from proletarian revolution, which they had advocated from 1928 to 1934. This fell in line with the new policy of the Comintern, adopted in 1935. Now, in the early 1940s, they promoted broad, reformist electoral coalitions in the name of anti-fascism. (The Comintern – Communist International – had been founded by Soviet Communist leaders in March 1919 with the aim of fighting for the overthrow of the international bourgeoisie and for the creation of an international Soviet republic.)

Led by the centrist Radical Party, the administration of President Pedro Aguirre Cerda's Popular Front had assimilated the Socialists and Communists into the established system, turning potentially revolutionary forces into relatively moderate participants in legal institutions. As in the rest of Latin America, the Great Depression and then the onset of the Second World War had accelerated domestic production of manufactured consumer items, widened the role of the state and increased Chile's economic dependence on the United States. However, the Socialists and Communists were beginning to quarrel incessantly, especially over the Communist Party's support for the 1939 Nazi-Soviet Non-Aggression Pact.

Early in 1941, the Socialist Party decided it could no longer live with the Communists and withdrew from the Popular Front coalition. To appease the Right, President Pedro Aguirre Cerda clamped down on rural unionisation.

But in November 1941, the President died suddenly in office. He was mourned by many, not least the country's intellectuals, who had thrived under his regime. Two Radicals then stood as candidates to replace Pedro Aguirre Cerda – Gabriel González Videla and Juan Antonio Ríos Morales. Ríos was preferred. The Socialists put forward Oscar Schnake. The Right was represented by Carlos Ibáñez del Campo. Faced with the possible triumph of Ibáñez, the Socialists withdrew their candidate, Schnake, and threw their backing behind Ríos. A Liberal faction, led by former President Arturo Alessandri Palma, did likewise. This helped Ríos to emerge victorious with 56 per cent of the votes on 2 April 1942.

Given the wide support which helped him to become President, it was no surprise that Ríos' government was a broad spectrum, from Socialists to Liberals. In 1943, under pressure from the United States and in need of the protection the US could offer Chile's vulnerable Pacific coast, the Ríos administration severed relations with the Axis – Germany, Italy and Japan. At the same time, it established relations with the Soviet Union – a move bitterly criticised by the Right. On 13 April 1943, Chile declared war on Japan, abandoning the policy of neutrality it had followed through two World Wars.[15]

Even before he made his formal allegiance to the Communist Party, Neruda was approached, in 1944, to stand as candidate for senator, representing the arid northern provinces of Tarapacá and Antofagasta in the Atacama desert, the driest region on Earth, where there was sometimes no rain for years on end. Neruda's initial response to the request that he should campaign was one of alarm: he was aware of his shortcomings as a political speaker. But he was reassured when the Party told him that reading his poetry would be his most effective political message to the masses.

Neruda campaigned in the north with Elias Lafertte, then president of the Communist Party, a former nitrate worker and, as an ex-actor, a highly accomplished orator. Here, for the first time, Neruda came into contact with the poorest, most desperate people in the whole of Chile.

> There are few places in the world where life is so harsh and offers so little to live for. It takes untold sacrifices to transport water, to nurse a plant that yields even the humblest flower, to raise a dog, a rabbit, a pig. I come from the other end of the republic. I was born in green country, with thickly wooded forests. I had a childhood filled with rain and snow. The mere act of facing that lunar desert was a turning-point in my life.[16]

Not for Pablo Neruda the cold, Anglo-Saxon detachment of George Orwell as he recorded the miners' existences. Where Orwell saw the coal miners and their daily hardships as 'different universes',[17] Neruda saw their life as part of his own. Strikes were breaking out in the nitrate fields of Humberstone and Mapocho. Neruda witnessed the conditions in which the miners lived:

> My heart is still shuddering with the memory of the poverty of those camps . . . Here in Pan de Azúcar, the camp was built on rubbish tips. As I enter one of the houses, a pampa woman tells me how suddenly, from under the floor of her room, dead mice and old shoe-soles appear. It's the rubbish dump which is swimming up to the surface [from beneath the floorboards]. I enter her house and she shows me the rickety old beds, one on the floor, other furniture, a table made out of shelves, a lone chair for the whole house. There was no kitchen. At ground level, a stove of corrugated iron and metal hoops acts as an oven. 'The food comes out black,' she tells me.[18]

Back in Santiago, Neruda was struggling to oversee another kind of chaos in his own two houses, especially the new Pacific coast home at Isla Negra.

There were major problems at Isla Negra, and these caused some friction between Pablo and Delia. When guests came to Isla Negra, they were met with huge boulders standing outside the house and they often had to put up with the fact that construction was going on all around them. Pablo had commissioned a Spanish architect, Germán Rodríguez Arias, to build the main room and a stone tower. At times, Pablo would get up, leave his friends and inspect the work operations, growing annoyed when the Ant didn't show the same degree of interest in how the house was progressing.

When Neruda's friend Tomás Lago visited the couple at Isla Negra on 21 February 1944, he found that they had clearly been arguing:

> They were not talking, and only Delia answered my questions. Then, from some faltering phrases, I could tell that Delia bitterly reproached him [Pablo] for blaming her for the upheaval around the house. And Pablo, for his part, was saying: 'How could you think of waiting until the very last minute to send the maid out for some milk?' The kitchen was unswept and would remain locked for several days with the pile of putrefaction inside. The WC had no running water and was dirty (like all the water at Isla Negra), etc.[19]

When another friend, Anita Lagarrigue, tried to lighten the mood by joking to Delia: 'So, you didn't cook breakfast for Pablo, eh?' Delia snapped back: 'And why doesn't he make *me* breakfast?'[20]

On the journey back from Isla Negra to Santiago, Neruda felt guilty over his irritability, said he hadn't slept well the previous night and begged for forgiveness. 'In truth, Pablo is kind-hearted,' said Lago. 'He gets cross, but only occasionally, and for very short periods, and he deeply regrets it afterwards.'[21]

On 4 March 1945, Neruda was elected a Communist senator for Antofagasta and Tarapacá – though he was still not a Party member. In his memoirs he said,

> I shall always cherish with pride the fact that thousands of people from Chile's most inhospitable region, the great mining region of copper and nitrate, gave me their vote. Walking over the pampa was laborious and rough. It hasn't rained for half a century there, and the desert has done its work on the faces of the miners. They are men with scorched features; their solitude and the neglect they are consigned to have been fixed in the dark intensity of their eyes . . . But my poetry opened the way for communication, making it possible for me to walk among them and be accepted as a lifelong brother by my countrymen, who led such a hard life.[22]

A misspelt reminder of Neruda's senatorial campaign can still be seen carved in the rock in the desert: 'Vote por Lafferte y Neftalis Reyes (Pablo Neruda) . . .'

Meanwhile, the world was changing shape politically. The Second World War was over. The Nazis had been defeated, and it was a good time to be on the Left, with the Red Army triumphantly entering Berlin.

May 1945 was a good month for Neruda, too. He won Chile's National Prize for Literature – a source of considerable pride to him because it was awarded for his entire body of work to date (and he was the first poet to receive it). Moreover, since he had now come out publicly as a Communist, even if not officially affiliated, he saw the prize as conferring some recognition on his political stance too, because the jury comprised government representatives as well as intellectuals.

He sensed that, as a well-known writer and parliamentarian, he had a double mission to fulfil. In his maiden speech as a senator, on 30 May 1945, he declared that 'the ideological, moral and legal responsibilities which all of us, or almost all of us, feel are much greater in my case.'

Giving the lie to his apprehensions about not being able to deliver a passionate political address, Neruda celebrated Hitler's death, the Allies' victory over the Nazis, and the triumph of the Left – and in particular, of Communism:

> Until a few days ago, a madman existed who, under the banner of anti-Communism, massacred and destroyed, defiled and blasphemed, invaded and murdered human beings, cities, fields and villages, peoples and cultures. This man gathered formidable forces which he guided into becoming the most immense torrent of hatred and violence that the history of mankind has ever seen. Today, next to the ruins of his nation, among millions of dead whom he dragged to the grave, he lies anonymously twisted like a piece of burnt, dried meat beneath the debris of his personal fortress, above which now flies a glorious red flag with a star and a hammer and sickle. And this flag, along with the others symbolising victory, means peace and reconstruction of our insulted human dignity.

He praised the USSR, not only for its courage in standing up to the Nazi menace militarily but for allowing culture to flourish: 'I have just read in the official statistics,' he told the Senate, 'a fact which fills my writer's heart with a flood of invincible joy. The fact is this: "During the war, one billion copies of 1,000 books in 100 different languages were published in the Soviet Union."'[23] What Neruda had not yet heard or read – or chose not to read – was that, after a brief wartime relaxation, writers were again being persecuted by the Soviet regime for refusing to follow the official Communist line.

Neruda put everything he could into his senatorial duties. He enjoyed meeting ordinary people in the streets, but some of the paperwork reminded him of the bureaucratic grind of his consular postings.

And his enemies remained all-too-prepared to snipe. During a speech on 24 June 1945, at the Santiago headquarters of the Society of Chilean Writers, where the PEN Club were honouring Neruda's award of the National Prize for Literature, he was constantly interrupted by various voices. One declared:

> You have betrayed poetry, poets, a whole system of humanist and disinterested poetry. You abandoned secret discoveries, you don't speak to us about magic or André Breton. You are a . . . propagandist. You are too comprehensible, too clear. Where is the myth, where is the magic? I have read Kafka, Apollinaire, the Marquis de Sade, Picasso and Paul Eluard, and they're sublime.

Undaunted, Neruda took up the challenge and responded to the heckler:

> I see all profound contributions to human culture as sublime. I venerate the mysterious musical secret of the totemic tribe, from the dazzling birth of the great poetic idiom with Chaucer, Villon, Berceo, Alighieri, through the gallant piano of Ronsard, the fury and the jewels of Shakespeare, the timber strength of Bach or Tolstoy, to Stravinsky and Shostakovich, and also Picasso and Paul Eluard. Magic and craft are the two permanent wings of art, but I believe that it is those who distance themselves from the bonfire on which culture is burning, instead of rescuing it (even if it means burning one's hands), who are traitors to poetry.

Another voice broke in from the hall, this time accusing Neruda of writing too obscurely.

You are a demagogue. And moreover, you are an obscure poet whom nobody understands. I've just read that in my favourite newspaper. You write in hieroglyphics ... You brought us the Spanish Reds. You are against the homeland, the family and the home. You obey orders from Moscow. You are an enemy of order, you have two houses which you are bound to have stolen, because this is a country of thieves. And what are you doing talking about the Nazis? All the films they're showing about concentration camps are pure propaganda. Germany is a great country. It must be respected. It is the nation of Beethoven ...

To which Neruda calmly replied that the speaker was talking like so many other

patriots who gnaw away at and destroy the homeland every day, narrow-minded and sterile egotists ... I have two houses, one of them paid for through my poetry, directly from the publishers to the owner, and the other paid by our Public Employees' Fund. They are two beautiful houses which give me pride and remind me daily of my duties.[24]

On 8 July 1945, Neruda officially joined the Chilean Communist Party at a ceremony in Santiago's Caupolicán arena. There can be no more telling expression of just how much this moment meant to him than his poem 'A mi partido' (To My Party), from *Canto general*.

You have given me brotherhood towards the man I do not know.
You have given me the added strength of all those living.
You have given my country back to me, as though in a new birth.
You have given me the freedom that the lone man lacks.
You taught me to kindle kindness, like fire.
You gave me the straightness which a tree requires.
You taught me to see the unity and yet diversity of men.
You showed me how one person's pain could die in the victory of all.
You taught me to sleep in the hard bed of my brethren.
You made me build upon reality, as on a rock.
You made me an enemy to the evil-doer, a rampart for the frenzied.
You have made me see the world's clarity and the possibility of joy.
You have made me indestructible, for I no longer end in myself.[25]

Joining the Chilean Communist Party helped Neruda to make a painful, decisive split from his old, protracted, adolescent identity. From now on, neither Neruda nor his poetry would 'end in themselves'.

Three weeks later, he flew to Rio de Janeiro to pay his first visit to Brazil. It was a joyous occasion: Luis Carlos Prestes had been freed from jail after more than a decade. On 31 July Neruda read his poetry to a packed Rio stadium. He found Brazil wonderfully life-enhancing. There was a cultural energy in painting and sculpture which made Argentina seem, in comparison, as he told a friend later, 'old and mean'.[26]

In September 1945, as Neruda began writing *Alturas de Macchu Picchu*, he was doing so from a new perspective: he was now a member of the Communist Party, and this became a form of warm, embracing womb. Even more importantly, as Jason Wilson has pointed out, Neruda now felt a closer affinity with the exploited workers, his pre-Columbian ancestors, who built the Incan fortress high in the Andes. The poem is infused, as Wilson puts it, with 'Stalinist steel'. Neruda's 'emotional Communist Party rebirth is at the heart of the poem', and the poem's title 'makes the poem seem more exotically Latin American than it actually is'.[27]

Alturas can be read a thousand different ways. And each time, new meanings can be discovered in it. In one sense, Neruda is acting as spokesman for his ancient forebears. He is speaking for them as he spoke for the victims of Franco's repression in *España en el corazón*. But *Alturas* is also drenched in an obsession with life through death. Quevedo's influence feeds him once again. It might seem strange that a profoundly pessimistic religious poet from Spain's Golden Age could exert so profound a hold over a twentieth-century, euphorically Communist poet. However, Neruda had explained this clearly in his important 1939 lecture, 'Viaje al corazón de Quevedo' (Voyage to the Heart of Quevedo):

If when we are born we begin to die, so every day brings us closer to a fixed finishing-point, if life itself is a pathetic stage towards death . . . do we not integrate death in our daily existence, are we not a perpetual part of death, are we not the most audacious part of what came from death? That is why, in so many uncertain regions, Quevedo has given me a clear and biological lesson . . . If we have already died, if we come from a profound crisis, we lose our fear of death. If the greatest step from death is birth, the smallest step from life is dying. Which is why life grows in Quevedo's doctrine as I experienced it, because Quevedo was not a reading for me, but a lived experience.[28]

So in *Alturas*, we find Neruda writing:

> Irresistible death invited me many times:
> it was like salt invisible in the waves.[29]

Significantly, he associates death here with themes he usually employs in positive terms: salt, the sea. It is when he reaches Machu Picchu that Neruda feels reborn, as if feeding off the power of his ancient forefathers. And these, crucially, were working ancestors, craftsmen, toiling with their hands, in the soil, like his great Spanish peasant friend, Miguel Hernández.

Once again, he feels an immediate, direct, sensuous rush, of present-day sensations mingling intensely with the past. Except that this time, this is not a personal nostalgia or memory but a new, more substantial link:

> And the air came in with lemon blossom fingers
> to touch those sleeping faces:
> a thousand years of air, months, weeks of air,
> blue wind and iron mountain ranges . . .

The temporary sensations meet the comfort of the permanent, the awareness of a new brotherly connection with his continent's remote history, with real human beings who had toiled like slaves to produce this mountain-top wonder, a task requiring so much energy and life that he can still feel that energy emerging from the rock:

> And yet a permanence of stone and language
> upheld the city raised like a chalice
> in all those hands: live, dead and stilled,
> aloft with so much death, a wall, with so much life,
> struck with flint petals, the everlasting rose, our home,
> this reef on Andes, its glacial territories.

This reference to the rose is a frequent theme in Neruda's poetry. The Chilean psychologist Luis Rubilar Solís suggests that it might here refer to Neruda's longing for someone just as unknown to him as his ancient ancestors – could he possibly have been thinking of his mother, Rosa Basoalto, who died shortly after giving birth to him, when he speaks of rebirth through death? In his 'Oda a la rosa', years later, he would write: 'It's not true, rose, I love you. You belong to me, rose.'

Alturas is a great love poem, every bit as a passionate as any of Neruda's *Twenty Love Poems*. He enjoys the idea that 'the dead kingdom is still alive', reaching out, perhaps, for something to survive him, since his sick daughter had not. If he was not looking back to his mother, he might have been imagining a form of salvation through a loving, almost filial entreaty to his anonymous forebears to live on through him, and beyond him.

The relationship that is most evident in *Alturas*, however, is brotherhood. '*Sube conmigo, amor americano*' (Come up with me, American friend). Writing now two years after his visit, the poet has acquired political duties. He is a Communist senator. He represents the underprivileged, the starving, the poor, the people of the arid Chilean north. And this awareness of his current, pressing responsibilities extends to those ancient brothers who worked so hard to build Machu Picchu.

There is no mistaking Neruda's genuine compassion for the sufferings of his fellow man:

> Stone within stone, and man, where was he?
> Air within air, and man, where was he?
> Time within time, and man, where was he? . . .
> Let me have back the slave you buried here!
> Wrench from these lands the stale bread
> of the poor . . .

Amid the monumental scale of the Inca city, Neruda wants to know every small detail of those ancient lives, just as in his role as senator he now listens to the laments of the drought-tormented peasants in the north of Chile, as if to live the details himself. 'Tell me how he slept when alive / whether he snored, / his mouth agape like a dark scar.' Finally, he wants these slaves to be reborn: 'Arise to birth with me, my brother'. And he, in turn, will be renewed with their help, nourished by their fellowship:

> And give me silence, give me water, hope.
> Give me the struggle, the iron, the volcanoes.
> Let bodies cling like magnets to my body.
> Come quickly to my veins and to my mouth.
> Speak through my speech, and through my blood.

With this poem, Neruda severed his ties, once and for all, with the quasi-enjoyment of melancholic alienation from society in which he had indulged in his protracted adolescence. He now felt an immense joy in communion with civilisation, both past and present.

In November 1945, two months after completing *Alturas de Macchu Picchu*, Neruda was delighted to learn that Gabriela Mistral had become the first Latin American to be awarded the Nobel Prize for Literature. Neruda's pride at the success of his compatriot breathes through his speech to the Senate, in which he praised Mistral's poetry as being 'saturated by an essential compassion which never reaches the point of becoming rebellion or doctrine but does go beyond the limits of charitable pity'. Just as the great Russian writer, Maxim Gorky, had established 'a human order and a system of justice based on tenderness', so Mistral, 'a great lover of our geography and our collective life', seemed to be mother to all Chileans – although she never had any actual children of her own.[30]

It was back to business, after that. Life was still chaotic at Michoacán in Santiago, as well as at Isla Negra. When Tomás Lago turned up for lunch at Michoacán on 17 November, he found Pablo enjoying an apéritif with Rafael Alberti and María Teresa León. Neruda's half-sister Laurita was also there. But Delia was nowhere to be seen: she was in the little workshop she had set up to do her painting. 'There were no chairs at the table, or plates or cutlery. Pablo had no idea what to do.'[31] The guests were used to this state of affairs, however, and, unperturbed, they accompanied Laurita to fetch their own chairs. When Delia did finally appear, Pablo chided her for neglecting the guests.

> [Delia] was not prepared to play the role of housewife. I believe she cannot see any reason why it should be the woman who deals with

these domestic matters when the man is perfectly capable of doing them himself (what with equality between man and woman), but Pablo always insists: his ideal is different, in accordance with the upbringing of our middle class in Chile. It was an insoluble problem between them both.[32]

In early 1946, Neruda was delighted to be honoured with the Order of the Aztec Eagle by the Mexican government. Neruda still felt grateful to the Mexican regime for its generosity in welcoming so many refugees from European fascism, when other Latin American nations had closed their doors.

He did not have long to bask in his enjoyment of the Mexican award. On 28 January 1946, demonstrators gathered in the square in front of the Moneda presidential palace in Santiago to express their solidarity with the ill-paid, ill-fed workers in the Humberstone and Mapocho nitrate fields. It was an entirely peaceful protest, but without warning, the authorities lost their patience and opened fire on the crowd with machine guns. At least five demonstrators were killed. Incensed, Neruda wrote a poem, 'The Dead in the Square', in which he condemned not only the murders themselves but the way the authorities tried to cover up the incident,

> as if nobody died, nothing
> as if they were stones falling
> on the ground, or water on water

and demanded that those responsible be brought to trial in the same square.

In 1946, Ríos, like his predecessor, died in office. Suddenly, Neruda received a surprising summons. The Radical Party presidential candidate, Gabriel González Videla, asked Neruda to act as head of information – basically, to be his propaganda chief in the forthcoming election campaign.

At the time, González Videla appeared to many on the Left to be the best hope for Chile. He was supported by a left-wing coalition consisting mainly of the Radical and Communist parties. According to Volodia Teitelboim, 'He was the most left-wing politician we had. We knew he was coarse and uneducated, but what could we do? He was so decisive – we thought. But he deceived us all.'[33]

Neruda worked tirelessly singing González Videla's praises the length and breadth of Chile. Indeed, he turned to his Temuco friend, the soprano Blanca Hauser (whose husband, Armando Carvajal, director of the Chilean Symphony Orchestra, had joined the Communist Party on the same day as Pablo) to help compose a hymn to depict the presidential candidate in the finest light. When Neruda went round to Blanca's Santiago flat to discuss the project, he met an attractive young singer who laughed a lot. Neruda indulged in the briefest of affairs with her, before she left Chile for Mexico. Pablo would meet her again, three years later, and this time their reunion would be far more significant.

On 4 September 1946, Gabriel González Videla stood against Dr Eduardo Cruz-Coke, a surgeon-professor, in the new presidential elections; González Videla won 192,000 votes to his opponent's 142,000. Since this did not constitute an absolute majority, negotiations began between the Liberal Party and González Videla, in which he asked the Liberals to back his candidature. Congress met on 4 October, and favoured González Videla, with 138 votes against 46 for Cruz-Coke.

The victorious President González Videla's first cabinet was an uneasy mixture of Liberals, Communists and Radicals – very unusual as the world entered the Cold War. But it did not take long for the peculiar coalition to show signs of cracking. The Right accused the Communists of pro-Moscow sympathies and, in response, the Ministries under Communist control – Agriculture, Public Works, and Land and Colonisation – called for protest strikes. This, in turn, led to the creation of the Chilean Anti-Communist Action (ACHA)[34], an unsavoury paramilitary group made up of all Chilean parties – including the Socialists. Videla was already showing signs of turning against the Communists, who had helped him to win power. But for the time being, he took no direct action against the Party.

Disillusioned, Neruda wanted to escape Chile again. Despite the growing political tensions at home, his literary fame was spreading. *Residencia en la tierra* had been translated into Danish and, in the United States, into English. The Portuguese-language edition of the *Twenty Love Poems* was proving as successful in Brazil as it remained in Chile. And in Eastern Europe, which would see so much of the poet over the next few years, readers now had access to *España en el corazón* in Czech. All these editions brought in royalties, much of which disappeared into lavish parties and Neruda's book and seashell collection.

On 28 December 1946, Neruda finally said farewell legally to the name he had been born with. No longer would he be known anywhere as Ricardo Reyes. He was Pablo Neruda officially, to his readers and to his friends. In his delightful posthumously published *Libro de las preguntas (Book of Questions)*, he impishly wrote: 'Is there anything sillier in life than to be called Pablo Neruda?' But just as that flippant line about a roast at Machu Picchu concealed the deep emotional impact, so his definitive break from his earlier, angst-ridden, inward-turning, father-fearing self was as important to him as joining the Chilean Communist Party.

Michoacán continued to be a magnet for the world's greatest writers: Miguel Angel Asturias, Rafael Alberti, the French poet Paul Valéry and the Cuban poet Nicolás Guillén. Soon, Pablo's old school-friend Diego Muñoz came to live with them accompanied by his new girlfriend, Inés Valenzuela, after separating from his first wife. Inés told me about their life at that time:

> Pablo loved Delia, despite the difference in their ages. He couldn't live without her. In the Avenida Lynch, Pablo would get up early and go to the nearby market to buy fruit and vegetables. Delia would get up later. When we got back to the house, the first thing he asked was: '*Hay Hormiga o no hay Hormiga?*' ['Is there an Ant or is there not an Ant?'] And she had to show herself. Pablo was very affectionate with Delia – not the other way round. I don't mean that she wasn't affectionate, but the initiative always came from Pablo.[35]

Among the many visitors was the eccentric Chilean composer Acario Cotapos, who had so enlivened Pablo's embattled existence in Madrid during the Spanish Civil War. 'Acario told us that the best way to die of hunger was to submit oneself to Delia's cooking. And it was true that Delia had not the slightest idea of how to cook, or what needed cooking when guests were expected,' recalled one of Delia's closest friends, Lavinia Andrade. 'But she had the gift of the most overflowing cordiality. She never seemed to get bored, and appeared to enjoy meeting every person she came across. And she also gave the impression that, despite the time that they had been together, each day was the first day that she was spending with Pablo. They went to all the public meetings and friends' parties. She attracted people. She seemed to possess a strange magnetism.'[36]

Lola Falcón said that Neruda 'could count on Delia, who didn't mind making any sacrifice if it would help Pablo . . .'

> Delia was charming with the visitors, but I don't think she was much good at administering the house. One day, in the garden, I found a [kitchen] fork. She told me: 'So that's where the forks get to.' And she didn't even bother to bend down and pick it up! Those were the kind of details that didn't concern her. But friends took charge of domestic matters and no one could possibly complain about the service or the cordiality they found at Michoacán . . . What made Delia tick was her generous heart, her sense of friendship, fraternity, love for others. Her admiration for Neruda's poetry was not exclusive. She also loved Lorca, César Vallejo, Alberti, Machado. And above all, she loved happiness, justice and freedom for mankind.[37]

In 1946 Delia received some good news that eased the couple's financial pressures: she had finally managed to sell her estate in Argentina, and a considerable monthly income could be expected. Delia was able take over full ownership of Michoacán – where she would live to the end of her life – at a cost of 2.5 million pesos, and pay off the entire debt which Pablo had incurred with the Public Employees' and Journalists' Pension Fund to make the initial down-payment on the house. The other half of the money which Delia earned from her Argentine property vanished into a mysterious black hole after a friend of Pablo's who had offered to invest the money wisely, went bankrupt and then died in a car crash. But according to Delia's biographer, Fernando Sáez, Neruda resented the suggestion that he was living off Delia's money.[38] Perhaps it was the awareness that he was still – despite his literary fame – relying, in part, on Delia's money that led Neruda to make occasional, very public and insensitive, snipes at her domestic incapacities. Once, when Tomás Lago visited on 10 May 1947, Neruda began to talk about how much he had admired the scrupulous organisation of the house of a bachelor he had met.

> He said that he had been to his house just the once, for some reason or other, and had found the furniture in perfect order, each drawer

was destined for a different thing, here were the shirts, here the socks, there the towels. The man opened a compartment and, marvel of marvels, a set of ties appeared laid out immaculately, in order of woollen, silk, red, blue, etc . . . We all looked at Delia during the conversation, since she was the target. As soon as they got married, men lost their natural order [Neruda was implying]. Pablo then recalled his life in India [the Far East], when he too had been a bachelor. He had had a 22-year-old 'boy' who arranged everything for him, called Brampy. When he got out of the bath every morning, he found a clean shirt ready for him, with the cufflinks on, creased trousers laid out so that he had only to put his feet in, the socks were as good as new, as was the tie, and the underpants on the bed were impeccable.[39]

But Neruda had more turmoil, much more, waiting for him than the occasional twinge of domestic discontent. On 21 October 1946, the President arranged a meeting with Volodia Teitelboim, then the Chilean Communist Party's emissary to the chief executive's office who headed the Communist delegation, and ordered the Communist government ministers to step down. When Volodia told the President that they would refuse to comply with this order, González Videla raged: 'I'll sack them anyway.' And this he did, to Neruda's utter fury.[40]

Once outside the government, the Communists intensified their protests. The Communists' success in the April 1947 municipal elections hardened President González Videla's resolve to rid himself of them once and for all. In October, mine-workers began another strike in Lota. González Videla denounced the move as a revolutionary step designed to cripple the Chilean economy and the first stage towards overthrowing the democratic government and installing a Communist dictatorship.

The Lota strike was perfectly legal and it was nonsense to suggest that the Chilean Communists were taking orders from Moscow. In fact, since the seventh Comintern congress in 1935, the Chilean Communist Party, unlike the Socialists, had actually embarked on a strategy of alliances with progressive political and economic sectors in an attempt to carry out the bourgeois-democratic revolution.

A Communist miner, Damian Uribe Cárdenas, had been secretary of the powerful Lota miners' union until 1941, when he was elected to the National Congress. After that, he was happy to exchange his filthy miner's uniform for a tie to do political battle with the Conservative and Liberal politicians. At the same time, it was clearly this kind of alliance between social and political players, between rural and urban forces, which González Videla considered the gravest threat to his regime. It was why he took such a dim view of the senatorial respectability of Pablo Neruda. At the same time as González Videla saw his own personal hegemony challenged, the Cold War gave him a suitable international pretext to take firm action against the Left. The Brazilian Communist Party, he must have noted with glee, had just been declared illegal.

The Communists and other critics of González Videla claimed that he was acting under pressure from the United States and out of a desire to forge closer economic and military bonds with the dominant superpower. The United States certainly encouraged a crackdown on Chilean Communists, and the two countries agreed to a military assistance pact while González Videla was President. However, no conclusive evidence has yet come to light that the United States directly pushed him to act. González Videla also hoped that, in turning against the Communists, he could find favour with the right-wing critics of his government – especially the landowners, to whom he guaranteed a continuing moratorium on peasant unionisation.

At the height of his former campaign alliance with the Communists and the working class, González Videla had paid numerous visits to Lota, assuring the people there of his support and his sympathies. This explains the depth of their bitterness when he turned so violently against them.

Using the new 'extraordinary powers' granted to him by the Chilean Congress, the President sent his forces into Lota and the surrounding areas. People were arrested and sent on navy warships to military prisons on the islands of Santa María and Quiriquina. Among the men responsible for rounding up prisoners was a certain Augusto Pinochet Ugarte. The majority were later transported to a concentration camp which had been set up in the port town of Pisagua, in the northern desert, where the coal miners were soon joined by hundreds of other prisoners arrested throughout the country. (In January 1948, Pinochet was named head of the Pisagua camp, and at the end of February, he was sent to the coal mining region in Lota, where he served as Chief Military Delegate of the Emergency Zone for a year.)

Some sources maintain that González Videla himself was present to oversee the final breaking of the strike. Others claim that Pinochet was in charge of the operation. It seems that when the last remaining miners resisted attempts by fifty or so soldiers sent into the Schwager pit in Lota to remove them, tear gas was pumped into the ventilating system. When the miners emerged, dizzy and choking, more than two hundred of them were arrested.

Astonishingly, the Socialists stood firm in their support for González Videla's vicious moves to break the miners' strike. They backed decrees 977 and 978, which legally obliged the miners to return to work, but did provide for a 40 per cent rise in basic salary for those who worked in the interior of the mines and a 30 per cent increase for those working on the surface. The Socialists considered that these decrees satisfied the demands of the workers far more adequately than anything the strike could have done. They saw the continued strike as a political (Communist-led) manoeuvre which, as González Videla himself claimed, put Chile's very 'democracy' in peril.

It is almost impossible today to believe that the Socialists could have supported a dictatorial regime which made the miners' refusal to work grounds for court martial, removed food provisions from workers' homes and, when it learnt that workers were living off fish caught in the sea, banned fishing.

In August of this year of turmoil, Neruda's volume of poetry called *Tercera residencia* (Third Residence) was published by Losada in Buenos Aires. The mood of the poems varies dramatically. The long second section, 'Las furias y las penas' (Furies and Sufferings), which was written much earlier than the rest of the book and originally appeared as a separate booklet, is reminiscent, in its embittered attitude to sex, of the second volume of *Residencia en la tierra*:

> I was a man put there by chance
> meeting a woman by some vague arrangement.
> We undressed
> as if to die, or swim, or grow old,
> and we put ourselves one into another,
> she circling me like a pit,
> I banging at her like a man
> striking a bell . . .

But other poems gathered together in *Tercera residencia* – especially those of his Spanish Civil War period, *España en el corazón*, Neruda's earliest collection of 'committed verse' – reflect his identification with a 'popular' cause.

Neruda's sadness at the direction Chile's politics were taking in 1947 prompted him to yearn once again for the freshness of foreign lands. He asked to be appointed Ambassador in Rome. At first, González Videla saw the idea as a good way of getting rid of one of the best-known figures on the far Left. But Videla also knew from personal experience how comfortable the life of an Ambassador could be (he had arrived in Paris to take up the post of Chilean Ambassador in November 1939) and it may be that comfort was not what he had in mind for Pablo Neruda. By now, González Videla was considering outlawing the Communist Party completely. In secret, he made a deal to this effect with Admiral William Leahy, US President Truman's emissary.

So that was that. Neruda was forced to stay in Chile, as the political situation grew more and more desperate. Tomás Lago recalled that Neruda was losing weight and sleeping poorly. If he lost his senatorial status 'Pablo knew that he could be arrested and deported, or imprisoned, at any moment. But he refused point-blank to go into hiding. He said he had to suffer along with everyone else.'[41]

Delia, Lago noted, prepared by spending an afternoon at the hairdressers, insisting that, if she were to be deported to Pisagua concentration camp, she wanted to be good and ready.

On 27 November 1947, Neruda could hold back no longer. Because the censorship of the press in Chile was so comprehensive, he looked abroad, and published a bombshell article in the Venezuelan daily, *El Nacional*, under the headline: 'The Crisis of Democracy in Chile is a Dramatic Warning for Our Continent.'

In it, he launched a ferocious attack on González Videla for handing Chile over to North American domination. Neruda pointed out that González Videla had told the correspondent of the London newspaper, the *News Chronicle*, on 18 June 1947, that he believed war between the United States and Russia was imminent – in a matter of months – and this belief had dictated his attitude to Chile's Communists 'against whom he has no personal objections'. González Videla had told the British paper: 'Chile must co-operate with her powerful neighbour, the United States of America, and when the war begins, Chile will support the United States against Russia.'

Neruda railed against the man he had served loyally as propaganda chief:

> The ideal of Señor González Videla's life can be summed up in one phrase: 'I want to be President.' In other places in our America, superficial, fickle politicians of this type resort to intrigue and *coups d'état* to attain power. This is not possible in Chile. The bedrock of democracy in our nation obliged Señor González Videla, in pursuit of his objective, to don the garb of a demagogue . . . The incumbent President used his friendship with the Communists as the foundation stone of his presidential career . . . [But] with the dismissal of the Communist Ministers, at the demand of the government, and the North American monopolies, the enactment of the popular platform, to which Señor González Videla had pledged himself, was conclusively abandoned . . .

Neruda then referred to the coal miners' strike in Lota. González Videla had 'found in this strike the pretext for his ultimate betrayal, an excuse to provoke a widescale international reaction and to unleash a persecution against workers such as had never been seen in my country.'

The poet emphasised the terrible conditions in which the miners worked, often squatting down, constantly

> threatened by the firedamp [methane] that periodically kills them – even more speedily than their work. It takes the workers four hours to get to the work site, and this is not paid time. Thousands of workers earn less than fifty cents for those twelve hours, and those who earn as much as two dollars a day are very few. Then, when they emerge from their caverns, they encounter a new tragedy, that of housing and food. Official statistics show the horrifying figure of six workers for every bed. At the site called Puchoco Rojas, they operate on a 'warm bed' system. This system – which reveals the terrible tragedy of the Chilean people – consists of a regular turn to use a bed, with the result that, for years on end, a bed never grows cold. Food, with such miserable salaries, is far below the norm. According to the North American expert, Señor Bloomfield, each

man daily consumes two thousand calories fewer than he needs for subsistence. Anyclomiasis, a terrible disease, produces a high percentage of deaths, added to those caused by endemic tuberculosis and by accidents.

It is only natural that such terrible conditions have generated heroic movements of workers' resistance, which have succeeded in bettering to a barely discernible degree these abysmal conditions. Nevertheless, now and for the first time, a President elected by these very same workers – who hoped that at least once someone would hear the voices rising from their hell – has declared in public that the strike is not due to the frightful conditions in the coal regions, but to an international plot, and on the basis of this falsehood, he has treated the strikers with a cruelty and savagery found only in Nazi systems of slavery and oppression . . .

They placed pistols to children's breasts to make them tell where their fathers were hiding. They filled trains – like the trains of the Nazi condemned – with families and workers who had lived as long as forty years in that area. Often, the trains served as jails for many days, and no one was permitted to go to the aid of the victims, who were kept isolated and without food. Children and adults died as a result of this treatment. Corpses of miners appeared on the hills, and no investigation was possible, because no one was allowed to enter the zone. And while the UN is debating the crime of genocide – and the delegate from Chile will surely make a few emotional speeches on the subject – Señor González Videla is responsible for that very crime, perpetrated against his own countrymen.

Neruda issued a warning for the whole of the continent:

The instigators of these crimes threaten not only the freedom of Chile but the order and integrity of our forsaken Latin America. Other governments will repeat these debilitating betrayals. The cruel and bloody dictators in some of our sister countries will today feel more firm and resolute as they tighten the noose around the necks of their peoples . . .

Neruda ended his article in *El Nacional* by thanking the Communist Party for its generosity in giving him time off from his political duties to devote himself to his writing. He said he had been on the point of getting ready to 'weave again the rhythm and sounds of my poetry. I was preparing to sing again to lose myself in the depths of my country, in its most secret roots,' when President González Videla's betrayal struck like a thunderbolt, forcing him to throw himself back into the political fray. He said he was 'proud of any personal risk suffered in this battle for dignity, culture and freedom'.[42] And the personal risks were huge. Neruda was aware that, but for his senatorial immunity, he would have been arrested and jailed, maybe even detained at Pisagua.

The day after the publication of Neruda's article in *El Nacional*, a furious González Videla turned to the courts, demanding the poet's *desafuero* – the revocation of his senatorial status. The court accepted the President's call, but Neruda immediately appealed against the decision.

As the New Year dawned, there was no sign of any let-up in the vicious repression. With the legal ruling pending, Neruda was not in any mood to let the tyrant off the hook. On 6 January 1948, Pablo Neruda rose to his feet in the Senate and delivered one of the bravest, most astonishing speeches in Chilean political history. It has come to be known as 'Yo acuso' (I Accuse), after Zola's denunciation of the French government's persecution of the Jewish soldier, Alfred Drey-fus, fifty years earlier. 'The President of the Republic has taken one more step in the unbridled political persecution which will make him notorious in the sad history of these days, by filing an action before the Supreme Court requesting my impeachment . . .'

And yet, as Pablo Neruda read out the names of 628 people, both men and women, who were being detained at Pisagua concentration camp, without having been interrogated or informed of the charges against them, Neruda seemed unaware that his hero, Stalin, was censoring the press in Russia and silencing his political opponents with the same foul, brutal methods as González Videla. One wonders if Neruda could have afforded, emotionally, to have made any such comparison, even if he *had* known what was happening in the USSR.

With tremendous shrewdness, mixed with his characteristic sense of mischief – despite the gravity of the risks he was taking – Neruda threw back many of the President's formerly pro-Communist actions in his face.

I am accused of having disclosed what is happening in Chile under the leadership of His Excellency Señor Gabriel González Videla, who governs by means of Extraordinary Powers and censorship of the press. They charge me with having spoken against my country because I did not agree with decisions taken by this same Exalted Leader. This argument is truly pitiful. If to disagree with His Excellency Señor González Videla is to turn against the nation, what can we say when we recall that Señor González Videla, as president of the Committee for Aid to the Spanish People, supported and defended the rights of expatriate Spaniards to attack from exile the same Franco government with which he is now on such good terms? Did he not authorise, for those Spaniards, the freedom that, through an act of impeachment, he is now attempting to deny me, the former head of his presidential campaign and a senator of the Republic? . . .

I am proud that his persecution has fallen on my shoulders. I am proud, because a people who suffer and endure may thus have an opportunity to see which of us have remained loyal to their public obligations and which have betrayed them.

Neruda then specifically accused the President of having ordered the Chilean delegation to the United Nations to vote against severing ties with Franco; of having ordered the same UN delegation to abstain and thus 'silence Chile's voice on the question of creating a Jewish state'; of setting the armed forces against Chilean workers, and of attempting to suppress freedom of opinion.[43]

A week later, on Tuesday, 13 January 1948, Neruda made his final speech in the Senate:

I am a persecuted man, and justly persecuted. An incipient tyranny must persecute those who defend freedom . . . But persecution will not lead anywhere, because the Communist Party is making history at this very moment. We will be isolated, apparently, but from all sides, like invisible threads, come the brotherhood and solidarity of the people and free men. They will not be silenced . . .[44]

From that day on, Neruda was a wanted man. He knew that he would have to flee Chile almost immediately if he were to evade imprisonment – or worse. The newspaper *El Imparcial* announced a reward if any of the 300 agents put on the poet's trail actually managed to arrest him. How was he going to escape? Who would stand by him, when the risks were so high?

9

'A year of blind rats' – Neruda in hiding

1948–49

On 27 January 1948, days after unknown assailants had attempted to set fire to Neruda's house on Santiago's Avenida Lynch, Neruda took refuge in the Mexican Embassy.

The ambassador, Pedro de Alba, was new to diplomacy. He was a great admirer of Neruda and feared for the poet's safety, knowing that Chilean Communist leaders were being arrested and jailed daily. He lent Pablo and Delia his car, and, accompanied by the military attaché at the Mexican Embassy, Colonel Dávila, they made their way east to the border in an attempt to cross into Argentina. However, the border police at El Cristo Redentor – although not yet instructed to arrest Neruda – sent him back because there was a discrepancy in his documents: while his passport bore his new name, Pablo Neruda, other identity papers still read Neftalí Reyes. The couple made their way back cautiously to Santiago – and once again found a diplomatic shelter at the Mexican Embassy.

As soon as the Chilean Foreign Ministry learnt where Neruda was hiding, it protested to Pedro de Alba. The Ambassador initially stood firm, insisting that he was lending the poet his personal assistance. Alarmed by the sudden diplomatic uproar, Neruda decided to apply officially for political asylum at the Embassy. But the Mexican Foreign Minister, Jaime Torres Bodet, telephoned de Alba to warn him not to start a diplomatic incident by granting Neruda's request, and as the poet wanted to save de Alba from further pressure, he withdrew his asylum request and left the Embassy.

Some have criticised de Alba for acceding too quickly to the Mexican government's request. Neruda himself insisted to his friend and later secretary, Margarita Aguirre, that this criticism was unfair: 'Don Pedro showed great generosity towards me.'[1] Aguirre believed that it may have been the fact that de Alba was new to the diplomatic game which caused him to follow orders so speedily from back home in Mexico City.

Neruda had always praised Mexico for its warm and open-armed welcome to thousands of refugees from Nazism and fascism during the Second World War. But he never forgave the way the Mexican authorities, in the shape of the Foreign Minister, Jaime Torres Bodet, had turned their back on him now in his time of greatest need.

He depicted this period vividly in a passage of *Canto general*, written while still in hiding and bitter at the double betrayal.

> Then they reproached
> me for crimes, that pack
> of flunkies and hired hoodlums;
> the 'secretaries of government',
> the police, wrote their murky insult
> against me with tar [. . .]
> They closed off Chile's mountain ranges
> so that I couldn't leave
> to tell what's happening here,
> and when Mexico opened its doors
> to welcome me and protect me,
> Torres Bodet, pitiful poet,
> demanded that I be delivered
> to the furious jailers.
>
> But my word's alive,
> and my free heart accuses.[2]

Amid his courageous and angry condemnation of the Chilean and Mexican governments, Neruda was nevertheless aware of the danger he was in. At any moment, he knew, he could be arrested and become one more Communist inmate of Pisagua concentration camp in this 'bleak year of blind rats' – with his voice for justice silenced for ever.

Where indeed was Neruda to go? If any policeman saw him, he would be arrested on the spot. Neruda caught a taxi and gave the driver, who did not look at his illustrious charge, the address of a friend: the well-known folklore specialist, Carmen Cuevas. When he tried to pay the driver, the man, still without looking at him, said: 'You don't owe me a thing, Don Pablo. Good luck.'

Once inside Carmen Cuevas's house, Neruda asked for some dark glasses and fled into the Santiago night. For a week, he managed to dodge the authorities. On the afternoon of 5 February 1948, three friends of Neruda – Andrés Rodríguez, Homero Arce and Augusto Carmona – visited him at his home at Isla Negra, carrying a dramatic message: he would have to go into hiding at once. Two days earlier, the courts had confirmed that Neruda was no longer a senator and had issued an order for his immediate arrest.

So began an astonishing adventure, with Neruda and Delia being moved from one secret hiding place to the next, often at a moment's notice in the middle of the night, after a tip-off that the police were on their scent.

Contrary to what has often been written, the Chilean Communist Party was not the main organiser of this operation, although it did provide cars and other services. The chief mastermind was actually a young man, Alvaro Jara Hantke, a 24-year-old history student, whose nom de guerre was 'Ignacio'. He was not a member of the Communist Party at the time – although he had been in the Communist Youth. He was asked by the Party to take on the operation to hide Neruda and Delia after successfully managing to conceal Volodia Teitelboim from the authorities. Jara told Robert Pring-Mill years later that the Communist Party was in a state of considerable disorganisation at the time, 'running around like rabbits', when González Videla struck out in search of Neruda.[3]

Jara handled the arrangements with almost military precision – too military and too precise for Neruda's liking. The poet did not enjoy being bossed around by a man twenty years younger than he. And Jara, it seems, did not have a much better opinion of Neruda: 'Pablo, as is well known, was a big child, very headstrong and accustomed to people agreeing to his demands without opposition. Moreover, life in hiding abruptly cut him off from the wide social world with which he usually surrounded himself every day.' In contrast, Jara had nothing but positive recollections of the Ant: 'Delia was such a charming, brave and refined woman, who would accompany [Pablo] all that time, without complaining once about their gypsy-like, hazardous and occasionally uncomfortable – and always potentially dangerous – existence.'[4]

Jara rightly pointed out that this enforced underground existence increased Neruda's poetic productivity, because it allowed him so much time to think and write, away from social distractions.

> I would even say that 1948 was the year of *Canto general* . . . I was a witness, on many, many occasions, when we were chatting, myself, Delia and [Neruda], when suddenly the poet stood up and slipped away in a hurry, without explanation, as if words were escaping or falling from him, and he settled in the room next door. Soon we could hear the clattering of the keys of his portable typewriter, which he pressed hurriedly and mercilessly. Sometimes, this clattering went on for quite a while; at others, it was short-lived. The Hormiguita was silent for moment, then explained with a smile: 'Pablo is writing.'[5]

It was at around this time that Neruda produced a clandestine leaflet, which he called *Antología popular de la resistencia* (Popular Anthology of Resistance). In fact, it is not an anthology at all – most, if not all, of the poems were written by Neruda, under various pseudonyms. Many consist of witty attacks on President Gabriel González Videla's act of betrayal and Alvaro Jara recalled that Neruda laughed out loud as he was typing them. Jara said that Neruda was heavily influenced in this enterprise by the French *résistance* productions still very much in vogue in 1948.[6] And Robert Pring-Mill has rightly pointed out that the spirit of this leaflet reflected Neruda's desire to forge connections between his poetry and Chile's *poesía popular*.[7]

Pring-Mill has investigated this clandestine 'anthology' and believes that two of the poems in it – 'Tendrá su farol' (He Will Have His Lamp), said to be by the Cuban poet Nicolás Guillén, and 'Tiempo americano' (American Times), purportedly by Julio Moncada – could, indeed, have been penned by those authors. (Moncada was a popular poet of the time and a member of the Chilean Communist Party.)[8]

According to Víctor Pey – whose life Neruda had saved on the

Winnipeg mission and who was soon to return the favour by harbouring Pablo and Delia himself – no one realised just how difficult hiding the poet was going to be.

> When the hunt for Neruda started, they weren't prepared. They had no idea where to take Neruda. No one has published this. Neruda himself told me later that he suggested some names. One of them was a civil engineer, a very close friend of mine, José Saitúa Pedemonte, who had been a militant Communist since his student days but he was not very well-known. When they asked Neruda what had called his attention to Saitúa's name, he replied that he was married to a Spanish Republican refugee, Gloria Nistal.[9]

So Saitúa and Nistal's apartment near Santiago's Plaza de los Leones became the first safe haven for Neruda and Delia. They arrived there at three in the morning on 6 February, three days after President González Videla ordered Pablo's arrest. Saitúa and Nistal 'were a couple with three young children and a maid. As a good Communist, Saitúa did what the Party ordered him to do and let Neruda and Delia into his house. But the police were after Neruda, and Saitúa could not tell his children who the strange couple were. It soon became clear that it was too dangerous for them to stay there.'[10]

Next Pablo and Delia moved to Víctor Pey's small apartment on the Avenida Vicuña Mackenna. Pey was living on his own, separated from his wife, Marta Jara.

> On the list of a hundred possible hiding places, Neruda chose me. I was living in a tiny kitchenette. I told the Party people: make sure no one telephones me . . . They complied with this impeccably. It was a tiny place. I only had one bedroom. Neruda and Delia and myself couldn't all squeeze in. So I left the apartment. I organised everything at this time . . . I kept up all the appearances of a normal lifestyle. The porter did not notice anything was wrong. I would bring food up, and the porter still thought I was living there. During his stay, Neruda wrote prolifically, attacking the regime. He ordered me to buy special paper. I made twenty or thirty copies of what he was writing and sent them to journalists. They were fabulous verses, against González Videla, some very filthy ones as well.[11]

Pey, who brought detective novels and whisky for Neruda, recalled that Pablo had a typewriter 'but he preferred to work by hand. I also had a small portable typewriter, and he would dictate poems for me to type. That was all he did, the entire day: write poetry.'

Pey said that, because of the age difference between Neruda and Delia,

> it was hard to imagine that they had a proper, compatible physical life together. She would cover her face with cream. She looked a disaster in the mornings. When I brought her food in the apartment, from the nearby Oriente restaurant, she would not do any of the washing-up. I had to do it myself – she said it hurt her hands. She made me buy her plastic gloves. In that aspect, she was very unattractive. All this time, Neruda was working on *Canto general*. In 'El fugitivo' [The Fugitive], part of *Canto general*, Neruda mentions an engineer (so as not to identify me) and says that he and Marta Jara were waiting for him (Neruda). Nothing of the sort. I was living alone. But while he was staying at my apartment, I brought Marta along to introduce her. That was how they met.[12]

There was one terrifying moment when it looked as though Pablo's cover had been blown. After a fortnight cooped up in Pey's tiny flat, Neruda was starting to feel extremely claustrophobic.

> One day, I asked Neruda whether he'd like to go up on the terrace. No one went up there. So we both went up (leaving Delia downstairs) at about ten at night, but precisely at that moment, the foreman was doing some repairs. Neruda was petrified. After all, his silhouette was unmistakable. Fortunately, the foreman was sixty or seventy and did not have a clue who he was. But Neruda panicked. He was a fearful man, very scared.[13]

Pey concocted a bizarre plan to show the foreman there was no one else in the flat. He informed the man that there was something wrong with the bathroom lock, and when he came down to fix it, Neruda and Delia hid in the only wardrobe in the apartment for half an hour, concealed by Pey's clothes. High farce indeed!

In the end, it was simply too risky to stay in one place for more than a few weeks. So, at the end of April or beginning of May 1948, Alvaro

Jara took over the operation. Pablo and Delia left Pey's apartment and were driven to the *parcela* (smallholding) of Julio Vega. He was chosen because he was totally uninvolved with the Communist Party and so unlikely to arouse suspicion: Vega was a *contador* (accountant) in a small business. In *Canto general*, Neruda recalled him fondly as a man who shared his love of nature.

The drive from Víctor Pey's apartment to the smallholding was a heart-stopping one. 'Suddenly, near the old airport at Los Cerrillos, out of the shadows emerged the figure of a policeman, making signals for me to stop,' Alvaro Jara recalled. Neruda and Delia were sitting in the back of the car, reclining as if they were asleep. 'I warned them not to move and I stopped the car. Fortunately, the *carabinero* was off-duty, and asked me whether I was going to Valparaíso and whether I could take him. I breathed a sigh of relief, and said I was sorry but we weren't going that far. It was lucky that it had been a false alarm, but it taught me to restrict journeys along streets and roads to an absolute minimum.'[14]

Once they arrived at the smallholding, Julio Vega greeted Pablo with great warmth and respect. The poet gave the place the name of Godomar de Chena, a mischievously pompous way of referring to the modest municipality of Maipú, in the Chena region. But the change of name was also a way of protecting Vega from the authorities' clutches – though Godomar was one of Julio's surnames.

Here, Neruda was known as 'Don Pedro' and Delia as 'Sara' – the name of Alvaro Jara's wife. Alvaro himself was 'off-duty' for two weeks as Neruda's minder while he went on honeymoon with Sara but, according to Robert Pring-Mill, he was rapidly whisked back to work when Pablo made a fuss about his replacement. Astonishingly, Jara's wife knew nothing about his undercover life as 'Ignacio' until he took her to visit Pablo and Delia at Julio Vega's smallholding. Sara was flabbergasted both to meet Chile's greatest poet and most famous fugitive – and to discover what her new husband was mixed up in.[15]

In early June 1948, Pablo and the Ant moved to the three-storey apartment of Sergio Insunza and his wife, Aída Figueroa, on the Calle Ismael Valdés Vergara. The couple were lawyers and both were members of the Communist Party, which did not make them a particularly discreet choice. But they were used to harbouring refugees from justice, especially miners' leaders fleeing the persecution in Lota. So they were not surprised when Alvaro Jara burst into the house of an aunt with whom they were having lunch and asked them to look after two more unnamed fugitives: the surprise came when they opened the door at ten the next morning to find Pablo and Delia on the doorstep. Sergio Insunza already knew Pablo a little, because, although very young, he had been helping to represent the poet in his legal fight against having his senatorial status revoked.

Pablo and Delia loved the place as soon as they saw it: it had a sensational view overlooking the Parque Forestal – even more pictur-esque that winter, as, for the first time in many years, Santiago saw snow. There was a large grand piano in the living-room, and as she and Pablo entered it for the first time, Delia, who could play a little, exclaimed: 'We're going to be very happy here. How lucky we are!' They rejected Aída's offer to move out of the big bedroom into her one-year-old daughter's: 'There is no way we will allow you to do that. We'll sleep here on the narrow bed, like teaspoons.'[16]

While Delia continued to dye her hair and paint her face, Pablo sat down at his portable typewriter to produce 'La lámpara en la tierra' (A Lamp on Earth), which would become the first section of *Canto general*. He sensed, as he sat in hiding in that Santiago apartment, a fugitive in his own capital, that he had a new mission: to decipher the mystery of America, ancient and modern, of man, ancient and modern. His daily struggles had given him both the strength and the drive to take on a civic duty – that same *civismo* he had criticised Mexican poets for lacking in the newspaper interview he gave soon after arriving in Mexico City in 1940.

> I am here to tell the story,
> from the peace of the buffalo
> to the pummelled sands
> of the land's end, in the accumulated
> spray of Antarctic light,
> and through precipitous tunnels
> of shady Venezuelan peace,
> I searched for you, my father,
> young warrior of darkness and copper,
> or you, nuptial plant, indomitable hair,
> mother cayman, metallic dove.
> I, Incan of the loam,
> touched the stone and said:
> Who

awaits me? And I closed my hand
around a fistful of empty flint.
But I walked among Zapotec flowers
and the light was soft like a deer,
and the shade was a green eyelid.
My land without name . . .

Neruda had a regular routine. He got up at about 6.30 every morning and cherished a soak in the bathtub. Over breakfast, he read the press and listened to the radio news bulletins, which often mentioned his name. Then he worked on poems until about 1 p.m., showing them to Delia, as always. She made him correct grammatical errors or historically inaccurate references to dates and also advised him to cut down on the repeated use of words like '*raíces*' (roots).

After a long siesta in the afternoon, Pablo arose with renewed strength. And in the evenings, he would recite the day's poems or recall experiences in Spain and Chile, even if it was very late. 'We could hardly conceal our drowsiness as it overcame us at midnight,' Aída recalled. 'At times, we were dropping off to sleep when Pablo was reading poems from "La lámpara en la tierra". So we sleepyheads became the first people to hear the *Canto general*.'[17]

Turning on the radio one day in 1948, Pablo was delighted to hear the presenter declare that the police had lost all trace of him, and that he was thought either to be in the south of Chile or to have escaped the country altogether. Astonishing – since Sergio Insunza's and Aída Figueroa's apartment was situated virtually in the centre of Santiago. And Pablo could not resist rowdy gatherings with his closest friends, even in hiding. These were sometimes so raucous that they earned Neruda a warning from the Communist Party to be less noisy in future, otherwise his whereabouts would be revealed. But this did not seem to dampen the poet's high spirits.

As far as anyone knew, Pablo had disappeared off the face of the earth. Yet this complicated his fight to retain his senatorial status. If it could be shown that he had absented himself from Chile without permission, he would lose his seat in the Senate permanently. So Alvaro Jara arranged another extraordinary meeting – between Neruda and the president of the Senate, Arturo Alessandri Palma so that he could confirm the presence of Pablo Neruda on Chilean soil.

At the appointed hour, Jara drove Neruda, almost unrecognisable behind a heavy beard, to a popular district of Santiago, near the old central railway station.

> Don Arturo arrived punctually in a big black car, with his chauffeur. As expected, the door opened immediately and he entered the house. Then Pablo did the same, while I waited behind the wheel . . . The district was very populous, we were fully visible and we could not risk hanging around. We had to avoid calling attention to ourselves. After a few minutes, Don Arturo came out and a minute later, Pablo did the same. The poet was radiantly happy . . .[18]

Like Jara, Aída Figueroa believed that the confinement of hiding was actually propitious to the writing of Neruda's most expansive poem, *Canto general*:

> I believe that, without Pablo's period in hiding, there would prob-ably have been no *Canto general*. In that book, he rewrites the way of looking at the history of America. He reclaims America, geographically, anthropologically, historically. But he achieved this gigantic process in the most restricted of conditions . . . He couldn't even walk out on to the street . . . But in hiding, the only thing he did was write poetry. It was his rebellion against these limitations that produced *Canto general*.[19]

What kept Neruda going, more than anything else, was the energy born from his sense of betrayal.

> And atop these calamities
> a smiling tyrant
> spits on the betrayed
> miners' hopes.
> Every nation has its sorrows,
> every struggle its torments,
> but come here and tell me
> if among the bloodthirsty,
> among all the unbridled
> despots, crowned with hatred,
> with sceptres of green whips,
> there was ever another like Chile's?[20]

As Neruda said later in his memoirs, 'The only course left was to bide one's time and go underground to fight for the return of democracy . . . Chile went through a malaise that wavered between shocked daze and agony. With the protection of the United States, the President whom our votes had elected turned into a vile, bloodthirsty vampire.'[21]

Aída Figueroa claims that Neruda and Delia stayed with them for several months. However, it is clear that they were never there for more than a few weeks at one time. They came and went. Robert Pring-Mill says Albertina Azócar told him that Pablo and Delia had stayed with her and Angel Cruchaga for about a week during the period between March and June 1948, during which time he was putting the finishing touches to 'Que despierte el leñador' (Let the Woodsplitter Awake), one of the most famous sections of *Canto general*, which he completed in May. This section is a love song to North American man and an angry attack on North American politics, as well as a hymn to Soviet courage.

> You're beautiful and spacious, North America.
> You're of humble stock like a washerwoman,
> beside your rivers, white.
> Built in the unknown, your honeycomb peace is your sweetness.
> We love your man with his red hands
> of Oregon clay, your black child
> who brought you music born
> in the ivory lands: we love
> your city, your substance
> your light, your mechanisms, the West's
> energy, the peaceful
> honey, from hive and hamlet,
> the gigantic lad on the tractor . . .

> A guest
> unexpected
> as a worn old octopus
> immense, all-enveloping,
> has occupied your house, poor soldier:
> the press distils ancient poison, cultivated in
> Berlin.
> The periodicals (*Time, Newsweek*, etc.) have been turned

into yellow leaves of indictment: Hearst,
who sang the Nazis a love song, grins
and files his fingernails so that you'll ship out again
to the reefs or steppes
to fight for this guest who inhabits your house . . .
Walt Whitman, raise your beard of grass,
look with me from the forest,
from these perfumed magnitudes.
What do you see there, Walt Whitman?
I see, my deep brother tells me,
I see how the factories run,
in the city that the dead remember,
in the pure capital,
in resplendent Stalingrad . . .[22]

This section also includes one of Neruda's anthems to Stalin, which would later win him the Stalin Peace Prize but would also lay him open not only to political enemies but to friends who believed that, when his poetry slipped into melodramatic propaganda, it was the poorer for it.

In three rooms of the old Kremlin
lives a man named Josef Stalin.
His bedroom light is turned off late.
The world and his country allow him no rest.
Other heroes have given birth to a nation,
he helped to conceive his as well,
to build it,
to defend it . . .[23]

Meanwhile, Aída and Sergio (unlike some of Neruda's other underground 'hosts') never felt that the presence of the fugitive poet in their midst was a burden. Insunza said he remembered Neruda's stay with them as

a continual party, and we learned to live like Pablo. We are grateful to him, for example, for teaching us to value the smallest things: the trees in the park, the stones in the sea, old books, textures, smells, tastes . . . He was a man of absolute simplicity. Any kind of pedantry bored him: it was useless to try and discuss any theory with him in academic terms. He preferred to talk about cooking recipes or old films. He had an inexhaustible sense of humour and a gentle, telling irony. He didn't understand the theses that literature students were writing on his poetry . . . He was up to date on everything, even the crimes in the tabloid headlines.[24]

What amused Insunza was the fact that Neruda did not know any of his own poems by heart – even the most famous ones such as 'Farewell' from *Crepusculario* or Poem 20 from the *Twenty Love Poems* – and yet he had no problem reciting large chunks of Rimbaud in French.

In June and July 1948, Neruda and Delia moved out of Santiago, and travelled north-west to Valparaíso, where they hid in a two-room house at 81 Calle Cervantes, preparing for an escape by sea. Here, Neruda was known as Antonio Ruiz Lapotegue and Delia as María.

> I had to keep to a part of one room, and a small section of window from which I could observe the life of the port. From that humble watchtower, my eyes took in only a fragment of the street. At night, I would see people bustling past. It was a poor area, and the narrow street, a hundred metres below my window, took up all the light in the neighbourhood. Dumpy little stores and junk shops lined it. Trapped as I was in my corner, my curiosity knew no bounds . . . Why, for example, would passers-by, whether indifferent or in a hurry, always pause at one store? What fascinating merchandise was displayed in that window? Whole families would stop for long minutes, with children on their shoulders. I couldn't see the rapt look on their faces as they gazed into the magic window, but I could imagine them. Six months later, I learned that it was just a shoe-store window. Shoes are man's greatest interest, I concluded.[25]

Alvaro Jara and the Communist Party were planning to ship Neruda out of Chile in the cabin of one of the sailors living in the Valparaíso house where he was hiding, and to put the poet ashore with the bananas when the ship reached Guayaquil in Ecuador. In his memoirs Neruda remembered the preparations for the trip:

> The seaman explained to me that, when the ship dropped anchor [in Guayaquil], I was to appear on deck suddenly, like a well-dressed

passenger, smoking a cigar, although I have never been able to smoke cigars. Since I was on the verge of departure, the family decided it was time that I had the right kind of suit made – elegant and tropical – and I was duly fitted. The suit was ready in less than no time. I've never had so much fun as I had when I received it. The women of the house took their notions of style from a celebrated film of the day: *Gone with the Wind*. What the boys, on the other hand, considered the last word in elegance was something they had picked up from the dance halls of Harlem, and the bars and cheap dance joints of the Caribbean world. The double-breasted jacket was fitted with a belt and came down to my knees. The trousers hugged me at the ankles.[26]

However, that escape by sea, for which Neruda had been so exquisitely fitted out, never took place. After drawing a plan of the wharf, Alvaro came to the conclusion that it would take 'a miracle even to get as far as the boat'. If Pablo was caught in Chilean waters he would immediately be handed over to the authorities. After having agreed with Neruda that the risks were too high, Alvaro returned to Santiago with his 'delicately explosive and precious cargo'.[27]

On 12 July 1948, to mark Neruda's forty-fourth birthday, Alvaro Jara took a risk and arranged a party at his Valparaíso hideout – a celebration he called the Fiesta de San Antonio, after Pablo's assumed name.

During his forty days in Valparaíso, Neruda wrote most, if not all, of 'El fugitivo' (The Fugitive) and 'El gran océano' (The Great Ocean) from *Canto general*:

Through the dead of night through my entire life
from tears to paper, from clothes to clothes,
I paced those trying days.
I was the fugitive from justice:
and in the crystal hour, in the fastness
of solitary stars,
I crossed cities, forests,
small farms, seaports,
from the door of one being to another
from the hand of one being to another being, and another . . .[28]

And he beautifully depicts his stay in hiding in Valparaíso:

> I went to the window: Valparaíso opened a thousand
> trembling eyelids, the nocturnal
> sea air entered my mouth,
> the lights from the hills, the tremor
> of the maritime moon on the water,
> darkness like a monarchy
> adorned with green diamonds,
> all the repose that life offered me.[29]

From his restricted hiding place, Neruda fell in love with the port.

> I love, Valparaíso, everything you enfold.
> and everything you irradiate, sea bride.
> even beyond your mute cloud.
> I love the violent light with which you turn
> to the sailor on the sea night,
> and then, orange-blossom rose,
> you're luminous and naked, fire and fog . . .
> Queen of all the world's coasts.
> [. . .]
> I declare my love to you, Valparaíso,
> and when you and I are free
> once more, I will live here at the crossroads
> of your throne of sea and wind
> and my wet philosopher's soil. We'll make freedom
> surge between the sea and the snow . . .[30]

And later, true to his word, Neruda would buy a house on the hill in Valparaíso, called La Sebastiana, with stunning views over the bay.

By the third week in July 1948, Pablo and the Ant were hiding in the Santiago apartment of Simón Perelman, on the Avenida Antonio Varas. Here Neruda completed 'Los conquistadores' (The Conquistadors) and began 'Los libertadores' (The Liberators) from *Canto general*, sitting under an old tree. As ever, Delia played a key role as critic and corrector of the poetry.

The couple had undergone another metamorphosis. To the children of Perelman and his wife, Elisa, Neruda was known as Uncle Pedro and Delia as Auntie Sarita. The children were, however, aware that something secret was going on, and respected this. One day, Elisa's sister paid a visit and wanted to go into the downstairs room where Pablo and Delia were hiding. One of the children, four-year-old Juan Carlos, insisted that his mother was upstairs and steadfastly refused to allow his aunt downstairs. This won Juan Carlos the nickname of 'El Pequeño Conspirador' (The Little Conspirator).[31]

On another occasion, Alvaro Jara brought a surprise visitor to Simón Perelman's house: Neruda's Buenos Aires publisher, Gonzalo Losada. Pablo made the adults in the household sit down while he read them the whole of *Canto general*, as it then existed. Since it already consisted of at least six parts – including *Alturas de Macchu Picchu* – the reading must have lasted at least four hours. Perelman told Robert Pring-Mill that Losada had brought a couple of bottles of whisky with him, knowing Pablo's fondness for this, and these had gradually been consumed as the reading wore on, with Perelman and Losada struggling to stay awake.

It was while he was writing 'Los libertadores' – between 27 July and 17 August 1948 – that Neruda gave a remarkable interview, providing written answers to a journalist from his hiding place. Remarkable, because there is not a trace of self-pity, or even the bitterness that infuses much of *Canto general*. In fact, Neruda refers only briefly to his own predicament. Most of his answers relate to the political and economic failings of the Chilean government, but intriguingly, he wrote: 'I will not agree to any other interview until next January [1949], because I want to keep my whereabouts in exile unknown for many, appreciable reasons – among others, the FBI operates throughout the Americas. And I also want to complete a vast literary work which I must hand over to my publishers in December of this year.' This is an obvious reference to *Canto general*, although in fact no such contract with a publishing house had been signed.[32]

He told the journalist: 'Every day, I have a profound sense that I am fulfilling a duty. I was a nocturnal writer who spent part of his existence clinging to the walls on empty nights. Now I am happy. We must walk down the middle of the street, meeting life head on.' This reference to the empty nights of drink with his friends reinforces the regret for valuable time lost to vacuous bohemianism, to which he had indirectly alluded in *Alturas de Macchu Picchu*.

From his hiding place, Neruda added: 'The apolitical writer is a myth created and given impulse by modern-day capitalism. This species simply did not exist in the times of [Dante] Alighieri.'

On 3 September 1948, President González Videla introduced the ludicrously misnamed Law for the Permanent Defence of Democracy. It soon came to be known to its enemies as the Accursed Law (*Ley Maldita*). Under the new legislation, not only was the Chilean Communist Party outlawed, but thousands of people were removed from the Chilean electoral roll, and thereby deprived of a fundamental right of citizenship. Nationwide, 26,650 people lost the right to vote, to participate in politics in any way or to belong to a trade union.

In his memoirs, in a section entitled 'My Historic Vindication', González Videla wrote: 'Among the great satisfactions destiny has brought me . . . is to see through my vision as a leader – to put a halt to Communism in our country . . . Without my inexorable personal intervention in 1947, Chile might have experienced then the bloodbath that Communism brought on through its insane pretension to confront the Armed Forces with its paramilitary brigades.'[33]

González Videla also claimed in his memoirs that he had known all along where Pablo was hiding, and could have detained him at any moment, 'but I did not want to give him the pleasure of being a hero'.[34] Everyone I have talked to in Chile finds this idea preposterous. They all maintain that, if the authorities had known Neruda's whereabouts, they would not have hesitated to arrest him.

Neruda himself, in his memoirs, said that the only person 'who always knew where I would eat or sleep each night was my young and radiant leader', the secretary-general of the Chilean Communist Party, Ricardo Fonseca.

With Neruda still in hiding, González Videla was at least right in saying that Chile was quickly becoming immersed in the Cold War, as both the Soviet Union and the United States attempted to intervene in its affairs. The Chilean Socialists turned definitively against the Communists and aligned themselves with the American Federation of Labor-Congress of Industrial Organisations (AFL-CIO). Some Socialists had even approved of the *Ley Maldita*, even though it had deprived thousands of miners of the vote.

Neruda spent most of September 1948 at Julio Vega's smallholding. In the middle of the month, Pablo approached his friend, Manuel Solimano, to ask whether he and Delia could stay at his house on 18 September. Solimano's home had already been raided by the police seeking Neruda, and was being watched. Solimano told him: 'Pablo, I'll welcome you with open arms, and for me it will be the very best 18 September I could possibly hope for, but I warn you that my house is being watched and has been raided.' Neruda replied: 'You can tell that you don't know Chile yet, even after so many years living here. No one looks for anybody in Chile on the 18th.' Solimano, an Italian, had forgotten that 18 September is a national holiday in Chile: it marks the country's independence from Spain in 1810. Solimano recollected: 'I called all Pablo's available friends. He made me spend a pile of money on noodles.'[35]

At the end of September or the beginning of October, Pablo and Delia returned to Julio Vega's smallholding, where Neruda completed 'Los verdugos' (The Executioners) for *Canto general*. The house contained a large, multi-volume encyclopaedia to which Neruda frequently referred in order to check geographical and botanical facts that he incorporated into *Canto general*. He also made full use of the standard two-volume history of Chile by Barros Arana.

Pablo and Delia may also have returned to Aída Figueroa and Sergio Insunza's apartment again – they did go back and forward to this flat several times over a two-month period – but Robert Pring-Mill believes they could have found refuge at the house of Tomás Lago, Pablo's friend from bohemian Santiago student days, since Pablo dedicated the draft of 'La arena traicionada' (Sand Betrayed), which he was writing at the time, to 'Tomás'.[36]

Neruda and Delia spent at least a month, from October to November 1948, in the holiday home of Francisco Cuevas Mackenna, former president of the National Mining Society, at Los Vilos, a village just beyond Isla Negra. Here, Neruda felt particularly restless. One day, Alvaro Jara received a telephone call from Pablo containing a coded message which was to be used only in the gravest of emergencies. Fearing the worst, Alvaro persuaded a friend to drive him to Los Vilos as fast as possible. They arrived to find the house in darkness. When Alvaro tapped gingerly on the window, the sleepy face of Delia peered out. It quickly became clear, to Alvaro's considerable annoyance, that Pablo had merely been feeling bored and craved company.[37]

On another occasion, Alvaro Jara was preparing to take a Communist Party friend to see Pablo at Los Vilos, but was suddenly alarmed to discover that the friend had eluded his minder and had made his own way to the house. Not only that – he had spirited Pablo and Delia away to Santiago for a merry evening. An enraged Jara tracked them down in the capital, and gave them 'exactly ten minutes' to get ready to move to a new house. It was moments like this which prompted Neruda later to refer to himself – only half in jest – as Alvaro Jara's 'former prisoner'.

The house to which they were whisked next was the home of Julita Mackenna (Francisco's sister) in San Juan de Pirque, where they may have spent November and December 1948. However, some sources claim that Pablo and Delia were taken straight to the small home of Lola Falcón in Santiago's Calle Ana Luisa Prats. Lola had recently returned to Chile with her son, Poli, from New York, where her husband Luis Enrique Délano was Chilean consul.

In the kitchen was an object which enchanted Neruda: a huge, US-made Philco refrigerator. He stopped in front of it and stared in amazement. He then examined it from all angles, and even tried to get at the back to look at the mechanism, but it was too close to the wall. Finally, he bowed down before the fridge and proclaimed it 'the White Elephant'. And from then on, every time he passed the fridge, he would emit a litany of praise.

On the radio, news bulletins repeated the latest details of the massive police search for Chile's greatest poet. It was an edgy time for Lola, still waiting for her husband to return from the United States, to be harbouring the fugitives on her own. Every day, people would arrive at the apartment: Communist leaders or Pablo's friends. Sometimes, she had to improvise meals for several visitors.

Pablo – despite the fact that he could be arrested at any moment – made not the slightest attempt to restrict his gastronomic obsessions: he insisted on some of his favourite dishes: *arroz a la valenciana* (Valencia-style rice), *angulas al pil pil* (eels in garlic), *tripes à la mode de Caen*, *cauques* (langoustines) or beef with béarnaise sauce. According to the Chilean writer and journalist José Miguel Varas, Pablo even suggested that Lola prepare an Indian curry.[38]

Christmas itself with Lola Falcón, however, was not extravagant. Pablo did not demand special seasonal foods although he did persuade his host to prepare peach with kirsch as a tasty dessert. But, Neruda did have a special request for Christmas Day. He wanted to see his friends. All of them. And there had to be a party with plenty of food and drink. Reluctantly, Alvaro Jara agreed. He chose the Santiago apartment of Sergio Insunza and Aída Figueroa. It was to prove the most delicate of operations, as Alvaro Jara recalled:

> I arrived with Pablo and Delia when it was already getting dark. To camouflage himself as if behind a trench, he had concocted an enormous bunch of flowers, which hid both his face and his corpulence. Protected by the huge flowerpot, we entered the building and went straight to the lift. Pablo was happy and trembling with laughter at his trick. Once we were safely inside, I asked [Aída] to lock the door and I stayed there on guard. I didn't let anyone leave the party before we did. I stuck firmly to this, despite a few protests – even though the guests had been warned that this was a condition of their invitation.[39]

Aída Figueroa still has fond memories of Pablo's Christmas party at her flat, into which Juvencio Valle, Rubén Azócar, Volodia Teitelboim, Diego Muñoz, Luis Enrique Délano, Carlos Vasallo and Manuel Solimano, among many others, smuggled themselves. After the Christmas Day party, Neruda and the Ant returned to Lola Falcón's house.

January 1949 was stiflingly hot. It was at around this time that Pablo also told Lola that a woman (he didn't name her) would be paying him a visit at the house while Delia was at the dentist, and he asked Lola to pass on a message. Lola refused outright and the woman visitor, whoever she was, was never mentioned again.

Poli Délano remembers Neruda's state of mind at this time as easy-going. 'He seemed pretty calm to me. He went around in shorts and shirt, and his only disguise was a heavy beard,' Poli told me. His mother, Lola, would not take any nonsense from Neruda during his stay. 'She was not at all complaisant with Pablo. Pablo needed his court, his followers. I remember that he once wanted to eat eels, and my mother told him: "We simply don't have the money."'[40]

A few days into the stay at Lola's, Pablo's friend Rubén Azócar arrived in a very agitated state to inform them that the police were looking for the poet nearby. At two o'clock in the morning, Alvaro Jara turned up with his wife, woke Neruda up and forced him to get dressed hurriedly (and ill-humouredly), and then tossed all his belongings back into his suitcase or into an improvised sack made from one of Delia's sheets. Delia returned to Víctor Pey's apartment for a while.

Pablo was taken to the apartment of Nana Bell, daughter of his friend Graciela Matte, on Providencia. Nana Bell had been receiving Neruda's typewritten versions of *Canto general* – passed on by Alvaro Jara via at least one intermediary (at some point, this 'cut-out' may have been Tomás Lago) – which she would type out again neatly; Alvaro would then show Neruda Nana's version and the poet would make new corrections. The corrections were sent back and forth to Nana until the poet was completely happy.

Those bravely helping Neruda at this time went through their own nightmares. Once, as Lola Falcón was returning to her apartment from Nana Bell's flat, she was alarmed to find that she was being followed by a thin man in glasses. Had she inadvertently revealed Pablo's whereabouts? Had the poet's luck finally run out? But her pursuer soon made his amorous intentions abundantly clear. Quickening her stride, she ran into two policemen, who managed to separate her from her assailant.

From January to February 1949, Pablo and the Ant returned to Julio Vega's smallholding for the third and last time. It was here that Alvaro Jara finally lost his patience with Pablo and withdrew his services as the poet's minder. Neruda had given Alvaro a shopping list of eighteen items to buy in Santiago – including cosmetics for Delia. However, Jara's car suffered a puncture on the journey, delaying him, so that he had managed to obtain only fifteen of the items on the list. When he returned to the smallholding and gave Neruda the news about the three missing objects, the poet angrily chided him, as if telling off an inefficient office boy. Alvaro, in turn, lost his temper and said he would no longer be responsible for the operation to hide Neruda from the police. It took a personal visit by Galo González, soon to become secretary-general of the Communist Party, to persuade Pablo to stop sulking, shake hands with Alvaro and make up.[41]

From this anecdote, a very different picture emerges of Neruda in hiding, far from the life-enhancing fugitive described by Sergio Insunza and Aída Figueroa. Of course, he had now been living underground for nearly a year, but it is hard to escape the feeling that the poet was beginning to behave like a self-indulgent child.

It was here, at Julio Vega's smallholding, nevertheless, that Pablo wrote the wonderful final section of *Canto general*, 'Yo soy' (I Am). In it, as Chile's security forces were combing the land in an increasingly ferocious attempt to arrest him, Neruda for the first time looked back in verse on his 44-year-old life, recalling the smells and the colours, the sensations and the friends he was missing.

> My childhood is wet shoes, broken trunks
> fallen in the forest, devoured by vines
> and beetles, sweet days upon the oats,
> and the golden beard of my father leaving
> for the majesty of the railways . . .
> To what lost archipelagoes
> did my father slip away with the land's
> dark daybreak, in his howling trains?
> Later I loved the smell of oak in smoke,
> oils, axles of frozen precision,
> and the solemn train crossing winter stretched
> over the earth, like a proud caterpillar.
> Suddenly the doors trembled.
> It's my father . . .
> Then I arrived in the capital, vaguely impregnated
> with mist and rain. What streets are those?
> The clothing of 1921 pullulated
> in an atrocious smell of gas, coffee and bricks.
> I circulated among students bewildered,
> concentrating the walls within me, seeking
> every evening in my poor poetry the branches,
> the raindrops and moon that had become lost . . .

Love and friendship prompted the first stirrings of maturity:

> O you, sweeter, more interminable
> than sweetness, carnal beloved
> amid the shadows . . .
> From the violent
> night, night like streaking
> wine, purple night
> I fell to you like a wounded tower,
> and between the poor sheets your star
> pulsed against me, burning the sky . . .
> I bit woman, plunged in fainting away
> from within my strength, I treasured clusters,

and set forth, walking from kiss to kiss,
tied to caresses, bound
to this grotto of cold hair,
to these legs ranged by lips:
hungering amid the earth's lips,
devouring with devoured lips . . .

There was the desolation of his years in the Far East and his escape from
protracted adolescence through the agonies and pleasures of Spain and
his true companion at this time, Delia. His desire to maintain ties with his
past does not prevent him from expunging others. Although he lovingly
depicts Delia, he does not even mention his first wife, Maruca.

You gave me firm love, Spain, with your gifts.
The tenderness that I waited for joined me
and the one who brings the deepest kiss
to my mouth accompanies me . . .
My sweet love,
struggling beside me, like a
vision, with all the signs
of the star . . .
your fine shade
cast over my pages, my bride . . .
I no longer recall when you begin:
you were before love . . .

His three years in Mexico brought him closer to the ancient roots of
the American continent, as well as his contemporary brothers – and
distasteful literary feuds. He recalls his return to Chile, and to the dry
north as senator:

I returned . . . Chile welcomed me with the yellow face
of the desert.
I wandered suffering
from an arid moon in a sandy crater
and encountered the planet's barren dominions,
unadorned light without tendrils, empty rectitude.
Empty? But without vegetation, without talons, without
manure the earth revealed its denuded dimension to me.[42]

He concludes this section, which was to be the final section of *Canto general*, with thoughts about death. Was he fearful of immediate arrest and murder by the authorities, as he sat writing in hiding at Julio Vega's smallholding? Or was he looking ahead, to a more natural end? He boldly calls a tiny segment 'I am going to live (1949)' and declares: 'I am not going to die. I am departing now / on this day full of volcanoes / for the multitudes, for life.' Did he write these lines after learning of the escape plan to bring him out of Chile to safety? Or is it a general declaration of defiance?

In the segment entitled 'Testament', Neruda says he will bequeath Isla Negra, his home by the Pacific,

> to the labour unions
> of copper, coal and nitrate.
> let them rest there, those abused children
> of my country

And there he wants to be buried. Whether or not he was preparing for his possible capture and death, or the chance that he could die during his attempted flight, he wanted to make it clear that:

> I write for the people, even though they cannot
> read my poetry with their rustic eyes.
> The moment will come in which a line, the air
> that stirred my life, will reach their ears,
> and then the farmer will raise his eyes,
> the miner will smile breaking stones,
> the brakeman will wipe his brow,
> the fisherman will see clearly the glow
> of a quivering fish that could burn his hands,
> the mechanic, clean, recently washed,
> smelling of soap, will see my poems
> and perhaps they will all say: 'He was a friend.'[43]

In February 1949, Pablo and Delia moved for the last time, to the apartment of Graciela Matte on Providencia. By now, the final arrangements for a remarkable, and extremely hazardous, attempt to smuggle Neruda across the Andes from Chile into Argentina were virtually complete. The main players were Víctor Pey and Jorge Bellet, a man whom Neruda refers to in his memoirs as 'a former aviation pilot, a mixture of practical man and explorer'. At that time Bellet ran a timber mill at Hueinahue in the south of Chile, near the border with Argentina.

Pey had realised Neruda could not go on hiding indefinitely.

> It was too dangerous for Neruda. I was a very good friend of Jorge Bellet. I asked Jorge how things were in the south, what the crossing points were like. He wasn't surprised by my question. I telephoned the secretary-general of the Communist Party, Ricardo Fonseca, and then told Jorge Bellet: 'I have two Communist comrades that you have to get out of the country.' We discussed the way to do it, and when the operation was ready, I phoned Fonseca to say that we were prepared.
>
> In his book, Volodia [Teitelboim] alters what happened. He said that the entire operation was conducted by the Communist Party. They *were* involved in the sense that they provided the car and contacts. But I arranged it and Bellet carried it out – with the full knowledge of the Communist Party, of course. It is not out of vanity that I say this. I had a night-time meeting in a car with Fonseca and Bellet to finalise the arrangements. Bellet was a very loyal, extraordinarily brave man. He returned to his sawmill.[44]

Here Jorge Bellet takes up the story. The absentee owner of the timber mill where he worked was a businessman called José Rodríguez Gutiérrez. Bellet saw the place as a good final hiding place for Neruda before the Andes crossing – Rodríguez was close to the government of President González Videla and so would not come under any suspicion.

One Tuesday, Bellet was telephoned and told that he should drive that night, at eleven, to the north-eastern corner of Santiago's Parque Forestal. He did so, and found another car in which sat the two Communist Party leaders, Ricardo Fonseca and Galo González.

> They informed me of their programme to take Pablo to Valdivia. In short, there would be fifteen or twenty men in a bus, all armed and ready to face any problem and hand over Pablo to me at Lake Ranco, in a little village called Futrono [at the foot of the Andes]. I told them that I didn't think that was a good plan, that it was a

mistake to move so many people around. I said I preferred a car in very good mechanical condition, carefully checked, with all kinds of spare parts in case of a breakdown and with a chauffeur-mechanic who was not informed of his mission until the last possible moment. I also asked for addresses of long-standing, solid [Communist] militants in the various towns which we would be forced to pass through, so that, if we did hit mechanical failure or other obstacles on the journey, I would have a place to hand Pablo over until I could pick him up again.[45]

'The Party then provided me with another contact: Manuel Solimano,' Pey told me. 'He was a car salesman with an office in the Alameda in Santiago.'

Manuel Solimano himself recalled a friend of Pablo's, Fernando Silva, coming to his house and telling him that Neruda had a chance to leave Chile, and needed a good car. 'I bought a 1946 Chevrolet, and I handed it over. He left, and the car reappeared two-and-a-half months later.'[46]

Solimano could never have imagined the extraordinary events which had occurred in those two-and-a-half months. 'There was a delay, because Bellet could not deal with matters on the days we'd arranged: there were terrible storms in the south,' Víctor Pey told me.

As the weeks passed and nothing happened, and we had heard nothing from Bellet, I drove out to find him. I didn't know where Neruda was hiding at the time. I headed southwards. I met Bellet at the Hotel Schuster in Valdivia. He told me that the roads were impassable because of the dreadful weather. I accompanied him down south to inspect the situation for myself. I returned to Santiago with Bellet, informed Fonseca that no one had let him down, but that the rains were too heavy, and we had to arrange a new date. So Solimano produced another car. The Party provided us with a chauffeur who was also a good car mechanic.[47]

At this point, there was very nearly a disaster. 'The chauffeur arrived and took me to a store to buy spare parts for the car in case there was a breakdown,' Pey recalled. 'People coming into the shop recognised the chauffeur. The chauffeur suddenly blurted out: "I need spare parts for the car because I'm going on a very important journey, a very risky journey!" I thought we were both going to be arrested on the spot. But nothing happened. We were very lucky.'[48]

Meanwhile, Jorge Bellet had gathered together his best cowhands and, without mentioning Neruda, discussed the possibility of crossing the Andes to San Martín de Los Andes in Argentina. Bellet claimed that the purpose was to explore the possibility of exploiting timber there. The cowhands rejected the idea: they said it would be too expensive and that San Martín de Los Andes was not a suitable place for exploiting timber. 'I insisted, and I proposed to go and explore the area. They told me that the route was tough but viable. We would have to use a path that cattle-rustlers used, crossing the cordillera from the Lilpela Pass on the west bank of Lake Lacar . . .' They had until the first half of March at the very latest to carry out the operation. 'It wasn't much time. We had to turn a poet into a horseman, and a horseman capable of crossing the Andes along a route used by smugglers.'[49]

At dusk in early February, Neruda kissed goodbye to Delia in Santiago and climbed, heavily bearded and wearing dark glasses, into a car driven by his friend, Dr Raúl Bulnes. Pablo Neruda was no more: his papers, which he had obtained from the Argentinian consul, named him as Antonio Ruiz Lagorreta, aged forty-five, born in Santiago, a bachelor, and an ornithologist by profession. Neruda loved this touch: he did know a great deal about birds (and would write a book called *Arte de pájaros* (The Art of Birds) in 1966).

On the outskirts of Santiago, Neruda/Ruiz changed cars and Jorge Bellet took over as chauffeur. They drove south through the night: the poet, the chauffeur and a comrade who would return the car to Santiago. Bellet recalled that he was kept from falling asleep at the wheel by Neruda's love of nature, down to the smallest detail: 'He knew the name of the insect which had just died on the windscreen; how and when the beautiful tree along the side of the road had arrived in Chile . . . This admirable Don Antonio knew everything, and he explained it all with infinite tenderness.'[50]

Bellet also remembered Neruda explaining to him on this journey how he had lost some of his usual joie de vivre during his time in hiding. But during this car trip, he seemed to come to life once more. At noon the next day, the car swept through Temuco, passing the street where he had spent his childhood. Neruda would have loved to stop, but it was far too dangerous. The police had already raided the houses of many of his relatives hunting for the poet.

Juan Carlos Reyes, Neruda's great-nephew – whose father was the son of Pablo's brother, Rodolfo – remembers one such raid:

When the soldiers came to raid our house on the corner, they tried to look over my father's bread shop. They wanted to check the top of the ovens. Well, up there, there was a thick layer of sand which was used to isolate the temperature of those old brick ovens – that was where we smoked our first cigarettes. The ovens were lit – as they were almost all year round – but the soldiers, as usual, did not think. They asked: 'Are these ovens big?' My father was trying hard not to burst out laughing. 'Right,' they said, 'we're going to take a look inside.' So my father gently took them down and opened up the stoves, which let out a blast of heat which I'm sure put them off their senseless search. They did check out our house later, but after finding nothing, they left.[51]

Neruda himself recalled how it felt to leave Temuco behind him, covered by a blanket in the back of the car:

We halted a fair distance from the city and sat down on a rock to have a bite to eat. There was a creek far down the slope, and the sound of its waters came up to me. It was my childhood saying goodbye. I grew up in this town. My poetry was born between the hill and the river, it took its voice from the rain, and like the river, it steeped itself in the forests. And now, on the road to freedom, I was pausing for a moment near Temuco and could hear the voice of the water that had taught me to sing.[52]

A few miles further on came the only tense moment of the journey south. A police officer flagged the car down, and asked if the chauffeur could drive him a few hundred miles along the road. Fortunately, the policeman sat in the front seat and did not take any notice of the blanketed bundle in the back.

Yet, after that, there were no further problems and the car arrived at its destination: a water-lapped timber estate shrouded by trees, near Lake Miahue. Neruda was introduced as the ornithologist, Antonio Ruiz, who was joining Bellet's administrative staff as an advisor in a pioneering enterprise to exploit wood in Chile. In reality, Pablo had to be prepared – and quickly – for a perilous journey on horseback. He had not been on a horse since his rides along the beach at Puerto Saavedra as a child.

Pablo was in enormously good spirits. But one Saturday, a few days later, Bellet found a telegram waiting for him at Valdivia which spelt trouble. It was from the owner of the estate, José (Pepe) Rodríguez Gutiérrez, announcing that he would be arriving to inspect affairs with his father and three friends. While it was useful that the estate was owned by a González Videla supporter from the point of view of not attracting the attention of the police, to have the man actually on the premises meant that Neruda would have to disappear. But where could he go?

Pablo and Bellet discussed the matter long and hard, and, despite Neruda's initial protests that it would mean violating the Party's demands for absolute secrecy, they came to an astonishing conclusion: 'After analysing [Pepe Rodríguez's] cultural background, and his human qualities, we decided that the best thing to do would be to tell him that Neruda was hiding on his estate. In the worst-case scenario, when Pepe Rodríguez left again, [Pablo] would still have four days before the police had time to reach [such a remote spot], even if he were immediately denounced.'[53]

It was a gamble. Neruda waited, with some anxiety, for the moment when he would have to reveal his identity to the owner, and tried to make himself comfortable in his makeshift room. As soon as the owner arrived at the estate, Bellet sat down and had lunch with him, before inviting him to inspect the sawmills. It was now or never: 'The poet Pablo Neruda is hiding on this estate,' he told Rodríguez, and then held his breath. Rodríguez was stunned at the news: 'Really? Where is he? Let's go and see him right away.' Bellet feared the worst.

We left and in less than two minutes, we reached Neruda's lodgings. I stopped, and at the sound of the engine, Neruda, now once more Neruda, came out into the doorway of the hut. Pepe Rodríguez approached him with his arms wide open and said: 'You are Pablo Neruda, a man whom I have always wanted to meet, a poet I admire so greatly, whom I have read so much.' We had crossed the first hurdle. And after that, everything was easy. They talked without stopping. Pepe recited poems by Neruda which he knew by heart, and Pablo took out some drafts and read some poems he had written recently. Without our noticing it, night drew quickly in. We separated at two in the morning.[54]

On the way back to the estate, Pepe Rodríguez told Bellet: 'This has been one of the most beautiful nights of my life. I've just met the greatest poet of this century. What do I care if he's a Communist! You did very well to hide him and I don't hold it against you that you didn't consult me before bringing him here. What a pity that I can't tell my father about this. Make sure that he is given everything he needs.'

The next day, owner and fugitive met again, and they were soon the best of friends. The day before Pepe Rodríguez was due to return to Santiago, he promised Neruda faithfully that the authorities would hear nothing about it: 'I give you my word of honour, Pablo, that however much I would love to tell people with pride that I have been at your side here in my estate, you can count on me: I am a capitalist, with all the defects of a capitalist, but I know how to be a friend to my friends – and I feel proud to have you as a friend.'

Indeed, in his memoirs, Neruda claimed that Rodríguez gathered his subordinates together around the poet and commanded them: 'If any obstacles come up within the next week to keep Señor Lagorreta from crossing into Argentina through the smugglers' pass, you will open another road so he can get to the border. Drop all work on the timber, and open that road. Those are my orders.'[55]

José Rodríguez died two years later, bankrupt and persecuted for allegedly leading a major smuggling operation.

There was one more serious hurdle before the Andes crossing could be attempted – a Mapuche Indian working at the sawmill had accidentally been shot. The Indian court in Valdivia had claimed compensation, and Bellet, as the man in charge, was indicted. A telegram informed him that he would have to meet the representative of the Indian court the following day. Bellet returned to the estate at Hueinahue downcast, and went straight to Neruda, afraid to announce that there might be a further delay in the escape plan, or even a cancellation.

Clearly, Pablo could read trouble in Bellet's face. 'Are you bringing me another Pepe Rodríguez?' the poet asked. 'Yes,' Bellet replied, and asked Neruda whether he knew the Indian court representative, a man named Víctor Bianchi Gundián. Pablo's face brightened: 'Of course I do. Not only do I know him, he's one of my closest friends. Víctor is a superb fellow, cheerful, cordial, open – a great friend.'[56]

The next day, 1 March 1949, Bellet and Neruda took the boat linking Lake Ranco and Llifen to meet Bianchi. Astonishingly, Víctor recognised the heavily bearded Neruda immediately but, since he had no idea whether Bellet knew who he was, he did not dare greet Pablo. It was yet another moment of French farce. Poor Bianchi went pale and silent. But Neruda shook him out of his confusion by embracing him warmly. Bellet had to do the same.

Not only was the Mapuche Indian case settled satisfactorily, Víctor Bianchi also joined the team conducting the escape operation across the Andes. He was a useful addition being an experienced explorer used to dangerous physical environments: he had been one of the few survivors, Neruda recollected in his memoirs, of a successful ascent of Chile's highest mountain, Aconcagua.

In his own illuminating diary, Víctor Bianchi wrote that he now subjected Neruda to an interrogation:

> How many hours was he capable of riding a horse? When was the last time he'd ridden a horse? Who had explored the pass? Who would our guides be? His replies were soul-destroying. No one knew anything, and as for the riding, the entomologist [sic, Neruda] had only the vaguest idea that they would need horses. On 2 March, I went out with my victim and forced him to get on a horse for three hours.[57]

Things were not going well. A storm on 5 March put the boat they were planning to use out of commission. Two days later, the whole jetty was washed away. Jorge Bellet had not yet returned from Valdivia as he had promised. And Neruda, wrote Bianchi, 'had given up riding the horse, preferring his whisky'.

Eventually, everything was in place. On 7 March, 1949, the day before he was due to make the crossing, Pablo arranged a party in the moonlight. The following day, they set out in the launch boat from the extreme west of the lake, where it joins the Curringue. There, they found the three loyal cowhands, to whom Neruda would always refer as Los Tres Juanes (The Three Juans – he was disguising their real names), with three horses. (Two of the cowhands are still alive. At a meeting in Futrono in 1999 to celebrate the fiftieth anniversary of the escape operation, one – 88-year-old Juvenal Flores, who still works as a cowhand despite his advanced age – confirmed that he had no idea who he was taking across the mountains; he had been told by Bellet only that their guest was an important timber-buyer, and that they must take great care of him on pain of their lives.)

In his diary, Bianchi wrote: 'Our poet-entomologist looked more like a bearded sack of potatoes in his saddle, and I suspect the horse had a similar opinion.'[58]

Their first major task was to cross the Curringue River. Neruda's horse was carrying precious cargo on its back: Latin America's most famous poet, a bottle of whisky and the typescript of *Canto general*, as heavily disguised as its author. It had a false cover, bearing an equally false title: *Risas y lágrimas* (Laughter and Tears) by Benigno Espinoza. Pablo also insisted on bringing his typewriter with him.

In this first phase of the lazardous journey, Neruda nearly died. He described the experience when he accepted the 1971 Nobel Prize:

> We had to cross a river. Those small streams born in the peaks of the Andes head down, discharging their dizzy, overpowering force, forming cascades and stirring up earth and rocks with the energy and the speed that they bring from those famous heights. But on this occasion, we found a pool, a great mirror of water, which could be forded. The horses splashed in, lost their foothold and began to swim towards the other bank. Soon my horse was almost completely covered by the water, I began to plunge up and down without support, my feet fighting desperately while the horse struggled to keep its head above water. Then we made it across. And as soon as we got to the other side, the peasants who were accompanying me asked with a smile: 'Were you very afraid?' 'Very. I thought that my last hour had come,' I said. 'We were behind you with our lassos at the ready,' they replied.[59]

On another occasion, Neruda's horse stumbled again and was badly hurt. As Bianchi noted in his diary, 'The wound unleashed the poet's compassion and a moment later, the forest bore witness to the most unexpected scene of tenderness in the midst of our escape. Pablo stroked the horse, smothering it with words of comfort and promising that he wouldn't ride it again for the rest of the journey.'[60]

Neruda was eventually persuaded to continue the journey but their way was soon blocked by giant trees brought down by strong winds. After much hacking away with machetes, they eventually found a way through and suddenly saw a burning light, a sure sign of human life. It was the Chihuio baths – pieces of adobe with roofs made from straw and mud and doors made from tree-trunks. It was not quite dusk when they arrived, so 'we splashed around happily, washing, cleansing ourselves of the heaviness of our long ride' in the thermal baths. 'We felt refreshed, born again, baptised.'[61]

Neruda/Ruiz, Bellet, Víctor Bianchi and the three Juans then sat around a fire and drank wine and dined on meat and cheese. And as Neruda began to talk about memories from his childhood, a group of strangers gathered around, listening with fascination, unaware of the identity of their famous narrator.

The following day, as Neruda had always anticipated, was the hardest part of the crossing: the so-called smugglers' route through the mountains. As they stood at the foot of the Andes, Pablo turned smiling to Bellet and asked him: 'What did you say this place was called?' 'The Lilpela Pass,' Bellet replied. And Neruda asked Bellet to engrave with a knife a verse on a tree trunk next to them. Neruda's verse – written in the popular *cuarteta* form, which contributed to the atmosphere and the humour – went:

> How good the air smells
> in the Lilpela Pass
> because the shit has not yet arrived
> from traitor González Videla's arse[62]

As the horses made their way gingerly through the Andes Neruda had a second brush with death.

> We went on, eventually entering a natural tunnel perhaps opened up in the impressive rocks, either by some powerful river that has since disappeared, or by a spasm of the earth that created this formation in the mountains, dug this canal in the hinterlands, excavated from the rock, the granite which we were now entering. A little further on, our horses began to slip when they tried to gain their footing in the rocky depressions, their legs buckled, sparks flew from their shoes. I was thrown from my horse and left sprawled out on the rocks more than once. My horse was bleeding from the nose and legs, but we stubbornly continued on our vast, magnificent, gruelling way.[63]

Suddenly, in a clearing, they came across a bull's skull. The cowhands dismounted and left a few coins in its eye-sockets. Then, in an unforgettable ceremony, they began a strange dance around the skull.

Soon afterwards they reached the Argentinian side.[64] They had made it. But difficulties remained. Manuel Solimano was told later that, after crossing the border into Argentina, when Pablo and his fellow adventurers tried to check into a hotel at Llau Llau posing as lumbermen, the owner took one look at them and said they couldn't stay. After four days on horseback, they were filthy, ill-shaven and they stank. Fortunately, the local police chief was a friend of Chile and persuaded the hotel-owner to relent. The policeman later lamented that he had not recognised Pablo Neruda at the time: 'I'm a great admirer, and I would have loved him to sign some books for me.'[65]

The organisational problems continued, however. As Víctor Pey recalled, 'The Argentinian Communist Party had arranged to meet Neruda on the other side and drive him to Buenos Aires. Bellet was supposed to meet an Argentinian representative who was intended to oversee the handover. But although Bellet turned up at the hotel, the Argentinian didn't.'[66] In the end, the Argentinian contact, Benito Marianetti, a Communist deputy from Mendoza, did find Bellet. He had been waiting at a different hotel all along.

To celebrate the successful outcome of an outrageously daring escape, Neruda and his group enjoyed a feast at the inn in San Martín de Los Andes. It was a joyous occasion, full of flowing wine and food and chat – and, even though he could never recite his own verse by heart, Neruda came out with another of his impromptu poems, this time a ballad – taking liberties with mischievously misplaced emphasis to fit the rhyme and rhythm at the end of each line – which delighted his companions.

Pablo Neruda had escaped the clutches of the Chilean police. The next the world knew of him was when he surfaced a few weeks later, in public for the first time in a year, at the World Peace Congress in Paris, introduced by Pablo Picasso.

Delia and Matilde – an Eastern European juggling act

1949–52

If Neruda thought that he was safe in Buenos Aires, after his escape across the Andes, he was much mistaken. The Chilean authorities – who still had no idea where the poet was – had nonetheless already alerted the Argentinian police to arrest him in case he did manage to negotiate the frontier. So Pablo had to remain in hiding.

Then a huge slice of luck came his way. His old friend, the Guatemalan novelist Miguel Angel Asturias, happened to be in Buenos Aires at the time. He had been appointed cultural attaché at the Guatemalan Embassy in 1947 and was then given a ministerial position there. The two men were fairly alike physically. As Neruda recalled in his memoirs, 'By common consent, we had classed ourselves as *chompipe* – an Indian word for "turkey" in Guatemala and parts of Mexico. Long-nosed, with plenty to spare in face and body, we shared a resemblance to the succulent bird.'[1]

Asturias came to visit Neruda in his Buenos Aires hideout and Pablo asked to borrow his friend's passport: 'Allow me the pleasure of arriving in Europe as Miguel Angel Asturias.' Asturias did not hesitate, and a few days later, Neruda crossed the River Plate into Uruguay as 'Miguel Angel Asturias'. The authorities never suspected a thing.

Neruda realised that he could never do the same with the French authorities. He would have to revert to being Pablo Neruda and this would lead to difficulties since, as an internationally renowned Communist, at the height of the Cold War, he was *persona non grata* in many countries.

Then an unlikely saviour stepped in: the painter Pablo Picasso. Just a few months earlier, Picasso had made a bold decision: he had chosen to dedicate his first and only public speech, at the first World Congress of Intellectuals for Peace held in Wroclaw, Poland, in July 1948, to an impassioned appeal in defence of the fugitive poet, Pablo Neruda. 'I have a friend who should be here with us, a friend who is one of the best men I have ever met,' Picasso had said. 'He is not only the greatest poet in his country, Chile, but also the greatest poet in the Spanish language and one of the greatest poets in the world. Pablo Neruda.' Picasso had probably first met Neruda at or around the time that Neruda delivered his famous tribute to Lorca in Paris on 21 January 1937.

Picasso personally dealt with all the bureaucratic hassle in Paris as soon as Neruda checked in at the George V Hotel in Paris. 'He spoke to the authorities, he called up a good many people. I don't know how many marvellous paintings he failed to paint on account of me. I felt very badly that he was losing time that was so precious to him.'[2]

A similar conference, the first World Congress of Peace Forces, was taking place in Paris when Neruda arrived, at which scientists and artists were joined together in the name of peace: Frédéric Joliot-Curie, one of the fathers of modern nuclear science, mingled with Picasso, Paul Eluard and Louis Aragon. The black American Communist, Paul Robeson, whose records Neruda had listened to in Rangoon with his lover, Josie Bliss, gave a speech and sang to the assembled delegates on 20 April 1949. But it was at the concluding session, on 25 April, that Pablo Neruda was presented to a stunned audience at the Salle Pleyel. Most had believed him to be dead. He gave a brief speech apologising for 'my slight delay in arriving at the meeting' which, he said, was due to 'a number of difficulties I had to overcome'. Neruda warned of the threat of a new war and pledged to place his poetry in the service of peace. Then he read his poem 'Un canto a Bolívar' (A Song to Bolívar) to huge applause and hugs from delegates.

The following day, asked by an interviewer from the French news agency, Agence France-Presse, what he should write to counter the Chilean government's furious denials that Neruda had escaped their clutches and was safely in Paris, the poet replied, paraphrasing Mark

Twain's famous comment about Shakespeare: 'Say that I am not Pablo Neruda, but another Chilean who writes poetry, fights for freedom and is also called Pablo Neruda.'[3]

Despite the efforts of Picasso and Neruda's two great French Communist poet friends, Paul Eluard and Louis Aragon, Pablo had to remain in hiding in Paris. He could not be sure that his safety was guaranteed. Indeed, he later claimed to have discovered that there was a file on him at the Quai d'Orsay containing ludicrous allegations.

So, just as in Chile, so in Paris, Neruda found himself being moved secretly from house to house. One of these was an apartment next to the French writer, Colette. This contained a huge Picasso painting, from his pre-Cubist period, featuring a long loaf of bread on a table. One day, Picasso himself came to visit and Neruda led him over to the painting:

> He had forgotten it completely. He started going over it very earnestly, sinking into an extraordinary and rather sad absorption very seldom seen in him. He spent more than ten minutes in silence, stepping up close to the forgotten work and then back. 'I like it more all the time,' I said to him when he ended his contemplation. 'I'm going to suggest that my country's national museum buy it.' . . . Picasso turned his head towards the painting once more, his eyes piercing . . . 'It's not bad at all'.[4]

Ilya Ehrenburg was living in Paris, and Neruda wanted to meet him finally. It was easy, he was told: the Russian writer took a late lunch at the famous restaurant and literary haunt, La Coupole, every day.

'I'm Pablo Neruda, the poet, from Chile,' said Neruda, sitting down at Ehrenburg's table. 'According to the police, we're close friends. They claim that I live in the same building as you. Since they're going to throw me out of France because of you, I wish to meet you, at least, and shake hands.' Ehrenburg looked out from under his thick, untidy hair and replied: 'I also wanted to meet you, Neruda. I like your poetry. But for starters, try some of this *choucroute à l'Alsacienne*.'[5]

Neruda later said he believed Ehrenburg began translating his hymn to Spain, *España en el corazón*, into Russian that very same day. 'I must admit that the French police unintentionally provided me with one of the most gratifying friendships I have ever had, and also presented me with the most eminent of my Russian translators.'[6]

Ehrenburg was prepared to criticise Neruda's poetry to his face. 'You have too many roots in your poems. Too many roots!' the Russian frequently protested, with a smile. Neruda conceded this point: 'It's true. The frontier regions sank their roots into my poetry and these roots have never been able to wrench themselves out. My life is one long pilgrimage that is always turning on itself, always returning to the woods in the south, to the forest lost to me.'[7]

Shortly after this first encounter with Ehrenburg, Neruda was called in to see the chief of police, who gave him bad news: 'I've received a request from the Chilean Ambassador to take away your passport. The Ambassador claims that you are using a diplomatic passport and that would be illegal. Is this information correct?' Neruda replied that he did not have a diplomatic passport. He had an official one, as a Chilean senator, but since it was private property, no one had the right to remove it from him. The chief of police, who was an admirer of Neruda's poetry, examined the passport, picked up a telephone and told the Chilean Ambassador that he refused to take away the poet's papers. Hanging up the telephone, he turned to Pablo and told him: 'You can stay in France as long as you wish.' Yet again, Neruda had found a surprising friend. His poetry seemed to disarm even those who might normally be considered his political or personal enemies.

From this moment, Neruda was able to emerge into the open in France. Picasso invited him to visit Villauris, the little village on the French Riviera where he spent much of his time. There, the two Pablos became firm friends. They shared the same political views and the same childish sense of mischief. At one dinner in Villauris, they were growing increasingly annoyed by the frequent interruptions by auto-graph-hunters. So Neruda suggested to Picasso that they swap signatures. This they did – and nobody noticed. On another occasion, the two men were sitting alone in a restaurant. At the precise moment when the waiter was bringing them a chicken, a photographer emerged out of nowhere, snapped a picture, and disappeared as quickly as he had arrived. Picasso stood up, indignant, but Neruda calmed him, saying: 'Sit down, he only wanted to photograph the chicken!'[8]

In June 1949, Neruda accepted an invitation to visit the Soviet Union for the first time. It was trip made long after most of his other Communist friends had travelled to witness the results of the Bol-shevik Revolution. That month, the commemorations began in the

USSR for the 150th anniversary of the birth of one of their greatest literary figures, the poet Alexander Pushkin, whom Neruda admired immensely. Neruda arrived in Leningrad on 8 June, and there he visited the Winter Palace and the seventeen-room National Pushkin Museum inside.[9]

While in Moscow, Neruda is said by some sources to have met Stalin himself. According to these accounts, Stalin presented him with a magnificent astrakhan coat lined in red silk for Delia, and Neruda gave Stalin one of his books. Neruda was curiously unforthcoming in his memoirs (and to his friends) about this encounter – perhaps because it never took place. The closest Neruda claims he came was hearing the news relayed over the telephone, the year before he actually won the Stalin Peace Prize, that Stalin had been shown a list of that year's candidates and had said: 'And why isn't Neruda's name among them?' Certainly, one of Neruda's closest Russian friends, his translator Vera Kuteishikova – a critic who, a month earlier, had written one of the very first studies of Neruda's poetry, *Pablo Neruda's Fate* – vigorously denied that the poet had ever met Stalin when I raised this with her in Moscow.[10]

Neruda was thrilled to be able to stand in the white house at Mikhailovskoye where Pushkin wrote *Boris Godunov*, and look out on the same scene that Pushkin would have seen: 'the green valley, criss-crossed by quiet rivers'. He was delighted to find that many of Pushkin's favourite books were also his own. He visited the 'beautiful city of Leningrad, with the majestic memory of the empire of Peter the Great floating by the slow river along Nevski Prospect, street of old dreams, a place of pathos and sleepwalking, straight out of the pages of the old Russian novels'.[11]

Vera Kuteishikova recalled the atmosphere of expectation in Moscow at the time.

> The truth was that, at that moment, we were more up to date with the extraordinary vicissitudes in Pablo's life than with his marvellous poetry, which was still barely known in our country . . . I will never forget that day, that wait at the airport. Among the people who came down the steps was Pablo, a corpulent man of forty or so years . . . Meanwhile, the solemn ceremony had begun at the Bolshoi Theatre [in Moscow] and we were still at the airport, carrying out the strict formalities. On top of that, we still had to

pass by the hotel. As you would expect, we arrived late and they led us on to the stage through the wings. We saw Paul Robeson sitting on the podium. In a break in the proceedings, Pablo and Paul would have their first hug – at last![12]

Another of Neruda's great Russian friends was Lev Ospovat, who first met Neruda at the huge event held in the Chilean's honour on 27 June 1949, in the Great Hall of the Moscow Conservatory.

All Moscow's media representatives were there, as well as cultural personalities and simple readers . . . And what was he like? On that first occasion, I saw a tall, solidly built man who seemed immobile – remember that Ehrenburg compared him to Buddha – who sat there with half-closed eyes and gave the impression that he was dozing off. I remember that it was Fadeyev who opened the ceremony and that Ehrenburg declared: 'There are many lines of poetry in this world and few poets – if you'll forgive me that truism.' In fact, I often saw Ilya Ehrenburg and Neruda together later on. I knew full well that Ehrenburg, far from being sentimental, was a sarcastic man, with a stiletto for a tongue. But Pablo was one of the few people by whom he was genuinely moved and for him he felt real admiration.[13]

On the matter of Russian poets persecuted in that very year under Stalin, Neruda was entirely silent. A year after this visit, in a speech in Guatemala City in 1950, Neruda referred obliquely to what he called a 'rumour' that 'in the Soviet Union, writers and musicians and scientists must shape their creations to the demands of a few leaders. This is one more calumny of international reaction.'[14]

No doubt Neruda hoped that this was so. What is more surprising is that, even twenty-five years later, he made no mention, in his post-humously published memoirs, of the fact that the regime was oppressing his fellow writers in 1949. What he said was this:

In Moscow, writers live in constant ferment, a continual exchange of ideas. There, long before the scandal-mongering West discovered it, I learned that Pasternak and Mayakovsky were the best Soviet poets, Mayakovsky was the public poet, with a thundering voice and a countenance like bronze . . . Pasternak was a great poet of evening shadows, of metaphysical inwardness, and politically an honest reactionary who, in the transformation of his country, saw no further than an enlightened deacon. Yet the severest critics of his static political views often recited Pasternak's poems to me by heart.[15]

However, Vera Kuteishikova informs me that, during that first visit to Russia in 1949, 'Neruda was told by many people that Pasternak was a reactionary, and, since Neruda was still an innocent and Pasternak was no more than a name to him at the time, he believed them.'[16]

Artistically, Neruda maintained his independence from the Socialist realism espoused by Andrei Zhdanov who, at the first Soviet Writers' Congress in 1934, had called on writers to 'counter the vestiges of bourgeois influence on the proletariat'. Neruda felt uncomfortable with literary schools or dogmas. Nevertheless, in stark contrast to André Gide, who as long as thirteen years earlier, had already discerned serious defects in the Soviet system during his visit and whose criticisms had cast such a heavy pall over the Valencia writers' congress in 1937, Neruda saw nothing but positive aspects. Indeed, as Vera Kuteishikova noted, from his very first encounter, 'Neruda always showed an intense desire to seek an echo in Russia of his Chilean experiences. The rain during our visit to Mikhailovskoye reminded him of the rain in Chile. The landscape, likewise.'[17]

Meanwhile, back in Chile, Delia – who had been hiding in the Santiago apartment of Víctor Pey's mother – was finally preparing to leave to join her husband in Europe. She and Neruda had been apart for six silent, anxious months which had taken their toll on her.

As Tomás Lago recalled later: 'Since Pablo left, her situation had been a hell, hidden in various houses of people she hardly knew, with the immediate fear of stirring up a fuss there . . . That was no life for a person who was as attached to her partner as she was, at the critical age she found herself.'[18]

She rejoined Pablo in Poland in July 1949. Neruda had been there since the beginning of that month. On his forty-fifth birthday, 12 July, he visited the coal mines at Katowice and went underground to see for himself the conditions under which 350,000 miners worked. He also visited other Polish cities and admired the rebuilding of Warsaw from the ashes of the Nazi bombardment. An indefatigably dynamic Polish publisher, Jerzy Boreszja, took Neruda to the lake region around the Baltic.

From Poland, after their reunion, Pablo and Delia travelled to Hungary on 23 July 1949. It so happened that at precisely this time, Hungarian translators were working on an anthology of Neruda's work, and when they asked him which poems he wanted to include, he decided to turn his back on the melancholy of *Residencia*. He had become an outward-looking messenger of the joys of life, speaking to the ordinary people. So strongly did he feel about this that he would not allow anyone to publish *Residencia* for long afterwards. As he explained in an interview published years later, 'The tone of that book was deliberately gloomy, though it came from a hopelessness which was quite real . . . But joy doesn't kill anybody . . .'[19]

Neruda, who had suffered so much persecution at the hands of the so-called free world, naturally wanted to believe that Soviet Russia was a human triumph. And he also shared the official Soviet view of the poet's responsibilities. At a poets' gathering in Budapest, the case of Boris Pasternak came up. Some present condemned him for not taking a more active role politically. One of the poets protested: 'Don't attack Pasternak; he's a good poet.' Neruda's position was clear. It was no longer sufficient for a poet to produce beautiful verse: he or she had to take a concrete political position.

> How long is the list of our matryrs, our bitter Poes, Verlaines, Daríos, not to mention the more recent deaths of the murdered García Lorca and Miguel Hernández? Today, a new world is being built, and in this new world of man, the poet is at the centre of his homeland, at the foot of the flag, at the centre of the harvests watching and singing, fighting and defending, assuming, for the first time in history, the true role of poetry.[20]

As they moved on to Romania, Delia, now aged sixty-five, and more aware than ever of the twenty-year gap between Pablo and herself, dived headlong into a treatment of mud baths and vitamins offered by Dr Ana Aslan, the founder and scientific director of the State Institute for Geriatric Research and Medicine in Bucharest. Dr Aslan, who dedicated her life to the research of decaying cells, claimed to have discovered a method that slowed down the ageing process, which she called Aslan Original Therapy. She alleged that among those who had benefited were Charlie Chaplin, Salvador Dalí, Marlene Dietrich, Pablo Picasso and John F. Kennedy.

From Budapest, Pablo and Delia travelled to Prague on 16 August 1949, before returning to Paris for a few days. Tragic news reached them from Chile: police had shot dead seven student demonstrators in Santiago. President Gabriel González Videla continued to accuse the Communists of trying to overthrow his regime, even though the Party was banned and many of its leaders were detained at Pisagua concentration camp.

In August, Neruda and Delia left Europe for Latin America, heading across the ocean to Mexico, where Pablo had been invited to represent the newly formed World Peace Council at the American Peace Congress in September. He and Delia were joined on the boat by the recently widowed Paul Eluard and his new companion, Dominique, and the French writer and philosopher Roger Garaudy.

They arrived in Mexico City on 28 August. Neruda was delighted to be back in the country where he had served for three years as Chilean consul, although the Mexican authorities had let him down in hiding. A week later, the 1949 congress was opened by the Mexican poet and physician, Enrique González Martínez. It was a remarkable gathering. Chaplin had sent a public statement in support both of the Paris meeting of the World Congress of Peace Forces and the Mexico congress. Neruda was widely fêted in Mexico City and made new friends, including the Venezuelan journalist Miguel Otero Silva, and the Cuban writer Juan Marinello.

In his closing address – which many of those present considered the high point of the Mexico City congress, such was his reputation as both a poet and a refugee from fascist oppression – Neruda stressed that the writer could not afford to remain passive in the face of war. He denounced the 'servile' Chilean tyrant, Gabriel González Videla, who was at the beck and call, he said, of North American mining interests.

> If I could have returned to my country, I would have brought other stories with me, other experiences, different truths. I would have carried with me the truth of Pushkin: Pushkin's song, his banner, that of an old poet, his people's main poet, which another nation would have forgotten but which the Soviet Union, far from forgetting, has raised over its vast land . . .

Neruda's father, José del Carmen, in Temuco.

Neruda's mother, Rosa Neftalí Basoalto Opazo, who died two months after giving birth to him.

The beach at Puerto Saavedra where Neruda played as a child.

Neruda at the age of two at the Fundo Belén in Parral, belonging to one of his uncles, before the family moved to Temuco.

Neruda (*far right*) during a visit to
Temuco, with (*left to right*): his
father, José del Carmen; Neruda's
half-sister, Laurita; his brother,
Rodolfo, and his stepmother,
Trinidad (Mamadre).

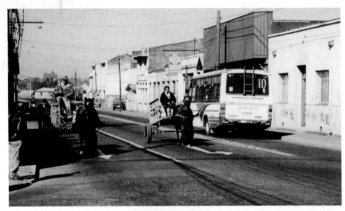

Temuco today.

Laurita and Neruda
in Temuco.

Sketch of Laura Arrué (Milala), 1925, one of Neruda's Santiago girlfriends from his student days, by an unknown artist, with an inscription by Neruda, and included in Laura's diary.

Neruda in his black cape as a student in Santiago in the 1920s.

Neruda as a student in Santiago in the 1920s.

Alberto Rojas Giménez, the poet who introduced Neruda to the bohemian student life in Santiago.

Alvaro Hinojosa and Neruda (*right*), pictured in 1927 shortly before leaving Chile on their long boat journey to Rangoon.

Neruda (*right*) with his friend, Tomás Lago, in Santiago in 1927 before Neruda's departure for the Far East.

Neruda in Ceylon, 1929.

Letter from Neruda to Héctor Eandi, 25 October 1927, in which he thanks Eandi for a review the Argentinian had written of the *Twenty Love Poems*, which 'effortlessly delved in great depth into the anxieties I experienced [in writing] that book – something I will never forget'.

One of Neruda's first loves,
Albertina Rosa Azócar.

Official announcement of
the wedding.

Neruda and his first wife, María Antonieta
Hagenaar (Maruca), pictured on their wedding
day in Batavia, 1930.

The Chilean writer, María Luisa Bombal,
who stayed with Neruda and Maruca in
Buenos Aires in 1933.

The Spanish poet, Miguel Hernández, one of
Neruda's closest friends around the time of
the Spanish Civil War. He died in prison in
1942.

Neruda with his friend, the Spanish poet,
Federico García Lorca (*left*), in Madrid, 1934.

Some of the two thousand
Spanish Republican
refugees rescued by Neruda
on the fishing-boat the
Winnipeg pay an on-board
tribute to Chile's President
Pedro Aguirre Cerda in
1939.

Neruda with Delia del Carril.

Death notices of Neruda's
daughter with Maruca,
Malva Marina Reyes,
1943, aged eight.

Neruda at Machu
Picchu, 1943.

Neruda pictured during his
visit to Colombia in 1943,
dancing on one leg with
Raquel Tapia Caballero, wife
of the Chilean poet, Juan
Guzmán Cruchaga.

Neruda's official accreditation as a Chilean
senator from 1945.

Víctor Pey, Santiago, 2000. One of the
Spanish refugees rescued by Neruda and
shipped to Chile aboard the *Winnipeg* in
1939, Pey returned the favour by hiding
Neruda and Delia at his Santiago
apartment in 1948.

Aída Figueroa and Sergio Insunza, in front of one of
Delia del Carril's horse paintings, Santiago, 2000.
The couple hid Neruda and Delia at their apartment
in central Santiago in 1948.

The first draft of 'Los libertadores', a section
from *Canto general* which Neruda typed
while in hiding in 1948. It shows Delia del
Carril's comments – including her criticism
of the repeated use of the word '*raíces*'
(roots) – on the right-hand side.

Este es el árbol de los libres.
El árbol tierra, el árbol nube,
el árbol pan, el árbol flecha,
el árbol puño, el árbol fuego.
Lo ahoga el agua tormentosa
de nuestra época nocturna,
pero su balancea
balancea su poderío,
otras veces de nuevo caen
las ramas rotas por la cólera
y la ceniza amenazante
cubre su antigua majestad;
así pasó desde otros tiempos,
así salió de la agonía,
hasta que una mano secreta,
unos brazos innumerables,
el pueblo, guardaba raíces,
escondía troncos inmensos,
y sus labios eran las hojas
del inmenso árbol sumergido
derramado por todas partes,
caminando con sus raíces.

Este es el árbol, el árbol
del pueblo, de todos los pueblos,
de la libertad, de la lucha,
asómate a su cabellera,
toca sus rayos renovados,
hunde la mano en las usinas
donde su fruto palpitante
su luz propaga cada día,
levanta esta tierra en tus manos
participa de este esplendor,
toma tu pan y tu manzana,
tu corazón y tu caballo
y monta guardia en la frontera
en el límite de sus hojas,
defiende el fin de sus
comparte las noches hostiles,
vigila el ciclo de la aurora,
la altura estrellada,
y el árbol, el árbol
que crece en medio de la tierra.

Neruda's false identity paper naming him as
Antonio Ruiz Lagorreta during his year in
hiding, 1948-49.

A heavily bearded Neruda on horseback during
his daring escape across the Andes, March 1949.

An extract from Víctor Bianchi's diary of the escape across the Andes, including a drawing of
himself and Neruda pacing up and down in exasperation at the delays to the crossing.

Neruda with the Chilean poet, Nicanor Parra, during a poetry recital in Chile, 1950s.

Neruda receives the applause of his Turkish friend, the poet Nazim Hikmet (*right*), 1950s.

Picasso embraces Neruda, Warsaw, 1950.

Neruda (*second from left*) with his Chilean friends (*left to right*) Rubén Azócar, Homero Arce and Orlando Oyarzún, pictured at Michoacán, Santiago, in the 1950s.

Neruda with the Chilean poet Gabriela Mistral – the first Latin American to win the Nobel Prize for Literature – in the 1950s.

Neruda during one of his many visits
to the Soviet Union.

Neruda and his friend, the French poet,
Paul Eluard, in Budapest, 1949.

Neruda with his Russian friend
and translator, Ilya Ehrenburg
(*right*), during their visit to
China in 1951.

David Alfaro
Siqueiros, Diego
Rivera and Pablo
Neruda signing
the first copy of
the Mexican
edition of *Canto
general* in Mexico
City, 1950.

Neruda with Matilde Urrutia, later to become his third wife, with their dog, Nyon, on Capri.

The cover of the first, anonymous edition of *Los versos del capitán*, printed in Naples, 1952.

La Sebastiana, Neruda's house in Valparaíso.

Neruda with the Chilean poet and journalist, Sara Vial, at her house in Valparaíso, 1958.

Neruda signing autographs during his first visit to Venezuela, 1959.

Neruda at the time he received an honorary doctorate from Oxford University, 1965.

Neruda with Matilde.

Neruda with the American writer, Arthur Miller, in a New York bookshop during the visit Neruda made to attend the PEN Club meeting, 1966.

Neruda as Chilean Presidential candidate, 1970

Neruda reading his poetry in Valparaíso, 1971, his last recital before leaving Chile to take up his post as Ambassador in Paris.

Neruda enjoying a joke at Isla Negra with Salvador Allende (*left*) and Volodia Teitelboim.

Neruda on the presidential campaign trail, 1970.

The Moneda presidential palace in Santiago engulfed in flames after the military coup on 11 September 1973.

Neruda receiving the Nobel Prize for Literature from the King of Sweden in Stockholm, 1971.

The beach at Isla Negra.

He proceeded to provide his own vision of the role of poetry, which he said had 'grown up' along with him:

A short whole ago, after travelling around the Soviet Union and Poland, I signed a contract in Budapest for the publication in Hungarian of all my poems. After I'd signed the contract, at a meeting of translators and publishers, I was asked to indicate, page by page, what I wanted included in that book. . . . After so many years of not reading my old poems, I ran my eyes over those pages in which I had put so much effort and care, in front of those translators waiting for orders to start their work, I suddenly saw that they were useless, that they had aged, that they bore the wrinkles of bitterness of a dead era. And I rejected them. I didn't want old pains to dishearten new lives . . . So I didn't allow a single one of those poems to be published in the people's democracies. And even today, as I return to the Americas, I confess that I do not want those old songs to be reprinted here . . . Why should the mark we leave on this earth be like the mark left on wet clay by the desperation of the hanged man?

He said that it was very easy to fall into the trap of drinking from the 'bitter brew', a mixture of all poisons. And it was not only his early poetry that he now rejected:

When Fadeyev declared in his speech in Wroclaw that, if hyenas used a pen or a typewriter they would write like T.S. Eliot or the novelist Sartre, I think that was an insult to the animal kingdom. I do not believe that creatures endowed with intelligence and the power of expression would make such an obscene religion out of annihilation and repugnant vice, as those two so-called 'masters' of Western culture have done.[21]

In his Mexico City speech, Neruda also initiated an unsavoury spat with a Mexican writer, José Revueltas (brother of Silvestre), who had recently published a novel, Los días terrenales (Earthly Days). Neruda said that Revueltas had cruelly disappointed him, partly because of the novel's apparent anti-Communist stance but mainly because Revueltas had renounced his membership of the Mexican Communist Party after thirteen years over what he saw as the Party's dogmatism.

Revueltas, according to his daughter, Andrea, was left emotionally paralysed by such a public attack on him by Neruda, whom he had considered an 'elder brother' and whenever he heard the Chilean's name mentioned, 'all he could do was to let out a pained groan'. The two men never met again, though they were reconciled at a distance when Revueltas was arrested after the massacre of Mexican students at Tlateloco in 1968 and Neruda wrote a very moving letter to Mexico's then-President, Gustavo Díaz Ordaz, assuring him of Revueltas's innocence and calling for his release 'because he has the genius of the Revueltas [family] and because we love him greatly'. Profoundly touched, Revueltas dedicated his book, *Al apando*, to Neruda and, after Neruda's death, he told an audience: 'We weep for you, Pablo Neruda, and we beg you – don't rest in peace!'[22]

Neruda pointed out to his Mexican audience in 1949 that there was one very important absentee: the mural painter, José Clemente Orozco, who had died three days earlier and whose funeral Neruda had just attended. Pablo himself was ill with the phlebitis that, a few days later, was to force him to be confined in bed with his leg in plaster. Nor did he yet know that his bedridden state was soon to bring a new love into his life.

Not that anything could stop him working. When he was asked to write a prologue to a Mexican book called *González Videla, the Laval of Latin America*, he leapt at the chance to renew his assault on 'this ridiculous *pelele* (puppet), this tiny bloody *cacique* (tyrant) . . .'

In a letter to Laurita from Mexico City on 13 October 1949, Delia wrote:

> Our life has been so constantly busy, and not even being forced to stay in bed with a fever has stopped your brother working and organising things with tremendous success. His performance at the Peace Congress was a sensation and it is very touching just how immense is the affection and respect people hold for him throughout the world. Here, they have looked after him very tenderly, and the house has been one big party, almost twenty-four hours a day. They even send an emissary from the presidential palace every day to ask after his health. Today I think he is finally making a firm recovery. For the first time in a month and a half, last night, we were able to sleep normally with only the obligatory interruption every four hours for him to take the sulphanilamides . . . It seems that all Pablo's problems come from his tonsils. We'll see.[23]

As Delia said in her letter, Neruda's apartment on Mexico City's Reforma had indeed become a magnet for friends. On 18 September (Chile's national holiday), 300 guests came to the apartment, small as it was, in spite of the fact that Pablo himself was still confined to bed.

Neruda and Delia were soon joined by another compatriot: the Chilean painter and sculptor, Nemesio Antúnez, who arrived from New York with his wife, Inés Figueroa, and their one-year-old son, Pablo. Antúnez had, however, found himself in trouble in Mexico: he could not renew his visa. 'Come and stay here with us,' Pablo said. At which Delia exclaimed 'But Pablo, where's he going to sleep? This apartment's too small.' 'In the wardrobe,' Neruda replied. Perhaps he was recalling the time he and Delia had hidden in a wardrobe in Víctor Pey's Santiago flat. They emptied the wardrobe of clothes and suitcases and laid a mattress down there for Nemesio. Inés, meanwhile, returned to New York with their baby.

'It was like love at first sight. They loved each other deeply, for life,' said Inés. 'When Nemesio woke up every morning in the tiny wardrobe, he stretched out (as far as he could) on his mattress and called out: "May the Painter in the wardrobe come out into the house of the Poet?" To which Neruda replied from the bed he shared with Delia: "Go ahead! The Poet gives the green light to the Painter." '[24]

At around this time, a nurse arrived to help Pablo deal with his phlebitis. And the nurse seemed vaguely familiar. Where had he seen this beautiful woman before, this woman with thick black hair and a dazzling smile, with the same first name as Verlaine's wife?

Matilde Urrutia certainly remembered Neruda. She was the Chilean singer who had had a brief affair with Pablo after their encounter at Blanca Hauser's Santiago apartment in 1946. It had clearly meant more to Matilde than Neruda. 'I looked sideways at Pablo and I thought I'd never seen eyes like his. I asked Blanca who it was beside her and she replied: "Ignorant thing! It's Pablo Neruda." I looked more closely at him. What strange eyes, they seem to be looking inwards! I want them to look at me. At that moment, he turned his face and looked at me and I looked at him. A little while later, he said something to Blanca, and she told me, in a low voice: "Pablo asked me who you were." I was so happy. He had asked about me. And I remembered his poems. When the concert in the park ended, Blanca invited us both to her house for tea.'[25]

In Mexico City, right under Delia's nose, they resumed their affair – just as in Madrid Neruda had begun his affair with Delia in front of Maruca and their newborn daughter. Delia was so vague that she apparently did not notice what was happening. But in any case, she apparently believed, quite wrongly, that Neruda no longer needed physical relations. That, at least, was what she had told Aída Figueroa in Chile.[26] Other friends, too, believed that sexual relations had cooled between the couple some time earlier, though great friendship remained.

Matilde Urrutia, who came into Neruda's life for good in Mexico City, at the age of thirty-seven, was born in 1912 in Chillán, in southern Chile, a town which had been devastated by several earthquakes, not far from Neruda's own birthplace of Parral. Her parents were poor, and Matilde, by nature every bit as independent as Delia, but also encouraged by her mother, sought to escape this poverty by taking up a career as a singer. She left the provinces to study singing in Santiago. Her teacher was Blanca Hauser, at whose home she began her brief affair with Neruda in 1946. But she also made frequent tours of Latin America. It was in that same year, on 5 July 1946, that a film, *La Lunareja*, shot in Peru, was premièred in which, according to the Peruvian film critic Ricardo Bedoya, Matilde sang (contralto) a song called 'Mal de Amores' (Love Sick). Inés Valenzuela, widow of Pablo's schoolfriend, Diego Muñoz, suggested to me that Matilde had been Orson Welles' mistress for a time when she was a young starlet.

Unlike Delia, who was an ardent Marxist, Matilde was not overtly political at all. She came from a humble, but conservative, family which nevertheless, according to Jorge Edwards, fitted 'a Communist tradition which exists in Chile, one in which Christian names could be found as extravagant as Pravda, El Siglo, Lenin or Stalin'.[27]

But Matilde had a very potent reason to feel antipathy, not to say hatred, towards the Chilean Communist Party. She told Edwards that one of her brothers, who had been a lifelong Party militant, had been expelled over some internal struggle and accused of dissipation and alcoholism. Distraught, he committed suicide. Matilde never forgave his brother's accusers, and every now and then she would bitterly reproach the Party leaders for bringing about his death.[28]

Matilde was not a cultured woman, but she was, in stark contrast to the Ant, a superb housekeeper: a good cook, careful with clothes and a fine organiser of financial and other affairs. Pablo had for some time been growing impatient with Delia's complete lack of domestic skills, and Matilde's abilities in this area were a powerful draw, quite apart from the strong sexual attraction he felt for her.

On 28 January 1950, Neruda's constitutional permission to remain outside Chile – which had been granted by the President of the Senate, Arturo Alessandri Palma, after that extraordinary secret meeting in Santiago – expired. This solidified Pablo's exile; he now knew that if he returned to Chile, he could be arrested immediately, since he no longer enjoyed the status of senator with its accompanying immunity from arrest and prosecution. The news came as a blow, even if it was expected. Would he ever be able to return to his beloved homeland? Fortunately, his new love for Matilde was sustaining him in exile, as was his growing reputation and success as a poet around the world. By this time, translations of his poetry were available in languages as diverse as Korean, Vietnamese, Japanese, Arabic, Turkish, Ukrainian, Uzbek, Portuguese, Slovak, Hebrew, Yiddish, Georgian and Armenian.

From his Mexican bed, Neruda was now engaged in a major undertaking: the secret publication of his great epic, *Canto general*. This involved a group of people preparing a text of the book from the typescript he had smuggled out on horseback across the Andes in March 1949. Diego Rivera and David Alfaro Siqueiros produced the illustrations for this sumptuous limited edition of 341 copies, which was published in March 1950 and offered to readers by subscription. The members of this editorial 'committee' included Wenceslao Roces (the Spaniard who had translated *Das Kapital*); Miguel Prieto, who would be responsible for the wonderful typography, and a Chilean Communist teacher called César Godoy Urrutia. It is doubtful that this last name would have been included had Neruda known that Godoy, a cousin of Matilde's, was having an affair with her until she dropped him for Pablo.

Inés Figueroa was heavily involved in the operation.

I helped give advance notice of the book to future subscribers in 1949. We charged 15 dollars. We advertised it among friends, in Mexico. It proved very popular, I even received a letter asking for a copy from the American composer, Aaron Copland! It was a huge book. There were considerable problems printing it because of its

Communist associations. But the whole process was magical. People couldn't wait to see it – and it eventually came out in early 1950, despite the fact that Pablo kept wanting to add bits, especially the polemical attacks on González Videla or on the United Fruit Company.[29]

A truly clandestine edition of the book was being prepared in Chile at the same time, with engravings by José Venturelli. But Mexico was the birthplace of the first edition of *Canto general*, and since it was illustrated by the country's two greatest surviving mural painters, it is not surprising that many Mexican critics have claimed it as their own, maintaining that the influence of the muralists was paramount.

One of these critics, Hugo Méndez-Ramírez, went so far as to suggest, in a fascinating, if not entirely convincing book, that *Canto general* must be read in the light of the murals, with the murals, even as a mural in itself.[30] He is right to point out that Neruda's social agenda had expanded crucially during his three-year stay as Chilean consul, when the poet did indeed become immersed in the philosophy, goals and consequences of the Mexican Revolution and was well acquainted with *muralismo* and its proponents. The early sections of *Canto general* contain Rivera-like images of ancient Aztec religious ritual and myths, as well as references to the slavery inherent in the Aztecs' social system. And like Rivera, much of Neruda's book exalts the 'Libertadores' – those who freed South America from its imperialist oppressors, both past and present. Like the Mexican muralists, too, Neruda's poem is, as Roberto González Echevarría has noted, 'monumental, in the sense that it covers a vast span of history and focuses on transcendental persons and deeds, as well as on the humble masses. One has the sense of being in a crowd when viewing one of Rivera's great murals. The self is dwarfed by the size and by the transcendence of the historical figures: one is properly reduced to being a member of the mass of spectators or victims (they are sometimes both). The same is true of Neruda's poem.'[31]

However, Méndez-Ramírez and others seriously underplay the importance of Neruda's personal biography, his condition as fugitive and exile, and the physical conditions under which *Canto general* was actually written – in confined rooms, in constant fear of discovery.

Just days before the Mexican edition of *Canto general* appeared, Neruda gave his friend, the Mexican critic Alfredo Cardona Peña, his own version.

> I wanted to give a sense of our continent's struggles through a revolutionary romanticism which is not out of tune with the realism to which I aspire in the book. It will come as a surprise to read names without historic importance . . . I did it deliberately so that a symbolic stigma falls on them. I know that this is rather harsh and will astonish and upset quite a few readers. But I want them to remember how bitter it was for me to make the realities of this time concrete. I believe my book, from the beginning, is a cheerful, sane, optimistic work, despite the sadness which partially surrounds it. For a whole year's work, I felt an intoxicating joy, because life gave me the chance to conquer all the enemies of the people just when I was believed to be at rock-bottom.[32]

The secret Chilean edition of *Canto general*, which appeared just after the Mexican one, on 3 April 1950, was every bit as dramatic in its production, and the team did not have the author around to guide them. This was not the same text as the Mexican edition. Into the Mexican edition, Neruda not only wove a number of new poems (which could not be inserted in the same place in the Chilean edition because, by then, it had been sewn up) but he also made numerous alterations to the typed version of what he had written 'underground' in Chile.

The Chilean text was taken from a typescript which Neruda had left in Chile before his escape across the Andes. Venturelli received the manuscript from Luis Corvalán, who at that time was the Chilean Communist Party's propaganda chief. Venturelli planned the layout and the illustrations which, astonishingly, he took quite openly to a commercial business to have made up from plates. Neruda himself did not have any opportunity to see them, being far from Chile at the time. The printing was handled by Manuel Recabarren from hand-set type. The sewing (stitching the binding mechanically would have been too noisy not to give them away) was done by hand in the cellar of Venturelli's house.

Another of the team, Américo Zorrilla, who had been manager of the Communist daily *El Siglo*, recalled that the Party had summoned him to a meeting where he was informed of the operation. 'At first sight, there is a flagrant contradiction between what had to be a clandestine printing and that book, which was big and voluminous and had a cover with huge letters on it. When you do a clandestine printing, you normally try and reduce size to the minimum. In this case, for a number of political and practical reasons, this audacious format turned out to be a success . . .'[33]

Zorrilla said that, just as with the Mexican edition, the Chilean team faced tremendous obstacles, many of them deriving from the fact that the Communist Party was still banned. Although the Party was very experienced in producing underground propaganda, this was something quite different: 'We had to publish 5,000 copies of a book of 468 pages and in big format (27 × 19 cms). We used about four tons of paper . . . The dictator's police could not be allowed to know where the book was produced and this necessarily reduced our options as to what type of paper to use.' In the end, they used a yellowish, harsh paper for the 3,000 'ordinary' copies and the other 2,000 were produced at a higher price on the superior 'pluma' paper.[34]

Canto general is Neruda's vast emotional response to, and celebration of, Latin America, past, present and future. The Cuban critic Enrico Mario Santí views the book as prophetic, with the numerous biblical allusions providing evidence – as he sees it – that the poet's political vision was mediated by a Christian conception of history.[35]

I prefer Jaime Alazraki's view, in another context, that Neruda laicised traditional religious language, 'loading the cliché with new, expressive resonances'.[36] If Neruda was a prophet, he was a secular one, and it is in this context that he sometimes refers to himself as a 'sacerdote' (priest). As Judy McGinnis has noted, Neruda playfully, even ironically, chose Christian terminology for the title of his memoirs, *Confieso que he vivido* (I Confess I Have Lived), but she, too, goes much too far, like Santí, in suggesting that Neruda 'took on the role of Christ' and 'wanted to enact the Christian promise in a Marxist Utopia in this life'.[37]

Neruda believed the book had a harmony which allowed it to coalesce as one work. It is difficult to agree: the epic and the personal elements do not always hold together smoothly. In themselves, they both contain poems of breathtaking beauty. And a theme of betrayal runs through the work – both Latin America's and Neruda's own. But, as the Argentinian critic Saúl Yurkiévich has written, there are two languages in use in *Canto general*: one, the irrational and mythic, is inherited from *Residencia en la tierra*, and tries to encapsulate a vision of both the poet's subconscious and the natural world; the other, the rational, is rooted in concrete political history and aimed at the future. Yurkiévich believes that in *Canto general* these two languages – and the 'stories' they tell – are essentially in conflict.[38]

But does this matter? This conflict also lends the work a creative tension which would have been absent if Neruda had achieved an overall unity.

After overseeing the Mexican edition of *Canto general* in March 1950, Pablo and Delia left Mexico City for a brief visit to Guatemala. To Neruda's delight, Matilde accompanied them as his nurse. At this stage, Delia was still unaware of any impropriety between her husband and Matilde.

In fact, Delia herself seemed happy to have someone around to care for Pablo's health. She remained touchingly concerned for his well-being. According to the Ant, Pablo had had a tooth removed at this time which had been troubling him since childhood, and was on a diet. ('He looks great,' she wrote excitedly back to Laurita on 4 June 1950.)[39]

Europe beckoned again. Neruda was still a fugitive, but the Communist Parties and writers' unions there provided him with a safe haven. Reluctantly abandoning Matilde and promising to meet up with her again as soon as he could possibly arrange it, Neruda set sail for Lisbon with Delia in July 1950. In an interesting letter written to Laurita from on board ship on 8 July, Pablo sought information on how his family in Temuco were coping with life under the González Videla dictatorship. 'I want you to tell me about the family: what's the news on my uncles and aunts and the nephews and nieces? How did the Reyes behave in the whole business of the traitor, G.V.?'

In Paris, the couple settled in an apartment beside the Seine, overlooking Nôtre Dame. 'Sand barges, tugboats, laden convoys as slow as freshwater whales, pass before my windows. The cathedral is an even larger ship raising its arrow of chiselled stone like a mast. Every morning, I look out to see whether it is still there beside the river, the cathedral ship, or whether, while shadows cover the world, the sailors carved in ancient granite have given the order to weigh anchor, to set sail across the seas. I want to go with her.'[40]

They visited Prague in June 1950, where the Czech Writers' Union offered him a room at Dobriss Castle, which he could use whenever he chose. 'Near Prague is the most beautiful castle in Czechoslovakia, a little Versailles, by a lake of marvellous groves. Dobriss Castle has been assigned by the state as a residence and refuge for writers. I spent a week with them.'[41]

Oddly, when Delia wrote to Laurita in Santiago on 28 June 1951, the writing paper was headed 'Hotel Esplanade, Prague'. Were they already living separately? According to the Ant, Neruda's feet were continuing to give him trouble. 'Your brother's health is good, but his legs are still swelling up and his circulation isn't completely regular. He has great satisfactions, because there are no words to express the affection with which he is treated in this noblest and grandest part of the world. But his desire to see his homeland is immense.'[42]

Neruda enjoyed his stay in the Czech capital, and delightedly asked to be given a tour of the district where his namesake Jan Neruda had lived.

In August 1950, Pablo and Delia returned to Paris, but the poet was soon on his travels once more. The French nuclear physician, Joliot-Curie, who was also the world president of the organisation Partisans for Peace, entrusted Neruda with an important mission: Pablo was to travel to India and attempt to strengthen the peace movement there. Joliot-Curie gave him two letters, one for a scientist in Bombay and one to be delivered in person to the Indian Prime Minister, Jawaharlal Nehru.

It turned out to be an unpleasant trip. Travelling without Delia, he flew first to Rome, where he stayed for a few days before boarding the plane for India. When he arrived at Bombay airport, officials went through his luggage with a fine-tooth comb:

In Rome, I had wrapped my shoes, so as not to soil my clothes, in a wrinkled newspaper I had found in my hotel room. I believe it was the *Osservatore Romano* [the Vatican newspaper]. They spread the page on a table, held it up to the light, folded it as carefully as if it were a secret document, and finally put it aside with some of my papers. My shoes were also studied inside and out, like unique samples of fabulous fossils.[43]

He found out later that the police had interrogated all the people whose names appeared in his contact book – including his sister-in-law, Delia's sister, who was living in Bombay.

Neruda's exasperation over this two-hour search was eased a little by lunch the same day with Nehru's sister. 'She was a woman of great beauty, made up and dressed like an exotic actress. Her sari flashed with colour, gold and pearls heightened her air of opulence. I took to her immediately. It was quite a contrast to see such a refined woman eating with her hand, sticking her long, jewelled fingers into the rice and curry sauce.'[44]

However, soon after Neruda arrived in New Delhi to visit Nehru himself, the Chilean Ambassador, Dr Juan Marín, called to inform him that the police authorities were keen to see him leave India as soon as possible. The Indian government was concerned about his activities. Pablo replied that he was equally eager to leave a country that, 'in spite of my proven sympathy for its causes, treats me so discourteously, without any reason whatsoever'.[45]

Neruda had met Nehru's father, Pandit Motilal, thirty years earlier at an independence rally during his last visit to India. But when he informed Nehru of this fact, 'it produced no change in his face. He replied in monosyllables to everything I said, scrutinising me with his steady, cold eyes. There was something high and mighty about him, something stiff, as if he was accustomed to giving orders but lacked the strength of a leader.'

Neruda handed him the peace letter, but Nehru still said nothing. Neruda felt obliged to discuss his mission to India. He expressed his concern that the Cold War could turn 'red hot' at any moment. Nehru's only reply was: 'As a matter of fact, both sides are pelting each other with arguments about peace.'[46]

Neruda claimed in his memoirs that he had made one final request before leaving: to visit the Taj Mahal. But by the time permission to do so reached him, Neruda was totally fed up with India and he took the first flight back to Paris.

Yet, five years later, while acting as a member of the committee awarding the Lenin Peace Prize in Moscow, a smile came over Neruda's face as the Indian delegate put forward Nehru's name. Bearing no grudges over his treatment, Neruda voted in favour of Nehru, who duly won.

In Paris, Pablo and Delia – known locally as 'Madame de Carril' –

moved into the first floor of a charming, three-floor chalet at 12 rue Pierre-Mille, in the 15th arrondissement. It was a workers' district, which Neruda adored, full of his beloved markets, fairgrounds with fire-eaters and plenty of bistrots where he could relax with a drink. Above them, on the second floor, to their delight, the Chilean painter Nemesio Antúnez, Inés Figueroa, and their young son, Pablo, came to live. Delia also rented the third floor, to prevent any unwanted vistors, strangers or even police informers from moving in.

Neruda was forced to make frequent trips abroad in order to renew his documentation. Because of the Cold War climate, the French government would still allow him only a limited tourist visa.

There were, as usual, joyous social occasions at the house, stretching long into the night. Paul Eluard's companion and future wife, Dominique, helped with the cooking. Louis Aragon was another frequent visitor, and he often made fun of Pablo's insistence on Chilean wines. Aragon was accompanied by his Russian-born wife, Elsa Triolet, sister of Mayakovsky's great love, Lily Brik.

In November 1950, Neruda and Delia returned to Poland, where Neruda took part in the second World Peace Congress in Warsaw. This was originally due to have taken place in London, before being moved to Sheffield in northern England. However, the British government of Clement Attlee considered the congress to be little more than a Communist front and, in the atmosphere of incipient Cold War, refused visas or entry to so many 'suspicious' foreign delegates that the conference was reduced to chaos and hurriedly switched to Warsaw by the organisers, the World Peace Council. Neruda was one of the names placed on the British Home Office blacklist.

He condemned the British authorities for what he saw as turning the country into a police state, in a poem written three years later, 'Londres':

> They wanted to bury
> that word 'peace' . . .
> They covered it in darkness,
> in police fog,
> they arrested it and locked it up,
> they beat it to a pulp,
> they spattered it with a martyr's blood,
> they interrogated it,

> and threw it into the deep sea,
> weighing it down with a stone
> tied to every syllable . . .[47]

In Warsaw, Neruda read his poem, 'Que despierte el leñador' (Let the Woodsplitter Awake), from *Canto general*. It contains one line which was misunderstood, at the time, as the Chilean journalist and critic José Miguel Varas has pointed out:[48]

> Peace for my right hand which only wants to write Rosario

This was not a reference to a rosary, as most people assumed, bewildered by such a religious image from a Communist poet. In fact, Rosario was Neruda's secret nickname for his new lover, Matilde, whom he was burning with desire to meet again after their Mexican affair. Very few people outside his closest circle of friends were aware of this relationship, and certainly not of the nickname.

At this same Warsaw congress, Paul Robeson sang and Neruda praised him as 'both a great artist and a great conscience . . . the most eminent man in the United States of North America. That is why they prevent him from leaving the country at the same time as they prevent Shostakovich from entering.'[49] Pablo Picasso presented his famous dove of peace, and in the closing ceremony on 22 November 1950, the two Pablos were jointly awarded the World Peace Prize, along with (in his absence) the great Turkish Communist poet, Nazim Hikmet, then languishing in a Turkish jail.

An international committee, including Picasso, Robeson and Jean-Paul Sartre, had been established during the peace congress in Paris in 1949 to campaign for Hikmet's release from prison. The Turkish Communist Party had been outlawed, and Hikmet had spent most of the 1920s and 1940s in jail on a variety of trumped-up charges. But he had still managed to publish nine books between 1929 and 1936, as well as working – when out of prison – as a bookbinder, proof-reader, journalist, translator and screenwriter to support an extended family which included his second wife, her two children, and his widowed mother. But in January 1938, Hikmet had been arrested again for inciting the Turkish armed forces to revolt and sentenced to twenty-eight years in prison on the grounds that military cadets were reading his poems, particularly 'The Epic of

Sheik Bedrettin'. In 1950, Hikmet started an eighteen-day hunger strike, despite a recent heart attack.[50]

In his Warsaw speech, Neruda lashed out at North American writers for failing to denounce what he saw as political atrocities, including the Korean War, which had just begun.

> Hemingway, you painted the lives of many gangsters in your inimitable style. Now, can't you draw sufficient inspiration from the destruction being wrought by a wave of bandits on our beloved Korean Republic? Doesn't MacArthur resemble the portrait of gangsters that you depicted in your books, engraved with a chisel? And why don't you talk of peace? Do you want war? Steinbeck, great Steinbeck, author of great books, what can you tell us of Howard Fast? Do you agree that a great writer from Jefferson's country should be writing his novels from a prison cell? Steinbeck, what have you done for your brother?[51]

What, it may well be asked, was Neruda doing for his own victimised 'brothers' in the Soviet Union? He appeared too blinded by his love for the Communist Party to acknowledge or even recognise his own double standards.

At the end of the Warsaw congress, an impatient Pablo Picasso turned to Neruda and whispered, 'The money. Where's the money?' Neruda was shaking with silent laughter. In fact, they were not paid their prize money, the massive sum of five million old French francs, that year. It would only happen the follow year, in Paris. When Neruda heard that Picasso had lost a large portion of the prize in income tax to the French authorities, Neruda insisted that his own share of the prize must be delivered in cash – in huge, old notes. This created a problem that Neruda had not anticipated. He did not have a suitcase or anything else to put the money in. Unwilling to go and collect the money himself, he sent Delia and Nemesio Antúnez, who, according to one story – which others have since denied to me – returned in a large overcoat on a boiling hot day, with the coat pockets stuffed with notes. At this time, most of Pablo's economic affairs – including the author's rights which Neruda should have been receiving for the many editions of his poems which were now appearing all over Europe and beyond – were being handled by Inés Figueroa. She was alarmed when the prize money first arrived back at the chalet in the rue Pierre-Mille, but then decided that Pablo must open a safe deposit in which to place the prize money. In future years, when awarded prizes in Russia, he was never able to take the money out of the country and insisted on being paid in caviar, which he would hand out generously to friends on his arrival back home.

Meanwhile, Neruda's literary fame was continuing to spread worldwide. While a tribute to the poet was organised in his absence by the Chilean Writers' Society and the Writers' Union in Santiago on 14 January 1951, collections of his poetry were being published in the United States, China, Czechoslovakia, Poland, the Soviet Union, Sweden, Romania, Italy and even in the Middle East, in Israel and Syria.

On the same day that he was being honoured in Santiago, Neruda was in Italy, reciting his poetry to equally warm applause at the Unione Culturale in Turin. While he was there, he visited the offices of the Communist daily, *l'Unità*. Two days later, on 16 January, he left for Venice, where he was received at the Palazzo Ducale. It was here that Neruda was reminded how delicate his position remained: the police banned him from discussing political themes. He obeyed, knowing that he risked expulsion. Sticking to poetry, he stayed for more than a month in Venice, a city he adored. On 20 February, he moved on to Genoa, where he was received by the Mayor, Professor Gelasio Adamoli, at the Palazzo Turso. He was delighted to be reunited with Gabriela Mistral once again in Genoa. However, back in Venice, bad news – never too far away – quickly arrived. The Italian government, falling into line with the Cold War climate, was unhappy with Pablo's presence on Italian soil, and the police – who had been stationed at the doors of his hotel day and night – now informed him that he must leave the country immediately. Undaunted, he remained in Venice for a further two days, reading his verse once again at the Palazzo Ducale on 23 February. Later Neruda described his hounding by the Italian police – including a gondola chase on Venice's canals – as 'slapstick comedy'.[52]

Although he responded instinctively to the food, the beauty and the people of Italy, Neruda left with the same sour taste in the mouth with which he had left India. There was nothing he wanted more than to be with his new love, Matilde. And he had plans to see her again soon.

In early August, Pablo received a warning that he could be expelled from France. On 5 August 1951, he flew from Paris to Prague to attended the Sixth Karoly Vary Film Festival. It was here that Neruda received one of the most welcome gifts of his life: José Venturelli, the illustrator of the clandestine Chilean edition of *Canto general*, handed a copy to him in person.[53]

A film festival was a paradoxical place to find Pablo Neruda. He had, at best, an ambivalent relationship with the cinema, unlike many of his friends – Rafael Alberti and Manuel Altolaguirre, among them – who had collaborated on film scripts. In fact, he was frequently dismissive of what he believed film had become in the capitalist world: a much lower art form than literature, designed to make as much money for its producers as possible.

And yet, at the same time, as a youth he had loved visiting the cinema in Santiago. And it was this enthusiasm that he was keen to transmit to his audience at the Karoly Vary Film Festival. He began his speech by saying: 'I am the man who enters the dark cinema hall seeking fascination, in any place and at any time . . . Cinema demands a total, paralysing attention, as no other art does. We can turn off the music, close the book, we can grow tired of a museum of great art, but few of us rise from our cinema seat before the end of a film, even if it depresses or irritates us.'[54]

The next day, 6 August 1951, Neruda took the train with Delia from Prague to East Berlin to speak at a major youth festival. It was here that he was finally reunited with Matilde. (On her arrival in Europe, she had tried to telephone him at his Paris apartment, but José Venturelli – who was staying there at the time – answered instead. Their voices were similar on the telephone, and Matilde initially thought she was talking to her lover.)[55]

Pablo had secretly persuaded the East German authorities to grant Matilde a visa to allow her to participate as a singer in the youth festival.

'I arrived at the festival after it had already started,' Matilde recalled in her own memoirs.

> Pablo had sent me telegrams, and thanks to one of these, I received the visa which had been refused me. I wasn't a political woman, I didn't know anything about all of that. I came from another world. I had never cared for the slightest sign of a fight . . . I arrived in Berlin, and friends waiting for me told me that Pablo was due to be at a theatre and had asked me to go there immediately. I felt radiant. I

arrived at the theatre and there he was. His face lit up when he saw me. We embraced and he said: 'That's it – I don't want to be separated from you ever again.' I have never been able to forget that sentence . . .[56]

Also in Berlin was Pablo's fellow Communist fugitive from justice, the Turkish poet Nazim Hikmet, who had been released from jail but had been forced to flee Turkey across the Bosphorous at night. It was the first time that the two men had met, but they both recognised a kindred spirit, embraced warmly and quickly became the closest of friends.

Matilde recalled Hikmet as 'a fascinating man, tall, fair, very handsome, with eyes that sparkled and a mouth that was always ready to laugh. He took a long look at me and said: "I approve of you, I approve of you. You're an Araucanian Chilean woman, I like you a lot." And with his immense hands, he lifted me up to his face to give me a kiss.'[57]

That same night, Neruda told Matilde there would be a gift waiting for her in her hotel room. When she opened the door to her room, she found Nazim Hikmet and Pablo Neruda inside, laughing like naughty schoolboys. 'Madame, your gift,' said Nazim, handing Pablo over to Matilde and leaving the room to the lovers.

In her memoirs, Matilde wrote: 'Pablo explained to me that he had gone to his hotel and told them to tell Delia that there was an urgent meeting of the [Communist] Party which would last until dawn. So the whole night would be ours . . . When I rested my head on his chest and closed my eyes in repose, I remember I told him: "You smell of tenderness." He replied: "Careful. That's poetry. You're not turning literary on me, are you?" '[58]

Thus began a remarkable double life, a juggling act conducted by Neruda between two women, all the way across Europe.

Just how was Neruda able to manage what, at times, was a truly Machiavellian operation, without the Ant even beginning to suspect him of infidelity? Clearly, he benefited from his close connections to Communist Party functionaries in Eastern Europe, as well as loyal friends all over the world who were willing to act as accomplices. (It would not be until he returned to Chile that he discovered, to his great sorrow, how strongly many of his friends disapproved of the way he was treating Delia.)

The next day, Matilde sang, as planned, with a group of Chilean dancers and was well received by the festival delegates. And she and Pablo seized every spare moment to be with each other. But as far as the world outside their intimate circle knew, Pablo was still happily married to Delia.

At the end of the Berlin youth festival, Pablo was very keen to be on his own with Matilde, but Delia's presence made this impossible. So he suggested that he and Delia should go on holiday to Romania with the Cuban poet, Nicolás Guillén, with Matilde making up a foursome. According to José Venturelli, during the train journey to Bucharest in late August 1951, Guillén tried to make a pass at Matilde, which initiated a lifelong antipathy between the Cuban and Neruda.[59]

Arriving on 28 August 1951, the four of them lodged in a large house in the Romanian capital. That same day, Neruda began writing the first poem of what would be a mysterious collection of highly charged, extremely erotic poems to Matilde – *Los versos del capitán* (*The Captain's Verses*) – which would be published anonymously in Naples the following year. The poem in question, the harrowing 'La pródiga' (The Prodigal), was a significant one in the life of the two lovers. Matilde insisted that it referred to her first miscarriage, which she claimed had occurred back in Mexico in 1949.

> I chose you from among all the women
> so that you could echo
> on earth
> my heart which dances in the corn
> or fights to the finish if it must.
>
> I ask you: where is my son?
>
> Wasn't he waiting for me inside you, recognising me,
> and telling me: 'Call me out across the land
> to continue your struggles and your songs.'
>
> Give me back my son![60]

Neruda appears to be resentful and bitter, and in her own memoirs, Matilde implied that he had blamed her miscarriage on her not taking sufficient care of herself. But he was just as angry with himself for not being there to nurse the baby through to term. Despite Pablo's promise to Matilde that they would never be separated, they could not be seen openly together. As he travelled through Europe, he continued to write these overtly sexual love poems to his new mistress, even when his wife was sitting at his side. Some of 'El amor' was written on the Trans-Siberian Express on 10 and 11 September 1951, as he crossed the Urals with Delia on the way to Mongolia.

On that train journey Pablo and Delia were also accompanied by his Russian friend and translator, Ilya Ehrenburg, who kept them entertained during the week-long trip with anecdotes about his time in the Red Army.

'With his unruly locks, deep wrinkles, nicotine-stained teeth, cold grey eyes and melancholy smile, Ehrenburg was the old sceptic, the great disillusioned man,' wrote Neruda in his memoirs, at the end of his life. Neruda then significantly continues: 'I had recently opened my eyes to the great revolution and was blind to sinister details. I found little to quarrel with in the general poor taste of the time or in those statues [of Stalin, which were mounted at each station where they stopped] smeared with gold and silver. Time would prove that I was not right, but I don't think even Ehrenburg fully realised the immensity of the tragedy. Its magnitude would be revealed to us all by the Twentieth Congress [in 1956 when Khrushchev disclosed the extent of Stalin's crimes].'[61]

Neruda was wrong about Ehrenburg: he was aware of what was going on in the Soviet Union, but it would not have been something he could risk talking about, even to his closest friends.

When Ehrenburg wasn't talking on that long train journey, he was finishing his novel, *The Ninth Wave*. With Delia beside him, Neruda was writing some of the most passionate of the love poems to Matilde from *Los versos del capitán*. By now, clearly, Pablo had dropped his regular habit of showing whatever he was writing to the Ant for her opinions, as he had always done in the past.

They left the train at Irkutsk and from there flew to Mongolia. The arid landscape reminded Neruda of his time as a senator in the north of Chile. He tasted Mongolian rice whisky in magnificent silver cups. It was made from fermented camel's milk. 'Shivers still run up and down my spine when I recall its taste.'[62] From Mongolia, he continued on to China. In Peking, Neruda had been invited to deliver the 1951 Lenin Peace Prize to Madame Soong Ching-Ling, widow of Sun Yat-Sen.

Among the people waiting to meet Neruda, Delia and Ehrenburg at Peking airport were the Chinese poet, Ai Qing, later to be a victim of the Cultural Revolution. The visit to China went smoothly, apart from difficulties arising from Neruda's desire to buy a pair of socks. 'When we reached the store, our Chinese friends jumped out, quickly herded all the customers out of the store, halted traffic, formed a barrier with their bodies, a human passageway through which Ehrenburg and I passed with our heads down, to emerge fifteen minutes later, our heads bowed once more, each with a little package in his hands, firmly determined never to buy another pair of socks in China.'[63]

There was one other awkward moment. When they were told that it would be 'almost impossible' to offer them Chinese food, Neruda turned to Ehrenburg and declared: 'Comrade, please prepare my papers for my return to Paris. If I can't have Chinese food in China, I'll have it in the Latin Quarter, where it is not a problem.' Neruda's anger produced quick results. They were escorted to a famous restaurant which happened to be situated right next to their hotel, where they were treated to an 'exquisite, memorable' dish of glazed duck.

By October 1951, Neruda and Delia were back in Europe, living in Prague. The Czech Writers' Union had offered him a room, once again, at Dobriss Castle. And as a member of the World Peace Council, to which he had been elected in Paris in 1949, Neruda joined Nicolas Guillén, Ilya Ehrenburg and the Brazilian novelist, Jorge Amado, in preparing for the World Peace Congress the following year in Vienna.

After a brief visit to Vienna in November 1951, Pablo and Delia settled for a while in Switzerland, in the Geneva suburb of Grand-Saconnex. While he was here Neruda managed to slip away at the end of November 1951, to spend a week alone with Matilde in the picturesque Swiss village of Nyon.

How did they manage this, with Delia still in Europe? Inés Figueroa told me that it may have happened during one of Delia's frequent trips back to Paris alone. (Neruda's limited tourist visa still meant that he had to remain out of France for extended periods.) However, the Nyon stay may have occurred after the Ant returned to Latin America.[64]

There is no mention whatsoever of this exceptionally happy Swiss interlude in Neruda's autobiography. But Matilde dwelled on it lovingly:

We went to Nyon. It was the first time that we had lived together. Nyon is a little town open to the blue sky of Lake Leman . . . Pablo was still a political fugitive, and Nyon was the perfect refuge. I seemed to have entered a security zone, where we breathed freedom and life was easy. Switzerland gave us a feeling of cleanliness and trust in all respects. They didn't ask for our documents at the hotel. No one doubted that we were husband and wife. Nobody knew us and we did not mean anything to anybody . . . If they could give me any moment to relive, I would choose this one without the slightest hesitation.[65]

On that very first night, they headed out to find a restaurant, only to discover that the Swiss dine much earlier than Latin Americans and there was nowhere open. They returned cheerfully to the Hotel du Lac, where they also found the restaurant closed. In the end, the management took pity on them and gave them a tray of cold food and a jug of wine.

'There, in Nyon, we bared not only our bodies but our souls,' wrote Matilde. Pablo talked at length about his childhood. He told Matilde how he had not turned out to be an ideal son for his father, being physically weak, introverted and silent. But he fondly remembered the train trips with his father in the forest. He bemoaned the fact that, as a child, he had had no one to share his tears when he cried while reading a book and that, even as an adult, his poet's sensibility was misunderstood. He recalled that the first time he'd seen the sea was the most memorable moment of his youth. And Matilde told Pablo all about her own impoverished childhood in Chillán. She, like Neruda, had worn her shoes until they had holes in them.

He continued to write *Los versos del capitán* in their room at the Hotel du Lac, blissfully in love with his Rosario. On one draft, he wrote: 'Nyon, December 2, facing Lac Leman, with Rosario opposite me and two camparis, at 12.04 in the morning.' The poem he was writing was the remarkable, jealousy-laden 'Si tú me olvidas' (If You Forget Me). Whenever Pablo was apart from her, or so Matilde claimed in her memoirs, he felt increasingly jealous. She said he needed to be with her all the time, to ensure that he was her sole lover. And Matilde herself acknowledged that Pablo had some reason to feel concerned: 'I had a past which he did not know about, and he was capable of uncontainable jealousy and fury. They were like storms which whipped his soul and mine – but they never had the power to destroy the chains which linked us together.'

Matilde believed it was Pablo's insecurity about her which had impelled him to write *Los versos del capitán*. 'What drove him on in writing this book was the idea that he could never be entirely sure of me. My independence upset him a lot. And that was behind the dreadful fights we had . . . When he was with me, he never used violence. It was when I was not with him that he imagined terrible things . . . Since I liked singing, laughing and going out, he was never totally sure of me.'[66]

That jealousy, Matilde insisted, lay behind the ferocious lines in the poem 'El desvío' (One False Step), from *Los versos del capitán*:

> If your foot strays again
> it will be cut off.
> If your hand takes you
> on another path
> it will rot and fall off . . .
> If you separate me from your life
> you will die,
> even while you live.
> You will remain dead or a shadow
> wandering the earth without me[67]

For her part, Matilde claimed that she was never jealous of Pablo's wife, Delia. 'Pablo never thought of separating from her. We were a totally happy couple. For us, marriage was not important at all . . . I knew that Pablo belonged more to me when he was at her side. I don't think it was the difference in their ages. It was simply the security I felt right from the beginning. We were a couple that no one was going to destroy. I didn't want to get married. I was too happy being Pablo's lover.'[68]

The lovers' passionate Swiss idyll soon came to an end, however. They could not be alone together long, with Delia still in Europe. But while Matilde was due to return to Paris, and Neruda was continuing on to Rome, they now realised that they could not bear to be apart. Matilde decided that she would join him in Rome. She had Mexican friends there, singing students, and she could stay with them at their boarding house.

On their last evening in Nyon, Neruda rushed to his writing desk, wrote the 'Carta en el camino' (Letter for the Road) which would form the final part of *Los versos del capitán*, and handed it to Matilde in an envelope, on condition that she did not break the seal and read it until she was on her way to Paris the following day.

> Farewell, but you will be
> with me, you will be inside
> a drop of blood flowing in my veins
> or outside, a kiss burning my face
> or a belt of fire around my waist . . .
> I found you after
> the storm,
> the rain washed the air
> and in the water
> your sweet feet glimmered like fish.
> Adored one, I am leaving for more combats
> I will scratch away the earth to make you a cave
> and there your Captain
> will wait for you with flowers on the bed . . .

True to his word, even after they separated, Neruda kept writing the love poems which would make up *Los versos del capitán*. He wrote everywhere. Drafts of one poem show that he was writing on plane trips from Basle to Prague and from Lvov to Prague, and on a train between Switzerland and Italy.

Robert Pring-Mill, who has produced a brilliantly detailed chronology of the writing of *Los versos del capitán*, points out that Neruda occasionally made errors in the date and place in which a poem was written when he wrote his notes in the margin. Some of these notes – scrawled, unusually for Neruda, in purple ink, rather than green – are decidedly misleading (such as confusing Bucharest with Budapest).[69]

Neruda was in Rome on 12 December 1950. On New Year's Eve, he had to leave Rome for Naples. He returned to Rome two days later, then went on to Florence on 9 January 1951, where he was received by the Mayor at the Palazzo Vecchio. On 11 January he read his poems at the Palazzo dell'Arte della Lana and the following day at the Palazzo di Parte Guelfa.

During these exhausting reading tours, Pablo also found time to continue work on another collection of poems, *Las uvas y el viento* (The Grapes and the Wind), which he had begun writing in 1950. It is a very different book from *Los versos del capitán*. Neruda himself always counted it among its favourites, but it is, in fact, one of the most uneven works ever written by a great poet and contains some extremely poor poems. What *Las uvas y el viento* does present is a personal account of a Communist poet's travels around Eastern Europe at the height of the Cold War. It is infused with his love for Socialism as he saw it functioning (and functioning well, in his eyes) in the new 'People's Democracies', as well as with his love for friends, both alive and dead.

Looking back on the book in 1964, Neruda said that he wrote it primarily as a *cronista* (chronicler). He had intended it to be 'a poem of geographical and political content. This was a frustrated effort, to some extent, although it does sometimes attain the intense and expansive tone that I seek in my songs.'[70]

Las uvas y el viento is, indeed, a chronicle of Neruda's twin passions at the time: the reconstruction of the Soviet bloc nations from the rubble of the Second World War and his love for Matilde. In the sixth section, 'Regresó la sirena' (Return of the Mermaid), the poet explicitly and graphically conflates these two passions. He tells Matilde:

> I dug
> and dug
> night and day
> on your grave
> and I rebuilt you.
> I raised your breasts from the dust,
> the mouth I adored from its ashes,
> reconstructed
> your arms and your legs and your eyes,
> your hair of twisted metal
> and I gave you life . . .
> And that, my love, is just the way
> they rebuilt Warsaw . . .
> Now you can understand how
> love built the avenues,
> made the moon sing in the gardens.[71]

Robert Pring-Mill has noted that section seven of the book – 'La patria del racimo' – does contain work which is 'up to the level of *Los versos del capitán* and is indeed virtually a continuation of it. And many other parts show the incipient development of the apparently simplistic techniques which will dominate throughout the four collections of the *Odas* phase: these parts of *Las uvas* seem to me to represent the outcome of the "Socialist Realism" with which, I believe, Neruda had been experimenting while in the Soviet bloc.'[72]

The fact remains, however, that many of the poems in *Las uvas y el viento* strive too hard to express Neruda's political solidarity with his European comrades, and this leads to uncharacteristically clumsy expression.

Take the poem, 'Vuelve España' (Spain Returns), in which he attempts to describe how deeply his experiences in Spain still influenced him.

> What am I without your crucified beacon? Where am I without the
>   water
> from your rock? Who are you if you did not give me blood?

The use of religious symbols does not ring true here, any more than in another poem from the same collection, 'Sólo el hombre' (Man Alone) in which he talks about himself as having broken a tree with an axe.

Still worse are his hymns to the modern machinery of socialist Europe. There is no hint of Zola's romantic attachment to technology and progress. Take this moment from 'Construyendo la paz' (Building Peace) where Neruda depicts his visit to a Poland recovering gallantly from Nazi destruction:

> In Gdansk I saw life repopulating itself.
> Engines kissed me
> with their lips of steel.

Occasionally, lines of true beauty shine out, as in his poem 'Aquí viene Nazim Hikmet' (Here Comes Nazim Hikmet):

> When Nazim laughs,
> Nazim Hikmet, it is not like when you laugh;
> his laugh is whiter.

> In him the moon is laughing,
> a star, wine, undying earth . . .

When Neruda turns away from Eastern Europe and yearningly back
to his homeland, there is a potent poignancy. In 'Cuándo de Chile', he
writes:

> Oh Chile, long petal
> of sea and wine and snow,
> when,
> when,
> when
> will I see you again

But such moments are all too rare in *Las uvas y el viento*. The book
did not actually appear until 1954 – two years after *Los versos del
capitán*.

By late 1951, relations between Delia and Neruda had become
strained. But a letter written by Delia to Laurita from Paris on 25
November – possibly when Neruda was in Nyon with Matilde –
shows that the Ant had lost none of her generosity of spirit. She was
concerned for Laurita's own state of mind (she was still grieving for
the death of her young husband, Ramón):

> Oh Laurita, don't lose heart or worry too much. We find ourselves
> in a moment of great indecision because we have to liquidate our
> affairs here. But your brother has said that, wherever we end up, you
> will be. We still don't know where that will be. But it won't be Paris.
> Could it be Italy? Or Ecuador or nearby? Wait calmly.[73]

But Delia still had one more extraordinary adventure to live with
Neruda in Europe. On 11 January 1952, the Naples police arrived at
their hotel and calmly informed him that he must leave Italy that very
same day. The Communist Party daily, *l'Unità*, reported the news with
indignation: 'All the writer's documents, and those of his wife, who was
with him, were perfectly in order. The police burst into the hotel where
Neruda was staying at 5.30 this morning, virtually in the middle of the
night. Agents ordered the poet and his wife to follow them to the
Prefecture. Here, Neruda was also subjected to a lengthy interrogation.'

As soon as the news broke of Neruda's impending expulsion from Italy, many of the country's intellectuals expressed their horror and anger. In Naples, they issued a statement declaring: 'We, intellectuals and artists of Naples, hearing the grave ruling against the famous poet and patriot, Pablo Neruda, a great friend of Italy, who has been ordered to leave our country immediately, despite possessing a valid permit for three months, vehemently protest . . .'

At 5 p.m., friends and supporters gathered at Naples railway station to wave Neruda and Delia off. Surrounded by police guards, the couple made their way to Rome, where they would change trains to head for the border. But as the train drew into Rome station, an amazing sight met them. The platform was full of people shouting 'Pablo, Pablo', and hurling flowers at the train. As he clambered down the train steps, thousands of anonymous arms pulled him away from the clutches of the police guards, who were helpless in the face of such numbers. And suddenly, Neruda recognised a few faces in the crowd: the Italian novelist Alberto Moravia, and his wife, Elsa Morante; the painter, Renato Guttuso. Carlo Levi, author of *Christ Stopped at Eboli*, was holding out a bouquet of roses. And somewhere, discreetly hidden in that crowd, was Matilde, who was living in Rome in any case and who had rushed to the station immediately.

In the chaotic scenes that ensued, people were throwing punches at the police, and at one point, Elsa Morante struck a policeman with her umbrella. And all the while, the crowd was shouting slogans: 'Neruda stays in Rome!' 'Let the poet stay!' It was only when a police superior arrived and pledged to ensure Pablo would be allowed to remain in Italy for the full three months of his tourist visa that Neruda's hundreds of Roman supporters were finally appeased.

Matilde could not approach Pablo publicly. Neruda was taken first to Rome's Hotel Inghilterra. Guttuso, who knew about Matilde, contacted her to inform her of Pablo's whereabouts. Neruda himself then telephoned her from his hotel to say that it was considered too dangerous for him to remain there (his friends had told him: 'If they grab you in the night and take you to the border, there's nothing we can do for you') and that he was being moved to the house of an Italian Socialist senator. Neruda asked Matilde to visit him there the following day.

The next day, it was officially announced that Pablo could remain in

Italy. Once again dodging Delia, the two lovers escaped into the Rome streets to celebrate the news. Stopping in front of a pet shop, they saw a tiny dog in the window, who looked back at them sleepily. They entered the shop and bought the dog, which they named Nyon, after the Swiss village where they had enjoyed their idyll.

Days afterwards, Neruda received a telegram from Italy's greatest living historian, Edwin Cerio, expressing his disgust at the Italian authorities' behaviour and offering Neruda and his wife the use of his villa on Capri. Actually, Cerio was responding to a letter from the Italian Communist Senator, Mario Alicata, on 8 January 1952, asking him to help Neruda who was looking to 'spend three months on Capri to finish his book on Italy'.[74] A second letter to Cerio from Alicata on 11 January referring to Italy's 'noble tradition of hospitality and generosity' seems to have done the trick.

Although Neruda would shortly take up Cerio's offer of his Capri villa with relish, he still had unfinished business to take care of. He knew he could no longer live without Matilde, and he disliked the necessity of deceiving Delia – yet he still found it impossible to hurt her by telling her the truth about the situation. So he tried to convince her, gently, that he needed her to return to Latin America to prepare his triumphant return to Chile from exile. By now the Left was initiating a resurgence in Chile. On 25 November 1951, Salvador Allende had announced his candidacy for President of Chile representing the PSCH (the Socialist Party of Chile) in the 1952 elections. Allende's manifesto openly condemned the imperialism of the Gonźalez Videla regime and called for the nationalisation of Chile's basic resources. Delia initially resisted Neruda's request. She still loved Pablo deeply, and could not understand the urgency of his pleas for them to separate. The Ant did not yet have the slightest inkling that her husband was even seeing the woman she herself had hired to look after his phlebitis in Mexico City three years earlier.

However, in late January 1952, she finally agreed to Neruda's request. She left for Argentina from Gothenburg harbour, in Sweden, on 30 January 1952. Pablo wrote a rather chilly letter from the Hotel St Gotthard, in Zurich, Switzerland, to Laurita in Santiago, telling her that she would have to wait a while to see him again:

> Dear sister, I'm sorry to have to dash your hopes a little, but the truth is that your sister-in-law [Delia] is returning to her country for

various reasons on 15 January on the Danish steamer, *Bío-Bío* . . .
You must by force of circumstances put off your trip to Europe,
which will wait for another occasion . . .[75]

Soon after Delia left Italy for Sweden, Neruda moved to Cerio's
villa, the Casetta Arturo, on Capri with Matilde. Later he would write:

We came to the marvellous island on a winter night. The coast
loomed through the shadows, whitish and tall, unfamiliar and silent
. . . It was the first time we had lived together in the same house. In
that place of intoxicating beauty, our love grew steadily, we could
never again live apart. There I finished *Los versos del capitán*, a
book of love, passionate, but also painful, which was published later
in Naples, anonymously.[76]

There was almost immediately a crisis: Cerio's only condition to
Neruda was that he did not indulge in any political activities while on
the island. However, on 28 January Cerio wrote to Pablo in French to
protest that the poet had infringed this condition. Cerio noted,
pointedly: 'I have the defect (which I'm sure you find unforgivable)
of hating all politics, but that is my way of loving humanity.'[77] It
seems there had been a misunderstanding: Cerio had received a
telephone call from a Chilean in Naples asking to speak to Neruda,
and had immediately become alarmed that Pablo was indeed indul-
ging in politics. The following day, 29 January, Pablo hastened to
write back to Cerio to reassure him that the messenger had merely
wanted to inform him of the presence on Italian soil of his dear
Chilean friend, José Venturelli. And there the matter ended.
    Edwin Cerio's wife, Claretta, has left charming portraits of both
Neruda and Matilde at this time:

I saw a portly man, tall, olive-coloured, with dark eyes who
observed everything carefully, his head almost bald . . . He seemed
older than his forty-eight years, or perhaps not older but rather of
indeterminate age, like the impression we get from the faces of pre-
Columbian sculptures . . .

while Matilde was

a gentle, affectionate woman, very attentive, but discreet and always ready to give way to others. Of few words and measured movements, she showed none of the capricious temperament associated with her actress profession . . .[78]

Los versos del capitán appeared in a limited edition of just forty-four copies on 8 July 1952, under the auspices of the Italian painter, Paolo Ricci, at the print house of Naples. It was printed L'Arte Tipografica on ivory paper made by hand, with illustrations by Ricci. On the cover was a Medusa's head remarkably reminiscent of Matilde's. The production costs were assumed by the Italian Communist Party as a homage to the 'exiled comrade and poet'. Each one of the distinguished collaborators is mentioned on the last page of the book: Luchino Visconti, Giulio Einaudi, Carlo Levi, Renato Guttuso, the poet Salvatore Quasimodo, Elsa Morante and Jorge Amado, among others.

The book bears a prologue in the form of a letter dated 3 October 1951, addressed to an unknown individual in Havana, Cuba, and signed Rosario de la Cerda. (De la Cerda was Matilde's second surname.) 'I have all the originals of these verses,' the fake letter reads.

> They were written in the most varied of places, such as trains, aeroplanes, cafés, and on peculiar little pieces of paper in which there are hardly any corrections. In one of these last letters came the 'Carta en el camino'. Many of these papers were almost illegible because they were so wrinkled or cut up, but I think I've managed to decipher them. My identity is not important but I am the protagonist of this book and that makes me proud and satisfied with my life.[79]

Rosario/Matilde goes on to invent a story about how, when and where her love affair had begun, clearly with the aim of making it still harder to identify the author. Matilde told Robert Pring-Mill years later that the Rosario de la Cerda letter had actually been written by her, not Neruda: the lovers had concocted the basic cover story together but Pablo had asked her to write the letter 'because you will get the tone right' – and they had chortled together over the result.[80]

Neruda wrote: 'it remained a secret for a long time, for a long time it did not carry my name on its cover, as if I were disowning it or as if the book itself did not know who its father was.'[81]

> A few suspicious critics suggested political motives for the appearance of this book without a signature. 'The Party is against it, the Party doesn't approve,' they said. But it wasn't true. Fortunately, my Party is not against expressions of beauty. The real truth is that I did not want those poems to wound Delia, whom I was leaving. Delia del Carril, sweetest of consorts, thread of steel and honey tied to me during the years when my poetry said most, was my perfect mate for eighteen years. This book, filled with sudden and burning love, would have struck her like a rock hurled against her gentleness. That, only that, was the profound, personal, respectable reason for my anonymity.[82]

Pablo and Matilde celebrated the publication of the mysterious volume with a party at a table laden with flowers, seafood and Capri wine. Matilde's own favourite of the poems dedicated to her in this book was 'La reina' (The Queen):

> I have named you queen
> There are taller women than you, taller.
> There are purer women than you, purer.
> There are more beautiful women than you, yes, there are.
> But you are the queen.

The Capri life of paradise continued, though Neruda was beginning to miss his homeland, which he had not seen for three years. Matilde recalled, 'When we arrived at the Marina Piccola, Pablo said to me, longing perhaps for Isla Negra, "If only the sea would roar here. Its feeble waters are almost silent by the time they reach the shore. And it doesn't smell like our sea, either." '[83]

But whenever they opened the windows of their white bungalow, they discovered a small terrace and a forest. And how reviving it was for Neruda to come out into the daylight, a free man at last, after a year underground in Chile and the concealing of his love for Matilde from Delia. Capri, with its natural beauty, was the perfect setting for this rebirth. As he told an interviewer many years later: 'The sea, fish and birds have a material existence for me. I depend on them just as I depend on daylight.'[84]

Meanwhile, Delia had arrived back in Santiago from Argentina, and there, awaiting her, were piles of letters from Pablo on Capri expressing his love: 'My Ant, here I am, all alone, your wild cicada, in the cold sun of Capri', 'A thousand kisses from your Pablo'. But he was anything but alone.

In fact, it seemed that soon there would not just be the two lovers on the island but a third newcomer: Matilde was sure that she was pregnant for a second time with Pablo's child, and this time she was determined to look after herself. She sent the pregnancy test to Naples and sat edgily at a café while Pablo walked over to the post office to collect the letter confirming the result. 'I saw him coming back, radiant. I got up to ask him, but I never had a chance to say a word. A long, long kiss forced my mouth closed. We laughed, we sang. In the square, people were looking at us, and we felt so happy about our secret.'[85]

Returning to the villa, neither of them could find their keys. They could hear Nyon, their dog, howling at the door. It was a cold night, and there was no choice but to look for a hotel. They eventually found an icy room, but even the frustrating knowledge that they had a fire burning in their own locked villa did not matter: they were so happy about their impending parenthood. Matilde remembered:

> One day, Pablo said to me: 'In a few days' time, at full moon, I want us to get married, because we are going to have a child. We will have a party and the moon will marry us. Today I'm going to get a ring made that you will wear for the rest of your life.' On Capri, there was an old jewelller who made us the ring, which said: 'Capri, 3 May 1952, your Captain.'[86]

When the day came for the celebration, they invited their friend Sara Alicata over from Naples, and gave their maid, Amelia, the day off. Matilde cooked a duck à l'orange and various fish dishes in different sauces. The walls were covered in flowers, and on coloured paper Neruda had written: 'Matilde, I love you.' On the terrace, Neruda asked the moon to marry them. He explained that they couldn't be married on earth, but if the moon married them, they would respect this as just as sacred a rite. As Pablo put the ring on Matilde's finger, he swore to her that he had seen the moon's mouth move giving them its blessing.

How could anyone be so in love? What a joyful meal! And all the time, he told me: 'You are the queen of the kitchen. How happily married I am.'[87]

But what could the date on the ring mean? Full Moon fell on 9 May in 1952, not 3 May – so maybe Pablo had inscribed the latter date to mark the day Matilde's pregnancy was confirmed?

While the Italians called Matilde 'Medusa' because of her thick curly hair, Pablo called her his 'Patoja'. This was a strange choice of endearment. As José Miguel Varas has noted, it is not a common word in Chile, especially when used as a term of affection to a loved one. 'Among us, it has a derogatory nuance. It seems to refer to a short person with short legs. It's even worse in Spain, according to the Real Academia [Spanish Royal Academy] definition: "That which has twisted or malproportioned legs or feet and, when walking, wobbles its body from side to side like a duck [pato]." '[88]

As Varas points out, Matilde 'had none of these defects, and she didn't wobble when she walked. And yet Matilde didn't mind it when Pablo called her that. It is quite likely that, in their years in Mexico, both, or at least one of them, had come across the meaning that the [masculine version of the word], patojo, has in neighbouring Guatemala: something like "boy, chap", and when the boy refers to his girlfriend, he speaks with some tenderness and a protective air of "my patoja".'[89]

Then sorrow clouded their happiness: the child which Neruda had already named Neruda Urrutia was lost. 'A shadow descended on our surroundings and threatened to wrap us in sadness and anxiety.'[90]

Pablo told her: 'I'm going to give you a child. It's just been born, and its name is Las uvas y el viento.'[91]

But this book, which Neruda had started writing in 1950, was not actually published until 1954.

From that moment on, Matilde said, she began to feel a 'sweet dependence' on Pablo, in a way she had never depended on anyone before. 'Every day, Pablo was my light, my joy.'[92]

On 5 June the lovers travelled to Venice, which Neruda knew well by now but which was competely new to a dazzled Matilde. When they returned to Cerio's villa on Capri's Via Tragara, they found Nyon pining for them. But they also found that tourists were beginning to interrupt their relaxed walks, even after they moved to a smaller house on Capri – a beautiful home at number 7 Via Gli Campi.

In this new house, Neruda sat down at his desk to work, and discovered, to his horror, that he could not find any of his latest manuscripts of *Las uvas y el viento*. The whole of the section on China had gone missing. He was inconsolable: it was such a long section that he knew it would be impossible to recover from memory. 'All right,' said Matilde. 'I can remember some of the poems and the structure. I'm going to tell you how the poem goes and you can write it.' And so the whole section was rewritten – though Neruda was never convinced that it was as good as the original.

Eventually, the tourist invaders began to make the lovers' life too uncomfortable. It was time to abandon Capri. The couple sought refuge in the small fishing village called Sant'Angelo, on the island of Ischia, which was completely unspoilt. They stayed at a hotel over-looking the sea, from where they could watch the fishermen and their children at work, with their wives carrying the baskets.

It was here, in June 1952, that Neruda received joyous news. In the dying months of the González Videla dictatorship, the arrest warrant issued four years earlier against him by the Chilean authorities had been dropped. (Neruda still had many enemies in Chile, however. On 10 July, a conservative senator, Sergio Fernandez, made a speech in which he argued against the idea of an amnesty for the poet, adding acidly that Neruda's breathing should be synchronised with the orders reaching him from Moscow.)

Neruda had been invited to a writers' congress in Berlin in July. He had intended, of course, to take Matilde with him, but he learnt that the police had visited their Sant'Angelo hotel while they were on the beach. Matilde, delighted to be able to teach Pablo something, was giving him swimming lessons. The police had left without their prey.

Reluctantly, Neruda left Matilde behind in Italy to sort out doc-umentation, arranging to meet up in Geneva. It was fortunate that Matilde could turn to Pablo's friend and fellow poet, Gabriela Mistral. She was now Chilean consul in Rome, and she arranged for Matilde's visa to be renewed. She also signed a second form – granting Nyon a visa, allowing his owner to take the dog out of Italy to Chile.

An incident at the Berlin congress indicates Neruda's new, self-confident attitude, which could alienate those who who took it for arrogance. Pablo met the East German writer, Stefan Heym, who was living in the United States and had arrived in Berlin with an impressive Swiss-made Hermès typewriter. Neruda was captivated by the machine, and wanted to exchange his own typewriter for Heym's. When Heym refused, he went into a rage and asked whether the German knew who he was. 'Of course I do,' Heym replied and, excusing himself, returned to his room with his treasured typewriter, leaving Pablo forlorn.[93]

Meanwhile, back in Chile, rumours were growing that Neruda was about to return to Chile. But repeated telephone calls to Europe could not produce any confirmation of the poet's whereabouts. In fact, a Spanish writer friend, José Herrera Petere, had secretly invited Pablo to stay at his house outside Geneva, in a pretty little village called Vézenas. Matilde was to join him there.

Delia eventually did manage to get through to Herrera Petere, but he lied to her, saying that Pablo had left 'in a car', without saying anything more.

The González Videla dictatorship was in its death throes, collapsing under the weight of corruption allegations. The Chilean Socialists were in the process of putting forward Salvador Allende as their candidate for the presidential elections due in September 1952. They were very keen to have their most prominent left-wing literary figure – a legend worldwide – back in Chile to support the Allende candidature.

Neruda was waiting for Matilde in Vézenas, as arranged, seemingly oblivious to what was going on back in Chile. Their fortnight together was another mini-idyll. Pablo could not stop laughing when he heard about Gabriela Mistral's help. 'A visa for a dog! And why not a passport?'

Pablo was, indeed, on his way home – but he had not informed anyone back in Chile of how, or when. In fact, it was not by air, as they all assumed in Santiago, but by boat. There were two weeks to spare before the *Julio Cesare* was due to set sail for Chile from Cannes.

In Cannes, Neruda suggested to Matilde that they should go and eat in Villauris, Picasso's village. The next day, they returned to Cannes and to the shipping office to pick up their tickets. To their astonishment, they saw Paul Eluard coming towards them, with an invitation to lunch with Picasso. It was an irony that the ever-social Neruda would, for once, have preferred to enjoy his last moments on French soil with Matilde alone. Their plan was for her to remain in Uruguay while he continued on to Santiago.

Matilde could not show herself at the lunch, even though Picasso and Eluard both knew about her relationship with Neruda. Moreover, Matilde still did not have a visa for Uruguay. The Uruguayan consul in Cannes turned out to be a young boy in a T-shirt and shorts, who took one look at Matilde's passport, which read 'Profession: Singer' and replied: 'I'm also a singer. In the opera. In a few days' time, I'm singing Pinkerton, in *Madame Butterfly*.' He then tried to persuade Matilde to stay in France with him. In the end, Matilde had to pay him 200 dollars to persuade him to issue her visa.

The lunch was a mixture of joy and sadness. Round the table were Picasso and his mistress, Françoise Gilot; Eluard, Eluard's wife, Dominique, Nemesio Antúnez, Inés Figueroa; Inés's sister, Carmen, and her scientist husband, Philip Meyer. It was a beautifully positioned restaurant on the beach, and there on the sand played Picasso's two children, Paloma and Claude. Inés Figueroa recalls Neruda as being 'very nervous'.[94]

At one point during the lunch, Picasso stood up, removed his shirt and then reached down to remove a pendant of a minotaur, which he placed lovingly around Neruda's neck as a farewell present. Pablo thanked him, but he could not reveal the reason for his edginess: he feared that Matilde might not obtain her visa.

The lunch companions wanted to accompany him to the docks to see him off, but in the end they all went their separate ways. It was the last time Pablo would see Eluard. The Frenchman died on 18 November that year.

The lovers were still not safe. As they were preparing to get into one of the small launches taking passengers out to the boat, a loudspeaker announced: 'Señor Pablo Neruda is requested to present himself to the International Police.' At this, a woman passenger's voice could be heard shouting: 'That man's a Communist, an agitator. I know, because I'm Chilean.' Another woman's voice shouted even louder: 'I should teach you a lesson for being Chilean and attacking the greatest writer in Spanish. I am a Uruguayan, and we would love to have that agitator, as you call him.'

Matilde feared their trip might be scuppered at the last minute. Eventually, a boy came up to her and said that Neruda had told her to board the ship and that he would join her shortly. Suspicious, Matilde refused to move anywhere until she could speak to Pablo. Suddenly, another launch appeared in the sea, and in it was a man waving a white handkerchief. It was Neruda: the police were taking him out to the boat on his own.

Reunited, the lovers hugged each other with relief, but Pablo's face revealed a new sadness. 'Something very painful happened today,' he told her. 'They've expelled me from France. That's why they called me in.' Then the officials had asked for his autograph.

It was a profound emotional blow. 'That country has everything that I love most,' he told Matilde, as the boat slipped away from the French coast. 'Its natural science stores have so many shells that they look like an immense sea. The *bouquinistes* are the best in the world . . . It's the model of a civilised country – and they expelled me as if I were its enemy. Me, who learnt French as a child by reading its authors.'[95]

They had separate cabins on board ship, but Neruda ordered a bottle of champagne and they drank to the lascivious Uruguayan consul and to the poetry-loving officials who had unwillingly expelled Pablo from France.

When Pablo accompanied Matilde to her tiny, second-class cabin, she found that her companion was a good-looking woman called Antonia. As soon as she saw the poet, she exclaimed: 'What! Neruda here!' and gave him a huge kiss. It turned out that she had been one of the Spanish refugees Neruda had saved on the *Winnipeg* in 1939. 'Come in,' she said. 'We'll arrange things somehow.' And though the cabin quickly resembled the stateroom scene from the Marx Brothers' film, *Night at the Opera*, Pablo and Matilde settled in a corner and found room for him to set up an improvised desk.

On Sunday, 26 July 1952, the Chilean Communist Party daily, *Democracia*, appeared with huge red letters on its front page: *Hoy llega Neruda* (Neruda Arrives Today). In a few hours, a vast crowd had made its way out to Santiago's Los Cerrillos airport, where Volodia Teitelboim had arranged a welcoming party. The aircraft landed, but Pablo was not among the passengers coming down the steps. There was no sign of the returning hero.

A group of lawyers, including Jorge Jiles and Alejandro Pérez, boarded the plane but emerged a few minutes later shaking their heads disconsolately. Teitelboim told a journalist: 'This is not the first time he's done this to me, but it's the last time I come and wait for him.'[96]

Wild rumours were starting to spread. Delia was weeping with nerves alongside her friend María Maluenda as they waited at the airport. The Ant had hardly slept for days in anticipation of seeing her husband again. But where was he?

II

Return the conquering hero

1952–59

We now know where Neruda was on that Sunday, 26 July 1952, as half of Santiago gathered at the airport to welcome their hero home – though this remained a secret for many years afterwards.

The Uruguayan architect and film-maker, Alberto Mántaras Rogé, and his wife, Olga, who had travelled on the *Julio Cesare* steamer from Cannes with Pablo and Matilde, had invited the poet to stop off with them in Uruguay for a few days, staying at their luxurious chalet by the sea at Atlántida. The two couples had become immensely fond of each other during the long sea voyage from Europe, and Neruda found the invitation impossible to resist – although he knew Matilde would have to continue on to Buenos Aires.

Pablo Neruda arrived back in Chile more than a fortnight later at 1.22 p.m. on 12 August 1952. It was the first time he had trodden Chilean soil in three and a half years. There waiting for him at the airport were his wife, Delia, many close friends and other admirers. When finally Neruda emerged, after a brief radio interview with his friend, the journalist Lenka Franulic, he walked over and joyously hugged Delia and his friends on the airport tarmac, to the cheers of 'Neruda, Neruda!' from the crowd. Tomás Lago noted that 'He had put on weight, more than I'd thought, probably due to the boat trip, but he looked fine. He was wearing a sports suit and a little green hat, with a narrow ribbon. He looked like an Argentinian detective.'[1]

Pablo and his friends made their way to Michoacán, the house in Los Guindos, Santiago. Neruda shut himself away to freshen up, while others tried to organise lunch. The problem was that the house was overcrowded. Orlando Oyarzún (who had shared tiny student lodgings with Neruda and Tomás Lago in Santiago), came up to Tomás and said that not everyone could be allowed to stay to eat. But the difficulty was that many of the people thronging the house were among Neruda's closest friends – it would be impossible to tell any of them to leave. Lago came up with an unusual solution: Pablo's very best friends would have to be the ones to leave!

The same day, a crowd of about 5,000 people gathered in Santiago's Plaza Bulnes for their first glimpse of the poet since he had disappeared into hiding in 1948. Tomás Lago recalled the scene. After some dancing, when Pablo at last appeared, a huge commotion broke out in the crowd and then a prolonged, electrifying ovation: ' "Neruda, Neruda, Neruda!" was the sustained cry. Handkerchiefs, hands, hats were raised in the air, and still they cried: "Neruda, Neruda!" By now . . . his face was a little tense, fixed in an emotional half-smile, and I saw tears starting to run down his cheeks . . ."[2]

Lago addressed the crowd, followed by Clotario Blest, Inés Moreno, Olga Poblete and José Miguel Varas. Then Neruda clambered to his feet and told his adoring audience:

> I owe Santiago a few drops of madness and wisdom. I also owe it the most important thing: the discovery of my party, the Communist Party of Chile. I owe it my pride in being a Communist. That is why I have returned to Chile, to repay my debt to the whole of Chile, and all the people. I come to express my gratitude to you, because I know how hard you have worked for my return . . . Over these past years, many simple people have suffered more than I have . . . [Chile is] one of the richest countries in the world; our people are one of the poorest in the world. We have more copper than anywhere else on the planet. But our children do not have shoes . . . Instead, fifty-floor buildings were erected in New York City.

He explicitly condemned US economic imperialism, its control over so many foreign industries. 'If our telephones stop being in foreign hands, we are not going to stop communicating with each other by telephone. And if electricity stops being owned by foreigners, we are not going to live in darkness. I believe that, on the contrary, we are going to have more electricity, and there will be enough for all of us.'[3]

The government of González Videla was moribund, but the Chilean Communist Party was still banned and Neruda's words were not the kind of message the right-wing authorities wanted blaring out in the main square of the capital. Yet, so large was the crowd they were powerless to intervene.

Neruda was reunited with Delia at Michoacán. Pablo was delighted to be living there, savouring the return to the 'rambling house. It has corners where, after such a long absence, I like to lose myself . . .' The smell of the library was one of the things Neruda had most profoundly missed, 'that book aroma, which is almost alive, going straight to the nostrils'. And he was back with his huge collection of seashells, 'the most silent residents in my house . . .'[4]

Suddenly, a totally unforeseen and very unpleasant development arose: a further act of betrayal and political vindictiveness on the part of President Gabriel González Videla. The President contacted Neruda's first wife, Maruca, in Holland and personally paid for her to be brought over to Chile to start legal proceedings against Neruda, claiming that his second marriage to Delia del Carril was bigamous, because she (Maruca) had not been allowed to contest her divorce from Pablo and so was still legally married to him. Neruda and Delia had married in Mexico in 1943, but it was argued that this marriage was not recognised in Chile because divorce was not recognised in Chile.

'González Videla wanted Pablo behind bars,' Neruda's friend and lawyer Sergio Insunza told me in Chile. 'The two lawyers involved were Carlos Vicuña Fuentes and Carlos Vasallo. But the case was badly handled. Maruca came to my office a couple of times. She was in a filthy mood. She spoke to me, in Spanish, complaining bitterly about Pablo's behaviour. She protested that she had been left penniless. She was a very curt woman.'[5]

We have a tantalising glimpse of this unsavoury legal tussle from Tomás Lago. Delia had called him[6] to say that Pablo's lawyer needed him to testify in person on Neruda's behalf. When Lago arrived at the lawyer's office, he found Maruca filling in forms.

> She was dressed . . . like an unhappy woman, as if the victim of a gutless man, wearing a coat of worn fur which looked as though it belonged to someone else, and a faded dress of a neutral colour . . . [The lawyer's] questions related to the extent of Pablo's wealth, and

I had been summoned to testify that he had no regular income, nor riches, which would allow him to give more money to that woman. They asked me whether I knew about his house by the sea, when he'd bought it, whether it was his or the Ant's, if his collection of seashells was very valuable, how much it was worth, if he had a car, if he paid for his foreign trips or whether he was a guest, how much he received for author's rights, the works of art he had in his house . . .[7]

In the end, the case never reached the courts. Maruca was paid off with the sum of 300,000 pesos – she had been demanding a million – on condition that she never attempt to make any legal representations again.

What happened to Maruca after that remains a mystery. Margarita Aguirre, Neruda's future secretary and biographer, recalled an incident which appeared to show that she still felt some loyalty to Neruda, despite her bitterness at what she saw as his shabby treatment of her. 'She was a very good person,' Aguirre told me in Chile. 'I'm going to tell you something which I'm not sure anyone else knows. When President González Videla brought her over to Chile in 1952 to fight the bigamy case, it didn't work out because of *her*. She did receive money, but she was [also] robbed of it.'

She spent a few months here in Chile afterwards. My mother received Maruca a lot in her house. . . . Once, I was with Maruca in a tram in Santiago, and she saw that someone had written on a wall, in big letters: 'Neruda traidor' [Neruda traitor]. Maruca was beside herself. She told me: 'Margarita, when I see things like that, I feel like getting off and rubbing it out.' Maruca spoke Spanish correctly – but with a Dutch accent, of course. The interesting thing is that, despite the hatred Neruda had shown her, Maruca retained her affection for him. Remember that, when Malva Marina, their daughter, died with her in Holland in 1943, she sent Neruda a cable, but he never replied – something like that would make you stop loving anyone.[8]

Some sources state that Maruca stayed on for a while in Chile, giving private tuition. Tomás Lago provides another, bizarre version. He claims that Maruca was still in Chile in late February 1954, and that the newspaper, *Ultima Hora*, reported that she had been detained and interrogated by the Chilean police. The police refused to confirm the report, and after Neruda made a lengthy telephone call to find out the truth, he turned to Lago and said, enigmatically: 'Drugs . . . It's incredible how little we know the people we've lived with. I always wondered what she was living on.'[9]

Eventually, Maruca did return to Holland. She was certainly living in The Hague in January 1958 and died there on 27 March 1965.[10]

To uninitiated observers, Pablo and Delia now became a close couple once again, working hard side by side in support of the presidential candidature of Salvador Allende. Neruda urged the banned Chilean Communist Party to emulate the attitude of the Soviet model. He told a meeting of the Chilean Party's central committee in September 1952: 'In Stalingrad, I went to a shop. The curtains were half-closed. I knocked on the door. They opened up, and I saw that all the shop assistants were taking part in a class on Marxism . . . One day, I watched a ballet. The Soviet Union's top ballerina was dancing. One of my companions invited me to meet her the next day. We waited for her with tea. And that same ballerina, who the night before we had seen dressed in butterflies or a flower, now came to us straight from a Marxism class, her books still under her arm. I believe that, if they study so hard in the Soviet Union, [there is] still more reason for us to do the same.'

In another section from this same speech, Neruda added, 'I have changed my style. I'm writing more simply. Little by little, I have shed complicated forms so that everyone understands my poetry. With the publication of my books in the Soviet Union, and China, in almost every country and language, I see that we must write so that everyone understands us.'[11]

In his memoirs, Neruda wrote: 'The years between August 1952 and April 1957 will not be detailed [here], since I spent almost all this time in Chile and nothing out of the ordinary happened to me, no adventures that would amuse my readers.'[12]

We now know that nothing could be further from the truth. Neruda's memoirs are among the most alluring ever written, but you will not find constant veracity – or anything like the full story – within their pages. (After Neruda's death, Matilde, along with Miguel Otero Silva, edited out repetitions and tidied up the structure, but – as

Matilde firmly insisted to Robert Pring-Mill when they met in Paris in the late 1970s – she added nothing which had not been written by Pablo. She pointed out that, since the memoirs, as Neruda left them, did not contain anything about Delia, people might believe that she – Matilde – had removed any positive references to the Ant, so she and Otero Silva had prosified a brief extract from one of the poems he had dedicated to Delia in his collection, *Memorial de Isla Negra*.)[13]

Neruda was still officially married to, and living with, Delia. He still loved her, too, but the relationship was almost certainly no longer physical, and he adored Matilde. His devotion to both women caused him considerable anguish.

By now, Matilde was back in Chile, living in a tiny apartment opposite Santiago's military hospital. Neruda resumed the juggling act between the two women that he had conducted in Mexico and Eastern Europe from 1949 to 1952. While Delia spent almost all her time at Michoacán – when she was not travelling abroad on her own – Neruda met Matilde at the house at Isla Negra on the coast. It seems that Neruda trusted the staff at Isla Negra to be discreet (a trust, as it turned out, that was ill-founded). Neruda also saw that Matilde had a separate love-nest: an apartment on Santiago's Avenida Providencia, number 2457.

A new house was being planned for Matilde: La Chascona, situated in Santiago's Calle Fernando Márquez de la Plata, in the Bellavista district of the capital (which today is the headquarters of the Neruda Foundation). On 5 November 1952, Matilde signed the deed of purchase for the land, although the construction work did not begin for another year.

On 18 November 1952, Margarita Aguirre brought Pablo a cable announcing the death of Paul Eluard: 'I saw him suddenly go pale and punch the desk with his fist, murmuring with rage: "Merde, merde".'[14]

If Delia remained blissfully unaware of Matilde's existence in her husband's life, some people had begun to suspect that Neruda was in love with another woman after the anonymous *Los versos del capitán* had been published in Italy earlier in 1952. Others, of course, already knew the true story, but not many.

A good friend at the time was Aída Figueroa, who with her husband, Sergio Insunza, had hidden Neruda and the Ant from the Chilean authorities at their central Santiago apartment in 1948.

Neither Pablo nor Delia knew how to drive, so Pablo often asked Aída to drive him in Sergio's car to his meetings or poetry recitals, or to wander around markets and antique shops. Aída would arrive at Michoacán in the morning after taking her husband to his lawyer's practice.

'On many occasions, the poet asked me to take him as far as the Bellavista district [of Santiago], where, he informed me, the Party central committee – of which he was a member – held its meetings. It was only later that I learned that this wasn't true. He was actually going to meet Matilde Urrutia at La Chascona, which they were building at the time . . . I was aware of the poet's extra-marital affairs, and I turned a blind eye . . . I saw the affairs as natural escape valves, considering the age difference between [Pablo and Delia]. Delia was not jealous. She accepted that a large number of ladies hovered around her husband. The Ant celebrated them all: the pretty, the well-dressed, the talented women. She didn't remotely consider that they had any intentions other than friendship or literary ones.'[15]

Other friends were less forgiving. On 27 July 1953, Tomás Lago noted: 'There are murmurings among the women that [Pablo] goes out every night at dusk, on various pretexts, and leaves Delia alone. And it's true. Who is he seeing?'[16]

There were plenty of people willing to stir up trouble in the Neruda household. One of these was María, wife of Matilde's cousin and former lover, César Godoy Urrutia, a senator and one-time friend. María began to spread gossip about Neruda's love for Matilde to anyone willing to listen. Pablo shrugged off the rumours as idle tittle-tattle. But he knew he would eventually have to make an agonising choice.

The dilemma could so easily have come to an abrupt, tragic resolution on 27 October 1952, when Pablo and Delia were nearly killed in a car crash. They were returning on a hot day from a lunch at the Maison de France in honour of Guillermo Pedregal, who was stepping down as president of a Chilean solidarity group working for the rights of Spanish Republicans. Pablo's normally cautious chauffeur, Jorge Palacios, was at the wheel when, just after midday, at the junction of Suecia and Simón Bolívar streets, their vehicle was hit by a heavy lorry. Neruda was left with a fractured right arm, while Delia had multiple injuries, a fractured heel and a temporary loss of memory. Neruda was taken to hospital at the Posta de Ñuñoa, where he remained for seven hours, before being allowed to return home to Michoacán, with his leg in plaster. Delia was more seriously hurt and was forced to stay in hospital for two more days.

Many people visited the house, concerned for Neruda's health. One of these was Matilde Urrutia, who – just as she had done in Mexico City, when Pablo suffered a lengthy bout of phlebitis – stayed to nurse Neruda until the Ant was released from hospital.

Once they had both fully recovered from their injuries, Pablo and Delia undertook more tours of Chile campaigning for Allende. However, the result of the presidential elections was a blow: the victor was the old dictator, General Carlos Ibáñez del Campo, who had ruled Chile with an iron hand from 1927 to 1931. Ironically, one of the platforms which won Ibáñez re-election was his promise to lift the ban on the Chilean Communist Party, which had been outlawed since 1948. It seems that the electorate forgot the authoritarian nature of Ibáñez's first presidency and, indeed, recalled the prosperity he had introduced. It also appears likely that money may have flowed in from Argentina, from President Juan Perón himself, to persuade people to vote for Ibáñez. However it came about, the victory was a severe disappointment to Neruda – but at least the Party was free once more to meet openly.

In December 1952, Neruda and Delia visited Moscow again, attending the Second Writers' Congress. They stayed in sumptuous rooms at the Hotel Metropol, where they received Russia's leading writers and intellectuals. However, while they were there, Neruda came down with a fever. To Delia's surprise, he expressed the desire to return to Chile immediately. The Ant advised him against moving anywhere in his condition, but Pablo insisted. The true motive for his haste, of course, was his impatience to be with Matilde. She was his nurse and his lover. And according to Delia's biographer, Fernando Sáez, Matilde had issued Neruda with an ultimatum: 'If you take another long trip to Europe without me, at least make sure you're back by the end of the year. If not, I will leave Chile for Mexico.'[17]

In fact, Neruda did not return immediately to Chile with Delia. While Delia went on to Santiago alone, Neruda flew from Zurich to meet Matilde at Alberto and Olga Mántaras's house in Uruguay. Matilde arrived there from Chile on 29 December – the same day as Pablo – and the delighted couple were driven by Alberto to his chalet, some twenty miles east of Montevideo.

'They spent all of January 1953 there alone and happy,' Mántaras told José Miguel Varas years later.[18] It was here at 'Datitla' (Pablo's near anagram of Atlántida) that a piece of Neruda folklore was born: the Nikolaska – a potent cocktail invented by the poet's Russian friend and translator, Simyon Kirsanov, consisting of good cognac, lemon slices and sugar. Neruda adapted it as the Coquetelón, using cognac, cointreau, dry champagne and orange juice.

During this stay, the couple composed an extraordinary book, *Oda a las flores de Datitla* (Ode to the Flowers of Datitla), which, in a remarkable piece of publishing history, was not to appear until nearly half a century later, in November 2002. This luxury edition, limited to 1,500 copies, and produced by Santiago's Corporación Sintesys, which promotes the arts and sciences in Latin America, was published simultaneously in Santiago, Havana, Paris and Buenos Aires.

It features Neruda's verse, with drawings of wild flowers and plants which Pablo and Matilde had lovingly gathered from the garden of the Mántaras's chalet. There are also photographs and facsimiles of letters which Neruda and Mántaras exchanged. According to Neruda's godson, Ramiro Insunza, the book was a present to the Mántarases in gratitude for their generosity.

Neruda had wanted to publish the book soon after it was written, but the timing was too delicate: he was still married to Delia. Mántaras kept the manuscript in a drawer until 1992, when he visited Chile and handed it over to Ramiro. 'Do something with it, even if it takes you until the twenty-first century,' Mántaras told Insunza. Sadly, Mántaras died in 1994.[19]

The original can be seen in the Paseo de Neruda Museum at Atlántida. The book's subtitle reads: 'Versos de Pablo Neruda; herbario de Matilde' (Verse by Pablo Neruda; Flower Collection by Matilde).

Neruda did not return to Chile until 22 January 1953. He quickly embarked on three more projects: the Continental Congress of Culture, to be held in Santiago in May; the building of the house for Matilde, La Chascona; and the completion of a very different book of poems, the delightful *Odas elementales* (Elementary Odes), on which he had already been working, intermittently, for some months.

Neruda worked hard, too, on the congress, despite the obstacles the Chilean government put in his way (including an attempt to prevent the Soviet delegation from attending). Writers and artists – many of them Neruda's personal friends – were invited from all over the world, including Diego Rivera, Nicolás Guillén and Jorge Amado.

But on 5 March 1953, Stalin died. When Neruda heard the news, he was at Isla Negra, and it came, as Neruda put it in the only poem he dedicated entirely to Stalin, 'like a blow from the ocean'. Five days later, Neruda wrote an article published simultaneously in the Chilean Communist Party daily *El Siglo*, and the Moscow newspaper *Gazeta*, declaring: 'The greatest of simple men, our master, has died. With his passing, a blow falls on our knowledge and intelligence, on the culture of our glorious, tormented times.'[20]

Here is how a leading Soviet poet, Yevgeny Yevtushenko, recalled the reaction in the USSR to the death of their leader: 'A sort of general paralysis came over the country. Trained to believe that Stalin was taking care of everyone, people were lost and bewildered without him. The whole of Russia wept. So did I.'[21]

Did Neruda feel he had lost a father figure when Stalin died? It seems so. In the poem he wrote on Stalin's death, Neruda refers to him as 'the Captain'. How odd. Neruda had seen himself as the Captain while living on Capri with Matilde. And he himself embraced the role of leader. Neruda would not have agreed with Boris Pasternak, who once told Yevtushenko: 'I didn't intend to lead anyone anywhere. I think a poet is just a tree – it stands still and rustles its leaves.'[22] Pablo Neruda never stood still.

On 26 May Neruda got to his feet at the Teatro Caupolicán to address the Continental Congress of Culture and began a rousing speech with a quote from Walt Whitman. He recalled the difficulties in which he had written *Canto general*: 'I believe that we are writing for a continent where everything is being done and above all, where we want to do everything . . . Our cities must be born. We need houses and schools, hospitals and trains . . . We are writing for modest people who, very, very often, cannot read. And yet, on this earth, poetry existed before writing and printing. That is why we know that poetry is like bread, and must be shared by everyone, the literate and the peasants, by all our vast, incredible, extraordinary family of peoples.'[23] Significantly, in the midst of the Cold War, Neruda recalled Walt Whitman's 1881 call to recognise that, different as Russians and Americans were, they had a certain characteristic vastness which made them similar to one another.

Despite Stalin's recent death, optimism breathes from every sentence in Neruda's speech. The ship could move forward without the original skipper at the helm, because the route ahead had been so firmly plotted. 'I believe in the splendour to come. I believe in man and in men . . . I know that our beloved friend, one of the greatest artists ever to tread this earth, Paul Robeson, has been forcibly prevented from attending our congress . . . I know that in Spain, in Turkey, in Greece, for years, writers, artists and teachers have been living in prison. I know that, on the island of Macronissos, for many years, the great Greek poet Yannis Ritsos has been writing behind barbed wire. I believe all this will come to an end . . .'[24]

On 27 November 1953, work finally began in earnest on Matilde's house, La Chascona. The plans were based on those of the Catalan architect, Germán Rodríguez Arias, although the restless Neruda apparently made changes to the sketches on an almost weekly basis. 'I didn't want to meet [Pablo's] friends. I told him never to introduce me to them,' Matilde wrote later. 'But this friend was the man who was going to build the house, so I had no choice.'[25]

Rodríguez Arias 'burst out laughing when he saw the land. "You'll spend all your time going up and down stairs," he predicted. And it was true that the spot wasn't horizontal, but vertical. That fascinated us. Our love had rejuvenated us; we were behaving like two adolescents . . . A few days later, the architect brought us a draft. Like any good architect, he looked at the sun and the view towards Santiago. Pablo took one glance at the draft and said: "Don't be stupid! I don't want to be looking out at Santiago. I want a view over the Andes." . . . The architect told him that there wouldn't be enough sunlight, and that, since it would mean building it up higher, they'd have to put more stairs in. "Great!" Pablo replied. "Put lots and lots of stairs in." '[26]

Much of the money for the construction work came from the Stalin Peace Prize, which Neruda was awarded on 20 December 1953. But Neruda's constant changes to the building as it went along meant that there was a shortage of funds, leading to some difficult decisions.

'My money had shrunk considerably,' recalled Matilde. 'So we began to sell all my possessions. The weekly anguish of how to pay the workers began every Monday, but our willpower, and luck, enabled us to pull through . . . We were a happy couple. We met up at all hours of the day. Pablo was like a house-ghost: he always arrived with a laugh, telling a joke. Sometimes he came in in a hurry, gave me a kiss, and left again.'[27]

Meanwhile, rumours were strengthening that Chile's foremost poet was conducting a passionate affair with another woman – and that he was indeed the author of the anonymous *Los versos del capitán* celebrating their life together on Capri. María de Godoy Urrutia continued her smear campaign against Matilde. If Delia knew about these rumours, she pretended not to be aware of them, or not to care. Neruda's main concern was that the news of his affair did not reach the ears of the Chilean Communist Party, which ironically had very bourgeois and puritanical views on extra-marital affairs.

Desperate for more time alone with Matilde, Pablo persuaded Delia to take a trip to Europe on his behalf – just as he had persuaded her to return to Chile the previous year when he needed breathing space with his new love. On this occasion, Neruda insisted that, since Delia had worked with the great French painter, Fernand Léger, it would be ideal if she could now persuade him to do the illustrations for a new, luxury edition of the *Canto general*.

Dutifully, Delia did indeed travel to Paris. She enjoyed the trust Pablo had placed in her, and was thrilled to be reunited with Léger. But by now, she had been affected by the constant rumours of her husband's passion for another woman. Could it really be true? Could he have been lying all this time?

As a new year dawned and Pablo approached his fiftieth birthday, he found himself free to enjoy the physical love with Matilde which he craved, and continued to make speeches in praise of Stalin. At a reception at Santiago's Teatro Caupolicán on 17 January 1954, in honour of his being awarded the Stalin Peace Prize, he said: 'Receiving this great honour, which people from many countries have conferred on me, I think of the name that it bears, the name of Stalin. In the Soviet Union, I have often seen small, gold, national Stalin Prize medals on the chests of engineers and musicians, scholars and poets. But nothing was more moving than seeing them on the chests of the worker heroes, the miners, the train workers, the women peasants.'[28]

That same month, January 1954, Neruda survived what could have been another very serious car accident. This time, the chauffeur was Alberto Mántaras, who was driving a second-hand car Neruda had hired from Manuel Solimano (the man who had played such a key role in arranging Pablo's escape across the Andes in 1949). Approaching Valparaíso from Santiago, the car's brakes failed. Fortunately, Mántaras managed to steer off the road on to some open land.

Not that Neruda learned from this hair-raising experience. Just a week later, he and Matilde asked Alberto to take them out again, in another run-down car. This time the engine died completely and they had to return to Santiago by train.

Pablo's time alone with Matilde was coming to an end. In March 1954, Delia caught the steamer *Andes* in Cherbourg bound for Buenos Aires. It seems likely that she expressed her anxieties about her marriage to her sister, Adelina, while in the Argentine capital, before travelling on to Santiago. She was clearly troubled – during one reading of a love poem from *Las uvas y el viento* to friends at Isla Negra, some of those listening happened to look across at Delia, and tears were streaming down her face.

Soon after she returned from Europe, Delia uncharacteristically ordered a clear-out of the house at Isla Negra. As the staff were clearing bookshelves, they found a number of whisky bottles hidden away. This upset the Ant – not because it showed that Pablo had held many parties at the house in the three months she had been away in France, but because he had bothered to conceal the signs.

It was at around this time that Pablo formally introduced Matilde to some of his friends, although he continued to call her Rosario and clearly expected them to conceal her existence from Delia. Tomás Lago observed that, 'During the meal, he came up to her [Matilde] all the time and held her, touched her knees, hugged her to him with real pleasure and delight. He called her "my love" again and again.'[29]

In June 1954, Neruda took a significant decision: he would donate his entire, extremely valuable, collection of books and seashells to the Universidad de Chile. It was an enormously generous gesture. Neruda loved his books. He once told his friend Jorge Edwards that he wasn't interested in books about books: he liked books that looked like chunky, juicy steaks. At the ceremony at the Universidad de Chile on 20 June Neruda exclaimed: 'I'm not a thinker, and these collected books are more reverential than investigative. Here is a collection of the beauty which dazzled me . . .'[30] The donation included a precious gift from the late Paul Eluard: two letters written by Rimbaud's sister, Isabelle, from a Marseille hospital to their mother, recounting his death throes.

But a more momentous milestone was on the horizon: Pablo's fiftieth birthday on 12 July 1954. Delia gamely busied herself drawing up a long list of guests: friends and writers from all over the world.

One of these friends, the Chinese poet Ai Qing, left this description of his visit to Isla Negra for the birthday celebrations:

> We walk into
> the home of a navigator
> The ground is strewn with seashells
> Perhaps the tide came in last night . . .
> Pablo Neruda
> looks out at the ocean waves,
> his language quarried from a mine . . .
> Gathered around the blazing fire
> are a dozen sailing companions
> drinking wine, sharing tales . . .
>
> We come from many countries . . .
> but we are the closest of brothers . . .[31]

At another ceremony at the Universidad de Chile to mark his birthday, Neruda described 'how poetry is born: it comes from invisible heights. It is secret and obscure in origin, solitary and fragrant and, like a river, it will dissolve anything that falls in its path . . . It will irrigate the fields and will provide bread for the hungry . . .'

On 11 August 1954, Ilya Ehrenburg travelled to Santiago to award Neruda the Stalin Peace Prize. Neruda told Ehrenburg that Chile had always welcomed the Russian with open arms. This was scarcely the welcome that Ehrenburg received when he arrived at Santiago airport. Far from it. According to Neruda, the Chilean authorities, on US instructions, rifled through all Ehrenburg's luggage at the airport. Among the Russian's papers, they found the proofs of the first Russian translation of Neruda's *Canto general*. 'The learned functionaries showed [the proofs] in triumph to the journalists. "They're instructions from Moscow. We'll have them translated." And so the *Canto general* was going to be translated back into Spanish again . . .!'[32]

What other incriminating evidence lay in Ehrenburg's luggage? A list of Chilean plants, with their Latin names, and a Scandinavian Airlines prospectus. 'The North American employees don't know any Latin, and they thought they were dealing with a secret language . . . The diploma granting me the Stalin Prize, in Spanish, also created a

mood of drooling anticipation in police circles. They took photos of it
– rather like photographing the Eiffel Tower – as a secret document.'[33]

Eventually, the Chilean President intervened directly, ordering the
authorities to return the documents to Ehrenburg, but the right-wing
media continued to launch smear campaigns against the Russian while
he remained on Chilean soil.

That year, 1954, which ushered in Neruda's half-century of life,
also saw the publication of two books: the unsatisfying *Las uvas y el
viento* and the wonderful *Odas elementales*. Neruda was always fond
of *Las uvas y el viento*, coinciding as it did with his full political
commitment and his love for Matilde. What is surprising is that he did
not recognise its serious literary shortcomings. He thought that he had
fulfilled the primordial duty of the poet as he expressed it in 'Todo es
nuevo bajo el sol' (All is New Under the Sun), the prologue to the 1953
anthology of his *Poesía política* (Political Poetry):

> There is no poetry without human contact . . . The path of poetry
> leads outwards, through streets and factories; it listens at the doors
> of all the exploited, runs and warns, whistles and gathers, threatens
> with the heavy voice of the future, is everywhere that men are
> struggling, at all the battles, in all the bells announcing a world
> being born, because with strength, with hope, with tenderness and
> toughness we will make sure it is born.[34]

One critic, Jaime Concha, believes that *Las uvas y el viento* represented a transformation of Neruda's poetic vision as dramatic as that
of his 1926 collection, *Tentativa del hombre infinito*. 'In this book
[*Las uvas*] the edifying and numinous celebration co-exists with the
spectacle of ruins and rubble . . .'[35]

Concha draws special attention to Neruda's many allusions to the
battle of Stalingrad: 'Stalingrad, more even than the October Revolution in this moment of Neruda's poetry, represents a fundamental
turning-point in contemporary history, towards the irrevocable construction of a new social order. It is the victory that ensures the
peace.'[36]

The fact that the *Odas elementales* was a very different book
highlights Neruda's willingness to change and experiment, to enrich
his poetry. Some observers – like the bestselling Chilean novelist, Luis
Sepúlveda – see this lack of unity of tone and attitude in his work as a

whole as a weakness. Sepúlveda told me in Spain: 'I share Borges's view of Neruda that he was uneven. All poets are uneven, of course, but Neruda's poetry underwent some peculiar leaps. How could the same man write both *El hondero entusiasta* and the *Odas elementales?*'[37]

But Neruda was always eager to renew himself with each book. The *Odas elementales*, published five months after *Las uvas*, in July 1954, praise simple objects like onions and tomatoes. The lines are often very short – the poem 'Oda a las Américas' even contains a one-letter line, 'y' (and) – as if attempting to distil the essence of the world around him.

Neruda was probably unaware of what his Russian hero, Pushkin, had written about odes in an 1824 note: namely that odes were the lowest form of poem, because they lacked a 'plan' and because mere 'rapture' excluded the kind of 'tranquillity' which, Pushkin said, was 'an indispensable condition of the highest beauty'.[38] Neruda does, however, achieve both rapture and a sense of tranquillity in many of these poems.

The book proved a huge success with its readers and even won over literary and political opponents such as Alone, who wrote: 'Some say this clarity of expression was imposed by the Soviets so that Neruda would be able to reach the masses. If that were true, we would have to forgive the Soviets an awful lot . . . Bitterness gone, complex obscurity banished, it was to be feared that the poetry would go too far . . . and fall into prose. Well, never has Neruda's poetry seemed more authentic. We would like to place a limit on this praise. They say that no judgement is good without reservations. But we can find none. We even forgive the poet his Communism.'[39]

Buoyed by the critical and public acclaim, Neruda brought out two more books of odes for the same publisher, Losada: *Nuevas odas elementales* (New Elementary Odes) in 1956 and the *Tercer libro de las odas* (Third Book of Odes) in 1957. He later wrote that he considered these three books, plus the 1959 collection, *Navegaciones y regresos* (Voyages and Homecomings), to be part of a single book – indeed, the last was subtitled 'the fourth column of the elementary odes'.

A few of the 150 odes were first published in the Venezuelan daily, *El Nacional*, the newspaper edited by Neruda's friend, Miguel Otero Silva. Otero Silva had invited Pablo to contribute a weekly poem, and

Neruda stipulated the unusual condition that it must appear on the news pages, not in the arts section. 'In this way, I managed to publish a history of time, of diverse things, trades, people, fruits and flowers, of life and my vision, of the struggle, in fact of all that I could take in through this vast cyclical urge of my creation . . .'[40]

In the *Odas elementales*, René de Costa has written, 'The poem is designed as a didactic artifice, helping us to see, to witness and to speculate on the marvellous significance of the world in which we live, all of us.'[41] I do not agree with de Costa that the *Odas* are didactic or artificial: many seem genuinely full of Neruda's awe at the beauty around him. But there is certainly no anguished soul-searching, and de Costa is right to point up Neruda's generous desire to share his glorious sense of oneness with the natural world around him. And his enthusiasm is, indeed, irresistible. We enjoy the world anew through his eyes: yes, a simple artichoke can be seen as a soldier, wrapped in armour and ready for battle; an onion is 'more beautiful than a bird / with blinding feathers'.

Neruda's aim in the *Odas* was to speak to the ordinary people in the street about ordinary things using the language of the street. His *Odas* have a refreshing spontaneity which brings the world alive. Now he explicitly rejects poets (including himself) who indulge in self-absorbed misery. In the first poem in the book, 'El hombre invisible' (The Invisible Man), which Neruda actually wrote in Europe as far back as 1952, he says:

> I laugh,
> I smile
> at the old poets . . .
> They're always saying 'I'
> . . . no one suffers,
> no one loves,
> apart from my poor brother,
> the poet . . .[42]

'Oda a la alegría' (Ode to Joy),

> It merely happens
> that I'm happy

is an almost conscious rebuttal of the first line of Neruda's
famously pessimistic poem from *Residencia en la tierra*, 'Walking
Around':

> It so happens that I'm tired of being a man

In 'Oda a la soledad' (Ode to Solitude), he again turns his back on the
romantic loner who had sought creativity in loneliness:

> It's not true what they say about
> creative solitude . . .
> The desert is solitude
> on earth, and it is as sterile
> as a man's loneliness.

In later years, he would come to embrace solitude as a friend once
again. But not yet.

The drive for fraternity with his fellow human beings in 'Oda al
hombre sencillo' (Ode to the Simple Man) contains strong echoes of
his wish in *Alturas de Macchu Picchu* to know everything about the
daily life of the pre-Columbian slave labourers who had built the
Andean mountain fortress:

> I want to know who you are,
> how much you earn,
> where you work,
> which mine,
> which pharmacy.
> I have a terrible obligation
> to know it all,
> to know it all,
> day and night, to know
> your name.
> That's my job . . .

And the influence of Proust can be felt in Neruda's fiercely sensual
memories of his childhood in Temuco. The 'Oda al pasado' (Ode to
the Past) begins, startlingly, with the Proustian

> Today, I was talking
> when, like a mother,
> the past emerged,
> my past . . .

But other odes in the three books have a different function. Some are overtly political. As the Korean War was raging, Neruda wrote his 'Oda al átomo' (Ode to the Atom) condemning North American military aggression. The 'Oda al cobre' (Ode to Copper) hits out at the United States for taking over much of the Chilean copper industry. ('My people / Chile mastered the material / separated the minerals / from the stone / and they went to Chicago.') The 'Oda a Guatemala', written much earlier, is an attack on the 1954 overthrow, with US help, of the democratically elected regime of Jacobo Arbenz in that country.

But as Neruda's literary success soared, the tension of living his double life was becoming too much to sustain. 'Delia once showed me a copy of Los versos del capitán and said "Eso tiene bastante de Pablo, pero no es Pablo" (This is quite like Pablo, but it isn't Pablo),' Aída Figueroa told me. 'Pablo kept leaving, suddenly, saying, "I'm off, I've got things to do." And Delia started to wonder what he was doing. But she had no idea what it was. It was a terrible time for her. She thought it might be some fling.'[43]

One day, a gardener, whom Neruda had sacked after accusing him of stealing several bottles of fine wine, approached Delia and said: 'I'm a Communist, señora, and we don't accept these things.' He had been at Michoacán while Delia was convalescing in hospital after the car crash in 1952, when Matilde had arrived to nurse Pablo. Delia told the gardener to hold his tongue, but she had heard enough.[44]

Neruda's friends, Francisco Velasco and Marie Martner, told me that Pablo would also take Matilde to Valparaíso, where he presented her, very indiscreetly, as his niece, Rosario. Rosario was the name he had given Matilde in the anonymous Los versos del capitán. 'Pablo liked to have a siesta in the afternoon. I offered him my son's bedroom which had a little bed in it. And he went to sleep with Matilde, his "niece". He had no problem with this, and nor did I!' Martner recalled.[45]

Meanwhile, friends of the Ant recollect her becoming very nervous. She was even more absent-minded than usual. Her dress sense had become extravagantly misplaced, her hats were enormous, her make-up piled on in heavy layers.

By now, most friends were aware of what was going on. Knowing that it was only a matter of time before the Ant herself found out, two of her closest friends – Diego Muñoz, Neruda's schoolfriend from Temuco, and his wife, Inés Valenzuela – decided to reveal the truth as tactfully as possible. Delia immediately tackled Pablo, who denied everything: 'So just who is this Matilde Urrutia?' she asked him. 'But you know her, Ant – she's the woman who ironed your blouses in Mexico.'[46]

Delia became more suspicious than ever. She began sifting through his clothes for any sign of proof that the rumours were true, and one day, she found it. It was a letter from Matilde which Pablo had carelessly left in a jacket pocket telling him that she was pregnant for the third time.

There followed a horrific scene: Neruda and Delia had a meeting with Galo González, the secretary-general of the Chilean Communist Party, in an effort to avoid a public scandal. In tears, Pablo begged Delia to stay with him, but her mind was made up: 'This is not a bourgeois marriage, Pablo. If there's no love, there's no marriage.'[47]

Desperately, Neruda continued to try and win the Ant back – through intermediaries. His argument ran like this: 'Matilde has done nothing worse than what Delia did in Madrid when I was married to Maruca: she got me into bed. Why can't she understand? But she's being badly advised, that's the problem.'

The last time Pablo and Delia saw each other was at the end of the Chilean summer, 1955, at Michoacán. As on almost every other morning, Diego Muñoz and Inés were there, as was Galo González. Delia took Inés to one side and informed her that she had decided to leave: 'I can't accept what Pablo is proposing. Would you accept such a thing?'

There was nothing Inés could say in response.[48]

Delia left and initially stayed at the house of her friend, Graciela Matte. Then, at the end of March 1955, unable to bear living in the same country as the man she had loved and trusted for so long, she left Chile for Buenos Aires. Margarita Aguirre and her then-husband, Rodolfo Araoz Alfaro, who accompanied her to Santiago airport, found her calm and determined to go on with her life.

Delia spent just two days in Buenos Aires before taking a boat to Europe. In those two days in Argentina, she wrote a stinging letter to Margarita and Rodolfo, condemning them – and others – for concealing Pablo's affair with Matilde from her. It was a letter dripping with hurt pride.

'The fact is that Pablo was very much in love with Matilde, but he also felt great anguish in separating from Delia,' Inés Figueroa told me. 'Pablo was *not* a man of the world, he was not a cynical *sinverguenza* (scoundrel). He was almost a child in the face of such a difficult situation. Pablo planned nothing serious with Matilde at first, but it grew into a great passion. She had a very strong character, and she became indispensable to Neruda. But it cost him a great deal because he had loved Delia a lot, and the fact is that La Hormiga was very lovable. Pablo lost a bit of himself when he lost Delia.'[49]

Some took against Matilde because she was not a cultured woman, as Delia was, not 'refined' in the same way, and could seem cold to outsiders. She tried to protect Neruda from unnecessary distractions, and this meant cutting him off from visitors. Others, however, approved of the order which Matilde was trying to impose on her lover's life and the fact that, at her new home – amidst the construction work at La Chascona – she was a good cook and housekeeper.

What is painfully true is that the final separation of Pablo and Delia created a dramatic split in Neruda's closest circle of friends. Some, like Tomás Lago, announced that they never wanted to see or speak to Neruda again for the rest of their lives.

Tomás Lago's daughter, Victoria Lago, told me in Chile: 'Things were so bad between them that, when one found out that the other was going to a place, the other avoided going there. They were both severe men, in that way. But later, when my father was very ill, Pablo got someone to telephone to ask after his health. The same happened in reverse when Pablo became ill.'[50]

Yet for all Pablo's distress at what was happening, he knew that Matilde could give him the things he craved, which Delia, who was now seventy, could no longer offer: a fulfilling sex life and an ordered existence allowing him to concentrate fully on his writing. It was not going to be an easy transition.

Aída Figueroa told me:

What really hurt Delia when she found out was that Pablo had taken Matilde to Isla Negra and slept with her in Delia's bed. I believe that, unlike Pablo, Matilde always planned to stay permanently with him. Not Pablo. He wanted to keep Delia as an intellectual companion and Matilde as his sensual passion. When I first met Matilde, she was very coarse, primitive. Even though she had already led a full life, Pablo took great efforts to educate Matilde, making her read, even memorise things. He encouraged her to sing in public – even though she sang very badly! Eventually, he realised it was not a good idea, and he stopped asking her to do that. So she then became his great administrator – of his physical well-being, his health, his household. She changed his whole lifestyle. Pablo gained a lot – but he also lost a lot. He lost dynamic friendships. Matilde invited some people into the house and eliminated others from the list. While he was with Delia, we could simply walk into the house and talk to Pablo. It was a very spontaneous, disorganised life. But Matilde changed all that.[51]

Victoria Lago's view is harsher:

Matilde Urrutia entered Neruda's life riding roughshod over the Ant. She set herself up at [Delia's] home in Mexico and in Italy, making friends with her, and Delia was such a good person that she never realised what was going on. My father knew about everything and he did not agree with it. Matilde did all she could to separate them and keep old friends, like Diego Muñoz and Acario Cotapos, away. She wanted to be in the foreground. She could not accept playing second fiddle.[52]

After his separation from Delia, Neruda moved into La Chascona, now completed, with Matilde, but he was clearly shaken by his marriage break-up. He did not write much poetry for the rest of 1955.

He kept active, however: he launched the *Gaceta de Chile*, which was printed three times a year. A selection of Neruda's poetry appeared in Arabic that year and another in Persian. Nascimento published his collection of lectures, *Viajes*, in Santiago. And he travelled widely – now with Matilde openly at his side. He visited the Soviet Union again, China and then further Eastern Bloc countries. On his return to Latin America, he gave readings in Brazil and Uruguay, before staying at the home of Margarita Aguirre's husband, Rodolfo Araoz Alfaro, in Totoral, Argentina. There, in December 1955, he wrote two of the odes which form part of the *Tercer libro de las odas*: 'Ode to the Butterfly' and 'Ode to the Black Panther'.

In January 1956, the second book of odes, *Nuevas odas elementales*, was published in Buenos Aires by Losada, and the following month, Neruda and Matilde returned to Chile.

February 1956 shook the world of every Communist – Nikita Khrushchev stood up at the Twentieth Soviet Communist Party Congress and condemned Stalin's crimes. Neruda made no public comment at the time. On 4 November that year, the Soviet tanks rolled into Budapest. Neruda, once again, did not say a word to denounce the Soviet system. Some friends insist that Neruda felt deeply pained inside by these events, but others have criticised him strongly for not speaking out openly in condemnation.

He wrote about it only later – much, much later – in his memoirs:

> Many have believed me a die-hard Stalinist. Fascists and reactionaries have described me as a lyrical interpreter of Stalin. I am not particularly put out by this. Any judgement is possible in a diabolically confused era. The private tragedy for us Communists was to face the fact that, in several aspects of the Stalin problem, the enemy was right. This revelation, which was staggering, left us in a painful state of mind. Some felt that they had been deceived. Desperately, they accepted the enemy's reasoning and went over to its side. Others believed that the harrowing facts, implacably brought to light during the Twentieth Congress, proved the integrity of a Communist Party which survived, letting the world see the historical truth and accepting its own responsibility. This has been my stand: the darkness, unknown to me, of the Stalin era. Stalin rose before my eyes, a good-natured man of principles, as sober as a hermit, a titanic defender of the Russian Revolution. Moreover, this small man with his huge moustache had become a giant in wartime. With his name on its lips, the Red Army attacked and demolished the power of Hitler's demons.[53]

Neruda sought solace in his own country's Communist Party, in which, he said, 'I found a large group of simple people who had left personal vanity, despotism and material interests far behind. I felt happy knowing honest people who were fighting for common decency, for justice.'[54]

Many people down the years have tried to explain why Communism exerted such an enduring hold over intellectuals. The Portuguese writer, José Saramago, a Nobel Prize-winner and a Communist, has described Communism as a hormone which, once it takes hold in a body, is very difficult to expunge.[55] Louis Aragon declared that 'There are only two sides to a barricade' – echoing Neruda's belief that if you withheld your loyalty to one side, you were falling into the other camp. The Party, in the words of the British Communist, Eric Hobsbawm, 'was what our life was all about. We gave it all we had. In return, we got it from it the certainty of our victory and the experience of fraternity.'[56]

This loyalty was sorely tested by Khrushchev's revelations. As Yevtushenko has written: 'After the text was read to them at Party meetings, they went away in distress, their eyes on the ground. Probably many among the older people tortured themselves with the question: had they lived their lives in vain? The gifted writer Fadeyev shot himself with the gun he had carried as a partisan in the Civil War. His death was another of Stalin's crimes.'[57]

Jorge Edwards noted that the poet's work showed signs of the effect of the calamitous news of 1956, even if he remained publicly silent on the issue:

> The author of the third book of odes, published at the end of 1957 is, in contrast, an entirely different poet, an intimate, voluptuous, nostalgic contemplator . . . of nature, of creatures, of objects whose use has been degraded but at the same time humanised: a flying albatross, a bicycle, a village cinema, an old railway station . . . If you compare those poems with *Las uvas y el viento*, you have the immediate sensation that the poet, whose eyes had been fixed on the future, is focusing once again on the things that surround him, big or small, on the immediate landscape, on omnipresent nature [without clear-cut messages] such as the one transmitted by the waves of the Pacific Ocean solemnifying the death of Joseph Stalin, or the wind from Asia which was the wind of revolution.[58]

In a sense Neruda is indirectly reaffirming his opposition to Sartre's 'nausea', the French philosopher's disgust at the world around him. Not for nothing had Neruda singled out Sartre for his contempt in public speeches. For Sartre, objects and nature have no meaning. For Neruda, they are imbued with life-enhancing meaning.

Nuevas odas elementales, published that year, contains the wonderful 'Oda a los calcetines' (Ode to Socks), in which Neruda sees his feet as 'two woollen fish, two long sharks . . . two gigantic blackbirds, two cannon: my feet were honoured in this way by these celestial socks.' In this love affair, he resists the temptation to place the socks in a 'gilded cage / and feed them . . . pulp of pink melon'.[59] Humour, mischief – the same sense of mischief that led him to dress up in disguises at parties well into his sixties.

The 'Oda a Paul Robeson' honours the great American Communist singer, and emphasises Neruda's love of his fellow man.

> . . .
> powerful
> voice
> of water
> on fire,
> the solemn, deliberate, hoarse, pure
> voice of the earth
> reminding us
> that we were
> still men,
> that we shared
> pain and hope . . .

He contrasts the silence after Hiroshima with Robeson's voice, which emerges once more,

> filling
> the sky with your sacred voice,
> not just
> for blacks,
> for the poor blacks,
> but for the poor
> whites,
> for
> the poor Indians,
> for all
> peoples.

And the 'Oda a Walt Whitman' returns to another great poetic
influence:

> I don't recall
> at what age,
> nor where,
> whether in the great wet South
> or on the
> fearful coast, beneath the shrill
> cry of seagulls, I touched a hand and it was
> Walt Whitman's hand . . .

In his superb study of the *Odas*, Robert Pring-Mill rejects any
attempt to divide up Neruda's work into mutually exclusive stages and
points out that the *Odas* are as politically committed, lyrically, as
Canto general was epically.[60] Pring-Mill notes that many of the lines
from Neruda's poetic explanation of his devotion to the Communist
cause, the poem 'A mi partido' (To My Party) in *Canto general*,
provide the key ideas in the *Elementary Odes*, especially:

> You made me build upon reality, as on a rock

and

> You have made me see the world's clarity and the possibility of
> joy . . .

The problem for the poet, Neruda summed up, was that 'it is much
easier to writer difficult poetry than simple poetry'.[61]

On 10 January 1957, Gabriela Mistral died. The next day, the
Chilean Communist daily, *El Siglo*, published a tribute by the man
who, as a boy, had timidly walked into her office at the Temuco girls'
school. And now, with her loss, wrote Neruda, 'Chile's heart is in
mourning'.[62]

That spring, Pablo began to write the *Cien sonetos de amor*, one
hundred love sonnets dedicated to Matilde, but he interrupted this
work, first to undertake a disastrous trip to Argentina, and then to
take Matilde with him on a remarkable return to the Far Eastern

setting for those desolate years of his youth. The couple would be away from Chile for most of 1957.

On 1 April 1957, he travelled to Buenos Aires where he hoped to give a series of readings. However, on 11 April he was arrested and spent a day and a half in the National Penitentiary.

> An encounter with the secret police may not seem dangerous, but if it's the secret police of Argentina, that is something else again – not without humour, but with unpredictable consequences. This particular night, just arrived from Chile and en route to far-off lands, I fell into bed exhausted, I was just starting to doze off when several policemen burst into the house. They ransacked the place: they picked up books and magazines, they rummaged in closets, and went through the underwear. And they had already taken away the Argentine friend in whose house I was staying, when they discovered me in my room at the back of the house.

Matilde told the police agents that the man was Pablo Neruda and that he was sick and very tired after his trip. An hour later, they returned with an ambulance.

> Matilde protested, but this had no effect on them. They had their orders. They were to take me in, weary or fresh, healthy or sick, dead or alive. It was raining that night, thick drops came down from the heavy Buenos Aires skies. I couldn't understand it. Perón had already been ousted. In the name of democracy, General [Pedro Eugenio] Aramburu had overthrown tyranny. Yet, without knowing how or when . . . I was on my way to prison. The stretcher on which the four policemen were carrying me became a knotty problem as we descended stairways, entered elevators, crossed hallways. The four litter-bearers suffered and puffed. To make their distress even greater, Matilde told them in a honeyed voice that I weighed 110 kilos . . .
>
> Finally, they deposited me upstairs, in the farthest cell, with a tiny, very high window. I wanted to rest, to get some sleep, sleep, sleep. I couldn't . . . Some hours later, the community of writers and friends had gone into action in Argentina, Chile and several other countries. They took me from my cell, carried me to the infirmary, returned my belongings, and set me free, I was about to leave the prison when

one of the uniformed guards came up to me and put a sheet of paper on my hands. It was a poem he had dedicated to me. Written in crude verse, filled with careless errors, innocent like all popular art, I imagine few poets have received a poetic homage from the men assigned to guard them.[63]

The Chilean consul secured Neruda's release, but the poet left Argentina without completing his schedule of readings.

He and Matilde continued on to the Orient. Neruda had been invited to Colombo in Ceylon to attend a peace congress. They found a conference hall full of hundreds of Buddhist monks. Then they went off to look for the house where Pablo had lived in the suburb of Wellawatta.

I had a hard time finding it. The trees had grown, the face of the street had changed. The old place where I had written so many painful poems was going to be torn down soon. Its doors were worm-eaten, the tropical dampness had damaged its walls, but it had stood there waiting for this final moment of parting.[64]

While in Ceylon, Neruda placed an advertisement in a local paper seeking news of his old servant boy, Brampy. He heard nothing. From Ceylon, Pablo and Matilde flew with Jorge Amado and his wife, Zelia, through a thunderstorm, the rain leaking into the aircraft, to Rangoon. It was the thirtieth anniversary of Neruda's residence there, as an unhappy consul, in a town 'delirious with colour, a torrid and fascinating place, [whose] languages were impenetrable'. Back in 1927, 'the colony was being exploited and preyed on by its English rulers, but the city was clean and luminous, its streets sparkled with life, the shop windows displayed their colonial temptations'.[65]

In 1927, Neruda had succumbed to the temptations of Josie Bliss. Now, three decades later, with his new love, Matilde, at his side, he set about trying to find out what had happened to his Burmese lover. 'No one could supply me with information about her life or her death. The neighbourhood where we had lived together no longer even existed.'[66]

Neruda's friend, Inés Figueroa, recalled: 'He told me Josie had broken his heart. He was very sorry, because she had been a great earth-woman, very primitive, and she had ended up asphyxiating him with her extreme emotions.'[67]

From Rangoon, Neruda and Matilde flew on with Jorge and Zelia to China. There they were met by Neruda's friend, the Chinese poet Ai Qing. Neruda described him as one of those poets 'whose voices were natural and lyrical . . . very gentle in their poetry, but iron-fisted in politics, they had come home in time to carry out their destinies'.[68] But Ai Qing's fate was out of his hands.

While in China, Pablo and Matilde visited a bizarre forest made of stone, each rock shaped either like a needle or 'like a wave in a still sea'. Neruda said he felt at home in post-revolutionary China but noted that some things had changed since his visit five years earlier with Ilya Ehrenburg: 'I miss the colour blue.' On his previous visit, 'everyone was dressed in proletarian blue then, some kind of twill or light workmen's tweed. Men, women and children wore it. I liked this simplified dress with its varying shades of blue. It was a beautiful thing to see innumerable blue specks crossing streets and roads.'[69] The reason for the absence of blue was not sinister, Neruda discovered: it was simply that China's textile industry had grown sufficiently to allow the Chinese people to be clothed in all colours.

With Matilde and Jorge Amado at his side, he sailed down the Yangtse River, but although Neruda loved the poetry of the Chinese landscape, it was not an entirely happy trip. Something had changed, Neruda recalled later, in his friendship with the great Brazilian writer:

In truth, the revelations about the Stalin era had snapped a coiled spring deep within Jorge Amado. We are old friends, we have shared years of exile, we had always been united by a common conviction and hope. But I believe I have been less sectarian than he; my nature and my Chilean temperament inclined me towards an understanding of others. Jorge, on the other hand, had always been inflexible . . . The report of the Twentieth Congress was a tidal wave that drove all revolutionaries to take new stands and draw new conclusions. Many of us had the feeling that, from the anguish produced by those painful revelations, we were being born all over again . . . Jorge, on the other hand, seemed to have started a different stage of his life on board that ship, between the marvellous cliffs of the Yangtse. I don't believe he lost faith in the revolution, but he fell back on his work and divested it of the direct political character that had marked it until then.[70]

If we take this version as authentic, then Khrushchev's revelations appear to have hardened Neruda's Communist convictions, rather than thrown him into inner doubt, and he seems here to condemn Amado for his wavering.

Neruda turned fifty-three in China. Zelia and Matilde asked Ai Qing to try to persuade the Chinese authorities to allow them to prepare a special banquet on board the boat. They were disappointed: the country might be able to afford multicoloured costumes, but it was in the midst of austere cut-backs: even Mao Tse-tung had renounced celebrations for his own birthday.

Somehow, however, Ai Qing prevailed. 'On that 12 July, my birthday, we had our roast chicken on the table, the golden booty of the controversy. A couple of tomatoes and slices of onion brightened a small dish. The huge table stretched on beyond it, embellished, as it was every day, with dishes gleaming wth luscious Chinese food.'[71]

Tragically, later in the trip, Ai Qing did not turn up for a meeting in Peking. The so-called 'anti-rightist' struggle had just begun and the exiled Ai Qing was among its first victims. Neruda was distraught. As another Chinese poet, Xi Chi, recalled:

> I was chairing a poetry symposium in Peking and Pablo Neruda was there. Suddenly, he left his seat and started wandering along the corridors of the big hall, alone. I ran up to him and asked: 'What are you looking for?' He replied, tactfully: 'I'm looking for . . . you.' But I knew who he was really looking for. We went back into the poetry session, but he never returned to China after that.[72]

Clearly, Neruda left China profoundly disillusioned. There is a very intriguing passage from Neruda's memoirs in which he attacks personality cults – an attitude that was to get him into trouble with Fidel Castro not long afterwards.

> What has estranged me from the Chinese revolutionary process has not been Mao Tse-tung but Mao Tse-tungism. I mean Mao Tse-Stalinism, the repetition of a cult of a Socialist deity. Who can deny Mao the political personality of a great organiser, of the great liberator of a people? How could I fail to be impressed by his epic halo, his simplicity which is so poetic, so melancholy, and so

ancient? Yet during my trip, I saw hundreds of poor peasants, returning from their labours, prostrate themselves, before putting away their tools, to salute the portrait of the modest guerrilla fighter from Yunnan, transformed into a god now . . . In Stalin's case, I had contributed my share to the personality cult. But in those days, Stalin seemed to us the conqueror who had crushed Hitler's armies. The saviour of all humanity. The deterioration of his character was a mysterious process, still an enigma for many of us.[73]

Neruda's Russian friend, Vera Kuteishikova, told me in Moscow that Pablo's disenchantment with the cult of Mao marked one of the first genuine steps in his private change of attitude to Stalinism.

From China, Neruda and Matilde travelled to Moscow and from there spent several months touring the Soviet republics of Abkhazia and Armenia. In Abkhazia, it struck him that, unlike the Russia he had seen before, 'this land of sunlight, wheat and huge vineyards has another tone, a Mediterranean accent. These men walk differently, these women have the eyes and hands of Italian or Greek women.'[74]

The couple then flew to the Armenian capital, Erevan, which Neruda described as 'one of the most beautiful cities I have seen. Built of volcanic tuff, it has the harmony of a pink rose.'[75] He had an unforgettable visit to the astronomical observatory of Binakan – where he noted that 'each star has its own distinct way of writing, tremulous and fascinating, but unintelligible to the eyes of an earth-bound poet'[76] – followed by a joyous encounter with a swimming tapir at the zoo.

From Erevan, Pablo and Matilde flew back to Moscow, where they met Ilya Ehrenburg and enjoyed his hospitality ('I could never tell whether he knew more about Stendhal or about *foie gras*'[77]) before making a brief visit to Paris. When they returned once again to Moscow in October 1957, they found the capital in festive spirits: it was the fortieth anniversary of the Russian Revolution. Leaving Moscow by train for Finland, they gazed up at the sky, which was lit up with fireworks, 'like volleys of cheers, like signals of mutual understanding and friendship'.[78]

In Finland, Neruda renewed his love affair with the whale, buying a narwhal's tooth, before he and Matilde continued on to the Swedish port of Gothenburg, where they caught the liner *Bolívar* at the beginning of December, bound for Valparaíso. Pablo wanted to pay a brief visit to Venezuela when the boat stopped off there, but was prevented from doing so by the Venezuelan dictator, Marcos Pérez Jiménez, who had sent 'enough soldiers to fight a war'.[79] By the time Neruda reached Chile, the dictator had been deposed.

On 18 December 1957, Losada published the *Tercer libro de las odas* – a reminder that Neruda had kept up his astonishingly energetic output. The first complete works of Pablo Neruda had been published by Losada in January of that year. Some critics have held this productivity against him. A fellow Chilean poet, Gonzalo Rojas, addressing a Madrid gathering in 2003 to commemorate the thirtieth anniversary of Neruda's death, called him a great poet but also 'a tree, and a tree needs a lot of pruning'.[80]

Pablo and Matilde spent the New Year at Isla Negra. March 1958 brought sombre news: the death of the Chilean Communist leader, Galo González. Neruda then took part in the second presidential campaign in Chile, once again travelling the length and breadth of the country and speaking at packed political meetings. But all his efforts proved ultimately fruitless, as Salvador Allende again lost out, this time to Jorge Alessandri Rodríguez, son of the late Arturo Alessandri Palma. Advocating draconian state intervention to restructure Chile's economy, Allende came within a hair's breath of victory.

That same year, Neruda changed tack again, with the publication of another extraordinary book, *Estravagario*. Like the title of *Crepusculario*, his first book, *Estravagario* is a neologism; but this latest work – basically an extended autobiographical sketch – is full of witty self-doubt and self-deprecating irony.

'I want just five things,' Neruda writes in the poem 'Pido silencio' (I Call for Silence) in *Estravagario*:

> One is love without end.
> The second is to see the autumn.
> I can't live without leaves
> flying off and falling back to earth.
> The third is the seriousness of winter,
> the rain I loved, the caress
> of the fire in the wild cold.
> In fourth place comes summer
> as round as a watermelon.
> The fifth are your eyes,
> My beloved Matilde.

> I do not want to sleep without your eyes,
> I don't want to live without you looking at me.
> I'd give up spring
> to be sure you were looking at me.
> Friends, that's all I want.
> It is virtually nothing and practically everything . . .[81]

The self-doubt in this book is playful, and without anguish, as if in acknowledgement of his own complexities and contradictions:

> Now I realise that I've been
> not one man but several[82]

And there are flashes of humour. In 'Sobre mi mala educación' (On My Bad Upbringing), he makes fun of his own social clumsiness and is jealous of the natural ease of fish, guests of the sea but always immaculately dressed, without a single scale out of place. In contrast, formal dinner parties horrify him and Neruda acknowledges his shyness and physical awkwardness at public gatherings:

> I don't know what to do with my hands
> and I thought about coming without them, but where would I put
>   the ring?
> . . . And then I don't know anyone.
> I don't remember their names.

Other poems mingle darkness with the humour. 'El miedo' (Fear) is a great poem, expressing the difficulty of living with himself, and with the demands imposed on him:

> Everyone asks me to leap in the air,
> to tone up, to play football,
> to run, swim and fly.
> Very well, then.
>
> Everyone advises me to rest,
> everyone sends me doctors,
> looking at me strangely
> What's up? . . .

> Everyone picks at my poetry
> with unbreakable forks,
> looking, no doubt, for a fly.
> I'm afraid.
>
> I'm afraid of everyone,
> of cold water, of death . . .
> That's why, in these short days,
> I'm not going to listen,
>
> I'm going to pen myself up
> and lock myself away
> with my most perfidious enemy,
> Pablo Neruda.

It is as if one part of him is full of joy and another part is starting to think of death and of the beauties of the world coming to an end for him.

In her memoirs, which are often no more reliable than Neruda's, Matilde claimed that she fell pregnant with Neruda's child for the third time in Santiago while Pablo was writing *Estravagario*. This would fit the story that Delia had found a letter in Pablo's jacket from Matilde announcing that she was pregnant. But friends have expressed scepticism that, at Matilde's age (forty-six), she would have been likely to have conceived again. Matilde wrote that they were ecstatic at the thought of being parents at last, but that, once again, their hopes were dashed by another miscarriage. After that, Pablo said they should stop trying for a baby.

Where does the truth lie? Look at the poem 'Repertorio' (Repertory) in *Estravagario*. Could this not be read as a poem to his child (a son?) to be?

> I will look for someone you can love
> before you're even a child
>
> . . .
>
> I want them to love you
> and for you never to know death.

Another poem from the same book, 'Al pie desde su niño' (To the Foot from its Child), could be seen as written after the third miscarriage. Elsewhere in *Estravagario*, there are many references to birth and to growing.

On the other hand, Pablo's friend Inés Figueroa does not believe that there ever was a third pregnancy: 'I don't think Matilde had as many miscarriages as she claimed. She was too old. It was simply her way of holding on to Pablo. She did have one miscarriage, to my certain knowledge', Inés told me in Chile. 'It affected both of them. At around that time, in 1955, I gave birth to a daughter and that moved Pablo greatly.'[83]

If *Estravagario* is often obsessed with birth, it is also obsessed with death. Neruda was ill off and on with throat infections while writing the book, and these led at one point to a complete loss of his voice for several weeks. In 'Laringe' (Larynx) he asks death:

> What do you want with my skeleton?
> Why don't you take away the sad,
> the cataleptic, the astute,
> the bitter, the disloyal, the hard,
> the assassin, the adulterous,
> the prevaricating judge,
> the lying journalist,
>
> the tyrants on the islands,
> those who set fire to mountains,
> the police chief,
> along with jailers and thieves?
> Why take me away with you?
> What have I got to go to in heaven?
> I don't fancy Hell either.
> I feel just fine on earth.

Indeed, the final, lengthy poem in the collection is called 'Testamento de otoño' (Autumn Testament) in which he leaves his worldly goods to the Communist Party and to the people; he has too much joy to leave behind, but his sadness he bequeaths to those who made him suffer ('but I've forgotten who they were') and he leaves Matilde 'all I had and did not have'.

Another poem, 'Itinerarios', contains one of his few references (and the last) to his first wife, Maruca:

> Why did I get married in Batavia?
> I was a knight without a castle,
> inadmissible passenger,
> a person without clothes or . . . a pure wandering idiot

There is a restlessness fuelling much of this book. When he is in his beloved Paris (as in 'Adiós a Paris'), he wonders why he's not back home in Chile where he's needed. And he moves back and forward in time, perhaps reflecting the continuing hold Proust exerted over him. In 'Dónde estará la Guillermina' (Where Can Guillermina Be?), Neruda recalls being fourteen in Temuco and living 'with the spiders / dampened by the forest / the beetles knew me and the tricolour bees . . .'; 'Carta para que me manden madera' is a moving poem to his father.

Yet despite his doubts, Neruda is fundamentally content with what he has. In 'El perezoso' (Lazybones) he writes:

> My house has sea and land
> my wife has big eyes
> the colour of wild hazelnuts.
> When night falls, the sea
> dresses up in white and green
> and the moon in the foam
> dreams like a marine bride.
> I don't want to change planets.

This belief in the primacy of what is physically present, what is available to all five senses, is, I believe, intimately linked with Neruda's Marxism. That is, his political beliefs affected his love poetry powerfully. No more would Neruda write lines like the ones he once wrote to his girlfriend, Albertina Azócar: ('I like you when you're silent, because it's as though you're absent'). Marxism had taught him that only things you could sense physically were real. He would never again feel the faintest attraction to Rilke's *Sehnsucht* – the sense that longing for a loved one is superior to possessing her.

Extravagario was a mature book by a man paradoxically sure of his doubts. He has finally grown up, although his friends always told me they considered him 'un gran niño' (a big child), meaning that he never lost his infectious love of life.

Neruda was delighted when Boris Pasternak was awarded the 1958 Nobel Prize for Literature. According to Jorge Edwards, Neruda welcomed the decision as marking the end of the isolation of Soviet literature. A few days later, however, he heard that the Kremlin had banned publication of Pasternak's novel, *Doctor Zhivago*, and had prevented him from travelling to Stockholm to receive the prize. Neruda, writes Edwards, 'could have protested, without a doubt, but that protest would have provoked a considerable political scandal and would have served, as they put it at the time, to "lend ammunition to the enemy's arguments". So he opted for swallowing his initial enthusiasm and maintaining a strict, uncomfortable silence.'[84]

It is very difficult to admire this silence. Neruda shrewdly realised the importance of playing the Cold War game of offering no ammunition to his right-wing opponents. Still, his mute acceptance of the Soviet mistreatment of Pasternak leaves a sour taste in the mouth. Neruda's attachment to the USSR remained undiminished. In December 1958, Pablo and Matilde left for Moscow, where Neruda was a member of the jury for the Lenin Peace Prize. The following month, they returned to Latin America, undertaking a lengthy visit to Venezuela. In fact, the couple remained there until April 1959 and Neruda became the first Chilean to be made an honorary citizen of Caracas. During this stay, Neruda met Fidel Castro at the Cuban Embassy in the Venezuelan capital, beginning a very troubled relationship with the Cuban leader, who had taken power at the beginning of the year and was overseeing a revolution on the island, a development not only watched closely by politicians and intellectuals in Latin America but with great alarm in Washington. Indeed, when a photographer surprised Neruda with Fidel in a Caracas hotel and tried to photograph them together, Castro, apparently desperate to avoid any evidence of the encounter, erupted in a fit of rage and pushed the hapless photographer out of the room.

Little could Neruda – the greatest literary warrior of the Cold War – imagine that he was himself becoming the target of a secret international battle to drag his name through the dirt.

12

The new regime

1959–66

The years in enforced exile between 1949 and 1952 had not been entirely happy ones – but they were enriching, and coloured the books that Neruda wrote for years afterwards.

The critic James Nolan believes that each volume of Neruda's poetry presents a new persona. In Nolan's words, 'Neruda's major personae include: the lost child (1923) [*Crepusculario*], the adolescent lover (1924) [*Veinte poemas de amor y una canción desesperada*], the anguished somnambulist (1933) [*Residencia en la tierra 1925–1931*)], the witness of war (1947) [*Tercera residencia*], the politicised American singer (1950) [*Canto general*], the poet of simple objects (1954) [*Odas elementales*], the whimsical private man (1958) [*Estravagario*], the autobiographical older poet (1964) [*Memorial de Isla Negra*], and the naturalist and metaphysician of his late work.'[1]

But *Estravagario* was also – as Neruda himself put it in an interesting, and little-known, interview with a Cuban newspaper, 'a new attack on dogmatism'.[2] This struggle against narrow and petrifying dogmatism, he said, was 'an inherent quality of all poets . . . which explains the difference in style, manners and often the very basis of almost all my books'.[3]

Robert Pring-Mill believes that there was a steady progress in Neruda's poetry from *Estravagario* onwards. That book, Pring-Mill has written, marked the autumn of the poet's work. A basic pattern began to emerge in his life as well, with the solidifying of his relationship with Matilde, the assumption of public duties and deepening preoccupations.

After Losada, in Buenos Aires, published Neruda's fourth collection of odes, under the title of *Navegaciones y regresos* in November 1959, the poet brought out a private, 300-copy subscription edition of a new book, *Cien sonetos de amor* (100 Love Sonnets), in Chile dedicated to Matilde on 5 December 1959. The *Cien sonetos* is a neglected work. It is a lesser collection, but it again demonstrates how the materialism of Marxist thought made its mark even on Neruda's love poetry. In Sonnet 8, Neruda writes to his beloved *Patoja*:

> In your embrace, I embrace what exists,
> sand, time, the tree of rain,
> and all lives for me to love:
> I can see it all without going far,
> I see in your life all that lives.

Many of the *Cien sonetos* are physical:

> I'm hungry for your mouth, your voice, your hair . . .
> I'm hungry for your slippery laugh . . .
> I want to eat your skin like a whole almond[4]

Intriguingly, in Sonnet 29, he does acknowledge that, while he himself cannot believe in religion, other, good-hearted people, joined in their bond of goodness – in this case Matilde's mother and his own *mamadre* – are, in his vision, washing clothes together 'in their heaven'.

The importance of Matilde for Neruda's emotional and professional stability and well-being cannot be exaggerated. Among the poet's closest friends in the last decade and a half of his life was Sara Vial, a beautiful young poet and journalist. Neruda told Sara that Matilde 'has patience with my whims and co-operates so that I can live as I want, and write comfortably . . . I'm not always an easy person . . . I don't give myself any peace. She [Matilde] solves my problems. Anything practical complicates my life: she helps to free me of everything unpleasant and tiresome, like signing cheques (I've no idea how to sign them). She organises my trips. She deals with all the accounts, and that is very good for a poet, isn't it? Good for a husband

and even better for a poet. And that's how she helps me in my literary work. The truth is, I have a lot to be grateful to her for.'[5]

Pablo would write regularly from eight to eleven in the morning. And when he wasn't working, Matilde, unlike Delia, kept a close watch on his activities, especially where other women were concerned. For there were still women lining up to throw themselves at the poet's feet.

One of Neruda's persistent admirers, who rarely took no for an answer, was the poet Stella Díaz Varín, red-haired like Matilde. Stella had taken the opportunity, during a busy meeting at the headquarters of the Society of Chilean Writers, of which Neruda had been appointed president in May 1958, to declare her love for Neruda: 'The next time I see you, things will go a lot further,' she told him in front of dozens of witnesses.[6]

Many people found the new, less relaxed, Matilde-led regime oppressive. Rodolfo Reyes, the son of Neruda's brother, Rodolfo, and now a successful businessman in Santiago, told me that as children, he and his brothers

> would visit and play with Pablo's toy trains. He wasn't a famous poet to us – he was the man who gave us toys to play with. But once he had met Matilde, and went to live with her at La Chascona, the situation changed completely . . . When I turned up with my father to say hello to him, she would say to us: 'Pablo's asleep.' And we had to wait. I clearly remember once when Pablo came out of his room and my father was downstairs. Pablo said: 'Rodolfo, why don't you come up? Matilde, how could you make him wait?' And she replied: 'But Pablo, you were sleeping.'[7]

As Aída Figueroa's husband, Sergio Insunza, put it to me, 'Matilde came into his world from outside. She wasn't a writer, a poet. So she had to undergo a process of introduction into this world. At times, Matilde felt very cautious, reserved, careful, as if walking on eggs!'[8]

Inés Valenzuela observed:

> Matilde had had quite a life outside Chile before she met Pablo. When they met, Pablo was about fifty – an age when men start to question themselves, wondering whether they're still as much of a man as ever! At this time, Delia was quite old, and Matilde excited him . . . He was a timid man. Women came to the house in the

Avenida Lynch and threw themselves into his arms. He should have rejected them – but no Hispanic man could have done that. It would have been very bad form! But Matilde attracted Pablo for her looks, for her experience of life. Pablo was actually very naive in many things. And Matilde was a revelation – she opened up a world that he didn't know.[9]

If Neruda's home life was peaceful and satisfying – at least to him – his country was entering a period of growing tension. The Chilean government of Jorge Alessandri Rodríguez, which came into office in 1958, quickly ran into difficulties. The attempt to hold down wages led to union protests, culminating in a series of strikes in 1960. In November of that year, there was a national strike as well as a series of demonstrations all over the country in which two workers were killed. Under pressure from the United States – anxious to avoid another Cuba in Latin America – Jorge Alessandri Rodríguez announced the first steps towards land reform.

On 12 April 1960, Neruda and Matilde left their troubled homeland bound for Europe on board the steamer, the *Louis Lumière*. On the ship, Neruda finished his hymn to the Cuban revolution *Canción de gesta* (Song of Protest). He could never have imagined how much turmoil this one book would stir up in a few short months.

Neruda and Matilde travelled to the Soviet Union. This was actually supposed to be an annual duty for Neruda, as a permanent member of the Lenin Peace Prize jury (formerly the Stalin Peace Prize), but according to Matilde, in her memoirs, they went only every other year. The prize was always handed out on 1 May.

Early on 3 May 1960 – Matilde's birthday – the telephone rang in their room at Moscow's National Hotel (they almost always stayed here because the rooms were large and overlooked Red Square). It was the Turkish poet, Nazim Hikmet, who now lived in Moscow. He suggested that he and Matilde should go out to buy her a present. When Pablo heard this, he got dressed hastily, exclaiming: 'You alone with a Turk – I'd never allow that!'

Matilde's birthday present turned out to be the painter Ilya Glazunov. Or rather, Glazunov was to paint Matilde's portrait. It took about twenty minutes, and a delighted Neruda, who always thought Matilde looked young, said: 'That's how you'll look in ten years' time.'[10] (There is only one other known painting of Matilde: the famous portrait by Diego Rivera. It shows Matilde with two faces. A cascade of red hair tumbles over her shoulders – but if you look more closely, you see the unmistakable silhouette of Neruda – his nose, pate and double chin – in the tangles of Matilde's hair.)

Travelling on from Moscow, Neruda and Matilde visited Yalta, Poland, Bulgaria, Romania and Czechoslovakia. In Prague, Pablo, Matilde and a Chilean friend, José Miguel Varas, stopped to admire the houses where his namesake, Jan Neruda, had lived: the House of the Two Suns and the House of the Three Eagles. When they came to another building, the House of the Three Violins, Neruda was entranced. How strange that this instrument should be what most enticed Neruda during the visit.

From Prague, Neruda and Matilde settled in Paris for virtually the rest of 1960, though they still had to leave and return in order to obtain French tourist visas. His French friend Jean Marcenac translated his poem 'Toros' (Bulls), accompanied by sixteen etchings by Pablo Picasso.

Among the records of Neruda in Paris in 1960 we have this one, from Manuel Díaz Martínez, a Cuban writer now living in exile in the Canary Islands:

> We had been invited to meet Pablo Neruda that same morning at the residence of the Cuban cultural attaché . . . I can't remember why but he wanted the Cubans based in Paris to be the first to get to know [his book, *Canción de gesta*]. Our appointment with the poet . . . took place behind closed doors at the apartment which the cultural attaché at the Cuban Embassy, Roberto Fernández Retamar, occupied with his family in Passy. Neruda looked like an amiable, absent-minded mastodon, and I found him warm and tender to meet. [Matilde], on the other hand, gave me the impression of watching everything too carefuly while being too distant from everyone. Neruda moved in slow motion, as if each step cost him a huge effort . . . Neruda read us the whole of his *Canción de gesta*. No one reads poetry as badly as he does. Nasal, monotonous, his diction crushed the poems . . . Claiming that we couldn't find a seat, we slipped out of the reading with the utmost discretion.[11]

In Paris Pablo received terrible news: a huge earthquake had destroyed much of southern Chile – including his beloved childhood refuge by the sea, Puerto Saavedra, which had been swallowed up by a giant seaquake or tsunami. A long section of the coastal strip – from at least Concepción down to Puerto Montt – simply sank, as though hinged like a trapdoor, and the first effect was that the sea withdrew and then swept back with devastating results. In Concepción, it killed all those who had been attempting to escape by crossing the bare river bed towards the mainland.[12] La Sebastiana, the building which, before leaving for Europe, Neruda had chosen as their new house in Valparaíso, was severely damaged.

He wanted to return quietly to Latin America. On 12 November 1960, he and Matilde boarded a ship in Marseille bound first for Cuba. As Hernán Loyola has written, he 'could never have imagined that, as soon as he set foot on the island, there would be a whole string of misunderstandings and antipathies . . . which were to last until his death.'[13]

Neruda's second visit to Cuba was very different from his first, charmingly trouble-free trip in 1942, when he and Delia had explored Cuban forests and beaches and filled their suitcases with shells. Now, at the end of 1960, the atmosphere, a year after Fidel Castro's revolution, had changed indelibly.

Jorge Edwards has pointed out that, during Neruda's previous visit, the poet had recognised the poverty but had also enjoyed the nightlife. In Cuba, wrote Edwards, Neruda 'always insisted, on the need for the revolution to preserve the joy of night-time partying. The revolution, of course, never suppressed these shows entirely, but puritanism, ideological severity, especially from the neophytes, had made itself felt on the island from the very first day.'[14]

Edwards said that Neruda had told him how upsetting it had been to see Che Guevara sitting with his large boots up on the desk at the Banco Nacional de Cuba when he received Pablo. Neruda was appalled by Che's bad manners. (Paradoxically, Neruda was Che's favourite poet – he took a copy of the *Canto general* with him everywhere, and in 1965, before returning a volume of Spanish-language poetry to the Cuban writer, Roberto Fernández Retamar, Che took the trouble to copy out one of his favourite Neruda poems, 'Farewell' from *Crepusculario*. But when Neruda later heard of Che's assassination, in 1967, instead of expressing condolences, he told his rather shocked informer, Sergio Insunza: 'The people we should be admiring are the Recabarrens [Luis Recabarren was the founder of the Chilean Communist Party] and not these young dreamers who go around committing crazy acts.')[15] Publicly, however, it was different: Neruda wrote several articles regretting the loss of a great 'hero'.

Edwards was told by Carlos Franqui, then editor of the Cuban newspaper, *Lunes de Revolución*, that he, Franqui, had come across Neruda looking very disconsolate in his room at the Hotel Nacional in Havana during this 1960 visit. Franqui blamed the situation on the envy of Cuba's greatest living poet, Nicolás Guillén, with whom Neruda had uneasy relations – perhaps he was still harbouring a grudge towards Guillén for making advances towards Matilde on that train journey to Bucharest in 1951.[16]

It may also be that Neruda was unhappy that Fidel had not yet declared the Cuban revolution Socialist in nature. Indeed, in a speech on 21 May 1959, Castro had even stated: 'Our revolution is neither capitalist nor Communist . . . Capitalism sacrifices the human being, Communism, with its totalitarian conceptions sacrifices human rights. We agree neither with the one nor the other.' (It was not until May 1961, after the invasion of Playa Girón, that the Declaration of Havana proclaimed the Socialist character of the revolution.) Neruda told Jorge Edwards a few years later that Castro had been forced to destroy one of the strongest and best-organised Communist parties in Latin America in his quest for power.

What upset Neruda more than anything, however, was the total indifference the new Cuban regime seemed to show to his hymn to the Cuban revolution, *Canción de gesta*. He thought it amounted to an inexplicable snub.

He had actually started to write the book in 1958. As Sylvia Thayer, sister of Alvaro Hinojosa, has noted, the book began life as verses to the drama occurring in Puerto Rico, not Cuba. Thayer had introduced Neruda to a strange Puerto Rican, Antonio Santaella, who was attending a masonic conference in Chile. Santaella was an activist fighting for Puerto Rican political and economic liberation from United States control. Neruda was impressed and promised Santaella that he would write a few poems, perhaps even an entire book, on the situation in Puerto Rico. Pablo did indeed begin *Canción de gesta* with this other island in mind, but the Cuban revolution intervened and changed not only the whole course of Latin American history but the route the book took.

Why is it that *Canción de gesta* has never been republished in Cuba? Why is it that no one even mentions the book on the island? The fact that *Canción de gesta* was (officially, at least) ignored in Cuba clearly rankled with Neruda right to the end of his life. His memoirs recall: 'I cannot forget that I was the first poet to dedicate an entire book to exalting the Cuban revolution.'

The answer may lie in a far more serious quarrel between Neruda and the Cuban regime that was to blow up six years later, in 1966. For now, though, Neruda headed home to Chile, where another edition of *Canción de gesta* was published in February 1961, this time by the Santiago publishing house, Austral.

Neruda and Matilde dashed impatiently to Valparaíso to inspect the extent of the earthquake damage to La Sebastiana. 'The whole floor with the library had collapsed,' Matilde recalled.

> Pablo was desperate. His big horse from Temuco was open to the elements. That horse had been in an ironmonger's in Temuco. When Pablo went to school, he had to pass that street and whenever he saw it he stroked its nose. He lived and grew up seeing that horse – he considered it part of him. Every time we visited Temuco, he asked the owner to sell it to him, but it was no use . . . But one day, a fire broke out at the ironmonger's. The firemen arrived and naturally lots of people gathered, including friends of Pablo's. Later, they told us that only one cry could be heard: 'Save Pablo's horse. Don't let the horse be burnt!' And it was the first thing the firemen saved . . .[17]

The official house-warming at La Sebastiana took place on Chile's national holiday, 18 September 1961. As Sara Vial recalled:

> From above, on that spring morning, songs, guitars, voices of friends and the appetising smell of meat roasting on the grill would greet us . . . Narrow staircases, turning ever narrower, either wooden or carpeted, dragging footsteps upwards. The terrace (on the Maruri Theatre roof), decorated with paper Chilean flags. Neruda, wearing a 'huaso' outfit and a sash around his girth, welcomed us, handing out a glass of *chicha* (fermenting grape juice) with a slice of orange in it . . .[18]

The house was named in honour of Sebastián Collado, a Spaniard who had originally built it with the aim of living there when his children married. Collado actually wanted to convert the third floor into a bird sanctuary and the roof into a helicopter pad. The first and second floors belonged to Francisco Velasco and his sculptress wife, Marie Martner. Neruda adored the house, with its staggering views of the Valparaíso bay. He described it lovingly in several poems. In his 1962 book, *Plenos poderes* (Fully Empowered), he wrote:

> I built the house.
>
> I made it first of air.
> Then I raised the flag in the air
> and I left it hanging
> from the firmament, from the stars, from
> the lightness and the darkness.

On 3 June 1961, he founded a club in Valparaíso, the Club de la Bota (Club of the Boot). Its first 'meeting' was held at the city's Restaurante Alemán, better known to locals as the Schoenner Bar. As Sara Vial recollected in *Neruda en Valparaíso*, at that first meeting, surrounded by friends, Pablo placed a splendid heraldically decorated ceramic boot he'd bought in Mexico, which gave its name to the club, in the centre of the table. You could become a member of the club (a *botante*) only if you were able to draw a *chanchito* (piglet) with your eyes blindfolded with a napkin.

There were some very surprising members of this club, including two Cubans, Alejo Carpentier and Nicolás Guillén, suggesting that the 1960 trip to Cuba had not foundered through personal animosity. But Neruda's attitude to the Cubans remained ambivalent. According to Sara Vial, Guillén stayed at La Sebastiana and Pablo, in Vial's words, 'loved him like a brother'. However, Vial immediately goes on to admit that Neruda declared Guillén to be 'very pretentious . . . He made himself up carefully . . . before leaving the house. He looked himself up and down in the mirror and put all kinds of creams on his face to make himself look whiter.'[19]

As for Alejo Carpentier, whom Neruda described in his memoirs as the most neutral man he had ever met, he was made a member of the Club de la Bota on 17 August 1962. Vial remembers Carpentier as being, 'like all good Cubans, an inexhaustible talker. With his sing-song tone, he kept us captivated.' Until, Vial writes, Neruda suddenly lost patience and cried: 'Can someone shut that idiot up?'[20]

The books kept flowing in Neruda's green ink – and they needed to, in order to help finance the upkeep of Isla Negra and the continuing building work at La Chascona and La Sebastiana. In June 1961, the Buenos Aires publisher, Losada, published, *Las piedras de Chile* (The Stones of Chile). In the preface, Neruda said that the book was the delayed fulfilment of a project conceived twenty years earlier – in other words, while he was busy writing the *Canto general*. This new book was based on a series of photographs which Antonio Quintana had taken of the rocks around Isla Negra. As the Chilean critic, Marjorie Agosín, has pointed out, Isla Negra, for Neruda, 'functions as a geographic vision and as political discourse'.[21]

For Neruda – conscious of his own ill-health (gout or phlebitis seemed to be his constant companions, often making it difficult for him to walk) – the solidity of the stone, and the perseverance of the sea, were his comforts, together with his love for Matilde. Sixteen years earlier, *Alturas de Macchu Picchu* had shown how stone, for Neruda, could provide a link to the past, and also a route towards a hopeful future of love, peace and brotherhood. His new, underrated book reiterated these concepts, and also included a fascinating passage which gives credence to those critics who believe that Neruda was constantly seeking a return to his true mother, Rosa, who died soon after giving birth to him.

> I was a stone: a dark stone
> and the separation was violent,
> a wound in my alien birth;
> I want to return
> to that certainty,
> to the central rest, to the womb
> of the maternal stone
> from which I do not know how or when
> they detached me to break me up . . .

In October 1961, Losada brought out Neruda's *Cantos ceremoniales* (Ceremonial Songs), ten poems which Hernán Loyola astutely describes as impregnated by 'contradictory melancholy, debating whether to die or to be reborn'.[22] Chile, destroyed in part by the 1960 earthquake, becomes a symbol of both death and rebirth. In 'Cata-clismo' (Cataclysm), he thinks back to his early influence, Augusto Winter, the 'old poet with the yellow beard', who had founded the very first municipal library in Chile, in Puerto Saavedra, only for it to be swept away mercilessly in the 1960 tsunami.

1961 marked a milestone in Neruda's career: the millionth edition of the *Twenty Love Poems and a Song of Despair* was printed by his Buenos Aires publisher, Losada. As a love poet, his fame now had few equals around the world. Neruda was also delighted when Yale University decided, towards the end of 1961, to award him an honorary doctorate. He was fully aware that he was following in the footsteps of such poets as T. S. Eliot and Saint-John Perse.

In January 1962, Neruda undertook another ambitious project. The Brazilian magazine *O Cruzeiro Internacional* began to publish a series of twelve autobiographical articles by the poet, under the title 'Mem-orias y recuerdos de Pablo Neruda: Las vidas del poeta'. These would later form the basis of the poet's posthumously published memoirs.

Two months later, on 30 March 1962, Neruda gave a revealing speech at the Universidad de Chile to mark his becoming an academic member of the university's faculty of philosophy and education. In this address, he took his audience, as he would do more and more frequently in these autumnal years of his life, back to his childhood and upbringing.

> My southern timidity was based on the inseparability of solitude and expression. My people, my parents, neighbours, uncles and aunts and companions, hardly expressed themselves at all. My poetry had to be kept a secret, separated with an iron fist from its origins . . . But my faith in truth, in the continuity of hope, in justice and in poetry, in the perpetual creation of man, come from that past, accompany me in the present . . .[23]

Neruda was now the 'elder statesman' of Chilean poetry and in that same month, the poet Nicanor Parra paid a generous tribute to him. Their relationship had often been complicated. Not long before, Parra had attacked Neruda for using 'grandiloquent' language. But in the speech in Neruda's honour, Parra began: 'There are two ways to dismiss Neruda: one is not to read him, and the other is to read him with bad faith. I've tried both, and neither worked for me.' Parra hit back at those criticising the irregularity of Neruda's output: 'For some demanding readers, the *Canto general* is an uneven work. Well, demanding readers, the Andes themselves are also an uneven work.'[24]

The real reason for the friction between Parra and Neruda remains unclear. Parra himself told me in Chile that he remained grateful to Neruda for his financial assistance in helping him to rent an apartment in Santiago: 'Pablo Neruda was very generous. He told me he'd seen a chalet for sale in Los Guindos. I went to have a look at it, but I said to him: "I haven't got any money – and they've asked me for three months' deposit." "Don't worry," Pablo said, and he handed me a cheque.'[25]

Neruda's biographer and friend, Margarita Aguirre, told me in Santiago: 'Pablo loved Parra, and always spoke well of him. But Nicanor was very jealous. They did break off their friendship – actually, they were never really friends. Nicanor was much younger than Pablo, and there was always a distance between them.'[26]

In April 1962, Neruda and Matilde left Chile again. July saw them in Moscow. Even though the Cuban missile crisis was already brewing, Neruda praised the Castro-led revolution to his Moscow audience and attacked the United States' hostile stance. Later that year, at Santiago's Teatro Caupolicán, on 12 October 1962 – just four days before John F. Kennedy called together a group of his closest advisers at the White House to discuss detailed photographic intelligence identifying Soviet nuclear missile installations under construction on Cuba – Neruda would defend the Cuban position and condemn the 'aggressor, President Kennedy'.[27]

From Russia, Pablo and Matilde went on to Bulgaria, Italy and France before returning by boat direct to Valparaíso. From 1961 to the middle of 1962, Neruda had been working on another book, *Plenos poderes* (Fully Empowered), which Hernán Loyola has called 'one of Neruda's most multicoloured'.[28] The book, published by Losada in September 1962, does indeed include an eclectic mix: there is the neo-romantic 'Deber del poeta' (Duty of the Poet); his love poem to La Sebastiana, and an ode to his eccentric musician friend, Acario Cotapos, who refused to shake hands with any man in case he caught germs.

Plenos poderes also contains what Loyola calls 'not only Neruda's best "political" poem but one of the most beautiful "political" poems written in Spanish or any other language.' The poem, 'El pueblo' (The People), was actually Neruda's formal intervention at the twelfth congress of the Chilean Communist Party in March 1962, as a member of the Party's central committee. In it, Neruda sums up his attitude to human solidarity:

> I looked for him among the tombs, and I told him
> as I squeezed his hand which had not yet turned to dust:
> 'Everyone will leave, you will live on.
> You lit up life
> You made what was yours.'
> So let no one be upset when
> I seem to be alone and I am not alone.
> I am with no one and speak for all . . .[29]

Plenos poderes is, in some ways, an optimistic book. A theme of rebirth, of daily renewal runs through it. In the lovely little poem, 'Oda para planchar' (Ode to Ironing – an allusion to Neruda's call in the poem to 'stretch out the skin of this planet / to smooth out the whiteness of the sea'), he writes: 'Hands make the world each day.'

In some poems, there is a return to the vocabulary of his post-adolescent phase: in both 'En la torre' (In the Tower) and 'Serenata' (Serenade), he uses the word 'estrellada' (starry) which had been made famous – and remains so to this day – in Poem 20 of the *Twenty Love Poems*. But here, crucially, Neruda uses the word in poems of hope, not despair.

On 3 May 1963, Matilde's fifty-first birthday, Neruda wrote a love song to his *Patoja soberana* (Sovereign Patoja):

> You give me the light and you are illuminated,
> your midday is not a day older.
>
> And even if the stars go pale
> with this love, the years do not age:
> you're a year younger, my love[30]

But while his love for Matilde was a strengthening rock of permanence, the deaths of dear friends saddened him and reminded him that everything came to an end. *El Siglo* published Neruda's pained poem

to Nazim Hikmet, who had died of a heart attack in Moscow on 3
June 1963.

> Why did you die, Nazim? And what will we do now without your
>   songs?
> . . . Let me see, think,
> imagine the world without the flower you gave it . . .[31]

In 1963 the strongest indications yet suggested that Neruda was going
to receive the following year's Nobel Prize for Literature. This had
been a regular rumour for a number of years, and, like clockwork, a
Uruguayan writer, Ricardo Paseyro, came out with his routine vicious
attack (in the press and on the radio) on Neruda's poetry and his
worthlessness for any award, let alone the Nobel. That year Pablo's
Swedish friend Artur Lundkvist, a writer, translator and member of
the Swedish Academy, who was already pushing for Neruda to be
awarded the Nobel Prize, published a long article dedicated to the
poet in the Stockholm literary magazine, BLM (Bonniers Litterära
Magasin).
  This time, it seemed, the prize could, indeed, be coming the poet's
way. As he recalled in his memoirs:

> There's a long story behind my Nobel Prize. For many years, my
> name was always mentioned as a candidate, but nothing happened.
> In 1963, things got serious. The radio said repeatedly that my name
> was very strong in the voting in Stockholm and I would probably be
> the winner of the Nobel Prize. So Matilde and I put into effect home
> defence plan number 3. We laid on supplies of food and wine and
> hung a huge padlock on the old gate at Isla Negra. I threw in a few
> mystery novels by Simenon, expecting to be under siege for some
> time. The newsmen got there fast, but we kept them at bay. They
> could not get past the gate secured with the huge bronze padlock,
> which was as beautiful as it was powerful. They prowled behind the
> outer wall like tigers. What were they trying to do, anyway? What
> could I say about a debate in which only the members of the Swedish
> Academy on the other side of the world were taking part?[32]

But Neruda was wrong on this last point. In fact, an international
campaign had swung into action from the Right to prevent Neruda

from winning the Nobel Prize. This campaign was largely the work of the so-called Congress for Cultural Freedom.

The Congress for Cultural Freedom sprang from a conference which opened in 1950 – by coincidence on the day after North Korea invaded the South. The main theme of the conference was to find a way to oppose the view that Communism was more congenial to culture than bourgeois democracy. Delegates included the playwright Tennessee Williams, the Hollywood actor Robert Montgomery, and Arthur Koestler, the anglicised Hungarian writer who had broken with the Communist Party. Koestler declared, 'Freedom has seized the offensive,' as he read the Congress's freedom manifesto at the closing rally on 29 June 1950.

The Congress for Cultural Freedom, which was sponsored by the Central Intelligence Agency in the United States, operated in some thirty-five countries, including in Latin America. And one of its main targets was Pablo Neruda.[33] A report on the activities of the Latin American committee of the Congress for Cultural Freedom during the second half of 1954 said that, 'on the occasion of the fiftieth anniversary of Pablo Neruda and the visit to Chile of the Russian writer, Ehrenburg, and fifty Communist intellectuals from China and other countries, our Committee arranged for the publication of the article by Alexander on the enslavement of Soviet writers, as well as for the translation of a poem by Ehrenburg himself, written in 1921, and directed against the "Bolshevik Barbarians".' More surprisingly, the American poet, Robert Lowell, was despatched to Latin America to help this campaign – although he proved ineffective in the role.

Two of the Congress for Cultural Freedom's 'leading lights', John Hunt and Keith Botsford, began a vigorous campaign to undermine Neruda's reputation – especially after Hunt was tipped off that Neruda was a candidate to win the 1964 Nobel Prize. By December 1963, a 'whispering campaign' had been launched to discredit Neruda. Julian Gorkin edited the Congress's journal, *Cuadernos*, from Mexico. He had founded the Communist Party of Valencia, Spain, in 1921, and had worked in an underground network for the Comintern, before breaking violently with Moscow in 1929, alleging that the Soviets had tried 'to persuade him to become an assassin'. No friend of Neruda, Gorkin was happy to help in any smear campaign against the poet. He wrote to a friend in Stockholm about Neruda and told Hunt that 'this [unnamed] man is ready to prepare a small book in Swedish on "*Le cas Neruda*".'

Hunt did not think that such a book, with by definition a limited (Swedish) readership, would carry much weight, and instead he instructed a Congress activist, René Tavernier, to ensure that a fully documented report, written in both French and English, should be prepared for circulation to certain individuals. He asked Tavernier to organise the dual-language report in collaboration with Julian Gorkin and his 'Swedish friend'. When the report came out, it concentrated on Neruda's commitment to the Communist cause, and argued that it was 'impossible to dissociate Neruda the artist from Neruda the political propagandist'. The report accused Neruda of using his poetry as 'an instrument' of political engagement which was 'total and totalitarian' and it made great play of Neruda's having won the 1953 Stalin Peace Prize, which it described as 'poetic servility'.[34]

The report said Neruda had 'distinguished between the good and the bad bomb' – the atom bomb tested by the Soviet Union and the American atom-bomb attack on Hiroshima – and once again reproduced the old claim, staunchly denied by Neruda, that he had been an accomplice in the first failed attempt by the Mexican painter David Alfaro Siqueiros on Leon Trotsky's life in Mexico City in May 1940. The report concluded by quoting from Neruda's preface to his hymn to the Cuban revolution, *Canción de gesta*: 'I assume, once more with pride, my duties as a poet of public utility, that is, a pure poet.'

Neruda did not win the 1964 Nobel Prize. It went to Jean-Paul Sartre, who promptly refused to accept it. Some claim that Sartre declared that it should, by rights, have gone to Neruda. But this may well be apocryphal.

Neruda maintained his regular writing schedule – he always told younger poets that it should be a daily activity – but also fulfilled many speaking engagements and journalistic commitments, reinforcing his reputation as one of Latin America's best-known political figures. On the eve of Fidel's visit to the USSR, the Moscow daily, *Pravda*, asked Neruda to write a few words on the Cuban leader; there was still no hint of the split to come. Neruda sent in an article which he called 'Portrait of the Gladiator'. It was published in Spanish by *El Siglo*, on 28 July 1963.

Now that Moscovites have seen and heard, felt and lived, Fidel Castro, I will tell you that I also know him . . . He is very tall and you look up at him . . . It is also logical that we Americans look up to him, because this man has suddenly grown and made his country grow as well . . . [with] words of action and acts which sing.[35]

Yet shortly afterwards, in Santiago's Parque Bustamante, on 29 September 1963, Neruda gave an address in which – in marked contrast with his apparent lack of concern for the repression of writers in the Soviet Union – he condemned the Chinese authorities' treatment of their own intellectuals, especially personal friends of his, in the so-called Cultural Revolution.

And the poet, Ai Qing, who is known to all Chileans, the best poet in China, an old Communist who visited Chile on the occasion of my fiftieth birthday, where is he? Accused of being a Rightist because he knows the French language, and for other ridiculous accusations, he has been exiled to the Gobi desert . . . and has been forced to sign his poems using another name. In other words, he has been morally executed. The Chinese leader who informed me gave me a frozen smile. I'm not smiling, comrades . . . Why go through this stage of disorientation, division, persecution? . . . We Communists do not accept terror. Beneath the oppressive government of the personality cult, all ideas are deformed.[36]

Having previously denounced President Kennedy for his role in the Cuban missile crisis and for, in his eyes, bringing the world to the brink of nuclear catastrophe, Neruda was as shocked as the rest of the world by Kennedy's assassination on 22 November 1963. In a radio statement on 1 December, Neruda once again found a connection with North America through the poet Walt Whitman, recalling his remarks on 14 April 1879, on the assassination of Abraham Lincoln. Whitman had been present, as a journalist, in the theatre where it took place.[37]

Neruda turned sixty in 1964. To mark his birthday on 12 July, *El Siglo* published a long interview with him. 'The poet looks young, agile, smiling, animated,' wrote the paper. 'He writes from seven in the morning. The telephone calls begin at eight. They hardly leave him time to get dressed.'

Did he consider that he had fulfilled his dreams? the interviewer asked.

If by dreams you mean ambitions, then I can say that I have fulfilled them all, because I never had any practical ambitions: I never wanted to be a parliamentarian or President of the Republic, nor even Mayor of Isla Negra. In that sense, everything has gone just fine. As for my work as a writer, this never felt like a dream or an ambition, but has always been a kind of extension of my physical organism. For me, writing poetry is like seeing and hearing – it's something inherent in me.

Asked for his response to those who protested that Communism prevented artists from fully realising themselves, Neruda merely replied: 'There are few artists as accomplished as the Communists Bertolt Brecht, Aragon . . . Picasso . . . There are many anti-Communist writers and artists who are not accomplished.'[38]

Many critics were now queueing up to write essays and books on his verse. One of the most important appeared in 1964, by Raúl Silva Castro, a Chilean critic and academic. There was a series of lectures at the Biblioteca Nacional in Santiago, by such Neruda specialists as Fernando Alegría, Mario Rodríguez, Hernán Loyola, Hugo Montes, Nelson Osorio, Luis Sánchez Latorre, Volodia Teitelboim, Manuel Rojas, Jaime Giordano and Federico Schopf. Three Chilean magazines – *Aurora, Mapocho* and *Alerce* – published special editions dedicated to Neruda.

On Neruda's sixtieth birthday, Losada, in Buenos Aires, published Neruda's poignant and revealing five-part collection, *Memorial de Isla Negra*. It is largely autobiographical, and contains very moving poems to his father and his stepmother, but especially to his real mother.

> As I never saw
> her face
> I called out to her among the dead,
> but like the others buried there
> she does not know, or hear, or answer,
> and there she stays, alone, without her son,
> shy and elusive
> among the shadows.[39]

There is also a pair of poems recollecting life with Josie Bliss in Burma and two others to Delia del Carril, to whom he continued to feel grateful long after his separation from her nine years earlier. (Delia outlived both Neruda and Matilde, and continued to paint up to her death, in 1989, at the age of 104.) Delia, he said, had been

> a gentle
> passenger,
> a thread of steel and honey which bound my hands
> in those sweet-sounding years . . .
> It is not adversity that separates
> a man from a woman, but
> growth.[40]

In *Memorial*, Neruda seems to move between his roles of private poet and public prophet – between his memories of love for Terusa and Albertina and his love for Spain and fears for the future of Chile (in 'El fuego cruel'). The critic Luis González-Cruz believes that Neruda had, by this time, developed a view of himself as an individual, a member of a minority singled out from the masses, even though this idea was fundamentally at variance with the Communist philosophy he embraced so fervently. Like Romantic poets such as Wordsworth, writes González-Cruz, Neruda believed his spirit was purest in childhood and sought in adulthood to regain that purity. This is an intriguing, if not entirely convincing view. I believe that Neruda felt he had truly 'grown up' only when he joined the Communist Party. But at the same time, this break with his childhood and adolescence was, in a very real sense, a wrench away from his roots, and in *Memorial de Isla Negra*, some of the finest – and frankest – poems seek to reach back to those earlier days.

In one of the most significant sections of *Memorial de Isla Negra*, 'El episodio' (The Episode), Neruda welcomes humanity's return to reason. In a clear allusion to Stalin's crimes, he laments the fear which had ruled people's lives and condemns the statues erected to a man of terror whose police spelt danger for everyone. A few years earlier, these statues would have earned his unstinting praise – an indication that Neruda had moved away from idolising Stalin after the Khrushchev revelations of 1956.

In 'Nosotros callábamos' (We Were Silent), he writes: 'Knowing hurts. And we knew.' But in the following poem, 'Los comunistas'

(The Communists), he promises with renewed, steely determination, that, even though a dark moon had eclipsed the star,

> Now you will see what we are truly worth.
> Now you will see what we are and will be.

In other words, the Stalinist period had been just a temporary aberration whose 'cancerous nature we never suspected, or refused to recognise', in the words of a fellow Marxist and French Neruda specialist, Alain Sicard, 'a tumour that history had generated, but which history – in its infinite wisdom, and through the god of Dialectics – had already extirpated.'[41] But Stalinism was much more than an aberration. For Neruda, Stalin had been the one leader willing to lead his country against the evil of Hitler's fascism.

Metrically, as Giuseppe Bellini has pointed out, the poems of the five books comprising *Memorial de Isla Negra* generally feature the endecasyllable or the irregular metre which had marked the *Odas* and *Estravagario*. The exception, writes Bellini, is the hymn to Matilde, in which Neruda – like a modern-day Petrarch praising his Laura – allows himself an expansive metre 'to celebrate the fullness of his feelings and to emphasise the excellence of the woman he was praising'.[42]

In this final section of the book, too, Neruda's love for Matilde and for his homeland become almost inseparable (she was the only Chilean among his three wives).

> You, light and dark, Matilde, dark and golden,
> you are like the wheat, the wine, the bread of the homeland . . .
> you made your thighs sing out and, ancient earthly Araucanian,
> you resembled the pure amphora burning with the local wine . . .[43]

That hectic year, 1964, was also the four-hundredth anniversary of the birth of William Shakespeare. To mark this, Neruda was asked to translate *Romeo and Juliet*.

> I accepted this request with humility. Humility and a sense of duty
> . . . I came across a new discovery. I understood that behind the plot
> of infinite love and horrific death, there was another drama, another
> . . . main theme. *Romeo and Juliet* is a great argument for peace

among men. It is the condemnation of useless hatred, it is the denunciation of barbaric war . . .⁴⁴

The accomplished translation was published on 9 September by Losada, and, as Neruda again travelled up and down Chile campaigning for the new presidential candidacy of Salvador Allende, a company at the Universidad de Chile's Instituto de Chile prepared to give the Neruda version of the play its first performance on 10 October.

Neruda had high hopes that this time, finally, the Left would win the elections in 1964. Even the entrepreneurial sector's support for the government of Jorge Alessandri Rodríguez had begun to wane, especially when inflation accelerated after the 1962 devaluation. Demonstrations against the government in that year had led to six people being killed. The Communists registered small gains in the 1963 municipal elections. But Neruda was disappointed again: Eduardo Frei was elected President in 1964. The shadow of Cuba – and the fear of Communism – had hung heavily over the election campaign.

In February 1965, Neruda and Matilde travelled to Europe, where, on 5 June, Neruda was given an honorary doctorate at Oxford University. It was the first time this honour had been bestowed on a Latin American. The invitation to Oxford was also significant because, although Neruda was still on the British Home Office's blacklist, Robert Pring-Mill (responsible for the invitation) had made some telephone enquiries to the Foreign Office, which had not only expressed its willingness to see Neruda's visit go ahead but had positively approved of the idea as it would enable them finally to remove the poet from the blacklist.⁴⁶

From England, Pablo and Matilde moved to Paris, where they lived for the whole of July. While there, the French Communist daily, *Humanité*, fêted the hero in their midst. As always, however, enemies were ready to pounce.

A snide article in the November 1965 edition of the French journal, *La Brèche*, denigrated Neruda's talent. While admiring his 'combative ardour', the article referred to the earlier derogatory remarks made by the Spanish poet, Juan Ramón Jiménez, and raised the old accusation that he had helped the painter David Alfaro Siqueiros to escape after his attempt on the life of Trotsky in Mexico City. The article concluded: 'And his greatest literary glory? The Stalin Prize. As a Com-

munist senator and then a wandering minstrel of the Kremlin, Neruda
has distinguished himself for the past ten years through his punctilious
obedience to orders dictated from above.'[47]

Of course, the magazine neglected to mention that, years earlier, in
1942, Juan Ramón Jiménez had written to Neruda to apologise and to
call him the greatest writer in Latin America.

From Paris, Pablo and Matilde flew to Budapest. Here, in 1965,
Neruda joined forces with his Guatemalan friend Miguel Angel
Asturias to write a sumptuous little book – composed in alternating
prose and verse – about the delights of Hungarian food and fine wine,
Comiendo en Hungría (Eating in Hungary).[48]

For one critic, María Salgado, Neruda and Asturias are commenting
on Western discourse, 'characterised by the dogmatic capitalism/Com-
munism polarisation of the Cold War. I believe it was precisely the
political tensions of this historical period which motivated Asturias and
Neruda to imagine Hungary as "the confluence of chillis and paprika,"
a telling image used by Asturias to introduce Hungarian culture in his
first poem in the book.'[49]

Whether or not one accepts this extravagant interpretation, there is
an almost utopian feel to much of the book, as if a love of good food
can ease some of the world's major tensions.

In order for the book to be published in Spain, the authorities were
forced to disguise the authors. The cover is seemingly innocent: a
white cloth and a large fork and spoon. And the only way to identify
who wrote what is through icons on each page: a fork for Neruda and
a spoon for Asturias. It is amusing to think that a book co-authored by
a Stalinist poet slipped through the censor's net into Franco's Spain.

Neruda's peace congress travels in 1965 took him from Hungary to
Yugoslavia, Finland and Russia, where as a member of the Lenin Prize
jury, he was delighted to see the prize go to his old friend Rafael
Alberti, now living in exile in Rome. In Bled in Yugoslavia, he
attended the PEN Club's thirty-third Congress. Here, the American
playwright Arthur Miller, who had just been elected the new president
of International PEN, invited Neruda to the following year's congress
in New York. Miller promised to do everything in his power to
persuade the United States authorities to lift their entry ban on
Communist intellectuals so that Neruda could attend.

13

The other Cuban crisis

1966–68

In the Chilean summer of 1966, Pablo's lawyer and friend, Sergio Insunza, had the unenviable task of delivering his petition for divorce to Delia del Carril, who by now was back in Chile. She refused point-blank to grant Neruda what he wanted. She would not even discuss the matter.

'Neruda actually claimed that his marriage to Delia was null and void because, at the time he had contracted marriage to Delia, he still had marital ties to María Hagenaar,' Insunza told me in Chile. It was a bizarre argument, the same one employed by President González Videla when he summoned Maruca to Chile to take Neruda to court for bigamy in 1952, alleging that he was not legally married to Delia because he was still married to Maruca. 'In Mexico, they accepted the divorce from Maruca, but here in Chile, they did not.'[1]

It took months of tense conversations to persuade Delia to agree to the divorce – and then only on the strict condition that she would not have to take part directly in proceedings. She gave her proxy to Luis Cuevas Mackenna to represent her.

On 16 June 1966, a Santiago court finally ruled in favour of Neruda and declared his marriage to Delia del Carril Iraeta annulled. He was free to marry Matilde – but the wedding would have to wait for later in the year. That same month, June 1966, Neruda was due to attend the thirty-fourth International PEN Congress in New York.

This was a move of some significance, and there were misgivings expressed – usually anonymously[2] – that Neruda would face an uncomfortable time during the meeting because delegates were likely to bring up the issue of Andrei Sinyavsky and Yuli Daniel – two young Soviet writers who had been sent to labour camps in February 1966 for smuggling their works out to the West under the pseudonyms of Abram Tertz and Nikolai Arzhak.

The United States authorities were initially very reluctant to grant Neruda and Matilde visas. Neruda was automatically barred from the US as a Communist. But as he had promised, Arthur Miller worked hard behind the scenes to convince the government of President Lyndon Johnson to bend the rules. In the end, as Miller told me, 'they became nervous that it would not be good to be seen banning such a famous figure and realised that it would be wise to relax the ban for Neruda.'[3] Miller feels that, if the United States had made a point of being more open to people like Neruda, 'the whole pro-Soviet line would have been mitigated. If they had been given the choice, many would have chosen the United States. But they had no choice.'[4]

Neruda 'loved New York passionately', according to Miller – the streets, the adoring public who packed his readings, the bookshops, where he bought copies of Shakespeare and Walt Whitman, 'and he was positive about the US, although we did not talk politics, because he seemed more interested in literature. He had read the contemporary US writers.'[5]

Neruda may have enjoyed being in New York and later in Washington (where he recorded some poems for the Library of Congress) and California, but he pulled no punches in his condemnation of US foreign policy – especially the continuing war in Vietnam – while he was in the US.

Roaming the bookshops with Neruda, Arthur Miller felt 'baffled more than ever how a man of such all-embracing spirit could continue to countenance Stalinism. I could only think that, once again, the depth of alienation from bourgeois society had locked a man into a misconceived, nearly religious loyalty to the dream Russia of the believing thirties, a country whose sheer human reality he felt it dishonourable to acknowledge.'[6]

But there was a portent of problems to come while Neruda was in New York. 'When I got there, I was told that the Cuban writers had also been invited. At the PEN Club, they were surprised that [Alejo] Carpentier had not come, and I was asked if I could clear this up . . .

Evidently, there had been a higher-up, last-minute decision against him attending.'[7]

The chairman of one of the sessions at the PEN meeting was the Uruguayan critic, Emir Rodríguez Monegal, then editor of the magazine, *Mundo Nuevo*.

> I chaired a Latin American round-table discussion in which Neruda, Parra, Mario Vargas Llosa, Carlos Fuentes, Haroldo de Campos and Victoria Ocampo all spoke. Alejo Carpentier, the Cuban novelist, had promised to attend, but at the very last minute the Cubans boycotted the meeting because they were trying to 'isolate' the United States culturally. In any case, any Latin American who visited the United States in the sixties was immediately branded a traitor [in Cuba].[8]

At one of the sessions of the PEN meeting, Neruda became embroiled in a heated discussion with the Italian novelist, Ignazio Silone, about the treatment of writers living under totalitarian regimes. According to press reports of the congress,[9] Silone insisted that these writers were mere instruments of the state, condemned the treatment of Boris Pasternak in the Soviet Union and enthusiastically cited the role played by Hungarian writers in the 1956 uprising. French and Chilean reporters quoted Neruda as responding that Silone was rekindling a Cold War which he (Neruda) believed was over. According to the same reports, Neruda told Silone that he was 'proud' to accept the label of 'propagandist' and that, during his many trips to countries on both sides of the Iron Curtain, he had met 'happy writers and unhappy writers'.

There was another incident of note at the PEN congress: Valery Tarsis, a Soviet writer who had been stripped of his citizenship and was living in exile, proposed that the Cold War be replaced by a hot war. (Neruda later told the Chilean weekly *Ercilla* that the presence of the 'clown' Tarsis may have been the reason that there were no writers from the USSR at the New York meeting.)[10] As for the Sinyavsky-Daniel case, Neruda did refer to it – but only on his return to Chile. *El Mercurio* quoted him on 16 July as saying: 'I do not agree with writers being persecuted for their literary work anywhere. But I believe it is also my duty not to contribute – by taking up this cause, which may be questionable – to fuelling the Cold War . . .'

On their way back to Chile from New York, Neruda and Matilde stopped off first in Mexico, where the poet gave a number of recitals at the Universidad Nacional Autónoma de Mexico (UNAM). This was to prove Neruda's last visit to Mexico. When they met Pablo at the home of the Mexican writer Javier Wimer, José Revueltas and the poet Eduardo Lizalde had a long conversation with Pablo in which they tried to persuade him that

> he could not go on deceiving himself and others, knowing full well what the USSR was like, and that he must – in view of his great intellectual and moral prestige – denounce the criminal existence of the Gulags, the groundless persecution of dissidents, the suffocating lack of freedom and the mishandled economy in the [Soviet] republics.[11]

A Mexican journalist present, Marco Antonio Campos noted that 'Neruda listened, not without a certain apprehension', and with good reason. His position was powerful enough by now for him to have spoken out against the Gulags.

In Peru, Neruda read his poems to fanatical crowds at Lima's Teatro Municipal and at the Universidad de San Marcos, as well as at the Universidad de Ingeniería in Arequipa. He and Matilde were also received by President Fernando Belaúnde Terry, who, at the request of the Peruvian Writers' Association – chaired by the novelist, Ciro Alegría – decorated Neruda with the Orden del Sol del Perú for his poem, *Alturas de Macchu Picchu*.

Little could Neruda have imagined the storm this short visit to the US – and the stopover in Peru – would provoke. The problem was that the Peruvian government was opposed to the new Fidel-led regime in Cuba. Neruda's astonishingly successful visit to New York and the West Coast, followed by his apparently friendly meeting with President Belaúnde Terry, was seen in Cuba as a betrayal of their version of Communism. The Mexican novelist Carlos Fuentes, writing in *Life en español* – the Spanish-language edition of the American photo-magazine – echoed Neruda's belief that the PEN conference had marked the beginning of the end of the Cold War.

There now occurred one of the bleakest events in Neruda's life which would leave a scar on him to the end. In July 1966, a group of more than one hundred Cuban intellectuals – apparently on the personal orders of Fidel Castro – published the 'Carta de los Cubanos'

(Open Letter from the Cubans) condemning Neruda for his willingness to indulge the enemy, which it called a perfect example of the tepid, pro-Yankee reformism prevailing in Latin America as an alternative to Castrismo.

The letter appeared over several pages of the official Cuban Communist Party newspaper, *Granma*, on 31 July 1966. It began by asking why the United States had granted visas to Neruda and other left-wing intellectuals after refusing to issue such documents for twenty years. 'Is this proof that we have entered a period of harmonious cohabitation on the planet?' the letter asked. The Cuban signatories answered their own rhetorical question with a no. 'So there must be other explanations: in some cases, because such Leftists have stopped being Leftists, and have become quite the opposite, leaders collaborating with North American politics.' In other cases, the letter said, they were, indeed, men of the Left, such as Neruda, but the fact remained that 'the United States could benefit from their presence'.

The letter continued,

> Jean-Paul Sartre, some time ago, turned down an invitation to visit the United States, in order to avoid being used, and moreover to give concrete shape to his repudiation of the North American aggression in Vietnam . . . It is unacceptable that we speak highly of a supposed peaceful co-existence and of the end of the Cold War, at the same time as North American troops, which have just attacked the Congo and Santo Domingo, are savagely assaulting Vietnam and are preparing to do the same in Cuba . . .

Of Neruda the letter demanded: 'We need to know that you are unequivocally on our side in this long battle, which will not end until we have achieved a decisive liberation,' and insinuated that the Neruda of 1966 would have been condemned by the Neruda who had written *Canto general*. What would Neruda have said, the Cuban writers asked, if a friend of his had dined with President González Videla and been decorated at the presidential palace in Santiago?[12]

The letter had been drafted by Roberto Fernández Retamar, Nicolás Guillén, Lisandro Otero, Edmundo Desnoes and Ambrosio Fornet, and among the signatories were Alejo Carpentier, José Lezama Lima and Virginio Piñera. Only one Cuban writer, Enrique Labrador, had refused to sign the document.

Hernán Loyola called the letter 'the most unhappy document in the whole history of Latin American culture. It was an unjust, unjustified and gratuitous act of aggression.'[13] Jorge Edwards felt that this letter was one of the most hurtful wounds Neruda ever experienced.

> No attack from the Right would have caused him so much pain . . . He knew perfectly well that no Cuban writer would have dared to write and sign that message without having received orders from above. He did not have the slightest doubt that the inspiration, when it came down to it, had come from Fidel Castro.[14]

Publicly, Neruda said nothing at the time, except for a brief reply in *El Siglo*, on 2 August 1966, coolly defending himself against the accusations and insisting that, 'in the United States and the other countries I visited, I maintained my Communist ideals, my unshakeable principles and a revolutionary poetry. I have a right to hope and demand that you, who know me, do not harbour or spread unacceptable doubts in this regard.'[15]

In private, however, he was very willing to express his bitterness. He was convinced that Fidel had a personal reason for hating him. Neruda told Edwards that Castro had not taken kindly to his only half-veiled warning to the Cuban leader to avoid making a cult of his public persona. The warning appears in the poem 'A Fidel Castro' in *Canción de gesta*. In the poem, Neruda invites Fidel to share a bottle of Chilean wine with him and, as he drinks, to realise

> . . . that your victory
> is like the old wine of my homeland:
> it is not one man who makes it but many men
> and not one grape but many plants
> and it is not one drop but many rivers:
> not one captain but many battles . . .[16]

Neruda never returned to Cuba, even though he was invited to do so in 1968, and he never forgave those who had signed the letter. He expected a public correction and apology, but they never came.

'Neruda was a disciplined chap, a Party man,' said Jorge Edwards. 'That's why he never admitted publicly that he didn't like Castro. But in fact, deep down, he didn't like him, he couldn't stand him. And the feeling was mutual.'[17]

Edwards recalled a reception in the 1970s when Fidel received a book of Chilean poetry in Havana. The Cuban leader flicked through the book, made a comment on a Nicanor Parra poem, cracked a joke about a Gabriela Mistral poem but, when he came to a page containing a Neruda poem, he looked at it and quickly and silently turned the page.[18]

The whole Cuban affair was a saddening event, because Neruda had clearly loved Cuba. In 1960, he had written a poem in the Cuban newspaper, *Lunes de Revolución*, to mark his visit, called 'Pez en el agua' in which he said that, when asked on the streets of Havana how he felt being there, he replied,

> I feel
> in Cuba
> like a fish in water.[19]

On 28 October 1966, Pablo and Matilde were legally married. The wedding took place at Isla Negra, in the presence of friends and the civil registrar. Photographers were kept well away by a fence around the house – although some tried to invade, insisting that Neruda was infringing the freedom of the press in Chile. Neruda sent Volodia Teitelboim out to talk to the journalists, and he somehow appeased them with the offer of a good picture taken at the moment the marriage was pronounced.

The photographer, as it turned out, was not a professional at all. He was Manuel Solimano, the used-car salesman who had helped Neruda out of Chile in 1949. But the picture was a good one: Pablo, wearing a black suit, and Matilde, wearing a white one, are flanked by the witnesses to the marriage, Matilde's singing teacher, Blanca Hauser, and Blanca's husband, Armando Carvajal.

1966 saw the publication of Louis Aragon's *Elégie à Pablo Neruda* in Paris, and Rodríguez Monegal's study of Neruda: *El viajero inmóvil*. Then, on 1 November, Neruda published *Arte de pájaros* (The Art of Birds), printed in a private edition by the Chilean Society of Friends of Contemporary Art. It had been written largely in 1962 and 1963. Neruda himself claimed that the idea had come to him while he was standing in Red Square, Moscow, during the festivities to mark the simultaneous space flights of Soviet cosmonauts aboard *Vostok III* and *IV*. Neruda was a genuine expert on Chilean birdlife – the choice of ornithologist had been an apt profession for his false documents with which he escaped, bearded, across the Andes in 1949.

The book's illustrator, the Chilean painter Julio Escámez, described the book's gestation to Hernán Loyola:

> We set out, accompanied by the indefatigable Matilde, I with my binoculars, notebooks and pencils; Pablo with his cap and an old sailor's telescope. Infallibly, the poet guided us to a hidden place where the *teruterus* were swarming. We settled down for long hours to observe them from a distance . . . For a painter, working with Pablo means forging a contact with a whole world of stimuli . . .[20]

But just as *Eating in Hungary* was no traditional recipe book, so this is no ordinary bird-watching guide. Real birds ('pajarintos') alternate with imaginary ones ('pajarontes'). The invented ones include the 'Tontivuelo – *Autoritarius Miliformis*' (The Stupid Winged Military Dictator Bird), which

> couldn't fly, just couldn't fly
> but gave orders for others to fly.
> It grew up sitting down and
> this sad, unfeathered bird
> never had wings, nor song, nor flight.
> But the dictator dictated . . .

There is great fun and mischief here. One of the most revealing poems in *Arte de pájaros* is 'El pájaro yo – *Pablo Insulidae Nigra*' (The I-Bird – Pablo of Isla Negra). The sense of his own contradictory nature here echoes some of the poems in *Estravagario*:

> My name is the Pablo bird,
> bird of a single feather,
> a flyer with a clear shadow
> and confused clarity . . .
> I fly, and I fail to fly, but I sing.
> I'm the furious bird
> of the tranquil storm.[21]

Una casa en la arena (A House in the Sand), also published in 1966, is a prose paean to the beauties of life at Isla Negra. Neruda remembers his dead friends, whose names he has carved on the beams of his roof: Alberto Rojas Giménez, Joaquín Cifuentes, Federico García Lorca, Paul Eluard, Miguel Hernández, Nazim Hikmet. 'Why did they leave so soon? Their names will never slip from the beams.'[45] He tells the story of the famous ship's masthead, which now resides in one of the main rooms of his house at Isla Negra. It had belonged to a ship wrecked off the coast of Valparaíso while he was in hiding there in 1948. There is the anchor, brought from Antofagasta, in the north of Chile, where it had been 'slumbering in the dry sands', and now lodged in the plants and sand outside Isla Negra. And there is the locomotive in front of the house, a reminder of the wonderfully inspiring trips he took with his father through the forest as a child.

By now, Neruda's health was beginning to fail and he was haunted by death: his own and Matilde's. In *Una casa en la arena*, he recognises that 'everything will remain firm without us, everything will be prepared for the new days which will be beyond our destiny'. The sea, fittingly, has the last word in the book: with its 'worrying . . . blue belly . . . It can't be tied up or locked in.'

In May 1967, Neruda attended the Congress of Soviet Writers in Moscow. He was in fine spirits. Vera Kuteishikova recalled a memorable visit he made to the new apartment she had moved into that year with Lev Ospovat: 'The first thing that happened was that we all got stuck in the lift! But Pablo kept totally calm, totally Chilean, until they came to free us. I never saw him angry or flustered.'[23] One of the first people to greet the poet at the apartment was an old floor-polisher, who carefully wiped his hand before shaking Neruda's and then, to Pablo's delight, began to recite one of Neruda's poems by heart.[24]

Lev Ospovat remembers Neruda as a man with a great sense of humour and affection for his friends. At one Moscow party, Pablo rose to his feet and said: 'Here among us sits my friend Lev, who wrote a whole book about me. They say it's not a bad book. I've no idea, because I haven't been able to read it, for obvious reasons. So I raise my glass: may all my books come out in languages I don't understand.'[25]

A mini-crisis occurred in this, the first year of the official Neruda marriage. The couple were in Viareggio, in northern Italy (on their way home from Moscow), where Neruda was due to receive a new prize inaugurated that year for international personalities working for culture and understanding between peoples. Matilde was usually eagle-eyed when women came near her husband. But not this time. Before the prize-giving ceremony, Pablo had gone to the house of the Italian sculptor, Marino Marini. Sitting next to him there was 'the most beautiful of Florentine women'. At one point in his conversation with her, he later recounted, the name of the British sculptor, Henry Moore, came up. The 'golden-eyed enchantress' made him a magical offer: to find Moore for him, even though he lived in England. ' "I'll be waiting for you in my car. You can see Henry Moore. Just say goodbye, don't say where we're going." I followed in the wake of her splendour.'

She drove him for many miles until they came to a country estate – and there stood Henry Moore, 'short, stout, genial and strong . . . For the half-hour I spent with Henry Moore, all we talked about – heaven knows why – was Death, I had the sensation of being with a great stonecutter who knew the extremes of hardness – that is, infinite stone.'

Meanwhile, the television lights were burning brightly at the Gran Teatro in Viareggio, waiting for Neruda to walk up to receive his award. Matilde sat forlornly in the audience, wondering where Pablo was. Neruda and his mysterious beauty were heading back, but by the time they arrived the Mayor and his committee had already vanished. 'I waited in the shadows until everyone had left. Once the place was deserted, I went to look for Matilde. She is still angry with me.'[26]

From Italy, the couple made a secret stop-off in Spain. It was June 1967, and the visit, which was revealed by the Barcelona daily *La Vanguardia* only in 2002,[27] had to be kept quiet, because Neruda remained unwelcome in Franco's Spain. It was not his first visit to Spain since Franco's victory – Neruda had briefly passed through Cádiz in 1960,[28] but that had been a totally anonymous visit of a few hours, during which he had met no one. This time, his Spanish publisher, Esther Tusquets, using methods she has never been willing to reveal, managed to smuggle Neruda and Matilde off the boat and on shore for their very secret visit to Barcelona.

During his brief stay in Barcelona, Neruda met the Colombian novelist, Gabriel García Márquez, who gave this wonderful fictionalised portrait of the poet in a book written in 1992:

Pablo Neruda . . . devoted a morning with us to major book hunting in second-hand bookshops. He walked among the crowds like an invalid elephant, with a childish interest in the internal mechanisms of every single thing. The world, to him, seemed like an immense wind-up toy . . . I have never met anyone closer to the idea we have of a refined gluttonous Renaissance Pope . . . Matilde, his wife, put a bib on him which looked more like something out of a barber's shop than a dining-room. But it was the only way to stop him bathing himself in sauces. That day . . . was a typical example. He ate three whole lobsters, pulling them apart with a surgeon's mastery, and at the same time devoured everyone else's dishes with his eyes, and picked at a bit of everybody's, with a delight in eating that was contagious: Galician clams, Cantabrian barnacles, Alicante prawns . . . And all the while, just like the French, all he talked about was other exquisite dishes, especially the prehistoric seafood of Chile which he carried with him in his heart.[29]

From Barcelona, Pablo and Matilde travelled first to France, then to England. During the Poetry International conference in London in August 1967, two poets who had once loved each other, but had refused even to meet for nearly thirty years, were finally reunited. 'One day, I was invited to an international poetry festival in London,' Octavio Paz recalled later, 'and Pablo Neruda read his poems the day before me.'

It went well, and I was rather worried. The day I was due to read, I met a woman. It was Matilde Urrutia. She looked at me and said: 'You're Octavio Paz.' 'Yes I am,' I replied, and added: 'And you are Matilde Urrutia. I know you from your photographs.' 'Me too,' she replied. 'Pablo's upstairs. Say hello to him, Octavio. It'll really make him happy. Go on, do it.' . . . We went up three floors to Neruda's room. He was with a reporter, giving an interview. Matilde Urrutia interrupted it. Without explanation, he got rid of the reporter. Matilde quizzed him: 'I bet you can't guess who's here?' 'Who?' Neruda asked. 'Octavio Paz,' replied Matilde. 'My dear boy, come here,' Neruda exclaimed, and he gave me a hug. We hugged each other. 'But you look great, Octavio!' 'And you look magnificent, Pablo,' I responded. 'Don't I look a lot older to you?' Neruda asked, worried. I replied: 'To me, you couldn't look better.' The truth is, Neruda did look old. The years had taken their toll . . .[30]

Robert Pring-Mill, who was unaware of the two men's meeting upstairs, tells me he was present when they met again later in the lobby and gave each other a public hug 'which did not strike me as heartfelt at all, but looked very artificial'.[31] And the fact remains that, for years afterwards, Paz continued to snipe at Neruda's political 'errors'. In a 1980 essay on Sartre, called 'Jean-Paul Sartre: A Memento', Paz wrote: 'Why did he [Sartre] strive so, in order not to see and hear? I exclude, of course, the possibility of complicity or duplicity, as in the case of Aragon, Neruda and so many others who, though they knew, kept silent.' In another essay, on Solzhenitsyn ('Considering Solzhenitsyn: Dust After Mud'), Paz went even further, writing: 'When I consider Aragon, Eluard, Neruda and other famous Stalinist writers and poets, I feel the gooseflesh that I get from reading certain passages in [Dante]'s *Inferno*. No doubt they began in good faith . . . But insensibly, commitment by commitment, they saw themselves becoming entangled in a mesh of lies, falsehoods, deceits and perjuries, until they lost their souls. They became, literally, soulless . . .'[32]

Yet when his Mexican journal, *Vuelta*, published an article on the Chilean in September 1993, Paz called it: 'Mi enemigo más querido' (My Dearest Enemy). And his admiration for Neruda as a poet was vast. In 1990, he told Jorge Edwards in a telephone conversation that he had been re-reading the whole of Neruda's work. 'My conclusion,' said Paz, 'is that Neruda is the greatest poet of his generation. By far! Better than Huidobro, better than Vallejo, better than Borges. And better than all the Spanish poets.'[33]

Neruda himself, when he referred to that London poetry congress a couple of years later, made no mention of Paz at all. In fact, in a self-deprecating way, Neruda recalled groups of autograph-hunters gathering around 'Spender, Olson, Magnus Enzensberger, Auden, Ungaretti, Berryman and myself . . . until the North American *beatnik* poet, Allen Ginsberg, arrived, hair down to his shoulders, mystical smiles falling from his beard to the ground, amulets, rosaries and Tibetan trinkets hanging round his neck,' and took all the crowds away with him.[34]

Neruda and Matilde returned to Chile in August 1967. That same year, Neruda was named an 'illustrious citizen of Parral' by the town in southern Chile where he had been born sixty-three years earlier.

On 4 December Neruda's next collection, *La barcarola* (The Barcarole), was published. It is largely an extended love poem to Matilde:

> I loved you without a why, without a whence, I loved you
> without looking, without measure . . .
> I did not know, Chilean woman, that you were my own roots . . .[35]

This is one of the most surreal books Neruda produced in his later years. He writes, for example, in the poem 'Resurrecciones' (Resurrections)

> Friend, it's your kiss that sings like a bell in the water
> of the submerged cathedral, through whose windows
> entered eyeless fish, dissolute seaweed . . .

In the second episode of *La barcarola*, Neruda lovingly recollects his life in the rue de la Huchette in Paris. He recalls, too, his reaction to the news of the death of his old friend, Rubén Azócar, 'con la risa y la rosa en la mano' (with a laugh and a rose in his hand).

La barcarola also introduces the first version of Neruda's account of the legend of the bandit, Joaquín Murieta, which he would soon turn into his first and only play. Neruda had originally become fascinated with this mysterious outlaw while in hiding from President González Videla in Chile in 1948. An article about Murieta in the magazine *National Geographic*, and especially a picture of the bandit's head emerging from the glossy pages, had haunted Neruda. Murieta, whom both Mexicans and Chileans have always claimed as their own, and who joined the California Gold Rush in the 1840s, had been killed and his severed head displayed at the San Francisco Fair.

In 1966, almost regretfully (because he said: 'Experience has taught me that when you talk a lot about something before doing it, the odds are that it will never get done'), Neruda had described his plans for this poem about Murieta.[36] His interest in the whole legend had increased during the 1964 presidential campaign on behalf of Salvador Allende, when his friend, the Chilean writer Fernando Alegría, told him in Concepción about a novel he had written about Chilean gold-hunters in California in 1849. Then, during his trip to the United States in 1966, Neruda read the poem from *La barcarola* to a group of friends, including Alegría, in Berkeley, California. He asked them for their views. 'Some enthusiastic ladies quickly exclaimed that it was a wonderful play,' Alegría recalled. It was not what Neruda had wanted to hear; he had intended it as a poem. 'I thought it was more honest to tell him that he didn't yet have a work of theatre, but rather a libretto that a daring and imaginative director could convert into a spectacle.'[37]

Neruda had never wanted to write for the theatre even though, in 1943, he had asked his Catalan architect friend, Germán Rodríguez Arias, to build a little theatre in the patio of Isla Negra. But in the fascinating interview he gave to the Cuban newspaper, *Lunes de Revolución*, in 1960, during his troubled Havana visit, he said:

> Theatre directors have often suggested that I write for them (in my country there are many companies and theatre is very advanced). . . . I have always rejected this idea, through lack of ability. I simply do not know how to do it. Just as I would not be able to write a story or a novel. [Apparently, he had forgotten the novella, *El habitante y su esperanza*, he had written in 1926] . . . I have to say that poetic theatre bores me profoundly, even some of Federico [García Lorca]'s plays . . . I prefer a work of genuine action, which overpowers the audience, which carries it away, transports it . . . I would exclude Brecht from my criticism – he often puts his poetry [into his plays] but always with an intensity of dialogue and such a great knowledge of the theatre that he is the greatest writer for the theatre of the last few years.[38]

When the French director and actor, Jean-Louis Barrault, a friend, asked Neruda to write something that he could perform on stage, he replied, 'I'm just a poet, and I'm only interested in writing verse and anyway, I wouldn't know how to write for the theatre.' ' "You're wrong," Barrault replied. 'You write your poem and I'll turn it into a play.' I was disconcerted. As I am a person who mulls things over very slowly – don't forget that I come from the south – this conversation went round and round in my head for several years, until one day I said – why not?'[39]

The very first read-through of Neruda's play, *Fulgor y muerte de Joaquín Murieta* (Radiance and Death of Joaquín Murieta), took place at La Chascona. The parts were read by Pablo, Matilde, the Chilean writer-actress María Maluenda and her actor husband, Roberto Parada. Most of the songs were sung by the great Chilean singer-songwriter, Víctor Jara.

Neruda handed over the manuscript of the play to the director, Pedro Orthous, who turned to Sergio Ortega to add music. Orthous 'put his oar in and cut here and there and asked me for changes. And if I protested, I learned that Lope de Vega had done exactly the same with Shakespeare . . .'[40]

Sergio Ortega, who became a good friend of Neruda's, said that the poet had 'transformed the hero, Joaquín Murieta, into a universal figure fighting for justice'.[41] Ortega stayed with Neruda at Isla Negra while the final touches were being put to the play. 'He was extremely human, open, generous . . . Joaquín Murieta was a kind of Robin Hood figure, and Neruda must have identified with him.'[42]

It is interesting that Neruda chose to look to the past. I believe that this reflected a growing disenchantment with the present. In an earlier book, he had written that he would never choose another planet to live on. But *La barcarola* contains a poem called 'El astronauta' (The Astronaut), which reflects a need to escape from the Earth.

It is also fascinating that Neruda, the great peace-lover, was attracted to the legend of a violent bandit. But the story, like *Romeo and Juliet*, has elements of justice in it as well – Murieta was seeking to avenge the murder of his wife. Neruda had often faced this inner dilemma: he condemned war, but also believed that some wars were just, which is why he admired the Republicans' struggle against Franco and the Russians' defeat of the Nazis at Stalingrad. Murieta was a perfect hero in this sense. Neruda adopted him as his own although there is no evidence whatsoever to prove that he was actually Chilean. However, as his friend, Aída Figueroa told me, Neruda would often protest: 'Why must the Mexicans have all the bandits? Murieta was Chilean!'

Fulgor y muerte de Joaquín Murieta was given its first performance in Santiago on 14 December 1967, by the Instituto de Teatro de la Universidad de Chile. Fernando Alegría called it 'a brilliant epic with elements of opera, comedy, *zarzuela*, pantomime and even ballet'. At the same time, the Chilean publishing house Zig-Zag printed the first edition of the play.

Some critics have seen echoes in *Joaquín Murieta* of García Lorca's farces. The play is an uneasy, sometimes stunningly beautiful, hybrid of epic poetry, love dialogue and burlesque. Robert Pring-Mill detects the influence of Bertolt Brecht on the play, which, he says, would have been a different work if there had been no *Threepenny Opera,* no *Mother Courage.* Speaking to Pring-Mill at Isla Negra in 1968, Neruda said that what he had found so fascinating about writing for the theatre was that being intimately involved with director, cast and composer had made him feel, for the first time in his life, that he was not a lone-wolf writer but actually working as a member of a team. 'It was the collective nature of the creative participation which enchanted him.'[43]

In April 1968 Neruda was honoured with the Joliot-Curie medal, which he received at the Municipal Theatre in Santiago. The award was named after the man who had sent Neruda to India on a peace mission in 1950 for that unhappy interview with Nehru. Neruda spent much of his acceptance speech remembering his Soviet friend, Ilya Ehrenburg, who had died in Moscow on 31 August 1967: 'Every nation, every airport saw this grey-haired man in wrinkled trousers expending his strength and intelligence in the battle against terror and war. With his death, I lost one of the men I have most admired and respected . . .'

He also took the opportunity to attack the US involvement in Vietnam once again, as well as the newly imposed US embargo on Cuba and the 'cruel and cold' murder of Martin Luther King in Memphis, Tennessee, just four days earlier. Neruda called for President Lyndon Johnson's speedy resignation – but he also condemned the silence of some Latin American countries on Vietnam: 'We believe in peace, and we will knock at every door to achieve its sovereignty.'[44]

As Neruda had said in a speech at the University of Concepción in southern Chile: 'Perhaps the duties of the poet have been the same throughout history . . . Poetry is rebellion . . . We poets hate hatred and make war on war.'[45]

In May 1968, he was named an honorary member of the North American Academy of Arts and Letters. In a letter from Isla Negra to the Academy's president, George F. Kennan, on 12 March, he said:

I feel both uncomfortable and honoured to figure with my small poetic oeuvre alongside such enlightened personalities from the past and present as Braque, Chagall, Isak Dinesen, T. S. Eliot, Gide, Malraux, Matisse, Miró, Henry Moore, Nehru, Orozco, Bertrand Russell, Bernard Shaw, Schweitzer, Shostakovich, Villa-Lobos and H. G. Wells.[46]

14

The Nobel Prize – and a last, passionate love

1968–72

In his mid-sixties, Neruda could have been forgiven for quietly enjoying his many achievements. Instead, he was entering a final decade as full of turbulent upheaval as ever.

In July 1968, Losada published the third edition of Neruda's complete works. By now, there were enough of them to make two volumes. And this new edition included a thorough bibliography by Hernán Loyola.

A new work, *Las manos del día* (The Hands of the Day), appeared on 8 November 1968. In some ways, this is an uncomfortable, unsatisfying, even disingenuous and unconvincing book. It reads like a 'guilt trip'. Neruda regrets the fact that he has done nothing useful with his hands; he calls them 'las manos negativas' because he kept them clean, away from the grime. He would have liked to have been a Miguel Hernández, working off the land. Or even one of his pre-Columbian forebears working the stone of Machu Picchu.

> Yes. I'm guilty
> of all I failed to do,
> of what I didn't sow, cut, measure,
> of not having incited people to populate lands.
> of having remained in the deserts,
> my voice talking to the sand.[1]

He even goes as far as to say, in 'El hijo de la luna' (Child of the Moon), that

> I feel the world never belonged to me;
> it belongs to the hewers and hammerers . . .
> I no longer have the right to proclaim
> my existence: I was a child of the moon.

The self-indulgence of this poem feels reminiscent of the tormented posturing of his protracted adolescence.

The critic Jaime Alazraki reads this book differently. He sees *Las manos del día* as an apology for not doing something useful with his poetry, for having forgotten that poems should be as utilitarian as flour.[2]

Another specialist, Manuel Durán, goes further. He says it is a book that

> reveals the deep and harrowing conflict in Neruda's mind – a conflict between his public persona and the privacies of a lifetime that was anything but private . . . Politically, his goal was unabashed, programmatic, affiliated: to further the cause of the workers, the peasants, the proletariat. Yet *Las manos del día* makes clear that, in his daily life, he was intimately aware of the fact that he was an 'escritor culto' like Quevedo before him, a 'mandarin' who had never been able to construct anything with his hands, who had created only words, sentences, images, paragraphs, poems . . .[3]

I do not believe Neruda seriously thought of his poetic craft as altogether pointless at this time. There are too many examples of Neruda telling friends how touched he had been to see the effect his words had on ordinary people – including, as he said to Alain Sicard, a whole crowd made up entirely of appreciative sheep-shearers.

And Neruda would have been pleased, even surprised, to hear his fellow, much younger, Chilean poet, Raúl Zurita, tell a journalist in 1980:

> Personally, I believe, unlike many others, that his greatest work lies in his political poetry and not in the *Residencias* . . . Neruda can be found there and any work – including my own – has to pass through

him. It is not a problem of writing – he has already had enough imitators, as Parra has. You cannot imitate Neruda – to do that, you would have to write better than him, and I do not know anyone who writes better than Neruda.[4]

It would seem that Neruda could please both manual workers and his fellow intellectuals. And yet Neruda told the French news magazine, *L'Express*, in 1971, 'My greatest defect is laziness. I've never worked. That's why I have had a certain admiration for my father, who was a great worker . . . He just spent his life working, while I can't do anything. Perhaps a little poetry.'[5]

But *Las manos del día* may have a broader message: that a lonely, loveless life without solidarity with one's fellow man – the kind of solidarity and collaboration which had made Neruda's one launch into playwriting such an enjoyable experience for him – was an empty, meaningless existence. He was conscious that the act of writing poetry was essentially an isolating one – until his words were read by others.

After a brief visit to Caracas in 1968, Neruda undertook a series of weekly articles for the Santiago magazine, *Ercilla*. He was in the midst of this commission when the Warsaw Pact troops invaded Prague in August 1968, brutally ending the 'Prague Spring'.

The official justification, upheld by Fidel Castro and by Communist parties around the world, was that the Czech authorities had asked for the tanks to intervene in order to avoid being overrun by the counter-revolutionary insurgence. This was denied by others, including the Czech Ambassador to Chile.

Jorge Edwards has written of how strange he found it that Neruda made no public comment – or even remarks to friends – about what was going on in Czechoslovakia, a country he knew very well. He actually visited Neruda on the day of the invasion, 21 August, and was astonished to find that nothing was said: they talked about books and friends, there were spontaneous jokes but Prague did not come up. It was only as Edwards was leaving, and he asked Pablo about his forthcoming trip to Europe, that Neruda told him: 'I don't think I'm going. I think the situation's too Czechoslovak.'[6]

Neruda's silence – even in private – on the Prague invasion does seem peculiar, even shocking.

That was his only reference to Prague 1968. The following year, however, brought Neruda's 1969 collection, *Fin de mundo* (End of the World), first brought out in Santiago with illustrations by Mario Carreño, Nemesio Antúnez, Pedro Millar, Marie Martner, Julio Escámez and Osvaldo Guayasamín. In this book, we learn something of Neruda's inner response to the news of the Soviet tanks crushing the Prague Spring the year before:

> The hour of Prague fell
> on my head like a stone,
> my fate was uncertain,
> a moment of darkness . . .
> I ask forgiveness for this blind man
> who saw and didn't see.[7]

The assault on a city where Neruda had shared so many memorable experiences, and whose greatest writer, Jan Neruda, had given him his name, left him genuinely disillusioned and confused. If we compare the section '1968' from *Fin de mundo* with the euphoria of *Las uvas y el viento*, we can see how Neruda's simple faith in the Socialist revolution had been shaken.

In private, he had serious misgivings. His Russian friend Vera Kuteishikova told me that, during one of his visits to Moscow, he had asked her: 'How can they persecute a great poet like Joseph Brodsky?'[8] (Brodsky had been tried in 1963 on charges of 'social parasitism' – he had written poetry without being a member of the Soviet Writers' Union – and sentenced to five years' hard labour in Archangelsk, in northern Russia, though a campaign successfully secured his release after eighteen months.) Significantly, Neruda never voiced this protest publicly, just as he had never publicly protested over the treatment of Boris Pasternak in 1958. His refusal to stand up and condemn the persecution of his Soviet colleagues, while understandable, given his emotional attachment to the Party, must still be deplored.

But Neruda was also horrified by what had happened to the United States. It is important to be aware of this double disenchantment embittering his sixty-fifth year. The country which had produced Abraham Lincoln and Walt Whitman had, he wrote, been transformed into a country whose people were loved by no one on earth. 'They're not the Estados Unidos but the Estados Estúpidos.'[9]

The senselessness of the Vietnam War continued to appal and sicken him:

> Why go so far to kill?
> Why go so far to die?[10]

In 'Artes poéticas (1)' (The Art of Poetry (1)), Neruda seems to retract the self-abasement of *Las manos del día*. Here, in *Fin de mundo*, he calls himself a 'poeta carpintero' (poet-carpenter) passing his hands lovingly over wood, then cutting it with a saw. And he is the 'poeta panadero' (poet-baker), preparing the oven, the flour and the yeast. He calls himself a 'ferretero solitario' (lonely ironmonger). Even if these could be construed as symbols of poetic craft, in 'Resurecciones' (Resurrections) his tone is very far from the regretful timbre of *Las manos del día*:

> If I ever live again
> it will be the same way . . .

Unevenness, an ability to evolve and change, is what makes Neruda's poetry so vibrant, fresh and enriching. But there is a valid question here: how genuine was his regret in *Las manos del día*, if it could fade within a year?

Similarly, it seems reasonable to question how seriously we should take his attack on the cult of Stalin in *Fin de mundo's* poem, 'El Culto II' (The Cult II):

> A million horrible portraits of Stalin covered the snow
> with his jaguar's moustache.
> When we learned and bled
> to discover sadness and death
> beneath the snow on the meadows
> we took a break from his portrait
> and we breathed without his eyes on us,
> eyes which suckled such fear . . .

After all, Neruda does go on to say:

> Forgetting is better
> in order to sustain hope . . .

> We found the light
> and we recovered our reason

The Chilean critic, Federico Schopf, has written very thoughtfully on Neruda's attitude to Stalinism from Khrushchev's 1956 revelations onwards.

The content, and even the style, of *Estravagario*, published in 1958, would begin to reflect – in a curious game of 'reveal and conceal' – the impact of these revelations on the poet who at that time was going through a particularly happy period of his life . . . The poet declares himself prepared to assume the enormous weight of this dark story, but he warns that he considers it just one more burden to add to the heavy sack of 'huge stones' which he has been dragging around for some time. This declaration is, of course, a way of minimising the political seriousness of Stalinism. But the poet tries to reduce the extent of his responsibility in other ways, as well: by claiming that he was unaware of the real magnitude of the Stalinist crimes and, above all, through the humorous and light style which characterises the book [*Estravagario*] . . . And yet Neruda's worries about Stalinism will be constant from now on and will re-appear at various moments of his extensive late works. By the time he wrote *Memorial de Isla Negra* (1964), he admits that he had been singing only the positive aspects of Soviet society during the Stalinist period. He also confesses that he had received some news of the crimes during this period – 'Every detail emerging from the shadow made us suffer as much as necessary' – but that, like so many others, he kept silent for tactical reasons. And in the poems of *Estravagario* a distinction begins to emerge (one which Neruda never abandoned) between two periods in the life of Stalin and his policies: the one which 'embodied the direction of the day / when he asked opinions of the light' and the one in which Stalin usurped absolute power, destroying the Party and separating himself from the people.[11]

Hernán Loyola has claimed that Neruda was originally thinking of calling *Fin de mundo* by another name: *Juicio final* (Final Judgement), because of its apocalyptic tone.[12] Neruda himself wrote, in a letter to another Italian critic, Giuseppe Bellini, that *Fin de mundo* was a 'bitter' book, 'a kind of nightmare about the cruelty and evil of the twentieth century'.[13] But, as Bellini adds, despite the anguish, Neruda reaffirms his duty, his mission, to take an active part in the life of man and rebuild hope for the future.

But it was to love that Neruda returned again and again, as if it sheltered him from political disillusionment. In his 1971 interview with *Marcha*, Neruda was asked for his views on Arthur Koestler, the Anglo-Hungarian author who had so noisily broken with Communism. Neruda replied in a very interesting, and surprising, way:

> He seems to have felt a great fatigue. I don't feel that fatigue, because I haven't only written about politics. I have written, perhaps, seven thousand pages of poems. Well, I believe you won't even find four pages on political matters! That's why I have many reasons not to be tied to this order of things. My poetry comes from other sources . . . I prefer love. Politics is an obsession for others, not for me . . . Politics is not an essential aspect of my poetry. What is essential? To write what one really feels, at every moment of one's existence . . . I do not believe in schools – not in symbolism, realism nor surrealism . . .[14]

But what is politics? In another interview, this time with the Mexican newspaper, *Excelsior*, Neruda declared, 'You cannot be happy if you do not fight for other people's happiness. You can never abandon the sense of guilt of having something if others do not. Man cannot be a happy island.'[15]

True to this spirit, Neruda showed enormous generosity towards younger artists – not only poets but those working in other areas of the arts. One of today's best-known Chilean singer-songwriters, Tito Fernández ('El Temucano'), told me that he had been astonished when Neruda sat down with him during a visit to Temuco on 14 December 1969, and listened to him reciting his poems for several hours. 'I will never forget that gesture – and the fact that Neruda himself offered to help get me a record contract. He said I should be a singer, not a poet!'[16]

Neruda also continued to demonstrate his adventurous spirit. In 1969 he started a script for a film, *Babo*, based on the short novel *Benito Cereno*, by the nineteenth-century American novelist and fellow sea-lover, Herman Melville. The novel, published in 1865 but set in 1799, features Captain Amasa Delano as the commander of a large vessel in the harbour of St Maria – a small, deserted uninhabited island towards the southern extremity of the long coast of Chile – and concerns a slave rebellion.

Neruda had long yearned to work on Melville, and began his script, in verse, with an amusing invented dialogue between Melville and himself in which Melville protests at Neruda's attempts to resuscitate

> the cold story which I told
> and no one bothered to listen to or read . . .
> I made a blaze from their rancour.
> Let's not talk about it. The fire went out.

In a moment oddly reminiscent of *Alturas de Macchu Picchu* in its optimistic belief that man can rise from the dust like a phoenix, Neruda tells 'Melville':

> Good comrade, I think there's still time,
> time from the ashes, because those
> who disintegrated with time
> will emerge from the dust, will exist again
> if you blow on the ash . . .[17]

Sadly, Neruda never completed this intriguing project, and few are even aware of its embryonic existence.

At the same time as he was writing *Fin de mundo*, Neruda was writing what was to prove his shortest book, a shining little jewel called *Aún* (Still) – a single poem of 433 lines.

According to Robert Pring-Mill, *Aún* was written in just two days, on 5 and 6 July 1969, and rapidly printed in 500 copies by Neruda's first publisher, Nascimento, in Santiago. *Aún* contains some of Neruda's most touching poetry:

> If on your travels you come across
> a boy
> stealing apples
> and an old deaf man
> with an accordion,
> remember that I am
> the boy, the apples and the old man.[18]

On 3 September Luis Corvalán, the secretary-general of the Chilean Communist Party, arrived at Isla Negra on an important mission: to offer Neruda the conditional candidacy for President of Chile in the 1970 elections. His name would be put forward – along with those of three other 'pre-candidates' – to the six parties making up the Unidad Popular (Popular Unity) coalition. They would then decide whether to choose him as their presidential candidate in the forthcoming September 1970 elections.

In the end, he *was* approved as the Communist candidate, 'on condition that my resignation would be accepted when I rendered it. My withdrawal was inevitable, I felt. It was far too improbable that everyone could be rallied around a Communist.'[19]

In his memoirs, Neruda claims his heart was not set on becoming President. He was asked by one journalist whether he was willing to take on the onerous responsibility of running the country. He was, he replied, provided that they allowed him to continue to take his daily siesta. 'My nap is non-negotiable.'[20]

From the balcony of the headquarters of the Communist Party's central committee in Santiago's Calle Teatinos, Neruda told a cheering crowd that he accepted the pre-candidature: 'I have never conceived my life as being divided between poetry and politics.'[21]

His nomination naturally made the front pages of all the Santiago newspapers. Only one launched a personal attack on Neruda: *La Nación*. The paper contrasted what it called 'the artful, elegant and bourgeois presence of Pablo Neruda' with the austere appearance of other Communists like Luis Corvalán. Their comments concentrated on 'the cloud of smoke coming from the candidate's pipe' and even charged Neruda with having an '*agringada*' voice (a voice like that of a foreigner).[22]

But most of the media viewed the sight of Chile's most famous personality throwing his hat into the heavyweight political ring with interest – although they did not, on the whole, give much for his chances of defeating the party of the incumbent, President Eduardo Frei.

Despite poor health, Neruda set off, once again, to cover the whole of Chile on behalf of the Party, this time campaigning for his own 'pre-candidature'. As often as he could, because of his difficulty walking, he travelled by plane. His friend, Aída Figueroa, said that he took on the role despite the fact that 'he was loaded down with work at Isla

Negra. He had . . . commitments he had to meet because he had huge debts. There was a false idea that he was a man who earned a lot of money, but that was not true . . .'[23]

Ultimately, the coalition did indeed decide that it was Salvador Allende, a Socialist, who was the appropriate candidate. The poet could be left to do what he did best: write luminous verse.

It is generally assumed that Neruda was entirely happy to hand over the reins at this point. But just a few months later, Neruda told his friend, José Miguel Varas, in Moscow:

'I always knew that my presidential candidature was a salute to the flag. A necessary sacrifice. Someone else would be the candidate. Allende was the best, without a doubt. But what can you expect?' he added with a self-critical little smile. 'When you start out on an electoral campaign, you almost inevitably get caught up in the excitement. And the terrible thing is that, in the end, when my companions told me that they had achieved their objective and were withdrawing my candidature, I felt sorry. Can you understand that? Six months earlier, I swore that I had no other wish than to live a quiet life at home, writing.'[24]

Though Neruda had fought four elections on behalf of Salvador Allende, he was not impressed by Allende's skills as an orator, or by his tone – and says as much in his memoirs. But the two men shared a love of the Mexican muralists and pre-Columbian art. '[Allende] knew the *Canto general* very well and surprised the poet by reciting stanzas which he himself had forgotten,' recalled Aída Figueroa.[25]

Neruda himself declared:

None of those who accompanied Allende could keep up with his stamina. He had a knack worthy of Churchill himself of being able to fall asleep whenever he felt like it. Sometimes we would be travelling over the infinite arid stretches of the north of Chile. Allende slept soundly in a corner of the car. Suddenly, a small red speck would appear on the road, and, as we approached, it would become a group of fifteen or twenty men with their wives, their children and their flags. The car would stop. Allende would rub his eyes to face the high sun and the small group, which was singing. He would join in and sing the national anthem. And he would speak to them – lively, swift and eloquent. Then he would return to the car and we would continue on over Chile's long roads. Allende would sink back into sleep effortlessly . . .[26]

At the end of 1969, Neruda wrote a letter from Europe to his friend, Jorge Edwards, then counsellor at the Chilean Embassy in the Peruvian capital, Lima. He told Edwards that he and Matilde would be returning to Chile by boat and would like to stop off in Lima to give a recital. Could they stay at Edwards' house? Edwards panicked a little at Pablo's request. Neruda was not an easy guest: he needed the palest of whiskies and fine wines. 'Some people were scandalised by the fact that a Communist poet had such expensive tastes, but the theoretical justification was pretty simple: no one was seeking abso-lute egalitarianism, which had been discarded since the earliest days of the Revolution, but rather equality of possibilities. Socialism was built precisely, among other things, so that poets and creators could consume a magnum of Dom Perignon every now and then . . .'[27]

Neruda did indeed stop off in Lima and read his poems to a packed enormous amphitheatre at the Ursuline Nuns' College.

Neruda liked to declare, in private and even in press interviews, that his most popular book, the *Twenty Love Poems and a Song of Despair*, was the most mediocre of his works. That afternoon, in front of that fervent crowd, time passed and there was no sign of him reading any of the *Twenty Poems*. A question hung in the atmosphere, an unformulated request. And suddenly, the poet, when the applause which followed each reading died down, began to recite, in that unmistakable voice of his: '*Puedo escribir los versos más tristes esta noche . . .*' A gigantic sigh ran through the hall, a great collective breath, largely feminine in tone but in which every-one took part: men and women, young and old. It was something which, until that moment, it seemed, had been repressed. The poet smiled broadly . . . and went on reciting, this time in a sacrosanct silence . . .[28]

In April 1970, Neruda and Matilde left Chile once more for Europe. They were in Moscow again for Matilde's birthday on 3 May. José Miguel Varas had lunch with them at Moscow's luxurious National Hotel, where the Nerudas had been given their usual large suite on the second floor 'with clouds and little angels painted on the ceiling, with balconies and windows opening out on to a splendid view of the Kremlin . . .' Yet although Pablo kept up his usual high-spirited conversation, Varas observed that '[he] seemed melancholy to me. Matilde looked at him with concern and I think she made an oblique reference to some pending medical tests. And then, of course, we talked about politics.'[29]

Later in May, Neruda and Matilde were in Italy, where they watched the Italian première of *Fulgor y muerte de Joaquín Murieta* at Milan's Piccolo Theatre.

Returning to Chile, Neruda stopped off in Venezuela in early July 1970, and gave a speech to the third congress of the Latin American Community of Writers in Puerto Azul which reflected his continued optimism about a 'brilliant generation of writers' but condemned the repression taking place in Guatemala and Santo Domingo, and the

> humiliating condition of Puerto Rico, the criminal darkness which is enveloping Haiti, the ever-open wound of Nicaragua, the torture which is the bread of every day in Brazil. Writers remain in prison in Bolivia. Cuba is cut off by a boycott imposed by the North on our republics, a boycott which prevents food, medicine or books from getting through. In Paraguay, the jails are full of forgotten inmates. In Chile, my homeland, it has become usual to see shots fired on groups of writers and students.[30]

The period leading up to the 1970 presidential elections in Chile was indeed marred by increasing violence in Chile. The worst example occurred when police fired on a group of squatters in the southern town of Puerto Montt, killing nine people (an event commemorated in a famous song by the Communist singer-poet, Víctor Jara).

That same year, 1970, Neruda was made an Illustrious Son of Valparaíso by the town's municipality. In his speech of thanks, intriguingly, if perhaps unwittingly, he provided an insight into why he now saw those early bohemian years in Santiago as empty ones: 'Always, for a southerner like me, a provincial arriving in the city of Santiago as I awoke from adolescence, Santiago was too succulent a dish or an over-bitter drink in which there was no room for moments devoted to dreams and illusions.'[31]

Also in 1970, Matilde – increasingly anxious that, at fifty-eight, she might be beginning to lose her looks – took a dramatic decision. She told Pablo that she wanted to go to Buenos Aires to have plastic surgery on her face. Neruda was astonished, at first. As he saw her off at Santiago airport, he turned to his friend, Marie Martner. 'He asked, concerned: "Marie, I suppose she'll be able to smile after the operation, won't she?" The fact is, Matilde had a very attractive laugh. And Pablo did not know how to laugh – it was a silent laugh! Matilde had a loud laugh, and Pablo loved that.'[32]

But while Matilde was under the surgeon's knife in Buenos Aires, Neruda found a new, final passion. At the age of sixty-five, he fell in love with his wife's niece, Alicia Urrutia, whom Matilde had invited to stay with them at Isla Negra, along with her young daughter. Alicia was in her thirties, and her daughter – who was sent to a school at Isla Negra – was called Rosario (the name Neruda had initially given Matilde to disguise their relationship).

What came out of Pablo's relationship with Alicia was an astounding late burst of energy: his book, *La espada encendida* (The Flaming Sword). At the time, it read as an extraordinary, Bible-like epic of spiritual renewal, which begins with a quotation from Genesis telling of the expulsion of man from Paradise. When asked about the book by a journalist soon after he had finished it, Neruda described *La espada encendida* as 'about the myth of Adam and Eve, punishment and guilt, in reality, a new Adam and a new Eve. The world has come to an end, the bomb and the war have destroyed it and Adam, the only man on earth, meets Eve. Life and humanity begin once again with them.'[33]

Gabriel García Márquez once said of Neruda that he was loyal to Matilde, rather than faithful. This is a frequently voiced distinction in Latin America – and Latin culture in general. However, Neruda's attitude to women was very different from his friend Picasso's. When Picasso painted one of his wives or mistresses, he believed that he was performing a mystical, almost occult operation. They were not usually paintings of love: the act of painting appeared to give him a sense of power over his subject. Not with Neruda. As often as not, the object holds power over the artist. Indeed, in *La espada encendida*, Neruda makes Rosía (Alicia Urrutia) the first woman on Earth. There could be no more empowering position.

Hernán Loyola claims that, quite apart from the emotional energy which Neruda gained from this final love affair, he drew on another 'precise – though not declared – literary source: *L'Incendie terrestre*, a prose text by Marcel Schwob [a French writer who died in 1905], which Neruda had translated in his youth'.[34]

I have asked some of Neruda's friends whether his relationship with Alicia represented an attempt to recover something which had gone out of his marriage. They insist that Pablo continued to love Matilde as passionately as ever. And when I rather impudently asked his friend, Francisco Velasco, whether he thought Neruda had ever consummated his relationship with Alicia, he was happy to reply (though, presumably, without evidence): 'No. It was an entirely platonic love.'[35]

This is difficult to believe when we read the descriptions in the book of the relationship between Rhodo/Neruda and Rosía/Alicia, which are at once tender and vividly sexual:

> Rosía naked in the
> tangled field,
> Rosía, white and blue, fine-petalled,
> clear-thighed, dark-haired,
> she opened up to let Rhodo into her . . .[36]

When Matilde returned from Argentina and found out about Pablo's love for her niece, under her own roof, at Isla Negra, she flew into a rage and threw Alicia physically out of the house, with all her belongings. Pablo had betrayed her with her own niece. Alicia, like Matilde, was red-headed. Unlike Matilde, she was half Neruda's age.

It is hard to imagine that the marriage would have survived if Matilde had realised that Rosía in *La espada encendida* was based on Alicia – that Neruda had given his final love the ultimate accolade of being Eve, the mother of all humanity. Especially as Neruda makes his Eve supremely fertile, while Matilde had apparently suffered at least two miscarriages:

> Says Rosía: We broke the chain
> Says Rhodo: You will give me a hundred children
> Says Rosía: I will populate the light
> Says Rhodo: I love you. We will live[37]

Matilde threatened to leave Pablo – the idea of staying with him at first seemed impossible. She talked to friends who persuaded her to calm down. But there was a new, unspoken, gnawing tension between them which made them both unhappy.

Neruda had other problems that he also wanted to be kept quiet. On 12 July 1970, on his sixty-sixth birthday, he secretly spoke to his doctor friend and La Sebastiana neighbour, Francisco Velasco: 'Look, Pancho, I'm worried. There's blood in my urine.' Velasco advised him to consult the best urologist in Santiago immediately. Pablo took his advice – but only partially. 'He went to a specialist and came back saying that they had found some small thing and that he should return within a month to have some tests done. But he never went back. He was too scared,' said Velasco, who used to be director of the Hospital Salvador in Valparaíso.[38]

Velasco believes Neruda could have avoided the prostate cancer which eventually killed him. 'It was neglect on his part. He didn't go back to have the tests and the illness progressed.'[39]

In the midst of this physical and emotional turmoil, Chile's presidential election took place on 4 September 1970, and in a result which staggered the world, Salvador Allende won most votes: 36.3 per cent, just ahead of Jorge Alessandri Rodríguez with 35.3 per cent. The vote would still have to be put to the Chilean Congress for approval – and the United States would do its utmost to make sure that Senate vote went against Allende – but for the moment, it seemed that the world might have its first ever democratically elected Marxist head of state. On 24 October the Congress approved Allende as President.

Just days later, Neruda telephoned him with an urgent request: 'Get me away from here. Make me ambassador to France.' Neruda, the man who had written, in Canto general, that all Chilean idiots were made ambassadors, needed an excuse to escape from the homeland he loved. He needed to repair his marriage, and distance from Alicia seemed the only way to do this. Allende agreed that Neruda would be an ideal ambassador in the country he knew so well. He quickly appointed Neruda to the post, and asked the Chilean Foreign Minister, Clodomiro Almeyda, to present the move to the Senate for official approval.

Another version, as told to Robert Pring-Mill, was that the Chilean Communist Party had hinted to President Allende that the appointment would avoid a scandal.[40]

Francisco Velasco believes that the poet 'chose France because, apart from being one of his favourite countries, it boasted the best specialists in urology'.[41] Velasco disagrees with Matilde's contention in her memoirs that Pablo never knew the precise nature of his illness. 'He pretended he didn't know. I tried to hide the cancer from him, saying it was arthritis. But he knew what was wrong and he knew I was lying to him.'[42]

New Year 1970–1971 was not the customary cheerful affair for Neruda. He knew his health was deteriorating, and relations with Matilde remained tense. We also know, from private comments to friends, that he was uneasy about the prospects of a smooth ride for the new government – even though he declared Allende to be the greatest Chilean President since the nineteenth-century José Balmaceda. He was afraid that the Allende regime could befall a similar fate to that of the Spanish Republic before the civil war.

Fortunately, Neruda was kept busy. On 7 January 1971, he and Matilde paid their first visit to Easter Island, the mysterious Chilean territory thousands of miles out in the Pacific. Neruda had agreed to make a series of documentary programmes for Chile's Canal 13 television station, to be called *Historia y geografía de Pablo Neruda* and broadcast in mid-1971.

One woman who still remembers Pablo's only visit to Easter Island well is his 'Rapa Nui muse', María Ignacia Paoa Languitopa, whose identity was revealed more than two decades later, in 1999. 'Neruda called me Ignacia,' she told the island's newspaper, *La Gaceta de Isla de Pascua*. 'Apparently, he never found out that everyone on the island calls me Makaoa – meaning skinny – because I was always very slim.' She believed that she was the 'innocent beauty dancing Rapa Nui's rhythm' to whom Neruda refers in a poem from the book he wrote about this visit, *La rosa separada* (The Separate Rose). She recalled that Neruda himself had danced on the island 'but he was not a good dancer'.[43]

La rosa separada was first published in a luxury edition of 99 copies in Paris in 1972. In it, he compares the enduring mystery of the island and its stone statues with the ordinary lives of the tourists – himself included – with their 'hypocritical smiles', like 'Sinbads and Columbuses', who discover nothing more magical than the 'bar-bill' before they leave again on jets and boats back to their mundane jobs. I believe that this uncharacteristic misanthropy was partly fuelled by Neruda's unhappiness at the interruption of his love affair with Alicia and the continuing friction in his marriage to Matilde.

While still on Easter Island, Neruda heard, on 21 January, that the Chilean Congress had approved his appointment as Chilean Ambassador to Paris. He was about to take up a post which had once been occupied by his arch-enemy and persecutor, Gabriel González Videla. To add to the irony, Pablo was taking over from the veteran diplomat, Carlos Morla Lynch, whom he blamed – wrongly, it seems – for having contributed to Miguel Hernández's death by refusing to grant him diplomatic asylum at the Chilean Embassy in Madrid.

On 2 March 1971, Pablo and Matilde left Chile to take up the Paris posting. They stopped off in Buenos Aires for a week and there Neruda defended the fledgling Allende government against the growing criticism of its policy of nationalising key industries, and, at the same time, condemned the United States.

> We know that oil was nationalised in Mexico under Cárdenas more than thirty years ago, that the Suez Canal was nationalised in Egypt by Nasser. There's a nationalisation every day somewhere in the world. In Chile, a country so well-developed politically and intellectually . . . foreign companies were permitted to own the telephone and electricity companies, not to mention copper, which produces a million dollars a day for the North Americans. Please! Why be scared if we try to clothe our people, build hospitals, schools, roads, with those million dollars a day which we want to – and shall – recover?[44]

In April 1971, safely in Paris, Neruda told his friend, Jorge Edwards, who had now joined him as second-in-command at the Embassy, that he would be receiving a number of letters with Edwards' name on, and that he should hand them to Pablo immediately and very discreetly. These letters, we now know, were from Alicia, who continued to write to Neruda from Chile. 'The letters began to arrive regularly, at a rate of about one or two per week,' Edwards recalled, 'and once, when I made the mistake of handing one of them to another person, someone we both trusted . . . Pablo gave me a serious dressing-down: "You must never do that," he said. "For any reason." '[45]

Edwards suggests that Neruda continued to send presents back to Alicia's daughter in Chile, and even that he was making plans for Alicia herself to come over to live in Paris – though Edwards adds that he considered this to be the fantasy of an ailing man.

Not long after arriving in Paris, Neruda underwent his first surgical operation, at the Cochin Hospital. He insisted that one of the doctors present should be his Chilean friend Raúl Bulnes. By 1971, Matilde was told the news: Neruda had prostate cancer. She refused to inform her husband, but felt the need to confide the truth to close friends, on condition that they, too, vowed to keep it a secret from Pablo.

'In 1971, we were confidentially informed that he was ill with cancer,' said Aída Figueroa.[46] 'But he didn't know, he didn't even suspect it, even though he was much thinner.'

Neruda continued to fulfil his diplomatic functions in Paris. 'He was an excellent ambassador in France and his mission was not easy,' said Aída. During his stint there, 'Chile's external debt was renegotiated . . . and then he was obliged to hold more meetings with bankers and economists than with artists . . . I visited him there in 1971 . . . The Embassy was full of life, of visitors. We went to see the RER [the regional metropolitan train line] in Paris, which was just being built, and the workers recognised him and surrounded him.'[47]

Pablo's sixty-seventh birthday, on 12 July 1971, was a subdued occasion. Neruda was still recovering from his operation and still reeling, too, from his affair with Alicia. He showed a totally atypical indifference to any kind of birthday celebration. Gone were his childish pranks, or any desire to disguise himself. He had written back to his friend Volodia Teitelboim in Chile the day before to say that he had a fever 'which doesn't matter, except that tomorrow is my birthday, which doesn't matter either'.[48]

Then Pablo, Matilde and their Venezuelan friend Miguel Otero Silva – with whom Matilde would collaborate after Neruda's death to bring his memoirs to fruition – made a decision which was very nearly fatal to Neruda. They chose to spend the summer holiday of 1971 in northern Italy. When they arrived in Tuscany, they found the region in the midst of a record-breaking heatwave. As they were watching the famous Palio horse race in Siena in mid-August, Neruda suddenly felt very ill and fainted. He was soon in a state of semi-coma. The doctors recommended his immediate transfer to Florence by ambulance. Recovering in hospital, and then at Florence's Hotel Baglioni, Neruda was visited by his friends, the Chilean Ambassador to Italy, Carlos Vassallo, and Carlos's wife, Carmen. He reassured them, in a sonnet written on 18 August,[49] that 'I no longer remember my suffering / loyal friends' – but it had been a close thing.

Shortly after returning to Paris, Neruda learned of the death of Nikita Khrushchev on 11 September from a heart attack at his dacha on the outskirts of Moscow. According to Jorge Edwards, Neruda had long been an admirer of Khrushchev and was appalled at the way the Soviet Communist apparatus had dealt with him. In particular, Neruda disapproved of the low-key funeral for Khrushchev. A visiting Hungarian government Minister agreed with Neruda but exclaimed in French: 'Pablo, Socialism will triumph, even so!' Neruda replied, also in French: 'I have my doubts.'[50]

In an important interview with the French weekly news magazine, *l'Express*, in September 1971, the journalist Edouard Bailby asked him about Stalin and his crimes. Neruda's reply was concise but telling: 'Je me suis trompé' (I was mistaken).[51]

Early that autumn Artur Lundkvist, a member of the Swedish Academy and a friend, visited Pablo in Paris and announced privately that the Academy had decided to award him that year's Nobel Prize for Literature. Neruda reacted, at first, with disbelief. There had been so many previous false alarms.

While waiting for the official announcement later the same month, Neruda asked Jorge Edwards to accompany him to Normandy to find a place to live. Perhaps Paris, like Santiago in Chile, had begun to pall – he needed to be closer to nature. As Edwards recalled:

> At the end of that Saturday morning, we found the house in Condé-sur-Iton – an old saw-mill attached to the local stately home, a property presided over by a Renaissance castle which couldn't be seen from the village, because it had been built on low land, but whose grilled front gates looked out on to the main road. As always happened in these cases, Pablo took his decision immediately and began to think about the house as if his life depended on it . . . He signed some papers . . . handed over a cheque as a deposit, and the whole affair was signed and sealed before two in the afternoon . . . I told him that he had found Temuco in Normandy, and I think that he agreed, though he didn't say a word. The house was pure wood . . .[52]

On 21 October 1971, Neruda was officially awarded the Nobel Prize for Literature. Journalists gathered at his Paris residence eager for a response. President Allende sent a message expressing the 'joy' of the Chilean people, who were 'celebrating their compatriot, their brother'.

In the statement, Allende said that Neruda 'could and should have won this extraordinary and significant distinction years ago . . . His books and poems have been translated into all the languages of the world for some time, but it is worth pointing out that this prize goes to the poet who is committed to his people . . .'[53]

What few people knew – because Neruda insisted that it be kept scrupulously secret – was that the poet was to undergo more medical tests in the next few days. To his annoyance, this would prevent him from representing the Chilean government at an act of homage at the Palais des Sports in Paris to celebrate the ninetieth birthday of Pablo Picasso.

In December, Neruda and Matilde travelled to Stockholm to receive the Nobel Prize. They were met at the airport by Arthur Lundkvist, who confirmed to journalists that he had worked long and hard for many years for this moment.

Virginia Vidal was the only Chilean journalist who covered Neruda's Nobel Prize ceremony. She recalled Neruda coming down the aircraft steps at Stockholm airport on 10 December in a raincoat.

> He walked unhurriedly, and he wasn't smiling. The journalists surrounded him and started firing off questions. Sober, experienced, he irradiated serenity as he replied: 'My hobbies are shells, old books, old shoes. In Paris, I feel like a cocktail of diplomatic poet and Socialist.' There was a silence and then he said, with simplicity: 'I'm so afraid of you and now it seems as though you're afraid of me.' . . . Someone asked him: 'Which is the prettiest word?' 'I'm going to reply in a fairly vulgar way, like in a radio song, with a word which is extremely hackneyed: the word *love*. The more you use it, the stronger it gets. And there's no harm abusing the word, either.'[54]

After which, he was taken to his Stockholm hotel, where he was thrilled to hear that he and Matilde would be joined by their friends Miguel Otero Silva and his wife, María Teresa Castillo. He was also happy to be reunited with his old friend and diplomatic colleague, Luis Enrique Délano, who was now Chilean Ambassador to Sweden.

In those three days leading up to the Nobel ceremony, a rumour began circulating around Stockholm that Neruda had received anonymous threats, condemning him for being about to take part in an imperialist event, wearing a tailcoat, and promising that, during the ceremony, his tailcoat would be cut to shreds with scissors. The Swedish police took the threats very seriously. It was only later that it emerged that the threats had been a prank organised by Miguel Otero Silva.

On the day itself, 13 December 1971, as Virginia Vidal pointed out, Neruda looked totally at ease as he sat in the Stockholm Filadelfiakyrkan in his tailcoat, which he had worn on numerous occasions at ambassadorial events.

When the King of Sweden came to shake his hand, they fell into an animated conversation. Matilde asked Pablo later what they were saying to one another. Neruda replied: 'We started talking about stones. Stones are his passion. And then I told him about our Easter Island . . . I told him how its great figures face the sky, with their gaze lost in the ocean. We talked so long about that and he was so impressed that, in the end, I told him that I would invite him to visit the island. He answered that he would like nothing more, but that his strength was failing him.'[55] The King died later that year.

In his long Nobel Prize acceptance speech – one of the most powerful he ever gave – Neruda first took his audience back to his extraordinary escape over the Andes into Argentina in 1949. Then he turned to what that experience had taught him for his poetry:

> I did not learn from books any recipe for writing a poem, and I, in my turn, will avoid giving any advice on mode or style which might give the new poets even a drop of supposed insight . . . The poet is not a 'little god' . . . He is not picked out by a mystical destiny in preference to those who follow other crafts and professions. I have often maintained that the best poet is he who prepares our daily bread: the nearest baker who does not imagine himself to be a god. He performs his majestic and humble task of kneading the dough, consigning it to the oven, baking it in golden colours and handing us our daily bread as a duty of fellowship. And, if the poet succeeds in achieving this simple awareness, this too will be transformed into an element in an immense activity, in a simple or complicated structure which constitutes the building of a community, the transformation

of the conditions which surround mankind, the handing over of mankind's products: bread, truth, wine, dreams. If the poet joins this never-completed struggle to extend to the hands of each and all his part of his commitment, his dedication and his tenderness to the daily work of all people, then the poet must take part in the sweat, in the bread, in the wine, in the dream of all humanity . . . Each and every one of my verses has chosen to take its place as a tangible object, each and every one of my poems has claimed to be a useful working instrument, each and every one of my songs has aspired to serve as a sign in space for a meeting between paths which cross one another, or as a piece of stone or wood on which someone, some others, those who follow after, will be able to carve the new signs . . .

In a veiled admission that Stalinism had been an error, Neruda spoke of offering his services to

an honourable army which may, from time to time, make mistakes but which moves forward unceasingly and struggles every day against the anachronism of the recalcitrant and the impatience of the opinionated. For I believe that my duties as a poet involve fraternity not only with the rose and with symmetry, with exalted love and endless longing, but also with unrelenting human occupations which I have incorporated into my poetry.[56]

During a dinner hosted that night in Stockholm by Luis Enrique Délano's wife, Lola Falcón, Matilde informed Lola that Pablo had cancer – but insisted that he should never know this.

The next day, Neruda gave a recital of his poems at Stockholm's Museum of Modern Art to a crowd of young people sitting or lying on the floor of the museum, alternating with Swedish translations read by the actor Max von Sydow.

There was one final surprise before Pablo left Sweden: the invitation to an exhibition which left the poet open-mouthed with joy and fascination. The star of the show was a seventeenth-century Swedish boat, the *Wasa*, which had sunk on its maiden 'voyage' in 1628 without even leaving the harbour. The vessel, built from a thousand oak trees, had been preserved in immaculate condition when it was lifted to the surface again.

Not everyone, of course, was happy with the choice of Nobel Prize-winner. The Argentinian writer, Jorge Luis Borges, told the journalist, Ramón Chao:

> He [Neruda] had written a poem opposing the tyrants of America, devoting several stanzas to the United States, but not a single one about Perón. People thought that he was filled with noble indignation . . . He was married to an Argentine woman and he was well aware of what was going on, wasn't he? But he didn't want his poem to do any harm. When I went to Chile, he slipped away to avoid seeing me, and he was right to do that. People wanted to pit us against each other. He was a Chilean Communist poet, and I, a conservative Argentinian poet, was against the Communists. I cannot agree with a theory which preaches the domination of the State over the individual. But everything I've just said has nothing to do with the quality of Neruda's poetry. When the Nobel went to Miguel Angel Asturias in 1967, I immediately said that Neruda had deserved it. And he finally won it in 1971. I do not think it is fair that a writer is judged by his political ideas. It's true that Rudyard Kipling defended the British Empire. But we must also recognise that he was a great writer.[57]

From Stockholm, Pablo and Matilde headed for Poland, where Pablo was looking forward to watching the Polish première of *Joaquín Murieta*, under the direction of the Chilean Boris Stoicheff. Neruda and Matilde then travelled on to make a secret visit to the Soviet Union. It was towards the end of 1971; a belated celebration was held in Moscow for the Nobel win, but Neruda was mainly there to allow top Soviet doctors to examine him again.

The Moscow visit was marked by a memorable party given by Neruda's friend, the Soviet poet Simyon Isaakovitch Kirsanov, who had been a friend of Mayakovsky. 'When he and Pablo met, it was like standing next to fireworks letting out sparks of wit and joy,' Matilde said. During the party, Simyon presented Pablo with a beautiful wine glass and told him, 'When you drink a toast, I will be with you.'[58] And then it was back to bureaucratic duties in Paris.

Despite his general weariness, Neruda continued to take his diplomatic functions seriously. Jorge Edwards recalls how Neruda would go up to his offices on the third floor of the Embassy, which Neruda always referred to as 'The Mausoleum', at about ten in the morning.

He would discuss the telexes and letters with Edwards and receive two or three visitors.

> At around 12 midday, he was already very tired. He would stick his head into my office, which was right next to his, and say: 'I can't take any more. I'm going out for a walk.' 'Off you go,' I would say to him. 'Don't worry about anything.' Or I would say: 'Remember that you have a lunch at such and such a time.' But he was not the type of person, except in the worst moments of his illness, to forget his commitments . . . In the afternoon, he shut himself away in his vast bedroom on the second floor, where, as he wrote in his memoirs, a knight from the times of the Crusades could have lodged – and with room for his horse, as well. At the end of the siesta, after six or even later, I came down and told him what had happened during the day. Neruda would be lying on his back, with a cup of tea on the bedside table, the bed covered with books and magazines, and with his fat, naked feet emerging from the sheets, since at that time, Matilde would be massaging his feet and legs – I suppose to counter phlebitis or the signs of gout, from which he also suffered. ('The gout stops me from eating caviar,' he told me one day – which, as a complaint from a Communist poet, has its funny side.) Later, when he got up and dressed, Matilde had to crouch down and tie his shoes, because the poet was unbelievably clumsy with his hands . . . Once I saw him, dressed up to the nines in white, ready to go out to a reception . . . with an expression of anguish, shouting out for Matilde. If she didn't arrive to tie his laces, he had to wait there, immobilised, like a heavy boat which could not raise anchor.[59]

On 7 December 1971, Neruda held a house-warming party at his new home in Normandy, which he called La Manquel, a Mapuche Indian word for 'condor'. Immediately, a furore broke out. The Right in Chile claimed, ludicrously, that Neruda had bought a castle in France. In fact, it was a disused mill attached to a big mansion. Some maintained that Neruda had spent his Nobel Prize winnings in advance – but he had not even been officially awarded the prize when he signed the deposit cheque on the house.

At La Manquel, Neruda celebrated what was to be his penultimate New Year's Eve party. They had brought back copious quantities of goose meat and fresh caviar from Moscow. After looking through a whole list of possible guests with whom to see in the year 1972, Pablo, Matilde and Jorge Edwards reduced the list to just two: the Colombian poet Arturo Camacho Ramírez, his country's representative at UNESCO, and his wife. Neruda liked Arturo. He was good-humoured and, significantly, was uninterested in politics. But the fact that the guest-list was stripped down to two reflects both Neruda's declining health and his new preference for quieter social gatherings. As it happened, Camacho himself arrived suffering from a severe attack of bronchitis and spent the whole evening prostrate on a sofa.

Many friends passed through La Manquel over the following months. In February 1972, the Argentinian novelist Julio Cortázar and his then-wife, Lithuanian-born Ugné Karvelis, arrived in a large van. They stayed the whole weekend, along with Volodia Teitelboim, who was also visiting, and not once was Pablo's illness mentioned. Cortázar regaled his host with descriptions of a journey around Europe, sleeping in his van. Neruda had once told Sara Vial that he valued one thing above any other in a human being: 'Never intelligence, always goodness.'[60] He loved Julio because he had both. During his stay, they talked happily about literature, travels, memories of the past.

Neruda returned to Normandy from Paris every Friday to rest over the weekend. It was at La Manquel that Neruda continued work on his book, *Geografía infructuosa* (Fruitless Geography), which was published by Losada in March 1972. Although the book's dedication claims that it was written in 1971 in Chile and France, much of it had been written much earlier: partly during his travels around Chile in 1969 campaigning for his own pre-candidature for the presidency of Chile (particularly the first poems mentioning towns in the south of Chile), partly between March and June 1970, during his trip to Italy; and we know that he wrote four poems – 'De viajes' (Trips), 'Sonata de Montevideo' (Montevideo Sonata), 'Paisaje en el mar' (Sea Voyage) and 'A plena ola' (On the High Sea) – on the boat returning to Chile from Italy in 1970.

Hernán Loyola has rightly pointed out that *Geografía infructuosa* is surprisingly free of references – direct or indirect – to the political turmoil taking place in Chile. Nor is there any sign here of the passion he felt for Matilde's niece, Alicia. Loyola believes that Alicia – who was by then in Arica in northern Chile, where she still lives with her daughter and three grandchildren, refusing even today to talk to anyone about her relationship with Pablo – is very likely to own secret erotic texts written by Neruda at around this time.[61] Indeed, Neruda wrote a poem called 'Tal vez me espera' (Perhaps She's Waiting for Me), probably in 1973, which was published for the first time in 2002. In it, he says that in Iquique (near Arica),

> I forgot
> a love, an umbrella and
> whatever else.
> I've lived thinking
> about
> this love
> or about an object
> or about an object without
> any destiny . . .
> I want to see
> whether I can find
> what I lost,
> what perhaps is
> waiting for me still . . .[62]

Geografía infructuosa reveals a poet who no longer hides his physical decay.

> I felt naked
> after so many medals,
> ready to return to where I'd come from
> to the damp beneath the soil . . .

and this same poem immediately continues with the bitter line:

> There is no mercy for man among men[63]

March 1972 saw Pablo and Matilde in Milan again. This time, they were there to attend the thirteenth congress of the Italian Communist Party. In the evening, Neruda gave a recital at the Milan Academy. He was also proud to see a bookshop displaying Italian translations of his three *Residencias, Canto general* and *Fin de mundo*, all of which had been brought out at the same time.

From Italy, Neruda and Matilde returned to Moscow in May. Pablo knew he needed more medical tests, and though he once again had a room at the National Hotel, he spent most of his stay in hospital.

Vera Kuteishikova and her husband, Lev Ospovat, visited him there. She told me that he was clearly very ill.

> We did not talk about his health, but it was impossible to hide his condition and he definitely knew what was wrong with him. He was quiet, but we spoke about the new Italian editions of his work. Lev showed him a list of contents of a collection he was preparing of Neruda's prose. We also talked about the political situation back home in Chile, and he told me something I have never forgotten: 'I am pessimistic about the present, but optimistic about the future.' He had no illusions about the fragility of the Allende government, but he remained hopeful.[64]

It was to prove Neruda's final visit to Russia.

Back in Paris, despite his deteriorating health, he held more meetings – including one with President Georges Pompidou, to whom he presented a copy of *Arte de pájaros* – aimed at renegotiating Chile's external debt. (The Mexican novelist Carlos Fuentes has confirmed to me that Neruda told him he spent most of the three-hour meeting with President Pompidou discussing Baudelaire's poetry.) When the Soviet leader, Leonid Brezhnev, paid an official visit to France in 1972, he received Neruda privately at the Soviet Embassy in Paris. During this meeting, Neruda asked Brezhnev to intervene to stop the mistreatment of the Soviet writer, Alexander Solzhenitsyn. The Soviet leader 'listened to me, silently, with a wooden face, and I had no choice but to change the subject'. As Neruda told Jorge Edwards: 'Solzhenitsyn's a bore, an unbearable idiot, but they have to leave him alone. Because it will be us, the Communist writers on the other side, who will carry the can.'[65]

Another distinguished visitor to the Chilean Embassy in those last months of Neruda's stint in Paris was Dolores Ibarruri (La Pasionaria), the Spanish Communist heroine of Civil War times, living in exile in Moscow. 'Neruda sat her down in an armchair which he had just acquired at the Galeries Printemps ... La Pasionaria spoke with enthusiasm of Spanish democratisation which, in her view ... was inevitable.' Much amused, Neruda told Jorge Edwards later that La Pasionaria had become so animated in her praise of the progress being made in Spain that her armchair had overturned, throwing its occupant on the floor, 'covering her with a grotesque shell, like a gigantic tortoise, amid the cries of alarm of the poet and the three or four other people in the room'.[66]

On 7 April, Neruda flew to New York, where he had been invited back to address the PEN Club. Fernando Alegría, who had accompanied him on his previous, troubled trip in 1966, was with him again, staying in the room next to Pablo at New York's Algonquin Hotel. 'I knew that Neruda was suffering from a grave illness, that he had already been operated on in Paris, but he refused to talk about all that,' Alegría recalled. 'And yet the truth of his condition showed through in insignificant details . . . Matilde looked after him gently but firmly.'[67]

A drink at the hotel bar had to be cancelled, but still Neruda did not complain. 'He endured a horrible session with a dentist. Then we took a taxi and went to buy seashells. On the way, the conversation took on an unexpected tone. He was getting old. But of course, people do get old. You don't have to be reminded of that.'[68]

On 10 April Neruda gave a speech at a dinner in New York to mark the fiftieth anniversary of the founding of the PEN American Center. He pointed out that, while he was required to negotiate Chile's external debt, he personally had a huge debt to the US:

> As for myself, now a man of almost seventy, I was barely fifteen when I discovered Walt Whitman, my primary creditor. I stand here among you today, still owing my marvellous debt that helped me to live . . . Greatness has many faces but I, a poet who writes in Spanish, learned more from Walt Whitman than from Cervantes. In Whitman's poetry, the ignorant are never humbled, and the human condition is never derided.[69]

Neruda's debt to Whitman was indeed vast. When his carpenter, Rafita, noticed a portrait of the bearded American poet hanging on the wall at Isla Negra, he asked Pablo: 'Is that your grandfather?' Without hesitation, Neruda replied, 'Yes.'

In contrast to the sad, defeated note of much of his late poetry, Neruda's public pronouncements, were overtly optimistic. In New York, he said he hoped that colonialism in Africa and Asia would come to an end, and that black writers in Africa and America were 'beginning to communicate the true pulse of their hapless, long-silent race. Political struggle is an integral part of poetry. Man's liberation has often flowed in blood, but always in song . . .'[70]

It was as if he were bravely trying to conceal the truth in public, but it forced its way out in his verse.

Neruda was weak. He no longer craved constant attention, no longer wanted to be emperor of any court. He wanted peace. Not just world peace. His peace. Peace he could not find in New York. As Fernando Alegría noted:

> There were too many people crowding around him. I saw Neruda turning grey . . . They besieged him, they crumpled him, they cornered him, until he was forced to disappear. He found himself in an elegant, velvet-lined room where [he was given] air and mouthfuls of champagne like an exhausted boxer in the final rounds . . . As he slowly made his way to the bathroom, he passed me and told me that he was not feeling well, that he would be returning to Chile in November, and no one must find out. Everyone knew.[71]

During this second visit to New York, Neruda again enjoyed visiting the city's antique shops, particularly those that sold seashells. The British biologist, Sir Julian Huxley, had once arrived at Santiago airport and asked for Neruda, who was a friend. 'Neruda the poet?' the journalists enquired. 'No, I don't know any poet by the name of Neruda', said Sir Julian. 'I want to speak to Neruda the malacologist [specialist in molluscs].'

Neruda gave two recitals in New York, at the United Nations headquarters and at the Poetry Center, and he addressed teachers and students at Columbia University on 13 April. The following day, he flew back to Paris.

Soon afterwards, he was contacted by Mikos Theodorakis, a famous Greek composer living in exile in Paris, who had been setting Neruda's *Canto general* to music. He told the poet that he was ready to start rehearsals. Pablo sat dutifully in a corner as he heard soloists, chorus and orchestra sing his poems 'Algunas bestias', 'Vienen los pájaros', 'Los libertadores', 'América insurrecta' 'A mi partido' and 'Voy a vivir'. To his own surprise, perhaps – he had no ear for music – Neruda found the experience pleasurable and, after dedicating a signed copy of *Canto general* to Theodorakis, he asked the composer to include other poems in the oratorio: the newcomers were 'A Emiliano Zapata', 'Lautaro' and 'Sandino'.

On 12 July, his sixty-eighth birthday, Neruda was in remarkably good spirits, despite his frailty. At the party at La Manquel in Normandy, he dressed up in a top hat, a red barman's jacket and a false moustache. But after carefully arranging the different coloured wine glasses on the table and cheerfully sharing out the caviar he had brought back from his last trip to Moscow, he suddenly turned to one of the guests – the Chilean writer Poli Délano – and said: 'Poli, congratulate me.'

> I thought he was referring to the the layout of the table, but he went on: 'I've just pissed, and when I manage to piss, I feel that everyone should congratulate me.' This all sounded rather odd to me, because at that time I had no idea he was suffering from prostate problems, nor that his last trip to Moscow had been for medical reasons.[72]

On 19 September 1972, Neruda reaffirmed his commitment to Communism in an upbeat greeting written for the seventh congress of La Jota – the Communist youth group representing workers, students and other professionals. He wrote:

> Young people must learn to be young, and that is no easy task. I was a boy in mourning. The sadness of the poor peoples of the south, the cry of the rain, the intransigent solitude, fell on my life. Later on, I found that the more serious the problems life throws at us, the more difficult the discovery of our path, the more serious our sense of social injustice, the more reasons we have to feel worthy of our responsibility. That's how we discover the road to joy . . . We fight to make sure that our joy can be shared and handed out all over the world . . .

It was that joy of being alive which made him such a life-enhancing poet, and it was his generosity in wanting to 'share' this joy which gained him so many loyal friends – even among political foes.

However, in this same address, Neruda warned the youth of the day that capitalism and imperialism mask themselves under the guise of the 'free world', and beneath this mask hide terror, class repression, social perversity . . . Today, immense nations live in revolution. The Communists were martyred, assaulted, slandered. Today, they have a major say in the fate of the world . . . History moves forwards, leaving behind the stragglers and the impatient . . . I was already a man when I joined the family of Chilean Communists. I had been through solitude. I had felt and understood tragedies, misfortunes, catastrophes. I had been through wars and defeats, blows and victories. I thought I already knew it all. But I found, within my Party and walking among peoples and along roads throughout America and Chile, that I had a lot to learn, and that every day, nameless men, whom I had never met before, taught me the greatest lessons about wisdom, rectitude, firmness.

Then, in a revealing final passage, 'No one should consider himself superior to the Party. This sense of modesty does not mean vassalage, but rather overcoming the personal, learning a discipline which will always lead us to truth.'[73] Even in his final year of life, the Communist Party was all-important to him.

In late October 1972, UNESCO held a vote to decide whether to co-opt Neruda on to its executive board. When delegates voted in favour, a frail Neruda forced himself to attend the ceremony where he was loudly applauded. In his speech, he told UNESCO delegates about that key moment in his career when he had read poems from his book, *España en el corazón*, to the porters at the Santiago market and realised, from their response, that he had to write for the common man and avoid 'difficult' verse.

A few days later, on 27 October 1972, Neruda underwent a second operation at a Paris clinic. Again, he insisted that the surgery must be kept an absolute secret. Privately, Neruda had now made up his mind, reluctantly, to resign his post of Ambassador, despite his promises to many friends that he would not. His ill-health meant that he needed to return to Chile; that was where he wanted to spend whatever time was left to him on Earth.

He wrote to his friend Volodia Teitelboim in Chile to tell him to postpone a planned welcoming ceremony for him back home until 2 December, to give him time to recover from the surgery. As yet, any return to Chile must be presented to the world as temporary.

To Mikos Theodorakis, Neruda gave what he hoped would be the official reason spread to the media and other friends: President Allende had warned him that Chile was facing grave problems and his presence back home was indispensable.

Just before Neruda left Paris for good, he acquired a new habit: he would gaze from his Embassy bedroom out on to the golden dome of Les Invalides, through a cheap telescope. Significantly, it was a child's telescope: to the end, he never lost his curiosity about the world.

15

The final years –
and a posthumous gift

1972–73

Pablo and Matilde finally left Paris in November 1972. They stopped off, as usual on the flight from Europe, in Buenos Aires, and arrived back in Chile on 21 November. When he stepped off the aircraft at Santiago's Pudahuel airport, after two years away, the poet looked ill at ease, in stark contrast to his radiant appearance when he had returned from exile twenty years earlier. He knew, this time, that he was returning home to die. And he was also returning to a Chile in the grip of severe political violence.

'He was tired and his skin was sallow,' said Aída Figueroa.

> It was a great physical sacrifice for him to participate in the homage they paid him at the Estadio Nacional [National Stadium] at which General Prats – then vice-president of the republic – spoke. I remember that Neruda had to cross the whole stadium in an open car standing up, as if his legs were normal. Then he gave a beautiful speech. He did not want to show the authorities, the people, the journalists that he was ill. He got very annoyed when people felt sorry for his physical condition, and that is why, as soon as the event was over, he immediately returned to Isla Negra and never appeared in public again.[1]

Santiago's National Stadium was not full for the ceremony on 2 December. There were empty seats – rare for any event involving

Pablo Neruda. The reason was fear. Fear to be seen out on the streets, fear to be seen at such an overtly political gathering. In his address, Neruda pointedly warned of the dangers of fascism in Chile. With foreboding, he compared the atmosphere there to that before Franco's uprising which had brought about the bloody Civil War in Spain. He promised to work hard for the important forthcoming congressional elections in March 1973 which the opposition were hoping would unseat Allende – and still, Neruda refused to reveal publicly how ill he was. These words told a covert story: 'Life, struggle, poetry will continue to live when I am nothing more than a tiny memory on the luminous Chilean road.'

How much *did* Neruda know of the exact nature of his illness? Matilde had made all his friends promise not to tell him that he had cancer. On 28 December 1972, Neruda wrote to Jorge Edwards from Isla Negra referring to the 'rheumatism' in his hip. And a couple of months later, he wrote again to Edwards to say: 'My rheumatism is improving every day, but I am walking with a stick and I don't like showing myself. I have practically not gone to Santiago at all.'[2] In fact, he was going quite frequently to the capital – for urgent medical check-ups.

Edwards reflected:

> The Chilean doctors had told Matilde that Pablo's cancer was evolving slowly, and that he could still live for a number of years, and they had insisted on the importance of him keeping in good spirits. If he were allowed to slide into a depression, his organism, the doctors explained, would give off adrenaline, which in turn would precipitate the cancerous process. This was more than a good enough reason to justify hiding the true seriousness of his ailments from him.[3]

Chile's political situation was extremely precarious. Salvador Allende's Popular Unity government had transformed all aspects of public life in Chile. The government had planned to nationalise the economy and implement a massive programme of income redistribution, and to allow popular participation in the nation's economy. However, Chilean society was becoming increasingly polarised. The murder of a leading Christian democratic politician, Edmundo Pérez Zukovic, by an extreme leftist group in June 1971 had intensified a climate of political tension. The sheer breadth of the six-party ruling coalition was a major obstacle to smooth policy-making. The Radical Party was a moderate, social democratic party, while the left-wing section of Allende's own Socialist Party was Leninist. Although the government intended to implement its sweeping policies in the Constitution, the Socialists and the Communists within the coalition disagreed about how quickly this should happen. The Socialists believed that 'revolutionary violence' was essential, whereas the Communists – though loyal to Moscow in foreign policy – were more cautious domestically and saw the need to reassure the middle classes. And within the Socialist Party itself, there was factionalism and increasing ill-discipline.

The Unidad Popular government achieved some admirable advances: the distribution of free milk to all school children, reform of the tax system. But lack of wage restraints and other economic failures led to growing disputes. In what was hoped to be a more co-ordinated approach, in July 1972 a Socialist, Carlos Matus, was appointed Minister of the Economy, and a Communist, Orlando Millas, as Finance Minister. But relaxation of price controls and devaluation sent inflation spiralling upwards.

Meanwhile, while internal strife deepened, we now know, thanks to previously classified documents released by the United States Senate in November 2000, the full extent of the involvement of the US in Chile at this time. As early as 1964, terrified of another 'Cuba' in Latin America, the US Committee for the Study of Government Operations had authorised the channelling of US$3 million to ensure the election of the Christian Democratic presidential candidate, Eduardo Frei. Frei was duly elected President on 4 September 1964. On 25 March 1970, the same US committee allocated $125,000 for an operation to discredit Allende's Unidad Popular coalition in the months leading up to the elections. On 27 June, a further $400,000 was authorised with the same aim. On 16 July, John McCone, a former CIA director, arranged an interview between William Browne of the CIA and Harold Geneen, head of the American multinational, ITT (International Telephone and Telegraph Company), to discuss the possibility of channelling ITT funds into reinforcing the campaign against Allende.[4]

After Allende's election victory on 4 September 1970, the US Committee approved a further $250,000 to help the American Ambassador in Santiago influence the crucial vote in the Chilean Congress, on 24 October 1970, on the election results. In the meantime, Geneen informed McCone on 9 September that he was prepared to pay up to $1 million to collaborate in any US government plan aimed at forming a coalition in the Chilean Congress which would prevent confirmation of the Allende triumph. A few days later, McCone met the US Secretary of State, Henry Kissinger, and the CIA director, Richard Helms. On 15 September, President Richard Nixon instructed Helms to prevent Allende taking power in Chile by helping a military coup to take place. The following day, Kissinger told a White House press conference that an Allende victory would create 'massive problems' for the US and Latin America.

In October 1970, the ITT had presented an eighteen-point plan to the White House aimed at guaranteeing that 'Allende does not get through the next crucial six months'. The ITT plan was rejected. Although he had survived assassination attempts on 19 and 20 October, René Schneider, head of the Chilean armed forces, who had supported the democratic election of President Allende, was fatally wounded on 22 October. Two days later, the Chilean Congress approved Allende's election victory by 153 votes to 35. Admitting defeat, the Nixon government in the US now tried to discredit the new Marxist regime by channelling hundreds of thousands of dollars into the main right-wing daily in Santiago, *El Mercurio*. Some $700,000 came the paper's way.

Allende had other problems. On 21 August 1972, he had to declare a state of emergency in the province of Santiago, after a 24-hour shopkeepers' strike came to a violent end. Opportunistically, on 26 October, the US Committee authorised $1.4 million to support the opposition parties and the private sector in Chile in advance of the congressional elections in March 1973. President Allende, in a speech to the United Nations General Assembly in New York on 4 December 1972, claimed that Chile was the victim of 'a serious aggression' and had been subjected to 'pressures from abroad on a vast scale'.

This process formed the backdrop to Neruda's time in Paris – and as he grew progressively sicker his condition was not helped by profound concern for the future of his country. His desire to see Chile back on the right track and free of US intervention soon manifested itself in his most controversial book, called *Incitación al nixonicidio y alabanza de la revolución chilena* (Incitement to Nixonicide and Praise for the

Chilean Revolution). Neruda wrote it between December 1972 and January 1973, and it was printed in February 1973 by the Santiago publishers, Quimantú, in a special 1,000-copy run. The following month, a larger edition came out in Lima, published by Grijalbo.

Many admirers of Neruda have condemned *Incitación al nixonicidio* for abandoning lyricism and turning to blatant polemic. But it is important to see the book as part of Neruda's contribution to Unidad Popular's campaign in the March 1973 congressional elections in Chile. As Robert Pring-Mill has said in his invaluable study of the book,

> Those were months of crisis and the poet was prepared to put his art totally at the disposal of UP in order to make an appeal to the masses, writing a book which was deliberately pamphleteering. He did so fully aware that his efforts would be viewed in a negative light by most of the admirers of his poetry and knowing that the work would be so contingent that it would probably not transcend the immediate circumstances of its composition.[5]

The Unidad Popular won 43 per cent of the votes in the 4 March 1973 elections in Congress despite the money from the US Committee, which continued to flow in.

The prologue to *Incitación al nixonicidio*, which Neruda called a 'Peremptory Explanation' and which he dated January 1973, is very revealing. In it, he says that he had no choice but to write the book.

> My song is a tough attack on the enemies of my people, as hard as Araucanian stone. This may be an ephemeral function. But I am fulfilling it. And I am resorting to the oldest weapons avaliable to poetry: song and pamphleteering, used by the classics and the romantics with the aim of destroying the enemy. So stand firm, I'm about to fire the first shot![6]

Even more revealing, in its way, is a letter Pablo wrote from Isla Negra to Robert Pring-Mill on 15 February 1973 – his last letter to the British Neruda specialist – in which he described *Incitación al nixonicidio* as 'pamphleteering like *Canción de gesta*', his 1960 hymn to the Cuban revolution. 'They are poems deliberately written to be read by big crowds.'[7] Pring-Mill believes that Neruda saw a clear distinction between those two works and the rest of his poetry, however political his poems might be, 'through their form (absence of sophistication, expressive delicacy, hermeticism) . . .' The letter also seems to suggest that these were the only books that Neruda believed had any 'direct effect on the social struggle.'[8]

What a long way Neruda had come from 1929, when he wrote to his Argentinian friend Héctor Eandi, that the poet had a 'mandate' to 'penetrate life and make it prophetic: the poet must be a superstition, a mythical being . . . poetry must load itself with universal substance, passions and objects.'[9]

Now, the dying, pacifist Neruda showed a willingness to promote violence. He himself did not see this as a paradox. As he told Rita Guibert in January 1970:

> There is violence and violence. In the countries dominated by terror and fascist violence . . . I believe that all means are justified to escape from this situation. What other possibility is there when the government is run by criminals like Papa Doc in Haiti? The jails are full of political prisoners, as in Paraguay. Every people must choose its path. You cannot say 'I don't believe in violence as a general political axiom.'[10]

Neruda had planned to talk about *Incitación al nixonicidio* during another visit to Oxford, at the end of October and November 1972. Pring-Mill had invited him to recite his verse and take part in a debate on 'The Role of the Poet in the Third World'. Sadly, Neruda had been forced to cancel that trip to undergo the second operation in Paris – after which he resigned as Ambassador and returned to Chile to recuperate. It was his intention to travel to Oxford again once he had fully recovered – he believed that his first visit to the university city in June 1965, when he was given an honorary doctorate, had been a vital step on the path to winning the Nobel Prize, and he relished the chance to develop the ideas which he had begun to explore in his 1971 Nobel acceptance speech.

In that 15 February 1973 letter to Pring-Mill, Neruda added:

> The people aren't interested in sophisticated poetry, even if it calls itself 'fighting' poetry, nor does it serve them in any way. It is merely a luxury object to be debated among professionals. My multifarious

experience has taught me a lot. And above all, in the separation of intimate poetry and public expression, there is no reason for the latter to fear debate – indeed, it should appropriate it, invade it.[11]

In November 1972, Talleres Gráfica García published a book, *Antología popular de Pablo Neruda* (Popular Anthology of Pablo Neruda) which had been an initiative of President Allende, who wrote the prologue, to celebrate Neruda's Nobel Prize. The book specifically stated that Neruda would not receive any royalties. The choice of poems had been decided by Neruda's friend and secretary, Homero Arce, in conversation with the poet, at La Manquel in Normandy in September 1972.

That pleasurable collaboration with Arce is recalled in Neruda's book, *Defectos escogidos* (Chosen Defects). The title sums up Neruda's feelings, but there is none of the whining self-accusation of *Las manos del día*. Rather, Neruda returns to the genuine, and genuinely attractive, self-mockery of *Estravagario*.

'El incompetente' (The Incompetent One) is a scintillating poem, surprisingly self-deprecating for a man who was such a success with women throughout his adult life:

> Oh, those girls!
> I had never seen princesses like those . . .
> And I went around
> puny and concealing with pride
> my condition of idiot in love
> without daring to look at a leg
> or at that hair which fell from their heads
> like a cataract of dark water
> on my desires.
> And later, ladies and gentlemen, the same thing happened
> everywhere I went,
> with an elbow or two cold eyes,
> they eliminated me from the competition.
> They did not let me join their meal
> and went off with their blondes . . .[12]

Yet ill-health hangs over the book. Neruda is almost delirious in the startling poem 'Parodia del guerrero' (Parody of the Warrior). He had written before (in 'Ritual de mis piernas' [Ritual of My Legs] in *Residencia en la tierra*) about the amusement it gave him to contemplate parts of his body, especially his legs, which almost seemed as though they were separate from their owner. Now, in the midst of one his increasingly frequent fevers, he perceives his gout-riddled legs as useless.

> From up here I can see them:
> how clumsy my feet are,
> without my advice,
> how poorly they move on the pavement,
> they know nothing of the sun
> or dust,
> they have to learn to be children,
> to eat, to invade,
> to climb mountains,
>
> to organise notebooks,
> to kill fleas,
>
> to decipher territory,
> to discover islands.

The embattled government of Salvador Allende still had the interests of its most famous supporter in mind. At the beginning of 1973, the government announced that there would be a national celebration on 12 July 1974, to mark the poet's seventieth birthday. Writers would be invited from all over the world and the Chilean people would also take part.

'To reward them in some small way for these signs of affection, Pablo began to prepare his surprise – the gift that he would make to all those he had loved,' recalled Matilde.[13]

There is considerable disagreement over the order in which he wrote the eight books (the seven collections of poems and the memoirs) that ended up being published posthumously. We know that he often wrote several books at once. We also know from Matilde that six of the eight books were ready before Neruda's death. The other two – *El mar y las campanas* and *Defectos escogidos* – were unfinished. An additional complication comes from the fact that Neruda liked to publish part of his books in advance in limited editions. He also had a habit of slipping isolated poems into newspapers, especially the Venezuelan daily, *El Nacional*, edited by his friend, Miguel Otero Silva. Some of *Defectos escogidos* and *El corazón amarillo* appeared here.

The books Neruda was working on for his seventieth birthday contain some of his most beautiful lyrical poetry. They are filled with anguish, fear of death, awareness of physical deterioration, a quest for peace, for solitude, for understanding. It is remarkable that he was able to write at all.

In mid-January 1973, Neruda was at La Sebastiana in Valparaíso, cheerfully entertaining some visiting Soviet friends. He showed them the box with a glass in it and explained that it was a present from Simyon Kirsanov. One of the visitors, after a moment's hesitation, asked Pablo: 'Why are you talking about Kirsanov in the present tense? Didn't you know that he died more than a month ago?' Kirsanov had died in Moscow on 10 December 1972.

'It's very difficult to describe that moment,' Matilde remembered.

> Pablo stopped with the glass in his hand, staring at it. After a few minutes of painful silence, he left the room, withdrawn and wordless. I went out and watched him from a distance. With his eyes fixed on the glass, he was walking up and down, oblivious to reality. I didn't want to get any nearer. I looked on from far away and wept for our dead friend, but more for Pablo's pain. Only I knew how great it was. After a few moments, he returned to the room. There was a silence which locked up any words. We looked at each other, and he found the courage to smile. I smiled too. 'This was a joke by the great Kirsanov,' he said with a rather listless voice. 'The last thing he would want right now is to interrupt the toast.'[14]

There were other losses. Neruda was in Valparaíso, receiving cobalt treatment, when news arrived of the death of Pablo Picasso at the age of ninety-one on 8 April 1973. The Chilean journalist Luis Alberto Mansilla interviewed Neruda in his room at the Hotel Cap Ducal in Valparaíso:

> He was lying down. There were no chairs. He offered me a space at the foot of his bed. He was just waking up from his . . . unmissable

siesta . . . He got up . . . and wandered around the room, which looked out on to the sea. Of course, he wasn't the Neruda we knew, but he seemed to be in excellent spirits. He talked a lot. He spoke about his seventieth birthday. He referred to Allende with sympathy, saying he considered him a President who was genuinely a friend of culture. . . . He had a lot to say about Picasso. Serious things and anecdotes. They had been united by a long friendship and a political affinity. . . . Only the cortisone, which left its inevitable trace on his face, was a reminder that Pablo was seriously ill.[15]

Neruda somehow remained optimistic. On 13 April, he wrote to Jorge Edwards to express his belief that the Allende government was holding out, despite all the pressures on it. Once again, he referred to his illness as rheumatism, and said that living in Chile was 'a tonic, a stimulant, like no other'.

On 29 June 1973, the so-called 'tanquetazo' occurred: right-wing forces, led by Lieutenant Colonel Roberto Souper, took over the centre of Santiago and assaulted the Ministry of Defence and the presidential palace. Although troops loyal to the government crushed the rebellion, which had been the first attempted coup against a legally elected President in Chile for forty-two years, the country was collapsing.

Pablo's friend and lawyer, Sergio Insunza, was the Chilean Justice Minister at the time. He could see that those who wanted to bring down the constitutional government were determined to do everything in their power to achieve their aims. 'Pablo followed every step of the events from Isla Negra. He was avid for information . . . The first thing he asked his visitors was: "Tell me. Tell me what's going on."'[16]

On 12 July 1973, Neruda celebrated his sixty-ninth birthday – although 'celebrated' was not exactly the right word. 'Very few of us went to see him,' Aída Figueroa recollected. 'We found him in bed. I brought him a basket of fruit, I helped him to his feet and said: "Hugs and kisses and fruit, as well."'[17]

Aída's husband, Sergio Insunza, and a couple of friends sat around the bed, and everyone else ate downstairs with Matilde. 'We didn't feel in the mood for jokes. The situation in the country was at fever pitch . . . We expected the worse,' said Aída.[18]

Neruda was very frail. Many of the friends who visited him at

Isla Negra suspected that this would be Pablo's last birthday. A mini-delegation, comprising Volodia Teitelboim, the Communist deputy, Gladys Marín, and Gonzalo Losada, son of Neruda's Buenos Aires publisher, arrived; Losada presented him with a thick Patagonian jacket on behalf of his father to keep him warm. In return, Neruda asked Matilde to bring the manuscripts of seven unpublished books – one for each decade of his life. He handed them to Losada who promised to publish them immediately. Neruda told him to wait until the following year: 1974, after all, would mark his seventieth year.

As José Miguel Varas has pointed out, 'the handwriting of these final manuscripts is different. The calligraphy shows that the author was ill.'[19] He wrote these last books lying in bed, with a board spread across him.

In a letter to Juan Loveluck, dated 25 February 1975, Matilde confirmed:

> Pablo chose the titles for all the posthumous books himself. With the poems that were left untitled, I used the first line. I would never have dared to put a title to a book or a poem by Pablo, nor would I allow anyone else to do so. In September [1973], Pablo told me that he would spend two more months working on the memoirs. In his notebook, there are several annotated chapters which he did not manage to produce. But the memoirs were ready to go from the beginning right up to the last chapter, which he wrote after the 11th [the military coup in Chile of 11 September 1973] which in any case, was the definitive ending decided by him.[20]

We know that Neruda began to revise his memoirs in 1973. He used the ten articles he had written for O Cruzeiro Internacional in 1962, and other sources.

Hernán Loyola believes that Neruda wrote 2000, one of the first books to be published posthumously, at the beginning of 1971, during the same period that he wrote the Easter Island book, La rosa separada, and revised the poems later. Indeed, 2000 appeared in an Italian edition edited by Pablo's friend, Giuseppe Bellini, a Neruda specialist at the University of Milan, in 1974, together with other so-called 'Opere postume' – an error, because it included La rosa separada, which had been published in France in 1972. Neruda's

Buenos Aires publisher, Losada, brought 2000 out first in a separate edition on 8 January 1974.

The critic Luis Sainz de Medrano contends that, in 2000, Neruda 'aligns himself more closely with [George] Orwell's position in his conception of a future world – seen from the present – no more or less dehumanised and unjust than the twentieth century. There are also reasons to think of the [César] Vallejo of "Me moriré en París con aguacero" [I'll Die in a Paris Downpour] who was capable of envisaging himself after his death and listening to the voices of those lamenting his unjust treatment.'[21]

I believe that this concern with a time after death makes 2000 more redolent of Quevedo than of anyone else – and we know Neruda repeatedly expressed his gratitude to the Golden Age poet for the lessons he had taught him. What could be more Quevedoesque than these lines?

> I've arrived at this above-mentioned year 2000
> and what do I get out of it,
> and what will I scratch myself with, what have I got to do
> with those three zeros preening themselves in all their glory
> over my own zero, my non-existence?[22]

Another critic, Selena Millares, has pointed out that Neruda's younger compatriot, Nicanor Parra, had also used this technique of speaking in the voice of the dead.[23] But it was Quevedo who first realised that the voice emerging from death had purity and truth.

In 2000, Neruda ruthlessly exposes his lack of faith in any utopia – the logical climax to a process of disenchantment which had been deepening in him for fifteen years – at least since 1956. We are looking at a very different Pablo Neruda from the one who, the Spanish poet Jorge Guillén once said, had been taught the playfulness of life by Federico García Lorca. 'Lorca invented Neruda,' Guillén had said – but political disillusionment was now chipping away at him. It was this Neruda who, angered at the Cuban poet Nicolás Guillén for signing the famous 1966 letter against him, referred to his namesake, Jorge Guillén, as 'the good one, the Spanish one' in his memoirs.

And yet Neruda remains, fundamentally, an optimist in this book. He clings to what he perceives as the success of the Soviet Union –

though, as his Sainz de Medrano correctly notes, this is more for 'sentimental than ideological reasons'.

This was not the first time he had tackled the thought of the coming century. *Canción de gesta* had included a poem called 'Escrito en el 2000' (Written in 2000). But this book shows a Neruda determined to survive in some form, even though he must have sensed that only a medical miracle would allow him do so physically. So, like Shakespeare in his famous eighteenth sonnet, Neruda explicitly expresses the hope that he will live on through his writings.

> Today is today and yesterday passed – that much is certain.
>
> Today is also tomorrow, and I left
> with some cold year that passed,
> that year left with me and took me with it.
>
> This, too, is certain. My skeleton
> was made up of words as hard
> as bones exposed to the air and the rain,
> and I was able to celebrate what was happening
> leaving behind, not a song or a testimony,
> but a stubborn skeleton of words.[24]

The next of Neruda's 'birthday books', *Elegía*, contains many moving tributes to his friends who had died in Moscow – including the Spanish sculptor Alberto Sánchez; the Turkish poet Nazim Hikmet; and the Soviet writers Ilya Ehrenburg, Simyon Kirsanov and another of Neruda's Russian translators, Ovadi Savich.

> Where is the smile,
> or the communicating paint,
> or the word that teaches,
> of the laughter, the laughter,
> the clear laugh
> of those I lost in those streets?[25]

Stalin, he writes, was caught between God and the devil living in his soul. And yet mysteriously, perhaps sentimentally, Neruda still refers to him as

> that wise, tranquil Georgian,
> an expert on wine and many other things

as if his crimes were somehow not of his own doing.

Hernán Loyola believes that Neruda wrote much of his next book, *El corazón amarillo* (The Yellow Heart), in a state of shock after Matilde had discovered his relationship with her niece Alicia and his efforts to patch up his marriage in France. Whether that is true or not, we do know that Matilde considers this collection the one that had most of her in it.

In fact, it is a book in which Neruda is very honest about both his state of mind and his body:

> From time to time I'm happy! . . .
> And with my melancholy prostate
> and the whims of my urethra,
> they lead me unhurriedly
> to an analytical end . . .[26]

In the Chilean winter of 1973, Neruda invited the journalist and future novelist, Isabel Allende (niece of President Salvador Allende), to visit him at Isla Negra.

> The poet was not well . . . The wind was whistling among the pines and eucalyptus, the sea was grey, and it was drizzling in that seaside town of closed houses and empty streets . . . Pablo Neruda, with a poncho around his shoulders and a cap crowning his great gargoyle head, welcomed me without formality. He told me he enjoyed my humorous articles and sometimes photocopied them and sent them to friends. He was weak, but he found the strength to lead me through the marvellous twists and turns of that cave crammed with his trove of modest treasures and to show me his collections of seashells, bottles, dolls, books and paintings . . . He also liked his food. For lunch we had baked sea bass, that white firm-fleshed fish that is king of Chile's seas, and dry white wine. He talked about the memoirs he was trying to write before death bilked him of the opportunity. . . . He talked for a long time about the political situation, which caused him great agony, and his voice broke when he spoke of his country's being divided into violent extremes.

Rightist newspapers were publishing six-column headlines: 'Chi-leans, save your hatred, you'll need it!', inciting the military to take power and Allende either to renounce the presidency or commit suicide, as President Balmaceda had done in the past century to avoid a civil war . . .

After lunch, it began to rain . . . I realised then that the poet was weary, that the wine had gone to my head, and that I must hurry.

'If you like, we can do the interview now,' I suggested.

'Interview?'

'Well, that's why I'm here, isn't it?'

'Interview *me*? I'd never put myself through that,' he laughed. 'My dear child, you must be the worst journalist in the country. You're incapable of being objective, you place yourself at the centre of everything you do, I suspect you're not beyond fibbing, and when you don't have news, you invent it. Why don't you write novels instead? In literature, those defects are virtues . . .'[27]

Osvaldo Rodríguez has called the poet's next book, *Jardín de invierno* (Winter Garden) one of 'Neruda's most profoundly lyrical'.[28] Another critic, Jaime Alazraki, has an intriguing theory about this and Neruda's other final works. Neruda claimed to have been unmoved – even alienated – by the Eastern religions he encountered while consul in the Orient. However Rodríguez maintains that the cyclical shape in these late poems, as well as the need to withdraw within himself, and some of the symbols reminiscent of Brahmin philosophy. In 'Un perro ha muerto' (A Dog Has Died) he communes with his pet dog after his death:

> For this dog and all other dogs
> I believe in heaven: yes, I believe in a heaven
> where I will never enter – but he'll be waiting there for me,
> waving his tail like a fan
> to make sure I have a friend if I do turn up[29]

and with nature in 'La estrella' (The Star):

> . . . the sand decided
> and, as part of the landscape and waves,
> a syllable of salt, a water louse,

> I, sovereign, a slave to the shore,
> surrender myself, shackle myself to my rock . . .

The right-wing Chilean critic Ignacio Valente has drawn attention to the fact that 'Neruda kept, right to the end, his magnificent ability to reveal the face of nature, a certain quality of light, the fleeting mystery of an instant, an hour of the day, a season . . . and all couched in sumptuous, fluid language, which makes the verse run with . . . that spontaneous musical sense which never failed Neruda.'[30]

That spontaneous musical sense might indeed never have failed him but, as his friend Aída Figueroa told me in Chile:

> When he was very ill, he said to me in Isla Negra: 'Aída, how much it would have helped me to be able to listen to music.' Pablo was a very charming man. He valued the person he was talking to. I never heard him talk ill of anyone. He was a genius, not only as a poet but in everything relating to human relationships. The only thing he didn't have was an ear for music! He couldn't understand music. He could hear the sound of birds, people's words. But not music.[31]

Neruda himself wrote in his memoirs: 'My ear could never recognise any but the most obvious melodies, and even then, only with difficulty.' Significantly, the first piece of music to which he felt genuine attraction had a 'purely literary' reference: Marcel Proust. The music was a three-record album of César Franck's Sonata for Piano and Violin.

> Proust, the greatest exponent of poetic realism, lingered with passionate indulgence over many works of art, paintings and cathedrals, actresses and books. But although his insight illuminated whatever it touched, he often went back to the enchantment of this sonata and its renascent phrases with an intensity that he probably did not give to any other descriptive passages . . . I wanted to see in that musical phrase Proust's magical narrative and I was swept away on music's wings.[32]

By now, Neruda was very isolated. Only a few very close friends continued to visit him. He looked back increasingly, in private and in public, to his childhood. His friend Sara Vial told me:

Neruda spoke a lot to me about his childhood. He talked about his 'padre rudo', a hard man whom he seemed to admire and for whom – perhaps having forgotten his childhood fears – he felt great tenderness. But perhaps Neruda had an idealised vision of his childhood. [His half-sister] Laurita told me that Pablo had been deadly bored in Temuco as a child and had spent much of the time in bed.[33]

A doctors' strike had meant that Neruda was deprived of the cobalt treatment he had been undergoing in Valparaíso, which had held out hope of controlling his illness. He told Aída Figueroa that he had only two choices left to him: 'to put on a "moon face" or to die'. The reference to the moon face was the result of the swelling he knew would occur after he switched back to cortisone. 'Pablo . . . didn't complain nor did he talk of illness. He went on writing with the same timetable and rigour as ever. Sometimes, he remained in bed and continued writing from there. He loved to shuffle around plans for the future,' recalled Aída.[34]

One of his visitors at this time was the Chilean Communist leader, Luis Corvalán, who reassured Pablo that Allende was full of energy, despite all the pressure on him, and as determined as ever to continue along the path he had chosen for Chile.

The Chilean poet and diplomat Humberto Díaz Casanueva also visited Neruda at Isla Negra and left this testimony:

I had never felt him so intimate, so fraternal. I said to him: 'I saw the names of our dead friends on the beams of your house, and other beams are clean, waiting . . .' He told me: 'Yes, Humberto, what a terrible thing death is, and without any pity.' I reminded him about Rilke, whom he had translated in his youth. Years later, he spoke against the Rilkistas, including myself. He laughed. 'Humberto, I now see that there is no such thing as pure or impure poetry. I had to make mistakes, but I was honest enough to admit it . . .'[35]

Sick as he was, Neruda was determined to push ahead with his plans for the money he had won with the Nobel Prize. Sergio Insunza remembered that,

Soon after returning to Chile at the end of 1972, he called me – I was then Minister of Justice [under Allende] to get to work on a project which he had been mulling over for quite a while. He had acquired

some land near Isla Negra, at Punta de Tralca, and he planned to
found a comfortable residence for Chilean and foreign writers who
could go there and work for up to six months. It would be financed
with part of his Nobel Prize winnings and his author's rights, plus a
contribution from the State . . . The Unidad Popular government
appointed a commission, headed by myself . . . There would be
small bungalows, where the writers on grants would live and work,
and a central house, which would serve as a library and a place for
conversation and social meetings. The poet planned to donate his
library – including first editions of Rimbaud [and other books he
had not given] to the Universidad de Chile in 1954 – to the
foundation. Moreover, at Isla Negra, in front of the poet's house,
they were going to build a House of Culture, in which there would
be permanent exhibitions of tapestries from the famous weavers of
Isla Negra and elsewhere . . . This really fired up the poet in the first
months after he returned to Chile. He shut himself away at Isla
Negra and did not want to receive anybody, but if it was about
discussing these projects, his door was open . . . [He] said: 'They can
say I'm a bad poet, but never a bad architect.'[36]

Neruda also planned to help establish a university where tuition
would be offered exclusively in the Mapuche language.

It is sad to think of Pablo Neruda – once the most gregarious of
human beings, his houses open to anyone – becoming an ailing
recluse. And it is also sad that Neruda's euphorically pursued plans
for the Cantalao writers' foundation were never brought to fruition.
Vandals destroyed some of the building materials, and the project died
with Neruda.

And yet Neruda kept on writing, to the end. He was determined to
produce his eight books for the nation. *Libro de las preguntas* (Book
of Questions) is full of all his old wit, mischief and childish joy in life,
as well as a highly original way of looking at the world around him.

> Why don't the huge aeroplanes
> go for walks with their children?
>
> If I died and I'm not aware of it,
> of whom do I ask the time?

> Where can a blind man live
> if he's pursued by bees?
>
> Tell me, is the rose naked
> or is that its only dress?
>
> Is it true that hopes
> have to be watered with dew?
>
> Why couldn't Christopher Columbus
> discover Spain?[37]

There are sudden shifts of tone:

> Isn't our life a tunnel
> between two clarities?

but then he returns to the glorious self-deprecation of fifteen years earlier:

> Is there anything more stupid in life
> than to be called Pablo Neruda?

The book *El mar y las campanas* (The Sea and the Bells) features some the last poems Neruda ever wrote. The British critic, Christopher Perriam, who has written perceptively on Neruda's posthumous works, believes that the images of places which had previously confirmed the poet's identity – 'the land as a source of images and memories, the sea as a metaphor of purity'[38] – began to fail him in the final years of his life. The memories associated with the land, Perriam writes, while becoming more potent, are also associated with pain, and the sea, while revitalising the poetry, threatens to demolish the very structures on which it is based.[39]

Giuseppe Bellini, in his excellent study of the posthumous works, has pointed out the similarities between this book and the second part of *Residencia en la tierra*, especially its climate of despair. Bellini specifically compares the poem 'El reloj caído en el mar' (The Bell Fallen in the Sea) from *Residencia* with 'Hoy cuántas horas . . .' (Today How Many Hours . . .) from *El mar y las campanas*. But while the first poem had surreal tones, in the late poem the tone is one of solemn reflection. And here, the image of the sea is as black as it had ever been in Neruda's work.

El mar y las campanas ends with 'Final', which may have been the last poem Neruda ever wrote. It is a stunningly moving song of love to Matilde:

> It was so beautiful to live
> when you were alive!
>
> The world is more blue and more earthly
> at night, when I sleep,
> enormous, within your tiny hands.

When he was not writing his poetry, Neruda spent days with a tiny radio stuck to his ear, his eyes gazing at the television screens, anxious for the latest news. And the latest news was terrifying. The Americans were pouring money in to help to promote a new coup. On 2 August, Chilean bus and taxi owners declared a strike. On 23 August, General Prats González resigned as Defence Minister and commander of the Army and recommended that Allende replace him with Augusto Pinochet, believed at that time to be loyal to the government. It was to prove a disastrously misguided choice. On 27 August, shop-owners called another anti-Allende strike. Government supporters fought back, demonstrating 100,000-strong through the streets of Santiago on 4 September to celebrate the third anniversary of Allende's election. However, three days later, Admiral Raúl Montero was dismissed as head of the navy. This removed the last obstacle to the coup. It seems that the allegiance of General Pinochet to the plot came very late. However, when it did come, it signalled the beginning of the final arrangements.

Towards the end of August 1973, Neruda summoned the journalist Luis Alberto Mansilla to Isla Negra to dictate a few lines for a special supplement in *El Siglo* celebrating the ninetieth birthday of the scientist Alejandro Lipschutz (whom the poet had once called 'the most important man in my country').

> I found him in his library, facing the fireplace. He seemed sombre and downcast. On his knees lay a copy of Gabriela Mistral's collection,

Desolación. He told me that he had been impressed once again by her 'Sonetos de la muerte' [Sonnets of Death] and he read me a few verses . . . He watched all the TV news bulletins, listened to the radio, read all the newspapers. 'Don't you think,' he said, 'that we're just about to see a civil war?' I calmed him down: the situation was tense and delicate, but there was a way out. Then he asked me to talk to some writers, and to Dr Lipschutz himself, to create a committee which would call a big international meeting to support the Unidad Popular government. He gave me some possible names: Sartre, [Roberto] Matta, [Ernesto] Sábato, [Mario] Vargas Llosa, García Márquez, Arthur Miller, etc. The pretext would be his seventieth birthday, but the aim would be to garner support of major world cultural personalities for the government of President Allende.[40]

That same month, Neruda published an article in the *New York Times* condemning the International Telephone and Telegraph Company (ITT) for what he called its constant interference in the constitutional government of Chile. When the newspaper published a reply, Neruda, now mortally ill and just a month away from death, mustered the strength to plan a counter-response which, as he told José Miguel Varas, would be 'as hard as a kick in the snout, but with the precision of a Florentine stab'.[41]

It was too late. Varas telephoned Neruda at around seven o'clock on the morning of Tuesday, 11 September 1973, to tell him that there had been a military coup in Valparaíso. Varas said he would have to postpone his visit to Isla Negra planned for that day.

'See you later, perhaps.'
'See you never, perhaps,' he said with a weary voice.
And so it turned out.[42]

On 11 September, the armed forces rose and brutally overthrew the government. The presidential palace was taken and Salvador Allende died in circumstances still not clarified – he either killed himself or was murdered. Thousands of ordinary Chileans were also killed.

Matilde maintained that Neruda – desperately ill though he was – would have recovered if Allende's government could somehow have survived. She said that Pablo had been in a good mood on the day of the coup – until he heard of Salvador Allende's death.

Others disagree. Pablo's friend and Allende's Justice Minister, Sergio Insunza, said:

> The cancer had already progressed too far, and the end was just a question of time. But how much time? The doctors treating him performed miracles to keep him alive. Sometimes, he was surprisingly well, as if in the best times. I don't think that he knew that his death was imminent until the coup. He was making plans for a whole decade to come. New titles for books came to him and he wanted to write his memoirs in several volumes without forgetting anything or anyone. I believe his indomitable will to live ended on 11 September 1973. He watched on television the . . . bombing of La Moneda and the famous, sinister image of the four coup generals announcing the formation of the military junta. He felt very ill the next day and Matilde decided to take him to Santiago, and put him in the Santa María Clinic. She also wanted to avoid the chance of the military raiding the house in Pablo's presence.[43]

On 14 September 'he felt better and he told me that he wanted to dictate something,' Matilde recalled. 'I searched for paper and a pencil feverishly, and almost immediately I was at his side receiving the dictation by hand. It was the last chapter of the memoirs. I was very happy because, during the dictation, we would shake off the terrible tension which we had been living under since the 11th.'[44]

> Chile has a long civil history with few revolutions and many stable governments, all of them conservative and mediocre. Many little Presidents and only two great ones: Balmaceda and Allende. Curiously enough, both came from the same background, the moneyed class, which calls itself the aristocracy here. As men of principle bent on making a great country out of one diminished by a mediocre oligarchy, the two were steered down the same road to death. Balmaceda was driven to suicide for refusing to deliver the nitrate riches to foreign companies. Allende was murdered because he nationalised the other wealth of Chile's sub-soil: copper . . .
>
> Allende's acts and works, whose value to the nation can never be obliterated, enraged the enemies of our liberation. The tragic symbolism of this crisis became clear in the bombing of the government palace. It brings to mind the blitzkrieg of the Nazi war against

defenceless foreign cities – Spanish, English, Russian. Now the same crime was being carried out again in Chile. Chilean pilots were dive-bombing the palace, which for centuries had been the centre of the city's civic life. I am writing these quick lines for my memoirs only three days after the unspeakable events took my great comrade, President Allende, to his death. His assassination was hushed up, he was buried secretly, and only his widow was allowed to accompany that immortal body. The aggressors' version is that they found clear signs of suicide on his lifeless body. The version published abroad is different. Immediately after the aerial bombardment, the tanks went into action, many tanks, fighting heroically against a single man: the President of the Republic of Chile, Salvador Allende, who was waiting for them in his office, with no other company but his great heart, surrounded by smoke and flames. They couldn't pass up such a beautiful occasion. He had to be machine-gunned because he would never have resigned from office. That body was buried secretly, in an inconspicuous spot. That corpse, followed to its grave only by a woman who carried with her the grief of the world. That glorious dead figure was riddled and ripped to pieces by the machine guns of Chile's soldiers, who had betrayed Chile once more.[45]

As they were working, Matilde recalled, 'We heard voices. Who could be there? At that moment, the chauffeur entered in a state of great shock and said: "It's a raid."' A bus loaded with helmeted soldiers had arrived at Isla Negra late at night and ordered everyone out of the house. Neruda was in bed upstairs. From his bedroom window, he could see the soldiers, holding lanterns, examining the trees and plants in the garden. It must have been the most miserable experience to see the military, whom he loathed, invading what he thought of as the closest place to paradise on earth.

The commander of the unit asked for Neruda. They told him where he was and he went up cautiously, his weapon in his hand. Then something extraordinary occurred. The young soldier suddenly found himself face to face with Neruda, and this disconcerted him. Neruda looked at him and said: 'Look around – there's only one thing of danger for you here – poetry.' The soldier removed his helmet, respectfully, muttered 'Forgive me, Señor Neruda,' and withdrew, taking his soldiers with him. They had not broken anything in the house.

The army also raided La Chascona, the house in Santiago's Calle Fernando Márquez de la Plata, and this they left in ruins. Matilde learnt about it quickly, but refused to tell Pablo.

On 18 September, Chile's Independence Day, his health deteriorated. Matilde decided that he needed urgent medical care. He was taken by ambulance to the clinic on an incongruously warm, sunny day.

> On the way, they were stopped by a military patrol, who paid no attention to Matilde's telling them that she was accompanying the sick Pablo Neruda. They were both made to get out of the ambulance and to wait for about thirty minutes, while the soldiers carried out a meticulous examination of the vehicle, the papers, the clothing. Pablo did not say a word. Suddenly, Matilde saw that tears were streaming down his cheeks. He asked her: 'Wipe my face, Patoja.'[46]

One of the most significant early visitors to Room 402 of the Santa María Clinic in Santiago was the Mexican Ambassador, Gonzalo Martínez Corbalá. He told Matilde that the Mexican President Luis Echeverría had personally put a DC8 aeroplane at their disposal to fly Pablo and Matilde immediately out of Chile to safety in Mexico. When she discussed the idea with Neruda, his initial reaction was to reject the idea. 'I'm not leaving Chile. This is our country, and this is my place.'[47]

On 20 September, the Mexican Ambassador returned to try to persuade Neruda to take up the offer of a flight out of Chile on the Saturday (22 September) By now, Matilde had told Pablo about the raid on La Chascona, and he agreed that they would leave for Mexico, but not until the Monday (24 September), and even then only for a brief stay. They would be back in Chile soon, he said.

What is not generally known is that Neruda also handed the Mexican Ambassador the last thing he ever wrote: a short, handwritten note introducing a dazzling exhibition of works by Neruda's three Mexican muralist friends – Diego Rivera, David Alfaro Siqueiros and José Clemente Orozco – which President Allende had been due to inaugurate in Santiago on 13 September and which was, of course, cancelled after the coup and Allende's death. In his note, which he had entitled 'Tres Hombres' (Three Men) Neruda wrote: 'The fire in these paintings can never be extinguished, and it is alive here [in Chile]: we need its telluric potency to reveal the power of our people.'[48]

After Neruda had agreed to leave Chile for Mexico, Matilde went to Isla Negra with a list of books which he wanted to take with him.

> I was collecting some things together for the journey when the telephone rang. It was Pablo. He asked me to return immediately. 'I can't say anything else,' he said. I thought that the worst had happened. Feverishly, I closed the suitcase and set off . . . I dashed up to his room and sat down beside him. I was exhausted with nervous tension. Pablo is very agitated. He says he has spoken with many friends and that it is incredible that I don't know what's going on in the country. 'They're killing people,' he tells me, 'they're handing over bodies in pieces. The morgue's full of the dead, the people are outside in their hundreds, claiming the bodies. Didn't you hear what happened to [the Chilean singer-songwriter] Víctor Jara? He was one of those they tore to pieces, they destroyed his hands.' As I had tried to avoid his finding out about all the hair-raising news those days, he thought I was ignorant of everything. 'The body of Víctor Jara in pieces. Didn't you know that? Oh my God, that's like killing a nightingale. And they say he kept on singing and singing and that drove them wild.'[49]

Neruda insisted on watching the news bulletins, though Matilde eventually managed to have the television set removed from his room at the clinic – not, however, before Pablo had learned, to his sorrow, that bodies of youths who had been shot were being picked out of the nearby Mapocho River.

Aída Figueroa visited Pablo at the Santa María Clinic the day before he died.

> For the first time, I heard him complain of pains. He said: 'It hurts from my toenails all the way up to my hair.' And noting the absence of Matilde, who was doing chores, he added; 'And La Patoja's not here. She's the only one who knows how to move me, to prop me up in bed.' He was reading a book, a French novel which Delia Vergara [a friend] had brought him. He was unable to hold the book in his hands and he had torn it up into bits to read it in booklets. Meanwhile, in the next room, Homero [Arce] typed out a clean copy of some poems or part of his memoirs with the recent events. He brought him the papers and Pablo corrected them.[50]

Homero Arce himself died in mysterious circumstances a few years later, after being kidnapped and brutally beaten by the DINA (Pinochet's secret police).

Pablo was desperately concerned for the fate of his friends. Aída's husband, Sergio, had already sought refuge in the Honduran Embassy in Santiago. 'These people kill,' Neruda kept repeating to Aída. He still hoped to leave for Mexico and denounce events in Chile from there. But Aída could see how difficult it was for him even to breathe.

The Chilean painter, Nemesio Antúnez, also visited Neruda on 22 September. He found the poet in pain, but perfectly lucid and resigned. Had the final spark of that optimism which he had maintained throughout his life been extinguished? 'These soldiers,' he told Nemesio, 'are acting with great brutality at the moment, but later they are going to try to make themselves popular, make themselves look like the goodies. They're going to kiss the children and the old people in the public squares, in front of the television cameras. They're going to hand out houses, baskets of sweets, medals. And they're going to be around for many years. And in culture, art, television, everything, the most complete and utter mediocrity is going to prevail.'

On the night of 22 September, Neruda was left alone with Matilde. 'He was very tender with me that last night,' Matilde told Hernán Loyola later.

> I asked him to sleep a little, because he knew that helped him recover his strength. 'We've got out of worse messes than this,' he told me. He slept for a few hours, but when he woke up, he was no longer the same. He was never the same again. As the fever took over, he no longer recognised me. He was delirious. His conscience and his heart were with his persecuted and tortured friends. And in the midst of his incoherent speech he would cry: 'They're shooting them. They're shooting them.' And then came the drowsiness and the delirium again until, on the morning of the Sunday, he fell into a coma.[51]

Pablo Neruda died at 10.30 in the evening of Sunday, 23 September 1973. At his bedside were Matilde and his half-sister, Laurita. Also in the room was their friend, Teresa Hamel. His last words were 'Me voy' (I'm going). They had felt his body tremble. And then he was gone.

Hernán Loyola joined Matilde the next morning.

Matilde had promised that she would not separate herself from Pablo's body because of the risk that the authorities could take control of it for some masquerade of an official ceremony, or for some even worse purpose. She spent the night in that sinister corridor of the Santa María Clinic, which I will never forget because I found her there very early, in the midst of her abandonment and loneliness, when the suspension of the curfew allowed me to reach the clinic. When the foreign journalists arrived later, Neruda's body had been moved to a kind of antechamber of the chapel, a grey, bare area which looked more like a morgue. The poet, dressed in a sports jacket and an open-necked shirt, seemed to be resting on the stretcher and his expression was placid, almost smiling. It took a couple of hours for the coffin to arrive, and all that time, I remember Matilde standing by the stretcher, gazing at Pablo's face, without saying a word, very serene in her pain. From time to time, she said something to a journalist. The coffin finally appeared. It was a grey steel colour. Matilde said; 'I don't know anything about funeral arrangements. Teresa took care of the coffin. I only asked for it not to be black. Pablo hated the colour black at funerals.'[52]

Aída Figueroa went to the clinic early on the Monday.

Pablo's body was in a corridor on a stretcher, covered by a sheet. It was near the chapel. The staff at the clinic passed by, indifferent, dedicated to their chores. When I heard about his death, I immediately called Matilde to offer her our house for the wake. It seemed impossible that his body could be taken to his house [La Chascona], which had been sacked and burned. Matilde refused: 'They also offered to hold the wake at the Society of Writers, but I think I must take him to his house,' she told me. I asked her why she should put herself through such pain, when the house was a pile of rubble, broken glass, overturned furniture. She replied: 'Don't you think that the worse state the house is in, the better Pablo will be?' She realised that diplomats and foreign correspondents would go and they would confirm the brutality of fascism, which did not stop even in the face of the winner of a Nobel Prize for Literature, Chile's greatest literary glory.[53]

It had rained heavily in Santiago, and it was difficult to get Neruda's body into the house through the mud. A makeshift bridge had to be built to allow the coffin in. Someone laid down the first plank, and others followed suit. In ten minutes, a 'bridge' had been created.

While this operation was taking place, Hernán Loyola recalled,

up in the house, they were trying to clear the main room of rubble and the traces of the raid. It looked like a bomb had hit it. That was where the coffin was installed. Many nameless people brought flowers and tears . . . At midday, two representatives of the junta arrived – a Colonel Ibáñez and another soldier. But Matilde refused to receive them. There were many foreign journalists and, at around six or seven in the evening, the house was full of people, a permanent flow of people who wanted to express in some way or other Chile's pain. It was obvious that some of them had entered still full of terror that they could be caught in that place, and they left again rapidly . . . There were only nine people at Neruda's wake: Matilde, Laura Reyes, a married couple – the Cárcamos – Aída Figueroa, Elena Nascimento, Juanita Flores, Enriqueta Quintana (widow of the photographer, Antonio Quintana) and myself. Matilde slept for a while. It was incredible that she had been on her feet for so many days and nights without sleep. But less than two hours later, she got up again, vigilant, and returned to her guard of honour by the poet's body, looking at him intensely as she had done the whole day . . . Spring had just begun, but the cold was intense and it invaded easily through the broken windows.[54]

Among the visitors who arrived to pay their respects was an old man in a dark suit and equally dark glasses. It was Hernán Díaz Arrieta (Alone), who had lent Neruda money to help him publish his first book, *Crepusculario*, at the age of nineteen but whose hatred of Communism had driven him to write articles calling for the fall of the Allende government. In death, as in life, Pablo Neruda attracted affection and admiration from all parts of the political spectrum.

Uniformed soldiers and policemen entered the house, not bothering to remove their helmets. One of them said that he had come on behalf of General Augusto Pinochet: 'I want to speak to the widow and relatives of the great poet, Pablo Neruda, the glory of Chilean literature,' he said, 'to express condolences.' He was interrupted by a friend of Pablo's, Chela Alvarez: 'Everyone here is a relative of

Neruda.' Pointing to the remains of books and paintings strewn across the floor, Chela told him: 'In these ruins which you left, we are conducting a wake for Neruda. We demand respect and peace to pay him the final homage, and a guarantee that we will be left alone tonight.' The official announced that the government was decreeing a period of three days' mourning for the poet. But it had been back-dated, to begin from the day of his death – which meant, in effect, that the period of mourning would end in just a few hours' time.

On Tuesday the 25th, at nine in the morning, once again the sad task began of taking the body out across the water that was flooding the entrance and the ground floor . . . When we managed to get the coffin out, a considerable group of workers and students had gathered outside in the street, and I heard the first shouts: 'Comrade Pablo Neruda!' someone screamed and all the others answered: 'Present!' The cortège left in a defiant column (any massive demonstration was, of course, forbidden [by the military authorities]) . . . and the column grew along the way. Arriving at the General Cemetery along the Avenida de la Paz, the funeral became an impressive popular protest, the first since 11 September. . . . I confess that I was frozen with fear, because the people began singing the Internationale in a crescendo. Suddenly, I found that I had my fist in the air and was singing. Soldiers, armed to the teeth, surrounded the square opposite the cemetery and I sincerely believed that, in a matter of seconds, they would let off a round of machine-gun fire. When someone in a loud voice began to shout: 'Comrade Pablo Neruda!' we all answered 'Present!' The cry was repeated two or three times, and the responses grew in strength. Then suddenly, the cry was 'Comrade Víctor Jara!' All at once, our voices cracked: this was the first time that Víctor had been named in public to denounce his vile murder. 'Present!' Then the voice shouted: 'Comrade Salvador Allende!' Then the response was a hoarse, broken howl distorted by emotion and terror and the desire to shout it out so that the whole world could hear: 'Present!' I believe that was when we lost our fear, because they couldn't do anything to us there: it was better to die with our fists in the air and singing the Internationale. And singing at the top of our voices, all of us crying, we entered the General Cemetery. Perhaps the presence of so many foreign journalists saved our lives . . . Inside the cemetery, something strange happened. As we approached the graveside, the cortège began to accelerate . . . Everyone wanted to be close to the grave for the burial ceremony itself, and that was when those outside the column started to speed up. Suddenly, I saw Matilde and the rest of the cortège virtually breaking out into a run. The pall-bearers had also started to hurry, doubtless infected by the haste of the people beside them and by the absence of anyone able to impose an element of ceremony which no one needed, in any case.[55]

Someone opened a copy of Neruda's *España en el corazón*, and read the poet's attack on Franco's destruction of Spain: 'Generals / traitors / look at my dead house / look at broken Spain . . . Jackals which even a jackal would reject . . .'

And still the soldiers watched, their machine guns loaded. As Matilde noted later, 'What a police presence for the most peaceful man in the world, for a poet!'[56] Roser Bru, who was one of the mourners, told me: 'There was a very violent atmosphere. We were surrounded by policemen and soldiers. It was terrifying.'[57]

Neruda had always said he wanted to be buried at Isla Negra, so he could look out over the sea. But that was not possible. And there was not even a niche ready for Neruda's body. At the last minute, the writer Adriana Dittborn made her own niche in the family mausoleum available. Before Neruda's body was buried, an unnamed young man read his own words which he had written the night before, Chela Alvarez read some verses from the *Canto general*, and Neruda's friend Francisco Coloane called attention to Pablo's love of the sea and Chile. In his eulogy, Dr Yolanda Pino Saavedra declared: 'Now that the body of Pablo Neruda is leaving its residence on earth, his immortal spirit rises up to the glory of the homeland.' Then a whole line of anonymous, unidentified people spoke a few words on behalf of a man and a poet they had loved without ever meeting.

One morning, soon after Neruda's death, his friend Francisco Velasco was returning to La Sebastiana – the house in Valparaíso which he and his wife had shared with the poet and Matilde – when he found the place in uproar. A crowd was pointing up to the top of the house, where Pablo had lived. 'Doctor!' called a young man who helped around the house. 'Something strange is happening in Don Pablo's rooms. It looks like there's something inside.' They went up cautiously and, as they entered the living-room, as Velasco recalled later, 'we saw a huge eagle, with a fierce look and talons ready to attack'. How could the eagle have entered the house, when everything had been locked up for months? Velasco suddenly recalled the time Pablo had confided to him, that, 'if there was another life, he would like to be an eagle'. Velasco telephoned Matilde at La Chascona. 'That was Pablo,' said Matilde, without hesitation.[58]

Soon afterwards, Matilde set to work to bring Pablo's birthday present to the world. She sat down with Miguel Otero Silva in Venezuela to oversee the completion of Neruda's memoirs. And the following year, 1974, just as Neruda had asked, Losada brought out the seven books of verse he had been writing through his long and final illness.

As Neruda had said in one of his *Cien sonetos* to Matilde:

> If I die, survive me with so much pure strength
> that you arouse the pale and the cold to fury,
> from south to south raise your indelible eyes,
> from south to south let your guitar mouth sing.

She spent the next decade striving to keep Neruda's memory and works alive. She wanted to create a Neruda Foundation but was unable to do this in her lifetime, under the Pinochet dictatorship. Instead, she set up a committee of executors who did, in effect, begin to establish the Foundation. Over the next few years, she would attend ceremonies in his honour – some of them spectacular, such as the one in which the great French mime artist, Marcel Marceau, broke his habit of a lifetime and spoke for the first time in public to praise his friend, Pablo Neruda.

Veinte poemas de amor y una canción desesperada remains the most frequently reprinted book of poetry in the Spanish language, and translations of the collection continue to be made in every major tongue, as well as many obscure ones. But, as one critic put it, 'If you own the complete works of Neruda, you can converse with him in any state of mind: you can find hope in solitude, in the midst of an unhappy love affair or simply in the act of thinking. Neruda develops so many facets of his life and his poetry that he has a message for each of us in any circumstance. He embodied human beings in all our goodness, badness, mediocrity and contradictions.'[59]

On a cold, misty morning at the end of May 1974, Neruda's body was transferred to the General Cemetery in Santiago. Matilde died on 5 January 1985, when cancer claimed her, too. At the time of her death, La Chascona – the house which Neruda had built for his Patoja – was still run by the executors of the state and Isla Negra remained sealed up and inaccessible to anyone. It was not until June 1986 that the Fundación Pablo Neruda finally received government approval and Matilde's executors became its Board of Directors. And it was only in 1992, with democracy finally restored in Chile, that Pablo and Matilde's bodies were reburied in front of the house at Isla Negra, to the accompaniment of the Pacific waves.

Man dissolves into the ocean like a grain of salt.

Notes

Abbreviations used in the Notes

PN Pablo Neruda
AF Adam Feinstein

Unless otherwise stated, all translations from the Spanish are by Adam Feinstein.

Introduction

1. Yevgeny Yevtushenko, 'The Face Behind the Mask', trans. Arthur Boyars and Simon Franklin, *New Poems* (Marion Boyars, London, 1979).

1 Secrets, shadows, wine and rain 1904–20

1. From 'Nacimiento' in *Memorial de Isla Negra* (Losada, Buenos Aires, 1964).
2. This and other new information was supplied by Rodolfo Reyes's grandson, Bernardo Reyes, in his book, *Neruda – retrato de familia, 1904–1920* (Editorial de la Universidad de Puerto Rico, San Juan, 1996). Rodolfo would become a lover of women and opera, marry three times and drift restlessly from one job to the next.
3. Jaime González Colville, quoted in 'Doña Rosa Basoalto, Mariano Latorre y Neruda' in *Cuadernos*, Fundación Pablo Neruda, Santiago, No. 29, 1997, pp. 11–21.
4. Mario Latorre Elordouy, 'Anécdotas y Recuerdos de Cincuenta Años', in *Revista Occidente,* Santiago, No. 81, October 1952, pp. 37–44, and No. 82, November 1952, pp. 25–24.

5. Neruda's memoirs, *Confieso que he vivido*, translated by Hardie St Martin as *Memoirs* (Souvenir Press, London, 1977) p. 10.
6. Isabel Allende, *Paula* (Flamingo, London, 1996), p. 6.
7. Ibid., p. 61.
8. Quoted in the cultural magazine, *La Bicicleta*, Santiago de Chile, July 1983, p. 5.
9. Lidia Herrera, in conversation with AF, Temuco, April 2000.
10. Rodolfo Reyes, in conversation with AF, Santiago, March 2000.
11. Reyes, *Neruda – retrato de familia*, p. 46.
12. Ibid.
13. Lidia Herrera, in conversation with AF, Temuco, April 2000.
14. From 'La Mamadre', in *Memorial de Isla Negra*.
15. PN, 'Infancia y poesía', published in the Colombian daily, *El Tiempo*, Bogotá 31 October 1971.
16. Gilberto Concha Riffo (Juvencio Valle) quoted in *La Bicicleta*, p. 6.
17. PN, *Memoirs*, p. 14.
18. PN, 'Las vidas del poeta', in the Brazilian magazine, *O Cruzeiro Internacional*, Rio de Janeiro, 16 January 1962.
19. Ibid.
20. PN, 'Infancia y poesía'.
21. From 'El padre' in *Memorial de Isla Negra*.
22. PN, 'Las vidas del poeta'.
23. Ibid.
24. Reyes, *Neruda – retrato de familia*, p. 48.
25. Ibid., p. 50.
26. PN, 'Infancia y poesía'.
27. Concha Riffo, quoted in *La Bicicleta*, p. 5.
28. Ibid.
29. From Diego Muñoz, 'Pablo Neruda: vida y poesía', in *Ediciones de la Revista Mapocho*, Biblioteca Nacional, Santiago, Vol. 2, No. 3, 1964.
30. PN, 'Las vidas del poeta'.
31. Ibid., p. 24.
32. Pablo Neruda, *Para nacer he nacido*, edited by Matilde Urrutia and Miguel Otero Silva (Edicion Planeta, Santiago, 1978), translated by Margaret Sayers Peden as *Passions and Impressions* (Farrar, Straus and Giroux, New York, 1983), p. 241.
33. From 'Las Pacheco' in *Memorial de Isla Negra*.
34. Reyes, *Neruda – retrato de familia*, p. 64.
35. Irma Pacheco, in conversation with AF, Santiago, April 2000.
36. Ibid.
37. PN, *Passions and Impressions*, p. 241.
38. Ibid.
39. Ibid.
40. 'Amores: Terusa (1)' from *Memorial de Isla Negra*.
41. PN, *Memoirs*, p. 12.
42. Ibid.
43. Ibid, p. 20.
44. Ibid.
45. PN, 'Infancia y poesía'.

46. Ibid.
47. PN, *Memoirs*, pp. 27–28.
48. PN, *Cuadernos de Temuco* (Seix Barral, Barcelona, 1996).
49. Ibid, p. 174.
50. Ibid, p. 206.
51. Inés Valenzuela, in conversation with AF, Santiago, 2000.
52. PN, 'Infancia y poesía'.
53. From Diego Muñoz, 'Pablo Neruda: vida y poesía.
54. PN, *La Mañana*, 18 July 1917.
55. Muñoz, 'Pablo Neruda: vida y poesía', p. 188.
56. Volodia Teitelboim, *Neruda* (University of Texas Press, Austin, TX, 1991), p. 27.
57. PN, 'Infancia y poesía'.
58. Reyes, *Neruda – retrato de familia*, p. 46.
59. These early writings were collected in three notebooks by Neruda's half-sister Laurita. On her death in 1977, they were entrusted to a nephew of hers, Rafael Aguayo Quezenas, a teacher at the Universidad Católica in Temuco. The legacy was put up for auction at Sotheby's in London in 1982. Since then, the notebooks have been the subject of considerable controversy. The first time they were all published within one volume was in 2001, as part of Hernán Loyola's superb new five-volume edition of *Obras completas* (Galaxia Gutenberg, Círculo de Lectores, Barcelona, 2001, Vol. 4).
60. PN, *Ercilla*, Santiago, on 24 April 1968.
61. 'La hora del amor' included in *Obras completas*, Vol. 4, p. 153.
62. 'El liceo', ibid.
63. Volodia Teitelboim addressing the University of Stockholm, 20 September 2001.
64. When an interviewer, Rita Guibert, pointed out to him at Isla Negra in January 1970 that Pablo (Paul) meant 'he who says beautiful things' in Hebrew, Neruda replied: 'Are you sure? That must be the other Paul, Christ's companion.' Rita Guibert, *Seven Voices: Seven Latin American Writers* (Knopf, New York, 1973), pp. 3–78.
65. See Miguel Arteche, 'Opiniones: Sherlock Holmes admira a Neruda', *Hoy*, Santiago, No. 187, 18–24 February 1981, p. 42.
66. Enrique Robertson Alvarez, 'El enigma inaugural', an address given at the conference, 'Neruda, con la perspectiva de 25 años', held in Alicante, Spain, March 1999. Published in the *Boletín de la Unidad de Investigación*, University of Alicante, Alicante, December 1999.
67. PN, *Memoirs*, p. 158.

2 A bohemian in Santiago 1921–27

1. PN, *Memoirs*, p. 37.
2. Marcel Niedergang, *The Twenty Latin Americas* (Pelican Books, London, 1971), p. 21.
3. Interview with Pablo Neruda in the Uruguayan publication, *Marcha*, 17 September 1971.
4. Orlando Oyarzún, writing in *Aurora*, Santiago, July–December, 1964.

NOTES

5. Tomás Lago, *Ojos y oídos – Cerca de Neruda* (LOM Ediciones, Santiago, 1999), p. 24.
6. PN, 'Sexo' in *Claridad*, Santiago, 2 July 1921.
7. PN, interview in *Marcha*.
8. PN, *Cartas a Laura* (Letters to Laura), (ed. Hugo Montes, Ediciones Cultura Hispánica del Centro Iberoamericano de Cooperación, Madrid, 1978).
9. Homero Arce, *Los libros y los viajes – Recuerdos de Pablo Neruda* (Nascimento, Santiago, 1976).
10. Tomás Lago, 'Allá por el año veintitantos' in *Pro Arte*, Santiago, 15–31 July 1954.
11. Diego Muñoz, *Memorias: Recuerdos de la bohemia nerudiana* (Mosquito Editores, Santiago, 1999).
12. PN, interview in *Marcha*.
13. Ilya Ehrenburg, 'La poesía de Pablo Neruda', in *Poesía Política* (Austral, Santiago, 1953), p.11–14.
14. Ibid.
15. PN, *Memoirs*, p. 30.
16. Muñoz, *Memorias*, pp. 25–26.
17. PN, *Obras completas*, Vol. 4, 'Album Terusa'. pp. 271–278.
18. Ibid., p. 1238.
19. Quoted in *Buen Domingo*, Santiago, 12 August 1982.
20. Albertina Azócar interviewed in *Revista Intramuros*, Santiago, No. 9, 1978.
21. Ibid.
22. Ibid.
23. See Robert Pring-Mill's notes to his *A Poet for All Seasons*, (Catalogue for International Symposium on Pablo Neruda, Universities of Oxford and Warwick, 12–26 November 1993).
24. PN, *Memoirs*, p. 49.
25. Jean Franco, *Introduction to Spanish-American Literature*, 3rd ed. (Cambridge University Press, Cambridge, 1994), p. 280.
26. Hugo Montes, *Para leer a Neruda* (Ediciones Universidad Nacional Andrés Bello, Santiago, 1974), p. 21.
27. 'Morena, la besadora' from *Crepusculario* (Nascimento, Santiago, 1926).
28. 'Farewell' from *Crepusculario*.
29. 'Los crepúsculos de Maruri' from *Crepusculario*.
30. Montes, *Para leer a Neruda*, p. 23.
31. Muñoz, *Memorias*, p. 79.
32. PN, *Memoirs*, p. 49.
33. PN, *Memoirs*, p. 50.
34. Quoted in PN, *Memoirs*, p. 51.
35. Ibid.
36. Pring-Mill, *A Poet for All Seasons*.
37. Hernán Loyola's entry on Pablo Neruda in *Delal* (*Diccionario Enciclopédico de las Letras de América Latina*), Monte Avila Editores Latinoamericana, Caracas, 1993).
38. Robert Pring-Mill, ed., *Pablo Neruda: A Basic Anthology* (Dolphin, Oxford, 1975), p. xviii.
39. Muñoz, *Memorias*, pp. 38–39.

40. Ibid, p. 40.
41. PN, Lecture at the Biblioteca Nacional in Santiago, 1964, quoted by Alberto Cousté, *Neruda: El autor y su obra* (Ediciones Barcanova, Barcelona. 1981), p. 42.
42. Ibid.
43. Federico Schopf, in conversation with AF, Santiago, April 2000.
44. Orlando Oyarzún writing in *Aurora*, Santiago, July–December, 1964.
45. PN, *Cartas a Laura*.
46. Enrique Anderson-Imbert, 'La prosa vanguardista de Neruda', an address at the symposium devoted to Neruda at the University of South Carolina, 21–23 November 1974, whose proceedings were published in *Simposio Pablo Neruda*, Lévy, Isaac Jack and Juan Loveluck, eds (University of South Carolina Press, Columbia, SC, 1975), p. 305.
47. Sylvia Thayer, 'Testimonio', in *Aurora*, Santiago, Nos 3–4, July–December 1964, pp. 24–42.
48. Oyarzún, writing in *Aurora*, Santiago, July–December 1964.
49. PN, *Memoirs*, p. 64.

3 Asian desolation 1927–32

1. Laura Arrué recalled her days with Neruda in her memoirs, *Ventana del recuerdo* (Nascimento, Santiago, 1982). She died tragically in a fire at her house in 1986.
2. PN, *Cartas a Laura*, p. 32.
3. Volodia Teitelboim, in conversation with AF, Santiago, March 2000.
4. Muñoz, *Memorias*, pp. 145–146.
5. Ibid., p.149
6. PN, *Cartas a Laura*, p. 34.
7. From an interview with Jorge Luis Borges, *Le Monde Diplomatique*, Paris, August 2001, pp. 24–25.
8. PN, *Memoirs*, p. 95.
9. PN, *Para nacer he nacido* (Planeta, Santiago 1978), pp. 27–28.
10. Volodia Teitelboim, in conversation with AF, Santiago, March 2000.
11. PN, *Para nacer he nacido*, p. 28.
12. PN, *Cartas a Laura*, pp. 53–54.
13. Quoted in Alfredo Cardona Peña, 'Pablo Neruda: Breve historia de sus libros' in *Cuadernos Americanos*, Mexico, December 1950, p. 273.
14. Guillermo de Torre, 'Carta abierta a Pablo Neruda', in *Cuadernos Americanos*, Mexico, No. 3, May–June 1951, p. 278.
15. PN, *Memoirs*, p. 70.
16. Ibid.
17. Guillermo de Torre, 'Poemas en mapa', *La Gaceta Literaria*, Madrid, 1 August 1927, quoted in Edmundo Olivares Briones, *Pablo Neruda: Los caminos de Oriente, Tras las huellas del poeta itinerante 1927–1933* (LOM Ediciones, Santiago, 2000), p. 61.
18. PN, in a dispatch dated 2 September 1927, and published in *La Nación*, Santiago, on 20 November 1927.
19. Volodia Teitelboim, in conversation with AF, Santiago, March 2000.

20. PN, *Memoirs*, p. 74.
21. PN, *Cartas a Laura*, p. 35.
22. Lago, *Ojos y oídos*, p. 60.
23. PN, *Memoirs*, p. 86.
24. 'Religión en el este', from *Memorial de Isla Negra*, p. 107.
25. PN, *Memoirs*, p. 86.
26. Muñoz, *Memorias*, p. 163.
27. PN, *Memoirs*, p. 86.
28. Quoted in Olivares Briones, *Pablo Neruda: Los caminos de Oriente*, p. 93.
29. PN, *Cartas a Laura*, p. 80.
30. PN, *Memoirs*, p. 73.
31. Ibid.
32. PN, *Cartas a Laura*, p. 75.
33. PN, *Cartas a Laura*, p. 36.
34. PN, *Para nacer he nacido*, pp. 52–53.
35. *Veinte poemas de amor y una canción desesperada* (Losada, Buenos Aires, 1961).
36. PN, *Pablo Neruda, Héctor Eandi, Correspondencia durante Residencia en la tierra*, edited by Margarita Aguirre (Sudamericana, Buenos Aires, 1980) p. 32.
37. Volodia Teitelboim, in conversation with AF, Santiago, March 2000.
38. As he recalled in 1944 to Tomás Lago, see Lago, *Ojos y oídos*, p. 60.
39. Marco Antonio Millán, quoted in *La Crónica de Hoy*. Mexico City.
40. Inés Valenzuela, in conversation with AF, Santiago, March 2000.
41. PN, *Memoirs*, p. 76.
42. Quoted by Olivares Briones in *Pablo Neruda: Los caminos de Oriente*, p. 152.
43. Quoted by Emir Rodríguez Monegal in *Neruda: El viajero inmóvil* (Losada, Buenos Aires, 1966), p. 63.
44. Olivares Briones, *Pablo Neruda: Los caminos de Oriente*, p. 220.
45. PN, *Cartas a Laura*, p. 40.
46. PN, *Memoirs*, p. 87.
47. Ibid., p. 89.
48. PN, *Cartas a Laura*, p. 44.
49. PN, *Memoirs*, p. 92.
50. Ibid., p. 96.
51. Ibid.
52. Ibid., p. 93.
53. Ibid.
54. Ibid., p. 100.
55. PN, *Pablo Neruda, Héctor Eandi, Correspondencia*, p. 56.
56. Postcard published in the Chilean daily *La Tercera*, 1 August 1982.
57. PN, *Para Albertina Rosa*, with an introduction, notes and epilogue by Francisco Cruchaga Azócar (Editorial South Pacific Press, Santiago de Chile, 1992) pp. 338–339.
58. Ibid., pp. 345–348.
59. Ibid., p. 354.
60. Ibid., pp. 358–359.
61. Ibid., p. 357.
62. Albertina Azócar interviewed in *Revista Intramuros*, Santiago, No. 9, 1978.

63. Ibid.
64. PN, *Pablo Neruda, Héctor Eandi, Correspondencia*, p. 76.
65. Ibid., p. 78.
66. Ibid.
67. PN, *Pablo Neruda, Héctor Eandi, Correspondencia*, p. 81.
68. PN, *Memoirs*, p. 102.
69. Ibid.
70. Ibid., pp. 105–106.
71. PN, *Para nacer he nacido*, p. 177.
72. PN, letter reproduced in *La Nación*, 19 October 1930.
73. I am indebted, for this previously unknown information about Maruca, to the investigations of Kathleen Boet-Herbert in The Hague and to Anabel Torres in Barcelona.
74. Muñoz, *Memorias*, p. 182.
75. Margarita Aguirre, *Genio y figura de Pablo Neruda*, (Editorial Universitaria de Buenos Aires, Buenos Aires, 1967), pp. 119–120.
76. 'Itinerarios' in *Estravagario* (Losada, Buenos Aires, 1958).
77. PN, *Cartas a Laura*, p. 50.
78. PN, *Pablo Neruda, Héctor Eandi, Correspondencia*, p. 98.
79. 'Roxane', 'La isla de Java, Batavia, 1931' in *El Mercurio*, Santiago, 3 January 1932.
80. Jorge Edwards, quoted in *Literature in Exile*, edited by John Glad (Duke University Press, Durham and London, 1990), pp. 69–70.
81. Pring-Mill, ed., *Pablo Neruda: A Basic Anthology*, p. xxv. Neruda's relationship with surrealism was a curious one. He wrote his most surrealist verse before he met and befriended the leading French surrealist poets, Paul Eluard and Louis Aragon. In the late 1930s, the Chilean surrealist movement, La Mandrágora, would turn virulently against Neruda: its leader, Braulio Arenas, even leapt on stage during a Santiago poetry reading and ripped up Neruda's pages.

4 Back home, new battles – and Buenos Aires 1932–34

1. PN, *Pablo Neruda, Héctor Eandi, Correspondencia*, p. 111.
2. PN, *Residencia en la tierra*, edited by Hernán Loyola (Cátedra, Madrid, 1994), note p. 326.
3. Muñoz, *Memorias*, p. 180.
4. Ibid.
5. Quoted by Olivares Briones, in *Pablo Neruda: Los caminos de Oriente*, p. 348.
6. Arce, *Los libros y los viajes*, pp. 45–46.
7. Reproduced in Reyes, *Neruda – retrato de familia*, p. 118.
8. PN, *Pablo Neruda, Héctor Eandi, Correspondencia*, p. 113.
9. Sergio Fernández Larraín, *Cartas de amor de Pablo Neruda* (Rodas, Madrid, 1975), pp. 372–373.
10. Ibid.
11. Olivares Briones, *Pablo Neruda: Los caminos de Oriente*, p. 357.
12. Reyes, *Neruda – retrato de familia*, p. 119.

13. PN quoted in *El Mercurio*, 30 May 1932.
14. Hernán Díaz Arrieta (Alone), 'Critica literaria: Veinte poemas por Pablo Neruda', in *La Nación*, 18 September 1932.
15. Ibid.
16. PN, *Pablo Neruda, Héctor Eandi, Correspondencia*, p. 116.
17. Reyes, *Neruda – Retrato de familia*, p. 120.
18. Joaquín Edwards Bello in *La Nación*, Santiago, 10 November 1932.
19. Pablo de Rokha, 'Pablo Neruda, poeta a la moda', in *La Opinión*, Santiago, 11 November 1932.
20. Pablo de Rokha in *La Opinión*, 25 November 1932.
21. PN, *Lecturas*, 22 December 1932.
22. PN, *Pablo Neruda, Héctor Eandi, Correspondencia*, pp. 117–118.
23. PN, *Cartas a Laura*, p. 58.
24. Quoted by Rafael Aguayo in *Neruda, un hombre de la Araucania* (Ediciones Literatura American Rennida, Concepción, 1987) pp. 78–79.
25. *El Mercurio*, 5 February 1933.
26. PN, *Pablo Neruda, Héctor Eandi, Correspondencia*, pp. 115–116.
27. Neruda's comments to the Mexican critic, Alfonso Cardona Peña, in 1950 from 'Pablo Neruda: Breve, historia de sus libros 'in *Cuadernos Americanos* (Mexico City, No. 6, December 1950), pp. 257–289.
28. Pablo de Rokha, 'Epitafio a Neruda' in *La Opinión*, 22 May 1933.
29. Quoted by Olivares Briones in *Pablo Neruda: Los caminos de Oriente*, p. 423.
30. Luis Enrique Délano, 'Regreso de Pablo Neruda' in *El Mercurio*, 15 March 1932.
31. Quoted in Cardona Peña, 'Pablo Neruda: Breve historia de sus libros'.
32. Aguirre, *Genio y figura de Pablo Neruda*, p. 135
33. Letter to Giuseppe Bellini from PN dated 30 October 1959, and quoted by Bellini in his address to the conference 'Neruda, con la perspectiva de 25 años' held in Alicante, Spain, in March 1999. (Published in the *Boletín de la Unidad de Investigación* de la Universidad de Alicante, Alicante, December 1999).
34. Amado Alonso, *Poesía y estilo de Pablo Neruda* (Losada, Buenos Aires, 1940), p. 228. Although the book obviously omits Neruda's later works, it is essential reading for anyone seeking a detailed critical analysis of Neruda's early poetry.
35. Reyes, *Neruda – retrato de familia*, p. 124.
36. PN, *Pablo Neruda, Héctor Eandi, Correspondencia*, p. 116.
37. PN, *Cartas a Laura*, p. 61.
38. Aguirre, *Genio y figura de Pablo Neruda*, p. 156.
39. Ibid., p. 158.
40. Quoted by Virginia Vidal in 'Con tres sombreros puestos', *Cuadernos*, Fundación Pablo Neruda, Santiago, No. 31, 1997.
41. María Flora Yáñez, quoted by Gonzalo Vial in 'Los 10 chilenos mas importantes del siglo XX', *La Segunda*, Santiago, 17 September 1998.
42. Quoted in María Luisa Bombal, *Obras completas*, ed. Lucía Guerra (Editorial Andrés Bello, Santiago, 1996), p. 420.
43. PN, *Memoirs*, pp. 115–116.
44. Hugo Achugar, *Falsas Memorias* (LOM Ediciones, Santiago, 2000) pp. 87–88.

45. Hernán Loyola, in the introduction to his edition of PN, *Residencia en la tierra*, (Cátedra, Madrid, 1994), p. 43.
46. Bombal, *Obras completas*, pp. 418–421.

5 Spanish sorrow – the turning-point 1934–37

1. PN, *Pablo Neruda, Héctor Eandi, Correspondencia*, p. 133.
2. From 'Alberto Rojas Giménez viene volando' in *Residencia en la tierra* 1. (Ediciones de Arbol, Cruz y Raya, Madrid, 1935).
3. Luis Rosales, in his article, 'Distintos y admirables' in the Madrid daily, *ABC*, on 23 September 1983 (exactly ten years after Neruda's death).
4. Carlos Morla Lynch, *En España con Federico García Lorca* (Ediciones Aguilar, Madrid, 1957), p. 386.
5. PN, *Memoirs*, p. 116.
6. Quoted in PN, *Residencia en la tierra*, ed. Hermán Loyola, p. 52.
7. From 'Oda a Federico García Lorca', in *Residencia en la tierra*.
8. See Roberto Salama, *Para una crítica a Pablo Neruda* (Editorial Cartago, Buenos Aires, 1957), p. 77.
9. PN, *Memoirs*, p. 117.
10. From 'El culpable' in *Las manos del día*, (Losada, Buenos Aires, 1968).
11. María de Gracia in 'Neruda and Miguel Hernández', *Insula*, Madrid, Vol. 29, No. 330, 1974.
12. From 'Enfermedades en mi casa' in *Residencia en la tierra*.
13. Hernán Loyola, speaking during a round-table discussion at the conference, 'Neruda, con la perspectiva de 25 años', held in Alicante, Spain, in March 1999.
14. PN, *Residencia en la tierra*, ed Hernán Loyola, p. 334.
15. Ibid, pp. 48–49.
16. Pring-Mill, ed., *Pablo Neruda – A Basic Anthology*, p. xxiv.
17. From 'Josie Bliss', in *Residencia en la tierra*.
18. María Teresa León, *Memoria de la melancolía*, (Editorial Castilia, Madrid, 1998), p. 221.
19. 'Testimonios sobre Delia del Carril', *Boletín*, Fundación Pablo Neruda, Santiago, Spring 1991, pp. 33–37.
20. Ibid.
21. PN interviewed in *Marcha*, Montevideo, Uruguay, 17 September 1971.
22. Rafael Alberti, Introduction to *Pablo Neruda: Antología poetica* (Espasa-Calpe, Madrid, 1981).
23. Fernando Sáez, *Todo debe ser demasiado, Vida de Delia del Carril*, Sudamericana, Santiago, 1997, p. 98.
24. Reyes, *Neruda – retrato de familia*, p. 126–127.
25. PN, 'Confesiones desde Isla Negra' in *Ercilla*, Santiago, 24 April 1968.
26. Rafael Alberti, Introduction to *Pablo Neruda: Antología poética*, p. 22.
27. PN, in his prologue to *Caballo Verde*, 1935. Translated by Alastair Reid in 'A Visit to Neruda', *Encounter*, London, September 1965, p. 68.
28. Gabriel Celaya, 'El Poeta del Tercer Día de la Creación', *Revista de Occidente*, Madrid, No. 36, 1972.

29. PN, 'Las vidas del poeta'.
30. Luis Enrique Délano, *Sobre todo Madrid* (Editorial Universitaria, Santiago, 1970), p. 115.
31. Ibid.
32. Quoted in Sáez, *Todo debe ser demasiado*, p. 112.
33. PN, *Memoirs*, pp. 127–128.
34. Ibid., p. 128.
35. Reproduced in the anti-fascist magazine *Hora de España*, Valencia, March 1937.
36. PN, *Memoirs*, p. 130.
37. Octavio Paz, writing in *Reforma*, Mexico City, 7 April 1944, pp. 12–13.
38. PN, *Memoirs*, p. 132.
39. Jean Lacouture, *André Malraux – Une vie dans le siècle* (Editions Seuil, Paris, 1973), p. 253.

6 A life-saving mission 1937–40

1. Muñoz, *Memorias*, p. 217.
2. Ibid.
3. Robert Pring-Mill, in a note to AF.
4. Muñoz, *Memorias*, pp. 117–118
5. PN, 'Algo sobre mi poesía y mi vida', in *Aurora*, Santiago, No. 1, July 1954, pp. 11–12.
6. Ibid.
7. PN, *Memoirs*, p. 138.
8. Emir Rodríguez Monegal's book, *Neruda: El viajero inmóvil* (Neruda: The Immobile Voyager) remains one of the best studies of Neruda's poetry, despite the over-psychoanalytic thread running through it.
9. From 'Carta para que me manden madera' in *Estravagario*.
10. From 'La mamadre' in *Memorial de Isla Negra*.
11. From Neruda's article, 'César Vallejo is dead', in *Aurora*, Santiago, 1 August 1938.
12. John Gunther, *Inside Latin America* (Hamish Hamilton, London, 1942), p. 193.
13. Jordi Torra, interviewed by the Chilean Neruda specialist, Julio Gálvez Barraza, in *El Siglo*, Santiago, 13 July 2000.
14. Alonso, *Poesía y estilo de Pablo Neruda*, p. 359.
15. Monegal, *Neruda: El viajero inmóvil*, pp. 304 and 307.
16. Jaime Concha, *Tres ensayos sobre Pablo Neruda* (University of South Carolina Press, Columbia, SC, 1974), P. 85.
17. Octavio Paz, 'Neruda en el corazón' in *Ruta*, Mexico City, No. 4, 1938, p. 241.
18. Alberti, ed., *Pablo Neruda: Antología poética*, p. 24.
19. PN, *Memoirs*, p. 141.
20. Víctor Pey, in conversation with AF, Santiago, March 2000.
21. PN, *Para nacer he nacido*, p. 294.
22. Roser Bru, in conversation with AF, Santiago, March 2000.
23. Víctor Pey, in conversation with AF, Santiago, April 2000.
24. Roser Bru, in conversation with AF, Santiago, March 2000.
25. Víctor Pey, in conversaton with AF, Santiago, April 2000.

26. Ibid.
27. José Balmes, in conversation with AF, Santiago, April 2000.
28. PN, *Memoirs*, p. 148.
29. Ibid.
30. Delia del Carril, interviewed by Isabel Lipthay in the Chilean magazine, *Hoy*, in November 1979.

7 Mexican magic, marriage, a tragic telegram and a mordant badger 1940–43

1. This intriguing and little-known letter can be found in the Biblioteca Nacional José Marti in Havana, Cuba. The author's attention was drawn to it by an article in the Cuban journal, *Juventud Rebelde*, on 5 October 2003.
2. 'Open Letter to Pablo Neruda', reproduced in Juan Ramón Jiménez, *Guerra en España 1936–1953* (Seix Barral, Barcelona, 1985), p. 255.
3. PN, in an interview with *El Nacional*, Mexico City, 24 August 1940.
4. George Steiner, *Language and Silence* (Pelican Books, London, 1969), p. 310.
5. Quoted in 'Testimonios sobre Delia del Carril'.
6. Wilberto Cantón, 'Pablo Neruda en México (1940–1943)', *Anales de la Universidad de Chile*, Santiago, Nos 157–160, January–December 1971, pp. 263–269.
7. PN, *Memoirs*, p. 150.
8. Siqueiros himself hated the completed mural in Chillán. According to the Chilean muralist Julio Escámez, 'He wanted to destroy it as soon as he'd finished it. He threw a knife at it and left a scratch which no one noticed. He didn't want to attend the inauguration ceremony [for the mural]. But that was not unusual for him: he was rarely happy with his works when he'd finished them. That didn't stop him boasting about them later.' Julio Escámez, interviewed in *Cuadernos*, Vol. 10, No. 39, Fundación Pablo Neruda, Santiago, 1999.
9. PN, interview in *Marcha*, Montevideo, Uruguay, 17 September 1971, p. 3.
10. John Bart Gerald, in his book review of Pablo Neruda's *Winter Garden*, translated by William O'Daly, (Copper Canyon Press, Port Townsend, 1986) *New York Times Book Review*, 20 July 1990.
11. In a message intercepted by the US Army's signal intelligence organisation and translated as part of a project named Venona.
12. PN, 'Las vidas del poeta'.
13. Ibid.
14. Ibid.
15. From 'America' in *Canto general*, translated by Jack Schmitt (University of California Press, Berkeley, CA, 1991).
16. Octavio Paz, quoted in *Reforma*, Mexico City, 7 April 1994, pp. 12–13.
17. Enrico Mario Santí, in his Introduction to Octavio Paz, *Primeras letras 1931–1943* (Vuelta, Mexico City, 1988), p. 44.
18. Octavio Paz, *Laurel*, Seneca, Mexico, 1941.
19. PN, *Memoirs*, pp. 162–163.
20. Ibid.
21. Cantón, 'Pablo Neruda en México', pp. 263–269.

22. Poli Délano, 'Nerudeando con nostalgia' in *Cuadernos*, Fundación Pablo Neruda, Santiago, Vol. 10, No. 39, 1999, p. 27.
23. PN, *Memoirs*, pp. 159–160.
24. Ibid.
25. Octavio Paz, quoted by the Mexican daily, *Excelsior*, on 7 December 1990.
26. No one has previously revealed what happened to Maruca after she separated from Neruda in Monte Carlo in 1936. I am immensely grateful to Kathleen Boet-Herbert in The Hague and Anabel Torres in Barcelona for uncovering this remarkably detailed information for me.
27. Cantón, 'Pablo Neruda en México'.
28. Neruda's remarks were reproduced in *Excelsior*, Mexico City, 1 June 1943.
29. Julio Escámez, in *Cuadernos*, Vol. 10, No. 39, Fundación Pablo Neruda, Santiago, 1999.
30. PN, interviewed in *Hoy*, Mexico City, August 1943
31. Paz, 'Respuesta a un cónsul' *Letras de México*, Mexico City, 15 August 1943.
32. Jason Wilson, *Octavio Paz* (Twayne, Boston, MA, 1986), p. 23.
33. Octavio Paz speaking on the Spanish television programme, 'A Fondo', RTVE, 1977.
34. Octavio Paz, *Convergencias* (Seix Barral, Barcelona, 1991), pp. 129–130.
35. Raúl Arreola Cortés, *Pablo Neruda en Morelia* (Ediciones Casa de San Nicolás, Morelia, Michoacán, 1972).
36. Ibid.
37. PN, *Memoirs*, p.163.

8 From the rich heights of Machu Picchu down to the poverty of the driest place on Earth 1943–48

1. Reproduced in *Zig-Zag*, Santiago de Chile, 29 October 1943.
2. Neruda's response in *Zig-Zag*.
3. Pablo Neruda addressing the Law Faculty at the Universidad Nacional in Bogotá, Colombia, on 23 September 1943.
4. Robert Pring-Mill, in his Introduction to PN, *The Heights of Macchu Picchu*, translated by Nathaniel Tarn (Jonathan Cape, London, 1966), p. xi.
5. PN, *Memoirs*, pp. 165–166.
6. Quoted by Margarita Aguirre in *Genio y figura de Pablo Neruda*, p. 156.
7. PN, *Aurora*, Santiago, No. 1, July 1954, pp. 10–12.
8. Pring-Mill, ed., *Pablo Neruda: A Basic Anthology*, p. xii.
9. PN, *Obras completas*, Vol. 1, p. 1214.
10. Ibid.
11. PN, *Passions and Impressions*, p. 196.
12. From *The Heights of Macchu Picchu*, translated by Nathaniel Tarn.
13. Quoted in Sáez, *Todo debe ser demasiado*, pp. 141–142.
14. Inés Valenzuela in conversation with AF, Santiago, March 2000.
15. Even after breaking relations with the Axis powers, Chile was never satisfied with the amount of aid and military equipment it had received from the United States. The US, in turn, was unhappy with Chile's apparent slowness to act against Axis agents and firms.

16. PN, *Memoirs*, p. 167.
17. In 'Down the Mine' from George Orwell, *The Road to Wigan Pier* (Victor Gollancz, London, 1937).
18. PN, *Viaje al norte de Chile*, collected in *Viajes* (Nascimento, Santiago, 1955).
19. Lago, *Ojos y oídos*, pp. 45–46.
20. Ibid., p. 46.
21. Ibid.
22. PN, *Memoirs*, pp. 166–167.
23. PN, *Obras Completas*, Vol. 4, pp. 613–630
24. Ibid., pp. 549–555. Since this edition of Neruda's complete works was published, its editor, Hernán Loyola, has contacted AF to suggest that the interruptions to the 1945 address may well have been playfully invented or 'staged' by Neruda himself in order to liven up the speech.
25. Translation by Robert Pring-Mill in 'Both in Sorrow and in Anger: Spanish-American Protest Poetry', *Cambridge Review*, Vol. 91, No. 2195, 20 February 1970, pp. 112–122.
26. Lago, *Ojos y oídos*, p. 66.
27. Jason Wilson, 'In the Translator's Workshop', in *Poetry London*, Summer 2002, pp. 30–32.
28. PN, 'Viaje al corazón de Quevedo' collected in *Viajes*.
29. Translations here are by Nathaniel Tarn from *The Heights of Macchu Picchu*.
30. In his book, *Ojos y oídos*, Neruda's friend Tomás Lago mentions an occasion when Neruda spoke disparagingly of Mistral, especially criticising what he claimed was her lack of awareness of political events in Latin America (p. 66). Lago's daughter, Victoria Lago, went even further when talking to AF: she claimed that 'Pablo was annoyed that Mistral got the Nobel Prize before he did.' (Victoria Lago, in conversation with AF, Santiago, April 2000.)
31. Lago, *Ojos y oídos*, p. 68.
32. Ibid.
33. Volodia Teitelboim, in conversation with AF, Santiago, March 2000.
34. The Spanish word *hacha* means 'axe'.
35. Inés Valenzuela, in conversation with AF, Santiago, March 2000.
36. Quoted in 'Testimonios sobre Delia del Carril'.
37. Ibid.
38. Sáez, *Todo debe ser demasiado*, p. 148.
39. Lago, *Ojos y oídos*, pp. 84–85.
40. Volodia Teitelboim, Neruda, p. 288.
41. Lago, *Ojos y oídos*, p. 90.
42. PN, *Passions and Impressions*, p. 266.
43. Neruda's 'Yo acuso' speech is reproduced in *Obras completas*, Vol. 4, pp. 704–729.
44. Ibid., pp. 730–731.

9 'A year of blind rats' – Neruda in hiding 1948–49

1. Margarita Aguirre, *Genio y figura de Pablo Neruda*, p. 189.
2. From 'Acuso' in *Canto general*, 1950. Translation by Jack Schmitt from PN,

Canto general, fiftieth anniversary edition (University of California Press, Berkeley, CA, 2000), p. 198.

3. Robert Pring-Mill, Notes on the section of *Canto general* written underground. Notes kindly lent to AF.

4. Alvaro Jara, 'Neruda 1948: El poeta inalcanzable', an address to the International Symposium on Pablo Neruda at the Universities of Oxford and Warwick, 12–16 November 1993.

5. Ibid.

6. Ibid.

7. Pring-Mill, *A Poet for All Seasons*, p. 43.

8. I am grateful to Robert Pring-Mill for sharing his 1996 notes on the *Antología popular de la resistencia* with me.

9. Víctor Pey, in conversation with AF, Santiago, March 2000.

10. Ibid.

11. Ibid.

12. Ibid.

13. Ibid.

14. Jara, 'Neruda 1948'.

15. Pring-Mill, Notes on the section of *Canto general* written underground.

16. See Aída Figueroa, quoted in 'Vivir con Neruda: Conversación con Aída Figueroa y Sergio Insunza' by Luis Alberto Mansilla, *Araucaria*, Santiago, No. 26, 1984, pp. 89–105.

17. Ibid.

18. Jara, 'Neruda 1948'.

19. Aída Figueroa, in conversation with AF, Santiago, March 2000.

20. From 'El traidor' in *Canto General*, translated by Jack Schmitt, p. 197.

21. PN, *Memoirs*, pp. 172–173.

22. From 'Que despierte el leñador' in *Canto General*, translated by Jack Schmitt, p. 257.

23. Ibid., p. 267.

24. Sergio Insunza in Mansilla, 'Vivir con Neruda'.

25. PN, *Memoirs*, pp. 173–174.

26. Ibid., p. 174.

27. Jara, 'Neruda 1948'.

28. From 'El fugitivo' in *Canto general*, translated by Jack Schmitt, p. 273.

29. Ibid., p. 278.

30. Ibid.

31. Pring-Mill, Notes on the section of *Canto general* written underground.

32. This clandestine interview with Neruda appeared in *La Hora*, Buenos Aires, 19 October 1948.

33. Gabriel González Videla, *Memorias* (Editorial Gabriela Mistral, Santiago, 1975).

34. Ibid.

35. Robert Pring-Mill, Interview with Manuel Solimano, 27 June 1985.

36. Pring-Mill, Notes on the section of *Canto general* written underground.

37. Ibid.

38. José Miguel Varas, *Nerudario* (Planeta, Santiago, 1999), p. 104.

39. Jara, 'Neruda 1948'.

40. Poli Délano, in conversation with AF, Santiago, March 2000.
41. Pring-Mill, Notes on the section of *Canto general* written underground.
42. From 'Yo soy' in *Canto general*, translated by Jack Schmitt, pp. 373–387.
43. 'El testamento', ibid., p. 395.
44. Víctor Pey, in conversation with AF, Santiago, April 2000.
45. Jorge Bellet, 'Cruzando la cordillera con el poeta', in *Araucaria*, Santiago, Nos 47–48, 1990, pp. 186–202.
46. Pring-Mill, Interview with Manuel Solimano.
47. Víctor Pey, in conversation with AF, Santiago, April 2000.
48. Ibid.
49. Bellet, 'Cruzando la cordillera con el poeta'.
50. Pring-Mill, Interview with Manuel Solimano.
51. Juan Carlos Reyes, in conversation with AF, Temuco, April 2000.
52. PN, *Memoirs*, p. 177.
53. Bellet, 'Cruzando la cordillera con el poeta'.
54. Ibid.
55. PN, *Memoirs*, p. 180.
56. Bellet, 'Cruzando la cordillera con el poeta'.
57. Víctor Bianchi's diary is reproduced in *Cuadernos*, Fundación Pablo Neruda, Santiago, No. 51, 2002, pp. 9–17.
58. Ibid.
59. PN, *Obras completas*, Vol. 5, pp. 333–334.
60. Bianchi, Diary.
61. PN, *Memoirs*, p. 184.
62. Bellet, 'Cruzando la cordillera con el poeta'.
63. PN, *Memoirs*, pp. 182–183.
64. Is it too fanciful to wonder whether it ever occurred to Neruda that his escape over the Andes on horseback bore an astonishing resemblance to John Ferrier and his daughter's Lucy's escape from the Mormons in one of the poet's favourite Sherlock Holmes stories, *A Study in Scarlet*?
65. Pring-Mill, Interview with Manuel Solimano, 27 June 1985.
66. Víctor Pey, in conversation with AF, Santiago, April 2000.

10 Delia and Matilde – an East European juggling act 1949–52

1. PN, *Memoirs*, p. 186.
2. Ibid., p. 187.
3. 'It wasn't William Shakespeare who really wrote those plays, but another man who was born on the same day, at the same hour as he, and who died on the same day as he, and to carry the coincidence further, was also named William Shakespeare.' Ibid., p. 187.
4. Ibid., p. 188.
5. Ibid., p. 189.
6. Ibid., p. 190.
7. Ibid., p. 191.

8. Anecdotes recounted to Neruda's third wife, Matilde Urrutia, by Paul Eluard and reproduced in her own memoirs, *Mi vida junto a Pablo Neruda* (Seix Barral, Barcelona, 1986), p. 159.

9. Some of the details of this first Russian visit and subsequent tour of Eastern Europe come from a chapter of a sadly unfinished and unpublished biography of Neruda which the great Chilean scholar, Jorge Sanhueza, was writing at the time of his death in 1967.

10. Vera Kuteishikova, in conversation with AF, Moscow, September 2003.

11. From a speech Neruda read in Guatemala City in 1950. The text was originally published as 'El esplendor de la tierra' in *Viajes*, Santiago, 1955.

12. Ibid.

13. Ibid.

14. Ibid.

15. PN, *Memoirs*, pp. 194–195.

16. Vera Kuteishikova, in conversation with AF, Moscow, September 2003.

17. Ibid.

18. Lago, *Ojos y oídos*, p. 124.

19. Guibert, *Seven Voices*, pp. 3–78.

20. PN, 'El esplendor de la tierra'.

21. Pablo Neruda's speech to the Latin American Congress of Peace Supporters in Mexico City, September 1949. The text was originally published in a clandestine pamphlet by the Chilean Communist party in Santiago in 1949, and is reproduced in PN, *Obras completas*, Vol. 4, pp. 761–769.

22. Marco Antonio Campos, 'Los días terrenales de Revueltas', *La Jornada Semanal*, Mexico City, 11 June 2000.

23. Reyes, *Neruda – retrato de familia*, p. 142.

24. Inés Figueroa, quoted in Varas, *Nerudario*, p. 208.

25. Urrutia, *Mi vida junto a Pablo Neruda*, pp. 127–128.

26. Aída Figueroa, in conversation with AF, Santiago, March 2000.

27. Jorge Edwards, *Adiós, Poeta* (Tusquets, Barcelona, 1990), p. 69.

28. Ibid.

29. Inés Figueroa, in conversation with AF, Santiago, 2000.

30. Hugo Méndez-Ramírez, *Neruda's Ekphrastic Experience: Mural Art and Canto General* (Bucknell University Press, Lewisburg, NJ, 1999).

31. Roberto González Echevarría, in his introduction to Schmitt's translation of *Pablo Neruda: Canto General*, p. 7.

32. Alfredo Cardona Peña, *Pablo Neruda y otros ensayos* (Editorial de Andrea, Mexico City, 1955), pp. 37–38.

33. Américo Zorrilla, interviewed in *Aurora de Chile*, Santiago, No. 8, 1979.

34. A facsimile of the Chilean edition was made in 2000 to mark its fiftieth anniversary.

35. Enrico Mario Santí, *Pablo Neruda: The Poetics of Prophesy* (Cornell University Press, Ithaca, NY, 1982).

36. Jaime Alazraki, 'Observaciones sobre la estructura de la oda elemental' in *Mester* (UCLA) IV, No. 2, April 1974, pp. 94–102.

37. Judy McGinnis, in a text prepared for the 1997 meeting of the Latin American Studies Association in Guadalajara, Mexico, 17–19 April 1997.

38. Saúl Yurkiévich, 'Mito e historia: Dos generadores del *Canto general*' in *Revista Iberoamericana*, Pittsburgh, PA, 39, Nos 82–83 (1973), pp. 111–35.

39. Reyes, *Neruda – retrato de familia*, p. 150.

40. PN, writing in *Pro Arte*, Santiago, No. 117, 30 November 1950.

41. PN, 'El esplendor de la tierra'.

42. Reyes, *Neruda – retrato de familia*, p. 155.

43. PN, *Memoirs*, p. 199.

44. Ibid., p. 201.

45. Ibid. p. 202.

46. Ibid.

47. From 'Londres' in *Las uvas y el viento* (Nascimento, Santiago, 1954).

48. Varas, *Nerudario*, p. 118.

49. This speech to the second World Peace Congress in Warsaw was reproduced in *Pro Arte*, Santiago, 30 November No. 117, 1950.

50. When Turkey's first democratically elected government came to power after the May 1950 general election, Hikmet was released as part of a general amnesty, but the persecution continued. Hikmet escaped across the Bosphorous in a tiny motorboat on a stormy night, flagged down a cargo ship which picked him up half-dead, and found that the officers' cabin had an enormous photograph of him on the wall bearing the caption: 'Save Nazim Hikmet'. Taken to Moscow, he was given a house in the writers' colony of Peredelkino outside the city. The Turkish government denied his wife and child permission to join him. Although he suffered a second heart attack in 1952, Hikmet travelled widely during his exile, visiting not only Eastern Europe but also Rome and Paris. Neruda would meet him for the first time in East Berlin in 1951.

51. Howard Fast, a novelist blacklisted in America for his Communist sympathies, was awarded the Stalin Peace Prize in the same year as Neruda, 1953.

52. PN, *Memoirs*, pp. 211–212.

53. My immense gratitude goes to Robert Pring-Mill for affording me this and other details of the clandestine Chilean edition of *Canto general*, much of which he gleaned from two remarkable conversations he had with José Venturelli in 1986.

54. This speech was reproduced in *Democracia*, Santiago, 5 August 1951.

55. José Venturelli, in conversation with Robert Pring-Mill in 1986.

56. Urrutia, *Mi vida junto a Pablo Neruda*, pp. 46–47.

57. Ibid., p. 47.

58. Ibid.

59. José Venturelli, in conversation with Robert Pring-Mill in 1986.

60. From 'La pródiga' in *Los versos del capitán*.

61. PN, *Memoirs*, pp. 205–206.

62. Ibid., p. 207.

63. Ibid., p. 210.

64. Inés Figueroa, in conversation with AF, October 2002.

65. Urrutia, *Mi vida junto a Pablo Neruda*, pp. 65–66. Hugh Thomas points out that Nyon played a historic role in the Spanish Civil War. It was here that, on 10 September 1937, Britain and France invited Germany, Russia and all states with a Mediterranean frontier except Spain, to a conference aimed at preventing fascist

attacks off the coast of Spain. Hugh Thomas, *The Spanish Civil War* (3rd ed., Pelican Books, Harmondsworth, 1977) pp. 605–7.

66. Matilde Urrutia, interview with *La Tercera*, Santiago, 1982, reproduced in the same newspaper on 13 July 2002.
67. 'El desvío', from *Los versos del capitán*.
68. Matilde Urrutia, interview with *La Tercera*, 1982 (reproduced on 13 July 2002).
69. In the margin of the poem ' El jabón y la aguja', Neruda wrote: '2 to 3 in the afternoon, December 20, 1951', and then, tantalisingly, 'M . . . Krem . . . n'. Robert Pring-Mill believes this must refer to a visit to Moscow on those dates that has not been documented elsewhere. Robert Pring-Mill, Notes on the composition of *Los versos del capitán*.
70. PN, 'Algunas reflexiones improvisadas sobre mis trabajos', in *Mapocho*, Santiago, No. 3, 1964.
71. 'Regresó la sirena' from *Las uvas y el viento*.
72. Robert Pring-Mill, in conversation with AF, November 2003.
73. Reyes, *Neruda – retrato de familia*, p. 157.
74. Some of these details are taken from Teresa Cirillo Sirri, *Capri: Una tappa poetica di Neruda* (L'Orientale Editrice, Napoli, 2000).
75. Reyes, *Neruda – retrato de familia*, p. 159.
76. PN, *Memoirs*, p. 214.
77. Quoted in Cirillo Sirri, *Capri: Una tappa poetica di Neruda*.
78. Claretta Cerio, *Ex libris: Incontri a Capri con uomini e libri* (Edizoni La Conchiglia, Capri, 1999).
79. From the prologue to the first edition of *Los versos del capitán* (Imprenta L'Arte Tipografica, *Naples, 1952*).
80. Robert Pring-Mill, in a note to AF.
81. PN, *Memoirs*, p. 215.
82. Ibid., pp. 215–216.
83. Urrutia, *Mi vida junto a Pablo Neruda*. p. 105.
84. Guibert, *Seven Voices*, pp. 42–43.
85. Urrutia, *Mi vida junto a Pablo Neruda*, p. 108.
86. Ibid.
87. Ibid., p. 110.
88. Varas, *Nerudario*, p. 206.
89. Ibid.
90. Urrutia, *Mi vida junto a Pablo Neruda*, p. 129.
91. Ibid.
92. Ibid., p. 130.
93. Stefan Heym, *Nachruf* (Bertelsmann, Munich, 1988) p. 524.
94. Inés Figueroa, in conversation with AF, October 2002.
95. Urrutia, *Mi vida junto a Pablo Neruda*, p. 165.
96. Varas, *Nerudario*, p. 143.

11 Return the conquering hero 1952–59

1. Lago, *Ojos y oídos*, p. 160.
2. Ibid., p. 162.

3. Neruda's speech in Santiago's Plaza Bulnes was published the following day in *Democracia*, Santiago, 13 August 1952.

4. PN, *Vistazo*, Santiago, No. 12, 11 November 1952.

5. Sergio Insunza, in conversation with AF, Santiago, April 2000.

6. Lago, *Ojos y oídos*, p.175–6.

7. Ibid.

8. Margarita Aguirre, in conversation with AF, Santiago, March 2000.

9. Lago, *Ojos y oídos*, p. 198.

10. I am indebted, for this previously unknown information about Maruca, to the investigations of Kathleen Boet-Herbert in the Hague and to Anabel Torres in Barcelona.

11. The text of this speech was published in *Principios*, Santiago, September 1952.

12. PN, *Memoirs*, p. 224.

13. Confirmed to AF by Robert Pring-Mill.

14. Aguirre, *Genio y figura de Pablo Neruda*, p. 157.

15. Aída Figueroa, 'Delia y Matilde', in Carlos Orellana ed., *Los rostros de Neruda* (Planeta, Santiago, 1998), pp. 61–62.

16. Lago, *Ojos y oídos*, p. 170.

17. Sáez, *Todo debe ser demasiado*, p. 161.

18. Varas, *Nerudario*, p. 144.

19. *Qué Pasa*, Santiago, 4 October 2002.

20. *El Siglo*, Santiago and *Gazeta*, Moscow, 10 March 1953.

21. Yevgeny Yevtushenko, *A Precocious Autobiography* (Penguin Books, London, 1965), p. 95.

22. Ibid., p. 118.

23. This address to the Continental Congress of Culture in Santiago was reproduced in *El Siglo*, Santiago, 31 May 1953.

24. Ibid.

25. Urrutia, *Mi vida junto a Pablo Neruda*, p. 176.

26. Ibid.

27. Ibid.

28. The text of this speech was first published in *El Siglo*, Santiago, 18 January 1954.

29. Lago, *Ojos y oídos*, p. 188.

30. The text of this address was reproduced in PN, *Discursos del Rector de la Universidad de Chile, don Juan Gómez Millas y de Pablo Neruda* (Prensa de la Editorial Universitaria, Santiago, 1954).

31. From the poem 'On the Chilean Headland' in *Selected Poems of Ai Qing* (People's Literature Publishing House, Beijing, 1996), pp. 234–241. Poem translated by Liu Hongbin.

32. PN, *Aurora*, No. 2, Santiago, December 1954.

33. Ibid.

34. PN, Prologue to *Poesía política (discursos políticos) de Pablo Neruda*, ed. Margarita Aguirre (Editora Austral, Santiago, 1953), Vol. 1, pp. 7–9.

35. Jaime Concha, 'Neruda desde 1952; Nunca entendía lucha sino para que este termine' in *Texto Crítico*, Santiago, Nos 22–23, 1981.

36. Ibid.

37. Luis Sepúlveda, in conversation with AF, Gijón, Spain, May 1999.

38. Quoted in the introduction to Alexander Pushkin, *Eugene Onegin* (Penguin Books, London, 1964).
39. Hernán Díaz Arrieta (Alone), 'Muerte y tranfiguración de Pablo Neruda' (Death and Transfiguration of Pablo Neruda), in *El Mercurio*, 30 January 1955.
40. PN, *Algunas reflexiones sobre mi vida y obra*, January 1954.
41. René de Costa, *The Poetry of Pablo Neruda* (Harvard University Press, Cambridge, MA, 1979), p. 159.
42. PN, *Odas Elementales* (Losada, Buenos Aires, 1954).
43. Aída Figueroa, in conversation with AF, Santiago, April 2000,
44. Sáez, *Todo debe ser demasiado*, pp. 165–166.
45. Marie Martner and Francisco Velasco, in conversation with AF, Valparaíso, March 2000.
46. Sáez, *Todo debe ser demasiado*, p. 167.
47. Ibid.
48. Inés Valenzuela, in conversation with AF, Santiago, March 2000.
49. Inés Figueroa, in conversation with AF, Santiago, March 2000.
50. Victoria Lago, in conversation with AF, Santiago, April 2000.
51. Aída Figueroa in conversation with AF, Santiago, April 2000.
52. *La Tercera*, Santiago, 9 July 2002.
53. PN, *Memoirs*, pp. 318–319.
54. Ibid.
55. José Saramago interviewed in the *Guardian*, London, 28 December 2002.
56. Eric Hobsbawm, *Interesting Times – A Twentieth-Century Life* (Allen Lane, London, 2002), p. 134.
57. Yevtushenko, *A Precocious Autobiography*, p. 109.
58. Edwards, *Adiós, Poeta*, p. 86.
59. From 'Oda a los calcetines' in *Nuevas odas elementales* (Losada, Buenos Aires, 1956).
60. Robert Pring-Mill, 'El Neruda de las *Odas elementales*,' in *Coloquio internacional sobre Pablo Neruda (la obra posterior a Canto general)*, ed. Alain Sicard (Centre de Recherches Latino-américaines, Poitiers, 1979).
61. PN, in *Plática*, Buenos Aires, April 1956.
62. PN, *El Siglo*, Santiago, 11 January 1957.
63. PN, *Memoirs*, pp. 225–226.
64. Ibid., p. 229.
65. Ibid.
66. Ibid., p. 231.
67. Inés Figueroa, in conversation with AF, Santiago, April 2000.
68. PN, *Memoirs*, p. 231.
69. Ibid., p. 233.
70. Ibid., pp. 234–235
71. Ibid.
72. Xu Chi, Preface to *Selected Poems of Pablo Neruda* (Hunan People's Publishing House, Beijing, 1984).
73. PN, Memoirs, pp. 236–237.
74. Ibid., p. 240.
75. Ibid., p. 243.

76. Ibid.
77. Ibid., p. 246.
78. Ibid., p. 252.
79. Ibid.
80. Gonzalo Rojas, quoted in *La Tercera*, Santiago, 23 October 2003.
81. 'Pido silencio' from *Estravagario*.
82. 'Regreso a una ciudad' from *Estravagario*.
83. Inés Figueroa, in conversation with AF, Santiago, April 2000.
84. Edwards, *Adiós Poeta*, p. 90.

12 The new regime 1959–66

1. James Nolan, *Poet-Chief: The Native American Poetics of Walt Whitman and Pablo Neruda* (University of New Mexico Press, Albuquerque, 1994)
2. PN, *Lunes de Revolución*, Havana, Cuba, No. 88, 26 December 1960.
3. Ibid.
4. Sonnet 11 from *Cien sonetos de amor* (Prensa de la Editorial Universitaria, Santiago, 1959).
5. Neruda, in a written reply to a questionnaire from the poet and journalist, Sara Vial, which she quotes in her excellent book, *Neruda en Valparaíso* (Ediciones Universitarias de Valparaíso, Valparaíso, 1983), p. 215.
6. Varas, *Nerudario*, p. 217.
7. Rodolfo Reyes, in conversation with AF, Santiago, March 2000.
8. Sergio Insunza, in conversation with AF, Santiago, March 2000.
9. Inés Valenzuela, in conversation with AF, Santiago, April 2000.
10. Urrutia: *Mi vida junto a Pablo Neruda*, p. 250.
11. Manuel Díaz Martínez, Fragments from the unpublished book, *Sólo un leve rasguño en la solapa. Recuerdos*, published on the SISIB–Universidad de Chile website.
12. My thanks to Robert Pring-Mill for this graphic description of the tsunami's destructive consequences.
13. PN, *Obras completas*, Vol. 2, p. 1381.
14. Edwards, *Adiós, Poeta*, p. 146.
15. PN quoted by Pierre Kalfon in his book, *Che: Ernesto Guevara, una leyenda de nuestro siglo* (Plaza & Janes, Barcelona, 1997), p. 600.
16. Edwards, *Adiós, Poeta*, p. 146.
17. Urrutia, *Mi vida junto a Pablo Neruda*, p. 245.
18. Vial, *Neruda en Valparaíso*, p. 18.
19. Ibid, p. 184.
20. Ibid.
21. Marjorie Agosín, 'Neruda en Isla Negra, Isla Negra en Neruda', in *Nuevas aproximaciones a Pablo Neruda*, No. 39a.
22. PN, *Obras completas*, Vol. 2, p. 1391.
23. PN, 'Mariano Latorre, Pedro Prado y mi propria sombra', published in *Pablo Neruda y Nicanor Parra, Discursos* (Nascimento, Santiago, 1962).
24. Nicanor Parra's speech is reproduced in Pablo Neruda and Nicanor Parra: *Discursos* (Nascimento, Santiago, 1962) pp. 9–48.

25. Nicanor Parra, in conversation with AF, Las Cruces, Chile, April 2000. In 1981, Parra told the Uruguayan poet Mario Benedetti: 'Neruda was always a problem for me: a challenge, an obstacle in the way ...' (Mario Benedetti, 'Nicanor Parra o el artefacto con laureles' in *Los poetas comunicantes*, *Marcha*, Mexico, 1981, p. 46). But Parra seemed clear, when I met him, about how the dispute with Neruda had begun: it was, he said, after Neruda gave an interview in the Chilean magazine, *Ercilla*, around 1960. When asked what he thought of the other masters of Chilean poetry – Huidobro, De Rokha and Parra – Neruda had replied: 'I have other friends: Aragon, Eluard.'

26. Margarita Aguirre, in conversation with AF, Santiago, March 2000.

27. PN, 'Convenios católicos hacia la paz', published in *El Siglo*, Santiago, 14 October 1962.

28. Loyola, in the notes to PN, *Obras completas*, Vol. 2, p. 1393.

29. 'El pueblo' from *Plenos poderes* (Losada, Buenos Aires, 1962).

30. 'Un globo para Matilde', published as a leaflet by an anonymous printer in Valparaíso, 1963.

31. 'Winter Crown for Nazim Hikmet'. The poem was published in *El Siglo*, Santiago, on 9 June 1963.

32. PN, *Memoirs*, pp. 299–300.

33. I am grateful, for this and many other details of this campaign against Neruda, to Frances Stonor Saunders, for both conversations with her and material in her excellent book, *Who Paid the Piper? The CIA and the Cultural Cold War* (Granta Books, London, 1999).

34. Material kindly lent to AF by Frances Stonor Saunders.

35. The article was published in Spanish as 'Retrato de gladiador' by *El Siglo* on 28 July 1963.

36. The speech was reproduced in *El Siglo* the following day, 30 September 1963.

37. PN, radio statement on Kennedy's death, published in *El Siglo* on 1 December 1963.

38. PN, interview in *El Siglo*, Santiago, 12 July 1964.

39. 'Nacimiento' from *Memorial de Isla Negra* (Losada, Buenos Aires, 1964).

40. From 'Delia II', *Memorial de Isla Negra*.

41. Alain Sicard, in his address to the 'Simposio Pablo Neruda', 1975.

42. Giuseppe Bellini, in the introduction to his edition of *Memorial de Isla Negra* (Visor, Madrid, 1994), p. 13.

43. From 'Tú entre los que parecían extraños', *Memorial de Isla Negra*.

44. PN, *Anales de la Universidad de Chile*, No. 129, Santiago, January–March 1964.

45. From *Una casa en la arena* (Lumen, Barcelona, 1966).

46. Robert Pring-Mill, in a note to AF, September 2003.

47. *La Brèche*, Paris, No. 8, November 1965.

48. *Comiendo en Hungría* was published simultaneously in five languages in 1969 by, among others, Editorial Lumen in Barcelona and Editorial Corvina in Budapest.

49. María A. Salgado, 'La confluencia de ajíes y paprika: Hungría en el imaginario de Asturias y Neruda' (The University of North Carolina at Chapel Hill).

13 The other Cuban crisis 1966–68

1. Sergio Insunza, in conversation with AF, Santiago, March 2000.
2. See 'La otra cara de la medalla', in *PEC*, Santiago, No. 76, 10 May 1966.
3. Arthur Miller, in conversation with AF, November 2001.
4. Ibid.
5. Ibid.
6. Arthur Miller, *Timebends: A Life* (Minerva, London, 1990) p. 597.
7. Ibid.
8. Emir Rodríguez Monegal, 'The Boom: A Retrospective', Interview by Alfred J. MacAdam, in *Review*, No. 33, January 1984, pp. 30–34.
9. See *Le Figaro*, Paris, 20 June 1966, and *PEC*, Santiago, 28 June 1966.
10. *Ercilla*, Santiago, 20 July 1966.
11. Marco Antonio Campos, 'Los días terrenales de Revueltas' in *La Jornada Semanal*, Mexico City, 11 June 2000.
12. 'Carta de los Cubanos' *Granma*, Havana, 31 July 1966, reproduced in PN, *Obras completas*, Vol. 5 pp. 1390–1396.
13. Ibid.
14. Edwards, *Adiós, Poeta*, p.149.
15. PN, *El Siglo*, 2 August 1966.
16. From 'A Fidel Castro' in *Canción de gesta*. Translation by AF.
17. In *La Tercera*, Santiago, 17 March 2002.
18. Edwards, *Adiós, Poeta*.
19. From 'Pez en el agua', *Lunes de Revolución*, Havana, No. 88, 26 December 1960.
20. Julio Escámez, 'Testimonio' in *Aurora*, Santiago, Nos 3–4, 1964, pp. 225–226, quoted by Hernán Loyola in his notes to his edition of PN, *Obras completas*, Vol. 3, p. 949.
21. From *Arte de pájaros* (Edición de la Sociedad de Amigos del Arte Contemporáneo, Santiago, 1966).
22. From *Una casa en la arena* (Lumen, Barcelona, 1966).
23. Vera Kuteishikova, in conversation with AF, Moscow, September 2003.
24. As recalled by Lev Ospovat in *América Latina*, Moscow, July 1984, p. 91.
25. Ibid.
26. PN, *Passions and Impressions*, pp. 189–190.
27. *La Vanguardia*, Barcelona, 11 August 2002.
28. Neruda described this early visit to Cádiz in 'Elegía de Cádiz', one of the ten *Cantos ceremoniales* published in 1961.
29. Gabriel García Márquez, *Doce cuentos peregrinos* (Mondadori España, Madrid, 1992). p. 98.
30. Octavio Paz, interviewed in the Mexican newspaper *Excelsior*, 7 December 1990.
31. Robert Pring-Mill, in a note to AF, November 2003.
32. Octavio Paz, *On Poets and Others*, translated by Michael Schmidt (Carcanet, Manchester, 1987), pp 45 and 126.
33. Quoted in Edwards, *Adiós, Poeta*, p. 76.
34. *Ercilla*, Santiago, 4 April 1969.

35. From *La barcarola* (Losada, Buenos Aires, 1967).
36. PN, *Passions and Impressions*, p. 140.
37. Fernando Alegría, 'La Barcarola, barca de la vida', in *Revista Iberoamericana*, Pittsburgh, Nos 82–87, January–June, 1973, pp. 73–98.
38. PN, *Lunes de Revolución*.
39. Pablo Neruda, in a conversation on Radio Magallanes, transcribed in *El Siglo*, Santiago, 6 November 1966.
40. Ibid.
41. Sergio Ortega, interviewed in *La Tercera*, Santiago, 26 July 1998.
42. Ortega, interviewed in *La Montagne*, Clermont-Ferrand, 20 November 2002.
43. Robert Pring-Mill, in a note to AF, December 2003.
44. PN, published in *El Siglo*, Santiago, 10 April 1968
45. PN, in a speech published in *El Siglo*, 28 August 1966.
46. PN, letter to George F. Kennan, 12 March 1968. Reproduced in PN, *Obras Completas*, Vol. 5, pp. 1013–1014.

14 The Nobel Prize – and a last, passionate love 1968–72

1. 'Los soberanos' from *Las manos del día* (Losada, Buenos Aires, 1968).
2. Jaime Alazraki in his address to the 'Simposio Pablo Neruda'.
3. Manuel Durán, introduction to PN, *Late and Posthumous Poems, 1968–1974* (Grove Press, New York, 1988), p. xxii.
4. Raúl Zurita interviewed in *Revista APSI*, 16–29 December 1980, p. 441.
5. PN, interview with *L'Express*, Paris, 13 September 1971.
6. Edwards, *Adiós, Poeta*, p. 183.
7. From '1968' in *Fin de mundo* (Losada, Buenos Aires, 1969).
8. Vera Kuteishikova, in conversation with AF, Moscow, September 2003.
9. From 'Por qué, señor' from *Fin de mundo*.
10. Ibid.
11. Federico Schopf, 'Reception and Context of Pablo Neruda's Poetry' in *Pedro Lastux, la erudición compartida* (Prensa Editora, Mexico City, 1988) pp. 332–372.
12. Loyola, in his notes to PN, *Obras completas*, Vol. 3, p. 980.
13. Quoted by Bellini in 'Viaje al corazón de Neruda', an address given at the conference 'Neruda, con la perspectiva de 25 años', held in Alicante, Spain, March 1999. Published by the *Boletín de la Unidad de Investigación*, University of Alicante, Alicante, December 1999.
14. PN, interview with *Marcha*, Montevideo, 17 September 1971.
15. PN, interview with *Excelsior*, Mexico City, 23 October 1971.
16. Tito Fernández ('El Temucano'), in conversation with AF, London, May 2002.
17. From *Babo el rebelde*. The draft was preserved by Matilde Urrutia and published in *El fin del viaje* (Seix Barral, Barcelona, 1982).
18. Quotes from *Aún* (Nascimento, Santiago, 1969).
19. PN, *Memoirs*, p. 336.
20. PN, *La Segunda*, 3 October 1969.
21. This speech was published in *El Siglo*, Santiago, 1 October 1969.

22. *La Nación.* Ref to come.
23. Aída Figueroa, quoted in Mansilla, 'Vivir con Neruda'.
24. Varas, *Nerudario,* pp. 245–246.
25. Aída Figueroa, quoted in Mansilla, 'Vivir con Neruda'.
26. PN, *Memoirs,* p. 338.
27. Edwards, *Adiós, Poeta,* p. 206.
28. Ibid., pp. 207–208
29. Varas, *Nerudario,* pp. 244–245.
30. PN, speech in Puerto Azul, Venezuela, July 1970.
31. The text was published in a twelve-page booklet called *Soy un poeta de utilidad pública* as an appendix to *Neruda, Valparaíso* (Ediciones de la Universidad, Valparaíso, 1992).
32. Marie Martner, in conversation with AF, Valparaíso, March 2000.
33. Guibert, *Seven Voices,* pp. 3–78.
34. Loyola, in his notes to PN, *Obras completas,* Vol. 3, p. 987.
35. Francisco Velasco, in conversation with AF, Valparaíso, March 2000.
36. From 'El amor' in *La espada encendida* (Losada, Buenos Aires, 1970).
37. From 'Dicen y vivirán' in *La espada encendida.*
38. Francisco Velasco, quoted in *La Tercera,* Santiago, 23 September 2003.
39. Ibid.
40. Robert Pring-Mill, in a note to AF, January 2004.
41. Francisco Velasco, quoted in *La Tercera,* Santiago, 23 September 2003.
42. Ibid.
43. *La Gaceta de Isla de Pascua,* Easter Island, Year 4, No. 7, Summer 1999.
44. PN, in an interview in *Siete Días Ilustrados,* Buenos Aires, No. 200, 15 March 1971.
45. Edwards, *Adiós, Poeta,* p. 296.
46. Aída Figueroa, quoted in Mansilla, 'Vivir con Neruda'.
47. Ibid.
48. Teitelboim, *Neruda,* p. 434.
49. From 'Soneto Florentino', published in PN, *El fin del viaje.*
50. Edwards, *Adiós, Poeta,* pp. 272–273.
51. PN, Interview with *L'Express,* 1971.
52. Edwards, *Adiós, Poeta,* pp. 288–289.
53. Salvador Allende, 'Chile Vive', from Salvador Allende, *1908–1973 Obras Escogidas* (Editoria Crítica, Barcelona, 1989).
54. Virginia Vidal, 'La captura de un condor con cazamariposas' in Carlos Orellana ed. Mansilla, *Los rostros de Neruda* pp. 143–44.
55. Urrutia, *Mi vida junto a Pablo Neruda,* pp. 283–284.
56. PN, *Obras completas,* Vol. 5, p. 332–341.
57. Borges, *Le Monde Diplomatique,* August 2001.
58. Urrutia, *Mi vida junto a Pablo Neruda,* p. 309.
59. Edwards, *Adiós, Poeta,* pp. 251–252.
60. Sara Vial, *Neruda en Valparaíso,* p. 120.
61. In 2000, Volodia Teitelboim was signing copies of one of his books after a recital at Santiago's Biblioteca Nacional to mark the fiftieth anniversary of the first publication of Neruda's *Canto general,* when a woman in the queue announced

her name as Alicia Urrutia. 'I wrote, "With love for Alicia" and she kissed me on the cheek and left. Out of respect for her privacy, I never sought her out again. Physically, she looked just like Matilde.' (*Revista Intramuros*, No. 9, 2002, Santiago).

62. PN, 'Tal vez me espera', included by Matilde Urrutia in *El fin del viaje*.
63. 'No sé como me llamo' from *Geografía infructuosa* (Losada, Buenos Aires, 1972).
64. Vera Kuteishikova, in conversation with AF, Moscow, September 2003.
65. Quoted in Edwards, *Adiós poeta*, p. 273.
66. Ibid., p. 275.
67. Fernando Alegría, 'Neruda: Reflexiones y reminiscencias', an address given to the 'Simposio Pablo Neruda'.
68. Ibid.
69. The text of this speech was reproduced in *AuCh*, Santiago, 1971.
70. Ibid.
71. Alegría, 'Neruda: Reflexiones y reminiscencias'.
72. Poli Délano, 'Neruda: caracolas y elegías', *La Tercera*, Santiago, 27 September 2003.
73. PN, 19 September 1972, reproduced on La Jota's website: http://cipres.cec.uchile.cl/jjcc/jota/index-jota.html.

15 The final years – and a posthumous gift 1972–3

1. Aída Figueroa, quoted in Mansilla, 'Vivir con Neruda'.
2. Quoted in *La Tercera*, Santiago, September 2003, special Internet edition marking the thirtieth anniversary of Neruda's death. http://docs.tercera.cl/especiales/2003/30aniosneruda/obra/cartaedwards.htm.
3. Ibid.
4. In 1970 ITT owned 70 per cent of Chilteco, the Compañía de Teléfonos de Chile.
5. Robert Pring-Mill, 'Neruda and the Co-ordinates of the Poetry of Compromise' in *Nerudiana*, published by the Istituto di Lingue e Letterature Romanze, University of Sassari, Sardinia, 1995
6. From 'Peremptory Explanation', the prologue to Neruda's *Incitacíon al nixonicidio y alabanza de la revolucíon chilena* (Editora Quimantú, Santiago, 1973).
7. Quoted in Pring-Mill, 'Neruda and the Co-ordinates of the Poetry of Compromise'.
8. Ibid.
9. Letter dated 21 November 1929 PN, *Pablo Neruda, Héctor Eandi, Correspondencia*, p. 60.
10. Guibert, *Seven Voices*, pp. 37–8.
11. Quoted in Pring-Mill, 'Neruda and the Co-ordinates of the Poetry of Compromise'.
12. 'El incompetente' from *Defectos escogidos* (Losada, Buenos Aires, 1974).
13. Urrutia, *Mi vida junto a Pablo Neruda*, p. 249.
14. Ibid., p. 240.
15. Orellana, *Los rostros de Neruda*, p. 180.
16. Sergio Insunza, quoted in Mansilla, 'Vivir con Neruda'

17. Aída Figueroa, ibid.
18. Ibid.
19. José Miguel Varas, quoted in *Qué Pasa*, Santiago, 3 January 2000.
20. Matilde Urrutia, quoted in *Simposio Pablo Neruda*, p. 77.
21. Luis Sainz de Medrano, in his address to the conference 'Neruda, con la perspectiva de 25 años'.
22. From 'Los hombres' in *2000* (Losada, Buenos Aires, 1974).
23. Selena Millares, in her address to the conference 'Neruda, con la perspectiva de 25 años', Alicante, 1999. (Published in the *Boletín de la Unidad de Investigación*, University of Alicante, Alicante, December 1999).
24. The final lines of 'Celebración', the concluding section of 2000.
25. Section XVII from *Elegía* (Losada, Buenos Aires, 1974).
26. From 'Sin embargo me muevo' in *El corazón amarillo* (Losada, Buenos Aires, 1974).
27. Allende, *Paula*, pp. 180–182.
28. Osvaldo Rodríguez, *La poesía póstuma de Pablo Neruda* (Editorial Hispanoamérica, Gaithesburg, MD, 1995), p. 63.
29. From *Jardín de invierno* (Losada, Buenos Aires, 1974).
30. Ignacio Valente, 'Neruda's *Jardín de invierno*,' in *El Mercurio*, Santiago, 30 November 1980.
31. Aída Figueroa, in conversation with AF, Santiago, April 2000.
32. PN, *Memoirs*, pp. 97–98.
33. Sara Vial, in conversation with AF, Viña del Mar, Chile, April 2000.
34. Aída Figueroa, quoted in Mansilla, 'Vivir con Neruda'.
35. Humberto Díaz Casanueva, 'En el aniversario de la muerte de Pablo Neruda', a speech reproduced in *Casa de las Américas* XXIV, No. 144, May–June 1984, pp. 154–158.
36. Sergio Insunza, quoted in Mansilla, 'Vivir con Neruda'.
37. From *Libro de las preguntas* (Losada, Buenos Aires, 1974).
38. See Christopher Perriam, *The Late Poetry of Pablo Neruda* (Dolphin, Oxford, 1989).
39. Christopher Perriam, *The Late Poetry of Pablo Neruda: Some Patterns of Time, Place and Memory in the Creative Imagination* (D. Phil., Christ Church, 1985).
40. Luis Alberto Mansilla, 'Los últimos días' in *Anales de la Universidad de Chile Sexta Serie*, Santiago, No. 10, December 1999.
41. Varas, *Nerudario*, p. 247.
42. Ibid.
43. Sergio Insunza, quoted in Mansilla, 'Vivir con Neruda'.
44. Urrutia, *Mi vida junto a Pablo Neruda*, p. 10.
45. PN, *Memoirs*, pp. 348–350.
46. Aída Figueroa, quoted in Mansilla, 'Vivir con Neruda'.
47. Urrutia, *Mi vida junto a Pablo Neruda*, pp. 14–15.
48. PN, 'Tres Hombres', reproduced for the first time in *El Proceso*, Mexico City, on 9 September 1978.
49. Urrutia, *Mi vida junto a Pablo Neruda*, pp. 15–16.
50. Aída Figueroa, quoted in Mansilla, 'Vivir con Neruda'.

51. Hernán Loyola, *Ser y morir en Pablo Neruda*, Actas del Quinto Congreso, AIH, Bordeaux, 1974.
52. Ibid.
53. Aída Figueroa, quoted in Mansilla, 'Vivir con Neruda'.
54. Loyola, *Ser y morir en Pablo Neruda*.
55. Ibid.
56. Urrutia, *Mi vida junto a Pablo Neruda*, p. 29.
57. Roser Bru, in conversation with AF, Santiago, March 2000.
58. Recounted by Francisco Velasco in his book, *Neruda, el gran amigo* (Galinost-Andante, Santiago, 1987), p. 133.
59. Hernán Loyola, speaking during a round-table discussion at the conference, 'Neruda, con la perspectiva de 25 años', Alicante, 1999 (Published in the *Boletín de la Unidad de Investigación*, University of Alicante, Alicante, December 1999).

Select Bibliography

Principal works by Pablo Neruda

Obras completas, Galaxia Gutenberg, Círculo de Lectores, Barcelona, 1999–2001. This remarkable five-volume collection of Neruda's complete works – including his speeches and letters – is edited and annotated by the great Chilean Neruda scholar, Hernán Loyola, and is indispensable reading.

Earlier (and far less comprehensive) editions of the complete works were published by Losada, Buenos Aires, in 1957, 1962, 1968 and 1973.

For a full bibliography of books and articles about Neruda, though only up to 1988, the 600-page *Pablo Neruda: An Annotated Bibliography of Biographical and Critical Studies*, by Hensley C. Woodbridge and David S. Zubatsky (Garland Publishing, New York and London, 1988), is highly recommended.

The journal of the Fundación Pablo Neruda, *Cuadernos*, regularly contains many interesting articles by Neruda specialists and acquaintances.

Crepusculario, Editorial Claridad, Santiago, 1923; Nascimento, Santiago, 1926

Veinte poemas de amor y una canción desesperada, Nascimento, Santiago, 1924

By 1961, a million copies of this collection had been published around the world in numerous editions.

Tentativa del hombre infinito, Nascimento, Santiago, 1926

El habitante y su esperanza, Nascimento, Santiago, 1926

Anillos, (in collaboration with Tomás Lago) Nascimento, Santiago, 1926

El hondero entusiasta, Empresa Letras, Santiago, 1933

Residencia en la tierra 1925–1931, Nascimento, Santiago, 1933

Residencia en la tierra 1. 1925–1931; 2. 1931–1935, Ediciones del Arbol (Cruz y Raya), Madrid, 1935

España en el corazón, Ercilla, Santiago, 1937

Tercera residencia, 1935–1945, Losada, Buenos Aires, 1947

Alturas de Macchu Picchu, Ediciones Librería Neira, Santiago, 1948

Canto general, Imprenta Talleres Gráficos de la Nación, Mexico City, March 1950; Clandestine edition of the Chilean Communist Party, Santiago, April 1950

Los versos del capitán, Anonymous, Imprenta L'Arte Tipografica, Naples, 1952
Las uvas y el viento, Nascimento, Santiago, 1954
Odas elementales, Losada, Buenos Aires, 1954
Viajes, Nascimento, Santiago, 1955
Nuevas odas elementales, Losada, Buenos Aires, 1956
Tercer libro de las odas, Losada, Buenos Aires, 1957
Estravagario, Losada, Buenos Aires, 1958
Navegaciones y regresos, Losada, Buenos Aires, 1959
Cien sonetos de amor, Prensa de la Editorial Universitaria, Santiago, 1959; Losada, Buenos Aires, 1960
Canción de gesta, Imprenta Nacional de Cuba, Havana, 1960; Austral, Santiago de Chile, 1961
Las piedras de Chile, Losada, Buenos Aires, 1961
Cantos ceremoniales, Losada, Buenos Aires, 1961
Plenos poderes, Losada, Buenos Aires, 1962
Memorial de Isla Negra, Losada, Buenos Aires, 1964
Romeo and Juliet, translation by Neruda, 1964
Arte de pájaros, Edición de la Sociedad de Amigos del Arte Contemporáneo, Santiago, 1966
Una casa en la arena, Lumen, Barcelona, 1966
La barcarola, Losada, Buenos Aires, 1967
Fulgor y muerte de Joaquín Murieta, bandido chileno injusticiado en California el 13 de julio de 1853, Empresa Editora Zig-Zag, Santiago, 1967
Las manos del día, Losada, Buenos Aires, 1968
Comiendo en Hungría, Corvina, Budapest; Editorial Lumen, Barcelona, 1969
Fin de mundo, Sociedad de Arte Contemporáneo, Santiago, 1969; Losada, Buenos Aires, 1969
Aún, Nascimento, Santiago, 1969
Maremoto, Sociedad de Arte Contemporáneo, Santiago, 1970
La espada encendida, Losada, Buenos Aires, 1970
Las piedras del cielo, Losada, Buenos Aires, 1970
Geografía infructuosa, Losada, Buenos Aires, 1972
La rosa separada, Editions du Dragon, Paris, 1972; Losada, Buenos Aires, 1973
Incitación al nixonicidio y alabanza de la revolución chilena, Editora Quimantú, Santiago, 1973; Grijalbo, Lima, 1973
El mar y las campanas, Losada, Buenos Aires, 1973
2000, Losada, Buenos Aires, 1974
Elegía, Losada, Buenos Aires, 1974
El corazón amarillo, Losada, Buenos Aires, 1974
Jardín de invierno, Losada, Buenos Aires, 1974
Libro de las preguntas, Losada, Buenos Aires, 1974
Defectos escogidos, Losada, Buenos Aires, 1974
Confieso que he vivido, 1974. Neruda's memoirs, translated by Hardie St Martin as *Memoirs*, Souvenir Press, London, 1977; Farrar, Straus and Giroux, New York, 1977
Para nacer he nacido, a posthumous collection of miscellaneous Neruda texts, edited by Matilde Urrutia and Miguel Otero Silva, Planeta, Santiago, 1978; translated by

Margaret Sayers Peden as *Passions and Impressions* and published by Farrar, Straus and Giroux, New York, 1983

El río invisible, another posthumous collection of miscellaneous Neruda texts, Seix Barral, Barcelona, 1980

El fin del viaje, by Pablo Neruda and Federico García Lorca, Seix Barral, Barcelona, 1982

Cuadernos de Temuco, Seix Barral, Barcelona, 1996

Oda a las flores de Datitla, Corporación Sintesys, Santiago, 2002

Other works

Achugar, Hugo *Falsas Memorias*, LOM Ediciones, Santiago de Chile, 2000

Agosín, Marjorie *Nuevas aproximaciones a Pablo Neruda*, Fondo de Cultura Económica, Mexico City, 1987

Agosín, Marjorie *Pablo Neruda*, Twayne, Boston, 1986

Aguayo, Rafael *Neruda, un hombre de la Araucania*, Ediciones Literatura Americana Reunida, Concepción, 1987

Aguirre, Margarita *Las vidas de Pablo Neruda*, Editorial Zig-Zag, Santiago, 1967

Aguirre, Margarita *Genio y figura de Pablo Neruda*, Editorial Universitaria de Buenos Aires, Buenos Aires, 1967

Alegría, Fernando *Revista Iberoamericana*, Pittsburgh, 1973

Alazraki, Jaime *Poética y poesía de Pablo Neruda*, Las Américas Publishing Co., New York, 1965

Alberti, Rafael ed., *Pablo Neruda: Antología poética*, Espasa-Calpe, Madrid, 1981

Aldunate Phillips, Arturo *El nuevo arte poético y Pablo Neruda*, Nascimento, Santiago, 1936

Allende, Isabel *Paula*, Flamingo, London, 1996

Allende, Salvador *1970–1973 Obras escogidas*, Editoria Crítica, Barcelona, 1989

Alone (Hernán Díaz Arrieta) *Los cuatro grandes de la literatura chilena*, Zig-Zag, Santiago, 1962

Alonso, Amado *Poesía y estilo de Pablo Neruda*, Losada, Buenos Aires, 1940

Anguita, Eduardo, and Volodia Teitelboim *Antología de la poesía chilena*, Santiago, 1935

Arce, Homero *Los libros y los viajes – Recuerdos de Pablo Neruda*, Nascimento, Santiago, 1976

Arrué, Laura *Ventana del recuerdo*, Nascimento, Santiago, 1992

Beckett, Bonnie A. *The Reception of Pablo Neruda's Works in the German Democratic Republic*, Grove/Atlantic, New York, 1981

Bellini, Giuseppe *Introduzzione a Neruda*, Goliardica, Milan, 1966

Bellini, Giuseppe *La poesia di Pablo Neruda da Estravagario a Memorial de Isla Negra*, Liviana Editrice, Padova, 1966

Bethell, Leslie ed. *Chile Since Independence*, Cambridge University Press, Cambridge, 1993

Bizzarro, Salvatore *Pablo Neruda: All Poets the Poet*, Scarecrow Press, Metuchen, NJ, 1969

Bombal, María Luisa *Obras completas*, ed. Lucía Guerra, Editorial Andrés Bello, Santiago, 1996

Breton, André, and Louis Aragon *Surrealismo frente a realismo socialista*, ed. Oscar Tusquets, Tusquets, Barcelona, 1973

Brotherston, Gordon *Latin American Poetry: Origins and Presence*, Cambridge University Press, Cambridge, 1975

Cardona Peña, Alfredo *Pablo Neruda y otros ensayos*, Editorial De Andrea, Mexico City, 1955

Cerio, Claretta *Ex libris: Incontri a Capri con uomini e libri*, Edizioni La Conchiglia, Capri, 1999

Chisholm, Anne *Nancy Cunard*, Sidgwick & Jackson, London, 1979

Cirillo Sirri, Teresa *Capri: Una tappa poetica di Neruda*, L'Orientale Editrice, Napoli, 2000

Concha, Jaime *Neruda (1904–1936)*, Editorial Universitaria, Santiago, 1972

Concha, Jaime *Tres ensayos sobre Pablo Neruda*, University of South Carolina Press, Columbia, SC, 1974

Cortés, Raúl Arreola *Pablo Neruda en Morelia*, Ediciones Casa de San Nicolás, Morelia, Michoacán, 1972

de Costa, René *The Poetry of Pablo Neruda*, Harvard University Press, Cambridge, MA, 1979

Cousté, Alberto *Neruda: El autor y su obra*, Ediciones Barcanova, Barcelona, 1981

Délano, Luis Enrique *Sobre todo Madrid*, Editorial Universitaria, Santiago, 1970

Délano, Luis Enrique and Edmundo Palacios, eds *Antología de la poesía social de Chile*, Austral, Santiago, 1964

Durán, Manuel, and Margery Safir *Earth Tones: The Poetry of Pablo Neruda*, Indiana University Press, Bloomington, IN, 1981

Edwards, Jorge *Persona non grata*, Seix Barral, Barcelona, 1974

Edwards, Jorge *Adiós, Poeta*, Tusquets, Barcelona, 1990

Facio, Sara *Pablo Neruda–Sara Facio*, La Azotea, Paraguay, 1988

Fernández Larraín, Sergio *Cartas de amor de Pablo Neruda*, Rodas, Madrid, 1975

Ferrer Mir, Jaime *Los españoles del Winnipeg – El barco de la esperanza*, Ediciones Cal Sogas, Santiago, 1989

Ferrero, Mario *Neruda, voz y universo*, Ediciones Logos, Santiago, 1988

Figueroa de Insunza, Aída *A la mesa con Neruda*, Fundación Pablo Neruda, Santiago / Grijalbo Mondadori, Barcelona 2000

Flores, Angel *Aproximaciones a Pablo Neruda*, Ocnos/Libros de Sinera, Barcelona, 1974

Franco, Jean *Introduction to Spanish-American Literature*, 3rd ed., Cambridge University Press, Cambridge, 1994

Franco, Jean *The Decline and Fall of the Lettered City: Latin America in the Cold War*, Harvard University Press, Cambridge, MA, 2002

Furci, Carmelo *The Chilean Communist Party and the Road to Socialism*, Zed Books, London, 1984

Gabriel, González Videla *Memorias*, Editorial Gabriela Mistral, Santiago, 1975

Gálvez Barraza, Julio, *Neruda y España*, Ril Editores, Santiago, 2003
García Lorca, Federico, et al *Homenaje a Pablo Neruda*, Plutarco, Madrid, 1935
Gatell, Angelina *Neruda*, Editorial Espesa, Madrid, 1971
Gibson, Ian, *Federico García Lorca: A Life*, Faber, London, 1989
Glad, John ed. *Literature in Exile*, Duke University Press, Durham and London, 1990
González-Cruz, Luis F. *Pablo Neruda y el Memorial de Isla Negra*, Ediciones Universal, Miami, 1972
González Vera, José Santos *Cuando era muchacho*, Nascimento, Santiago, 1951
Goodnough, David *Pablo Neruda, Nobel Prize-winning Poet*, Enslow Publishers, Berkeley Heights, NJ, 1998
Gottlieb, Marlene ed. *Pablo Neruda and Nicanor Parra: A bilingual and critical edition of their speeches on the occasion of Neruda's appointment to the faculty of the University of Chile*, Edwin Mellen Press, Lewiston, NY, 1997
Guibert, Rita *Seven Voices: Seven Latin American Writers*, Knopf, New York, 1973
Gunther, John *Inside Latin America*, Hamish Hamilton, London, 1942
Heym, Stefan *Nachruf*, Bertelsmann, Munich, 1988
Hobsbawm, Eric *Interesting Times – A Twentieth-Century Life*, Allen Lane, London, 2002
Jiménez, Juan Ramón *Españoles de tres mundos*, Losada, Buenos Aires, 1942
Jiménez, Juan Ramón *Guerra en España 1936–1953*, Seix Barral, Barcelona, 1985
Lacouture, Jean *André Malraux – Une vie dans le siècle*, Editions Seuil, Paris, 1973
Lafourcade, Enrique *Neruda en el país de las maravillas*, Editorial Norma, Bogotá, Colombia, 1984
Lago, Tomás *Ojos y oídos – Cerca de Neruda*, LOM Ediciones, Santiago, 1999
de Lellis, Mario Jorge *Pablo Neruda*, La Mandrágora, Buenos Aires, 1957
Léon, María Teresa, *Memoria de la melancolía*, Castalia, Madrid, 1998
Lévy, Isaac Jack, and Juan Loveluck, eds, *Simposio Pablo Neruda*, University of South Carolina Press, Columbia, SC, 1975
Loyola, Hernán *Ser y morir en Pablo Neruda 1918–1945*, Editora Santiago, Santiago, 1967
Loyola Hernán *Introducción, notas y apéndices a Pablo Neruda, Residencia en la tierra*, Edición crítica, Ediciones Cátedra, Madrid, 1994
Lozada, Alfredo *El monismo agónico de Pablo Neruda*, Costa-Amic, Mexico City, 1971
Lundkvist, Artur *Elegi för Pablo Neruda*, Bonniers, Stockholm, 1975
Maluenda, María *Neruda y Arauco*, Ediciones ChileAmérica CESOC, Santiago, 1998
Marcenac, Jean *Pablo Neruda*, Seghers, Paris, 1954
Márquez, Gabriel García *Doce cuentos peregrinos*, Mondadori España, Madrid, 1992
Melis, Antonio *Neruda*, Castoro, Florence, 1970
Méndez-Ramírez, Hugo *Neruda's Ekphrastic Experience: Mural Art and Canto General*, Bucknell University Press, Lewisburg, NJ, 1999
Miller, Arthur *Timebends: A Life*, Minerva, London, 1990
Montes, Hugo *Para leer a Neruda*, Ediciones Universidad Nacional Andrés Bello, Santiago, 1974

Morla Lynch, Carlos *En España con Federico García Lorca*, Ediciones Aguilar, Madrid, 1957

Muñoz, Diego *Memorias: Recuerdos de la bohemia nerudiana*, Mosquito Editores, Santiago, 1999

Neruda, Pablo *Poesía política (discursos políticos) de Pablo Neruda*, ed. Margarita Aguirre, Editora Austral, Santiago, 1953

Neruda, Pablo *Pablo Neruda, Héctor Eandi, Correspondencia durante Residencia en la tierra*, ed. Margarita Aguirre, Sudamericana, Buenos Aires, 1980

Neruda, Pablo *Cartas a Laura*, ed. Hugo Montes, Ediciones Cultura Hispánica del Centro Iberoamericano de Cooperación, Madrid, 1978

Neruda, Pablo *Para Albertina Rosa*, ed. Francisco Cruchaga Azócar, Editorial South Pacific Press, Santiago de Chile, 1992

Neruda, Pablo *Discursos parlamentarios de Pablo Neruda (1945–48)*, Editorial Antártica, Santiago, 1997, ed. Leonidas Aguirre Silva

Niedergang, Marcel *The Twenty Latin Americas*, Pelican Books, London, 1971

Nolan, James *Poet-Chief: The Native American Poetics of Walt Whitman and Pablo Neruda*, University of New Mexico Press, Albuquerque, 1994

Olivares Briones, Edmundo *Pablo Neruda: Los caminos de Oriente, Tras las huellas del poeta itinerante 1927–1933* LOM Ediciones, Santiago, 2000

Orellana, Carlos ed. *Los rostros de Neruda, el poeta, el hombre*, Planeta, Santiago, 1998

Osorio, Nelson and Fernando Moreno *Claves de Pablo Neruda*, Ediciones Universitarias de Valparaíso, Valparaíso, 1971

Osses, Mario *Trinidad poética de Chile: Angel Cruchaga Santa María, Gabriela Mistral y Pablo Neruda*, Universidad de Chile, Santiago, 1947

Paseyro, Ricardo, et al *Mito y verdad de Pablo Neruda*, Ediciones Universitarias de Valparaíso, Valparaíso, 1971

Paz, Octavio *Laurel*, Seneca, Mexico, 1941

Paz, Octavio *Primeras letras 1931–1943*, Vuelta, Mexico City, 1988

Paz, Octavio *Convergencias*, Seix Barral, Barcelona, 1991

Paz, Octavio *On Poets and Others*, translated by Michael Schmidt, Carcanet, Manchester, 1987

Perriam, Christopher *The Late Poetry of Pablo Neruda: Some Patterns of Time, Place and Memory in the Creative Imagination* (D. Phil., Christ Church, 1985)

Perriam, Christopher *The Late Poetry of Pablo Neruda*, Dolphin, Oxford, 1989

Poirot, Luis, and Alastair Reid, *Pablo Neruda: Absence and Presence*, Farrar, Straus and Giroux, New York, 1990

Pring-Mill, Robert ed. *Pablo Neruda: A Basic Anthology*, Dolphin, Oxford, 1975

Pring-Mill, Robert ed. *A Poet for All Seasons* (Catalogue for International Symposium on Pablo Neruda), Universities of Oxford and Warwick, 12–26 November 1993)

Qing, Ai *Selected Poems of Ai Qing*, People's Literature Publishing House, Beijing, 1996

Reyes, Bernardo *Neruda – retrato de familia, 1904–1920*, Editorial de la Universidad de Puerto Rico, San Juan, 1996

Riess, Frank *The Word and the Stone: Language and Imagery in Neruda's Canto General*, Oxford University Press, Oxford, 1972

Rivero, Eliana *El gran amor de Pablo Neruda*, Plaza Mayor, Madrid, 1971

Rodman, Selden *South America of the Poets*, New Directions, New York, 1970

Rodríguez, Osvaldo *La poesía póstuma de Pablo Neruda*, Editorial Hispanoamérica, Gaithesburg, MD, 1995

Rodríguez Monegal, Emir *Neruda: El viajero inmóvil*, Losada, Buenos Aires, 1966

de Rokha, Pablo *Neruda y yo*, Multitud, Santiago, 1955

Rosales, Luis *La poesía de Neruda*, Editoria Nacional, Madrid, 1978

Sáez, Fernando *Todo debe ser demasiado, Vida de Delia del Carril*, Sudamericana, Santiago, 1997

Salama, Roberto *Para una crítica a Pablo Neruda*, Editorial Cartago, Buenos Aires, 1957

Santí, Enrico Mario *Pablo Neruda: The Poetics of Prophesy*, Cornell University Press, Ithaca, NY, 1982

Santí, Enrico Mario *El acto de las palabras: Estudios y diálogos con Octavio Paz*, Fondo de Cultura Económica, Mexico City, 1997

Sicard, Alain *La pensée poétique de Pablo Neruda*, Université de Lille, Lille, 1977

Sicard, Alain ed. *Coloquio internacional sobre Pablo Neruda (la obra posterior a Canto general)*, Centre de Recherches Latino-américaines, Université de Poitiers, Poitiers, 1979

Siefer, Elisabeth *Epische Stilemente im Canto general*, Wilhelm Fink, Munich, 1970

Silva Castro, Raúl *Pablo Neruda*, Editorial Universitaria, Santiago, 1964

Skármeta, Antonio *El cartero de Neruda (Ardiente Paciencia)*, Sudamericana, Buenos Aires, 1999

Stainton, Leslie *Lorca: A Dream of Life*, Bloomsbury, London, 1998

Stavans, Ilan *The Poetry of Pablo Neruda*, Farrar, Straus and Giroux, New York, 2003

Steiner, George *Language and Silence*, Pelican Books, London, 1969

Stonor Saunders, Frances *Who Paid the Piper? The CIA and the Cultural Cold War*, Granta Books, London, 1999

Suárez, Eulogio *Neruda total*, Ediciones Systhema, Santiago, 1991

Szmulewicz, Efraín *Pablo Neruda: biografía emotiva*, Editorial J. Almendros-Orbe, Santiago, 1975

Teitelboim, Volodia *Neruda*, translated by Beverley J. DeLong-Tonelli, University of Texas Press, Austin, TX, 1991

Teitelboim, Volodia *Voy a vivirme: Variaciones y complementos nerudianos*, Ediciones Dolmen, Santiago, 1998

Thomas, Hugh *The Spanish Civil War*, 3rd ed., Pelican Books, Harmondsworth, 1977

Tichonov, Nikolai, et al *Pablo Neruda: Poeta y combatiente*, Soviet Academy of Sciences, Moscow, 1974

Urrutia, Matilde *Mi vida junto a Pablo Neruda*, Seix Barral, Barcelona, 1986

Varas, José Miguel *Nerudario*, Planeta, Santiago, 1999

Varas, José Miguel *Neruda clandestino*, Editorial Alfaguara, Santiago, 2003

Velasco, Francisco *Neruda, el gran amigo*, Galinost-Andante, Santiago, 1987

Vial, Sara *Neruda en Valparaíso*, Ediciones Universitarias de Valparaíso, Valparaíso, 1983

Wilson, Jason *Octavio Paz*, Twayne, Boston, MA, 1986

Yevtushenko, Yevgeny *A Precocious Autobiography*, Penguin Books, London, 1965

Yurkiévich, Saúl *Fundadores de la nueva poesia hispanoamericana*, Seix Barral, Barcelona, 1971

Selected essays

Aguirre, Margarita 'La presentación de *Poesía política*', *El Siglo*, Santiago, 19 August 1953

Aguirre, Margarita 'Neruda y Margarita Aguirre – Conversaciones en Isla Negra', *Ercilla*, Santiago, 8 August 1973, pp. 34–38

Alazraki, Jaime 'Observaciones sobre la estructura de la oda elemental' in *Mester* (UCLA) IV, No. 2, April 1974

Alberti, Rafael 'De mon amitié avec Pablo Neruda', *Europe*, Paris, Nos 419–420, March–April 1964, pp. 71–75

Alegría, Fernando 'Two Worlds in Conflict', *Berkeley Review*, Berkeley, CA, Vol. 1, 1957, pp. 27–41

Aligher, Margarita 'Don Pablo at Home', *Soviet Literature*, Moscow, No. 11, 1977, pp. 88–100

Alone (Hernán Díaz Arrieta) 'Veinte poemas de amor y una canción desesperada', *La Nación*, Santiago, 3 August 1924

Alone (Hernán Díaz Arrieta) 'Tentativa del hombre infinito por Pablo Neruda', *La Nación*, Santiago, 10 January 1926

Alone (Hernán Díaz Arrieta) 'Critica literaria: Veinte poemas por Pablo Neruda', in *La Nación*, Santiago, 18 September 1932

Alone (Hernán Díaz Arrieta) 'Nuevo canto de amor a Stalingrado, por Pablo Neruda', *El Mercurio*, Santiago, 4 July 1943

Alone (Hernán Díaz Arrieta) 'El peligro que representa Pablo Neruda', *Zig-Zag*, Santiago, 24 July 1954

Alone (Hernán Díaz Arrieta) 'Pablo Neruda y Gabriela Mistral', *El Mercurio*, Santiago, 12 September 1954

Alone (Hernán Díaz Arrieta) 'Muerte y transfiguración de Pablo Neruda', *El Mercurio*, 30 January 1955

Alone (Hernán Díaz Arrieta) 'Estravagario, por Pablo Neruda', *El Mercurio*, 21 December 1958

Alone (Hernán Díaz Arrieta) 'Pablo de Rokha y Pablo Neruda', *El Mercurio*, 28 March 1964

Alonso, Amado 'Algunos símbolos insistentes en la poesía de Pablo Neruda', *Revista Hispánica Moderna*, Columbia University, NY, July 1939, pp. 191–220

Alonso, Amado 'La poesía de Pablo Neruda', *La Nación*, Buenos Aires, 5 November 1939

Amado, Jorge 'En veillant le poète du peuple', *Europe*, Paris, January–February 1974, pp. 31–33

Asturias, Miguel Angel 'Un mano a mano de Nobel a Nobel', *Revista Ibero-americana*, Pittsburgh, PA, Nos 82–83, January–June 1973, pp. 15–20

Bellet, Jorge 'Cruzando la cordillera con el poeta', *Araucaria*, Santiago, Nos 47–48, 1990

Bellitt, Ben 'Pablo Neruda and the gigantesque opinion', *Poetry*, Chicago, 1952

Bellitt, Ben 'The Burning Sarcophagus: A Re-evaluation of Pablo Neruda', *Southern Review*, Baton Rouge, LA, Summer, July 1968

Benedetti, Mario 'Vallejo y Neruda: dos modos de influir', *Casa de las Américas*, Havana, No. 7, July–August 1967, pp. 91–93

Bianchi, Manuel 'Pablo Neruda', *La Nación*, Santiago, 15 December 1946

Bly, Roger 'Pablo Neruda: An Interview' *Book Week*, New York, 14 August 1966

del Campo, Santiago 'Neruda está en Macchu Picchu', *Pro Arte*, Santiago, No. 17, 4 November 1948

Camurati, Mireya 'Significación del *Canto general* en la obra de Pablo Neruda', *Revista Iberoamericana*, Pittsburgh, PA, Summer 1972

Cantón, Wilberto 'Pablo Neruda en México (1940–1943)', *Anales de la Universidad de Chile*, Santiago, Nos 157–160, January–December 1971, pp. 263–269

Cardona Peña, Alfredo 'Pablo Neruda: Breve historia de sus libros', *Cuadernos Americanos*, Mexico City, No. 6, December 1950, pp. 257–289

Celaya, Gabriel 'El Poeta del Tercer Día de la Creación', *Revista de Occidente*, Madrid, No. 36, 1972

Chocano, José Santos 'Panorama lírico: a través de un recital poético', *La Prensa*, Buenos Aires, 12 March 1933

Coloane, Francisco 'Neruda y el mar', *Antártica*, Santiago, No. 4, December 1944

Coloane, Francisco 'Neruda como voz del cosmos', *Pro Arte*, Santiago, No. 95, 15 June 1950

Concha, Jaime 'Interpretación de *Residencia en la tierra*', *Mapocho*, Santiago, No. 2, July 1963, pp. 5–39

Concha, Jaime 'Los origines (la primera infancia de Neruda)', *Revista Iberoamericana*, Pittsburgh, PA, No. 72, July–September 1970, pp. 389–406

Concha, Jaime 'Neruda desde 1952; Nunca entendía lucha sino para que este termine', *Texto Critico*, Santiago, Nos 22–23, 1981

Concha, Jaime 'Sexo y pobreza', *Revista Iberoamericana*, Pittsburgh, PA, Nos 82–83, January–June 1973, pp. 135–157

Cortázar, Julio 'Carta abierta a Pablo Neruda', *Revista Iberoamericana*, Pittsburgh, PA, Nos 82–83, January–June 1973, pp. 21–26

Cortínez, Carlos 'Fidelidad de Neruda a su visión residenciaria' in *Fantasía y realismo mágico en Iberoaméricana*, Michigan State University, Lansing, 1975, pp. 177–283

Cruchaga, Angel Santa María '*España en el corazón* de Pablo Neruda es una obra de pólvora, sollozo y angustia', *Ercilla*, Santiago, No. 139, 1937

Délano, Luis Enrique 'Regreso de Neruda', *El Mercurio*, Santiago, 15 May 1932

Délano, Luis Enrique 'Metamórfosis de Pablo Neruda', *Aurora de Chile*, Santiago, No. 11, 1939

Délano, Poli 'Nerudeando con nostalgia', *Cuadernos*, Fundación Pablo Neruda, Santiago, Vol. 10, No. 39, 1999

Delogu, Ignazio 'Un inédito italiano de Neruda', *Nerudiana*, Istituto di Lingue e Letterature Romane dell'Università di Sassari, 1995

Díaz, Ramón 'Pasos entre las dos *Residencias* de Neruda', *Papeles de Son Armadans*, No. 54, 1969, pp. 229–242

Dussuel, Francisco '*Las uvas y el viento*, por Pablo Neruda', *El Diario Ilustrado*, Santiago, 21 March 1954

Dussuel, Francisco '*Odas elementales* de Pablo Neruda', *El Diario Ilustrado*, Santiago, 27 February 1955

Dussuel, Francisco 'Neruda y Stalin', *El Diario Ilustrado*, Santiago, 25 March 1956

Dussuel, Francisco '*Estravagario* de Pablo Neruda', *El Diario Ilustrado*, Santiago, 2 November 1958

Ehrenburg, Ilya 'Carta abierta ... a Pablo Neruda', *La Literatura Internacional*, Moscow, No. 6, 1942, pp. 29–31

Ehrenburg, Ilya 'La poesía de Pablo Neruda', in *Poesía Política*, Austral, Santiago, 1953, pp. 11–14

Ehrenburg, Ilya '7 días en Chile', *El Siglo*, Santiago, 26 September 1954

Elliot, Jorge 'Pablo Neruda', *Andean Quarterly*, Santiago, Christmas, 1944, pp. 5–21

Escorel, Lauro 'Poesía de Pablo Neruda', *O Estado de São Paulo*, São Paulo, 26 August 1943, pp. 4–5

Eshleman, Clayton 'Neruda: An Elemental Response', *Tri-Quarterly*, Evanston, IL, No. 15, 1969, pp. 228–237

Fast, Howard 'Neruda en el Congreso Mundial para la Paz', *Pro Arte*, Santiago, No. 48, 9 June 1949

Felstiner, John 'Neruda in Translation', *Yale Review*, New Haven, CT, Winter 1972, pp. 226–251

Ferrero, Mario 'Como nació *Las uvas y el viento* de Pablo Neruda', *El Siglo*, Santiago, 14 March 1954

Figueroa, Aída 'Delia y Matilde', *Los rostros de Neruda*, Carlos Orellana ed., Planeta, Santiago, 1998, pp. 61–62

Finlayson, Clarence 'Paisaje en Neruda', *Atenea*, Santiago, No. 160, October 1938, pp. 47–60

Franulic, Lenka 'Neruda', *Ercilla*, Santiago, 29 May 1945

Franulic, Lenka 'Cuatro años después llegó un nuevo Neruda', *Ercilla*, Santiago, 19 August 1952

Fuenzalida, Hector 'Odas elementales', *Anales de la Universidad de Chile*, Santiago, No. 100, 1955, pp. 172–175

Giordano, Jaime 'Introducción al *Canto general*', *Mapocho*, Santiago, No. 2, 1964, pp. 210–216

Gómez de la Serna, Ramón 'Neruda, grandísimo poeta', *Saber Vivir*, Buenos Aires, No. 37, August–September, 1943

Gómez Paz, Julieta 'Pablo Neruda, poeta realista', *Negro Sobre Blanco*, Buenos Aires, No. 2, June 1956

González Tuñón, Raúl '*España en el corazón*', *Literatura*, Havana, No. 2, 1938

González Tuñón, Raúl 'Neruda', *Cuadernos de Cultura*, Buenos Aires, No. 17, August 1954

Gorkin, Julián 'Pablo Neruda y el Congreso para la Libertad de la Cultura', *El Mercurio*, Santiago, 31 January 1959

Grindea, Miron 'Pablo Neruda with a portrait of the poet', *ADAM*, March–April 1948, pp. 180–181

Guillén, Nicolás 'Evocación de Pablo Neruda', *El Espectador*, Bogotá, 3 April 1949

Guillén, Nicolás 'Pablo Neruda en La Habana', *Hoy*, Havana, 3 July 1950

Gullón, Ricardo 'Relaciones Pablo Neruda–Juan Ramón Jiménez', *Hispanic Review*, Philadelphia, PA, No. 39, April 1971, pp. 141–166

Halperin, Maurice 'Pablo Neruda in Mexico', *Books Abroad*, No. 15, Spring 1941, pp. 164–168

Hernández, José Alfredo 'Pablo Neruda, poeta insignia', *La Prensa*, Lima, 3 November 1935

Holguín, Andrés 'Tres conferencias de Pablo Neruda', *Revista de Las Indias*, Bogotá, No. 56, August 1943, pp. 267–270

Kirsanov, Simyon 'Neruda, laureado con el premio Stalin', *El Siglo*, Santiago, 11 July 1954

Kuteishikova, Vera, and Lev Ospovat 'Venok Neruda', *Khudozhestvenaia Literatura*, Moscow, 1974

Labrador Ruiz, Enrique 'De la vida literaria, *Los versos del capitán*', *Alerta*, Havana, 17 December 1956

Ladrón de Guevara, Matilde 'Carlos Sabat Ercasty, ¿bebió su influjo Neruda?' *Zig-Zag*, Santiago, 2 February 1952

Lago, Tomás 'Pablo Neruda: tras el rostro de un perfil', *Antártica*, Santiago, Nos 10–11, June–July 1945

Lago, Tomás 'Neruda en la época de *Crepusculario*', *Pro Arte*, Santiago, 9 December 1948

Latcham, Ricardo 'Diagnóstico de la nueva poesía chilena', *Sur*, No. 3, Winter 1931, pp. 138–154

Lipschutz, Alejandro 'Pablo Neruda como indigenista', *Pro Arte*, Santiago, No. 157, 11 August 1952

Loveluck, Juan '*Alturas de Macchu Picchu*, Cantos I–V', *Revista Iberoamericana*, Pittsburgh, PA, Nos 82–83, January–June 1973, pp. 175–188

Loyola, Hernán 'A propósito de Neruda', *El Siglo*, Santiago, 24 November 1957

Loyola, Hernán 'Los modos de autorreferencia en la obra de Pablo Neruda', *Aurora*, Santiago, July–December 1964, pp. 64–125

Loyola, Hernán 'Neruda moderno/ Neruda posmoderno', *América Sin Nombre*, Alicante, No. 1, December 1999

de Luigi, Juan 'Pablo Neruda y su obra', *El Siglo*, Santiago, 2 August 1953

de Luigi, Juan 'Odas elementales, Nuevas odas elementales y Odas al pícaro ofendido', *Ultima Hora*, Santiago, 3 February 1957

Lundkvist, Artur 'Neruda', *Boletín*, Universidad de Chile, Santiago, No. 45, December 1963

Mancisidor, José 'Neruda en el *Canto general*', *El Nacional*, Mexico, 11 September 1950

Mansilla, Luis Alberto 'Neruda y el premio Nóbel', *Aurora*, Santiago, January–March, 1964

Mansilla, Luis Alberto 'Vivir con Neruda: Conversación con Aída Figueroa y Sergio Insunza' *Araucaria*, Santiago, No. 26, 1984

Mansilla, Luis Alberto 'Los últimos días', *Anales de la Universidad de Chile Sexta Serie*, Santiago, No. 10, December 1999

Marcenac, Jean 'El *Canto general* de Pablo Neruda hace de Chile la imagen del mundo', *Pro Arte*, Santiago, No. 120, 21 December 1950

Marín, Juan 'Madrid–Temuco, ida y vuelta', *Ercilla*, Santiago, 11 February 1938

Melis, Antonio 'Neruda, Petrarca e le officine galileo', *Nerudiana*, Sassari, 1995

Meo Zilio, Giovanni 'Influencia de Sabat Ercasty en Pablo Neruda', *Revista Nacional*, Montevideo, No. 202, October–November 1959, pp. 589–625

Meza Fuentes, Roberto 'Perfil de un poeta', *El Mercurio*, Santiago, 22 May 1932

Mistral, Gabriela 'Recado sobre Pablo Neruda', *El Mercurio*, Santiago, 26 April 1936

Monguío, Luis 'Introducción a la poesía de Pablo Neruda', *Atenea*, Mayaguez, Puerto Rico, No. 401, July–September 1963, pp. 65–80

Montes, Hugo 'La poesía política de Neruda', *Presencia*, La Paz, 3 July 1958

Morales, Leonidas 'Fundaciones y destrucciones: Pablo Neruda y Nicanor Parra', *Revista Iberoamericana*, Pittsburgh, PA, No. 72, July–September 1970, pp. 407–423

Muñoz, Diego 'Pablo Neruda', *El Siglo*, Santiago, 25 May 1945

Navas Ruiz, Ricardo 'Neruda y Guillén: un caso de relaciones literarias', *Revista Iberoamericana*, Pittsburgh, PA, No. 690, 1965, pp. 251–262

Neruda, Pablo 'Mi infancia y mi poesía', *Capricornio*, Buenos Aires, June–July, 1954

Neruda, Pablo 'Algo sobre mi poesía y mi vida', *Aurora*, Santiago, No. 1, July 1954, pp. 10–21

Neruda, Pablo 'Las vidas del poeta', *O Cruzeiro Internacional*, Rio de Janeiro, 1962

Neruda, Pablo 'Algunas reflexiones improvisadas sobre mis trabajos', *Mapocho*, Santiago, No. 3, 1964

Neruda, Pablo, 'Infancia y poesía', *El Tiempo*, Bogotá, 31 October 1971

Ogniev, Vladimir 'La lírica de Pablo Neruda', *Literatura soviética*, Moscow, No. 78, 1967, pp. 172–177

Osorio, Nelson 'Apuntes para un análisis marxista de la obra de Neruda', *Apuntes*, Santiago, No. 2, 1972, pp. 16–23

Osses, Mario 'La poesía erótico-panteista de Pablo Neruda, *Vértice*, Santiago, November 1946, pp. 50–53

Paseyro, Ricardo 'Noticia actual sobre Pablo Neruda', *Marcha*, Montevideo, 30 September 1949

Pastori, Luis 'Pablo Neruda', *Revista Nacional de Cultura*, Caracas, No. 39, July–August 1943, pp. 101–102

Paz, Octavio 'Neruda en el corazón', *Ruta*, Mexico, No. 4, 1938, pp. 24–33

Paz, Octavio 'Respuesta a un cónsul', *Letras de México*, Mexico City, 15 August 1943

Paz, Octavio 'Mi querido enemigo', *Vuelta*, Mexico City, No. 202, September 1993, p. 8

Picón Salas, Mariano 'Nueva poética de Pablo Neruda', *La Hora*, Santiago, 7 July 1935

Pinilla, Norberto 'Apuntaciones sobre Pablo Neruda', *SECH*, Santiago, December 1936, pp. 50–56

Préndez, Saldías 'Pablo Neruda y el comunismo chileno', *El Diario Ilustrado*, Santiago, 11 February 1951

Pring-Mill, Robert 'Both in Sorrow and in Anger: Spanish-American Protest Poetry', *Cambridge Review*, Cambridge, Vol. 91, No. 2195, 20 February 1970

Pring-Mill, Robert 'Neruda's Murieta', a talk for BBC Radio 3, broadcast on 8 April 1972

Pring-Mill, Robert 'The Poet and his Roots', *Times Literary Supplement*, London, 14 April 1970

Pring-Mill, Robert 'The Winter of Pablo Neruda', *Times Literary Supplement*, London, 3 October 1975

Pring-Mill, Robert 'El Neruda de las *Odas elementales*', *Coloquio internacional sobre*

Pablo Neruda (la obra posterior a Canto general), Alain Sicard ed., Centre de Recherches Latino-américaines, Poitiers, 1979, pp. 261–300

Pring-Mill, Robert 'Neruda y Oxford', *Araucaria de Chile*, Santiago, No. 45, 1989, pp. 137–154

Puccini, Dario 'Lettura del *Canto general*', *Società*, Turin, December 1950

Puccini, Dario 'L'ultimo Neruda. I sentimenti primordiali', *Il Contemporaneo*, Rome, 9 June 1956

Qing, Ai *World Literature*, Beijing, No. 3, 1980

Reid, Alastair 'A Visit to Neruda', *Encounter*, London, September 1965

Rodríguez Monegal, Emir 'Con Pablo Neruda en Montevideo', *Marcha*, Montevideo, 15 August 1952

Rodríguez Monegal, Emir 'Madurez de Pablo Neruda. Rasgos esenciales de las *Odas elementales*', *Marcha*, Montevideo, 26 October 1956

Rodríguez Monegal, Emir 'Pablo Neruda, el sistema del poeta', *Revista Iberoamericana*, Pittsburgh, PA, Nos 82–83, January–June 1973, pp. 41–71

Rodríguez Pérez, Osvaldo 'Del sentimiento de la muerte en la poesía última de Neruda', *Nerudiana*, 1995

Rojas Paz, Pablo 'Pablo Neruda – la poesía y su inseguridad', *Nosotros*, Buenos Aires, No. 19, October 1937, pp. 121–134

de Rokha, Pablo 'Pablo Neruda, poeta a la moda', *La Opinión*, Santiago, 11 November 1932

de Rokha, Pablo 'Epitafio a Neruda', *La Opinión*, Santiago, 22 May 1933

de Rokha, Pablo 'Retorno de Neruda', *Ultima Hora*, Santiago, 11 July 1952

Salomon, Noël 'Un événement poétique: *le Canto general* de Pablo Neruda', *Bulletin hispanique*, Bordeaux, 1974, pp. 92–124

Sanclemente, Alvaro 'La pasión en la poesía de Pablo Neruda', *Revista de las Indias*, Bogotá, No. 91, July 1946, pp. 41–58

Sanhueza, Jorge 'Pablo Neruda: ejemplo de tenacidad y progreso', *Paz*, Santiago, January 1954

Schopf, Federico 'Las huellas del poeta', *Araucaria de Chile*, Santiago, No. 2, 1984, pp. 114–127

Schopf, Federico 'Reception and Context of Pablo Neruda's Poetry' in *Pedro Lastux, la erudición compartida*, Prensa Editora, Mexico City, 1988, pp. 332–372

Sicard, Alain 'Neruda ou la Question sans Réponses', *La Quinzaine Littéraire*, Paris, 16 November 1971

Sicard, Alain '*La espada encendida* de Pablo Neruda, une fable matérialiste', *Cahiers du Monde Hispanique et Luso-Brésilien*, Toulouse, 1973

Silva Castro, Raúl 'Los nuevos: Pablo Neruda', *Claridad*, Santiago, 22 January 1921

Silva Castro, Raúl 'La poesía de Pablo Neruda', *Claridad*, Santiago, September 1924

Silva Castro, Raúl 'Una hora de charla con Pablo Neruda', *El Mercurio*, Santiago, 10 October 1926

Subercaseaux, Benjamín '*Las uvas y el viento*', *La Nación*, Santiago, 14 March 1954

Tarn, Nathaniel 'A Latin Walt Whitman', *The New York Times*, 22 October 1971, p. 34

Teitelboim, Volodia '*Las uvas y el viento* y la evolución de Neruda', *El Siglo*, Santiago, 28 March 1954

Teitelboim, Volodia 'Mirando desde la colina de los cincuenta años de Neruda', *El Siglo*, Santiago, 11 April 1954

Thayer, Sylvia 'Testimonio', *Aurora*, Santiago, Nos 3–4, July–December 1964, pp. 24–42

de Torre, Guillermo 'Carta abierta a Pablo Neruda', *Cuadernos Americanos*, Mexico City, May–June 1951, pp. 277–282

de Undurriaga, Antonio 'Neruda al senado', *Las Ultimas Noticias*, Santiago, 10 March 1945

Valente, Ignacio 'Residencias y Antipoemas', *El Mercurio*, Santiago, 23 February 1969

Valle, Juvencio 'Preguntas para el patriota Pablo Neruda', *Pro Arte*, Santiago, No. 157, 11 August 1952

Varas, José Miguel 'Presente, aquí estoy', *Pro Arte*, Santiago, No. 157, 11 August 1952

Varas, José Miguel '50 años de Pablo Neruda', *El Siglo*, Santiago, 11 July 1954

Varela, Alfredo 'Neruda en el Congreso Mundial de la Paz', *Pro Arte*, Santiago, No. 48, 9 June 1949

Vergara, Marta 'Ingenio y magnetismo de Neruda', *Pro Arte*, Santiago, No. 157, 11 August 1952

Vergara de Bietti, Noemi 'Evolución de Pablo Neruda', *La Prensa*, Buenos Aires, 7 January 1962

Vial, Gonzalo 'Los 10 chilenos mas importantes del siglo XX', *La Segunda*, Santiago, 17 September 1998

Vidal, Virginia 'Neruda en el corazón', *Hechos Mundiales*, Santiago, No. 60, November 1972

Vidal, Virginia 'Con tres sombreros puestos', *Cuadernos*, Fundación Pablo Neruda, Santiago, No. 31, 1997

Villegas, Juan 'Héroes y antihéroes en el *Canto general*', *Anales de la Universidad de Chile*, Santiago, No. 157–160, January–December 1971, pp. 139–151

Wilson, Jason 'In the Translator's Workshop', in *Poetry London*, London, Summer 2002

Wood, Michael 'The Poetry of Neruda', *The New York Review of Books*, 3 October 1974

Yurkiévich, Saúl 'Mito e historia: Dos generadores del *Canto general*' in *Revista Iberoamericana*, Pittsburgh, PA, Nos 82–83, 1973, pp. 111–135

Yurkiévich, Saúl 'Realidad y poesía', *Humanidades*, La Plata, No. 35, 1960, pp. 251–277

Newspapers and journals

ABC, Madrid, September 1973; 23 September 1983

l'Albero, No. 49, 1972

América Latina, Moscow, July 1984

Anales de la Universidad de Chile, No. 129, Santiago, January–March 1964

Revista APSI, 16–29 December 1980

Araucaria, Santiago, No 26, 1984, pp. 89–105; Nos 47–48, 1990

Aurora de Chile, Santiago, 1 August 1938; 1 July 1954; 1 December 1954; July–December 1964; Nos 3–4, 1964; No. 8, 1979

La Bicicleta, Santiago de Chile, July 1983

Boletín, Fundación Pablo Neruda, Santiago, Spring 1991, pp. 33–37

Boletín de la Unidad de Investigación, University of Alicante, Alicante, December 1999

La Brèche, Paris, No. 8, November 1965

Buen Domingo, Santiago, 12 August 1982

Cambridge Review, Cambridge, Vol. 91, No. 2195, 20 February 1970, pp. 112–122

Claridad, Santiago, 2 July 1921

Cuadernos, Fundación Pablo Neruda, Santiago, No. 29, 1997; No. 31, 1997; No. 39, 1999; No. 51, 2001

Cuadernos Americanos, Mexico City, No. 3, May/June 1951, p. 278

O Cruzeiro Internacional, Brazil, 1962

Democracia, Santiago, 5 August 1951; 13 August 1952

Ercilla, Santiago, 20 July 1966; 24 April 1968

Excelsior, Mexico City, 1 June 1943; 23 October 1971; 7 December 1990

L'Express, Paris, 13 September 1971

Le Figaro, Paris, 20 June 1966

La Gaceta de Isla de Pascua, Easter Island, Year 4, No. 7, Summer 1999

Gazeta, Moscow, 10 March 1953

Guardian, London, 28 December 2002

Hora de España, Valencia, March 1937

La Hora, Buenos Aires, 19 October 1948

Hoy, Mexico City, August 1943

Hoy, Santiago, November 1979; 18–24 February 1981

Insula, Madrid, Vol. 29, No. 330, 1974

La Jornada Semanal, Mexico City, 11 June 2000

Juventud Rebelde, Havana, 5 October 2003

Lunes de Revolución, Havana, Cuba, No. 88, 26 December 1960

La Maga, Buenos Aires, 1 November 1995

La Mañana, Temuco, 18 July 1917

Mapocho, Santiago, No. 3, 1964

Marcha, Montevideo, Uruguay, 17 September 1971

El Mercurio, Santiago, 3 January 1932; 15 March 1932; 30 May 1932; 5 February 1933; 30 January 1955; 30 November 1980

Le Monde Diplomatique, Paris, August 2001

La Montagne, Clermont-Ferrand, France, 20 November 2002

La Nación, Santiago, 20 November 1927; 5 February 1928; 19 October 1930; 18 September 1932

El Nacional, Mexico City, 24 August 1940

Nerudiana, Sassari, 1995

New York Times Book Review, New York, 20 July 1990

El Nuevo Diario, Managua, 7 June 1992

La Opinión, Santiago, 11 November 1932; 25 November 1932; 22 May 1933

Página 12, Buenos Aires, 28 July 2002

The Paris Review, Number 51, Spring 1971

PEC, Santiago, No. 76, 10 May 1966; 28 June 1966

Plática, Buenos Aires, April 1956

Principios, Santiago, September 1952

Pro Arte, Santiago, 30 November 1950; 15–31 July 1954

El Proceso, Mexico City, 9 September 1978

Qué Pasa, Santiago, 3 January 2000; 4 October 2002

Reforma, Mexico City, 7 April 1944

Revista del Domingo, Valencia, 22 August 1982, p. 6

Revista Occidente, Santiago, No. 81, October 1952, pp. 37–44; No. 82, November 1952, pp. 25–24

Revista Intramuros, Santiago, No. 9, 1978; No. 9, 2002

Ediciones de la Revista Mapocho, Biblioteca Nacional, Santiago, Vol. 2, No. 3, 1964

Ruta, Fondo de Cultura Económica, Mexico, Vol. 1 No. 16, 1939–9, p. 241

La Segunda, Santiago, 3 October 1969; 17 September 1998

Siete Días Ilustrados, Buenos Aires, No. 200, 15 March 1971

El Siglo, Bogotá, 29 October 1943

El Siglo, Santiago, 10 March 1953; 31 May 1953; 18 January 1954; 11 January 1957; 14 October 1962; 28 July 1963; 30 September 1963; 1 December 1963; 12 July 1964; 2 August 1966; 28 August 1966; 6 November 1966; 10 April 1968; 1 October 1969; 13 July 2000

Sucesos, Santiago, No. 5, October 1967

El Tiempo, 31 October 1971

La Tercera, Santiago, 1 August 1982; 26 July 1998 ; 17 March 2002; 9 July 2002; 13 July 2002; 23 September 2003; 27 September 2003; 23 October 2003

Times Literary Supplement, London, 16 April 1970

La Vanguardia, Barcelona, 11 August 2002

Vistazo, Santiago, No. 12, 11 November 1952

Copyright Acknowledgements

Index

NOTE: Works by Pablo Neruda (PN) appear directly under title; works by others under author's name

A NOTE ON THE TYPE

The text of this book is set in Linotype Sabon, named after the type founder, Jacques Sabon. It was designed by Jan Tschichold and jointly developed by Linotype, Monotype and Stempel, in response to a need for a typeface to be available in identical form for mechanical hot metal composition and hand composition using foundry type.

Tschichold based his design for Sabon roman on a font engraved by Garamond, and Sabon italic on a font by Granjon. It was first used in 1966 and has proved an enduring modern classic.

A NOTE ON THE AUTHOR

Adam Feinstein has published articles on Spanish and
Latin American literature in many newspapers and
magazines, and has translated the work of Frederico
García Lorca and Mario Benedetti for *Modern Poetry
in Translation*. He has worked for the Latin American
Service of the BBC and has been a London correspondent
for one of Spain's leading national daily newspapers,
El Mundo. During his work on this book, he received
awards from the Wingate Foundation and the
Leverhulme Trust. He lives in London with his wife
and three children.